I0188704

Johnson County, Kentucky

History and Families

Turner Publishing Company
Nashville, Tennessee

Turner Publishing Company

424 Church Street, Suite 2240
Nashville, TN 37219

445 Park Avenue, 9th Floor
New York, NY 10022

www.turnerpublishing.com

Library of Congress Control Number: 2001089727
ISBN: 1-56311-7568

Turner Publishing Company Staff:
Keith R. Steele, Publishing Consultant
Charlotte Harris, Project Coordinator
Shelley R. Davidson, Designer

Printed in the United States of America.

Contents

Johnson County Family History Book Committee

Rebecca Lewis Music, Chairman

Pat Patton
O.W. "Tubby" Harris
Ruth Salyer
Edna Mae Blevins
Jan Horne
Jim Trammel

John Sparks
W.H. "Pat" Pelfrey
June B. Rice
Harold L. Preston
Harry Holbrook
Burnett Music
Jim Hamilton

The Johnson County Historical and Genealogical Society strives to preserve the culture and heritage of Johnson County.

Publisher's Message

The people of Johnson County can be proud of the important role they and their ancestors have played in Kentucky history. The valuable heritage of Johnson County can now be more widely known as a result of the tremendous community support of this volume, *Johnson County, Kentucky Family History Book.*

This volume will allow today's generations to learn about their heritage and the events that shaped their lives. Future generations will benefit greatly from the wealth of information that has been recorded in this permanent hardbound book.

The Johnson County Historical & Genealogical Society is to be commended for their outstanding efforts and work during the initiation and completion of the project. We sincerely appreciate the work of Pat Patton, Jim Trammel, Rebecca Lewis Music, Jan Horne, Harold L. Preston, Harry Holbrook, Ruth Salyer, John Sparks, Burnett Music, O.W. "Tubby" Harris, Jim Hamilton, Edna Mae Blevins, W.H. "Pat" Pelphrey, and June B. Rice, who devoted their time to the gathering, recording, and organizing of materials for the book. We also appreciate the work of Bob Marsh in compiling the general history for the book.

We appreciate the many organizations and businesses who supplied histories, and their support to the society in publication of this book. Finally, we wish to acknowledge and thank each individual who contributed biographies and photos for publication, or had a part in this unique history.

Turner Publishing has created titles in many Kentucky counties, including *Anderson, Bell, Boyle, Breckinridge, Bullitt, Caldwell, Calloway, Christian, Clay, Edmonson, Floyd, Franklin, Fulton, Hardin, Hickman, Hopkins, Knott, Knox, Logan, Livingston, Marshall, McCracken, Muhlenberg, Oldham, Owen, Russell, Scott, Simpson, Todd, Warren, Washington, Wayne and Whitley* counties. It is with great pride that we now present to the people of Johnson County this volume, the *Johnson County, Kentucky Family History Book.*

Keith Steele
Publishing Consultant

Dave Turner
President

General History

A Brief History of Johnson County, Kentucky

by Robert L. Marsh

Any history of Johnson County must begin (and probably end) with the Big Sandy River. It was the Big Sandy, winding its way south-to-north from the Breaks of the Mountains to the Ohio River, which encourages the discovery and early exploration of the region. It was the Levisa (originally "Louisa") Fork of this sometimes blue-green, often muddy stream, meandering lazily through rich valleys and over treacherous shoals, which attracted such permanent settlements as Harmon's Station (1787), Leslie's Station (1789), Vancouver's Station (1789) and Paint Lick Station (1790), now Paintsville and Preston's Station (1797), now Prestonsburg.

As we will see, it was the Big Sandy River which attracted steamboats, railroads and highways to fuel the economy of the valley, market its produce and bring in manufactured goods. Finally, it was the river, at its junction with Paint Creek, which provided a broad alluvial plain for the permanent settlement which eventually became Paintsville, the county seat of Johnson County.

By archeological standards, the Appalachian Mountain chain is one of the nation's older mountain ranges and the Big Sandy River one of its older streams. Its channel is filled each winter and spring by the rain-choked torrents rushing out of such Johnson County tributaries as Johns Creek, Paint Creek, Jenny's (or Jennies) Creek, Miller's Creek, George's Creek, Frank's Creek, Tom's Creek, Buffalo Creek and Hammond Creek.

These smaller creeks and their even smaller tributaries provided the first roadways for early explorers and the settling families which followed between 1790 and 1820. Mostly English, Scotch-Irish and German in origin, they arrived from Virginia, the Carolinas, Pennsylvania and Tennessee.

However, when Johnson County was created by the Kentucky General Assembly by carving 268 square miles out of Floyd County, Lawrence and Morgan counties on February 24, 1843, the region's history was already several thousand years old. By the time of the county's first permanent settlement by families of European ancestry at Harmon's Station in 1787, mounds of the Adena Indians dotted the Big Sandy valley as they had for more than 2,000 years until their excavation by archeologists in 1938.

Meanwhile, although no tribe of native Americans made Eastern Kentucky its permanent home, the Iroquois, Delaware, Miami, Shawnee and Cherokee were among the native American

Big Sandy River, Paintsville, Kentucky; Greentown on the right, King Addition on the left.

Coal Tipples

Indians who traveled through, hunted in and fought territorial battles over the area drained by the Big Sandy River. Most violent encounters with Indians had vanished by the time Paintsville was platted as a permanent settlement and were unheard of after General Anthony Wayne's victory at the Battle of Fallen Timbers in 1794.

Early Court Street scene, Paintsville, Kentucky.

Although there is speculation that Spanish and French nationals may have made brief forays into what is now Eastern Kentucky, Dr. Thomas Walker, leading a band of explorers for the Loyal Land Company of Virginia on June 5, 1750, is generally identified as being the first white man to stand on the western bank of the Big Sandy River at the mouth of Paint Creek. His diary records that he found evidence of an early Shawnee village and of the prehistoric mounds.

Had Walker been as poetically inclined as historian Carol Crowe-Carraco, writing in her book *The Big Sandy* (UK Press, 1979), he might have penned as did she, "Like the ribs of a pawpaw leaf, the Big Sandy River with its Levisa and Tug Forks and tributary creeks veins the easternmost section of Kentucky. The river is both inviting and forbidding, inescapable and beautiful, The spring rains swell it beyond its banks and send it muddy and churning over the countryside."

It was the attraction of this river with its bountiful resource of deer, bear, beaver, squirrel, turkey and even buffalo which lured its initial permanent settlers. Soon, large land grants from the Commonwealth of Virginia further encouraged families from the Tidewater and Piedmont to make the hazardous and difficult journey across the mountains. They found the natural breaks and gaps which had been traveled by various Indian tribes for centuries and searched for the valley bottom lands and meadows near the essential waterways protected by nearby hills and mountains.

Not far from the point where Paint Creek drains into the Big Sandy River, a salt water artesian stream attracted wild game seeking salt and, in turn, the hunters who sought meat and hides. The salt rising from this spring, along with the colorful aboriginal tree markings, gave the future settlement its name –*Paint Lick Station*.

It is at this point that reference should be made to the important, fortress-like block houses built at the mouth of Johns Creek, near the present Johnson-Floyd County line. Matthias "Tice" Harman (or Harmon) and Samuel Auxier were equally responsible for this small frontier settlement just before and after 1790. Blockhouse Bottom, as it became known, was made famous by the heroic saga of Jenny (Virginia Sellards) Wiley. Her capture in 1789 by painted savages, the murder of her family and her eventual escape and return to Harman's Station has been immortalized by several authors, including Johnson County native, Dr. Arville Wheeler, in his popular book, *White Squaw*, and, thus, will not be re-told here, except to observe that Jenny (or Jennie) Wiley was the first of only two true legends claimed by Johnson County.

Paint Lick Station was founded in 1790 by Colonel John Preston, a Tidewater, VA, gentleman, land speculator and fur trader. Preston and a band of trappers and traders made their settlement, a one-story log structure, near the present Courthouse Square, and two nearby cabins. A high log fence surrounded the small structures and comprised a rectangular stockade. The land on which Preston established his trading station was patented to George Lewis in 1788 by the Commonwealth of Virginia.

Paint Lick Station trading post thrived into the early 1800s when Henry Dixon, a preacher/silversmith/farmer, purchased the land north of Paint Creek from Lewis, including the location of the trading post. Later, several tracts of the Lewis patent were auctioned to Isaac Hitchcock, John Auxier, Henry Dixon, James Stafford, John Iliff, Evan Evans and John Remy (Ramey). Other early property owners included William Remy, Andrew Rule, Electious Howes and Thomas Lewis, all patriarchal surnames which would have a profound impact on Johnson County.

Soon thereafter, Moses Preston, James Franklin, Francis A. Brown and William Barnett purchased parcels of land near Paint Creek from the earliest owners.

Shooting a well in the oil field.

According to J.K. Wells, writing in his small, but highly detailed book *The Gathering of the Trades People, The Early and Pre-History of Paintsville and Johnson County, Kentucky* (Gateway Press, 1992), observed that "(c)learing this land was a simple matter. From the willows and sycamores along the creek to the foot of the hills, both to the north and south of the creek, were few trees. The land was flat and marshy and covered with a thick, rank growth of reeds and Carolina cane, higher than a man's head. Rich black topsoil was overlaid on a good grade fire clay. Crops of corn and garden truck thrived, but the soil so marshy the settlers built their log houses back on the higher ground at the foot of the hills."

Soon, mills, ferries and taverns were operating near the mouth of Paint Creek. Henry Dixon installed a horse mill to grind corn into meal. John Auxier built a water mill and small dam near the present foot bridge at the west end of Paintsville's Main Street.

The arrival of new settlers between 1820 and 1830 prompted Dixon and Franklin to begin subdividing their property, recording plats in the Floyd County Courthouse and offering lots for sale. Records indicate that these lots, especially the creek bank lots, sold quickly.

The small trading post of Paint Lick Stations soon became a village and its name was changed to Paintsville to meet its new, more dignified status, In 1834 the state legislature issued Paintsville a formal charter as a "town" and its boundaries were established "upon the plat laid out by Henry Dixon."

By this time, other small communities had

Paintsville Hospital on Euclid Avenue, 1957 flood.

Church Street during the 1957 flood.

McKenzie Service Station, Third Street, U.S. 23 nd St. Rt. 40.

arisen. Flat Gap, with verdant rolling farm land, soon rivaled Paintsville in population and influence. Staffordsville and Oil Springs further west of Paintsville were joined by Buffalo and Greasy Creek east of the Big Sandy, as growing clusters of families choosing to make permanent homes where farming and business found markets at the juncture of Paint Creek and the Big Sandy.

The United States Postal Department recognized the importance of the former trading post when, on April 10, 1824, a new post office named Paint Creek was created with Charles Rumsey as postmaster. The post office was re-named Paintsville on June 21, 1843 and Jesse Wheeler was appointed postmaster that year.

As more families crossed into Kentucky and made homes along Paint Creek, Greasy Creek, Tom's Creek and other similar tributaries, residents became restless to have their own county. The absence of roads made travel to and from Prestonsburg difficult, if not impossible, at times. Furthermore, Paintsville was outgrowing Prestonsburg in population and economy between 1830 and 1840. By 1840 the cries for autonomy were heard in Frankfort and, in 1843, the General Assembly created a new county from portions of Floyd, Morgan and Lawrence counties. It was named Johnson County after Vice President Richard M. Johnson, a native of Scott County, KY, former congressman and hero of the Battle of the Thames. Johnson purportedly killed the great chief Tecumseh during this historically decisive Indian battle in the eastern United States.

Although created in 1834, the new county did not become a legal reality until April 1, 1844, when the first business of the county was transacted at the Paintsville home of James Franklin. One of the first acts of county government officials was the construction of a courthouse. John B. Harris and his brother, Henry C. Harris assumed the task and the building was completed in November 1846. However, the first fiscal court meeting was held in the building on March 3, 1845.

Five commissioners from other counties were appointed to establish the "seat of justice" in the new county. There was considerable pressure to name Flat Gap as the county seat. Like Paintsville, Flat Gap was a growing village and, except for the river, was as accessible as Paintsville. However, Paintsville had the advantage of

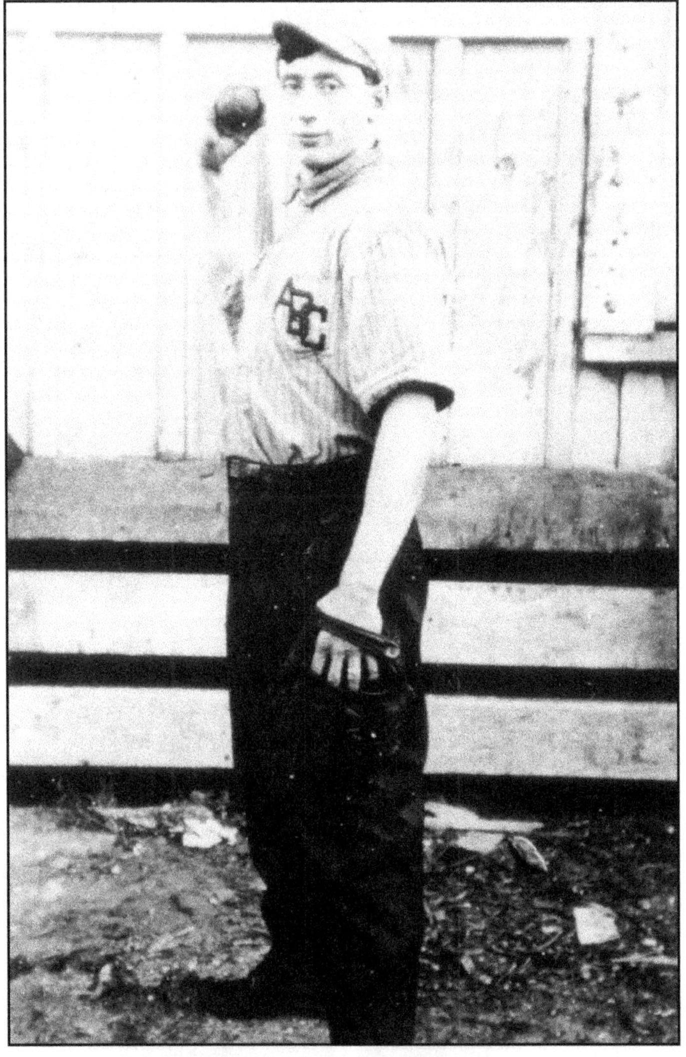

Red Blevins, Van Lear Baseball

location. Where Flat Gap was on the county's northwestern corner, Paintsville was situated near the geographic center of the county. In addition, its location at the point where Paint Creek joined the Big Sandy River was crucial.

The county's first officials were: Winston Mayo, circuit court clerk; Samuel K. Friend, state representative; James Remy (Ramey) county judge; John Howes, county court clerk; Daniel Hager, sheriff; William Dixon, jailer; and B.J. Livingston, county attorney.

Among the many duties of the Johnson County Fiscal Court was the maintenance of county roads. This was a simple task in the beginning because there were almost no county roads at the time. What few there were had been carved out of stream beds and forest land as wagon roads. Bridges were non-existent. Local citizens were expected to perform regular road maintenance by clearing fallen logs and rocks from the wagon roads. Ferries were licensed at strategic locations where existing roads met creeks or rivers too deep to ford. The ferries became continuations of the county road. Daniel Hager was granted a ferry license in 1857 and ordered to maintain Paintsville's Main Street leading to the ferry. Similarly, Henry Sherman was given a ferry license to cross the Big Sandy at Hell's Gate Shoals.

The county court set the rates for such ferries. Sherman was permitted to charge 10 cents for a man on foot, 10 to 15 cents for a wagon and, for each head of cattle, 3 cents. Likewise, the county court established the prices that local taverns could charge for food, lodging and drink. In 1854, one could have a meal at Daniel Hager's tavern for 18 cents. You could stay overnight for 12 cents. If you came on horseback you were charged another 12 cents for stabling and feeding the horse. Whiskey was 10 cents a pint or 21 cents a gallon. Other tavern owners and ferry keepers of this period included George W. Auxier, Ralph Stafford, Samuel Porter, William Meek, James W. Turner, Robert Borders and Edward Lavender.

Change was in the wind for residents of Johnson County and Eastern Kentucky, however, And it was announced by a loud shrill scream, not unlike that of a mountain cat, echoing from ridge to ridge along the Big Sandy River. It was the whistle of a steamboat.

Johnson County's isolation was ended. Economic, social and cultural intercourse with the rest of the nation and world was about to begin.

J.M. Feltner 4-H Club Camp, Fishtrap, near Paintsville, Kentucky.

Crossing Paint Creek

The first steamboat to travel up the Big Sandy as far as Paintsville arrived unannounced in 1837. The historic boat's name is lost in antiquity. It was soon followed, however, by a host of others. By the 1850s, the sternwheelers, sidewheelers, batwings and flat bottom boats brought the world to the doorstep of families in the county.

Manufactured goods, including tailored clothing, newspapers, furniture, hardware, building materials and farm equipment were brought up river while fur, hides, timber and other raw materials were sent down the river. New housing constructed with metal roofs soon began replacing log houses. Men and women adorned themselves with the latest finery from the north. Salesmen, entertainers, even evangelists, arrived at Paintsville's dock at the mouth of Paint Creek, along with manufactured cargo and brought with them a seamier side of a more refined civilization.

Manuel Slone (right), Verner Stambaugh, Irvin Arrowood (second from left), and Brown. Four salesman, 1938.

It was one of the most exciting times in the county's history. For those working on the steamboats, it was also one of the most dangerous. The Big Sandy River was treacherous at its best. In the long, dry summers the low water stopped almost all river traffic. In the winter and spring, shifting sandbars, rocky shoals, floating trees, packed ice and rushing creeks emptying themselves into the river, caused boats to ground and sink in the unforgiving waters. But the boats continued to make their runs up and down the Big Sandy from Catlettsburg to Pikeville. Numerous county entrepreneurs such as Green Meek and Dan Wheeler built, owned and operated boats of their own before the era ended.

Still, not even the railroad a half-century later had as much impact on Johnson County as did the steamboats. In addition, they represented a romantic way of life which those of us living along the Big Sandy today can only imagine.

By 1850, Johnson County had a population of 3,873 people, including 30 slaves. Early occupations and professions in the county included shopkeepers, cobblers, saddlemakers, silversmiths, physicians, attorneys, coal diggers, carpenters and cabinetmakers, in addition to tavern owners. There were blacksmith shops and general stores, as well as a brick kiln and gristmill, in Paintsville.

Although the people settling Johnson County were a religious, God-fearing people, the first church building was not erected until the 1830s. There were, however, numerous informal congregations of Methodists and Baptists which met in homes of their members throughout the county.

Church buildings rose in such disparate communities as Manila, Williamsport, Flat Gap and Staffordsville between 1837 and 1860. In 1867, Paintsville's first church building, now First United Methodist Church, was built and known as Vaughan's Chapel. This was soon followed by the Christian Church and a second Methodist congregation, the Methodist Episcopal Church, South.

In his significant book *History of Johnson County*, published in 1928 and now, sadly, out of print, C. Mitchell Hall reported that by 1867 there were no fewer than 15 churches in Johnson County.

As religious fervor appeared to be growing throughout the county so was its political counterpart.

The people of Johnson County, while isolated to a large degree, were not completely cut-off from events in the rest of the nation. The deep rifts occasioned by the anti-slavery movement and accompanying states' rights debates reached down into the hills of Eastern Kentucky. The first impact of this gathering storm was felt by local Methodists when their church separated into two distinct General Conferences, The Methodist Episcopal Church and The Methodist Episcopal Church, South, over the issue of slavery.

Hog killing time, 1932. Charlie Rice, Sitka, Kentucky.

Although Johnson County had only 11 residents who owned slaves (and these men held but 27 slaves among them) in 1860, strong opinions were held on the issue of state sovereignty and, more particularly, the mountain man's indomitable spirit of independence. As a consequence, the foundation for conflict was as strong in Johnson County as elsewhere in the nation.

Tension had been building among families and even between counties in Eastern Kentucky. The consensus throughout Kentucky was for staying in the Union but almost equally strong for permitting each state the right to run its own affairs. In fact, there had been many fights and quarrels around the courthouse in Paintsville as emotions overcame civility.

Still, it is surprising to learn that in October 1861, the county's fiscal court enacted a remarkable resolution ordering "that any person or persons who shall put up a flag upon the courthouse or public square representing the United States or the Confederate States shall be guilty of an offense and shall be fined the sum of $50.00." County officials had chosen to take a middle ground in any obvious effort to avoid clashes between opposing sentiments. It did not succeed.

As John David Preston notes in his detailed and highly informative book *The Civil War in the Big Sandy Valley of Kentucky* (Gateway Press, 1984), "(d)espite the well-intentioned efforts of the Johnson County Fiscal Court, neither Johnson County, Eastern Kentucky, nor the rest of the state could avoid the war."

Soon volunteers were donning Union blue or Confederate gray as they moved to join the 14th Kentucky Volunte Infantry (Union) or the Fifth Regiment Infantry (Confederate) which were organizing throughout the Big Sandy. The well-meaning but poorly trained men had little but enthusiasm to recommend them. By late 1861, each side was reinforced with more professional troops.

General Humphrey Marshall moved into the headwaters of the Big Sandy from Virginia with a large Confederate force in late 1861 and in January 1862, Colonel James A. Garfield marched up the Big Sandy from Catlettsburg. Garfield had orders to move Humphrey out of the state and back to Virginia.

On January 5, 1862, word soon spread throughout the valley that Garfield had crossed the Ohio River with a sizable Union force and was headed south toward Paintsville. Garfield's advance scouts came within sight of Paintsville late on that day. The following day, after a brief skirmish with opposing forces near the mouth of Jenny's Creek, Union troops entered Paintsville. They had made their way from Louisa through George's Creek and up Muddy Branch where they crossed Paint Creek.

Following a brief stay at the Vaughan home on Second Street, Garfield moved his troops further south along the Big Sandy where he encountered Humphrey at the Battle of Middle Creek in Floyd County. Soon Garfield was encamped in Piketon (Pikeville) and Humphrey was on his way to Virginia.

Three events of interest mark the early days of the Civil War in Johnson County and the Big Sandy Valley.

During Garfield's few days in Paintsville some of his more rambunctious Ohioans took advantage of the town's hospitality and returned the favor by vandalizing the town's young Masonic Lodge, stealing the Masonic jewels worn by lodge officials on formal occasions. Within days of their having arrived in Pikeville, however, Garfield became aware of the soldiers showing off their loot in camp. Soon, an armed escort from Garfield's headquarters company rode into Paintsville with the jewels and an apology from the man who would one day become president of the United States. As a Mason, himself, Garfield had recognized the jewels for what they were and for their significance to the lodge which had been formed only two years earlier.

As Garfield and Humphrey maneuvered for position near

Main Street, Paintsville, Kentucky.

Pikeville and the Kentucky-Virginia border, Mother Nature decided to take a hand and create her own conflict. In February 1862, one of the most devastating floods ever experienced on the Big Sandy struck the Union forces with particular ferocity. The Union commander reported that he had lost most of his food, equipment and supplies and that two steamboats had been left in the streets of Pikeville by the flood waters.

Garfield rushed to Catlettsburg for supplies and commandeered the steamboat *Sandy Valley*, owned by former Lawrence County Judge Archibald Borders. Traveling against the force of onrushing flood waters and subject to sniper fire from Confederate sympathizers along the shore, Garfield made the return trip in 48 hours, re-supplying his troops as well as the people of Pikeville.

Meanwhile, one of the leading southern supporters in Johnson County and one of its leading citizens, Daniel Hager, chose to move out of Paintsville to the isolation of his farm at Hager Hill. The gathering storm had already divided his family, taking son Daniel M. Hager to Union service and another son, John Hager, to a Confederate troop. The elder Hager ostensibly wanted to live out his life away from the war's discord, quietly and peacefully on his farm. He was 61 years old.

Remarkably, every historical account of the Big Sandy Valley agrees that Daniel Hager remained at his farm until the end of the war in 1865. They were all incorrect. More than 100 years after the death of this Eastern Kentucky scion Civil War amnesty records revealed that Hager had left his home with General Humphrey Marshall and served as a captain in the Quartermaster Corps of the Confederate Army until Lee's surrender at Appomattox in 1865. He was granted amnesty and a pardon, signed by President Andrew Johnson, at the age of 64.

The end of the war did not mean the end of strife and bitterness, however. As men in uniforms or in tattered homespun linsey-woolsey rode horseback or trudged on foot through the hills of Eastern Kentucky toward their homes, many more were killed or wounded by bushwhackers hiding in the woods along wagon trails. It would be several years before peace and harmony returned, especially to Johnson County, a border county in a border state.

Nevertheless, with the Civil War at an end, the citizens of Johnson County could turn their attention to improving their families and their communities. Education and the economy were among the most important needs crying for attention as the final quarter of the 19th century and the 100th anniversary of the region's settlement began closing in.

Industrial and economic changes were revolutionizing the nation, everywhere except in Eastern Kentucky. The telephone (1876), telegraph (1864), gasoline-powered automobile (1889) and the electric dynamo (1871), as well as a host of other inventions would not reach Johnson County until the arrival of the 20th century.

Schools, however, and the expansion of the minds of children throughout the county had already captured the imaginations of families across Johnson County.

At Flat Gap, Oil Springs and Paintsville, the earliest schools, called "subscription schools" began accepting students just before and just after the Civil War. Indeed, in 1867, Paintsville had two such schools. One, located on West Main Street, was called the Northern or Republican School and the other, housed in the M. E. Church, South, on lower Main Street, was called the Southern or Democrat School. Other early schools of note were the Enterprise Academy, founded by the Reverend William Jayne at Flat Gap and the Advance Seminary founded at Oil Springs by John R. Long.

The first schoolhouses, made of logs and axe-hewn shingled roofs, were few and far between. Pupils walked five or more miles to attend a school term which rarely lasted more than three months. Those students were blessed, however, with a number of dedicated teachers. Professor William N. Randolph, Lewis Mayo, Professor J.B. Wheatley, Professor T.J. Mayo and Charles Grim were among those who taught schools in Paintsville and Johnson County when bears, wolves and mountain lions were still a part of the local landscape. The title "professor" was honorary in most instances and conferred on those teachers who were most respected.

Paintsville's subscriptions schools closed with the state-approved creation of the Paintsville Graded School District in 1889. It first school building was built in 1892. Too soon the splendid frame structure burned, but not before Paintsville High School handed diplomas to its first two graduates, James W. Turner and Fred Howes. New buildings were built in 1918, 1926, 1951, 1958, 1968, 1972 and 1989 as the size and needs of the student body changed.

In 1905 a private, church-related prep school was organized in Paintsville. The Sandy Valley Seminary was created with the assistance of John C.C. Mayo and his wife, Alice, who contributed land and money to the school's founding. The Western Virginia Conference of the Methodist Church, South, assumed operating control of the school. The school's name was changed to John C.C. Mayo College in 1918 and continued to function until closing in 1929.

Meanwhile, county schools were advancing, as well. By 1927, there were more than 80 elementary schools scattered throughout Johnson County, along with high schools at Paintsville, Oil Springs, Flat Gap and Van Lear. High schools at Meade Memorial and Jennies Creek opened in the 1930s.

Among the noted teachers and administrators who established Johnson County's earliest educational traditions were B.F. Conley, Ella Webb, Calloway Hall, W.C. Brandenburg, W.H. Conley, Virginia Long, Jim Bailey, George Johnson, Mack Stapleton, Mollie Rice, Fred Meade, H.B. Rice, Beecher Stapleton, W.R. Conley and Mary Leslie to mention only a few.

The quality of the teacher is best judged by the academic accomplishments and personal achievements of his students. In this respect, the vast majority of teachers in both the city and county school systems deserve the highest accolades. Young men and women from Johnson County have gone on to post-graduate degrees and positions of highest responsibility and success in every major field of endeavor. Their careers span every worthwhile pursuit, including science, medicine, law, education, military, accounting, engineering, business, farming, banking, construction, sports, religion, transportation and, certainly not least, homemaking.

Educational programs, however, require an economy which can provide the financial base to support them. Prior to the advent of the 20th century, Johnson County was a rural, farming community with an agricultural based economy. The twin iron rails of the Chesapeake & Ohio Railway had made it up the Big Sandy as far as Richardson in Lawrence County by the 1880s. There it stopped for almost 20 years. Coal was being mined in relatively small quantities near the Lawrence-Johnson County line but it had no major economic impact as yet on the residents of our county.

Johnson County still had no banks, no railroad, no telephones, no electricity, no paved roads and a succession of unsuccessful newspapers which lasted anywhere from two weeks to six months.

There was, however, a young man living in Johnson County who had followed his father into the teaching profession. John Caldwell Calhoun Mayo had a vision of a Big Sandy Valley with a thriving economy based on the production, processing and utilization of coal. He foresaw coal as the catalyst of the county's future economy. Coal could bring new transportation, new industry and new convenience for both home and business.

John C.C. Mayo was to become Johnson County's second true legend.

Between 1890 and 1910, Mayo's feverish activity in buying, leasing, promoting, developing and selling coal from Eastern Kentucky had changed the face of Paintsville and Johnson County, as well as every other Eastern Kentucky county. It has also made him one of the wealthiest men in Kentucky.

Thanks to Mayo's enthusiastic importuning and his business acumen, the railroad arrived in Paintsville in 1904. A newspaper and a bank had preceded the C & O by only one and two years, respectively. The telephone and telegraph soon followed, as did electricity. Major underground coal mines were opened on Muddy Branch, Auxier and Van Lear. Mining towns, with their own houses, stores, schools and recreational facilities, sprang up along the railroad tracks. Hundreds of new families moved into Johnson County. They, along with an untold number of local men, were employed in bringing the abundant "black gold" to the surface for shipment to northern steel mills and other large industries.

As the North-East Coal Company and Consolidated Coal Company, the area's two largest coal operations, expanded, their management staff soon became integrated into the community. R.C. Thomas, Henry LaVries and other mine personnel joined Mayo, Dan Davis, H.B. Rice, Daniel M. Hager, Dr. I.R. Turner, Jim Auxier, C.T. Rule, H.S. Howes, James D. Johnson and others in boosting and building the community.

Wells Chapel Church

Mayo continued his support of Sandy Valley Seminary while beginning work on a new magnificent mansion. He paused in this endeavor only long enough to have his construction crews build the equally magnificent, cathedral-like church which today bears his name. He purchased the city's street paving and sewer bonds, thereby making these civic improvements possible.

By his 43rd birthday, Mayo could look with pride upon his accomplishments. He and his wife, Alice (or Alka), began to travel. Trips to New York, Philadelphia, Cincinnati, Chicago and Minneapolis were capped by a lengthy tour of Europe in 1913. Mayo had become involved in Democrat politics in the 1890s. This involvement not only earned him a seat on the state Democratic Committee and appointments as a delegate to two national conventions, but it almost got him killed.

In the midst of the turmoil over the election and assassination of Kentucky Governor William Goebel, Mayo was called to Frankfort to testify about election irregularities in Eastern Kentucky during the election of 1900. As Mayo sat in the lobby of the Capitol Hotel, a gunfight erupted between two feuding army officers. Seeing he was about to be in the line of fire, Mayo dropped behind a chair. He arose uninjured when the firing ceased. Several others were not so lucky.

Luck has been defined as that moment when preparation and opportunity meet. Thanks to his own hard work, preparation and seizing upon opportunities which he, himself, largely created, Mayo had been lucky throughout his life. Now, however, his luck was about to run out.

Soon after his friend and colleague John E. Buckingham threw a lavish party for Calhoun and Alice Mayo upon their return from Europe, Mayo learned that he had Bright's Disease. This malady, which afflicted the kidneys, was, in 1914, incurable.

Mayo consulted physicians in Cincinnati where he was hospitalized for a time. He was eventually transported by private rail car to New York City where the most eminent doctors available were consulted. Various treatments were attempted both in and out of hospitals to no avail. He was moved to the Waldorf-Astoria Hotel where he died on May 11, 1914.

The residents of Johnson and surrounding counties were devastated. John C.C. Mayo had been a friend and a benefactor. He had grown up in Paintsville and had taught school in Johnson County. In spite of his wealth and frenzied business activities. Mayo had never held himself aloof, or as his fellow Johnson Countians would say "he never got above his raisin'." The legacies of his life and its impact of Paintsville, Johnson County and the Big Sandy Valley would extend far into the 20th century.

Local grieving over Mayo's untimely death gradually began to wane while the demand for coal from Eastern Kentucky's coalfields opened by Mayo showed a dramatic increase over the next three decades.

Two world wars and nationwide industrial expansion, except for the Depression Era, saw coal production jump into the millions of tons per year. Jobs in mining were considered essential to the war effort as men from Johnson County went overseas in 1918 and 1942 to fight and die on strange soil with strange names like Belleau Wood and Chateau-Thierry in World War I and Guadalcanal, Okinawa and Bastogne in World War II.

Additionally, beginning in 1917, Johnson County became the center of an oil and gas boom which transformed communities like Flat Gap, Red Bush, Oil Springs and Barnetts Creek into beehives of activity. New families, many of them destined to make notable contributions to the future of their newly adopted county. Names like Jenkins, Roberts, Parrigan, Bailey, Maggard and a host of others chose this time to immigrate from Wayne, Jackson and Magoffin counties. They, along with uncounted others, made their fortunes in gas and oil development and its related businesses. Their descendants remain today.

On the home front during both wars, families gave their support by buying war bonds, raising Victory Gardens, knitting woolen garments for the troops, conserving electricity, stoically enduring the restrictions of rationing and reading each week of those who were wounded or killed in action. While Johnson County's fatalities were comparatively minimal in 1918, almost 100 local men lost their lives between 1942 and 1945 in World War II.

During the intervening years, as coal, oil and gas from Johnson County moved down the Big Sandy by rail and pipe, the wind of progress was blowing up the river to Paintsville.

New modern school buildings were erected throughout the county and in Paintsville. Meade Memorial High School was created at Williamsport in 1931 and was joined by Jenny's Creek

High School in 1935, as the Johnson County school system under the leadership of such administrators as Fred Meade, O.W. Cain, W.C. Brandenburg, Arville Wheeler, John Fred Williams and Verne P. Horne began to realize its full potential. Educational leaders in Paintsville during this period included, in addition to Brandenburg and Wheeler, W.B. Ward, H.R. Brown and R.G. Huey.

Riding on the wind of educational and cultural awareness, with Miss May Stafford handling the whip, Johnson County's Pack Horse Library, the forerunner to today's modern public library began making its rural rounds on December 20, 1938. The innovative book circulating enterprise initially occupied a room in the Mayo Mansion donated by E.J. Evans. Lumber for the shelves was donated by Paintsville mayor and lumberman F.S. Van Hoose. Books and magazines were carried in saddlebags to even the remotest sections of the county by workers who were soon known as "Book Women." Although books are now circulated throughout the county by a modern bookmobile, the lady driver is still referred to by some as the "Book Lady."

However, probably the most significant educational and industrial event of these decades was the establishment of Mayo State Vocational School in 1938.

After years of unsuccessful attempts, legislation introduced by State Representative John B. Mollett finally passed both houses of the Kentucky General Assembly and received the approval of Gov. A.B. "Happy" Chandler on April 14, 1938. Chandler was flanked by Mollett, along with city and county leaders J.N. Meek, Claude Buckingham, Forrest Preston, C.R. Cooper, Harry LaViers, Ray Turner, F.S. Van Hoose and J. Howard Frail as the legislation authorizing the purchase of a large portion of the John C.C. Mayo estate property and the creation of what is today Mayo State Technical College became a reality.

In the intervening 70 years, thousands of young men and women from Johnson and surrounding counties have been taught the skills and knowledge which opened the path to fulfilling lifetime careers in a variety of trades and professions. Under the leadership of such administrators as A.L. Pigman, James Patton, George Ramey and Bronelle Skaggs, vocational and technical education met a growing need for well-trained employees.

Great strides were taken in civic improvements throughout Paintsville and Johnson County, as well.

Paintsville was designated a Fourth Class City in 1926 and created its first fire department that same year. A series of annexations more than doubled the size of the city as Southside, Bridgeford and Stafford Addition were added to its boundaries. A succession of progressive mayors, supported by their respective city councils, set the pattern for continued growth. R.C. Thomas, J.N. Meek, Dr. E.E. Archer, F.S. Van Hoose, J.B. Wells Jr. and Escom Chandler paved streets and sidewalks, extended public water and sewer lines and eventually purchased the local water and natural gas systems. Fire and police departments were modernized and, in 1934, a new concrete bridge was built across Paint Creek, as the city attracted new businesses and an increased population.

Paintsville's second bank, Paintsville Bank & Trust, opened in 1910 and a third financial institution, Big Sandy Savings & Loan, opened in 1936. The competition and leadership provided by these and other major businesses were a necessary boon to Johnson County's economic stability. In their respective eras, J.B. Wells, C.T. Rule, William G. Bailey and the Dorton family, D.H., O.T. and Dennis T. Dorton of Second (now Citizens) National Bank; James W. Turner, Ross Lyons, Russell Meade, Robert Conley and James C. Witten of First National Bank; and F.S. Van Hoose, Dr. Lloyd G. Meade, W.H. Cox, B.E. Mullins, George Branham, Allen S. "Bud" Perry and Homer Short of Family Bank (formerly Big Sandy and First Federal Savings & Loan), each gave major impetus to the county's economic development.

Meanwhile, Paintsville Hospital, the county's first, opened in 1920. The Paintsville Golf Course was completed in 1929 and, on February 3, 1947, the Johnson County Public Library opened at the corner of Second and College Streets in Paintsville. In addition, the long-awaited completion of the Mayo Trail (or U.S. Highway 23) between Paintsville and Ashland was accomplished with the paving of what had come to be known as "The Missing Link." Ceremonies marking the end of more than 20 years of frustration, aggravation and irritation by angry motorists were held near the Johnson-Lawrence County border on September 14, 1946. However, ceaseless repairs and improvements, four-laning and upgrading, would seem to indicate that U.S. 23, like the National Cathedral, may never be entirely completed.

The demand for coal began to decline as the first half of the 20th century came to an end. Labor strife, foreign markets and changes in manufacturing plant design, as well as the increased cost of underground production, brought lay-offs and even the closing of local mines. After more than 35 years, the Auxier mine of North-East Coal Company ceased production. Consolidated Coal Company's Van Lear mines soon followed. For the next 20 years, until the advent of the strip or surface mining technique and the coal boom of the 1970s, small family owned mines, called "truck" mines or "punch" mines, were responsible for much of Johnson County's remaining coal production.

But, once again, the shifting sandbars of the Big Sandy River heralded change in the offing.

In 1939, with the encouragement of Congressman A.J. May, the U.S. Corps of Engineers began a study of building a flood control dam near the Johnson-Floyd County line. For more than 100 years, flooding by the Big Sandy had wreaked havoc with towns along the river. The 1937 and 1939 floods were particularly devastating

Timbering on the Big Sandy River.

as the water destroyed hundreds of homes and cost several lives. World War II interrupted the plans but, finally, on March 18, 1946 the contract for the construction of Dewey Dam in Floyd County was signed. Although the dam and its man-made lake would be situated entirely in Floyd County, it was hoped that, by controlling the waters running from Johns Creek into the Big Sandy River, future flooding could be significantly reduced. Johns Creek, a 100 mile-long stream, received much of its water from tributaries in Pike County, as well. Ironically, the Big Sandy reached a level of almost 39 feet in a flood which crested on January 9, 1946, little more than two months before the contract was signed.

(Because housing in Paintsville was in such short supply, the Corps of Engineers brought in 15 prefabricated housing units in which to locate many of its supervisory personnel and their families. These "quonset" huts were located in Stafford Addition and remained there for several years).

Throughout the late 1940s and until the dam's completion, successive congressmen, A.J. May, W. Howes Meade and Carl D. Perkins, labored to maintain funding for the project.

As this project was moving forward another movement involving the Big Sandy was causing local dissension. Federal legislation which would build locks and dams on the river from Pikeville to Catlettsburg, permitting barge traffic along the length of the Levisa Fork, hit a snag. Spurred by the opposition (and influence) of the C & O Railway, Big Sandy coal producers appeared before Congress to speak against the locks and dams. Their opposition succeeded and it is felt by many that the failure to make the river navigable was a serious economic blow to the future of Johnson County and Eastern Kentucky.

With brighter economic prospects provided by the Dewey Dam construction, Paintsville and Johnson County once again turned their sights on community improvements.

In 1949, the Paintsville Junior Women's League began a drive for an extensive park and playground system. Joined by members of Beta Sigma Phi, Rotary, Kiwanis, the *Paintsville Herald*, newly opened Radio Station WSIP, as well as local church and business organizations, the movement promoted every fundraising concept imaginable. From peanuts being pushed down Main Street on the noses of members of the Rotary Club to a performance of the popular musical hit "Mule Train," sung by Methodist minister Clarence W. Krebs over WSIP, funds slowly began to grow. With a bond issue from the city putting the drive over the top, the Paintsville Park & Playground was dedicated on July 2, 1953. The county's first Little League teams took the field that same year. Later donations of land by physician, philanthropist and sportsman Dr. Paul B. Hall, the Howes Land Company and Johnson County's fiscal court gave the city and county one of the finest public recreational complexes in Eastern Kentucky.

The biggest news to come out of the 1950s, however, was once again the Big Sandy River.

In March 1953, District Highway Engineer J.P. Noonan announced that the bridge over the Big Sandy connecting Greentown and Paintsville with the easternmost sections of the county would be closed April 1 for much-needed repairs. The faithful old structure, built 30 years earlier, had sustained some serious damage four years earlier when a state highway truck, carrying a bulldozer, collided with another truck in the middle of the bridge. Noonan proposed that traffic, meanwhile, be routed across the river at the West Van Lear bridge.

However, the objections of local business and school transportation interests persuaded State Highway Commissioner Curlin to overrule Noonan. One-way traffic was to be permitted while the repairs went forward.

On April 8, only a few days after the repairs began, a tractor-trailer rig hauling a bulldozer began moving slowly across the bridge. As the truck eased its way onto the center span of the bridge, the creaks and groans of the bridge turned into the grinding of twisting metal and the terrified screams of onlookers when the bridge collapsed. The driver and the bridge were doomed.

Now, the original plan was put into effect. All traffic was routed through Davis Branch and West Van Lear. By mid-January 1954, with the new bridge nearing completion, heavy rains and freezing temperatures caused a build-up of ice amid rising water. The pressure was too great. On Sunday, January 17, 1954, the bridge collapsed again. There were no injuries this time and a completely new bridge of concrete and steel was constructed.

With Dewey Dam in place, controlling the heavy run-off from Johns Creek and other up-river streams, the Big Sandy was thought to be under control. Apparently, no one told the river.

It was January once again, this time January 27, 1957, as typical winter rain began to fall. It fell for two and one-half days, as local emergency and disaster officials began to alert residents to prepare for a flood. By Wednesday morning, January 30, Paintsville was completely isolated by the still rising waters of the Big Sandy and Paint Creek. A state of emergency was declared by Mayor Ralph B. "Tiny" Preston and families were evacuated all across town.

Civil Defense Director Jim Tom Newman, assisted by William C. Martin, Cy Cooper and a host of volunteers from city and county government and Mayo Vocational School worked around the clock to coordinate the disaster relief effort while the raging torrent of the Big Sandy continued to rise. Seven hundred homes were under water. The flood had climbed the steps of First National Bank on Main Street and water was over the tops of most parking meters on Second Street.

Finally, at 3:00 a.m. on the morning of Thursday, January 31, the angry waters calmed and the river crested at a record height of 45.9 feet. The 1957 Flood was a major disaster across Johnson County and her neighbors to the south. Even with Dewey Dam, additional floods (although not of such record dimensions) would continue to plague the city and county in 1963 and 1964.

It is not surprising, therefore, to learn that as early as October 15, 1961, the concept of a new dam, this one on Paint Creek, was being proposed. The location, near Fish Trap and Barnetts Creek just beyond Staffordsville, was intended to assist in flood control and provide additional recreational facilities for the region.

It stirred up a hornet's nest of debate from the Johnson County Courthouse to the halls of Congress in Washington. The proposed dam was the subject of a local lawsuit by property owners near the Johnson and Morgan county lines, congressional hearings and even a front page article in the Wall Street Journal. Nevertheless, with the political power and might of Congressman Carl D. Perkins, the dam was built and in 1982 Paintsville Lake was opened to the public.

Not, however, before creating more headlines.

It was often referred to as "Exodus '78." What it really was the complete evacuation of the city of Paintsville and other downstream communities in the possible wake of the coffer dam at Paintsville Lake.

With eight inches of rain falling along the path of Paint Creek in a period of 36 hours, Paintsville Mayor James S. Trimble, Disaster Director Jim Tom Newman and Corps of Engineers commander, Colonel George Bicher, made a tough and courageous decision. Evacuate Paintsville!

Water backed up behind a temporary coffer dam at Paintsville Lake was threatening to breach the coffer dam. This much water had not been imagined in the dam's design. Officials noted a "seepage" through the coffer dam on the downstream side. If the seepage continued and began to seriously erode the earthen coffer dam, those living downstream, including residents of Staffordsville and Paintsville, would be in grave peril.

As a result of several meetings and detailed studies of years of

Nehi Bottling Company, Paintsville, Kentucky; W.H. Irvin, owner and manager.

data, city officials awaited the arrival of the water at a predetermined level, 675 feet above sea level, with the seepage continuing. That moment arrived at 8:58 a.m. Saturday morning, December 9, 1978.

Sirens sounded and Trimble and Newman went on WSIP radio and ordered the evacuation of the entire city of Paintsville, plus a strip of the county from Staffordsville to Thelma. It was not until 5:00 p.m. Sunday, December 10, that the "all-clear" was sounded and residents were permitted to return to their homes.

It had been a harrowing experience for all concerned. But for Paintsville Mayor James S. Trimble and Disaster & Emergency Services Director Jim Tom Newman, it was considered by many to be "their finest hour."

It must be said not everything that happened in Johnson County could be blamed on the Big Sandy River.

On October 6, 1962, in direct competition with the Johnson County Fair, the first Apple Day was held in Johnson County. Guided by Elmon Davis, an officer of Citizens National Bank and an orchardist at Flat Gap, one of the county's most enduring traditions got under way. Changing its name to The Kentucky Apple Festival of Johnson County, the three day event has continued for nearly 40 years, attracting crowds more than tripling the population of Johnson County on several occasions during the first weekend in October each year.

The Apple Festival began a move toward tourism as a viable economic option in Johnson County. The county was already known nationwide as the home of country music singing star Loretta Lynn, born and raised at Butcher Holler and considered by many to be the county's third true legend. Other country music stars, including Hilo Brown, also called Johnson County home. Still, tourism was not considered by everyone to be a true industry.

Consequently, local businessmen and women sought for several years to attract new industry to Paintsville and Johnson County. A sewing factory was begun on Broadway in Paintsville. It was a good effort but it failed. A wood products venture, called Kenwood, planned for an industrial site near Hager Hill on the banks of the Big Sandy, never got off the ground. Finally, due to the tireless efforts of such local business leaders as O.T. "Trigg" Dorton, Allen S. "Bud" Perry, Clarence Castle and many others, American Standard and international plumbing manufacturer, agreed in 1969 to locate a plant at the former Kenwood site, just south of Paintsville. By November 18, 1971, American Standard was reported to be employing between 380 and 400 men and women.

The capture of this solid industry brought about other local improvements. A new and modern motel was built in Paintsville. The Heart O'Highlands attracted many visitors, joining the Pritchard and Pride Motels as preferred hostelries in Johnson County. The advent of a new, more vibrant, economic era contributed to dramatic advances in education in Johnson County.

Beginning as early as 1962, the Johnson County Board of Education had begun discussing the consolidation of the county's high schools. In 1965, voters approved a tax levy for the construction of a consolidated high school to be built on the Mayo farm across Paint Creek from Paintsville.

On September 10, 1968, 1,200 students and 60 teachers assembled at the new Johnson Central High School. Harold L. Preston, a former principal at Meade Memorial High School and the new school's curriculum director, wrote, "In retrospect, one wonders in awe at the near normalcy for opening a school year. Here was a physical plant as large as probably all four previous high schools! Here was a freshman class as large or larger than the total enrollment in the student's previous school!"

Under the leadership of William Stapleton, Virgil Porter, Orville Hamilton, Hershell Conley and Frank Hamilton, Johnson Central High School soon established its own traditions of academic and athletic accomplishments. Within a few years, the Johnson County school system was one of the largest and most modern in Eastern Kentucky. It was a far cry from the days of a few subscription schools scattered throughout the county a century before.

At the same time, across the creek in Paintsville Oran C. Teater, a Paintsville High School graduate who had returned in 1946 as teacher and assistant coach, was named the Tigers' football coach upon the resignation of coach W.L. "Perk" Perkins. Superintendent R.G. Huey had been succeeded by J. Matt Sparkman and J.C. Edelman. Upon Edelman's resignation in 1955, Teater began the longest and most successful tenure ever achieved by a Paintsville Independent School superintendent. He submitted his resignation on January 21, 1978, after 32 years in the local school system.

In the Middle East, meanwhile, an oil embargo brought about a phenomenal resurgence in the local coal industry. Thanks to a new and highly controversial technique called "strip" or surface mining, coal once again began pouring out of Johnson County and down the Big Sandy River in 100 car unit trains and in large tractor-trailer trucks. The demand for coal was so great at the time that often the quality of the coal was not questioned. Some producers were even accused of mixing the finely ground coal with dirt to increase their tonnage. Prices for coal jumped over $60 per ton and it was not unusual for one local coal producer to pocket as much as $100,000 a week *after* taxes between 1970 and 1975. The new "coal boom" made a number of new millionaires in Johnson County. Among the more successful local coal operators at the time were Homer Short, James C. Witten, C.E. Hovatter, James S. Trimble, B.W. McDonald and J.W. Clifton.

William Lee Davis, George W. Davis, Tolby Hall, Johnny Hall, unknown; taken 1918 at Consolidated Coal Company in Jenkins, Kentucky. The car is a Model T.

Eventually, strict environmental regulations and a renewed flow of oil from the Persian Gulf area forces a sharp drop in prices and quantities of Eastern Kentucky coal. The boom was over as quickly as it had begun and only the scarred mountain tops and moonscape craters remained.

Nevertheless, in spite of its advantages and successes of many of its people, Johnson County was not immune from shock and violence.

It was not unusual for local residents to attempt to solve their grievances with a gun or knife. It had happened far too often with mournful consequences. The days of Prohibition in the 1920s saw its share of violence, as did other events of the decade which followed. Still, nothing quite prepared local residents for the shocking murder of Johnson County's young sheriff in 1966.

Walter Meek at 25 was the youngest sheriff in Kentucky on Saturday morning, November 26, 1966, when he responded to a call to serve a lunacy warrant on 34 year old, Jimmy Ward. Ward had apparently barricaded himself in his house on the hillside above Kentucky Route 40 just west of Paintsville.

Meek arrived, approached the house with caution, for he had been told that Ward had a shotgun and had twice been a patient at Eastern State Hospital. The sheriff, accompanied by his deputy Curt DeLong and a lifelong friend, Tucker Daniel, parked below the house. He instructed Daniel to wait at the car at the foot of the hill while he and DeLong walked toward the ramshackle house.

There was the blast of a shotgun. When Daniel rushed up the hill, Sheriff Walter Meek was dead and Deputy DeLong was wounded. He was the first sheriff of Johnson County known to have died in the line of duty. He was not to be the last.

On Wednesday, March 18, 1992, popular sheriff, Eugene C. "Gene" Cyrus was shot and killed by Flem Burchett, a man being tried in Johnson Circuit Court on a second degree rape charge. Burchett failed to return to court after a lunch break. Cyrus went after him. Approaching Burchett's residence on Caudill Fork at 2:55 p.m., Cyrus took a direct shotgun blast while standing on the porch of Burchett's house. Burchett shot himself, but survived. Johnson County Sheriff Gene Cyrus did not. He was pronounced dead on arrival at Paintsville's Paul B. Hall Regional Medical Center.

This brief summary of more than 200 years of the life and times of those who lived, worked and played in Johnson County, KY, has, of necessity, omitted many references to people and events which would otherwise deserve more than a passing notation. Included in this list would be the visit to Johnson County on April 24, 1964, by President Lyndon Johnson; the opening of the Mountain Parkway in 1963; the county's first viable television reception in 1954; the city's Urban Renewal Development project which resulted in Westview Manor, The Carriage House and Paul B. Hall Regional Medical Center and many others.

It has been 250 years since Dr. Thomas Walker stood on the west bank of the Big Sandy River near the mouth of Paint Creek and watched the raging, rain-filled waters rush by. Those who followed Dr. Walker and chose to settle here and cast their fortune and that of their families within the confines of the mountains of Eastern Kentucky have, as Shakespeare had Hamlet say, "...suffered the slings and arrows of outrageous fortune." They have also known the best of times in the best of places.

Hicks House at Williamsport, Kentucky; built in the 1850s.

FEATURE PAGES
CHURCHES, BUSINESSES, AND ORGANIZATIONS

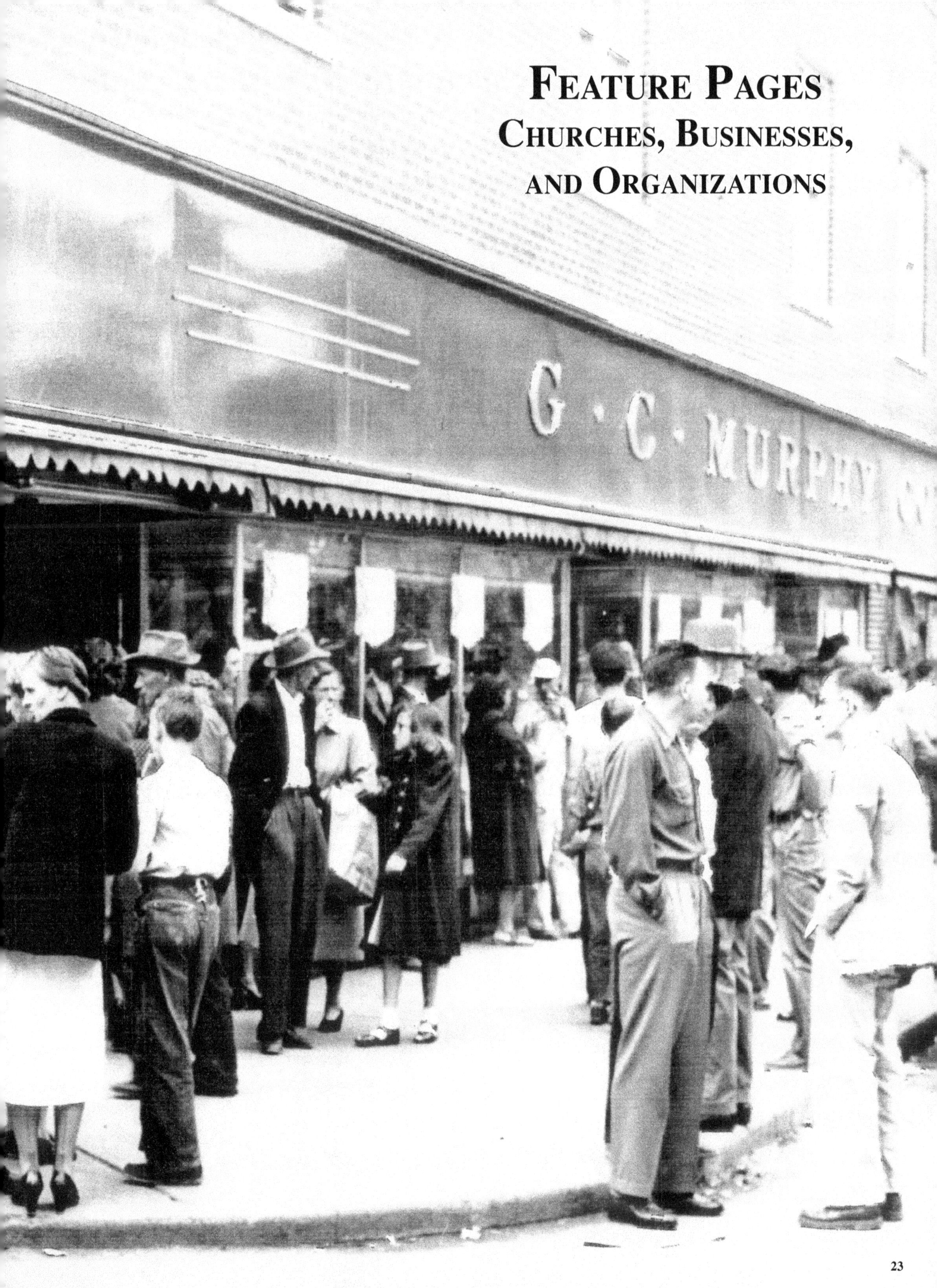

First Baptist Church of Paintsville

In the beginning, and until recently, the church was known as the Missionary Baptist Church. Under the leadership of Rev. Charles Martin, a State Mission worker for the Southern Baptist Convention of Kentucky, and with 18 charter members, the church was organized in November 1903. Names mentioned in the early days of the church and some of the charter members included the Blairs, Rices, Conleys, Chandlers, Prices and Wileys. Some of the charter members came from Liberty Baptist which was the oldest Missionary Baptist Church in the county.

The Freewill Baptists, the Missionary Baptists and the United Baptists owned a building on the corner of Church Street and Second Street. As the churches grew, each of the three Baptist denominations needed more time for services. The Missionary Baptists agreed to sell their interest to the United Baptists, and the transaction was completed in May 1906.

Soon thereafter, a lot on the corner of Fourth Street and College Street was purchased from W.H. Vaughan and the men of the church began work. A block-molding machine was purchased and the blocks to erect a building were molded and stacked, and in December 1906 the foundation and the walls were started. By April 1907, the outside structure was completed.

During this building period, the church met in the Paintsville School building. Charles Martin, who was called as pastor when the church was organized, served as pastor until October 1908.

The formal dedication of the church was held on Sunday, Feb. 2, 1908 with the other churches assisting in the dedication ceremonies. With the coming of the railroad up the Big Sandy and the organization of several mines, a number of new families moved to the Paintsville area. Many of these families were Missionary Baptists and contributed much to the growth of the church.

Pastors serving the church between 1903 and 1937 included Martin, Amerson, Partee, Petit, L.F. Caudill, Grumbles, Wright, Bell, A.H. Webb and R. Lee James.

The first parsonage, purchased in 1922, was the place known as the Abe Barber House on College Street beside the church. The White Brick, located directly behind the church on Fourth Street, was purchased January 1944 and used as a parsonage until 1950. It was then converted into Sunday School space.

The next purchase was the house on the East End of Fourth Street, bought in the spring of 1951 and used as a parsonage until the present parsonage on Court Street was built. The property used as the Bridgeford Mission was purchased December 1951.

The property on which the present church is located was bought December 1956 from the Southeast Coal Company. The church occupied the building on Fourth Street until October 1, 1967, at which time the church moved into the present structure located on the corner of Third and College streets. The church experienced its most successful growth between 1937 and 1999.

At various times and at various places, the church sponsored Missions, teaching Sunday School, conducting Vacation Bible School, revivals and worship services. In 1951 the church established a mission at Bridgeford which was in constant operation until the early 1990s. Many people passed through the Bridgeford Mission. Many moved on to new locations and many became faithful members of the local Baptist church.

In addition to local missions and activities, the church has been associated with the Enterprise Association of Southern Baptists, the State Convention, as well as the entire program of Southern Baptists. The programs of Southern Baptists include Foreign Missions, Home Missions, State Missions, the Baptist Children's Homes and various other divisions of mission work.

The local church has been very active in the teaching ministry, various mission classes and all church related activities. The Baptist Training Union has ministered to youth groups of all ages, the ladies of the church have maintained a strong Women's Missionary Union and the men participate in a Baptist Men's Fellowship which has been very active in the ministry of the church.

The following have served as pastors since 1937: Sam Slone, C.F. Smith, Ralph Webb, Roy Hamilton, C.H. Hockensmith, M.R. Thomason, James Wallace, Charles Milam, Don Yeager, Drew Martin and the present pastor, Donnie Patrick.

From 1903 until 1999, the First Baptist Church has been a strong influence in this community and has cooperated with other churches and organizations to make this part of Kentucky a place where the people worship and honor God, their country and their fellow man.

First Baptist Church Paintsville at College and Fourth streets.

First Baptist Church Paintsville at College and Third streets.

FIRST UNITED METHODIST CHURCH OF PAINTSVILLE

The Paintsville Methodist Society was organized in the summer of 1812. It met in the home of John Auxier, located in the east end of Paintsville. Among the most influential and zealous in organizing and maintaining the early Methodist Society were Lewis Mayo and Electious Howes.

In addition to the Auxier, Mayo and Howes families, early Methodist families in Paintsville included those of Samuel Friend, Daniel Hager, D.B. Wells and John Vaughan.

In 1844, Methodists adopted the Plan of Separation which, due to differences caused by the issues of slavery and abolition, divided the church between north and south thus creating the Methodist Episcopal Church, South (now known as Mayo Memorial United Methodist Church) and the Methodist Episcopal Church (now known as First United Methodist Church). However, in 1939 the Plan of Reconciliation was adopted which united the previous two factions.

First United Methodist Church of Paintsville was founded in 1865. Charter members included the Borders, Vaughan, Howes, Baldwin, Brown and Walker families. This congregation built the first church building erected in Paintsville in 1867. It was built of wood on the present site of the church at Main and Church Streets. The land had been purchased from Reuben and Amanda Patrick for $150.00 and the lumber and nails donated by Joseph Borders and the Vaughan family. In 1893 a church bell was purchased from Buckeye Bell Foundry of Cincinnati which rang faithfully for 74 years. The church was first called Vaughan's Chapel and then changed to First Methodist Episcopal Church when it became a "station" rather than a "circuit" in 1904.

The church building served the members admirably until 1914 when ground was broken for the present structure. A new parsonage had been constructed adjacent to the church the previous year. The cost of the new church building was $16,000 and the cost of the parsonage was $1,950. In 1956 the church purchased adjoining property from the J.A. Jones family on which an educational building was eventually constructed and opened in 1970 at a service with Bishop Roy H. Short presiding.

In July 1989 the church purchased the property of MR. and Mrs. Escom Chandler on 531 2nd Street for a new parsonage. In 1991 the old parsonage was finally razed. On Feb. 16, 1997, the church purchased the Stafford property adjacent to the church and the following year that dwelling was razed to make room for additional parking and eventually a family worship center.

Other notable events through the years include the addition of lovely carillon and Westminster Clock chimes in 1968; a new Allen organ replacing the older Hammond organ in 1979; a major renovation of the church interior in 1983 at a cost of $125,000; a new sound amplification and recording system in 1988; a handicap ramp in 1988; a new church directory in 1995 and a large illuminated sign on Main Street side of church that same year.

PASTORS OF THE FIRST UNITED METHODIST CHURCH SINCE 1904:

A.L. Williams	1904	O.J. Polley	1932	J.H. Burton	1964
A.H. Davis	1906	C.R. Garland	1936	W.A.E. Johnson	1974
J.D. Walsh	1908	G.W. Townsend	1938	Woodrow Church	1975
W.C. Stewart	1919	H.E. Trent	1939	Graham Abbott	1976
A.M. Harrison	1921	R.R. Rose	1942	James Powell	1985
E.J. Rees	1921	J.E. Savage	1944	David Ross	1989
W.B. Foley	1925	C.W. Krebs	1947	Wayne Sparks	1992
T.T. Ashley	1927	W.F. Pettus	1952	Terry Reffett	1995
L.D. Rounds	1930	Simmerman	1957		
O.C. Haas	1930	Hugh Smith	1960		
		Robert Hart	1961		

Information provided by First United Methodist Church from material previously compiled by E.J. Rees, W.H. Vaughan, H.B. Rice, H.S. Howes, G.H. Rice, Coke Williams and Mary Grace Rice Garland.

Flat Gap Baptist Church

This church was organized in 1909 and admitted into the Enterprise Baptist Association of Regular Baptist in the same year. Reverend R.H. Hayes served as first pastor.

There have been many pastors through the years. Brother Harold Salyer became pastor on January 18, 1964 and served as a devoted, faithful shepherd until November 11, 1991.

In 1979 a new church building was completed and the first worship service was held on Easter Sunday, April 15, 1979.

On August 23, 1985 the congregation, under the capable leadership of Brother Harold Salyer, voted to voluntarily withdraw from the Enterprise Association, becoming an independent organization.

On September 1, 1985 our new name, Flat Gap Baptist Church, was adopted.

In December 1986, baptistry and Sunday School rooms were added. Jack Lavender painted the baptistry mural February 1987.

First baptismal service in the new baptistry was Mar. 8, 1987. Candidates requesting baptism were Katrinka Cantrell, daughter of Gordon K. and Elaine Cantrell and Connie Roberts, daughter of Bill and Edie Roberts.

In 1991 after nearly 28 years of faithful stewardship to Flat Gap Church, Brother Harold Salyer was transferred by Ashland Oil to Grayson, KY.

In 1992 our church was blessed with another wonderful and capable pastor, Brother Johnny Estep.

In 1996, under the capable leadership of Brother Estep, the church voted to brick the church. Brother Luther Wright financed this project.

The information in this history was obtained from church records and older members of the church.

Thanks to everyone who contributed to this history.

Tidbits of Interest

Our two oldest living members are Verna Salyer Marshall, age 94, and Beulah Lyon McKenzie, age 87. Verna is the mother-in-law of Wanda Crislip Salyer. Beulah is the mother of Clista McKenzie Pelfrey. Both ladies are faithful Christians who attend our services when they can.

Our youngest member is Jacob Blanton, son of Jeff and Elizabeth Blanton, grandson of Tommy and Geraldine Blanton. Jacob is a student at Johnson County Middle School.

Brother Harold Salyer served 27 years, 9 months and 29 days, the longest term as pastor of Flat Gap Baptist Church (January 18, 1964 - November 17, 1991). Quite a record!

Emery Lemaster was the last person to be saved in the old building and the first person to be baptized in the new one.

Our most recent members are Jeff Blanton, Gary and Margaret Blanton and Randy Stapleton.

In 1938 our biggest revival was held by ministers H.T. Hamilton, E.L. Thomas, John Joseph and H.C. Green. Eighty-five people were saved and 70 were baptized.

In 1937 Augusta Williams served as church clerk.

In 1942 Sister Willie Cantrell was clerk.

In 1940s Sister Faye Fyffe was treasurer.

In 1958 Sister Prudence Bailey was clerk.

Brother Luther Wright donated new hymnals in memory of his late wife Angie.

Serving Flat Gap Baptist Church

Pastor
Johnny Estep

Clerk
Phillip Howard

Asst. Clerk
Lowell T. Blanton

Deacons
Lowell T. Blanton, wife Geraldine
Jack Holbrook, wife Jenny
Phillip Howard, wife Paula
Gary Mullins, wife Phyllis
Elwood Ramey, wife Jewell
Hobert Salyer, wife Ruby
Allen Blanton, wife Brenda

Sunday School Superintendent
Gary Mullins

Teachers
Adult Class, Jack Holbrook
Youth Class, Jeff Blanton
Primary, Brenda Blanton
Beginners, Rhonda Blanton

Youth Services
Willard Burton
Brenda Blanton
Karen Potter

Piano Players
Sue Ferguson
Paula Howard
Collista Pelfrey

Song Leader
Phillip Howard

Janitorial Personnel
Sheila Little
Karen Potter

Church Bulletin
Paula Howard
Peggy Cantrell

Prayer Warriors
Everyone in the church

Trustees
Bob Blanton
Orville P. Estep
Tall Hill
Lee Johnson
Charles Thompson
Hobert Salyer
Gary R. Ferguson

Jenny's Creek United Baptist Church

The Jenny's Creek United Baptist Church is one of the oldest churches in Johnson County.

The church was organized at the home of Brother James Spradlin on the third Saturday of July 1840. Elder John Borders and Elder Samuel P'Simer were the ordained presbytery. Records show Elder Elijah Bays, Brother Mark Trimble, Brother Asa Fairchild, and Brother James Spradlin were present for the organization.

The James Spradlin residence was located on what is now the Paul Caudill farm on Lower Twin Branch, Denver, KY.

The officers of the church were chosen at the organization and Elder Elijah Bays was chosen moderator and Brother Mark Trimble was chosen deacon and clerk.

At the April 1841 business meeting, the church changed their regular meeting to the fourth Saturday in each month and still meets that way today.

On July 13, 1845, Samuel Rice Sr. deeded the church property on his farm, 3/4 acre more or less. The church paid him 50 cents to make the transaction good.

Elder Elijah Bays had married Samuel's daughter Margaret "Peggie."

The first building was of logs with a large rock fireplace and no floor. The seats were made of split logs and tree stumps. This building was located in a large group of beech trees below the county road and near the creek. With so many beech trees on the property, the church became known as the Beechwall Church to all the people in the area. The Church is still called that today by many people. The building would flood on occasion and when the second building was built, it was built across the road up on the side of the hill

On April 17, 1871, Martin R. Rice gave to the church 1/2 acre joining the original property. On November 25, 1882, he gave the church an additional two acres.

The first communion and foot washing was held on Sunday after the fourth Saturday in July 1841. The communion and foot washing was changed to Sunday after the fourth Saturday in June. This meeting became known as "June Meeting" not only to people in Johnson County, but surrounding counties. Many people used this meeting not only to worship, but to visit with family and friends. There would be a large gathering on this day. People would ride horseback and come by horse and wagon. Those who lived longer distances could travel by train. A special train would run on this Sunday to bring people from neighboring areas. Merchants would come and set concession stands of food to sell to the people as this was a day long event. Many people used this day for a family reunion.

After 159 years, the Jenny's Creek (Beechwall) United Baptist Church is still located on the original grounds and still carries on the practice set up by our forefathers.

Johnson County Coal Camps
(Compiled from Dodrill's 10,000 Coal Company Stores)

Company	Community	County	Years	Employees
Preston Coal Co.	Alonzo	Johnson	1907-1913	50
Marylock Coal Co.	Auxier	Johnson	1912-1913	40
Royal Collieries	?	Johnson	1910-1910	30
Denver Coal Company	Denver	Johnson	1921-1923	40
Preston Coal Company	Emma (?)	Johnson	1909-1913	25
Whitehouse Cannel Coal	Louisa	Lawrence/Johnson	1903-1903	170
Royal Collieries	Greasy Creek	Johnson	1911-1913	65
Sandy River Coal Co.	Greasy Creek	Johnson	1905-1917	75
Yellow Chief Coal Co.	Greasy Creek	Johnson	1912-1913	30
Meek Coal Co.	Meek	Johnson	1906-1909	100
Yellow Chief Coal Co.	Meek	Johnson	1912-1913	30
Royal Coal Co.	Offutt	Johnson	1935-1938	135
Royal Collieries Co.	Offutt	Johnson	1914-1929	128
Royal Millers Creek Coal	Offutt	Johnson	1930-1934	175
Millers Creek Coal Co.	Paintsville	Johnson	1940-1940	100
North-East Coal Co.	Paintsville	Johnson	1907-1926	125
Northeast Coal Co.	Paintsville	Johnson	1908-1910	125
Green Rock Coal Co.	Riceville	Johnson	1921-1924	30
Tibbals Coal Co.	River	Johnson	1910-1910	77
North-East Coal Co.	Thealka	Johnson	1911-1952	296
Consolidation Coal Co.	Van Lear	Johnson	1910-1946	666
Fluhart Collieries	Whitehouse	Johnson	1911-1919	125
Tibbals Coal Co.	Whitehouse	Johnson	1910-1910	50
North-East Coal Co.	Whitehouse	Johnson	1911-1952	150
Sandy River Coal Co.	Williamsport	Johnson	1905-1907	40

Oil Springs United Methodist Church

by Mary Conley and M. Neil Price Jr., church historians, with information assistance provided by Mrs. Viva Mae Crace, Alice and Harold Conley, Neil Price Sr., Betty Stafford, Mrs. Peggy Adams and writings of W.R. Conley

Perhaps the best way to describe the Oil Springs United Methodist Church is the little church that not only could but did God's will by spreading his word through the ministers who sacrificed their lives to preach the word, the members who have served their God by serving their fellow man, and the church as a whole, that has served as the glue for the community at large.

While it is uncertain when and where this church began, it probably began in connection with other Methodist churches in the area (probably the Salyersville Methodist Church) with services starting at individual homes. The first permanent building was likely at its present location on land donated by Judge William Elzie Litteral and his wife the former Sue Witten. Mr. Literal was Sunday School Superintendent and a Sunday School teacher. His descendants like Jack Adams and Peggy Litteral Adams still belong to the church today.

In 1893 the church building was designed and built under the direction and hard labor of Ben F. Mahan. The building is known for its extraordinary construction and is in the National Register as a historical site in Kentucky. One such example of that construction is the two inch by six inch oak flooring that was installed on its edge. Many improvements have occurred over the years. In 1952 the church interior was paneled. In 1967, the fellowship hall was added. In 1974, new pews and pulpit furniture were installed. In 1975, the Sunday School rooms were constructed. In 1985, plastic siding was added to the exterior of the building. In 1988, a baptistry was installed. In 1991 a new roof was laid. Finally in 1999, the church purchased additional property from the sale of the Oil Springs School property under the direction of Rev. Joe Sublett. The additional property was necessary if the church was to expand at its present site. In addition to the church the property was occupied by a parsonage built in 1942 for $1,041 while building materials were scarce during WWII. The parsonage has housed the circuit ministers who served several other churches in the area including Rush Fork, Wells Chapel and Cannons Chapel.

However, no matter how well constructed a church is just an empty building without members. The founders like the Prater, Litterals, Staffords, Williams, Collins, Prices, Stapletons, Rices, Wards and many others must have received that wisdom from our Lord as many of their descendants remain as devout members. Mr. Mahan's descendants Betty Stafford and Mary Radcliffe are among the members who have belonged longest in this church. Other long serving members were the late Will Collins (who lived to over 100 years of age), Mrs. Virgie Williams, Mrs. Emma Stapleton Price, and Mrs. Parker West. Some were so noted for their Bible reading, witnessing, dedication to the church and community to such a degree like the Will Collins and Virgie Williams that the community adopted the Uncle and Aunt titles. Others like Mr. and Mrs. Harold Conley, Mr. and Mrs. Neil Price Sr. and Mr. and Mrs. Merle Pyles have given much time and devotion including the building of an assembly hall. Many like Ernestine Howard Rice, Cindy Blair, Catherine Sparks, Chris Fairchild, Mrs. Mary Lou Blanton, Mattie Craft Sublett, Viva Mae West Crace and Charlotte White Conley (the daughter of C.W. White, a former minister) have used their teaching skills to enhance the teaching of God's word. Others of God's family who made significant contributions to the ministry of the church include Mr. and Mrs. Harry Crace, Mr. and Mrs. Payne Rice, Mr. and Mrs. John Phillip Crace, Mr. and Mrs. Walter Stalker and family, Mrs. Brenda Cockerham and family, Mrs. Cathleen Trimble, Mr. and Mrs. Bob Stafford, Mr. and Mrs. Fed Conley and others too numerous to mention. To those members not mentioned, I sincerely apologize for a lack of memory but rest assured our Lord will not forget the service you gave.

Today's Oil Springs United Methodist Church provides the standard Sunday School classes at 10:00 a.m. every Sunday morning led by Mr. Walter Stalker, Sunday School Superintendent, who also organized a summer softball activity. Great church worship services held at 11:00 a.m. every Sunday morning are led by Rev. Joe Sublett who is extending his ample knowledge of the teachings of Jesus Christ at Asbury Seminary. Bible study is offered every Wednesday night at 7:00 p.m. led by Alice Rice Conley. A youth group is led by Mattie Craft Sublett. Choir is led by Jenny Robinson every Wednesday at 6:00 p.m. Mrs. Vicki Crace Rice compiles a monthly newsletter as an outreach to the community. There are many other outreach ministries to the community. One such effort is God's Pantry led by Mary Conley. God's Pantry helps feed those who fall upon hard times. Then there is my personal favorite outreach, church dinners. Maybe it's Ina Pyles' blueberry tort, Linda Hill's salad or any number of other cooks at our church but one thing you can be sure of is nowhere will you find better food.

Perhaps you can understand why the best way to describe the Oil Springs United Methodist Church is the little church that not only could but *did* God's will. You see, it may be the pearls of wisdom of Harold Conley, the kind words of Ida Stafford, the honesty of Viva Crace, the smile and handshake of Linda Collins, George Ward, Lois Ward or Ethel Colvin, or some small task no one ever notices but all make up our church family. That is why after over 100 years of faithful service the church continues to spread the love of our Lord who died on the cross for our sins.

Old Union Church and the United Baptists of Johnson County

by John Sparks

The story of Johnson County's oldest active religious congregation and the Community of Churches in Johnson County which sprang from it, actually begins in pre-Revolutionary times and many miles from the Eastern Kentucky mountains. In 1763 at Goshen Township in Orange County, NY a small Baptist church was organized under the leadership of Pastor James Benedist. The little congregation, which subsequently joined itself to Philadelphia Association, quickly prospered and among its regular attendants numbered the family of local landowners James and Abigail Wheeler. When the Wheelers and a large part of their family, including son Jesse and son-in-law and daughter Henry and Abigail Jayne, moved to the frontier of southwestern Virginia in the late 1780s to early 1790s, they brought their religious beliefs with them and the family actually appears to have influenced one northeastern Baptist minister, William Brundage, to pull up stakes and join them on the Virginia frontier. A New York native and Revolutionary soldier, Brundage had been connected with the King Street Baptist Church in nearby Fairfield, CT and he and the large Wheeler/Jayne family associated themselves with the St. Clair Bottom Baptist Church in present Smyth County, one of the oldest Baptist fellowships in that part of Virginia.

The Jaynes and Wheelers prospered in southwestern Virginia, with some of the younger family members marrying into the Ramey family in that region and one could wish that preacher William Brundage had prospered equally well. That, however, was not to be. Brundage had been raised up in the Philadelphia Association traditions of quiet, dignified worship, theological education and monetary compensation for services and his sudden exposure to the loud, emotional and earthly back-country Baptists of southwestern Virginia must have been quite a shock to him. The Virginia country Baptists, who had been bred in the "Separate Baptist" traditions and the loud, musical "New England Holy Tone" preaching cont of pioneer North Carolina ministers Shabal Stearns and Daniel Marshall must have appeared to Brundage as the antithesis of proper worship and he soon became embroiled in a bitter fight with the pastor of St. Clair's Bottom Church, Andrew Baker. As might be expected, separate "Brundage" and "Baker" factions soon had the congregation divided completely up, but the difficulty was solved for a time by the faction's mutual agreement to let Brundage and Baker preach on alternating weekends.

In a droll, rather charming bit of gossip to the famous Baptist historian Robert Baylor Semple, old Virginia preacher John Alderson related that this situation at St. Clair's Bottom continued until 1805, when Brundage and his faction moved north. And we Johnson Countians are eternally on debted to good old Alderson, whose gossip preserved just a bit of the circumstance under which William Jayne, Jesse and Stephen Wheeler and John Ramey and their families come to settle on the Big Sandy River near present Paintsville in that year and to organize their little Baptist church on the Wheeler property on Big Sandy River across from the Buffalo Shoal. The congregation which would come to be known as Old Union Church had been born.

For all his feistiness at St. Clair's Bottom, William Brundage appears not to have remained with his migrant friends very long; by 1807 he and his family had moved yet again, this time to Marion County, OH where they remained and where Brundage died at age 84 in 1825 and the "New England Holy Tone" preaching cont and the frontier religious customs he had eschewed, supplanted his influence. The little church on Big Sandy prospered rapidly, gaining members and congregants from among the nearby VanHoose, Preston, Mankins, Dorton, Picklesimer, Ward and Meek families and the groups found its next pastor about the year 1807 in a former Pennsylvania minister named Samuel Hanna. Originally having located in central Kentucky in the early 1790s Hanna had left the area due to trouble over conflicting land titles to settle in present Lawrence County, OH where he appears to have organized a church on the Ohio riverbank across from the mouth of Little Sandy. He still must have had a hankering to return to Kentucky though; when another minister, John Young settled on Little Sandy about 1804 or 1805, Hanna left the Ohio River Church in his care and proceeded to settle on State Road Fork of Licking River, then in Floyd County, where he subsequently began preaching work with the famous Daniel Williams. Despite the distance Hanna had to travel to the Big Sandy, he appears to have given the little church in his care faithful service and he eventually moved closer to it, a few miles away near the mouth of Miller's Creek. And though he, like William Brundage before him, finally moved away for good, settling first with some of his sons in Vernilion County, IL and later on the Arkansas frontier where he died in 1839 at the ripe old age of 83. Samuel Hanna's influence on the religious environment of this area was lasting.

Under Hanna's watch care the church raised up several ministers of its own, including such well-remembered names as Stephen and James Wheeler, Basil Lewis, Ezekiel Stone and Henry Dixon. As these younger preachers began to exercise their calling in company with Hanna, they rode an ever increasing circuit among the settlers of the Levisa and Tug Forks of Big Sandy and in accordance with the customs of the time. The church eventually established several other regular preaching places in addition to its home base near Paintsville. In time these "arms" of the congregation were organized as churches in their own right: Big Blaine in 1813 under the leadership of James Wheeler and Basil Lewis; George's Creek about 1817 under the care of Hanna; Rockcastle on the creek of the same name in present Martin County, in the early 1820s and Open Fork of Paint in present Morgan County, the products of the wide-ranging circuit of Henry Dixon; one named concord, at present Hager Hill, organized in 1823 under Hanna's leadership and which became the First Disciples of Christ congregation in present Johnson County during the so-called "Current Reformation" of 1827-1835; Bethel, located at Flat Gap, gathered in 1824; and later on Beechwall or Jenny's Creek and Fishtrap, organized in 1841 and 1843 respectively. These churches in turn grew and organized other congregations throughout Johnson County and thus Old Union Church may rightfully lay claim to being the "Mother Church" of nearly all both Baptists and Disciple or Church of Christ congregations in the county.

From early in its history Old Union Church has been associated with other congregations like-minded to it, first joining central Kentucky's North District Association in 1812. The messengers from the church to the association in that year, James Wheeler, Walter Mankins and William Meek, had to ride horseback more than 100 miles to represent their congregation at North District's 1812 session at Howard's Creek meeting house in Clark County. Shortly thereafter, though, the church joined with North District's other eastern Kentucky congregations to organize a new body, Burning Springs Association. Old Union Church, still known by the names either of "Buffalo Shoal" or "Paint" at this time, first hosted Burning Springs Association in 1816, at its new meeting house near the mouth of Big Paint Creek in the present Bridgeford area of Paintsville. On this occasion the church entertained as guest a rather famous, honored Virginia minister who had recently resettled in southern Ohio, John Lee. Lee was given the honor of preaching the first sermon of the association that year. Old Union Church remained a member of Burning Springs Association until 1837, hosting its last session of that association in 1836 and then joining the organization of newly-formed Union Association, which was named for the congregation. In 1840 the leaders of Union Association learned that there was another Union Association in Kentucky, so the group changed its name to Paint Union, which it still bears. Old Union Church, which by the time of the new association's organization had moved to its third meeting house on John Ramey's property near the mouth of Turner Branch, has since remained a consistent member of this body.

No one now really knows why before 1834 the church officially changed its name to "Union." Before that time it had been known by the location of its first and second meeting houses on Big Sandy across from the Buffalo Shoal and at the mouth of Big Paint Creek respectively. But a clue may be found in the 1820 minutes of Burning Springs Association wherein it was decided that the church should host an annual union meeting for the association every second weekend in May beginning in 1821. For that first 1821 meeting ministers Ambrose Jones, Daniel Duff, Simeon Justice and William Coffee were requested to come to the church and hold services and for many generations thereafter the "May Meeting" was maintained as a cherished tradition at the church although the old tradition has now been dropped. Over the years 1821-1834, the church simply may have been nicknamed "the Old Union meeting House" and the name stuck.

The associations to which Old Union Church belonged before 1837, North district and Burning Springs, were until about 1832-1835, members of the General Union of Kentucky Baptists which had brought regular and separate Baptists together in 1801 under the name of United Baptists. Though the General Union was state wide and nearly all Kentucky Baptist Churches were in fellowship with it through their association connections, it was a weak, loosely organized confederation extremely prone to splits and agitation by ambitious leaders who were skilled at manipulating mobs. The General Union suffered six splits in the first 25 years of its existence, some over doctrine and others over polity, but nearly all the result of bickering between powerful, ambitious men who commended docile followers. The seventh split, known then as the "Current Reformation" and alluded to earlier in this history, was the most disastrous and at its end most of the Baptists in Kentucky were desirous of a better organization and form of union that they had known under the old General Union. Consequently they formed the Kentucky Baptists Association in 1837, but North District and the other Eastern Kentucky Associations responded to the crisis in a different way. Meeting at Goshen Church in Clark County in 1830, North District Association established their code of conduct by the practices used by the Kentucky Baptists at the time of the formation of the General Union in 1801 and declared non-fellowship with all bodies which did not conform to the same standard. After a period of hesitation, Burning Spring Association followed suit in 1835. As did Paint Union when it was organized in 1837 as well as the various associations, Zion, Bethlehem, Mt. Zion, Blaine Union, Iron Hill and New Hope, which sprang from it. Most of the members of these groups no longer even know why they and their leaders praise "the old ways" so highly, but this historical circumstance was the actual reason.

Unfortunately, along with the tradition of "the old way" of the General Union, Old Union Church and its children have also maintained the tradition of splits. United Baptists, Primitive Baptists, Free Will Baptist, New Regular or "Enterprise" Baptists, some Southern Baptists and even Disciples of Christ and Church of Christ fellowships in Johnson County can all claim descent from Old Union Curch, but even among the several United Baptist Associations with churches in the county, only two very small groups maintain the old General Union-style correspondence: on faction of "Old" Paint Union Association which corresponds with the "Tri-State" Zion, "Union" Bethlehem and Iron Hill Associations and another faction of "Old" Paint Union which corresponds with Blaine Union Association. Even the faction of Paint Union Association to which Old Union Church presently belongs, known simply as Paint Union, declares non-fellowship with all other groups except itself. One wonders what the members of the Wheeler, Ramey, Jayne, VanHoose, Preston, Dorton, Picklesimer, Ward, Meek and other families who comprised the congregation of Old Union Church nearly 200 years ago would think. If they could have glimpsed into the future and seen the ups and downs to come perhaps, with characteristic frontier Calvinism and a wry backwoods sense of humor, they would have regarded some of the antics of their descendants as living proof of the depravity of man. Nonetheless, their hearts would be warmed by the knowledge that, as the presence of the little church of Route 40 at Staffordsville aptly indicates, in spite of the foible and antics of man, the faith in the Higher Power which they brought to this region, still lives on.

Thealka Freewill Baptist Church 1925-1999

The Thealka Freewill Baptist Church of Thealka, KY was established in 1935, primarily by brothers, Millard VanHoose and Dave Al Hayes. With Dave Al Hayes becoming the first pastor, 15 members were needed for a charter and they had 18. These are the recorded charter members: Sola Puckett, Millie Bowens, Milt and Grace Ratliff, Andrew and Lydia Lyons, Dora Preston, Foster and Rachel Burton, Jim and Callie Dale, Ambrose and Ellen Castle, Dewey, Pearl Lemaster.

According to the church historian, Mary Burton Rigsby, the church was built in the early 1920s by the North East Coal company for the Missionary Baptist Church, and was maintained by the company even paying their first pastors. They continued to pay their pastors until the great depression after which the church was used primarily for Sunday School, where most of the children of the community were taught their first Christian lessons by the family of Mr. and Mrs. Eugene B. Miller. After the Missionary Baptist membership declined, the church was offered as a gift to the Freewill Baptist through Foster Burton and R.C. Thomas a very influential person in the community and high official in the North East Coal Company. The building never to be used for anything except religious services. Some of the first officers of the church were the clerks: Ray Colvin being the first, Lizzie, Colvin, Roy Colvin, Jo Mills, Margaret Preston, Emogene Burton, Brenda Ratliff and Shawn Daniels.

The Deacons, Jim Dale, Ernest Dove, Bill Nichols, Bill Pack, Arnold Young, Foster, Burton, Roy Colvin, James Lyons, Johnny Castle, Clifford Burton, James Crider, Irvin Castle, Lacy Puckett, Paul Daniels, Luther Mills, Lonnie Blair, Dennis Blair, Everett Castle, George Conley, Ernest Taylor, Clarence Ratliff, Fr. Merri Preston.

The treasurers: Foster Burton, Johnny Castle, Clay Arnett, Lacy Puckett, Clifford Burton, Jeff Daniels and Merri Preston.

The Thealka Freewill Baptist has been blessed with many good pastors with brothers Don Fraley serving the longest (35 years), Dave Al Hays, Willie Horn, Al Castle, Filmore Gambill, Claude Preston, Charley Bailey, James Lyons, Kermit Preston, Scott Castle, Ervin Castle, Bob Lyons and Gary Blair.

God Blessed the old church with many hundred of souls being saved, under the preaching and teaching of brothers, Millard VanHoose, Scott Castle, Russell Kirk, Charles Isaac, Ted Green, Don Fraley, Charles Stapleton, James Lyons, Kermit Preston.

Between 1935 and 1959 two hundred and eleven souls were saved, since then at lest 100 more have been saved but not recorded in this church record.

In the early 1950s the old church building needed extensive repair and it was decided to build a new church. A new church was started in 1955 on the site we now occupy. Having very little money and needing financial help, a lot of the church was built with people buying only one block at a time.

The congregation moved into the new church before the floors were finished. Kermit Preston was the pastor; the word of God and the church progressed under his ministry with God's blessing many good things were accomplished in his name.

In 1950 the Ladies Auxiliary was organized. At this time it was called the Christian Charity Circle. Its goal was to promote missionary work. But the ladies have been and are a great asset to the church raising much money, through many endeavors. They were very instrumental in providing funds to build the new church.

The church tries to adhere and follow all the teaching and covenant of our faith. And the CTS has been a good part of teaching the young people in all aspects of God's word.

One part of our church that has had very positive influence in the community is the radio program for 35 years under the direction of Brother George Conley. Since its dedication to God in 1960 many good things have been added, new pews, piano, light fixtures, bathrooms. Bell-tower, carpet, new stove, refrigerator and cabinets.

In 1976 the outside of the building was bricked giving the beautiful appearance we see today. At this time the parking lot was paved and all these improvements were dedicated to God. This spring and summer 1999 God has blessed us to expand our basement for Sunday School and fellowship during our turn to host the conference.

During its 64 years the Thealka Freewill Baptist Church has shown alight in the darkness of sin and shelter from the storms of life, In this we give God the Glory.

The pews and chairs were rough and homemade. The only heat in the wintertime was a large pot bellied stove in front center of the church. In the summer the only relief from the heat was to open windows or personal hand fans usually furnished by the local funeral home.

There was a small table where a 10 quart water bucket set with a long handle dipper down the side. Everyone drank out of the same dipper. When some one needed to be baptized the little creek in front of the church was dammed up to form a pool deep enough to cover the saved in baptism.

The old church had a bell tower with a big bell with a very appealing sound. The bell was rung before each service by Uncle Bob Skeens and after his passing the honor was given to Uncle Jim Dale. Today in the new church brother Sanford "Shorty" Arms is the bell ringer, calling all the people to come to church.

THE PAINTSVILLE FUNERAL HOME

The Second Street of Paintsville has had many changes and also some constants. The Paintsville Funeral Home is one such business.

Lloyd H. and Julia A. Butler Preston bought out the Paintsville Funeral Home from Frank Conley July 1948. The funeral home was then housed in the Conley Furniture Company building which is now the Sturgill Furniture Company on Second Street. They stayed there until they bought the property located at 236 Second Street in the fall of 1954. In January 1955, they moved into the present home of the Paintsville Funeral Home after remodeling and during a big snow. The property was formerly owned by the Rule family and was built during the 1930s. During the big flood of Johnson County in 1957, the funeral home had approximately 10 inches of water in the first floor. Only quick thinking by Julia saved the new facility from mud and debris. She covered the floor furnaces and doorways with scatter rugs which filtered the back water.

At a time when women did not play a prominent role in the funeral industry, Julia began the tradition of "Lady Attendant" which has been a strong point of the Paintsville Funeral Home. Lloyd and Julia brought a special concept to the funeral home image, home and family. They believed in the family unit with the emphasis on the home and for many years all visitations were in the home. As the changes came it also affected the way family visitations were done. Families began moving their visitations to the funeral home and Lloyd and Julia stressed that concept by always suggesting that the families use the funeral home like they would their home. This tradition is still a vital part of the Paintsville Funeral Home.

In the early years, funeral homes in our area supplied our families with ambulance service. Lloyd saw a need for an outside entity to offer this service to the families. The Oil Springs Fire Department started the first ambulance service in this area with an ambulance donated to them by Lloyd. He felt that then and only then could the funeral homes eliminate that service to our area.

Along with Lloyd and Julia, their son, Russell started in the business in 1948. Jim Trimble worked for the Paintsville Funeral Home for many years and also served the area as coroner. Wendell Davis also was a part of the funeral home family for many years. A memorable figure at the funeral home was Gaius F., better known as "Tebe" Hampton. In 1963 Russell married Stella Vivian Rice who received her funeral director's license in 1968. Eugene Sturgill joined the staff in 1965 and his wife, Alberta, began working in 1967. Eugene got his funeral director's license in 1967 and is still an active member on staff. Larry Russell "Rusty" Preston, son of Russell and Stella, has been with the funeral home as an employee since 1985. In August 1995, Richard L. Childers joined the staff after graduating from Mid America College of Funeral Service. His wife, Almeta, also became part of the Paintsville Funeral Home family in June 1996. In the past 36 years, there have been several men who worked with the funeral home, Doug Hall, David Williamson, Lee Lemaster and Delano Cochran.

Lloyd died August 23, 1970, and Julie died February 29, 2000. Jim Trimble died in 1964 leaving the area with many stories to tell. Wendell and his wife, Ruth, moved to Ohio several years before his death. Tebe Hampton died June 27, 1999, closing a very colorful era of the Paintsville Funeral Home.

Currently the staff is Russell and Stella Preston, Richard and Almeta Childers, Eugene and Alberta Sturgill and Rusty Preston. They still maintain the quality of service and the homelike surroundings, with "Lady Attendant" a very important role in the day to day functioning of the funeral home.

The Paintsville Funeral Home has proudly served Johnson County since 1948, and still maintain that their service to families makes their HOME special. In the words of Julia Preston, "Come HOME to the Paintsville Funeral Home in your time of bereavement."

Paintsville United Baptist Church

On May 26, 1904, 16 members of various United Baptist congregations met for the purpose of organizing a United Baptist Church in Paintsville. As a result of that meeting, a committee composed of E.J. Harris, I.H. Rowland and Ransom Segraves was sent to area churches asking them to send their pastor and two of the brothers of the church to assist in organizing a new congregation. Those sent were Elder J. Powell Ferguson from the Bethel Church; Elder D. Grimsly from Blaine; Elder James Elliott; Elder A. Gibbs; Harry Vanhoose and James B. Preston from the Tom's Creek Church; Lick Springs Church sent Elder J.J. Prater; Friendship Church sent Elder William Honeycutt, Jesse Preston and John Butcher; Concord Church sent Elder Sam Preston, Mont Preston, U.S. Walters and James Davis.

The group met on Jun. 25, 1904 at 3:00 p.m. Elder E.J. Harris was elected its first moderator and T.S. Kirk was selected as Clerk. The first communion service was held at the church on Sunday, September 25, 1904.

Down through the years, the United Baptist Church of Paintsville has been led by a long list of the town's businessmen. They include C.C. Preston, W.L. Preston, Arthur Green, Lafe Walters, Sherman Wheeler, Guy W. Preston, McKinley Baldwin, F.F. Rigsby, Roscoe Lemaster, Lawrence Daniels and William Johnson, to name a few.

For a number of years the church property located at the corner of Second and Church streets was shared with both the Missionary Baptists and the Freewill Baptists.

In 1906 the Missionary Baptists sold their interest in the property for $500. In 1925 the local Freewill Baptist Congregation sold their interest to the United Baptists for $1,500. Twenty years later a new building was built on the site which today houses the Paintsville United Baptist Church. It is a congregation which will soon be 96 years young.

Pastors

John R. Pelphrey	1981-present
O.I. Williams	1963-1980
Charles Price	1978-1980
Foster Rigsby	1940-1969
Guy W. Preston	1929-1940
Roscoe Lemaster	1935-
Lafe Walters	1922-1928
Arthur Green	1920-1921
W.L. Preston	1918-1920
Ali Ward	1913-1915
J. Powell Ferguson	1907-1912
T.J. Collins	1906
E.J. Harris	1904-1906

Tom's Creek Free Will Baptist Church

Established 1876

Tom's Creek Free Will Baptist Church was the first Free Will Baptist Church in Johnson County and is the oldest continuing Free Will Baptist Church in Kentucky. The church was established on June 22, 1876, near the mouth of Sycamore Creek under a large oak tree, because a small group of Christians in the Mouth of Rush Community were dissatisfied with the United Baptist doctrine. A Free Will Baptist Church in Ohio whose beliefs were similar to theirs was contacted and Rev. William Calhoun was sent to help organize a church. Rev. Thomas S. Williams was the first pastor with Eliphas VanHoose as clerk.

The first church roll book did not record the date that members joined, but the first 25 members listed are T.S.Williams, Malissa Williams, E.P. VanHoose, Freelove VanHoose, Jasper Daniels, Rejoina Daniels, Marcum Castle, Catharine Castle, Nancy Castle, Martha Stambaugh, Susan Meadows, Levi Mead, Nancy Mead, Frederick Scarberry, Henry Scarberry, Sarah Wily, Lucinda Castle, Lois Ward, William Witten, Mary Daniels, James Dills, Sarah Daniels, Hanah Castle, Mary Castle and John Castle.

The first building was built of logs and served as a house of worship until about 1915. July 2, 1877 a deed was secured from George and Mary Daniels for a tract of land that was to extend for 2 feet on each side of this log building. The deed was made to the trustees of the Free Will, Missionary and United Baptist churches and their descendants. The United Baptists were to have the first and second weekends, the Missionary Baptists were to have the third weekend and the Free Will Baptists the fourth weekend. Small additions of real estate were donated or purchased as they became available until a total of six different deeds were acquired encompassing the land the church currently owns.

Over the years, through dedication and faithfulness to the teachings of the Holy Bible, the people of this church and community have seen Tom's Creek grow from a membership of 15 or 20 to a regular attendance of several hundred. As attendance increased, new buildings were built to accommodate the growing congregation. The present building was built in 1976 with the old sanctuary converted to a kitchen and fellowship hall. Classrooms were added in 1981 and the sanctuary enlarged in 1988.

First Pastor, Thomas S. Williams

The oldest existing Free Will Baptist Church in Kentucky, Tom's Creek has been instrumental in the establishment of numerous churches throughout the state. The Tom's Creek FWB Church also played a large role in establishing the Johnson County, Kentucky State and National Associations of Freewill Baptists.

The Johnson County Quarterly Meeting was organized in about 1879. The churches joining at that time were Tom's Creek, Hager Hill and Little Blaine (now Spencer). Tom's Creek hosted the first Kentucky State Association meeting on May 6, 1939. Rev. Millard VanHoose from Tom's Creek was the first moderator of the State Association and was a delegate to help organize the National Association of Free Will Baptists in Nashville, TN at the Coffers Chapel Church on November 5, 1935.

"Through the years this church has been blessed with faithful, God-fearing, dedicated men and women. Many sacrifices were made by these early pioneers that we might comfortably worship in this church. We thank the Lord that we are able by his mercy and grace to walk in the footsteps of our forefathers and to build on the same foundation with Christ being the chief cornerstone. May we continue to be part of the great commission; offering a living Christ to a dying world."

Pastors

Thomas S. Williams	1876-1891
James Lee VanHoose	1892-1893, Sep. 1912-Sep. 1913
H.B. (Burns) Conley	Sep. 1893-Jan. 1912, Sep. 1914-Feb. 1941
John Elliot Conley	Jan. 1912-Aug. 1912
W. Williams	Sep. 1913-Sep. 1914
Millard VanHoose	Feb. 1941-Jun. 1952, Sep. 1963-Sep. 1972
Nathan P. VanHoose	Jun. 1952-Jan. 1953
C.C. (Chick) Hall	Jan. 1953-Sep. 1962
Claude Preston	Sep. 1962-Sep. 1963, Sep. 1972-Sep. 1973
James Kelly Caudill	Sep. 1973-

Castle's Jewelry and Gifts, Inc.

In 1937, Clarence Castle opened a modest watch repair and jewelry store at the corner on Main and Church Streets in Paintsville. It was not the best time to launch a new business venture. America and Eastern Kentucky were still in the throes of the Great Depression.

One year (and six months of advertising) later, Clarence Castle moved Castle's Jewelry to a more visible location on College Street, now occupied by Baldridge Barber Shop.

Clarence and Cynthia Castle were in the jewelry business to stay. Today, 63 years later, Danny and Barbara Castle Pugh and their sons, Douglas, Darrell and David have the same commitment.

Thanks to the support of valued customers in every county in Eastern Kentucky and some in West Virginia, Castle's Jewelry has grown from a small watch repair shop to one of the most respected and reliable jewelry and gift shops in Eastern Kentucky.

After the death of Clarence in 1973, Barbara and Danny and family returned to Paintsville where their parents and grandparents had an important part of the business, social and civic community. Now their sons are assuming their own place in the future of Eastern Kentucky and in the future of Castle's Jewelry and Gifts.

Castle's Jewelry and Gifts now have a total of four locations: Prestonsburg Village, Prestonsburg, KY; Weddington Square, Pikeville, KY, and recently opened their fourth store at the South Side Mall, South Williamson, KY.

Castle's does jewelry repair and custom design work at all locations.

Johnson County Retired Teachers Association

The Johnson County Retired Teachers Association was organized in the 1970s when Johnson County's retired teachers became aware of the need for a local chapter. Its main purpose is to look out for the welfare of retired teachers, locally and statewide.

On Sep. 25, 1990, a scholarship fund was established with an initial bequest from the Vern P. Horne estate. Currently the scholarship fund accepts donations from not only retired educators, but the general public. Donations may be sent to Harold L. Preston, 7632 KY East Rt. 40, Williamsport, KY 41271.

The Johnson County Retired Teachers Association welcomes all retired teachers.

Citizens National Bank

Citizens National Bank was chartered on February 14, 1910 and first opened its doors for business on February 16, 1910. The frame building was located on Main Street in Paintsville, KY, and was originally named the Paintsville Bank and Trust Company. James W. Auxier, John E. Buckingham, Dr. J.H. Holbrook, A.J. Kirk, John C.C. Mayo, J.L. Patterson, George W. Preston, H.B. Rice, H.M. Stafford, John W. Wheeler and Dr. F.M. Williams were the charter Directors of the bank. H.M. Stafford served as the first president of the bank until 1919 along with H.B. Rice acting as the first cashier until 1915. Rice was succeeded as cashier by J.A. Williams from 1915 until 1919. That same year, Stafford was followed as president by H.S. Howes and Claude Buckingham began as cashier. In 1917, the building now standing on Main Street was erected and sits just 50 feet from the site of the original building.

The Paintsville Bank and Trust Company changed stockholders on July 1, 1922 and the new directors were W.B. Bailey, W.H. Conley, G.V. Daniel, R.A. Patrick, G.H. Rice, C.T. Rule and W.S. Wheeler. Ray Turner acted as cashier from 1922 until 1925, when he was replaced by D.H. Dorton Sr. Not only was C.T. Rule a director, but he also officiated as president beginning in 1924.

After 17 successful years, on January 3, 1927, Paintsville Bank and Trust Company became a national bank and was named The Second National Bank of Paintsville. In 1930 J.B. Wells Sr. began serving as president. Fred Howes became the first chairman of the board of directors in 1934.

The Second National Bank of Paintsville emerged as the principal bank in Johnson County and was completely remodeled in 1940. D.H. Dorton Sr. was replaced as cashier by his son, O.T. Dorton, in 1949. D.H. Dorton Sr. became president of the institution in 1958 in which capacity he served until 1963. Also in 1958, G.H. Rice became chairman of the board of directors and that same year, W.G. Bailey began as cashier. Since the Second National Bank of Paintsville was second to none and the oldest continuously operating bank in Paintsville, on June 30, 1959, they changed their name to Citizens National Bank of Paintsville.

Although the Main Office remained on Main Street, the second branch of Citizens National Bank was opened in Paintsville on February 15, 1960. It was known as The Motor Bank Branch and was located at the corner of Broadway and 10th Street at Stafford Addition. It was a convenient location of the bank because it was the first branch equipped with a drive-thru window for motorists. The Main Street location was once again remodeled in 1963. It received a new front and a complete addition was built on the building.

In 1964, O.T. Dorton succeeded his father as president and H.L. Mayo Jr. became cashier. Citizens National Bank purchased six lots adjacent to the Motor Bank Branch location and the Family Banking Center opened for business on March 29, 1971. W.G. Bailey once again served as cashier in 1971, but was replaced in 1972 by O.T. Dorton's son, Dennis T. Dorton. In 1976, the bank on Main Street was once again remodeled and redecorated and T.C. Meade replaced Mr. Rice as chairman of the board of directors. Growing at a rapid pace to meet the needs of Johnson County, the Mayo Plaza Branch location opened on Nov. 15, 1978 at the Mayo Plaza Shopping Center in Paintsville. Soon after, on August 7, 1982, the Village Plaza Branch in the Village Plaza in Paintsville was opened.

Later in the year, Citizens National Corporation, a holding company, was incorporated under the laws of Kentucky for the purpose of becoming the bank holding company for Citizens National Bank. Charles Patton became cashier in 1983 and Dennis Dorton replaced his father as president in 1986, becoming the third generation of Dortons to operate the bank.

On December 11, 1985, Citizens National Corporation sold two million dollars of Industrial Revenue Bonds for the purpose of constructing a new four story building adjacent to the Family Banking Center to serve as the new Main Office. The ground breaking ceremonies were held on June 17, 1986 and on January 17, 1988, the new Main Office was officially opened. Soon after the relocation of the Main Office from Main Street to the new building on Broadway, the Motor Branch was torn down.

In 1990, O.T. Dorton became chairman of the board of directors. He was followed by W.G. Bailey in 1994. Most recently, Charles Wells became chairman of the board of directors in 1996.

In October 1997, Citizens National Corporation purchased the Bank Josephine in Floyd County. This purchase made Citizens National Corporation the second largest bank holding company in the Big Sandy Area. As part of the expansion plan, the Bank Josephine opened a branch on March 1, 1999 in Salyersville in Magoffin County. The Corporation merged the two banks into one entity under the name Citizens National Bank on May 26, 1999. A new facility was built in Floyd County and the location on 8 Front Street in downtown Prestonsburg was moved to its new location at CentrePointe on September 7, 1999. The Salyersville location moved from its temporary location to its new facility on October 18, 1999. Presently, the board of directors consists of Paul D. Brown, Larry G. Conley, Robin Cooper, Dennis T. Dorton, L. Barfett Frederick, Bob Hutchison, Greg Meade, Lynn D. Mullins, Harold D. Ward and Charles Wells, chairman. Citizens National Bank currently serves three counties, including Floyd, Johnson and Magoffin counties with 11 locations.

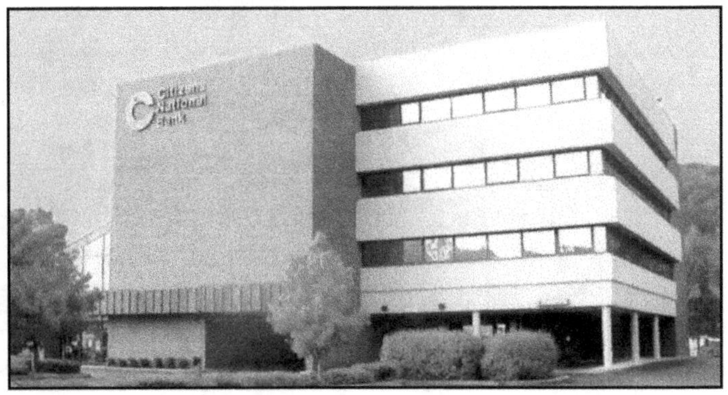

First National Bank of Paintsville

Now Classic Bank

A Century of Tradition

By 1902, Paintsville was a bustling town with nearly a thousand residents. For over a century people had conducted their business by using the barter system, trading livestock, homemade goods, dairy products an other handy items in exchange for what they needed. Because there was no banking facility nearby, a trip to Cincinnati or West Virginia was necessary if someone needed gold or silver.

Fortunately, the dawn of the new century brought with it a new prosperity for Eastern Kentucky. The Big Sandy coal industry was beginning to boom, and with the advent of a national railroad system making travel easier than ever, new residents made Paintsville and the surrounding villages their homes in unprecedented numbers. The need for a local banking system quickly became obvious.

On Mar. 17, 1902, the Paintsville National Bank opened its doors with Dan Davis at the helm as president and a capital investment of only $25,000. Founded by Davis, I.R. Turner, John C.C. Mayo, Daniel M. Hager, John H. Preston, James D. Johnson, John E. Buckingham and F.M. Williams, the fledgling bank relied on commitments Mayo had extracted from business connections in Baltimore and Pittsburgh for survival.

Its founders possessed uncanny business savvy and aligned themselves with up-and-coming rail and coal companies. Within 10 years, the bank's capital had increased nearly tenfold to $200,00 and the bank itself had earned the nickname "Old Reliable."

Business at Paintsville National Bank continued to flourish until the Great Depression hit America and the world like a sledgehammer. Even the great Appalachians couldn't shield Paintsville from the blow. From 1929 till 1933, loans were defaulted in ever-increasing numbers. On Mar. 6, 1933, President Franklin D. Roosevelt declared a bank holiday, closing the nation's banks for three days. Paintsville National Bank never reopened.

Six months later, through the diligence of residents like James W. Turner and Harry Davis, First National Bank of Paintsville was chartered and installed in the original building at the corner of Main and Mill streets. That building still stands today, the only example of Romanesque Revival Architecture in the city, and First National Bank still provides comprehensive banking services to Eastern Kentucky businesses and residents.

True to its Johnson County roots, First National Bank is run and staffed by local people today, just as it was at the turn of the last century. While much of its operations are housed at the original Main Street location, another full-service branch is now found on South Mayo Trail. First National is an independently-run member of the Classic Bancshares of Ashland family, providing customers with both its long-standing tradition of small-town service and the benefits of a regional banking network with state-of-the-art conveniences such as internet banking and debit cards.

Jenny Wiley Association

Descendants of Jenny Wiley and Hezekiah Sellards
Founded 1995

Jenny Wiley Association
P.O. Box 217
Auxier, KY 41602-0217
(606) 886-2865

The Jenny Wiley Association was formed October 1995 at Prestonsburg, KY during the Jenny Wiley Festival in order to represent descendants of Jenny Wiley.

We wish to help promote a better understanding of the Jenny Wiley Heritage, and let people know that our ancestor was a real live person who lived here, walked these roads and streams, and raised her family here.

Statistical information from Clayton Cox's *Appalachian Crossroads*, published in 1977, lists 27,938 descendants with 2,436 surnames. These people are known to have been born in most of the 50 states and many provinces of Canada, as well as many foreign countries.

Society Goals

To collect, preserve and share genealogical, biographical and historical data regarding our ancestor Jenny Wiley and her ancestors, the Hezekiah Sellards family

To encourage a greater understanding and appreciation of our common heritage

To provide a means for family members to become better acquainted and to keep in touch with each other.

Officers

President
Jim Daniels
P.O. Box 217
Auxier, KY 41602

Vice President
Betty Hazelett
319 F.M. Stafford Ave.
Paintsville, KY

Secretary
Russell L. Whitlock
28 10 Central Ave.
Ashland, KY

Treasurer
Brenda McKenzie
P.O. Box 57
Auxier, KY 41602

Board of Directors
Bertha Daniels
Proctor Conley
Robert Ewing
Jim Daniels

Charter Members

Betty Hazelett
Robert E. Small
Virginia E. (Jenny) West
Russell L. Whitlock
Ed Hazelett
Bertha Daniels
Madge Jennings
Brenda Wilson McKenzie
Barbara A. Wilson
Elba J. McClellan
Milicent Pritchard
Olive Smith Stone
Howard Stone
Elbie Prichard
Angela Pritchard
Ruth Alice Webb
Stephen Wiley
Wendell House
Emmagene McComas House
Robert Kalich
Clarence E. Wiley
Sharon Murrell
Lorene H. Wright
Bessie Adkins
Alex Buncy
Pamela Dee Doan
Karen Anderson
Shanna Gabrielle Anderson
Donna L. Baldwin
Callie Smith
Thelma Buncy
John W. Wiley
Juanita Fern Powell
Ray Wiley
Jewell W. Tussey
Cheryl Tussey Shepherd
Phyllis Wiley Conley
Aileen Sellards Hall
Alice Howard
Roberta W. Dixon
Kenneth Deboard
Delmas Saunders
Dorothy Tulla
Alberta Lyons Buckley
Rhoda Ramey
Betsy Jackson
Helen Welch
Marshall Welch
Helen Lynn Kassar
Virginia Edgel
V.M. Gott
Don Childers
Suzanne Childers
Jacob Earl Webb
Opal V. Morris
Geraldine Blankenship
Annette Kalich
Dottie Blankenship
Myrtie Bromley
Richard Bromley
Jennifer Lynn Brown
Emilie F. Lowe
Lisa R. Vinson Arvanitis
Elena M. Chafin
Carol Price
Helen Lynn Pavlik

Jones-Preston Funeral Home

Jones-Preston Funeral Home, formerly known as Jones Funeral Home, was founded by John Alfred Jones (b. January 13, 1885, d. January 18, 1952). John A., "One-Eared Jones" to all that knew him, came to the Paintsville area as an employee of Northeast Coal Company in 1914. In 1917, he became manager of Northeast Coal Company Commissary located at Auxier, KY. "One-Eared Jones" lost his ear as a result of an accident with a section cart on the railroad as a teenager.

As a consequence of the great flu epidemic of 1918, Mr. Jones saw a great need for personalized funeral care in the surrounding area. Somewhere around 1921, Mr. Jones left Auxier and came to Paintsville where he was associated with a group of local businessmen in the Paintsville Furniture and Funeral Company, becoming a licensed undertaker in 1925.

In 1941, at the age of 58, Mr. Jones left Paintsville Furniture and Funeral Company, located in the lower east end of Second Street in the building presently occupied by Sturgill Furniture Company. He then moved to Main Street and opened his own undertaking establishment under the name of Jones Funeral Home where he was assisted by his sons. Located beside the present First Methodist Church on Main Street, business operations continued until his untimely death in January 1952.

One of his sons, Edwin H. "Pinky" Jones followed in his fathers tradition and became operator of the Jones Funeral Home. In July 1948, a man by the name of James Richard Preston started in the funeral business and in June 1951 became a licensed funeral director and embalmer. In December 1951, his country called and he left for Korea where he stayed until June 1953, during which time John A. Jones died of cancer at the age of 68 at his home.

The funeral home continued operations under the supervision of the Jones family until February 1954 at which time the name of the funeral home became what today is known as Jones-Preston Funeral Home, Inc. The business continued on Main Street until December 1956 when the funeral home moved locations to the corner of Church and 2nd streets in Paintsville. In January 1957, the great flood destroyed the funeral home which they had just opened, so construction was started again. This operation stayed at this location until June 1972 at which time James R. Preston and Pinky Jones saw the need to increase the size of the funeral home. They constructed the first building that was built for a funeral home in Eastern Kentucky. This location which is to this day the location of the existing funeral home at the corner of 11th Street and Old U.S. 23 South in Paintsville, KY.

Only after two years at the new facility, Edwin H. "Pinky" Jones passed away at the age of 67 in August 1974.

After the death of her husband, Mrs. Sara Jones retained her husband's interest in the business with James R. Preston, along with three other licensed funeral directors: Dick Vanhoose, Bill Phelps and Bryan Fraley. In 1987 Bryan Fraley left the business, Bill Phelps retired in April 1988 and Dick Vanhoose is still with the funeral home.

In December 1983, following in his father's footsteps, James Andrew Preston began his career in the funeral business and to date is the present operator.

James R. Preston now has over 52 years in the funeral business and has the distinction of being the oldest and longest active funeral home director in Johnson and surrounding counties.

Jones-Preston Funeral Home has been a family owned and operated funeral home from their beginning on Main Street in 1942 through the present time.

Anna D. Melvin

Anna D. Melvin was the first woman elected to the office of Commonwealth's Attorney in the 24th Circuit. During her term in office, many successful programs were initiated.

When she began her service in 1994, the Office of Commonwealth's Attorney was a part-time position. And in 1997, after working closely with the Attorney General's Office and other Commonwealth Attorney's throughout the state, her office acquired full-time status, thereby assuring the people of the 24th Circuit a full-time prosecutor.

In 1994, Ms. Melvin began a voluntary multidisciplinary team to review and assess child physical and sexual abuse reports. The following year, Kentucky law mandated that all circuits convene a child sexual abuse multidisciplinary team to begin in January 1997. With this team in place, Ms. Melvin wrote a grant to employ a Crime Victim Advocate to work with victims of violent crime with a focus on child sexual abuse cases. That same year, Ms. Melvin asked the team to adopt a Growing Up Safe Protocol which involved members of the community in an educational effort to make the public aware of the issues surrounding child abuse. This grassroots endeavor was implemented in all three counties in the 24th Circuit and has grown into a highly recognized, non-profit organization.

Because of the high volume of child abuse cases, Ms. Melvin wrote and received a grant in 1996 from the Child Victim's Trust Fund to hire a Prevention/Education Specialist. This specialist was responsible for implementing a Child Assault Prevention Program in every grade school K-5 in the 24th Circuit. This program empowers children with skills to protect themselves in situations involving bullies, strangers and sexual assault. It also teaches basic self-defense techniques while teaching children conflict resolution and self-esteem.

Being a firm believer that early childhood prevention is the key to safer communities and that education is power, Ms. Melvin wrote yet another grant in 1997, from the Justice Cabinet for a Domestic Violence Advocate for Martin and Lawrence counties and instituted a Domestic Task Force for the circuit.

Ms. Melvin worked to form a non-profit advocacy center for child sexual abuse and adult sexual assault. Hope's Place opened its doors Oct. 17, 1998, and serves Lawrence County along with Boyd, Elliott, Greenup, Lewis and Carter. It is the first rural child advocacy center of its kind in the United States. Ms. Melvin is currently on the board of the center located in Ashland, KY.

In 1998, Ms. Melvin formed the D.A.T.A. (drug, alcohol, awareness, tobacco) Group. This voluntary group consists of individuals throughout the community who are interested in educating young children about the harmful effects of drugs and the problems associated with their use. Then in 1999, Ms. Melvin and her group acquired a Rotary International grant to form a theatrical troupe of young people to perform drug awareness vignettes throughout the Johnson County schools. The play won statewide recognition and received the Dorothy G. Mullen Arts and Humanities Award for 4th class cities.

During Ms. Melvin's term, the 24th Circuit presented its first capital murder case in 50 years, and successfully prosecuted its first case of welfare fraud in 30 years.

Ms. Melvin received her BA from the University of Kentucky in 1973. She also received an Elementary Education Certificate from Pikeville College in 1985 and a BS in Vocational Home Economics and a MA in Elementary Education from Morehead State University in 1985. She graduated from the University of Kentucky School of Law in 1988. She served as Johnson County Assistant County Attorney from 1990-1992, and entered private practice in 1993. She is active in local Republican Clubs and is a member of the First United Methodist Church where she serves as chair of the administrative board. Ms. Melvin is also very active in her community where she serves on boards for Mountain Comprehensive Care, the Big Sandy Chapter of the American Red Cross, Growing Up Safe, Hope's Place and the Rotary Club. Ms. Melvin is also a member of the Phi Beta Kappa Sorority, the Weslleyan Guild, Phi Alpha Delta-Clay Chapter, the Kentucky Bar Association, the National Association of District Attorneys, State Board for Domestic Violence, and the American Trial Lawyers Association. Melvin resides in Paintsville with her husband, Charles T. Melvin Jr., and is the mother of three children.

Paintsville Gas & Water

As early as 1924 plans were being made for Public water lines to all the homes in Paintsville, Mayor Jim Meek purchased the land from C&O Railroad in 1924 which is still the location of the water plant today. The city's plan called for drilling several wells around the city, placing the storage tanks on top of the hills to assure good water pressure, but later decided it was more economical to draw water from the Levisa Fork of the Big Sandy River.

By 1925, an eight inch line was being laid up Euclid Avenue, up Second Street and to Court Street and from there to the top of the hill to the storage tank behind Mayo Mansion.

The city purchased the Gas & Water Company from the Public Gas & Water Company of Ashland, KY.

Cy Cooper was the first superintendent serving from July 1, 1927 till September 1, 1940 with Public Gas & Water and from September 1, 1940 through March 1, 1964 for the City of Paintsville.

B.W. Cox was chairman.

D.H. Dorton was secretary/treasurer.

Herman Wheeler served as superintendent from January 1, 1964 through August 14, 1965, followed by Sidney B. Garland from August 14, 1965 through March 5, 1984.

James D. Hopson was appointed superintendent January 1986 through November 1996.

Gary Sellers served from December 1, 1996 through October 1998.

Larry Herald was appointed superintendent/general manager October 20, 1998 through the present.

The first office was located on Main Street in the building now occupied by Enchanted World Tours, later moving into the building which is now Paintsville Floral. After being purchased by the city the office was moved to city hall until the new office at 137 Main Street was completed February 1, 1997. Paintsville Utilities now serves 2,069 gas customers, 6,188 water customers and 1,700 sewer customers in Johnson, parts of Floyd and Lawrence counties, and hopefully Morgan County in the near future.

We are presently installing new water lines in the Jenny's Creek area and plan to expand the gas lines. A new waste water treatment plant at Johns Creek serving the new prison, Auxier, West Van Lear, and later the Van Lear area is planned for the future as well as a new water treatment plant at the Paintsville Lake area.

Paintsville Utilities Office, September 1, 1940 through February 1, 1997.

New building occupied February 1, 1997.

Paintsville Rotary Club

In 1999, the Paintsville Rotary Club celebrated its 77th Anniversary of following the Four Way Test of Rotary. Since the Ashland Rotary Club conducted our charter meeting June 1922, the Paintsville-Van Lear Rotary Club has contributed to the primary goal of Rotary International, stamping out polio, as well as playing a large part in the business and professional community locally.

It should be noted that a Paintsville native, John E. Buckingham, was in large measure responsible for the impetus resulting in the Paintsville-Van Lear Rotary Club. Buckingham had moved from Paintsville to Ashland and became a Rotarian there. He had three other Ashland members present for the charter night activities: Tim Fields, Walter Mayo and Ben Forgey. The name was changed to the Paintsville Rotary Club June 1, 1931 and the membership boundaries extended to all of Johnson County.

Indeed, the list of past presidents of the Paintsville Rotary Club and the Paintsville-Van Lear Rotary Club as we were initially chartered, reads like a litany of those who were in the forefront of every progressive movement which has made other cities and towns envious of our city and county.

From banking to insurance, law, religion, education, medicine, commerce and government...no beneficial field of endeavor has not been represented in the pantheon of members of the Paintsville Rotary Club.

Paintsville Rotary worked very hard for Mayo State Vocational-Technical School, city park and playground, Combs Field, Big Sandy Regional Airport, Dewey Dam and Paintsville Lake, American Standard, Kentucky Apple Festival, Paintsville Country Club, Johnson County Library, Depot Road, paving the missing link in Mayo Trail in 1947 and a host of other projects which could be named.

People projects include honor student luncheons for Paintsville and Johnson Central, Project Prom, supporting the Salvation Army, Boy Scouts, senior citizens, GUS, youth baseball and the children's clothing drive at Christmas. One of our most recent projects hand been participating in the American Cancer Society's Relay for Life, which we have also hosted for the past two years.

One of the Rotary's first community projects was to assist in the development and partial financing of the Rule Hole on Main Street. For many years, Rotarians held their weekly meetings in this hotel's dining room.

Paintsville Rotary Club concentrated on transportation for its first 25 years. Rotarians traveled to Frankfort, Pikeville and Ashland to support a better highway and still do. In 1947, the final section for the Mayo Trail at Lowmansville was finally completed.

There was fun and laughter along the way. There were baseball games against Kiwanis. We won some and lost some. They began in 1925. When raising money for the city's park and playground, Bill Bailey pushed a peanut down Main Street with his nose and Trigg Dorton got a cream pie in his face. Irvin Arrowood pushed Joe Radcliffe in a wheelbarrow. No one can forget the pancake day when William Johnson turned the mixer on without a cover and covered everyone and everything with batter.

Other events of historical note were the election of Paintsville Rotarian Luther Safriet as District Governor of Rotary in 1972, our 50th anniversary year, and the admission in August 1990 of Pat Patton as the first woman admitted to membership in the Paintsville Rotary Club. Pat was president in 1994.

Speaking of past presidents, at least two men are in competition as the youngest president, Henry Holbrook at 23 and John Edd Redd. At least four past presidents served two terms: Henry Holbrook, Henry Lewis Mayo, Joe Howard VanHoose and Bill Gibson. Three brother combinations were president: Paul B. and Lon Hall, Larry and Joe Brown, and Perk and Bill Bailey.

Currently we have four individuals, Dave Dorton, W.B. Bailey, F.S. VanHoose and Sidney B. Garland, named Paul Harris Fellows which represents a significant contribution to the Rotary Foundation. Sid also holds the current record for perfect attendance, 37 years.

When speaking about the Paintsville and Johnson County area, it may have survived and even thrived without Rotary the past 77 years...but we doubt it. Rotary's motto and influence is and always has been "Service above Self."

Paintsville Rotary Club, 1999.

Ramada Inn
Carriage House Hotel

An entourage of architects and dreamers left the mountains of Eastern Kentucky to search for a model that would match the dream that Blake and Bonnie Ratliff held for a new modern hotel to be constructed in Paintsville. The delegation's journey led them into the heart of the Louisiana Bayous in New Orleans. Here they meticulously searched the French Quarter for a protégé of what was to become known as the Carriage House Hotel.

In the heart of Louisiana, one particular establishment caught the eyes of the delegates. The group returned to the mountains with notes and ideas on paper. Shortly after returning to Paintsville, the group removed the first shovel full of sandy dirt from the banks of Paint Creek. Following years of arduous labor and countless hours, the hotel that Blake and Bonnie Ratliff dreamed of became a reality on December 2, 1981 with the grand opening of the Carriage House Hotel and Restaurant.

The new 160-room facility was an instant hit. The towering wrought iron balconies, inviting French doors, spacious garden atrium, tropical indoor/outdoor swimming complex and bubbling indoor fountain captured the mystique of France and placed it into the heart of the Appalachian Mountains within the confines of the hotel walls. Soon the large meeting rooms were filled to capacity with hundreds of convention goers and the glass-adorned elevators were carrying hundreds of guests to their sleeping quarters.

Blake and Bonnie Ratliff were owners of the hotel from December 2, 1981 to March 25, 1993. During this time the Ratliffs saw many changes. A year into the hospitality industry world, renowned franchises began to take notice of the new modern facility. The Holiday Inn began negotiations with the owners that would eventually fall through. The Carriage House would retain its name.

On March 25, 1993, after 12 years in the hotel business, Bonnie and Blake Ratliff sold the facility to Kay Booth. During the ownership of Kay Booth, the hotel underwent major renovations that would bring a whole new spirit to the hotel.

On September 29, 1997, a prominent businessman from Cynthiana, KY, and a Paintsville native, James A. Brown, acquired the hotel. He quickly began a complete renovation. On November 1, 1998, a milestone was reached in the history of the Carriage House Hotel. After 18 years, the Carriage House name was removed from the hotel, and the nation's largest franchise, the Ramada Inn, flew their flag over the skyline of Paintsville. Shortly following the acquisition of the Ramada franchise license, the hotel was awarded the "Gold Key Award" in 1999, indicating the facility to be one of the premiere hotels in Eastern Kentucky.

Under the years of the experienced leadership of Darl Music, general manager, the hotel has assured itself a place in the new millennium as one of the prime facilities of the industry. The hotel has far surpassed the threshold for hotel technology, employed a staff that serves guests with southern hospitality, and with the continued renovations the Ramada Inn will continue to fly the flag of success for years to come.

Words N' Stuff
Eastern Kentucky's Regional Bookstore

Located near the railroad's crossing of the Levis Fork of the Big Sandy River and adjacent to the site of the Van Lear Power Plant of the early 20th century, Words N' Stuff is continuing the effect of the site. While the power plant provided electricity for the homes of Van Lear, Van Lear Junction and Paintsville, it also provided power for the mines in the Van Lear seam of coal helping to rip thousands of tons annually from the hills surrounding Millers Creek.

The railroad bridge is now gone, the Van Lear seam is no longer mined in Van Lear and the power plant is no more. Electricity is imported on heavy wires from miles away. We still need the jobs that were with the railroad and the coal mining but they are gone nonetheless. The only electricity produced in Van Lear comes from the lightning that burns out our televisions.

Words N' Stuff is using the power plant site to distribute books to the region that received electricity produced here years ago. While the power of the books was not produced on site many were produced in the county and the region by some of the outstanding residents of our valley. Words N' Stuff's clientele is not limited to the immediate vicinity as was the power plant's. Some of our customers have come from the European and Asian continents and all parts of North America. Our product line has come from the ages and all parts of the world. We are honored that young minds have been enlightened by the product we sell.

We salute the historical society in the publication of this book and hope to add it to our ever increasing product line.

Visit us at the intersection of KY 302 and KY 1107, call us at 606-789-3592 or write us at P.O. Box 712, West Van Lear, KY 41268

Sawmill on Richmond Farm now Richmond Village, Route 40 E.

Foothills Rural Telephone Cooperative Corp., Inc.

Until the early 1950s, citizens of the rural areas of Johnson, Lawrence and Magoffin counties did not have a modern telephone system. Due to the foresight of some of the area citizens, Foothills Rural Telephone Cooperative was incorporated on September 10, 1951. The incorporators were Mort Mullins, Jim E. Jayne, J.W. Carpenter, J. Milton Kitchen, Sherman Bailey and B.E. Mullins, attorney. These men, along with other dedicated citizens in Magoffin, Johnson and Lawrence counties, under the leadership of Duell Williams, general manager, secured enough applications for service to satisfy the Rural Electrification Administration requirements to secure a loan of $398,000 in October 1952. The loan provided money to construct telephone lines and the most modern dial switching equipment available at that time. Also, included in this loan was money to purchase the Magoffin County Telephone Company which was bought on June 27, 1953.

The first pole was put into place on April 5, 1955, at Fritz Arnett's farm on Route 30 at Hendricks, KY. On November 12, 1955, at 5:00 p.m., foothills began cut over to the most modern dial telephone system available (at that time). The subscribers were offered either 8-party, 4-party, 2-party or 1-party service with selective ringing, which allowed the telephone of the person being called on the party line to ring without other party line subscribers being rung at the same time.

With the first dial telephone installed at the Edgar Paul Howard home on Route 30 in 1955 by Woodrow Ferguson, Foothills' employee, the next few years saw continuous line construction to accommodate applications for telephone service.

Other community leaders, such as Luther Carpenter, Stanley Gardner, Elmon Davis, Fred Arrington, Paul Gambill, John L. Burton and Stanley Fyffe served as trustees.

Beginning in 1969, Foothills Telephone eliminated 8-party lines and provided only a maximum of four parties on a line. Upon the retirement in 1975 of Duell Williams, with 24 years of service, Paul E. Preston became general manager. In 1977, the first planning started to convert all subscribers of Foothills Telephone to one party service, which required line construction throughout the entire system. With a loan from REA approved in 1978, construction began and the most modern digital switching equipment available was installed offering the new customer calling features, and by 1982, all subscribers had a private line in their home.

Other community leaders such as Gail Gillem, Roger Jordan, George J. Carpenter and Paul Williams, current trustees, helped the cooperative to continue to expand. Cellular Service, Inc., a subsidiary of Foothills Telephone, was formed, and cellular telephone and paging service were offered through general partnership with other small telephone companies in Eastern Kentucky. Internet service was started in 1995 with more than 2,850 customers by 1999. New class features such as caller name and number identification was added to the system. Voice mail was added in 1998.

Foothills serves more than 14,000 access lines and is continually expanding and offering new services to Eastern Kentucky. Foothills Telephone's staff of 53 has always and will continue to provide the best of telephone service.

Apr. 5, 1955, first pole setting at Fritz Arnett's farm on Route 30 at Hendricks, KY. L-R: Duell Williams, O.T. Dorton, B.E. Mullins, D.B. Garland, Ray Turner, Guss Moore, unknown, Milt Kitchen, Fred Arrington, Jimmy Carpenter, Mort Mullins, Elmon Davis, Lowell Edwards, unknown.

Bethel United Baptist Church

The Bethel United Baptist Church of Jesus Christ was organized or established January 24, 1924 at Flat Gap, KY, Johnson County. The charter members were John Lemaster, William Janes, Thomas Tackett, Francis Lemaster, James Sparks, Henry Janes, Joshua Pennington, John Lewis and N. Psimer. Pastors the first century were Elders Lewis Skaggs, James Pelfrey, David Daniel and J. Powell Ferguson.

Pastors for the second century were Elder J. Powell Ferguson serving into the second century his successor was Elder Dennis Williams, followed by Elder W.H. McKenzie, Elder Lonza Reed, Elder J.T. Bailey, Elder B.C. Ferguson, Elder Melvin Wright and at this date January 2000, Elder Bruce Howard pastor and Elder Ricky Curtis assistant pastor.

The deacons for the first century were Bro. Noah H. Williams, Bro. Hardin H. Williams, Bro. Isaac Fairchild, Bro. Hezekiah Fairchild, Bro. Joseph Stapleton, Bro. Joseph Salyer, Bro. E.E. Williams, Bro. Samuel Stapleton and Bro. John Harvey Williams.

Deacons for the second century are Bro. James P. Hall, Bro. P.P. Meade, Bro. Marian McKenzie, Bro. Columbus (Lumb) Salyer, Bro. K. Williams, Bro. Olive Cantrell, Bro. Blucher Lemaster, Bro. Chandler Salyer, Bro. Frank Pennington, Bro. Larry Lemaster, Bro. Johnny Curtis and Bro. Garry Curtis.

Bethel Church is still standing on its original faith and practices and is still prospering.

Johnson County Historical & Genealogical Society

The Johnson County Historical and Genealogical Society was organized March 1983 for the purpose of documenting and preserving the history of the area and the genealogy of the people. A number of people who were interested in history and family research came together to create the organization that has endured for nearly 20 years. Charter members include: Bob Young, Harry Holbrook, W.H. "Pat" Pelfrey, John Wells III, Pat Patton, Gail Spradlin, Jan Horne, Irene Adams and Mary Witten.

The organization has flourished over the years to include members in nearly every state. The interest of the group has been in compiling and preserving the past, for the present and future generations. The *Highland Echo* magazine, which is published quarterly, and is free to members, has been published four times per year since July 1983. Each issue features at least one family history, community history, cemetery listing and other articles of interest to researchers. The group has a very active Publication Committee and as a result have published three substantial volumes of cemetery listings.

Also, a volume on the *Historic Landmarks of Johnson County* was published. Many of the landmarks are gone today, but others have been restored and stand as monuments to generations past. Those include the Mayo's, Davis' Slone's and several businesses.

Presently, the members are working diligently on this, the *Johnson County Family History Book*.

Cando Steam Boat

Mill on Paint Creek

Ben Mollett Cabin

Officers Over The Years Include:

1984
W.H. "Pat" Pelfrey
John Wells III
Gail Spradlin
Pat Patton

June 12,1988
W.H. "Pat" Pelfrey, Vice President
Jan Horne, President

Sept 11, 1988
W.H. "Pat" Pelfrey, President

March 1990
Billie Edyth Ward, President
Ruth Salyer, Executive Secretary
Pat Wells, Treasurer

1991
David Wheeler, President
Jan Horne, Vice President
Pat Patton, Correspondence Secretary
Harry Holbrook, Chairman of Cemetery Committee
Irene Adams, Editor, *Highland Echo*

June 13,1991
Jan Horne, Treasurer
(A special election as Pat Wells resigned earlier in year)
Harry Holbrook elected Vice President

Dec 8,1994
Harold L Preston, President
Harry Holbrook, Vice President
Jan Horne, Secretary-Treasurer
Pat Patton, Correspondence Secretary

Jan 10, 1998
Rebecca Lewis Music, President
Harold L Preston, Vice President
Burnett Music, Treasurer
Jan Horne, Executive Secretary
Pat Patton, Correspondence Secretary
Harry Holbrook, Board Member

Nov 24,1998
Andy Keaton, President
Jim Trammel, Vice President
Burnett Music, Treasurer
Pat Patton, Correspondence Secretary
Jan Horne, Executive Secretary
Harold L Preston, Board Member
Becky Music, Board Member
John Sparks, Board Member
Sam Burchett, Board Member

Johnson County Fiscal Court

Connie Lynn Allen Commissioner District 1

Roger T. "Tucker" Daniel Judge Executive

Chuck Miller Commissioner District 2

Mike Adams Commissioner District 3

KENTUCKY APPLE FESTIVAL OF JOHNSON COUNTY
PAINTSVILLE, KENTUCKY

TRAILBLAZER
Kelly
Chevrolet Olds, Inc.
Sales, Service: 789-3585
Parts: 789-3615
830 Broadway
Paintsville, KY
1-800-589-7736

Family Biographies

ADAMS - George Washington Adams was born Mar. 11, 1875, in Johnson County, KY, the son of William J. and Rachel Baldwin Adams. He was the first of five children. John Q., Charity, Tom and Wiley followed. George W. was a teacher in one room schoolhouses in Johnson County and the surrounding area for 49 years. He was also a minister for the Freewill Baptist faith and learned to read Hebrew so he could read the Bible in its earliest form.

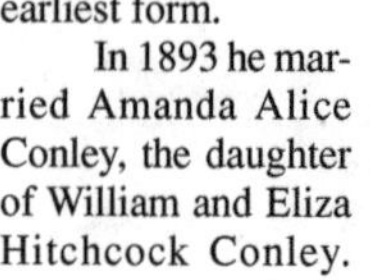

Front: Amanda, Alice Conley Adams and George W. Adams. Back: William R. Adams, Eliza Adams Kent, George Adams Preston and Elmer Adams.

In 1893 he married Amanda Alice Conley, the daughter of William and Eliza Hitchcock Conley. Alice was born Jul. 22, 1874.

George and Alice have five children: May (born 1895, died 1913), Elmer (born 1898, died 1987), Eliza (born 1900, died 1988), William (born 1904, died 1976) and Georgia (born 1909).

This family moved many times living around Johnson County and in Scioto County, OH, when George was assigned a new church.

ADAMS & CAUDILL - John Quincy Adams (born Aug. 18, 1878, died Aug. 24, 1904) married Apr. 21, 1898, Jincy Lou Caudill (born Sep. 7, 1884, died Feb. 3, 1970). John and Jincy lived on Lower Twin Branch at Denver. They had three sons: Miles (born Mar. 7, 1899, died Dec. 31, 1984); Frank (born May 2, 1901, died Jun. 6, 1966); and Bunk (born Sep. 14, 1903, died Jul. 17, 1904). John was a school teacher.

John Q. Adams, Jincy (Caudill) Adams, sons, Miles and Frank.

John was the son of William J. Adams (born 1851, died 1887) and Rachel Baldwin (born 1850, died 1883). William and Rachel were also the parents of George W. (born 1874, died 1962); Charity (born 1876, died 1955); and Thomas (born 1883, died 1883). Rachel may have died at the birth of Thomas. George W. Adams married Alice Conley and Charity married George B. Spradlin. William, Rachel and Thomas are buried in the Old Town Cemetery at Paintsville. William married second, Oct. 25, 1884, Rhoda Lemaster. They had one daughter, Maggie Adams (born 1885, died 1914) who married in 1908 to Johnson Leigh. Rhoda and Maggie are buried in the Blanton Cemetery on Blanton Branch.

William was the son of John Q. Adams (born 1829, died 1901) and Sarah Evans (born 1832, died 1886). "Grandpap Q" was born in Washington County, VA, and Sarah was born in Russell County, VA. They were married in Russell County, VA, in 1850. They came to Johnson County around 1855. They had 10 children. They are buried on Barnetts Creek.

Rachel was the daughter of Thomas Baldwin (born 1813, North Carolina, died 1902, Kentucky) and Charity Baines (born 1819, North Carolina, died 1882, Kentucky). Thomas and Charity had eight children. Thomas was the son of Anthony Baldwin and Elizabeth Stanley who were also the parents of eight. Charity was the daughter of Thomas Baines and Keziah Walton.

Jincy was the daughter of William Benjamin Caudill (born 1853, died 1884) and Elizabeth Spradlin (born 1859, died 1936). Ben and Elizabeth were married Jan. 17, 1878, in Johnson County. They had two sons, Jerry Franklin Caudill (born 1878, died 1907) who married Junie May; and John Elbert Caudill (born 1881, died 1943), single. Ben was the son of William Jackson Caudill (born 1822, died 1896 circa) and Rebecca Harris (born 1825, died 1904) who were married Feb. 5, 1846, in Morgan County.

Elizabeth was the daughter of James S. Spradlin Jr. (born 1824, died 1906) and Temperance Hitchcock (born 1826, died 1903) who were married Dec. 2, 1843, in Johnson County. Elizabeth and her parents are buried in the Spradlin-Hitchcock Cemetery on Lower Twin Branch. William Benjamin and his parents are buried in the Caudill Cemetery on Caudill Fork of Oil Springs.

Miles Adams passed the teachers exam before he was old enough to teach. He taught school one year. He and his brother, Frank, worked in the coal mines at Van Lear and in Paris Pelphrey's mines at Denver. Miles bought a store from a cousin and kept that store until his death. Miles never married. Frank Adams worked for the C & O Railway Co. for many years. He married Goldie Frazier and they had three children: Irene, Ralph and Mary.

Many of this family lived their entire lives at Denver, KY. *Submitted by Irene Adams.*

ADAMS - Mildred Howell Adams was born Dec. 12, 1935, in Floyd County, KY. Her father was William Adams, who was born Nov. 13, 1913, in Floyd County, KY, and died Nov. 5, 1955. Her mother was Samantha Mae Howell who was born Aug. 11, 1919, in Floyd County, KY. She had one sister, Ella Rose, who shared the same mother, but, her father was David Patierno. Ella Rose was born Aug. 21, 1938, in Floyd County, KY. She is married to Estes Breeding and lives in Ashland, KY. Samantha also lives in Ashland.

Mildred Howell Adams

Mildred lived most of her early years in the town of Martin. She attended school there and worked at the concession stand at the Martin Theatre. She enlisted in the Marine Corps in 1953 and after basic training in Parris Island, SC, she was stationed at Camp Pendleton, CA, where she worked as an office clerk.

While in California, she met her husband to be, Salomon Castro Jr. He was born Oct. 9, 1933, in El Paso, TX. They were married Jan. 14, 1956, in Yuma, AZ. While living in Los Angeles County, CA, they became the parents of three daughters. All three currently live in the Denver, CO, area. Linda Lee was born Nov. 25, 1956. She currently owns and operates a small business. Diana Lynn was born Mar. 26, 1962, she is a computer consultant. Susan Jane was born Aug. 6, 1963. She is currently a junior at the University of Colorado in Boulder. Her major is psychology.

Mildred received an AS degree from Santa Barbara Community College in Santa Barbara, CA. Majoring in nursing, she worked in the health care community until her retirement in 1997. She currently lives in Santa Barbara with her husband who was a designer for Raytheon Corporation until his retirement in 1996. Her hobbies include drawing, oil painting, acrylic tole painting, gardening and cooking.

Her great-grandmother, Samantha Roberson, was born about 1857 and lived in Johnson County, KY, until she married John G. Howell and moved to Floyd County.

Mildred's fondest memories are those of her childhood which she experienced when she spent her summers with her grandmother, Kizzie Mead Howell, on Abbott Creek. There were no fences then. With Grandma, aunt and uncles, she would roam the hills for hours and Grandma would tell them the names of all the plants and trees. They used to pick wild berries for canning and jams and gather Hickory nuts and walnuts for Christmas. One time they were out at night. There were no electric lights then. It was dark as you'd never see in towns or cities. All of a sudden they saw this huge display of lights in the sky. There were many colors and shimmering. The kids were really scared. They thought their mischief had finally caught up with them. Well, Grandma very calmly said. "Don't be afraid. It is only the Northern Lights." *Submitted by Mildred Castro.*

ADAMS - Ortie Adams, born on Jul. 15, 1913, to Thomas and Alice Hackworth Adams, and his wife, Dora Wright Adams, born Apr. 11, 1915, to Columbus and Hattie Frasure Wright, moved to Paintsville in 1938. They had been married on Feb. 7, 1935. Their first child, Jack Austin, was born in December 1935 but only lived 12 days; their second son, Wayne Gordon, was born in Floyd County May 27, 1937. Ortie got a job with Paintsville Grocery Co. and lived in Bristlebuck. Two daughters were added to the family, Alice Faye on Feb. 6, 1939, and Ruby Kaye on Oct. 12, 1940.

In 1945 Ortie and Dora bought a grocery store with living quarters and approximately 100 acres of land eight miles west of Paintsville at Barnetts Creek on Route 460, which later became Route 40. On Apr. 20, 1946, Carolyn Sue was born. She was named after Dora's grandmother, Caroline Qualls, who was a Cherokee Indian.

Ortie became a salesman for Paintsville Grocery, he and Dora ran a grocery store. They built a two-story home across from the grocery store and rented two apartments behind the store. In 1947 they added to the family by adopting a young girl from the community, Mildred Sluss. On May 29, 1949, Lynda Lou was born; on Feb. 26, 1952, Danny B. was born and on Jan. 25, 1958, Ricky Dean was born.

Ortie was a member of the Johnson County School Board from 1956-72 and believed very strongly in education, encouraging his children to pursue as much education as possible.

Dora Adams died Jul. 8, 1973, of multiple myeloma (cancer of the bone marrow) and Ortie Adams died Sep. 30, 1976, of a heart attack.

Wayne became a health technician for the state of Kentucky and married Gerry Adams of Magoffin County. They had one daughter, Celena Faye (born Jul. 14, 1962). Celina had Ortie and Dora's first great-grandchild, Adam Stephen Cummings.

Alice Faye married Paul Crace of Oil Springs. Their first son, Jeffrey Paul, was born Jun. 7, 1961. They moved to Lexington and Faye became a hairdresser. A second son, Gregory Neal, was born Apr. 13, 1963. Paul died in Lexington in 1978. Jeffrey spent four years in the Navy and settled in Los Angeles, CA. In 1994 Faye moved to Inverness, FL.

Ruby married Harold Dean VanHoose of Baker's Branch. She became an elementary school teacher. They had a daughter, Kara Paige (born Sep. 17, 1980). In 1993, they moved to western Kentucky.

Carolyn Sue became a business education teacher and married Paul Williams, a teacher and basketball coach in the Johnson County School System. They had two children, Bart Anthony (born Dec. 26, 1968) and Dora Suzanne (born May 17, 1974). In 1997 Carolyn Sue retired after teaching 30 years in Johnson County and in 1998 Paul retired as superintendent of the Paintsville Independent School System.

Lynda Lou married Scott Lafferty of East Point. They both worked for South Central Bell and had two children, Bryan Scott (born Apr. 15, 1969) and Kristi Lynn (born May 5, 1976). Lynda and Scott were divorced in 1993. Lynda later married Richard Hill, a CPA with the Internal Revenue Service.

Danny B. graduated from Morehead State University and married Sharon Stapleton of Hager Hill. They had two sons, Daniel Brent (born Nov. 25, 1975) and Derek Brandon (born Dec. 25, 1988). Danny became an entrepreneur owning B & B Distributors in Staffordsville.

Ricky Dean graduated from West Virginia Institute of Technology and became a mining engineer. He married Vicky Butler of Montgomery, WV. They had three sons: twins, Casey Ortie and Corey Butler (born Feb. 26, 1985) and Cody (born Nov. 17, 1988). In 1990 Ricky accepted a job with Arch Coal and moved his family to Logan, WV.

ANDERSON - Garnett Fairchild Anderson was born Apr. 30, 1932, at Pigeon, KY, in Johnson County. Her father was Orville Fairchild (born Dec. 7, 1909, at Oil Springs, KY). He worked with his father, James Henry Fairchild. They had a sawmill and grist mill in which they ground flour and cornmeal for the neighborhood. They also traveled through the countryside and threshed wheat for people. Later, he retired from the Union Fork and Hoe Co. in Columbus, OH.

Clyde Oakley and Garnett Fairchild Anderson

Her mother was Laura Edith Fairchild (born May 9, 1909, at Asa, KY). She was a seamstress. They were married Mar. 20, 1931, in Paintsville, KY, by Rev. Arthur Greene.

Garnett had two sisters and one brother: Loretta (born Sep. 9, 1934), Janice Marie (born Aug. 1, 1948) and Jimmie Ray (born May 30, 1947, died May 31, 1947).

Her first schooling was begun in a one room school house at Pigeon, KY. Her "primer" year was taught by her uncle, Wayne Fairchild, brother to her dad. Her first grade teacher was Willis H. Conley. This was his first year to teach. After that, in 1939 she moved to Ohio with her family. The rest of her school years were spent in and around Columbus, OH, except for one at Oil Springs Grade School.

At age 15, she met Clyde Oakley Anderson, who had just been discharged from the Army Air Corp. After a courtship of 15 months, they eloped to Flatwoods, KY, and were married there on Jul. 1, 1948, by Rev. E.L. Gallion. After living several years in Ohio, in the 1960s, they moved to California. Then in 1968 they moved to Kentucky.

Oakley was an aircraft-engine mechanic most of those years. After moving to Kentucky, he was self-employed as a plumber and electrician.

To them were born three sons and a daughter, all born in Columbus, Franklin County, OH.

James Oakley Anderson (born Jan. 20, 1949) married Pamela Sue Murphy Mar. 28, 1974, in Johnson County, KY. They have two daughters. Tracey Lynne Anderson (born Dec. 30, 1971) married Michael D. Salyer (born Sep. 21, 1971). They have one son, Tristen Michael (born Apr. 11, 1996) and Lauryn Elyse (born Jun. 12, 1998). Jamie Sue Anderson (born Oct. 6, 1975). One son, Daymion D.A.T. Anderson (born Feb. 24, 1996).

Michael Deane Anderson (born Apr. 15, 1952) was married to Bonnie Lee Salyer (born Apr. 20, 1953) on Jul. 28, 1973, at Flat Gap, KY, by Elder Arnold Reed. They have a son, Michael Paul Anderson (born Dec. 9, 1978) and a daughter, Sherri Lee Anderson (born Jan. 26, 1982).

Jackie Alan Anderson (born Dec. 11, 1954) married Norma Jean Wheeler Dec. 23, 1972, at Oil Springs, KY. They are divorced. They had a daughter, Amy Rose Anderson (born Nov. 5, 1975) married Chris Goslee of Ocala, FL. They have a daughter, Kristen Nicole Goslee (born Jul. 23, 1995, in Ocala, FL. A son, Alan Oakley Anderson (born Jan. 16, 1979). Jack married second, Patricia Spangler of West Virginia, divorced in 1997.

Judy Ann Anderson (born Oct. 10, 1956) married Danny Lewis Williams (born Mar. 10, 1955). Married on Mar. 24, 1973, at Oil Springs, Johnson County, KY. He is a United Baptist preacher. Ordained by Elder Lonza Reed on Mar. 26, 1983. They have two daughters and one son.

Christy Ann Williams (born Oct. 10, 1973) married Tony Burns (born Jun. 3, 1969) on Jan. 9, 1993.

Rhonda Lee Williams (born Jul. 22, 1976) married Michael Arthur Perry (born Mar. 19, 1975) on May 20, 1995. They have a son, Jerrod Michael Perry (born Aug. 18, 1997).

Bobby Lewis Williams (born Sep. 4, 1981).

Garnett and her husband, Oakley celebrated their 50th wedding anniversary in 1998 and live in Oil Springs on the farm formerly owned by her father. They have spent the last 20 winters in Florida.

ARROWOOD - Alonzo Arrowood was born in Johnson County, KY, Oct. 25, 1882, to Marion Arrowood and Deliah Price Arrowood. Alonzo (Lon to everyone who knew him) was the middle child of nine.

Lon married Dutch Gibbs Dec. 31, 1903, and she bore him eight children: Oberlin (born Nov. 1, 1904), Sylvia (born Jul. 7, 1906), John Lawton (born Oct. 19, 1909), Velma Etta (born in 1911, died in infancy), Frankie (born Mar. 9, 1912), James Arthur (born Oct. 11, 1914), Paul Matthew (born Mar. 21, 1917) and Georgene (born Jun. 27, 1920). After James was born, Lon built a new home for his family at Mingo, KY, where Paul and Georgene were born. Dutch Gibbs Arrowood passed away nine days after Georgene's birth. In 1924, he moved his family to Betsy Lane, KY (a coal mining town). He lived in Red Town for three years, moved on to Glo Glory and then to Wayland, KY, where he lived for 19 years and then moved to Maytown, KY, where he retired from Elkhorn Coal Co. Lon then moved his family back to Mingo, KY "to the Old Home place," where they truly felt at home.

Alonzo and Dutch Gibbs Arrowood

Lon was a hard worker. He made a living for his family by farming and raising livestock, selling pots and pans from house to house, and he was an accomplished photographer, too. He also worked as a slope miner for 44 years.

On Jul. 23, 1921, Alonzo married Anna Whitten Arrowood, a school teacher, and they had seven children. Only three of these children reached adulthood: Palmer Dillon "P.D.," Billie Marie and Raleigh Hamilton.

Oberlin Arrowood died in 1915 of a ruptured appendix.

John Lawton went to Springfield, MO, when he was 19 years old to live with his Uncle John Gibbs. He married Carolina Hern Oct. 1, 1934, in Joplin, MO. They had four children: Robert Bruce, Larry Wayne and the twins, Max Edward and Mary Lou Arrowood. John worked at the Hickory Hill Golf Course as greens manager.

Sylvia married Gaylord Pack from Williamsport, KY. They lived in Paintsville and had two children, Gaylord Euell and Deordena Rue Pack. Gaylord was part owner of the International Harvester Garage in Paintsville.

Velma Etta died at infancy.

Frankie married Frank Janow. They lived in Wayland and had two children, George Melvin and Leota Carol Janow. Frank was a coal miner in Kentucky and then worked for Sears, Roebuck Co. in Phoenix, AZ.

James Arthur worked in the Wayland coal mines and when Japan attacked Pearl Harbor and war was declared, James was one of the first three young men in Wayland to volunteer to fight for his country. He married Willa Dean Carver, and left Wayland to make their home in Phoenix, AZ. They had four daughters: Shirley Ann, Bobby, Judy Kay and Patty Arrowood. James also worked for Sears, Roebuck Co.

Paul Matthew married Lillian Pack Jan. 11, 1941. Paul served four years overseas during WWII. Lillian taught school in Van Lear and Paintsville and Paul taught electricity at Mayo State Vocational School in Paintsville. They had one daughter, Pamela Jane Arrowood.

Georgene married her childhood sweetheart, Forrest Oney, "the boy next door." Although she lived most of her early years in Wayland, she spent a lot of time in Paintsville with her sister, Sylvia Pack. Forrest served a brief tour in the USN, worked at the International Harvester Garage and for Ashland Oil Co. He retired after 35 years working for the Freeman United Coal Co. in DuQuoin, IL. They had two children, Forrest Lon and Saundra Lynn Oney.

Alonzo Arrowood passed on to his maker Jul. 2, 1970, and his family still misses him. He left 15 children (four are still living: Paul, Georgene, Billie Marie and Raleigh Hamilton), 15 grandchildren and 27 great-grandchildren.

ARROWOOD - Lillian Pack Arrowood was born Jun. 19, 1920, in Van Lear, KY, to James A. Pack and Bessie Meddings Pack.

Lillian was married in Pike County, KY, to Paul Arrowood on Jan. 11, 1941. They are the parents of one daughter, Pamela Jane Arrowood Owen (born Dec. 15, 1946).

Lillian attended first and second grades at Van Lear Elementary School. Her family moved to King Addition in Paintsville when she was in the third grade where she continued her schooling and graduated from Paintsville High School in 1937 at the age of 16. She attended Bethel Woman's College in Hopkinsville, KY, and earned her teaching certificate in 1939. She continued teaching and returned to Morehead State University where she completed her undergraduate work and later received her MA degree.

Lillian Pack Arrowood

At the early age of 18, Lillian began teaching in a one-room school in Upper Daniels Creek for the Johnson County School System. She later moved on to Thealka. It was at the Thealka School she met Paul Arrowood another teacher, who later became her husband.

Lillian's husband, Paul, trained for the Signal Corp and worked for the U.S. Government. During this time, they lived and worked in New York City, NY; Philadelphia, PA; San Bernadino, CA; Oklahoma City, OK; and Topeka, KS. With the declaration of WWII, Lillian continued traveling with Paul after his enlistment in the Army, where he was stationed in California, New Jersey and Texas.

When her husband was transferred overseas with the 82nd Signal Bn., Lillian returned to Paintsville where she continued teaching.

During the 37-1/2 years of her teaching career, she taught in Johnson County, Van Lear, Jenkins, Fairview in Ashland, and Paintsville. Lillian retired in 1983 from the Paintsville City Schools.

Lillian is an active member of the First Baptist Church where she has taught Sunday school, Vacation Bible School, and works in the Women's Missionary Union. Lillian taught a young girls' Sunday school class at the Bridgeford Mission. Because of her Christian influence and biblical teaching, many of those girls still correspond with her today.

She's also an active member of Johnson County Retired Teachers serving on the Scholarship Committee, Johnson County Homemakers and Eastern Star. Being a cancer survivor herself, Lillian has volunteered many hours, working with Reach to Recovery for the American Cancer Society, and is a council member of the Kentucky Cancer Program. Lillian is also a member of the Can-Survive Support Group. She, with the help of her husband Paul, collects aluminum can tabs to help children with cancer attend a week of camp at Camp Indian Summer in Irvine, KY.

Daughter, Jane, and husband, Tom Owen, both graduates of Morehead State University, live in Independence, KY. Jane teaches elementary school at Piner Elementary and Tom works for Baptist Life Services of Northern Kentucky. Granddaughter, Melissa Owen Willis, and husband, Kevin Willis, are graduates of Morehead State University and also live in Independence, KY. Melissa works as a mortgage loan originator for Third Federal Savings and Kevin is a manager of financial reporting for Continental PET Technologies.

Little Lindsey Brooke Willis, her only great-grandchild, was born Nov. 5, 1998.

ARROWOOD - Paul Matthew Arrowood was born Mar. 21, 1917, in Johnson County, KY, to Alonzo "Lon" Arrowood and Dutch Gibbs Arrowood. After his mother's death, he became the stepson of Anna Witten Arrowood. Paul was married in Pike County, KY, to Lillian Pack Arrowood on Jan. 11, 1941. They are the parents of one daughter, Pamela Jane Arrowood Owen (born Dec. 15, 1946).

Paul Arrowood

As a child, Paul attended elementary schools in Tutor Key, Betsy Lane and Wayland. Lon, his father, worked in the mines so the family returned to Johnson County. Paul played varsity basketball for the Meade Memorial Red Devils. At graduation in 1937, Paul was awarded a basketball scholarship to Center College, but chose instead to attend Morehead State University. Paul worked in the bakery there to put himself through school so he could become a teacher.

Paul taught his first year in Upper Van Lear in a three-room school. The next year after transferring to Thealka, Paul met another young teacher, Lillian Pack, who soon became the love of his life. Lillian is the daughter of the late James A. and Bessie Meddings Pack. She graduated from Paintsville City Schools at age 16 and Bethel Woman's College at age 18. After a year of "courting" Paul and Lillian married.

While Paul trained in electronics with the Signal Corp the couple lived in New York City, Philadelphia, PA, and San Bernadino, CA. Paul began working for the U.S. Government and they moved on to Oklahoma City, OK, and Topeka, KS.

The bombing of Pearl Harbor caused Paul to quit his job and return to Paintsville to enlist in the U.S. Army. During WWII, he was stationed in California, New Jersey and Texas. Then Paul's squadron, the 82nd Signal Bn., was sent overseas to Hawaii, the Philippines, and finally to Japan. They remained in Japan for five or six months after the end of the war.

Returning after the war, Paul worked as an electrician for Consolidation Coal Co. in Jenkins, KY, and for a mine in Breathitt County. Later he served as an agent for the Commonwealth Life Insurance Co. until joining the staff of Mayo State Vocational School. After teaching high school students industrial electronics for 20 years, Paul retired from Mayo in 1980. Many of his former students still keep in touch with him today. After 37-1/2 years, Lillian retired from teaching in the Paintsville City Schools in 1983.

As a strong Christian, who is active in First Baptist Church of Paintsville, Paul has led his family to serve the Lord. He is an active member of Kiwanis Club, Johnson County Retired Teachers Association and the Brotherhood of the First Baptist Church. He has a great love of hunting, fishing and doing volunteer work.

Daughter, Jane, and husband, Tom Owen, both graduates of Morehead State University, live in Independence, KY. Jane teaches elementary school at Piner Elementary School and Tom works for Baptist Life Services of Northern Kentucky. Granddaughter, Melissa Owen Willis, and husband, Kevin Willis, are graduates of Morehead State University and also live in Independence, KY. Melissa works as a mortgage loan originator for Third Federal Savings and Kevin is a manager of financial reporting for Continental PET Technologies.

Little Lindsey Brooke Willis, his only great-grandchild, was born Nov. 5, 1998.

AUSTIN - Isom Austin was born Oct. 14, 1899, in Johnson County, KY, to John Morgan Austin (born Apr. 12, 1878, died Mar. 10, 1919?, buried at the Collins Cemetery in VanLear, KY) and Fannie Jane Spriggs (born Sep. 9, 1881, died May 28, 1963, buried on the Dennie Pigg Cemetery at Boons Camp, KY). He was next to the oldest child of four born to his parents. He had one sister, Floria Austin Davis (born Apr. 13, 1897, died Dec. 21, 1987), and two brothers, Floyd Austin (born Jun. 21, 1906, died May 20, 1979) and Obie Austin (born Jan. 14, 1909, died Dec. 7, 1983).

Isom Austin and Bessie Bolen Austin

Isom married May 8, 1926, in Johnson County, KY, to Bessie Bolen (born Jun. 15, 1910), the daughter of Joe Bolen (born Oct. 6, 1875, died Jun. 29, 1967) and Allie Mae Bolen (born May 10, 1885, died Jul. 16, 1975), of VanLear, KY, both Joe and Allie are buried in the Austin Cemetery at Boons Camp, KY. They were the parents of one son, Alvin Austin (born Oct. 14, 1927) and one daughter, Lillie Mae Austin (born Sep. 21, 1929).

Isom worked his whole life as a coal miner in the Wheelwright and VanLear coal mines. He retired from coal mining in the 60s.

Isom and Bessie became members of the Meally Church of Christ, where they both remained until their death. Isom died of congestive heart failure at his daughter's home on Dec. 3, 1985. Bessie preceded him in death on Apr. 13, 1978, of congestive heart failure at her daughter's home. They both are buried in the Austin Cemetery that is located on their home place at the head of Greasy at Boons Camp, KY.

Isom and Bessie's daughter, Lillie Mae, married Mar. 29, 1947, to Herman Daniels, son of Joshie Daniels (born Sep. 8, 1903, died Oct. 16, 1985) and Clista Music (born Oct. 23, 1904, died Sep. 26, 1990), both Joshie and Clista were buried in Highland Cemetery at Staffordville. Herman was born Aug. 23, 1925, and died Nov. 16, 1990, of lung cancer, he was buried in Lakeview Cemetery, Staffordville, KY. Herman had one sister, Garnetta Daniels Austin (born Sep. 30, 1922, died Sep. 6, 1983), buried in Tip City, OH, and one brother, Arnold Haskel Daniels (born Oct. 23, 1927).

To Herman and Lillie Mae Daniels there was born four sons: Lon Cebert (born Jan. 5, 1948), Robert Dean (born Oct. 6, 1950), Calvin Bryan (born Feb. 15, 1954) and Herman J. (born Oct. 19, 1955); also four daughters: Marcella Mae (born Jan. 31, 1949), Garnetta Gay (born Aug. 8, 1957), Korletta Kay (born May 23, 1961) and Jannetta Joy (born Mar. 11, 1965), all of these children were born in Paintsville, KY.

Isom and Bessie's son, Alvin, married Dec. 21, 1953, to Jacqueline Ruth Lewis (born Nov. 21, 1933), of Pikeville, KY, daughter of John and Nancy Ponders Lewis. To this couple was born one son, Gregory Lynn (born in Paintsville, KY, Jan. 21, 1955) and two daughters, Janetta Ruth (born in Mount Carmel, IL, Aug. 31, 1958) and Teresa Sue (born in Mount Carmel, IL, Jan. 8, 1960).

AUXIER - The progenitor of the Auxier family is thought to be a man named Michael, born about 1685 at Auxerre, France. The name has undergone numerous changes of spelling, including "Oxer," "Oxar," "Oxier," and finally "Auxier" at the turn of the 18th century. Michael brought his family to America to escape the religious persecution of the Huguenots by the French government.

Dr. Dave Auxier, Memphis, TN, veterinarian and compiler of The Auxier Family

Arriving in Philadelphia on Sep. 24, 1742, Michael took the oath of allegiance to the Crown of England and immediately settled in Lancaster County, PA. Five of his grandsons: Simon, Michael, Abraham, George and Samuel, served in the Revolutionary War. Simon, the oldest, was at Valley Forge and at most of the major battles of the War. He reportedly witnessed the surrender of Cornwallis at Yorktown. Michael, was scalped by an Indian near Ft. Blackmore, VA, but survived and was known thereafter as "Baldheaded Mike." Abraham raised his family in Illinois, and George settled in the Kanawha Valley of what is now West Virginia.

The youngest of those five brothers was Samuel Auxier who was born in Hampshire County, VA in 1759 and moved his family to the Big Sandy Valley in 1795. Settling on a large fertile bottom between the present day towns of Paintsville and Prestonsburg, Samuel's family cleared land and built blockhouses which would give name to the now historic "Blockhouse Bottom." This was the same spot on which Mathias Harman had built hunter's cabins only to have them destroyed by Indians, and where Daniel Boone spent the winter of 1796-97 with Samuel's family, naming several creeks after himself and Samuel's son, Nathaniel. These locations are familiar to Johnson Countians as Boon's Camp, Nat's Creek, and Daniel's Creek. When Boone left the Blockhouse Bottom in 1797, he gave Samuel's wife, Sarah, a buffalo hide which was made into a swinging cradle, and to young Nathaniel, he gave a powder horn with the initials "D.B." carved into it. A section of the buffalo hide still exists and is in the care of Earnest Auxier of Madison, IN. Unfortunately, the powder horn has disappeared after being in the gun collection of Judge Jean Auxier of Pikeville for many years.

Samuel Auxier's family was hit by two tragedies soon after moving to Kentucky. First of all, Sam and Sarah's 4 year old son, Elijah, disappeared from the canebrake near the blockhouses and it was never determined if he was devoured by wild animals, captured by Indians, or drowned in the Big Sandy River. Then in 1799, Samuel died at the age of 40 after a horse threw him violently against a tree.

Despite these unfortunate happenings, the large family survived and prospered, and their descendants became respected in business and the professions. Several served honorably in the Civil War, including Maj. John B., Capt. David Valentine, and Sgt. George Washington Auxier, all of the 39th Kentucky Volunteer Infantry, U.S. Army. David Valentine was killed in the battle of Saltville, VA in October 1864, and will be the subject of a book to be published by his great, great nephew, Dr. Dave Auxier, in 2000. George Washington, Dave's great-grandfather, was a successful farmer and merchant who settled at Fishtrap on Paint Creek and was county sheriff for nine years. In 1984, the people of Johnson County elected him to the Hall of Fame.

The Auxier Family, a genealogy/history published in 1995 and scheduled for revision and republication in 2000, contains over 26,000 names and 10,000 marriages in 13 generations dating back to 1685 in France.

BAILEY - Col. James Arville Bailey was born Sep. 13, 1949, in Paintsville, KY, to Arville and Prudence Cottle Bailey. He is the grandson of the late James Crawford and Sarah Sparks Cottle and Wade Randall and Ollie Lyon Bailey. He grew up at Flat Gap and attended Johnson County schools graduating at Flat Gap High School in 1967. He earned a bachelor's degree in communications from Morehead State University, and a master's degree from Morehead in 1972. Professionally, he completed Squadron Officer School in 1979, Air Command and Staff College in 1982 and National Security Management in 1988.

Col. James A. Bailey

He was commissioned as second lieutenant in the Air Force following completion of Officer Training School in October 1973. He was transferred to Undergraduate Navigator Training, Mather Air Force Base, CA, where he was awarded the aeronautical rating of navigator in August 1974; he furthered his studies at Electric Warfare Officer School, graduating in March 1975. Col. Bailey's first operational assignment was as a B-52G electronic warfare officer, 62nd Bombardment Sqdn., Barksdale Air Force Base, LA, from July 1975-December 1979.

In January 1980, he was reassigned to RC-135 aircraft, Offutt Air Base, NE, where he served as flight instructor, evaluator and crew commander. His next assignment was as chief, Operational Analysis Branch, USCINCPAC Camp H.M. Smith, HI, from October 1982- May 1985. He was then assigned to the Office of Space Systems, Office of the Secretary of the Air Force, SS-9, director of Operations, through July 1988.

He was next assigned to Onizuka Air Force Base, CA, to serve with the Office of the Secretary of the Air Force, Special Projects, as director of Requirements, Operating Div. One, through March 1990, and as director of Mission Planning, Operating Division Four, through June 1993. In July 1993, he was assigned as the commander, Operating Div. Seven, Office of Space and Technology, Office of the Secretary of the Air Force. Col. Bailey assumed his present position in April 1997.

Col. Bailey's military awards and decorations include the Defense Superior Medal, Defense Meritorious Service Medal w/3 Oak Leaf Clusters, Air Medal w/2 Oak Leaf Clusters, Air Force Commendation w/1 Oak Leaf Cluster, Joint Meritorious Unit Award, Air Force Outstanding Unit Award w/1 Oak Leaf Cluster, Air Force Organizational Excellence Award, Combat Readiness Medal, National Defense Service Medal w/1 Oak Leaf Cluster and Humanitarian Service Medal. He has been awarded the Master Space Badge and has achieved a master navigator aeronautical rating accruing 3,079 flying hours including 1,396 hours in B-52G aircraft, and 1,498 hours in RC-135 aircraft.

Col. Bailey is married to the former Glenda Reed of Worthington, KY; they have two children, a daughter, Jami, and a son, Charles.

Their future plans include returning to Bailey Road at Flat Gap and building a new home to enjoy during their retirement years.

BAILEY - Maj. Gen. Maxwell C. Bailey was born in Paintsville, KY, May 20, 1947, the son of William G. and Jane Bailey. He and his wife, Joyce, are the parents of a daughter, Carolyn. Gen. Bailey entered the Air Force in 1969 after graduation from the USAF Academy. He has commanded a squadron, a tactical airlift wing, a special operations wing and provisional airlift forces at several locations on the Arabian Peninsula during Operations Desert Shield and Desert Storm. He is a command pilot with more than 5,500 flying hours.

Maj. Gen. Bailey's past assignments include: 39th Tactical Airlift Sqdn.; 48th Tactical Airlift Sqdn.; Air Force Board Structure, HQ USAF, Washington, D.C.; HQ Military Airlift Command, Scott AFB; U.S. Army Command and General Staff College; Air War College, Maxwell AFB; Council on Foreign Relations, New York City; 16th Special Operations Wing and director of Operations, U.S. Special Operations Command, MacDill Air Force Base, FL.

Maj. Gen. Bailey's awards and decorations include the Defense Superior Service Medal, Legion of Merit with Oak Leaf Cluster, Meritorious Service Medal w/2 Oak Leaf Clusters, Air Medal, Aerial Achievement Medal and the Air Force Commendation Medal. He has also been awarded the Parachutist Badge.

BAILEY - Thomas Murray Bailey was born Oct. 2, 1917, the oldest child of Sanford and Elsie Ferguson Bailey at Red Bush, KY. Dad and mother had one daughter, Janis, who married Okie G. Ferguson and another son, James H. Gerald, who married Ilene Williams. Brother passed away May 12, 1992, which was a sad time for the family.

Thomas M. was married to Opal Thompson Jun. 7, 1947, and they were parents of two children, Cynthia Carol (born Feb. 16, 1948) and Thomas J. Sanford (born Feb. 25, 1952). Cynthia was born in Louisa, Lawrence County, KY, and Thomas J. was born in Portsmouth, OH.

Thomas Murray graduated from Flat Gap High School in 1936 and Pikeville Junior College in 1938, attended Morehead State College the second semester in 1941 and graduated from Eastern State College in 1948 after serving almost four years in the USAAC. Prior to military service, he taught school in a one room school house at Red Bush and Upper Keaton, two terms at each place. After military service he taught one school term at Lower Keaton School and finished out one term at Paintsville City School, seventh and eighth grades. After graduation at Eastern, he was principal of the Mary Hellen Grade School for the years of 1948-49 and 1949-50. This was in a coal camp in Harlan County, KY. This ended his teaching profession.

In 1950 he joined the Pipefitters Union in Portsmouth, OH, and worked as a construction pipefitter and plumber until the last of December 1953 when he was elected financial secretary-treasurer and served in that capacity for eight years and was elected as business agent and served for six years ending in December 1957. He then went back to doing construction work until he retired in April 1983.

His daughter, Cynthia Carol, graduated from Green Township High School, Ohio State University, majoring in micro-biology, received her master's degree from Salisbury State University, Salisbury, MD, majoring in medical technology and she is teaching this subject matter at the University at the present time.

His son, Thomas J. Sanford, graduated from Green Township High School, went one year and one quarter to Ohio State, deciding college was not for him, joined the Air Force and when his enlistment was up, he started learning welding and became a member of the pipe fitter union and has made a proficient pipe fitter and welder. He is currently working at the Aristec Chemical Plant, Haverhill, OH, as a maintenance pipe fitter and welder.

His great-great-grandfather, John D. Bailey, was in Lawrence County, KY, Mar. 31, 1836, later became Johnson County. He bought 50 acres of land which was situated on upper Laurel Fork of Big Blaine Creek. This land was bought under the Kentucky Land Warrants Law for $20.00 per 100 acres. Some of John D. Bailey's children and grandchildren migrated to Lawrence, Elliot and Morgan counties.

Since Thomas M.'s retirement, he has been very active in tracing down his family history and gardening. He has the record of his family roots back to the immigrant Stephen Bailey, who received a land grant in 1657 in Northumberland County, VA, which is now Westmoreland County. He has been to the old homestead of Stephen Bailey on three occasions. It is located on the Yeocomico River, Kinsale, VA.

BAILEY - Wallace Ray "Wassie" Bailey was born Sep. 23, 1925, Tutor Key, KY, and died Jun. 20, 1989, Paintsville, KY. His parents were Zelda VanHoose Bailey and Hirst M. Bailey. His grandparents were Bascom VanHoose and Julia Helton VanHoose; and Dr. Thurman Britton Bailey and Martha Evans Bailey.

Wassie was the second child of the Baileys and attended Meade Memorial High School. His older brother, Fred, was in the U.S. Army, so Wassie left school to join the Army in 1943, as thousands of young men were doing during WWII. He volunteered for the newly formed U.S. Army Paratroopers and was assigned to the 551st Abn. Inf. Regt., Co. A, attached to the 82nd Abn. Div. During WWII, he participated in five campaigns, fighting in North Africa, France, Italy and Belgium.

He was injured in Southern France, Aug. 15, 1944, but later rejoined his outfit and returned to combat. His brother, Fred, was wounded in Southern France on Aug. 29, 1944, and returned to the USA.

Europe was experiencing a bitter cold winter, as the Allied Forces pushed toward Germany, expecting the war to end soon. The German Army trapped the Americans in the Ardennes Forest in December 1944 and demanded their surrender. The Americans refused and the battle that followed is known as the Battle of the Bulge (a major confrontation of WWII). This battle lasted from Dec. 16, 1944-Jan. 28, 1945.

Jan. 3, 1945, was one of the coldest and bloodiest days of the fighting. The 551st sustained 189 casualties, which was almost one-third of their battalion's strength. Almost half of these were from A Co., and Wassie suffered gunshot wounds that destroyed his right kidney and damaged his back, leaving him a paraplegic for the next 44 years. He awakened in England 30 days after the injury and did not know what happened to his outfit until in the mid-1980s. The 551st casualty rate for the Battle of the Bulge is listed at 94 percent. The remaining men were assigned to other outfits and the 551st was officially disbanded Feb. 10, 1945. (*Messengers of the Lost Battalion*, by Gregory Orfalea).

Wassie was discharged from the Army Mar. 31, 1946, but could not return to Johnson County for many months. After returning home, he became involved in sports. He supported the basketball, football, baseball and track teams of Paintsville High School. Although confined to a wheelchair, he played basketball, swam and bowled, while his health permitted. He was a member of the Paintsville Utility Commission at the time of his death.

BAILEY & CLAY - William Garland Bailey and Jane Clay Bailey were married at the Oak Cliff Methodist Church in Dallas, TX, on Sep. 9, 1944.

William "Bill" was born at Paintsville, Johnson County, KY, on Jul. 28, 1922, the third of three sons of Warrick B. Bailey and Suda Dixon Bailey. His two brothers are both deceased, Winifred "Colonel" Cox Bailey (born 1912, died 1986) and Maurice "Perk" Dixon Bailey (born 1914, died 1981).

William G. and Jane C. Bailey

Bill graduated from Paintsville High School in 1939. He attended Marshall College for two years and then worked for Kentucky West Virginia Gas Co. for one year before entering the USN in 1943. He served for 30 months in the Naval Air Corps as a flight instructor. After his discharge in 1945, he and Jane returned to Paintsville.

Bill began working at Citizen's National Bank in Paintsville in November 1945 and retired Dec. 31, 1988. At the time of his retirement he was executive vice president and continued to serve as chairman of the board until 1994.

Jane was born at Paintsville, Johnson County, KY, Sep. 28, 1922, the last of four children of Elmon Maxwell Clay and Carolyn "Carrie" Vaughan Clay. A brother, E. Maxwell Clay; and sister, Sarah Louise Clay Womack, are both deceased. Her only living sister, Lorraine Clay Wiley, age 92 and widow of Hansel Wiley, is presently residing at Bourbon Heights in Paris, KY. Lorraine will be remembered as a much-loved English teacher at Paintsville High School for many years. After graduating from Paintsville High School in 1940, Jane enrolled in Transylvania College in Lexington, KY, where she graduated in 1943.

Jane first began her teaching career at Meade Memorial High School in Johnson County in 1943 and 1944. After her children were born, she resumed full time teaching in 1960 at Paintsville High School where she taught English and related subjects. Jane retired from her teaching career in 1980. However, she is currently writing a column "... As I Was Saying" for the local paper, *Paintsville Herald*.

Jane and Bill have two children, Maxwell Clay Bailey (born May 20, 1947). After attending Paintsville High School, Clay graduated from the Air Force Academy in 1969. He is now a lieutenant general in command of the 21st Air Force in New Jersey. Clay is married to the former Joyce Gaye Preston and they have one daughter, Carolyn "Carrie" Clay Bailey, age 18, who graduates in June 1999 from Bayside Christian Academy in Tampa, FL, where her mother Joyce is employed.

Jane and Bill's daughter, Nancye Jane Bailey, was born Apr. 18, 1957. After graduating from Paintsville High School, she attended Sullins College in Bristol, VA, for two years then on to the University of Kentucky where she graduated in 1974. Nancye is married to James Harrah Thompson and they reside on their farm on Paris Pike where Jim is a farmer and insurance salesman. Nancye is employed in the development and publication department of Sayre College in Lexington. Nancye and Jim have two daughters, Sarah Walker Thompson, a sophomore at Agnes Scott College in Atlanta and Jane Collins Thompson, a sophomore at Sayre School.

Bill and Jane are very active in the First United Methodist Church in Paintsville, where Bill served for a number of years as treasurer and Jane as officer of the WSCS and Guild. Also, they have both been very active in the civic organizations in Paintsville.

They are now residing at 228 5th Street in Paintsville, Johnson County, KY.

BALDWIN & GREENE - Delmas Carrol Baldwin was born Oct. 11, 1927, in Paintsville, Johnson County, KY, to McKinley Baldwin and Nova Holbrook Baldwin. He was the third child of five children born to his parents, all of whom survived to adulthood.

Carrol, or "DC" as he was known to his friends, was married to Berneeda Joyce Greene on Jan. 15, 1945, and they were the parents of three sons: David Carrol (born Jan. 20, 1946), Timothy Duane (born Dec. 18, 1950) and Van Alan (born Nov. 6, 1954). David and Timothy were born in Johnson County and Van Alan in Carter County.

Carrol, after high school, went to work for the C&O Railway, as a freight agent and telegraph operator in various locations on the Big Sandy and Lexington Sub-Divisions. He worked for C&O until Nov. 15, 1957. At that time, he opened an office in Grayson, KY, as an agent for State Farm Insurance Companies.

He was very active in his profession during the 37 years he worked for State Farm and continued his formal education with supplemental classes in accounting, auditing, general business administration and insurance subjects.

He was active in the Republican political party and was appointed chairman of the Urban Renewal Commission of Grayson. He was also Carter County Disaster chairman and very active in amateur radio, where he held a general operators license. DC was an avid fisherman, who loved boating, reading and building computers.

Berneeda Joyce Greene Baldwin was born Jul. 28, 1928, at Stambaugh in Johnson County, the daughter of John Greene and Garnet Hanley Bayes Greene. She was the first child of a family of 12 children born to her parents.

Berneeda was very active in community affairs. She operated a business in conjunction with the financial institutions in Carter County for 25 years. She was president of the Homemakers Club, Carter Health Care Auxiliary and a volunteer with the University of Kentucky Cooperative Extension Service. She was always a loving mother, wife and faithful servant to her family and friends. She was undeniably the "best cook in any kitchen!"

Two of Carrol and Berneeda's sons, both graduates of Morehead State University, teach in the Carter County School System. David Carrol is head of the business department of East Carter High School and Timothy Duane teaches mathematics at East Carter Middle School in Grayson. Van Alan, also a graduate of Morehead State University, holds a degree in business administration, with a major in accounting and is employed as manager of a plumbing supply house in Grayson.

BALDWIN - My name is Fannie Baldwin. I am 86 years old and I want to tell my family story. I was born Dec. 22, 1912, to Andy Blair and Mintie Pelphrey. Mommy always told me that I was the best Christmas present she ever had. My parents already had a daughter, Bessie, who was born Jan. 31, 1907.

Andy Blair was born Oct. 17, 1886, and died Jul. 27, 1957. He was the son of James Fleming Blair (born 1864, died 1938) and Elizabeth Hitchcock (born 1866, died 1951). James Fleming, known as "Buddy Jim," was the son of George "Watt" Blair and Matilda Spradlin, who were the parents of 12. Elizabeth Hitchcock was a daughter of Parker D. Hitchcock and Sophia Salyer. Elizabeth was known to most people as "Liz" but to me she was "Ma." When I was small I liked to dress up and pretend. Ma often walked to the family cemetery. I remember dressing up in my hat, fur coat and someone's high heels to go with Ma to the cemetery on a hot summer day. I thought I was beautiful! Parker D. and Sophia Hitchcock were the parents of three daughters and two sons.

Andy and Mintie Blair

Mintie Pelphrey was born Jun. 18, 1887, and died Sept. 17, 1963. Mint was the daughter of Clark Pelphrey (born 1864, died 1929) and Martha McKenzie (born 1867, died 1893). Clark Pelphrey was the son of Daniel Pelphrey and Sarah Ann Hitchcock. Martha McKenzie was the daughter of Lemuel G. McKenzie and Mary Lemaster. Clark and Martha had five children. Martha died Jun. 23, 1893. Clark Pelphrey married second Jan. 17, 1894, to Clarinda Pelphrey, daughter of A.J. "Jeff" Pelphrey and Oma Salyer. Clark and Clarinda became the parents of five children. Martha McKenzie Pelphrey was buried on Slate Rock Branch, Clark and Clarinda were buried in the Old Tackett Cemetery on Barnetts Creek.

Mommy and Poppy started housekeeping on Upper Twin Branch, near the home of his parents. Poppy was a good carpenter and made some of our furniture. When I was very young we once lived in Castle Town while Poppy worked in the mines. One day Poppy told me if I would go with him to the commissary at Riceville he would buy me whatever I wanted. We walked the railroad with Poppy in front a couple of steps. While crossing a bridge I missed a step and one leg went through. I said "Poppy, I fell through the bridge!" He got me up and said "You're not hurt" and we went on our way. At the store I found what I thought was the most beautiful yellow hat and true to his word Poppy bought it for me. Mommy and Poppy often went to Beechwall United Baptist Church and I can remember attending many meetings there. Every year in June they held what was referred to as "the June Meetin" with dinner on the ground. These were very large gatherings of people from every where.

My sister, Bessie, married Crate Spradlin Dec. 22, 1921. Crate was born Mar. 4, 1903, to James Winfield Spradlin and Mary Jane Selvage. Crate and Bessie's household was blessed with three lovely daughters: Reba, Gegie and Betty, and one son, Leondas. Crate and Bessie lived on Lower Twin Branch and at Van Lear. They later moved to Ohio. I have many fond memories of their visits to our parents' home. We would cry when they came and we would cry when they left.

On Aug. 14, 1930, I was married to Bayless Baldwin, a mischievous, fun loving, never a dull moment when he was around, kind of person. I loved him so much and believed everyone else did too. Bayless was born Apr. 6, 1906, to Electrus Baldwin and Minnie Alice Blair. Leck and Minnie were the parents of three sons and four daughters. Bayless and I lived on Upper Twin Branch, Lower Twin Branch and Happy Hollow at Denver. We also lived at Collista and Hager Hill. We liked every place we ever lived and always had good neighbors. On Oct. 7, 1970, my beloved Bayless was taken from me. Life has never and will never be the same. I miss him so. Bayless is buried in the Mayo Cemetery at Paintsville, where I shall soon join him.

After Bayless' passing, I moved to Paintsville and lived there about 25 years. I became very ill at one time and had to retire to Mountain Manor where I now live and have a "big, wonderful family" who looks after all my physical and material needs. They treat me well and pamper me. I hope they forgive me when I feel frustrated and lonely and become cranky. I miss my home, my own couch to take a nap on, my coffee pot that was always full, my family pictures to look through and so many things one takes for granted until they are gone. Yes, it is sad and lonesome when you outlive everyone who cared for you and everyone that you loved so much.

BALDWIN - Joel Henry Baldwin was born Nov. 2, 1873, at Oil Springs to Shelby Anthony and Hannah Davis Baldwin. He was the oldest of 15 children: Joel Henry (born 1873, died 1957), James Wince (born 1875, died 1959), Eunice (born 1876, died 1962), Rhoda Talitha (born 1877, died 1878), Isaac Vincent "Doc" (born 1878, died 1970), Nora (born 1880, died 1974, Elec H. (born 1882, died 1952), John F. (born 1883, died 1962), Richard (born 1886, died 1887), Mary Susan (born 1887, died 1965), Cora A. (born 1890, died 1919), Luther P. (born 1891), Clinton M. (born 1892, died 1969), Guye (born 1894, died 1895) and Sherman McKinley (born 1896, died 1965).

Joel Henry Baldwin home, granddaughter, Eunice Pelphrey.

Joel Henry married Sarah Emily Fairchild Jun. 11, 1898. She was born Dec. 31, 1880, at Volga to Andrew and Cynthia Hitchcock Fairchild. Emily's family consisted of seven brothers and sisters: Mary, Alice, Alka, Nimrod, William, Jimmie and Branford.

Joel was a farmer and blacksmith. Sarah was a homemaker.

To this union was born nine children: Nellie May m. Tolbert McKenzie, Samantha md. Dord Bayes, Ora md. Mitchell Rice, Ruby Alice md. Trigg McKenzie, Louisa Hazel md. Ottis Holbrook, Talitha Hannah md. Ralph Burchett, Shelby Martin md. Stella Wheeler, Sherman Dencil md. Olga Picklesimer and Joel Henry Jr. md. Mary Blanton.

They lived and reared their family on a farm inherited from his mother. The farm later belonged to son, Sherman Dencil and is now owned by David Sherman Baldwin, Joel's grandson.

BALDWIN & HOLBROOK - McKinley Baldwin was born Nov. 4, 1896, at Oil Springs, Johnson County, KY, the last child of 15 born to S.A. (Shelby Anthony) and Hannah Davis Baldwin.

On May 1, 1920, McKinley Baldwin married Nova Holbrook, the youngest daughter of George Washington and Polly Johnson Holbrook of Red Bush, Johnson County, KY. Nova Holbrook Baldwin was born Feb. 28, 1903, at Red Bush and attended school there where McKinley taught for several years.

Shortly after their marriage, McKinley and Nova moved to Paintsville and McKinley worked a brief period for Williams Wholesale Grocery Co. before beginning work at the F.S. VanHoose Lumber Co. At the time of his death on Jan. 29, 1965, he was general manager of the company where he had worked for 43 years.

Nova was 78 years old when she died on Apr. 29, 1981. She was a devoted wife, mother and homemaker. She and McKinley were married for 45 years and lived at 79 Maple Street in Bridgeford Addition most of their married life. They were faithful members of the Paintsville United Baptist Church.

The children born to this union:

1) Imogene B. Baldwin (born Mar. 4, 1921, died Apr. 29, 1994) married Jess B. Ward (born October 1920, died December 1959). One child, Linda L. Ward Rice.

2) Lowell F. Baldwin (born Jan. 30, 1924) married Beverly E. Kern (born Feb. 23, 1927). Two sons, Steven and Michael Baldwin; and one daughter, Beth E. Baldwin.

3) Delmas Carrol "D.C." Baldwin (born Oct. 11, 1927) married Berneeda J. Greene (born Jul. 28, 1928). Three children: David Carrol Baldwin married Donna Grim and had Allyson; Timothy Duane Baldwin married Lisa ? and had Aaron Baldwin and Jill Baldwin; Van Alan Baldwin married first, Kathy Holbrook and second, Andrea ?. He had three children: Adam Baldwin, Hannah Baldwin and Ashley Baldwin.

4) Robert H. Baldwin (born Apr. 13, 1930) married Elizabeth "Libby" Matthew (born Feb. 9, 1932) and had six children: Robert Michael Baldwin married Edwinna Hamilton and had Laura Baldwin and Timothy Baldwin; Elizabeth Jeanne Baldwin married Russell Hackworth and had Rachel Hackworth and Aaron Hackworth; Mary Jane Baldwin married Barney Kinman and had Ben Kinman and Amy Kinman; James Mark Baldwin married Lynne Wheeler and had Erin E. Baldwin and Emma K. Baldwin; Jeffrey Matthew Baldwin married Georgia Auxier; and Nanci Lynne Baldwin.

5) Patricia R. Baldwin (born Feb. 25, 1936) married Ernest Morris Jr. (born Jan. 9, 1928) and had two children, Robert Keith Morris and Patricia Brett Morris.

BALDWIN - Robert H. Baldwin was born Apr. 15, 1930, at Paintsville, Johnson County, KY, the fourth child born to McKinley and Nova Holbrook Baldwin.

Robert married Elizabeth "Libby" Matthew Sep. 15, 1950. Libby was born to Clifford and Eliza Kozee Matthew Feb. 9, 1932, at Paintsville, KY.

Robert and Libby have six children:

1) Robert Michael Baldwin married Edwinna Hamilton and had a) Laura Baldwin and b) Timothy Baldwin.

2) Elizabeth Jeanne Baldwin Hackworth married Russell Hackworth and had a) Rachel Hackworth and b) Aaron Hackworth.

3) Mary Jane Baldwin Kinman married Barney Kinman and had a) Benjamin Kinman and b) Amy Kinman.

4) James Mark Baldwin married Lynn Wheeler and had a) Eryn E. Baldwin and b) Emma K. Baldwin.

5) Jeffrey Matthew Baldwin married Georgia Auxier.

6) Nanci Lynne Baldwin.

Robert and Libby attended Paintsville Elementary and Paintsville High School. Robert graduated from the University of Kentucky and became a teacher. At the time he retired from teaching, he was head of the Math Dept. at Paintsville High School. He has since become a certified appraiser and is presently working in that capacity.

Libby has been a housewife and homemaker, busy raising her children and actively participating in church and community affairs. She has become locally well known as a fabulous cook.

BAYES - Elijah Bayes was born in Pittsylvania County, VA, about 1800. His parents were John and Sarah (Owens) Bayes. Sometime before 1829 the family of John and Sarah Bayes, their child and grandchildren settled at what is now known as Salyersville. John, the oldest son of John and Sarah, died Jul. 17, 1826, in Virginia before they left.

On Feb. 14, 1833, Elijah was married to Margaret Rice in Floyd County, KY. Margaret Rice was the daughter of Samuel and Phoebe Rice. On Sep. 1, 1840, Elijah was chosen as moderator of the Burning Springs Baptist Church at Salyerville. He is listed on the Johnson County list of persons when it was formed covering the period 1844-48. Elijah signed as witness on Jul. 13, 1845, the deed for 3/4 acre on which to build a United Baptist Church on Jennys Creek. The church is known today as the "Beechwall Church." This land was sold to the church for 50 cents from Samuel Rice. Elijah served as an outstanding minister of this United Baptist Church.

He lived near Barnetts Creek in Johnson County. The Johnson County Court authorized him to keep a ferry at the mouth of Barnetts Creek. Elijah performed several marriages, one of the last being that of Jeremiah Salyer and Elizabeth Conley Sep. 17, 1845. Sometime before 1850 he died, his wife, Margaret, then married Araham Justice in 1852, later she married John Salyer in 1865.

The children of Elijah and Margaret were: Sarah (born 1834) married Henry Mckenzie; Phoebe (born May 11, 1836) married Daniel Lemaster; Joshua (born 1838) married Margaret Slone; William (born Feb. 10, 1841) married Lydia Pelphery; Samuel Edward (born Feb. 1, 1843) married Fanny Wheeler, the daughter of William R. Wheeler and Elizabeth Borders of Hood's Fork in Johnson County; and Mary Ellen (born Apr. 26, 1847) married Jasper Slone. *By Brenda (Bayes) Taber.*

BELHASEN - Charles "Charlie" Belhasen came to the U.S. around 1901, at about age 7. As a child growing up in his home town of Beruit, Lebanon, he probably had little chance in this world.

However, the fact that he grew up to become one of East Kentucky's leading citizens and wound up as the patriarch of a respected and prosperous family, with his children and grandchildren becoming a family which includes several doctors and lawyers, as well as other respected professional people, only shows that the USA truly is "The Land Of Opportunity."

Little is known about the circumstances of his emigration to the USA, but it seems clear that he was put on a ship by his mother and father, along with someone known to him as "uncle Abraham," who was escorting the young boy to the New World.

As was sometimes the case with parents who lived in "troubled lands," the child was put on the ship by them with the knowledge that they would possibly never see their son again. This proved to be true.

He landed in New York with his uncle, who died shortly after they arrived. As a result, he wound up on the streets of New York and was eventually sent, as a foster child, to Magoffin County, KY, to the home of Calloway Montgomery, where he lived until he was about 17.

It is not known exactly how long he was left "orphaned" in New York, before he was "adopted" by the Montgomerys, but he often told of making enough to survive by selling "shoestrings and pencils" as a little boy on the streets of New York City.

When I think of his existence as a New York City street urchin in the early part of the 20th century my thoughts sometimes go to the characters written about by Horatio Alger in "Mark The Match Boy" and other similar novels.

Charlie apparently grew up fast and married young. He went to West Virginia and married his first wife. They came to Paintsville and opened the Busy Bee Restaurant in about 1912. His first two children, Fred Belhasen and Hasen Belhasen, were born here.

Later, the family moved to Yeager, WV, where they lived for several years, until he was divorced from his wife and moved back to Kentucky. He continued to earn a living operating small department stores and selling from his car.

He was operating a small department store in Martin, KY, in the late 1920s when he met, courted and married Josephine Morgan, daughter of Rueben and Virgie Morgan of Wayland, KY.

They married and moved to Salyersville, where they opened a dry goods store. They later lived in Hazard where their first child, Ronald F. Belhasen, was born in 1932.

A few years later they moved back to Paintsville. They took up residence in what was then known as the "Bristlebuck" section of town. While living there their second child, Franklen Kemal Belhasen, was born in 1938.

During the early years in Paintsville and throughout the "depression years" Charlie was a salesman who traveled to the little general stores and small businesses all over the region selling anything from chewing gum and candy to punch boards, and the prizes that were given to punch board winners.

He was (and still is) remembered by the merchants and others who knew him at this time as "Chewing Gum Charlie" because of his visits to the little businesses that dotted the Eastern Kentucky countryside.

The family prospered in the years after the depression and purchased a home at 606 Frank Street in 1944. Their third son, Charles Keith Belhasen, was born there in 1944.

Charlie died in January, 1952, at the age of 56. Josephine is now 84.

BLAIR - Arnold Ray "Frank" Blair is a direct descendant of George and Mary Fairchild Blair through their son, John Goodwood, and Evaline Conley Blair. John's son, William Harlan, and Lydia Margaret Riggsby Blair were Frank's grandparents through their son, Samuel Mander, and Mary Alice Estep Blair.

Frank's siblings were: Amos Melvin, Escom Elton, William Marvin, Cecil Chalmer, Eula May, Major Jay Jennings, Ronald Junior and Richard Elmon. Frank was born in Opossom Hollow, he lived his early childhood on Jenny's Creek and he and his family later moved to Mudlick, KY. Frank had many occupations: miner, farmer, welder and ironworker. He has been a Mason for 40 years, master of the Chandlersville Lodge for two terms in 1965 and 1972. He is a most respected and well liked citizen of Johnson County. Frank married Malvrie Fields, daughter of Willis and Sophia Akers Fields, on Dec. 20, 1947. Malvrie was reared by her grandparents, William Robert "Bob" and Minnie Sublett Fields. Malvrie worked very hard during her early life. Bob Fields died in 1945 leaving Minnie in the care of Malvrie. Malvrie cared for her for many years before her death in 1961. Frank and Malvrie have lived at Sitka for the last 52 years.

Arnold Ray and Malvrie Fields Blair

Bob and Minnie were prominent citizens of Sitka, KY. At the time of their marriage, Jan. 25, 1903, Sitka was a thriving little community. Bob owned the general store and the boarding house. The home of Harold Witten is built on the foundation of the store. The boarding house was in the corner of Mr. Witten's yard next to the Sitka Freewill Baptist Church. Sola Rice, wife of Charlie Rice, was the postmistress. The post office was located in the off-set front room of their home. Millard Akers, Sophia's father, was the postman. The Rice's home set just the other side of the church and between the church and Castle's Garage of present day. The land around these public places was sold in lots. The road followed Tom's Creek (in and out of the water) until 1933 when construction of Kentucky Hwy. 201 began.

In 1894 the school was located on a lot, between the present home of Mrs. James Jarvis and the first drain of the ridge. A new school was built near the present Sitka Post Office. The blacksmith shop and sawmill were located just behind Frank and Malvrie's home. Bob Fields worked the mill in partnership with his brother-in-law, Dallas Sublett. Bob bought his land in sections. Besides his other endeavors he was an avid farmer. By the time of his death, Bob had acquired several tracts of the Philip Stambaugh property. Minnie, Dallas and John were the children of James and Charlotte Stambaugh Sublett. Charlotte was the daughter of Philip and Mary Jane McKenzie Stambaugh. Philip was the son of Samuel and Charlotte Rogers and the grandson of Philip Sr.

In an 1860 survey the Phil Stambaugh line bounded the Matt Clay property. Matt Clay's deed calls for 6000 acres to the Lawrence County border. The VanHoose Branch was originally the Matt Clay Branch. Philip Stambaugh Sr. and his sons, George Blair and his brother Noble, Preston Fields (Bob's grandfather), and Anthony Baldridge (Bob's great-grandfather on his mother's side) were among the very first settlers of this place we call home.

BLAIR & WARD - Dennis Vincent Blair was born Jul. 19, 1920, in Catlettsburg to Dee and Mary Ellen Blair (his siblings were Margaret, Anne, James Franklin and a half-sister, Linda Jane). Dennis was reared in the Jennie's Creek area of Johnson County and attended Meade Memorial High School. He joined the Army in October 1939; but with the advent of Pearl Harbor he found his stay in the service unexpectedly extended through July 1945. Dennis served in the HQ Btry., 46th Field Arty. Bn. with the 5th Div. Prior to the Allied Invasion of France he found himself stationed in such diverse and interesting places as Iceland, Ireland and England. But it was D-Day that presented him with the opportunity of "touring" continental Europe the hard way, mostly on foot and with a war going on all around. His service travels took him through France, Belgium and Germany during several theatres of action (including the Battle of the Bulge) all of which eventually earned him five Bronze Stars.

After the war Dennis took up the trade of "plumber," and then on Sep. 24, 1947, he married Iris Mildred Ward, daughter of Asbury and Mabel Williamson Ward. Iris was born on Dec. 8, 1926, at Chestnut, KY, in Johnson County. Her surviving brothers and sisters are: Wilma, Marie and Ralph Ward, all of whom attended Van Lear High School. Iris became a dedicated homemaker and mother, and worked for a number of years at Cox's Dept. Store in Paintsville.

Iris and Dennis have two sons, Ronnie Dee (born Jun. 20, 1948) and James Dencil (born Nov. 17, 1952), both born in Paintsville Hospital, and one deceased child, Donald Lee. They also have two grandchildren, Craig Matthew and Carrie Autumn Blair, from James' marriage to the former Mary Jane Hill, daughter of Edra Hamilton Hill and the late Fred Hill of Flat Gap.

Ronnie and "Jimmy" both attended all eight years of grade school at West Van Lear and later attended Meade Memorial High School from which Ronnie graduated in 1966. Jimmy graduated from the new consolidated Johnson Central High School in 1970. However, both boys hold bachelor degrees from Morehead State University. Jim now operates a successful monogramming business at Staffordsville, and Ronnie (a former art teacher in the Johnson County School System) tried his hand at acting out on the West Coast. After 20 years of stage, television and movie work, he has once again settled back home in Johnson County where during the summer months he continues to use his acting skills at the local Jenny Wiley Music Theatre in Floyd County. During the remainder of the year he works within the school system with an organization called C.A.P. (Child Assault Prevention).

Iris and Dennis, both now retired, are also active members in their respective churches, the West Van Lear Missionary Baptist Church (where Iris serves as pianist) and the Muddy Branch Freewill Baptist Church of Thealka.

As of this writing the Blairs still reside in West Van Lear in the same house they have called home for more than 45 years. But, if it's a pretty day and you want to find Dennis then look no further than the hollows of Paintsville Lake, a place this avid fisherman has adopted as his second home.

BLAIR - Elzie Blair was born Feb. 16, 1902, in Riceville, KY (Johnson County), the son of Leander Blair and Pearlina Elizabeth Lewis. On Apr. 17, 1925, at the United Baptist Church in Prestonsburg, KY, he married Connie Frances Ratliff, the daughter of Albert Ratliff and Margie Bell Rice. They are the parents of 10 children.

Their first, Edward Steward Blair, was born Jan. 19, 1927, at Paintsville, KY. The family then moved to McCuffey, OH, where their second son, Lee Edford Blair, was born Jul. 14, 1928. After a short stay in Ohio the family moved back to Paintsville, KY, where three more children were born: Elsie Pearl Blair (born Jan. 25, 1930), Arnel Glenn Blair (born Jan. 1, 1932) and Dwane Jack Blair (born Mar. 25, 1934). Elzie moved the family back to Ohio sometime in 1934 where five more children were born: Maudy Murrell Blair (born May 12, 1936), Randall Glee Blair (born Apr. 2, 1938) and Douglas Eugene Blair (born Mar. 4, 1939), all at Greenwich, OH; Elzie's last two children, Elberta Blair (born Oct. 28, 1940) and Caroline Elizabeth Blair (born Apr. 21, 1942) were born at North Fairfield, OH. In the mid-1940s Elzie moved to 17 Tilton St., Greenwich, OH, where he would spend the rest of his life.

Elzie Blair, son of Leander Blair and Pearlina E. Lewis.

Eight of the 10 children grew to be adults. Dwane Jack Blair and Rondall Glee Blair were just a few weeks old when they died, Douglas Eugene Blair was killed in an auto accident Apr. 30, 1960, and Elberta Blair died Jul. 11, 1970, they were never married.

Edward Steward married Ilene Failer, they have one son, Edward Allen.

Lee Edford married Julia Westbrook, they have a son, Roger Lee and a daughter, Nicky Kay.

Maudy Murrell married Robert Hamilton Maye, they have two daughters, Myra Lynn and Mary Lou.

Arnel Glenn married Marlene Westbrook, they have four daughters: Tammy Kay, Terresa, Constance and Patty; and one son, Chris.

Edward, Lee, Maudy and Arnel live in Greenwich, OH.

Elsia Pearl married Gerald Dwane Maye, they had two sons, Ricky Lee and Larry Dee. Elsia lives in Norwalk, OH.

Caroline married Boyd Rogers, they have a daughter, Bernice Ann and a son, Boyd Douglas. Caroline lives in Oberlin, OH.

Elzie was a very easy going, quite gentleman who loved to hunt and fish. He had many friends and was liked by all who knew him. He enjoyed music and played the banjo, guitar and mandolin.

As a young man he worked on the railroad in Johnson County, KY, and after moving to Ohio worked 17 years as a track man for the New York Central Railroad and seven years as security guard at the Akron Standard Co. in Greenwich, OH.

Elzie passed away Feb. 11, 1981. He is buried in

the Greenlawn Cemetery in Greenwich, OH. *Written Aug. 15, 1999, by Caroline E. (Blair) Rogers.*

BLAIR - Pauline Salyer Blair was the 11th child of Addison Salyer and Cora Bell Rice (born Oct. 1, 1920). She had eight brothers, namely: Ray, Roy, Tommy, Grady, Patrick, Jay Cecil, Addison Jr. and Billy Burton, all deceased; three sisters: Ruth, Bethel living and Reba deceased. She attended a one room school through the eighth grade and walked six miles per day to catch a school bus that took her 27 more miles to Meade Memorial High School at Williamsport, KY, and graduated in 1938 being one of 66 graduates, the largest group to graduate at that date. She continued her education by going to Pikeville College, Pikeville, KY. Then and there she decided to become a teacher. At that time, a legal certificate was issued on two years of college. She graduated in 1940.

Pauline Salyer Blair

She taught her first two years at Green Valley, a one room school on the Left Fork of Barnetts Creek, KY. Her salary was $84.00 dollars per month and out of this salary she had to pay $14.00 per month for room and board. The following year, she taught her home school at Upper Middle Fork. These school terms were only seven months.

During this time WWII was going on, she decided to help out in the war effort and went to Springfield, OH, and worked for International Harvester Co. There she packed spare parts for half tracks that were used in the war. She made as much there in one week as she made a month teaching in Kentucky.

She married Samuel Tollie Blair (a Kentucky native) in Springfield, OH, in 1943. To this union were born two sons, Larry K. and Wayde Douglas Blair. After marriage they continued to live in Ohio until 1946. In 1946 they moved to Kentucky. Here they built and operated a store and garage on route 460 at Barnetts Creek, KY. They ran this business until 1949.

Tollie Blair, her husband, died March 1954 leaving her with a 9-year-old son and a 6-year-old to raise. To support these two sons, she returned to teaching and taught at Van Lear school for one year and, then was placed at the Oil Springs School where she taught 34 more years and retired in 1985.

Her sons graduated from Oil Springs High School and from Berea College, Berea, KY. After graduating from college, Larry received a scholarship from the National Science Foundation to further his education in chemistry. He attended and graduated from Stanford University in California with a PhD degree in chemistry. He began his teaching at Sao Paulo University in Brazil, South America. There he taught one year and returned to Berea, KY, and began teaching chemistry at Berea College. He served one term as dean of the college. He married Linda Wear from Berea, KY. They have two sons, Paul and Peter. Paul is employed as an analyst for Providian Bank, San Francisco, CA. Peter is attending Notre Dame University, South Bend, IN.

Wayde Douglas lives and works in San Francisco, CA.

Since retirement in 1985 she has joined several clubs: Home Makers, The Quilters Guild and The Kentucky Retired Teachers Association.

She is a member of the Southern Baptist Church and resides at Staffordsville, KY, with her sister.

BLAIR - My name is Sandy Kay Blair. I was born Dec. 1, 1953. I am the daughter of the late James Orville Blair and the late Erie Collinsworth. I am the 12th child of 13, 10 of which are still living. Their names are as follows: Donald (born Dec. 15, 1934), Edgel (born Feb. 8, 1937), Delmar (born Mar. 3, 1938), Warren (born Jun. 16, 1940), these four were born in Johnson County, KY. They lived a while on Green Rock Fork, then they moved to East Liberty, OH, and had Judy (born Jan. 16, 1943), Linda (born Sep. 4, 1948), Rose (born at home Feb. 8, 1951), William "Bill" (born Apr. 24, 1952) and Shirley (born Dec. 29, 1954).

I have two sisters that died when they were babies, their names were Betty (born Aug. 20, 1946), she lived 10 days, the other was named Wanda (born Aug. 27, 1949), she lived for 10 weeks. Then my mother lost one in 1944 or 1945.

Mama and Dad were married Feb. 8, 1934, by Nolan Scott on Rockhouse in Magoffin County.

My dad was the son of Thomas Jefferson Blair and Sophia Lee Jackson. They are buried in the cemetery on the Willie Rice place at Oil Springs. James was born May 29, 1912, and died of cancer Sep. 15, 1956. I was only 2 years, 9 months and 14 days old. My brother, Donald, was married and had a baby girl named Diana. She was 6 months and 27 days old when my dad died. He is buried in the Blair Cemetery behind the Homer Blair place on 825. My great-grandparents were Britton Blair and Mary Watkins. Britton was the son of Noble Blair and Tabitha Stambaugh, Mary was the daughter of Reese Watkins and Sarah Stambaugh. Noble was the son of George Blair and Mary Fairchild. They lived at Big Mud Lick, Johnson County, KY. Sarah was the daughter of Phillip Stambaugh and mother unknown. My grandmother, Sophia Jackson, was the daughter of James Jackson and Mary Salyer Meade. James was the son of James W. Jackson and Mary A. Hall, as far as I know lived in Johnson County.

My mom was the daughter of Warren Collinsworth and Moncy Tackett. Mom was born Jan. 13, 1916, she died in a freak automobile accident Jul. 19, 1978, and was buried July 22, in the Fairview Cemetery at West Liberty, OH. Warren was the son of Evan Spencer "Doc" Collinsworth and Lydia Margaret Harmon. Evan Spencer was the son of George Collins/Collinsworth and Jemima Burke. Margarett was the daughter of William B. Harmon and Elizabeth Blair. My grandmother, Moncy, was the daughter of John Milt Tackett and Rebecca Lemaster. John Milt was the son of Hiram C. Tackett and Lucinda G. Shavers. Rebecca was the daughter of Thomas Lemaster and Mary Cantrell. Hiram C. was the son of Alsey Tackett and was born out of wedlock, his father was John Sizemore. Thomas was the son of Richard Lemaster and Bexy Christian. Mary was the daughter of Henry Cantrell and Rachel Blanton.

After my dad passed away Mom reared nine of us by herself, five of us were under the age of 10.

Ever since I was a little girl and we would come down here during the summer to visit my aunts and uncles, who still live down here, I always wanted to live in Kentucky. About 11 years ago my dream came true. I left Ohio and moved to Kentucky. I lived in Magoffin County for over a year, then I met and married my husband, Donald Ray Akers. I now live in Morgan County. I have lived in Wolfe County.

BLAND - John Elmon Bland, the youngest of seven children born to Morris and Norma Bland, is a native of Paintsville. On Jan. 31, 1964, John wed Nadine Stinson, the daughter of Albert and Vivia Stinson, of Flat Gap, Johnson County, KY.

Following their marriage, John and Nadine lived in various cities and on different naval bases in the fulfillment of John's naval career. He was selected as the sole representative from Naval Aviation to serve as an advisor to the chief of Naval Operations as a member of the Chief Petty Officer Advisory Board.

The Blands are the parents of one daughter, Stacy Renee, who is married to James Anthony Howard of Lawrence County. The Howards have one son, Dylan Anthony Howard (born Jun. 7, 1997). James and Stacy reside in Paintsville. John also has a daughter, Erin Lynn, who married Dan Rehberg, and lives in northern California. The Rehbergs have three children: Andrew, Jonathan and Christina.

Retiring after 20 years active duty, the Blands returned to Paintsville, where John was employed as the community development director, and later as the county planner for Johnson County. Nadine resumed her career as an administrative assistant with the Pepsi Cola Company.

John was employed for several years as a campus director and consultant to accredited proprietary educational institutions in Kentucky, West Virginia, Alabama and Texas prior to his retirement from active employment in 1995.

BLAND - John Wesley Bland was born Dec. 25, 1865, at Denver, KY, the son of William D. and Surrilda Bland.

On Dec. 4, 1889, John married Mary LeMaster at the home of her parents, Eli and Elizabeth Keaton LeMaster. Mary was born in Paintsville, where she remained a life-long resident until her death in 1956.

To John and Mary were born four children: Ora, who married Manuel VanHoose; Walter, who lost an arm while serving in the U.S. Army during WWI (Walter married Malta James and his family later moved to the state of Indiana); and Morris Benjamin, who married Norma Jean George. The fourth child was a daughter who died in infancy and is buried in the Old Town Cemetery in Paintsville.

A later marriage of John to Celia Ann Candle produced two children, Oscar, who married Virgie Smith; and Clara, who married Raymond Snoddy. Both Oscar and Clara made their homes in Flatwoods, KY.

During his work life, John was a farmer, coal miner, an inventory control manager for a coal company and did some work in the cement business. John died May 23, 1938, and is buried in the Melvin Cemetery at Raceland, KY.

BLAND - Morris Benjamin Bland (born Jul. 11, 1896, in Paintsville) was the son of John Wesley and Mary LeMaster Bland. He worked as a mine electrician, but most enjoyed being a policeman. He served as the chief of police in West Van Lear, and later as a deputy sheriff of Johnson County.

On Apr. 22, 1918, Morris wed Norma Jean George, daughter of John O. and Nevada May George, at Cliff, KY. Norma was born Jul. 12, 1900, in Floyd County.

Morris and Norma were the parents of seven children: Nancy Josephine, who married Lester W. Reed, and resides in Clarksburg, WV; Rena, who married Woodrow Frisby of Staffordsville; Helen, who married Clyde M. Bayes and resides in Paintsville; John, who married Nadine Stinson and resided in Paintsville; and Glenn, who died during a Navy career, the father of Phillip Bland of Cincinnati, OH. Morris and Norma had two other children, McKinley Avis and Dortha Francis, both of whom died at young ages.

Morris was shot to death Oct. 24, 1937, leaving Norma a single parent until the time of her death Nov. 12, 1979. Norma was a devout Christian, an ever caring mother, a neighbor in the truest sense and an inspiration to all who knew her.

BLAND - The name Bland dates well back into the 1500s and earlier in the history of London, England. The name was very prominent in the early settlement of the colonies in America, and Richard Bland was a member of the first Continental Congress which first met on Sep. 4, 1774, in Philadelphia.

The establishment of the Bland family in Johnson County, KY, is attributed to William D. Bland. Born Apr. 4, 1838, in White Gate, Giles County, VA, he was one of 11 children of James and Ida Dawson Bland, and the grandson of Robert and Anna Bland of Monroe County, WV.

During the Civil War, William served in the

Confederate States Army, Co. F, 11th (4th) Bn. Virginia Reserves. It was at Christiansburg, VA, that the command learned of Lee's surrender. After much discussion the battalion decided to disband Apr. 12, 1865. Most of the men either returned home or traveled to Roanoke, VA, or Charleston, WV, to officially surrender; but a few made their way into Kentucky, including William, and took the oath at Louisa, KY.

William married Surrilda Jane Evans Rice, widow of Martin Rice, with whom Surrilda had one daughter, Sarah Jane. To the Blands were born two children, Martha Ellen, who died in infancy; and John Wesley Bland.

The Blands lived in the Denver area of Johnson County. Records indicate that many marriages were conducted at the home of William and Surrilda. At the time of his death, Apr. 17, 1897, William was serving as a constable in Dist. 4 of Johnson County. He is buried in the Denver Hill Cemetery.

BLANKENSHIP - April (Barker) Blankenship was born Oct. 28, 1962, in Paintsville, KY, to Patty Sue (May) Barker and Ernest Barker of Johnson County. Patty was born Sep. 27, 1935, in Van Lear, KY, and Ernest was born Oct. 5, 1932, also in Van Lear. April was the fourth born to a family of eight.

April was married in Thelma, KY, in The Friendship Baptist Church, to Richard Duffy Blankenship on Dec. 5, 1980. They were parents of two children, Fawn Nicole Blankenship (born Apr. 27, 1982) and Richard Oscar Samuel Blankenship (born Jul. 18, 1988). They were both born in Highlands Regional Medical Center in Prestonsburg, KY.

April attended Van Lear Elementary, Porter Elementary and graduated from Johnson Central High School in 1980. She attended Mayo Vocational Technology School for two and a half years before dropping out to take care of her first born and to become a stay at home mom.

Her father served in the Army for four years and fought in the Korean War where he received medals. Her mother was a stay at home mom who reared six children: Jackie Ann May (born Feb. 6, 1953), Michael Ernest (born Dec. 4, 1956), Bernadine (born Jan. 26, 1958), Lundy Ray (born Sep. 7, 1965) and Martin Edward (born Oct. 26, 1965).

April's father-in-law was a preacher at the Church of Christ in Jesus Name for over 20 years. Her husband is now self-employed and they are currently residing in Thelma, KY, where they are preparing to put their oldest child through college.

BLANTON - Henry Frank Blanton was born Jul. 11, 1909, the third child of Hansford "Doke" (son of Elias and Minervia Ann McCarty Blanton) and Lousina Fairchild Blanton (the daughter of Thomas and Elizabeth Conley Fairchild). He had two brothers, Lasco and Ovid; and two sisters, Emma Blanton Curtis and Edna Blanton. Hansford and Lousina reared their family at what was then known as Kenwood, KY, but what is now Win Road, Oil Springs, KY.

Henry Frank's great-great-grandparents, George Blanton and Martha Shephard Blanton, migrated into eastern Kentucky, in the late 1700s, coming from the Powell Valley in Virginia, settling on what is now known as Blanton Branch. In the Blanton Branch Cemetery you can trace back generations of his ancestors.

Henry Frank and Lizzie Beth Williams Blanton

At an early age Henry Frank quit school, I believe after finishing the fourth grade, because his eyesight was so bad. While still a child and into early manhood he helped his mother run a grist mill, located on Little Paint Creek, while his dad and older brother worked in the logging and construction business. The mill washed out Jul. 4, 1929, during a flash flood. You can still see the holes carved out of solid rock, where the timbers stood if you want to make the climb down to "The Ole Mill Hole."

He married Lizzie Beth Williams, daughter of Luther and Ida Hunley Williams, of Flat Fork in Magoffin County, on Jun. 23, 1939. They were the parents of eight children, six of whom survived into adulthood: Adam Kanoah (born Jun. 14, 1940), Leo (born May 7, 1942), Sina May (born Feb. 23, 1946), Henrietta (born Oct. 25, 1950), Ruthie Lynn (born Nov. 28, 1956) and Pamela Lou (born Mar. 31, 1959). Two children died as infants, Mabel (born Mar. 2, 1945, died Mar. 2, 1945) and Hansford Victor (born Jan. 25, 1954, died Jan. 29, 1954).

Henry Frank was mainly a farmer even though he did work on the railroad for a few years. He also worked in construction and in the oil fields, anywhere he could find work. He was working for the Dept. of State Highways when he took sick in September 1965 and died a few weeks later in October 1965, from a kidney disease which through the years claimed most of his brothers and sisters.

Henry Frank always believed in education, and all his children graduated from high school and most went on to Mayo State Technical School for training. The exception was Adam who quit school when he was a freshman to join the Army and stayed to make a career of it. Leo died from cancer Aug. 15, 1993. Ruthie Lynn and her family moved to Urbana, OH, several years ago. The remainder of the children have reared their families in Johnson County. *Submitted by Henrietta Blair.*

BLEVINS - I remember as a young child pondering questions that dealt with my personal history and the origin of my surname. I knew that many families had taken their names from occupations or from the localities in which they lived. The name Blevins seemed shrouded in mystery. It has taken many years of research to accumulate the family history my records now contain, and much remains to be discovered.

Robert Blevins and Martha King Blevins. Children not identified.

The name, Blevins, is Welsh/English. It comes from the Celtic Welsh name, Bleddyn, which is a derivative of "ab Lawn" or wolf cub in the English language. The double "d" in the Celtic Welsh language has the same sound as the "v" in English. The earliest known usage of the name traces to a prince who ruled in northern Wales in the 11th century. This prince was Bleddyn ap Cynfyn. Bleddyn ap Cynfyn literally means Bleddyn, son of Cynfyn. Some researchers maintain that all Blevins families origins back to Prince Bleddyn ap Cynfyn, but the truth lies in the deep abyss of the past. There exists a tradition in my family that our true surname may actually be Williams, but I have yet found any concrete evidence to confirm this rumor.

Blevins are found in the early colonial records of Massachusetts and Rhode Island. One John Blevin arrived in Salem, MA, circa 1659. Later, others are found in Rhode Island, Virginia and North Carolina.

The early Blevins families were of a hearty stock. Many of them moved to the wilds of the Western Frontier. Several homesteads were established in western North Carolina and the southwestern portion of Virginia. It is a well documented fact that some of the Blevins were Long Hunters. These hunting bands were known for going into the wilderness of eastern sections of what became Kentucky and Tennessee and staying for several months at a time. On one occasion, Daniel Boone encountered a group of long hunters in Kentucky. The Blevins were numbered in this party. These hunters had preceded Boone's entry into Kentucky by five years. William Blevins was a long hunter and a contemporary of Elisha Walden and Henry Scaggs.

A great number of the Blevins from Johnson County trace their lineage to Elisha Blevins. Elisha was born circa 1809 in Lee County, VA. The identity of his parents has never truly been documented, but several hypothesis exist. One source is known to state that Elisha was the brother of a William Blevins who was the father of Capt. Daniel Blevins, CSA. It is also known that at one time the young Elisha lived on property owned by William in the Flat Gap section of what is now Johnson County. Elisha Blevins married Alsey Tackett, the daughter of Lewis and Susannah (Sumpter) Tackett. The wedding was held in Floyd County, KY, on Sep. 7, 1826.

The children of Elisha and Alsey (Tackett) Blevins are as follows:

1. William, the ancestor of Mr. Boone Blevins; 2. Lewis, the ancestor of Mr. Danny K. Blevins; 3. Solomon, the ancestor of many of the Morgan County Blevins including Kentucky state senator, Dr. Walter Blevins; 4. Mary; 5. John; 6. Martin (lived in the Ashland, KY, area); and 7. Sally.

Lewis Blevins, the son of Elisha and Alsey, was born circa 1830. He married Mary Ann "Polly" Meade, the daughter of Robert and Lydia (VanHoose) Meade. Alsey (Tackett) Blevins was living with Lewis and Mary Ann at the time of her death. The children of Lewis and Mary Ann Blevins are as follows:

1. Cynthia Ella; 2. Lydia; 3. Levi; 4. Samuel J. (also known as "Poor Bear," after combating a bear); 5. William Wallace McClelland "Clell"; and 6. Elisha Nelson, the father of three time Johnson County judge, Wayne Blevins and the grandfather of Clyde "Cousin Clyde" Blevins. Elisha Nelson was the Johnson County jailer 1946-50; 7. George W.; 8. John Elliott, the father of Russell Blevins, who sold produce in Johnson County for several decades; 9. Solomon, the ancestor of Lewis "Preacher" Blevins; and 10. Robert "Robbie," the ancestor of Danny K. Blevins.

Robert Blevins, the son of Lewis and Mary Ann (Meade) Blevins, was born in 1881. He married Martha "Dutch" King.

The children of Robert and Martha (King) Blevins are as follows:

1. Benjamin (born 1880); 2. Garfield "Dick" (born 1881, died Jun. 17, 1957, in Sorghum Hollow, Van Lear, KY); 3. Jesse Floyd (born 1884), made his home at Tram in Floyd County, KY; 4. William Harrison, lived for many years in Springfield, OH; 5. Maude (born 1865); and 6. Lewis Earl "Dock" married Alice Blevins of Lawrence County, KY.

Lewis and Alice lived in Wheelwright in Floyd County, KY. "Dock" is the ancestor of Dr. Soard of Inez, KY.

Garfield "Dick" Blevins, the son of Robert and Martha (King) Blevins, made his home in Van Lear, KY. He married Nora Meade, the daughter of Robert and Sarah Ella Mary Francis (Bush) Meade. The children of Garfield and Nora (Meade) Blevins are as follows:

1. Jesse (born 1908), the grandfather of Danny K. Blevins; 2. Minerva (born 1913); 3. Paul Martin (born Dec. 23, 1917); 4. William Harrison "Bill"; 5. Georgia (born Aug. 1, 1923, died May 31, 1995); 6. Bridgett Marie (born Oct. 30, 1927), currently lives in

Columbus, OH; 7. Richard Odell (born May 24, 1930); 8. Beatrice; 9. Audrey "Peggy"; 10. Macca; 11. Fannie; 12. Bertha; and 13. Helen.

Brigett Marie, Bertha and Helen are the only surviving members of this household as I write this article (1999).

Jesse Blevins, the son of Garfield and Nora (Meade) Blevins, married Eva Music, the daughter of Amos and Clara (Ratliff) Music. Jesse and Eva were the parents of Danny Eugene Blevins (born Feb. 9, 1939). Danny Eugene married Phyllis Jean Wells (born Feb. 13, 1942), the daughter of Beecher Jefferson and Marjorie "Margie" (Goble) Wells. Danny E. and Phyllis (Wells) Blevins had the following children:

1. Danny Keith, the author of this article (born Jun. 13, 1961, in Wabash, IN); and 2. Jessica Delene (born Nov. 2, 1964, in Wabash, IN).

Danny K. Blevins married Ida G. Butcher (born Oct. 26, 1964), the daughter of Heubert and Clarinda (Hampton) Butcher. Danny and Ida "Trudy" married Aug. 2, 1986, at the home of Danny E. and Phyllis in Van Lear, KY. The children of Danny K. and Ida Blevins are as follows:

1. Tracy Danielle (born Aug. 3, 1994, in Floyd County, KY) and 2. Daniel Trevor (born Dec. 26, 1997, in Floyd County, KY.

Jessica Delene (Blevins) DeBoard currently lives in Van Lear, KY, with her husband, Kennis DeBoard. Jessica currently has no children.

Anyone having additional information on this Blevins family is asked to contact Mr. Danny K. Blevins, P.O. Box 336, Van Lear, KY 41265. *By Danny K. Blevins.*

BOYD - Clifford Boyd was born on Aug. 11, 1923, in Floyd County, KY, to B. Palmer and Golda (Conn) Boyd. He was the first of five sons born to his parents.

Clifford and Winnie Staton Boyd

Clifford married Winnie Staton, a native of Bath County, KY, on Nov. 30, 1942, and they made their home in Betsy Layne, KY, until June 1961, when Clifford was transferred by his employer to Paintsville, KY.

Clifford grew up in Betsy Layne, KY, and is a graduate of Betsy Layne High School. He discovered early on what profession he wanted to pursue when he was almost electrocuted. After high school he served in the military (Army Air Force), attended Mayo State Vocational School studying electricity. He was employed by Kentucky Power Co. (American Electric) on Jan. 16, 1948, and held various positions within the company, one being area supervisor in the Paintsville, KY, office five years prior to his retirement in October 1988.

Clifford and Winnie are active members of the First Baptist Church in Paintsville, KY.

Clifford has been playing golf for over 40 years and continues to play as often as possible. He is also an active member of the Kiwanis Club.

They have three children: Nowana Sue Brown who lives in Paintsville, KY, and is employed by the Johnson County Board of Education; Lana Ann Russell who lives in Betsy Layne, KY, and is employed by an independent insurance adjustment company (GAB) in Pikeville, KY, and; Clifford Douglas Boyd who lives in Lexington, KY, and is employed by the Lexington Fire Dept. They also have five grandchildren and one great-grandchild to date (May 1999).

BOWLING - Clifford Bowling was born Nov. 5, 1932, near Van Lear in Johnson County, KY, to Clayton and Gracie Boyd Bowling. He had eight sisters and six brothers. Twelve siblings lived into adulthood, and six are still living.

Clifford and Mary Good were married Jan. 27, 1951, in a little town called Dora, IN, which is no longer there, since it is covered by the Salamonie Reservoir. They have two sons, Robert Lee (born Sep. 25, 1951, in Wabash, IN) and Gregory (born Jun. 19, 1962, in Rockford, IL); and one daughter, Helen Marie (born Oct. 30, 1957, in Wabash, IN).

Clifford and Mary Bowling

Clifford worked nine months in a coal mine at Legon, KY. Then in 1949 went to Wabash, IN, where he worked for General Electric for 10 years until they closed the factory and transferred the work to Rockford, IL. He worked at General Tire for a short while and decided to go to Rockford to work for General Electric again where he stayed for 16 more years until they closed that plant. He went to work at Quaker Oats Co. in 1976 as a millwright and stayed there until they closed in 1987. He retired then and has been having fun traveling and playing golf. He and Mary spend the winters in Phoenix, AZ, with their daughter, Helen, who is an architect. The rest of the year is spent in their home in Cherry Valley, IL, or on another trip to see more of the country. They have been in every state but Hawaii and Alaska and its just a matter of time until that is accomplished.

Clifford's sons live in the Rockford area. Robert is married to Ann Roberts, they have a daughter, Lisa (born in Rockford, IL, Apr. 23 1981). He also has a son, Steven (born in California May 15, 1973). Bob was in the Marines from 1969-79 and now has a business painting miniature war game figures.

Gregory lives in Loves Park, IL, with his daughters, Elizabeth (born in Rockford, IL, May 20, 1991) and Megan (born in Rockford, IL, Oct. 22 1992). Greg served in the Army from 1983-87 and now works as a machinist. *By Clifford Bowling.*

BROWN - About 1770, a little known pioneer in the "west" reared his family in the frontier areas of western Virginia and North Carolina. Valentine Brown is believed to have emigrated to this country from Ireland. He married Mary (unknown) in Lunenburg County, VA. He is listed on various Lunenburg and Grayson County censuses and the tax lists. At least one of Valentine's sons, John Quincy Brown, was already in Kentucky by 1820. George Brown (born about 1805) had remained in Ashe County, NC. His brother went to a part of Floyd County, KY, that became Letcher County.

John Brown and wife Lucinda Harman Brown

George Brown, son of Valentine, reared his family in Wilkes County, later Ashe County, NC. George married Abigail Osborne about 1824. George and Abigail had the following children: John, Isaac "Mac," William P., Alfred, Larkin, Benjamin B., Nancy, Catherine, George and Anna.

John Brown was born Feb. 24, 1831, in what is now Ashe County, NC. John Brown died Jul. 13, 1913, in Johnson County, KY. John married in about 1850, Nancy (Lewis?), by whom he had children named Henry, Caroline, Zilphie and Martha Brown.

Lucinda, Thoral and Arthie Daniels, granddaughters of John Brown

At age 31, John joined the Civil War effort at Jefferson, NC, on May 7, 1862, and fought for the Confederacy in Lee's Grand Army, Co. A, 1st North Carolina and 9th North Carolina Cav. Troops. He was wounded, at Second Manassas, or Bull Run (Aug. 28, 1862) then at the Battle of Paynes' Farm. He was with J.E.B. Stuart during the Battle of Gettysburg and rear guard when the war ended. He served from May 1862 till after April 1865. John, and his brothers: Larkin (age 20), Isaac (age 27), Benjamin (age 18), William (age 24) and Alfred (age 21), were all serving the south at the same time. All brothers: Alfred, Benjamin, Isaac MacDaniel, William P. and Larkin, served in the 21st Virginia, Robert E. Lee's Cav. in Co. K and other units as the war waged on. John Brown was wounded in the face. From that day forward he tried never to yawn by going to bed very early. When he yawned his jaw popped loose from his face bones requiring a painful maneuver to realign his jaw.

John Brown returned from the war to face possible unionist retribution at home due to his service in a new South filled with carpetbaggers. John also found his wife, Nancy, fraternizing with a unionist, relayed in my family with the term, "bushwhacker." John is reported to have slept in his Army coat on the floor until she delivered a son.

According to the oral tradition in my family, John, and his oldest son, Henry, cut wood for about two months to fill up a barn with wood. They fixed up flour, meat and other staples to ensure the woman was well taken care of prior to leaving to go to Floyd County, KY. The youngest of John's children, named Martha, about age 3, was left with her mother because she would not let go of her mother. The son born to this first wife kept the name Brown. He came to Kentucky when he was about 16 and lived with his half-brother, Henry Brown, until he was about 19 years old.

After migrating to Kentucky, John Brown married Angeline Blackburn Oct. 7, 1868, in Floyd County. In 1872, though John Brown put the fire out, Angeline died as a result of burns suffered when her dress caught on fire during a seizure. Two of their children grew to adulthood, Lettie Brown Sturgill and Louisa Brown. Two children, one named Bruce Brown, and an unnamed week old infant girl were taken to their mother's funeral by members of her family. Both young children died from whooping cough within two months of Angeline Blackburn's funeral.

John Brown's father, George Brown, and his mother, Abigail Osborne (Ausbourne), came to Kentucky sometime between 1870-80. Siblings "Katie" Catherine Brown, with her spouse, Thomas Osborne (also served in 21st Virginia Cav., Co. C), Larkin Brown, joined John Brown's migration. Abigail died in Johnson County and is buried on Tom's Creek. George Brown is buried in Ashe County, NC.

George Brown walked to Ashe County, NC, every year to visit his relatives; however, he became ill en route to Ashe County and died in North Carolina because he "took pneumonia."

John Brown remarried for the third time. Previously unmarried, Lucinda Catherine Harman, daughter of Aquilla Harman and Rebecca (Beavers?), married

John Brown in Floyd County, KY, Oct. 20, 1873. Aquilla was the son of Daniel Harman Jr., grandson of Daniel Harman, great-grandson of the widely respected Virginia long hunter, Heinrich Adam Harman (Herrmann).

John's brother, Larkin Brown, married Elizabeth Lewis in Floyd County. Other sons of George and Abigail Brown, William Brown married Tamsey Browning) and Alfred Brown (formerly a prisoner of war at the infamous Mt. Lookout Prison in Maryland) married Emaline Lewis in Ashe County then moved to Carter County, TN, some years after 1870.

Benjamin married Catherine Calhoun but he died before 1880 in the Farmville, VA, hospital for confederate soldiers. He is buried with other soldiers in graves next to the old hospital. Isaac MacDaniel Brown is listed in the 1880 federal census of Ashe County, NC. He married Elvira Goss and lived in Ashe County, NC, his lifetime.

John Brown and Lucinda Catherine Harman Brown lived in Floyd County, KY, for about 10 years, then moved to the Sitka and Tom's Creek communities, in Johnson County, KY, where they lived from 1882 till their deaths in 1912 and 1913.

They had the following five children, four of whom lived to adulthood: Minnie Rebecca Brown (born 1880) md. Artho Daniel, George M. Brown (born 1876) md. Minnie Rebecca "Sis" Daniel, Marion Brown (born 1874) md. Mary Ramey "Molly" Brown, Mary Alice Brown (born 1878) md. Willie Meadows, infant unknown name and date of birth.

John Brown wanted his grandchildren and great-grandchildren to know what he looked like, so he had a picture taken in about 1910.

In the family cemetery at the head of Tom's Creek, the family is reunited. John Brown, his wife, Lucinda Catherine Harman; his mother, Abigail Osborne Brown; his sister, Catherine "Katie" Brown Osborne; his brother-in-law, Thomas Osborne; his daughter, Minnie Rebecca Brown Daniel; and his son-in-law, Artho Daniel; as well as his son, Henry Brown, and wife, Margaret Baldridge Brown, are all resting on this hillside. Caroline Brown Jones, Marion and Mary Ramey Brown are interred there too. One of the granddaughters of John Brown, a daughter of Artho Daniel and Minnie Rebecca Brown Daniel, Lucinda Daniel, and her husband, Arlin Castle, complete three generations accounted for on this one site.

My grandmother, Rebecca Brown Daniel, always said we were of Irish people; she is "right-er" as the link to Ireland is the Virginian named Valentine Brown gets clearer, but, further proofs are still necessary. The legacy of John Brown is larger still than a hillside full of tombstones and a picture or a chart.

This farmer was known as a generous and kindly man, never asking much and caring for many on the fruits of his labor. My grandmother said there were four widowed women with no food for their children. John Brown had two log houses and built two additional log houses with kitchen out-buildings for these women who lived there with their kids. The women helped Lucinda with the cooking and other chores. No one went hungry on John Brown's farm.

That same kindly approach to life ran to the bone in my grandmother, Minnie Rebecca Brown, and still courses through the hearts of her daughters, my beloved mother, Arthie Daniel, and her sister, Thoral Daniel. This little biography is dedicated to the living memory of the Brown family as well as to my wonderful mother and dear aunt whose actions are examples of a life well lived through caring for others. *Respectfully submitted by Catherine Castle Kidd, great-granddaughter of John Brown, great-great-granddaughter of George Brown.*

BROWN & OSBORNE - Goldie Maxine Osborne was born Saturday, Aug. 7, 1937, at Loudean Ramey's house at Volga that her parents, Fred and Mae Osborne, were renting at the time. Dr. F.M. Picklesimer came out from Paintsville for the delivery. Her delivery cost $20.00 because the doctor had to return the next morning to set Maxine's broken arm.

Maxine grew up on Salyers Branch at Volga. She lived five years at the homeplace of her great-grandfather, Manford Salyer.

Maxine's first heart broken memory was when she was 3 years old and her grandmother, Beulah Salyer, died Jun. 20, 1941, at the age of 40.

Maxine Osborne Brown

When Maxine attended the one-room McKenzie Branch School she lived at the home of her grandfather, Kendrick Salyer, with her parents, two sisters, Beatrice and Ernestine, and her uncle, James Manford Salyer. Maxine remembers when Woodford Estep wired their home for electricity and her grandfather bringing home a radio one Saturday night so the family could listen to the Grand Ole Opry beginning Maxine's lifelong love for country, bluegrass and gospel music.

Maxine enjoyed hikes, picnics and visits to the huge rockland formation known as the "Big Rocks." At least five generations of the Salyer family saw the pictures and writings left by Indians when they occupied this land before the early settlers came. Most of these rocks have been destroyed by strip mining.

Maxine's ancestors came to Kentucky from Scott County, VA. Joe Salyer and his father, Levi, purchased government owned land and settled on Mudlick near Route 172 where the Indians had a sugar camp and where the Hope Valley Mennonite Church now sits. Joe's son, Logan Salyer, was Kendrick's grandfather.

Maxine is retired from the Sunman-Dearborn, IN, School System and a Kentucky retired teacher. She lives with her husband, Jonathan Brown, at Volga. Jonathan and Maxine are graduates of Morehead State University and Murray State University. They were married Jul. 14, 1968, at the First Methodist Church in Paintsville.

Jonathan Dan Brown was born Mar. 5, 1941, at Port Jefferson, NY. Jonathan grew up in the town of Eastport, NY, on Long Island near the Atlantic Ocean. Jonathan lived in the oldest house in Eastport. This house was built in 1775 by his Tuttle ancestors and still stands today.

Jonathan's father was Bartlett T. Brown and his mother was Josephine Lawrence Brown. Josephine (born Mar. 12, 1908), a retired teacher, resides at Volga near her son. Jonathan has two brothers. Robert Brown lives in Berkeley Heights, NJ, with his wife, Mary Margaret Bennett Brown. Richard Brown lives at Brown's Landing in Eastport, NY, with his wife, Barbara Harris Brown.

Jonathan and Maxine have a niece, Debbra Jean Brown DeLoma (born Jan. 14, 1967) who lives in Norwalk, CT, and a nephew, Thomas Lawrence Brown (born Jan. 2, 1971) who lives and works in New York City.

Their family is woven together with threads of love, warmth and kindness forever.

BROWN - Neva Evelyn Kerns Brown (born 1921), daughter of Clarence Kerns (born 1887, died 1950) and Ella Mae McKenzie Kerns (born 1900, died 1984). Clarence was the son of Lewis Kerns and Jennie Cooke Kerns of Lawrence County, OH; Ella, the daughter of William H. McKenzie (born 1862, died 1941) and Lydia Butler (born 1865, died 1948) of Johnson County.

Clarence Kerns worked at the Offutt Lumber Co. and Van Lear #5 coal mine. Ella moved to Columbus, OH, and took her first full-time job outside the home with the Southern Hotel at the age of 58. Clarence and Ella are buried in the VanHoose Family Cemetery at Tutor Key.

Neva Evelyn Kerns Brown

Evelyn's siblings include: Howard Leslie of Tutor Key, KY (married Olga Daniels), Jessie Irene, deceased (married Herman Eigensee), Louella Ruth of Teays Valley, WV (married first, Hobert Castle, married second, Homer Maddox), James Robert of Bob White, WV (married Marcelene Eskew), Minnie Grace of Paintsville, KY (married Bryan Barber), Clarence Richard, deceased (married Roma Schultz), Jack Dencil, deceased (married Ruth Kelly), Ray Douglas of Reynoldsburg, OH (married Madge Damron), Kenneth Herman of Columbus, OH (never married) and Doris Annette died in infancy.

In early life, Evelyn worked as a nanny for school superintendent, John Fred Williams and Carrie Bennett "Cecil" Cecil Williams. During WWII, she also worked briefly at an aircraft factory in Ypsilanti, MI, which produced B-24 bombers.

On Dec. 26, 1945, Evelyn married Claude Brown (born Apr. 3, 1916, died Jun. 15, 1988). Claude was the son of George M. Brown (born 1877, died 1962) and Minnie Daniels (born 1880, died 1948), both are buried in the Brown Family Cemetery at Volga. George was the son of John Brown (born 1830, died 1913), CSA veteran and Lucinda Harmon. Minnie the daughter of Joseph Daniel (born 1849, died 1923) and Sarah "Sally" Harmon (born 1853, died 1948). Claude's siblings include: Sally (born 1903, died 1986) married Everett Lemaster, Susie of Salyersville (born 1905) married Cecil Hitchcock, Charlie of Tutor Key, KY, (born 1907) married Mary Burchett, Carl (born 1910, died 1942), Clyde (born 1913, died 1980) married Georgia Lemaster, Clarence of Flat Gap, KY, (born 1918) married Frieda Patrick.

Claude briefly attended the University of Kentucky and served his country in Burma and China during WWII. He was employed for several years with North American Aviation in Columbus, OH, on the Vigilante Project. Claude was a member of Flat Gap Lodge F&AM and the Oleika Shrine.

To this union were born: Carlie Carma (born 1946, died 1972) married Judy Stapleton. Children, Christopher Michael; Carolyn Gay (born 1947) married Roger Owens. Children, Penelope Leigh (married first, Bryan Ward, married second, Edward Fernandez) and Elizabeth Ann (married Bryan Auxier); John Young (born 1949) married Diana Grace Booth. Children, Robert Jonathan (married Amy Tidball) and Heather Diane; Sandra Kay (born 1951) married Michael Wattenberger. Children, Michael L. Jr. (married Lillie Stambaugh) and Yetivia Noel.

Evelyn resides at Flat Gap and is currently a member of the Ramey Branch Church. As of this writing, Evelyn has three great-grandchildren: Wesley Paul Wattenberger of Winchester, KY; James Edward Fernandez of Austintown, OH; and Abby Ray Auxier of Paintsville, KY.

BURCHETT - Edward Grass Burchett was born Dec. 10, 1879, at Elna, KY, to David and Amanda Stapleton Burchett. He had 10 brothers and sisters. He married Idella Williams Jan. 5, 1903. Ida was born to Abraham and Miranda Blanton Williams Jun. 4, 1886, at Wheelersburg, KY.

Grass and Ida were the parents of 10 children which were: Ralph (born Aug. 19, 1904), Icy Mae (born Apr. 30, 1907), Amanda Melvie (born Dec. 24, 1909), Ethel (born Feb. 23, 1912), Fonzie (born Sep. 2, 1914),

Grass (Edward) and Ida Burchett, 1958.

Callie (born Jun. 24, 1917), David Winfrey (born Jul. 3, 1920), Virgil Willard (born Apr. 17, 1923), Louella (born Feb. 8, 1926) and Tera Emily (born Apr. 1, 1929), all in Johnson County.

Grass and Ida bought a farm from Sandy Phillips at Fuget, KY. They lived and reared most of their family there. In 1917, Grass got a job with Louisville Gas and Electric. While he worked at his job, Ida and the older children ran the farm. Grass retired from Louisville Gas and Electric in 1945. He then bought a small farm at Staffordsville, KY, and then sold the old home place to his son, Ralph, who reared most of his family there. Ralph's children still own the farm.

Ralph was married to Talitha Baldwin, Icy married Sonny Stapleton, Melvie married Payne Williams, Ethel married Bruce LeMasters, Fonzie married Maude Blair, Callie married Larry Williams, Winfrey married Earnestine Holbrook, Willard married Helen Dillon, Louella married Melvin Jayne and Tera married Walter Jackson Jr.

Grass and Ida were both members of the Cold Springs United Baptist Church for several years. Grass was a member of the Masonic Lodge and Ida was a member of the Eastern Stars.

Grass's grandfather, Leonard Burchett, ran a gristmill in the 1800s at McKenzie in Johnson County. Grass died Jun. 26, 1965, and Ida died Dec. 9, 1964. They are buried at the Patty Flat Cemetery in Johnson County along with five of their children. They have one girl buried in Delta, OH, and one buried in New Castle, KY. They still have three living children.

BURCHETT - Ralph Burchett was born Aug. 19, 1904, at Andy Lick Fuget, the oldest child of Edward "Grass" and Idella Williams Burchett. He married Talitha Hannah Baldwin Feb. 25, 1932, who was born Feb. 15, 1911, the daughter of Joel Henry Sr. and Sarah Emily Fairchild Baldwin. They were married at the Paintsville Furniture Store (Maggard's) by Guy Preston.

Ralph worked for Louisville Gas and Electric Co. from 1943 to retirement in 1969, seven of these years in Laconia, IN. He served on the Board of Education and was a member of the Cold Springs United Baptist Church since 1933. Ralph's Johnson County roots can be traced to great-grandfather, Leonard Burchett, who operated a grist mill at McKenzie Branch in 1800s.

Ralph and Talitha Burchett wedding, Feb. 25, 1932.

Talitha worked for elderly people during her youth, and in London, OH, at a steel wool mill during the war. She was an Avon representative and a homemaker. She became a member of Caudill Fork United Baptist Church in 1927. Talitha's roots are traced to great-great-grandparents, Electous and Sally Hudson Howes, and their parents, Richard and Mary Fugett Davis, Oil Springs, in 1700s.

To this union was born nine children:

Henry Edward (born Mar. 3, 1933) married Betty Trimble (divorced). Parents of two children, Vicky (born 1952) and David (born 1962). Later married Margie Stratton (divorced). Graduated from Flat Gap, served in Armed Forces, retired from Process Machinery, lives in Louisville.

Bernice Emily (born Aug. 8, 1935) married R.C. Stambaugh (deceased), parents of Gary (born 1963) and Lori (born 1970). Graduated from Flat Gap, attended Mayo, worked at *East Kentucky News*, lives at Wittensville.

Carroll Ishmel (born Dec. 11, 1937) married Carolyn Williams, parents of Julie (born 1963) and Leah (born 1967). Graduated Flat Gap and University of Kentucky, played basketball for Rupp, retired director of Carl Perkins Rehabilitation Center and Kentucky Rehabilitation agency, living at Red Bush.

Ida Eunice (born Nov. 8, 1940) married John "Leon" Pelphrey, 1963. Graduated Flat Gap and Mayo Business Schools, retired from Foothills Rural Telephone, lives at Elna.

Frecia Roszell (born Nov. 6, 1943) married George Spriggs, parents of Ralph (born 1963), Lisa (born 1966) and Dana (born 1968). Graduated Flat Gap and Mayo Cosmetology Schools, employed, Johnson County Board of Education, lives at Fuget.

Glenda Lee (born Oct. 8, 1947) married Dan Boone, parents of Jeffrey (born 1978) and Cortnai (born 1983). Graduated South Central and Mayo Business Schools, employed South Harrison School Corporation, lives at Laconia IN.

Anita Joyce (born Dec. 20, 1951) married Charles McMonigle, parents of Justin (born 1976) and Krista (born 1977). Graduated South Central and Mayo Cosmetology Schools, worked at Jo Mills Beauty Shop, now homemaker, living in Greenvile, IN.

Sandra Sue (born Dec. 26, 1953) married Bill Robinson, parents of Regina (born 1975). Graduated Johnson Central and Mayo Business Schools, employed Barker's Mobile Homes, lives at West Van Lear.

Ralph Neal (born Nov. 19, 1958), deceased.

The family home, a farm at Fuget, was Ralph's homeplace from age 13, and purchased from his parents in 1944. Ralph and Talitha lived there until their deaths; Ralph in 1992 and Talitha in 1996.

BURCHETT - Cuba is no more, once it was a thriving community with a school, church, stores and many families. Cuba is where Myrtle Estep Burchett was born Sep. 11, 1917, the daughter of Elzie Estep and Rachel Savannah Estep; the granddaughter of Lilburn Estep and Rachel Lemaster Estep and Margaret Estep. Lilburn Estep was born in Scott County, VA, in 1834, the son of Elijah Estep and Francis Chase Estep. Rachel Lemaster Estep was the daughter of Richard Lemaster and Rebecca Christian. Lilburn and Rachel are buried in the Estep Cemetery at Fuget; Richard and Rebecca Lemaster are buried in the Spice Cove Cemetery at Fuget, KY. Myrtle had five brothers: Lloyd Estep, William Estep, Lundy Estep, Glenn Estep and James Lowell Estep; and two sisters, Verna Estep and Claretta Estep. Five children died in infancy.

Ray and Myrtle Burchett

Myrtle married Ray Burchett, Apr. 3, 1937. They were married by Reverend Russell Wallin. Ray was born May 5, 1905, to James Burchett and Rose Castle Burchett. James was the son of David Burchett and Amanda Stapleton Burchett and Rose, the daughter of Harrison Castle and Lou Emma Salyers. Ray is buried at the Patty Flat Cemetery along with James and Rose Burchett. David and Amanda Burchett, Harrison and LouEmma Castle are buried in the Salyers Cemetery at Flat Gap, KY. Ray's brothers and sisters were: Earl Burchett, Darrell Burchett, James L. Burchett, Lionell Burchett, Ora Burchett, Maymie Burchett, Eula Burchett, Edna Burchett, Lillian Burchett and Virginia Burchett.

Myrtle is a housewife, mother, grandmother, great-grandmother, farmer, seamstress, Christian and friend. She and Ray were the parents of one daughter, Patricia Burchett Patton; one granddaughter, Michelle; and one great-grandson, Jon. She was the postmistress at Elna for many years. Following the death of Ray, she retired and moved to Flat Gap near her daughter.

Ray worked for the railroad in his early life, spending most of his time away from home and family. He later became an employee of Ashland Oil and Refining Co. as a member of the "Pipeline Gang" then becoming a "gauger" for the Low Gap, Red Bush area. Before roads were built he rode a bay mare "Ginger" up Paint Creek in rain, sleet, snow and blazing sun. He later drove a Jeep over roads most people would hardly walk on and before retiring he drove an International Scout. Ray was the general "Do-it-yourself- Man" after retirement. He was able to do a little bit of everything. He drove neighbors to the doctor, grocery store, cut hair (not using a bowl), never allowing a weed to become over two inches high. His pride was a great garden, free of weeds, and a lawn freshly mowed. He religiously mowed the Patty Flat Cemetery until his sudden death in August 1979. Ray and Myrtle were good neighbors and faithful Christians.

BURTON - Alex Harold Burton was born in Johnson County at Odds, KY, Apr. 12, 1925. He was the son of Roscoe Burton and Arena Goble and the grandson of James Patrick Burton and Margaret Montgomery, who were married in Johnson County in 1877.

Alex Harold Burton; Ella Robinson Burton

His family tree included many a noted pioneer such as John Walker, Patrick Porter, Daniel Boone and Jenny Wiley. Other surnames include Cook, Kozee/Keeze, Kitchen, Montgomery, Goble, Harless, Spears, Wells, Allieine, Auxier, Blair and Caudill, along with many others.

They came to Kentucky from the eastern ports and traveled the old wagon road through Virginia, homesteading until they found a place to call home.

Harold lived in Van Lear and at an early age developed a talent for music. At the age of 12, he was performing on the radio and could play any type of instrument. Harold played basketball and football at the Van Lear High School, graduating in 1945 while in Germany with Patton's Third Army. (I guess this was considered a field trip.) While in the 65th Div., he worked on communication lines and spotted for artillery. He received two Bronze Service Stars, a Good Conduct Medal, Victory Medal, European Theater Ribbon and the Occupation Medal for Western Germany at Rhine River.

After the war Harold attended Mayo Vocational School studying welding and machine shop. On Sep. 20, 1946, he married Ella Robinson from Auxier, in Floyd County, and started a family consisting of three children, and began a career in the number five mine at Van Lear.

Ray Burton was the first child born on Jun. 30, 1947, in the old Paintsville Hospital. Ray graduated from the Van Lear High School and Mayo Vocational School, entered the Air Force, married Shirlene Tackett, and had two sons, Michael Ray and Brian Christopher. He is employed by the General Telephone Co.

Harold L. Burton (born Jul. 7, 1951) graduated from Johnson Central High School, Mayo Vocational School and Morehead State University. Harold married Angela McCoart and had three daughters: Heather Leigh, Holly Elaine and Haley Rae. He has worked for the General Telephone Co., Island Creek Coal Co. and is now a teacher and coordinator at the Mayo Technical College.

Debra Kay graduated from Johnson Central High School in 1977 and married Mark A. Music. Mark was in the Air Force, so they traveled to bases in the U.S. and Germany. They had two children, Brandon and Danielle, and later divorced. Debra works for the Social Security Office in Prestonsburg.

Harold played music every Saturday night above the old Royal Theater, and for the Apple Day dance until his death in 1978 in a car accident. He spent 33 years as a union coal miner, was well respected in the community, and even ran for Johnson County sheriff. Harold was the kind of person that worked every day to provide for his family and instilled a strong work ethic in his children that will be his legacy to the community for years to come.

BUTCHER - Patsy Lois Butcher was born Jan. 12, 1944, in Johnson County, KY, to Gail Edward May (born Oct. 15, 1919, in Johnson County, KY) and Lucille Hitchcock May (born Feb. 20, 1914, in Johnson County, KY). Patsy was the third of four children born to her parents.

Patsy was married in Johnson County, KY, to Gene Arthur Butcher on Jun. 23, 1962. They were the parents of one son and three daughters: Sherrie Lynn (born Apr. 28, 1963); Rickey Eugene (born Sep. 23, 1964); Sheila Rose (born Sep. 3, 1965); and Vonda Lois (born Sep. 14, 1966). All were born in Johnson County, KY.

Patsy (May) Butcher

Patsy devoted her time to raising her children until they were all established in elementary school, after which she became employed by the U.S. Shoe Corporation, where she worked for several years. In 1983, at the death of her father, she took her invalid mother into her home and cared for her for seven years until her death in 1990. The years since her mother's death have been devoted to family and church.

Patsy's husband, Gene, was born Oct. 1, 1942, in Johnson County, KY, to Ashley Butcher and Nora (Webb) Butcher. He was the third of 12 children. In his early years he was employed in Indiana at a furniture factory. Later he worked on the railroad in Ohio and Michigan. He also was a long time employee of the Paintsville Heating and Roofing Co.

Gene and Patsy's daughter, Sherrie Lynn, lives in Baldwin, MI, and is employed by the Baldwin School System. She has two sons.

Their son, Ricky Eugene, lives in Johnson County, KY, and is employed by East Kentucky Hydro Seeding. He has one daughter and one son.

Sheila Rose lives in Mason, OH, and is employed by DA-Lite Screening Corp. She has one son and two daughters.

Vonda Lois lives in Johnson County, KY. She is a domestic engineer and is devoted to raising her two lovely daughters.

BUTLER - Lonnie B. "Lon" Butler was born Nov. 6, 1910, in Staffordsville, KY, to James Preston Butler and Mary Marie Molly Wheeler Butler. He was the seventh of eight children. Lon's father rode on horseback selling fruit trees. His mother was crippled due to arthritis and spent the last 18 years of her life confined in a wheelchair.

Lon grew up at Staffordsville and attended Paintsville schools. He married Nancy Opal Mckenzie Nov. 9, 1935, and they became the parents of four children: Della Mary (born 1936), Paul Edwin (born 1938), Delores Ann (born 1943) and Jerry Wendell (born 1950).

Lonnie B. and Nancy Opal Mckenzie Butler

For many years Lon was a truck driver for Williams Grocery of Paintsville, KY. Because he drove a food truck, Lon was exempt from the military service during WWII. Later Lon was a driver for Texaco Oil Co. After retirement from the trucking business, he worked part-time for Citizens National Bank.

Lon was a faithful Christian attending the Staffordsville Church of God. He loved to garden and was a dedicated husband, father and neighbor.

Lon passed away Feb. 19, 1988, from complications after brain surgery. He is buried at Highland Memorial Cemetery at Staffordsville, KY. He is survived by his four children and four grandchildren.

BUTLER - Nancy Opal Mckenzie "Opal" was born Feb. 5, 1917, at Cantrell's Creek in Flat Gap, KY, to William Edward "Bill Ed" Mckenzie and Della Mae Mckenzie. Her only sibling was her twin sister, Ocie Alice Mckenzie Ealey. Opal's father worked for Williams Grocery in Paintsville, KY, and her mother was a teacher in a country one-room school.

Opal was educated at her mother's elementary school at Cantrell's Creek and then at Flat Gap High School. She married Lonnie B. Butler Nov. 9, 1935, and spent the rest of her life at Little Mud Lick, in Staffordsville, KY.

Opal was a devoted mother to four children: Della Mary (born Sep. 3, 1936), first married Clyde King and second married, Edward Homer Ferguson; Paul Edwin (born Aug. 1, 1938) married Ann Wright; Delores Ann (born Apr. 27, 1943) married Bill Griffith; and Jerry Wendell (born Nov. 17, 1950) married Dinah Buchanan). Opal loved to crochet and was an excellent cook. She was a faithful Christian worshipping at the Staffordsville Church of God.

Opal was a full-time homemaker until her children were grown. Then she became a cook at Johnson Central High School. She retired after 19 years of service.

Opal died Feb. 20, 1993, from complications of brain cancer. She is buried at Highlands Cemetery at Staffordsville, KY. She is survived by her four children and four grandchildren: Tammy Ferguson Morris, Cygnet, OH; Marsha Butler, Knoxville, TN; and William Jarrod and Clay Thomas Butler, St. Cloud, FL.

CANTRELL - Burl "Whitey" Cantrell was born at Hargis in Johnson County, on May 2, 1921, to Thomas and Julia Ann Love Cantrell. Tom Cantrell was born Jul. 6, 1883, and lived his entire life at Hargis. He died there Jan. 3, 1969, and is buried in the family cemetery just above his home.

Julia Love was born about 1888 in Missouri and often told her family about moving to Kentucky in covered wagons. Tom and Julia were married in Magoffin County, Nov. 5, 1904. They were the parents of 12 children. One son, Henry Ford, was born in 1923 and died in 1925. Twins born in 1905 were stillborn. Other children of Tom and Julia are as follows: Robert (born 1907, died 1975) married Elna Frazier; Lennie (born 1909, died 1961) married Jeff Colvin; Bryan (born 1911, died 1986) married Ruie Blanton; Cal (born 1913, died 1963) was never married; Burns (born 1916, died 1977) married Mandy Blanton; Hazel (born 1920) married Charlie Cochran; Edna Merle married first to Junior Hudson, they divorced and she married second to Bill Cantrell from Tennessee.

Burl Cantrell grew up on Hargis and attended the one room school just below his home. He served in the Second Armd. Div. of the U.S. Army during WWII, a part of that time in France.

On Jul. 30, 1938, he married Gladys Marie Meade, the daughter of George Clinton and Martha Kathryn Williams Meade. To this union four children were born: Jackie Randall (born May 25, 1939); Sandra Sue (born Feb. 28, 1941); Burl "Skip" Jr. (born Feb. 24, 1943); and Wade Douglas (born Jul. 4, 1946).

Burl worked in the coal mines for several years before he began drilling in the oil fields. Later he worked as a pipe fitter at Ashland Oil Refinery until he was forced to retire because of a heart condition in 1976.

He died Jan. 24, 1990, at Paintsville. Gladys Meade Cantrell died at Paul B. Hall Regional Medical Center Nov. 4, 1995. Both are buried in Highland Memorial Park Cemetery at Staffordsville, KY.

CASTLE - Arthur "Artho" Castle was born Sep. 27, 1931, at the head of Tom's Creek at Sitka in Johnson County, to Arlin Castle and Lucinda Daniels Castle, the oldest of seven boys: Arthur, Clyde, Willie, Hayes, Richard, Nathan and Paul.

He attended Oil Springs High School, received a diploma in drafting from Mayo College and studied industrial arts and English at Morehead State University.

Arthur and Earlene Castle, Paul and Dianna.

He worked in the coal mines for a short time, on the railroad as a gandy dancer and at the golf course in Columbus, OH.

In 1951 he enlisted in the Air Force and was discharged in 1954. While in the Air Force he was stationed in such places as North Africa; Roswell, NM; and Lake Charles, LA. He was so influenced by the French-Cajun cooking of Louisiana that he still prefers it.

He worked for the Johnson County Library and taught school in Johnson County. He retired from the state of Kentucky having worked for the Dept. of Economic Security for 25 years as a social worker. He has served on many boards and committees, including past chairman of the Solid Waste Commission, Board of Assessments, he and others together were instrumental in getting the library tax passed, without which there wouldn't have been the new library built in early 1960s.

He has always been interested in preserving the heritage of Eastern Kentucky and has practiced that by the growing of cane and the making of sorghum on his farm at Stambaugh, cultivation of plants and wild flowers, making old time wooden toys and furniture and keeping old time banjo playing and folk music alive.

Arthur married Earlene Pack, who was born Jul. 17, 1936, the daughter of Walter Pack and Marie Stapleton Pack. They had two children, a daughter, Dianna (born Sep. 10, 1959). She married Bruce Radcliffe of Fayette County, KY. They have a daughter, Rebecca (born Feb. 4, 1993). Dianna attended Morehead State University where she received a degree in mining technology and a degree in applied sciences. She also attended the University of Kentucky where she received a degree in mining engineering and a degree in civil engineering. She has worked as an engineer for the state of Kentucky, Dept. of Highways located in Frankfort KY, for several years. Bruce is the manager of Hurst Office Supply in Lexington, KY. They live at Lawrenceburg in Anderson County, KY.

His son, Paul (born Oct. 22, 1969), married Sharon Collins from Pike County. They live in Ashland, KY. Paul attended Morehead State University where he took pre-med. He attended the University of Kentucky and received his degree in physical therapy. After doing his internship in Kentucky, Indiana and Tennessee, he worked at King's Daughters Hospital for a time before opening a Physical Therapy Clinic in Ironton, OH. He also has clinics in Huntington, WV, and Ashland, KY. Sharon attended the University of Kentucky and received a doctorate in pharmacology. She is a pharmacist at the Veterans Administration Hospital in Huntington, WV, at this time.

Arthur is a descendant of John Brown of North Carolina, who was in the Confederate Cavalry during the Civil War; the Harmans who founded Harman's Station; and Johann Kassel who was born in 1639 in Germany and came to America by special invitation of William Penn in 1686 on the ship *Jeffries*.

CASTLE - Cyrus Castle and Jemima Jane Castle were second cousins who married at Johnson County, KY, in 1892. Cyrus (born 1872, died 1945, Kentucky) was the son of Hezekiah "Kye" and Lavina Grimm. Jemima Jane (born 1872, Kentucky, died 1967, Ohio) was the daughter of Moses P. Castle and Julia Murphy. Jemima Jane's grandfather was William Castle, who happened to be an older brother of Hezekiah Castle. William Castle and Hezekiah Castle were the sons of Inman Castle and Nancy Davis. Brothers Zedekiah Alan Castle, Nathan Castle and Inman Castle migrated from Castlewood, VA (Russell County) to Floyd County, KY (section later became Johnson County) by 1820. Another brother, Benjamin Castle, migrated from Scott County, VA, in 1824. Another brother, John Castle, who had previously migrated from Castlewood, VA, to the state of Ohio, migrated to Johnson County prior to 1850. Meaning that all of the Castle families of southeastern Kentucky are actually related.

James Jay W. Castle

William Castle had been a Union loyalist during the Civil War, while his younger brother, Hezekiah Castle, had served in the Confederacy. Relations between the two lines were strained at best. Hezekiah Castle had already chosen a bride for his son, Cyrus, and it wasn't Jemima Jane Castle, as a result our successive lines have little knowledge or recollection of Hezekiah Castle.

Cyrus Castle and Jemima Jane Castle had 12 children, 10 of which were born in Johnson County, and they were: Homer B., Gloner, Sonnie, Hollie M., Ollie Mae, Blanche, Genoah, Estill Wendell, Dorman and Julia. Two children were born at Fleming County, KY, and they were, William Dallis and Stella Beatrice. Four of their children died young and they were: Gloner, Sonnie, Blanche and William Dallis.

Cyrus and Jemima Jane Castle migrated from Johnson County, KY, to Fleming County, KY, in 1917. They purchased a farm at Mt. Carmel.

Son, Homer B. Castle (born 1893), married Virgie Mineer and resided at Flemingsburg, KY, prior to his death in 1983.

Son, Hollie M. Castle (born 1900), married Kermit Hinton and resided at Fleming County, KY, prior to his death in 1981. This couple had two children, Dorman Lenox and Adalei.

Daughter, Ollie Mae Castle (born 1903), married Otto Hamm and resided at Bentonville, OH (Adams County) prior to her death in 1986. This couple had two children, Virgie B. and Francis Ruth.

Daughter, G/Jenoah Castle (born 1907), married LeRoy Hershberger Sr. and resided at Cincinnati, OH (Hamilton County) prior to her death in 1989. This couple had one son, LeRoy "Lee" Hershberger Jr.

Son, Estill Wendell Castle (born 1909), married Dora Mae Mineer (born 1906, died 1995) and resided at the family farm in Lewis County, KY, prior to his death on May 11, 1984. This couple had one child, William Lewis Castle Sr., who had 11 children. Estill Wendell's grandson, James "Jay" Wendell Castle, and namesake currently serves on the Ripley-Union-Lewis-Huntington Local Board of Education at Ripley, OH, Brown County (as he has for the last 12 years). James "Jay" Wendell Castle resides at Aberdeen, OH (Brown County).

Son, Dorman Castle (born 1911), married Margaret Dillon and currently resides at Aberdeen, OH (Brown County). This couple had the following children: Charles M. Castle, who has served as a teacher, principal and superintendent in the Ripley-Union-Lewis-Huntington Local School Dist. at Ripley, OH, for over 30 years and is now retired. Homer C. Castle, who served as a teacher in the Ripley-Union-Lewis-Huntington Local School Dist. and then went on to become county superintendent for the five local school districts that comprise Brown County. Homer C. Castle, who is retired, was recently elected to the Brown County Board of Education. James C. Castle Sr., served as a teacher and principal in the Ohio Valley/Adams County School Dist. for over 30 years (his daughters, Julie and Jonelle, currently teach at the Ripley-Union-Lewis-Huntington Districtwide Elementary at Ripley, OH). Mima Francis Castle-Manning, has taught in the Ohio Valley/Adams County School Dist. for over 30 years. Charles M., Homer C., James C. Sr. and Mima Francis, and their successive generations, reside at Aberdeen, OH (Brown County).

Daughter, Julia Castle (born 1913), married Lane Simpson and currently resides at Winchester, OH (Adams County). This couple had the following children: Mima Lee, Barbara Ann, Ronald Lane, Emma Kay and Daryl Wayne. Mima Lee Simpson married Larry Fulton (former mayor of Ripley, OH, and current Union Township Republican committeeman for Brown County) and resides at Ripley, OH (Brown County). She also has taught for 29 years in the Adams County/ Ohio Valley School Dist.

Daughter, Stella Beatrice Castle (born 1921), married Paul Wellman and currently resides at Batavia, OH, (Clermont County). This couple had one daughter named Jean. *By James "Jay" Wendell Castle.*

CASTLE - James Charles Castle (born Feb. 5, 1892, died Dec. 16, 1966), son of Charles Harrison Castle and Lizabetha Chandler Castle, married Amanda Ella Caudill Castle (born Sep. 28, 1898, died Feb. 6, 1987), daughter of E.E. Caudill and Sarah Ann Jenkins Caudill.

Their children were Ramey Castle (born Nov. 30, 1915, died Feb. 13, 1989) md. Ida Howard; Orville Castle (born Apr. 14, 1917, died Mar. 1, 1991) md. Lucy Montgomery; Sarah Castle Tackett (born Nov. 16, 1918) md. Fred Tackett; General Arnold Castle (born Apr. 20, 1920) md. Ola Gullett; Herbert Castle (born Jul. 8, 1922, died May 20, 1998) md. Edna Hawkins; James William Castle (born Apr. 2, 1927) md. Juanita; Clarie Castle Cantrell (born May 15, 1925) md. Cecil Cantrell; Rose Ella Castle (born Dec. 12, 1928, died Jul. 1930); Hubert Castle (born Feb. 14, 1924, died Feb. 14, 1924; Charles Harrison Castle (born Nov. 14, 1934, died Feb. 1925); Stella Castle Krigger (born Nov. 16, 1930, died May 16, 1996) md. Bud Krigger; Alma Castle Jenkins (born Sep. 15, 1932) md. Lloyd Jenkins; Emma Faye Castle Williams (born Feb. 25, 1937) md. Arnold Williams; Robert Frankie Castle (born Jun. 11, 1940) md. Leana Gay Phipps.

Herbert Castle was in the Army in World War II, went in Apr. 2, 1942 got out Dec. 5, 1945.

CAUDILL - Rev. Lewis F. Caudill began life in Johnson County, KY on Sep. 26, 1852 on Barnett's Creek. He was educated in the schools of Johnson County and became a teacher at about 18 years of age. He taught school for 28 years. He did not have an advanced education but he was a student all his life.

In 1871, he was married to Cynthia Conley of Denver, Johnson Co., KY, a school pupil of his. To this union nine children were born, four girls and five boys.

L.F. Caudill was saved at 30 years of age and united with the Missionary Baptist Church at Denver, KY. He became a minister of the Gospel and served in that capacity for 60 years.

"Brother Caudill," the name by which he was known, served as pastor of churches in Paintsville, Pikeville, Ashland, Salyersville and rural churches in Magoffin and Johnson counties.

With his family he moved from Jennie's Creek in Johnson County to Mash Fork in Magoffin Co., KY in 1887. He had preached there prior to moving there to live. At this time there was only one Baptist Church in Magoffin County, the Ivyton Baptist Church at Ivyton, KY. T.G. Riggs of Denver, KY organized this church in 1884.

Brother Caudill felt called of God to serve in Magoffin County. Some Christians in the Mash Fork vicinity were waiting for a Missionary Baptist Church. This church was organized in 1887. L.F. Caudill was called to be the pastor and served until 1906. He supplied and held meetings through the years after the pastorate was terminated. He became pastor of the Ivyton Baptist Church at Ivyton in 1888 and served intermittently until 1910.

Licking River Baptist Church at Sublett, Magoffin Co., KY was organized in 1900 by L.F. Caudill and he was pastor there for about 20 years. He organized the Lakeville Baptist Church at Lakeville, KY in 1906 and became its pastor in 1906, serving until 1908. He became pastor again in 1920 and served until 1925. After that he was supply pastor several times. He visited and preached until he became too advanced in age to serve.

He became pastor of the Mine Fork Baptist Church, Mine Fork, KY, Magoffin Co. in 1897 and served until 1917, the last record of a church meeting at that church.

Brother Caudill was pastor of the Pikeville Baptist Church, Pikeville, KY from 1907 until 1909. There was no church building at that time and services were held in the public school building. With his efforts, and the assistance of some friends, the lot on which the present church building now stands was purchased.

He preached at Salyersville before there was a Baptist Church there. Rev. Sledge held a meeting there in 1909 and a church was organized in that year. L.F. Caudill became its pastor in 1920 and served this church for two years.

He was a strong advocate of Vacation Bible Schools. They did not exist during his active ministry. He loved children and young people and always sought to help them to know the Lord. He visited a Vacation Bible School at the Ivyton Baptist Church with his pastor and other workers a few years before his home going. The pastor said, "Brother Caudill, how did you like the school?"

"It is the finest thing I know of, it is like a revival meeting," Brother Caudill replied.

Another monument to his memory is Magoffin Baptist Institute, Mountain Valley, KY, in Breathitt County and formerly Salyersville, KY. Dr. Brown of the Southern Baptist Home Mission Board came to Salyersville looking for a site for a school. He informed Brother Caudill that the Home Mission Board would build a school there if the Baptists in the vicinity would raise $1,800. Brother Caudill immediately went to work getting donations in cash and pledges. In a few weeks when the people met to find the results, he had $1,500 of the amount. He told them that he would mortgage his farm on Mash Fork to get the other $300. Three friends said, "We won't let that happen" and gave the remainder. They were methodists.

Magoffin Baptist Institute opened its doors to students in September 1906. It has stood through the years since that time as as institution of learning that has also trained young people spiritually for service in the Kingdom of God. Eternity alone will reveal the work that it has done. (This institution dissolved in the 50s, JBR).

In character as well as physical structure Lewis F. Caudill was dignified and erect. As a soldier of righteousness he was unconquerable. Figuratively speaking, he was born with a sword in his hand. In the old struggle between good and evil, he was the first to charge and the last to retreat. He was never conscious or confident of his own strength. He was a man of untiring efforts. The spirit of his long ministry manifests something of the heart of his Christ in behalf of the world. He was earnest, courageous and fearless in all his work. Many were the times he had to stand alone for the things that the Book stood for, yet he never wavered.

Over many counties of the eastern section of Kentucky there remains in memory of him many trails which he blazed that today fly the flag of Christianity. The churches that he helped to establish are now preaching his Christ to the world.

Most of his active ministry was before the days of the automobile. His black horse, Bill, carried him across hills and down valleys for about 20 years to his preaching appointments. The weather was never too cold or too hot for those appointments to be kept. Sometimes he would have to build a fire when he arrived at the church.

One could never estimate the number of people won to Christ by him. He preached to individuals as well as to crowds. He visited homes to minister to those in need of spiritual help. His mind was Scripture stored. His was a life lived for Christ.

When Brother Lewis F. Caudill was enfeebled with age, nearing his 90th birthday, the flickering candle went out. He slipped out of this earthly tabernacle into his heavenly home. He was reunited with loved ones and many of those whom he had won to Christ.

This biography of Lewis Caudill has been published in some Eastern Kentucky magazine. If I knew what magazine, I would gladly give credit. I am sure the author would be proud to have her research reprinted. In sincere appreciation, June Rice, for Liberty Baptist Church. Written by Jennie Williamson, submitted by June Rice

CHANDLER - Escom Chandler, widely known as Eck, was born Nov. 30, 1910, to Frank and Mary Hamilton Chandler. He was the first of six children. His father was a teacher, politician and banker and was elected Johnson County court clerk in 1918. Escom attended the Paintsville City Schools graduating in 1929. He was very active in sports, playing tennis, baseball, basketball and football. He excelled in football, serving as captain of the team during his senior year. He received a football scholarship to Western University. He attended Western two years until financial difficulties due to the depression forced him to drop out, get a teaching certificate and begin teaching. He taught at Flat Gap for two years, until he was able to resume his education at Morehead State University. He continued teaching and attending college until he graduated from UK in 1936. While walking across the platform to receive his diploma, Governor "Happy" Chandler stepped out to congratulate him, which made a lasting impression on Escom. After graduation, Escom became principal at Oil Spring School. He also taught at Paintsville High School before leaving teaching to enter the business world.

60th Wedding Anniversary, Escom and Katherine Chandler, July 19, 1937-1997.

Escom married Katherine Elizabeth Preston on Jul. 19, 1937. They were married almost 62 years until her death on Jun. 23, 1999. Katherine was born Mar. 17, 1913, the only child of Charles Clarence and Zora Daniel Preston. Her family moved to Milford, OH, when she was very young and she attended schools there. Her mother was a teacher and her father a farmer and businessman. Katherine graduated from Miami University in Oxford, OH, in 1935. She was a teacher at Paintsville High School and a helpmate in Escom's businesses.

When Escom left teaching he bought the Paintsville Bakery. He ran the bakery until he entered the Navy as a lieutenant junior grade. He served two years during WWII with 16 months aboard a ship in the South Pacific. During this time it was election time in Paintsville and even though Escom was on active duty, the people elected him as their mayor in 1946, in which capacity he served four years. During his term, he was responsible for putting in the first parking meters, appointing the first park commission and paving the streets of Stafford Addition. In 1946 he organized the Paintsville Dry Cleaner and Laundry along with other local businessmen. It was the first laundry service for Paintsville and the surrounding area. Escom was named Small Business Man of the Year in 1966 for his management of the business. He retired in 1973.

Escom has been a longtime member of both Paintsville Kiwanis and the Chamber of Commerce. He was elected president of the Chamber of Commerce twice. In 1959, his financial abilities and contributions were recognized by the Citizens National Bank when they elected him to their Board of Directors.

Mr. and Mrs. Escom Chandler have been longtime members of First Baptist Church of Paintsville. They were both Sunday school teachers. Escom has served as superintendent of the Sunday school and as deacon. Katherine was active in Womens' Missionary Union, holding offices on the local, district and state levels.

The Chandlers have been lifetime residents of Paintsville and Johnson County. Their personal high ethical standards have clearly influenced many lives.

CHESNEY & DANIEL - James Paul "Jim" Chesney was born in Donora, PA, Feb. 20, 1929, the son of Steven and Susanna Kral Chesney. His parents were both born in Hungary; they came to the U.S. in 1913. He had two brothers and three sisters: Julianne Chesney, Alex Chesney, Helen Chesney, Margaret Chesney and William Chesney.

Marilyn Sue (Daniel) Chesney was born in Allegan, MI, Sep. 30, 1937, the daughter of Simon and Ivel (Conley) Daniel. She grew up in the Paintsville area and first attended the two-room school at Concord, afterward attending Paintsville Elementary and High Schools, graduating from Paintsville High School in 1955. She is a member of the Paintsville United Baptist Church. She had three brothers and one sister:

Kerry Neil Daniel (born Sep. 25, 1934, in Johnson County, KY, died Jul. 11, 1936.)

Richard Lyle Daniel (born Sep. 12, 1943, in Prestonsburg, KY) married Ruth A. Johnson on Jun. 23, 1962. They have three children: Richard Alan (born Jun. 12, 1963), Kellie Renee (born Jul. 3, 1966) and Stacey Michelle (born Jul. 5, 1968). They have four grandchildren. They presently reside in Rome, GA.

Judith Ann Daniel (born Jan. 10, 1945, died Sep. 25, 1945).

Harry Lee Daniel (born Sep. 12, 1946, in Paintsville, KY) married Dorothy Bergstrom on Apr. 26, 1963. They have four children: Tammy Lea (born Feb. 6, 1964), Teresa Lynn (born Apr. 3, 1967), Kristi DeShawn (born May 14, 1968) and Gregory Mark (born Jul. 17, 1971). They have seven grandchildren. They presently reside in Suffolk, VA.

Jim and Marilyn had five children:

Kathleen Marilyn (born Aug. 15, 1960, in Riverside, CA) is a graduate of California State University, Long Beach, CA, and is a physical therapist. She married Jim Wiechelman on May 18, 1996; they have one son, Joseph Michael Wiechelman (born Dec. 8, 1998). They reside in Portland, OR.

Deborah Ann (born Aug. 8, 1961, in Orange, CA. She also is a graduate of California State University, Long Beach, CA, and is an elementary school teacher in the Temecula Valley (CA) Unified School Dist. She has two children, Edward L. Crain IV (born Sep. 4, 1986) and Kasie Michelle Crain (born Jul. 18, 1989). They live in Temecula, CA.

Michael Stephen Chesney (born Aug. 17, 1962, in Riverside, CA, died May 18, 1984, in Los Angeles, CA) was a senior, majoring in English, at the University of California, Riverside.

Mark Daniel Chesney (born Aug. 17, 1962, in Riverside, CA) is a graduate of California State University, San Diego, CA, where his major was computer science. He married Lisa Ann Beck Aug. 3, 1985; they have two children, Matthew James (born Feb. 27, 1990) and Melissa Rachel (born Jan. 10, 1994). He is employed by Zone Automation in Temecula, CA. They live in Murrieta, CA.

Mary Chesney (born Jan. 14, 1964 in Riverside, CA, died Jan. 14, 1964).

Jim and Marilyn reside in Temecula, CA, and are both retired from the city of Escondido, CA, where Jim was employed as a civil engineer and Marilyn as an administrative assistant for over 25 years. They are both now working part-time for the Temecula Valley Unified School Dist. and the Murrieta Valley Unified School Dist., Jim as a substitute teacher and Marilyn as a substitute secretary or computer/instructional aide.

Jim and Marilyn Sue (Daniel) Chesney and family.

CLATOS - In 1903, in Athens, Greece, Estrates Clatos, an only son, was born. At age 17, he made his way by ship to America. Despite the language barrier, he began to prosper in the restaurant business. By the late 1920s, he found himself in Paintsville, KY.

Now in 1915, Ison "Son" Fairchild and Bertha (McCloud) Fairchild had begun their family with a daughter, Irene. Two sisters followed later, Mary Elizabeth (Davis) Trimble and Agnus Pauline (H.C.) Burnette. Bertha and Ison were commonly known as "Big Mom" and "Daddy Son".

One of the first restaurants owned by Estrates Clatos was located on Court St. (now Maggards Furniture). The American translation of Estrates is Steve. Quickly, he became known as "Steve The Greek."

The first meeting of Steve and Irene was love at first sight. He told everyone in the restaurant that Irene would one day be his wife. On Feb. 22, 1934, his dream was realized with what was reportedly the grandest social event of that time. The marriage of Irene and Steve Clatos.

Estrates "Steve" and Irene Fairchild Clatos

The newspaper carried detailed accounts of the wedding feast Steve himself prepared. Including the beautiful cake and homemade ice cream. Their union produced three children: Lloyd Demetre Clatos, Penelopia Irene Clatos and Nicola Estrates Clatos. The Clatos' children were all delivered by a midwife, Ms. McKenzie, known as Ms. Mac. The family lived in an apartment above the restaurant for several years, and later moved to a part of town (Main Street) known as Bristle Buck. Today Paul B. Hall Medical Center and Johnson County Health Dept. occupy the area.

A plain spoken, kind hearted man, Steve regularly fed school children and adults for free in his restaurant. He continued to prosper through the 40s and 50s, despite difficult times.

Steve and Irene were members of the First Freewill Baptist Church. His life was spent caring for others and laying his treasures up in heaven. The names "Daddy Steve," "Little Mom," "Daddy Son" and "Big Mom" will always be remembered with love by his family.

Steve and Irene had three children: Lloyd Demetre Clatos, Penelopia Clatos Meade and Nicola Estrates Clatos. Following are their descendants:

Lloyd Demetre Clatos (born Jan. 6, 1935) married Betty Sue Witten (born Dec. 24, 1955) and had six children as follows.

Kathryn Louise Clatos married Robert Hutcherson, five children: Joshau Heath Callis, Cody McKay Callis, Christopher Derek Callis, Jennifer Ray Hutcherson and Robert Alan Hutcherson.

Steve Demetre Clatos married Ruth Davis, two children, Kristen Marie Clatos and Stephen Christopher Clatos.

Karen Sue Clatos married Johnny "Scott" Lefler, two children, Stacy Ann Lefler (married Fredrick Holst) and Thomas Scott Lefler.

Jerry Lloyd Clatos married Margaret McHargue, one child, Jeremy Shea Clatos.

Gary Nicola Clatos married Melissa Mitchell, one child, Tyler Nicolas Clatos.

Penelopia Irene Clatos married John Jude Osborn, one child, Megan Demetra Osborn.

Penelopia Clatos (born Jun. 20, 1936) married Billy Gene "Jack" Meade (born Jun. 18, 1955) had four children as follows:

Jackie Irene Meade married Jack Pelfrey, one child, Bryan Keith Pelfrey.

William Lindsey Meade married Leigh Anna Watson.

Michael Lee Meade married Michelle Leigh Ann Moore, one child, Michael Braden Meade.

Robert Allen Meade married Glenda June Hayden.

Nicola Estrates Clatos (born Jul. 18, 1938) married Alice Honeycutt (born Jul. 20, 1962) and had two children as follows,

Nikki Lynn Clatos McDowell married Gregory McDowell, two children, Rachel Shay McDowell and Wesley Sean McDowell.

Ronald James Clatos married Angie Pennington.

CLATOS & FAIRCHILD - A wedding of very unusual interest was solemnized on the evening of Washington's birthday at the home of Mr. and Mrs. Andrew Keourtis in Paintsville, when Miss Irene Fairchild became the bride of Mr. Steve Clatos. The marriage ceremony was performed by Judge H.B. Conley at 8 o'clock in the presence of a large number of guests, probably the largest crowd that ever attended a single wedding in Paintsville.

The bride is the daughter of Mr. and Mrs. Son Fairchild and a fourth year student in the Paintsville High School. The bride wore a white satin dress with accessories to match and carried a corsage of white and pink roses. The wedding cake was decorated with pink roses and contained the name of the bride and groom.

Mr. Clatos came to Paintsville four years ago where he engaged in the restaurant business had has been very successful and in known and respected as a good citizen. He is a native of Athens, Greece.

Irene Fairchild Clatos

After the wedding ceremony the time was spent in music, feasting and merrymaking, which continued until the early hours of the morning. There was no scarcity of refreshments, which were served abundantly throughout the night and the 250 guests who attended the wedding were loud in their praise of the entertainment accorded them.

One fat beef and one 250 pound porker were killed for the occasion, while ice cream, strawberries, cake and other delicacies were served to the assembled guests.

COLDIRON - It is thought by some that the word Coldiron comes from two German words, something like Colt or Cault meaning Coldiron and Isen meaning iron and that it has been translated literally into Coldiron. Johan Georg Kalteisen (George Coldiron) who came to America in 1750 from Goppingen, Wurttemberg, Germany, which is roughly the upper Rine. After starting his family in Berks County, PA, George moved his family to Rowan County, NC in California in 1767.

Conrad was the second son of George Coldiron and married Rachel Hendricks in Rowan County, NC in about 1783; removed from North Carolina about 1804/05 to Harlan County, KY and died between 1834-36.

A son of Conrad and Rachel Coldiron was William "Billie". He was born in 1802, Rowan County, NC and died Jan. 19, 1876. He married Feb. 20, 1830 to Leah Lewis who was born in 1808 and died Apr. 21, 1884. Her dad was Abner Lewis and her mother was Martha Nantz.

William and Leah Coldiron's second child was James Hiram (born Dec. 27, 1828). James married Rebecca Blanton Oct. 29, 1851. Rebecca was born in November 1832 and died after 1900 in Johnson County, KY. They were the parents of nine children: Gilbert (born Nov. 17, 1852); Nacharius (born ca. 1855); Jesse W. (born April 1857, died Dec. 7, 1878); Missouri Joseph; Radford (born Sep. 22, 1859); James G. (born February 1862); Sarah E.; George W. (born ca. 1866); John H. (born ca. 1869) and Mary M. (born ca. 1877).

James and Rebecca Coldiron's sixth child was Sarah Elizabeth (born Feb. 18, 1864, Magoffin County, KY, died Jan. 27, 1947 in Johnson County, KY). Marriage record for James H. McCarty and Sarah E. Coldiron on Feb. 6, 1879; James was 19 years of age and Sarah was 16. They married in Magoffin County, KY at the home of James H. Coldiron; witnesses were James Rice and William Rice and Wallis Bailey was the minister. James H. and Sarah were members of the Low-Gap United Baptist Church when it was a log church. Later the church burnt. They made their home on McCarty Fork of the Colvin Branch, Johnson County, KY and both are buried there. Their house is occupied by Carl McCarty and his wife. James and Sarah were the parents of 10 children: Forest W., Oscur, Gracie, Clifton, Mattie, Donna, Mollie, Dewey and James, all were born in Johnson County.

Every Coldiron descendant in America according to Otto Coldiron descend from this first immigrant, Johan Georg Kalteisen. He calls himself John George Coldiron in the body of his will, but he signed the same document as Johan Georg Kalteisen. He made the will in 1803 and it was probated in 1805, it was about the time of the probate that his son, Conrad, went through the Cumberland Mountains to a creek called Walled Creek and where it enters the Cumberland River and the town of Coldiron, KY now stands. *Submitted by James F. McCarty.*

COLLINS - My father, Arthur Collins, was born Mar. 1, 1915, in Johnson County, KY, the eldest son of Francis "Frank" Marion and Victoria Pennington Collins. His older sister, Fannie, was born in 1912. Ethel and Kelly followed. Frank and Victoria were loving parents who struggled to bring up their children in the rugged hills of Johnson County.

Frank worked as a coal miner until his death in a mining explosion at Pond Creek, KY, in 1922, at the age of 32. His widow was left with four young children ages 10, 7, 5 and 2. Three short years later, sadness came to the children again when their mother, Victoria, contracted tuberculosis and died leaving the four children orphans.

The children spent the rest of their remaining childhood living with aunts, uncles, grandparents and neighbors working the farms and performing chores to earn their food and lodging. Tragedy hit this family a third time when their sister, Fannie, died from tuberculosis when she was only 17. Arthur describes his older sister as a beautiful, kind and sensitive young woman.

Arthur and Kelly Collins taken 1946.

Ethel married young and had one son, Kenneth Collins, before she was stricken with tuberculosis and died at age 22.

Both Kelly and Arthur served their country in WWII. Arthur served in the Air Force from June 1943-January 1946. He served in the Islands with the 305th Fighter Control Sqdn., and also served in the Tinian Islands. He earned the Bronze Star, Marksman, Sharpshooter and Good Conduct medals. Kelly entered the Army Cav. and served in the European Theater, working with the infantry from 1942-46.

After the war Kelly and Arthur settled in Greenup County, KY. They married and reared families there. Kelly worked in construction and as a school bus driver where he was loved and respected by students, teachers and parents. He passed away at 54. He was survived by two children, Kelly Jr. and Ruby Riffe.

Arthur was employed and retired from Armco, Inc. and resides on a farm in rural Greenup County where he was reared by his father and his late mother, Doreen Linkous Collins.

His hobby and current vocation is raising fox hounds which he breeds and ships to buyers across the country. He and his wife, Wanda Castle Cook Collins, raise a garden, can and freeze the produce and keep several head of cattle. At this time his father is 84 and very active.

He is the sole surviving sibling. He returns to Johnson County frequently to visit friends and relatives and to tend the gravesites of his beloved family. He especially returns before Memorial Day to clear the graves at Sycamore Branch of Daniels Creek. He has been joined by his nephews, Kenneth and Kelly Jr., and his grandson, Vincent Cochran. My father wants to make sure someone will care for the resting place of the family taken much too soon. *Submitted by Tommie R. Collins.*

COLLINS & WELLS - Carl Collins (born Dec. 26, 1922, in Johnson County, KY), one of six children born to McKinley Collins and Callie Daniels Collins of Daniels Creek. Carl was a coal miner and farmer. He married Nov. 6, 1944, to Polly Wells (born Jan. 2, 1927), the daughter of Benjamin and Susanna Richmond Wells. Carl and Polly lived in Cleveland in the 50s where Carl worked with Park Drops Ford before returning to Kentucky and buying the farm that they presently live on. In Cleveland, Polly was employed at Precision Metal Smith, and in Kentucky Polly worked at a local sewing factor. Carl worked in the mines and farmed. They raised all types of vegetables and fruits and their own animals. The family always enjoys holidays since their children enjoy coming to eat their mother's dinners. She is known for her chicken dumplings.

Carl and Polly Wells Collins, Mike, Larry and Benette.

There were three children born to this marriage: Michael Collins (born Aug. 31, 1945, at Golden Rule Hospital, Paintsville) graduated from Morehead State University on a baseball scholarship and after graduation moved on to the Minor League with the New York Mets. He was traded to the Philadelphia Fillies where he remained for several years before returning to Kentucky. He married first to Judy Ward and they had one child, Tracy Collins (born Oct. 19, 1968, died Sep. 14, 1971). This marriage ended in divorce and Mike married Brenda Bailey and they had two daughters, Kelly Amanda Collins (born Aug. 4, 1976) graduated from Morehead State University May 1999 and Erin Allison Collins (born Aug. 30, 1980) will be a sophomore in the fall of 99 at Prestonsburg Community College.

Mike completed his master's degree at Morehead and is with the Johnson County Board of Education, and coaching baseball in the summers. His wife, Brenda, is a teacher at Flat Gap Elementary School. Mike and Brenda reside at Flat Gap, KY.

Carl and Polly's second child, Larry Collins (born Jul. 23, 1952, at Women's Hospital, Cleveland, OH) is employed with Booths Coal Co. He is married to Rita Griffith (born May 20, 1954) of Auxier, KY, she is with the Johnson County Education System as a teacher's assistant. Larry and Rita have two children, Tonya Collins (born Feb. 8, 1974) is a student at Eastern Kentucky University. She will graduate in the fall of 1999 with her master's degree in speech therapy. Adam Collins (born Apr. 26, 1982) is a student at Johnson Central High School where he is active in sports. Adam loves hunting and fishing. Larry and Rita reside on Rt. 3 Daniels Creek.

Benette Collins (born May 12, 1961, in Johnson County) married Harold Camden, two daughters were born to this marriage who were born in Johnson County. Cassandra Dawn Camden (born Aug. 30, 1979) graduated from Okechobie High School in 1998 and is working for a doctor. Cynthia Gail Camden (born Jan. 13, 1984) is a freshman at Okechobie High School where she is active in sports. Benette and Harold were divorced in 1994. Benette later married Charlie Ford from Okechobie, FL, where they reside.

COMBS - Benjamin "Ben" Franklin Combs was the son of William C. Combs (born about 1857, died about 1897). Ben's mother was Alice Armenta Witten. Born Jul. 17, 1849, married William C. Combs Apr. 10, 1872, died Dec. 6, 1920. William C. and Alice Armenta lived at Wittensville, KY.

Benjamin Franklin Combs (born Sep. 28, 1885) married Zora Mae Rice Oct. 9, 1913. Zora Mae (born Jun. 9, 1892) was native of Morgan County, KY. She spent most of her early life there. Zora Mae was the daughter of George William Rice and Marguaretta Osborn Rice. Ben and Mae lived all their married life at Wittensville, KY, at the old home place. They had 11 children: Hazel Louis Combs (born Mar. 12, 1914) married Carmel Witten. Hazel had three children: Wanda, Larry and Janice Witten.

Zora Mae Combs (born Jan. 4, 1916) married Wendell Ray Conley. They had one daughter, Brenda Conley.

Clyde Bennett Combs (born Apr. 8, 1917) married Goldia R. Preston, Oct. 6, 1945. They had three sons: Wendell Franklin Combs, Harvey Bennett Comb and Donald Gregory Comb.

Benjamin F. and Zora Mae Combs

Pansy Violet Combs (born Jul. 21, 1919) married Clarence Witten. They had one daughter, Myra Lorel Witten.

Daris Vincent Combs (born Jul. 21, 1919) (Pansy and Daris were twins).

Daris married Martha Stambaugh. They had one son, Mickell Combs. Daris died Sep. 14, 1981.

Bonnie Avis Combs (born Jul. 21, 1921) married Charles Castle July 1945. They had two children, Darell and Myra Castle.

George William Combs (born Nov. 30, 1923) married Earline Stapleton. They had five children: Debbie Combs, Kimberly Combs, Jeana Combs, Eric Combs and Mark Combs.

Bert Wendell Combs (born Apr. 26, 1925) died in WWII in April 1945.

Juanita Jean Combs (born Jul. 12, 1930) married Daniel Young, Harrison Weaver, Earl Johnson. Juanita had three children: Barry, Stephen and Marla Lovetta Joy Combs (born Jun. 9, 1932) married Harry Ronald Roach. They had two children, Mary Jane and David Roach.

Ermil Morris Combs (born Aug. 20, 1934) married Janice Blanton. They had two sons, Billy and Brian Combs.

Ben Combs was a merchant, farmer and Wittensville postmaster for many years. Ben was from a family of three brothers: Charley Combs, he married Dora Howard, they had 11 children: Gracie Eunice, Mable Lee, Sallie Arminta, Charles Ernest, Lexie Olive, William Virgil, Dora Lou, Howard Estil, John Carl, Lillian and Anna Louise.

Robert Combs (born 1883, died 1948) married Malinda Preston. They had seven children: Virlie, Arnold, Arbie, Shirley, Murley, Ruby and Jewell.

John Combs married Oatie Boure. They had five children: Esta, Thelma, Ann, Romaine and Charles.

Zora Mae Rice was from a family of seven children: Donald Rice, Winston Rice, Ted Rice, Ida Rice, McFinley Rice, Norton Rice and Eddie Rice. *Submitted by Clyde B. Combs.*

CONLEY - Henry Conley's ancestors migrated from Ireland in the early 1700s to Chester, PA. He was born there in 1751. During the Revolutionary War he served as a captain in the Cavalry Militia in North Carolina. He was married to Ann MacGregor. Their son, Thomas, was born in North Carolina in 1777. He married Susan Joynes (some say the spelling was later changed to Jaynes). Susan was said to be a close friend of Jenny Wiley.

The first Conley born in Johnson County was Thomas (Jr.?) in 1812. He married Mahala Davis in Floyd County. He passed away in 1877 and his grave is located at the mouth of Miller's Creek near a limestone cliff four to five miles above Paintsville on land known as "The Preston Farm."

Thomas and Mahala had a son, Matison (birth date not available). Matison married Elizabeth Colvin and both are buried at Abbott Creek in Floyd County.

John Milton, the son of Matison and Elizabeth, was born at Abbott in Floyd County in 1862. He married Marietta Woods in 1884 at the home of her parents, William and Lucina Stafford Woods, at Big Mud Lick. They had nine children: Forest, Harry, Everett, Ralph, William (Deke), Hobart, Ethel, Lillian and Ivel.

Forest was married to Clausie Picklesimer. He worked in Frankfort, KY, with the Department of Revenue until the time of prohibition. After that he moved to Philadelphia, PA, and worked with the American

1st row: Keith Conley, Hansel Picklesimer, Willis Pickelsimer, Warren Conley, Mary Conley, Eugene Conley, Anna Laura Picklesimer, Mary Forest Conley, Robert Earl Conley, Annabelle Dixon, Donald Conley and Arnold Conley. 2nd row: Hubert Picklesimer, Forest Conley Jr., Jesse Davis and Everett Fishel Conley. 3rd row: Harry Conley, Francis M. Picklesimer, Garland Dixon, Harry "Partee" Conley, John M. Conley and Maryetta Woods Conley, Charles Conley, Juanita Conley, Estil Picklesimer, Walter Picklesimer and Homer Picklesimer. Back row: William "Deke" Conley, Shirley Burke Conley, Hubert Conley, Bertha Barnett Conley, Ralph Conley, Everett Conley, Suna McKenzie Conley, Ivel Conley, Lucille Conley, Forest Conley, Otis Conley, Rolla Dixon, Gary Conley, Lilly Conley Dixon, Ethel Conley Picklesimer, Betty Picklesimer and Clausie Picklesimer Conley. [See Conley bio above, right)

Railroad Express until his retirement. They were the parents of six children.

Harry was a leading business man in Paintsville for several years. He was married to Bertha Barnett, and they had six children. They moved to Bloomfield, KY, and he held the position of government inspector with the State of Kentucky in Bardstown. Both he and Bertha are buried at Bloomfield.

Everett was a lifetime worker in the oil and gas business. He was married to Suna McKenzie. They were the parents of four. William, known as Deke, married Nellie Picklesimer. They had two sons. They divorced and he later married Shirley Burke; they had six children. He worked in the oil and gas fields. His last known address was Allegan, MI.

Hobert worked for the U.S. Postal Service in Paintsville for years. He was married to Ethel Preston. They were the parents of two sons. They were residents of Cincinnati, OH, at the time of Hobart's passing. Ethel continued to live there until her death and both are buried in Cincinnati.

Ethel was married to Homer Picklesimer. They reared 10 children. He was a grist and sawmill owner. The family played musical instruments and sang at local gatherings, and on a local radio station.

Lillian married Rolla Dixon. They had one son and two daughters. More information can be found elsewhere in this book about the Dixons.

Ivel married Simon Daniel. They had five children. After Simon's death Ivel married her childhood sweetheart, Marvel McKenzie.

Ralph was born Jul. 4, 1900 at Rocky Knob. He was reared on Big Mud Lick and attended a one room school for eight years. He was an accomplished pianist and teacher; self-taught in high school and college subjects through manuals and textbooks. He was an oil and gas well driller, and worked in several states, including Kentucky for over 50 years. In 1931 he married Ollie Blanton, born in 1915 to Walter and Sally Prichard Blanton. Ollie had three sisters and two brothers, Dixie, Mable, Monnie, James and Howard Paul.

Walter's parents were James Mac and Sarah McCarty Blanton. His grandparents were James H. and Mary Davis Blanton. His great-grandparents, George and Martha Shepherd moved to Johnson County from Powell's Valley, VA in the early 1800s. Sally's parents were Charley Prichard and Mary Ann Cantrell Prichard.

Ralph and Ollie reared seven children: Anita, born in 1932; Larry, 1934; Norvan, 1936; Janet, 1940; Paul, 1942; Karen, 1945; and Sharon, 1949. Anita married Kermit Picklesimer, son of Oakley and Mallie Hitchcock Picklesimer. Larry married Imogene Blair, daughter of Paris and Goldie Gullett Blair. Norvan's wife, Barbara, was the daughter of Bert and Lucille Pelphrey. Janet married Raymond Salyer, son of Millard and Martha McKenzie Salyer. Paul married Connie Risner from Magoffin County. Karen married and divorced Wayne McKenzie, the son of Russell and Berti McKenzie. She later married Van Duncan from the state of Indiana.

Sharon's husband, Wade Cantrell, was the son of Burl (Whitey) and Gladys Meade Cantrell. Ralph Conley passed away Jan. 9, 1994. He is buried at what used to be called the Persimmon Point Cemetery at Big Mud Lick and is now known as the Jayne Memorial Cemetery. His grandmother, Lucina Woods Stafford (born 1808, died 1904), is also buried there as is his great grandparents, John B. (born 1804, died 1869) and Calista Nott Stafford (born 1808, died 1865).

Ralph's family researched and gathered this information from family Bibles and other records.

CONLEY - Howard Conrad Conley was born in Johnson County, Flat Gap, KY, on Feb. 10, 1924. His father, Benjamin Franklin Conley, died when he was 9 years old. His mother, Dora Meade Conley, lived until 1958. Conrad attended elementary school and high school at Flat Gap. Having graduated from high school at age 17, he was off to Louisville, KY, where he was employed by the L&N Railroad Co. Realizing this type of work was not his calling, he enlisted in the U.S. Army in 1946. He served two years in Germany where he met his wife, Ada Lee Ritter, a civil service employee from Hobart, OK.

Howard Conrad Conley

After Conrad's two year stint in Germany with the U.S. Occupation Forces, he and Ada Lee returned to Washington, DC where they were married and Conrad enrolled in classes at the University of Maryland. Being well acquainted with public works, the Army and now with higher education, Conrad was able to make up his mind about his life's vocation. He decided the Army offered more opportunities, and at the same time he would be serving his country. He re-enlisted and again was on his way to Germany.

In 1951, the Flat Gap native was the first enlisted man chosen from the Garmisch Military Post to attend Officers Candidate School. The gold bars of second lieutenant were awarded Howard Conrad in 1952. With this step-up and other promotions to follow, he was admonished by his superior officers, "With increased rank goes increased responsibility." As his record shows, Conrad carried, with pride and valor, the responsibility entrusted to him. In just nine years, he had advanced to the rank of major.

The scope and magnitude of Conrad's assignments can be ascertained by the following 1965 news release from the 9th Logistical News: "Commanded by Major Howard Conrad Conley, the 172nd Transportation Detachment has personnel in Bangkok and Korat. The Detachment is responsible for all U.S. troop movement in Thailand."

Bob Hope recognized the skill with which the 172nd Detachment operated. He wrote the following note from Los Angeles, CA, on Jan. 5, 1965: "Thanks to the 9th Logistical Command for making our tour pleasant. I hope 1966 brings you much success and good health. Regards, Bob Hope."

Conrad held the rank lieutenant colonel when he retired in 1969. From an undocumented source, it was disclosed that Conrad was the fifth person to be commissioned lieutenant colonel in the 1950 year history of Johnson County.

Conrad and his family put their roots down in Charleston, SC where he worked as manager of the Hopkins Mayflower Moving and Storage Company. While working there, he was chosen Charleston's outstanding businessman of the year.

Using Conrad's priorities as criteria, one could conclude that he would want to be remembered as: (1) family man. He always managed to have his family with him wherever he was stationed. He wanted the best for his wife Ada Lee; daughters, Connie and Rachel; and son, John. (2) A loyal American - he served his country in uniform 23 years in both peace and war (WWII, Korean and Vietnam). (3) A community man - being a 32nd degree Mason is of itself an indication that he rendered outstanding service to his community. (4) A profound believer in God - through the years he never lost sight of his upbringing. His mother, whom he loved and respected, was his role model who believed and trusted in a living God. (5) A lover of life and humor - he was always a jovial fun-loving person. Conrad's love of life radiated to all those whom he met. He was revered by the company for whom he worked and respected by his competitors.

With all the high honors Howard Conrad Conley was privileged to experience, and with all the prestige that went with the rank of lieutenant colonel, his highest calling was from above when the Great Commissioner invited him to join his Army and Conrad accepted. Howard Conrad died May 25, 1986. He was honored with a full military funeral. After the 21 gun salute was fired and the bugler sounded the last call of the day, Lt. Col. Howard Conrad Conley was laid to rest in the land of his heritage, the Conley Cemetery in Flat Gap, KY. Conrad we salute you. *Submitted by Florence Conley Meade.*

CROTHERS - William T. Crothers was born Jul. 23, 1934, at Weeksbury in Floyd County, KY, to Thomas N. Crothers and Cloha Lee Price Crothers. He was the second of five children: Mary Crothers Hewlett (born Dec. 4, 1931) of Paintsville, KY; Lenore Crothers Eldridge (born Sep. 29, 1937) passed away Aug. 3, 1963; David Lee Crothers (born Aug. 25, 1950) passed away Dec. 4, 1986; and Carl Michael Crothers (born Feb. 26, 1952). Michael is now a resident of Mountain Manor Nursing Home in Paintsville, KY.

Thomas N. Crothers was born at Borderland, WV, Jan. 26, 1911. He was the son of William E. Crothers and Evaline Williams Crothers. The Crothers family came from Ireland in 1720 and settled in Cecil County, MD.

Cloha Lee Price Crothers was born Mar. 25, 1915, at Meally, KY, in Johnson County. She was the daughter of Clarence G. Price and Mary Hall Price. She is also a descendent of Moses Preston, a Revolutionary War soldier who settled in what is now Johnson County about 1799.

William graduated from the eighth grade at Van Lear School in Van Lear, KY, in 1947, and from Monterey High School in Monterey, TN, in 1951. He entered the USN Jan. 2, 1952, and served until Jul. 1, 1955. He is a combat veteran of the Korean War and served aboard the USS *Epperson* DDE-719.

He entered college in August 1957 and graduated from Eastern Kentucky University in June 1961 with a BA degree in social studies and in 1972 he completed the requirements for a master's degree in education from Eastern Kentucky University.

In 1961, William began teaching and coaching at Prestonsburg High School. He moved to Johnson County in 1967 and taught at Meade Memorial High School. After consolidation of the county high schools in Johnson County, he moved to Johnson Central and taught there until his retirement in 1993. While at Johnson Central he taught social studies, coached sports, drove a school bus and for eight years was the athletic director.

William married Ruby Shepherd Crothers Jun. 27, 1962, at Paintsville, KY. She was the daughter of Mort Shepherd and Lola Allen Shepherd of David in Floyd County. She was the third of eight children born to this union; five girls and three boys.

William and Ruby Crothers are the parents of two children, Judy Carol Crothers Huber and William T. Crothers Jr. Both reside in Paintsville, KY. They also have two grandchildren, Natasha Rose Huber and Craig Anthony Huber.

After William retired from teaching, he began working at Ed Spencers Law Office in Paintsville, KY, as a legal assistant. He is an avid fisherman and enjoys all sporting activities. He has also served as a member of the Paintsville Board of Education.

DANIEL - Arlie Ormond Daniel was born in Nashville, TN, Jun. 19, 1945, the son of Arlie Harmon Daniel and Mecleta Oeta (Kouns) Daniel. Arlie's mother, Mecleta, was born in Ashland, KY, Jul. 10, 1907. She was the daughter of William Henry Kouns and Hetti (Ransbottom) Kouns. Mecleta died Jun. 14, 1998, and is buried in the Daniels Cemetery on Daniels Branch near the Sugar Grove Church at Sitka, KY.

His father, Arlie, was born in Johnson County, KY, Aug. 10, 1901. He was the son of James Harrison Daniel and Venus (Slone) Daniel. They met in Ashland, KY, where he worked as a welder and she worked at Cress's Dept. Store. They were married Apr. 10, 1937, and moved to Johnson County in February 1947. He died in May 1966 and is also buried in the Daniels Cemetery.

Arlie and Betty Daniel

Arlie Ormond has two brothers, William Harrison Daniel (born Jan. 2, 1940) and Donald Lewis Daniel (born Feb. 11, 1953).

William Harrison Daniel lives in Covington, KY, along with his wife, Gerri. Donald Lewis Daniel and wife, Noi, live in Merrit Island, FL.

Arlie Ormond has two sisters, Elizabeth Ann Eagleston (born Mar. 30, 1947). She and her husband, Sidney Eagleston, live in Ashland, KY. Margaret Jean Wynn (born Jul. 30, 1947) lives in Frenchburg, KY, along with her husband, Roy Dale Wynn.

Arlie grew up on Daniels Branch at Sitka, KY, and attended Sugar Grove, a one room school, for two years, then he attended Flat Gap School until graduating in 1963.

He married Betty Lou McKenzie, Sep. 19, 1964. She was born in Johnson County, KY, Apr. 10, 1945, the daughter of Francis Marion McKenzie and Edith Mae (Stapleton) McKenzie.

Edith Mae was born in Johnson County, KY, Mar. 9, 1922, the daughter of Monterville Stapleton and Effie (Crider) Stapleton. She died Oct. 24, 1963.

Francis Marion was born in Johnson County, KY, Dec. 29, 1918, the son of Tobe McKenzie and Spicy (Tackett) McKenzie. He died Sep. 22, 1993. Francis and Edith are buried in the Stapleton Cemetery near the Kerz Church.

Francis and Edith were married Aug. 15, 1936. He worked in the coal mines and she was a housewife.

Betty was the fifth of 14 children. She attended Murray, which was a one room school, for five years. Then she attended school at Flat Gap until she graduated in 1964.

Arlie and Betty have two sons, Arlie Jr. (born Oct. 5, 1966) and Anthony Orban (born Dec. 23, 1968). They both attended Johnson County Schools and graduated from Johnson Central High School. Arlie Jr. attended Mayo College where he graduated in 1986 from the industrial electricity program. Anthony attended Eastern Kentucky University.

Arlie Jr. married Tonya Rene Rife, Dec. 23, 1997, the daughter of Dallas and Brenda Rife. He works as an electrician for a prep plant in Ragland, WV. They live at Stambaugh, KY.

Anthony married Dena Cornet, May 4, 1990, the daughter of Richard and Penny Cornet. He works for East Kentucky Power in Winchester, KY. They have a 3-year-old daughter, Emily and are expecting their second child in July 1999. They live at Winchester, KY.

Arlie has been employed by Big Sandy Rural Electric in Paintsville, KY, since September 1965 and plans to retire from there. He has held several positions there and is presently the maintenance superintendent. Arlie and Betty own a farm at Stambaugh, KY, where they have lived for 33 years.

DANIEL & DIXON - Buell Daniel was born Nov. 6, 1918, at Winfred, KY, to Edgar and Frona (LeMaster) Daniel. He was one of a family of five boys (i.e., Walter, Earl, Simon, Hubert and Buell) and one girl, Zona (Daniel) Songer. Buell and Annabelle Dixon were married Feb. 11, 1940, at Pikeville, KY.

Annabelle is the daughter of Rolla and Lillie (Conley) Dixon of Paintsville. Rolla is a descendent of Henry Dixon, one of the founders of Paintsville and one of Johnson County's earliest settlers. Annabelle's older brother, Garland, and sister, Dorothy (Dixon) Schroyer, are both retired and currently living in Paintsville, KY.

Buell and Annabelle Dixon Daniel

Annabelle was born Jan. 9, 1920, at Sitka, KY, and graduated from Paintsville High School. Buell, also a graduate of Paintsville High School joined the USAAC during WWII. He taught radar until his discharge in 1946. Annabelle worked for the Southern Bell Telephone Co. in Paintsville prior to transferring to Champaign, IL, during the war.

In 1952, Annabelle and Buell moved to Allegan, MI, where she still resides. Active in electronics, Buell was an owner of an appliance store before founding the Allegan TV System; the first cable television company in the Allegan area. After selling his share in the cable system, Buell designed and manufactured electronic programming equipment that was used by the cable television systems all over the U.S.

After moving to Allegan, Annabelle again worked for the telephone company until she accepted a position at Rockwell International as a receptionist and P.B.X. (switchboard) operator for 24 years. She retired from Rockwell in 1982.

A life-long member of the First Baptist Church, Buell also served as a member of the Masonic Lodge and Lions Club. He learned to fly small airplanes and became an accomplished pilot. He and Annabelle enjoyed flying and often flew to Paintsville to visit with their friends and family there.

An avid deer and goose hunter, as well as fisherman, Buell was artistically gifted and was taking oil painting lessons at the time of his death in March 1983. He passed away while he and Annabelle were in Florida, escaping the cold, snowy Michigan winter weather.

Annabelle is also a life-long member of the First Baptist Church. She continues in her love of travel and takes great pleasure in spending time with her friends and relatives who live in and near Grand Rapids, Hastings and Allegan, MI, as well as in Eastern Kentucky, Ohio and Florida.

Possessed of a green thumb, she, being especially fond of Kentucky White Half Runner Beans, plants gardens and raises beautiful flowers each summer. She also enjoys playing cards and reading.

DANIEL - Cecil Daniel Jr. (born Mar. 7, 1941) and Karen Lou Stumbo (born Aug. 5, 1955) were married Nov. 28, 1975, and have two children, Tara Anne (born May 8, 1978) and Johnathan Brett "J.B." (born Nov. 23, 1982). Cecil has two children, Cecil Dale (born Jan. 22, 1960) and Donna Lynn (born 1962), by a previous marriage.

Cecil's lineage is as follows: Father, Cecil Daniel Sr. (born Dec. 13, 1914, died Nov. 7, 1992), was a proud 23 year retiree of the UMWA and who was fondly called "Big Cecil" by his family and worked for Consolidated Coal at Van Lear. Mother, Edith Chandler (born Sep. 22, 1915, died Nov. 11, 1993), who at one time worked at the Castle Fork Nursing Home and was a housewife. Both are buried at Highland Memorial at Staffordsville, KY.

Cecil Sr.'s father, Alonzo Daniel (born Feb. 14, 1895, died Aug. 29, 1977), was also a retired UMWA Consolidated Coal miner who endured the tent camps in Chatteroy, WV. Mother, Alice Ward (born Aug. 16, 1889, died Nov. 14, 1959), worked during the war at Cincinnati and was a housewife. Both are buried at the Old Friendship Memorial Garden at Williamsport, KY.

Cecil, Karen, Tara and J.B. Daniel.

Edith's father, William Wesley Chandler (born Jul. 18, 1883, died Jan. 15, 1959), was a retired miner working in Betsy Layne and Whitehouse. Mother, Lydia Deboard (born Aug. 19, 1882, died Apr. 1, 1967), a housewife. Both are buried at the Chandler Family Cemetery at Lowmansville, KY.

Karen's lineage is as follows: Father, John Herman Stumbo (born Jan. 13, 1926, died Nov. 27, 1963), was a minister of The First Christian Church for 20 years. Mother, Helen Marie Bliffen (born Sep. 1, 1927, died Jun. 29, 1977), was a social worker for the Dept. of Human Resources. Both are buried at the Antioch Memorial Gardens in Liberty, KY.

John's father, Burns C. Stumbo (born May 4, 1905, died March 1973), was retired from C&O Railroad and a United Baptist preacher. Ethel Hall (born Mar. 30, 1908, died Oct. 15, 1984), was a housewife. Both are buried at Golden Oaks Memorial Garden, Catlettsburg, KY.

Marie's father, Ralph Dalton Bliffen (born Apr. 21, 1904, died Nov. 17, 1967), was retired from Huntington Herald Dispatch. Mother, Aleta Isabel Watrous was a housewife and became a missionary after her husband's death and served for a brief time in Africa. Both are buried at Ridgelawn Memorial Garden in Huntington, WV.

Cecil is a 22 year UMWA retiree of Arch Coal Co. and Karen works at the Johnson County Public Library. Tara and J.B. reside with their parents.

DANIEL - Mary Dutton was born Jan. 9, 1907, in Johnson County, KY, to Ben and Cynthia Perry Dutton. She had two brothers, Willie and Virgil, who preceded her in death.

Mary was married in December 1928, in Johnson County to James Lafe Daniel (born Jun. 16, 1910, died Jun. 20, 1969). They were divorced in 1952 and Mary never remarried. They had 13 children: Virginia (married Wilbur Loran Slone); Lafe Eugene (married Lena Burke); Clifford (married Sue Lemaster); Joshua (married Lois Dotson); Sarah (died in infancy); Benny McKinley (married Mary Lucille Hill); Callie (married Dean Johnson); Charles (married Emma Lou Fields); John Merman (married Judy Delong); Matilda (married Lowell Patrick, deceased 1962, married second, Harold Hughes); Kathleen (married Jimmy Ray Allen); Jackie (died in infancy); and Paul David (married Janet Foust). They have 41 grandchildren, 77 great-grandchildren and 18 great-great-grandchildren.

Mary attended school at the Boonescamp Grade School through the eighth grade. Although she had little formal schooling, she always managed to find a way to help support her family. After the divorce, times were hard but through hard work she managed to keep the family together and reared 11 children to be productive, self-supporting adults. She worked in Johnson County for several years as a waitress at Francis' Restaurant and Preston's Restaurant. They always had a garden and raised a lot of their own food to help make ends meet. Mary's first concern was always for others.

Even though she had a large family of her own, there were always a few extra children around that never went away hungry or without a smile and a kind word.

Mama, as she was known by family and friends, possessed a quiet inner strength that led her family through many hardships. Her favorite saying "Where there's a will there's a way; God will provide" has been a guide for her family that they will never forget.

Mary moved to Wabash, IN, in 1962. She was employed at Gackenheimer's Drug Store until she retired in 1979, at the age of 72. In February 1992, she returned to Johnson County where she resided until her death Apr. 22, 1993. She is buried at the Johnson County Cemetery. Mama was a blessing to all who knew her and her presence is sadly missed.

Family reunion, September 1992. Standing: Callie Johnson, Matilda Hughes, Kathleen Allen, Paul David Daniel, Charles Daniel and Benny Daniel. Sitting: Virginia Slone, Mary Daniel, John Daniel, Eugene Daniel, Clifford Daniel and Joshua Daniel.

DANIEL & CONLEY - Simon Daniel was born Feb. 15, 1913, in Kerz, Johnson County, KY, the son of Edgar Daniel and Frona Lemaster Daniel. He died Sep. 14, 1980, in Cambridge, OH. He had four brothers and one sister:

Earl Daniel (born Jan. 26, 1909, died Sep. 19, 1961) married (1) Lena Caudill, (2) Mabel Slone.

Walter L. Daniel (born Oct. 3, 1911, died Jun. 28, 1931) married Oena Grimm.

Hubert Daniel (born Oct. 11, 1915, died Mar. 6, 1997) married Helen Best.

Buell Daniel (born Nov. 6, 1918, died Mar. 13, 1983, married Annabelle Dixon.

Zona Daniel (born Oct. 8, 1921) married Jess Wakefield Songer.

He married Ivel May Conley Nov. 5, 1932. She was born Jul. 13, 1910, in Paintsville, Johnson County, KY, the daughter of John Milton and Marietta Woods Conley. She graduated from Paintsville High School in 1929 and attended Morehead State Teachers College for two years. She died Oct. 22, 1989, in Paintsville, KY. She had six brothers and two sisters:

Forrest T. Conley (born Jul. 1, 1885, died in 1972) married (1) Clausie Picklesimer, (2) Ethel ?.

Ben H. "Harry" Conley (born August 1888, died ?) married Bertha Barnett.

Ethel Conley (born Mar. 27, 1890, died in 1980) married Homer Picklesimer.

Everett M. Conley (born June 1892, died ?) md. Sunie McKenzie.

Lillian Conley (born Feb. 9, 1894, died Apr. 23, 1990) md. Rolla Dixon.

Ralph Conley (born Jul. 4, 1900, died Jan. 9, 1994) md. Ollie Blanton.

Hobart G. Conley (born Nov. 22, 1902, died Apr. 12, 1964) md. Ethel Preston.

William E. "Deak" Conley (born Oct. 19, 1904) md. (1) Nellie Reeves Picklesimer, (2) Shirley Burke.

Simon was an oil and gas well driller most of his life. He and Ivel were both members of the Paintsville United Baptist Church. They had five children:

Kerry Neil (born Sep. 25, 1934, in Johnson County, KY, died Jul. 11, 1936).

Marilyn Sue (born Sep. 30, 1937, in Paintsville, KY) md. James P. Chesney Sep. 26, 1959. They reside in Temecula, CA.

Richard Lyle (born Sep. 12, 1943, in Prestonsburg, KY) md. Ruth Johnson Jun. 23, 1962. Rick and Ruth presently live in Rome, GA.

Judith Ann (born Jan. 10, 1945, in Paintsville, KY, died Sep. 23, 1945).

Harry Lee (born Sep. 12, 1946, in Paintsville, KY) md. Dorothy Bergstrom Apr. 26, 1963. He and Dottie live in Suffolk, VA.

DANIELS - Remembering two people who were part of Johnson County are Lon (Alonzo) and Lora Daniels. They made their home in Tutor Key, KY, where they reared six children. Their names are Elizabeth (Betsy) Prince, Edna (Daniels) Daniel, Flora (Shug) Adams, Olga Kerns, Hobert Daniels and Loretta Nietubic. Two daughters, Edna and Flora, were teachers in the Johnson County School System for over 40 years.

My grandparents owned and operated the Daniels General Store with the Tutor Key Post Office inside the store.

Lon and Lora gave a helping hand to all who needed help. They never refused helping anyone who came to them for food, money or a place to sleep. The people living at Tutor Key were hard working people depending on farming or coal for their livelihood. Sometimes when these failed to provide food for their table my grandparents would supply them with the food from their store to keep their families alive. Times were very hard during the depression years and my grandparents almost lost their livelihood which was the general store from being so generous to other people in the community. *Written by Sandra Nietubic*

DANIELS - Terry Randall "Randy" Daniels was born Jan. 17, 1954, in Montgomery County, OH, to Earl Daniels Jr., the son of Earl Daniels Sr. and Savillar (Fairchild) Daniels (born in Johnson County, KY, Nov. 18, 1928) and Betty Jo (Colvin) Daniels, the daughter of Claude Colvin and Mary Ethel (Blair) Colvin Melvin (born in Johnson County, KY, Feb. 4, 1930).

Terry was the eldest of two sons born to his parents. The second son, Timothy Earl Daniels, died mysteriously Aug. 16, 1981, by single gunshot wound to the head. What is even more mysterious is the fact that his home burned to the ground the following night, Aug. 17, 1981.

Terry married in Johnson County, KY, Aug. 24, 1973, at the home of the Rev. Cline Salyer. He married Karen Sue Arrowood (born Mar. 11, 1955), the daughter of Wm. Frank Arrowood (born in North Carolina, Feb. 28, 1926), the son of Herbert Arrowood and Sally (Jackson) Arrowood; and Mildred Imogene (Wells) Arrowood (born in Floyd County, KY, May 8, 1928). She was the daughter of Paris Lee Wells and Alice (Goble) Wells.

Terry Randall "Randy" and Karen Sue Arrowood Daniels.

Terry and Karen had three children: one son, Terry Christopher "Chris" Daniels (born in Floyd County, KY, Jul. 14, 1976) and twin daughters, Stacey Michele (Daniels) Heuser and Shaunna Gail Daniels, born nine minutes apart, Stacey being the oldest, Aug. 2, 1977.

Terry was educated in the Johnson County School System. He attended Nancy Castle School; the Thelma two room school at Thelma, KY; the Colista one room school at Colista, KY; and the H.S. Howes School at Thealka, KY. He attended high school at Johnson Central High School in Paintsville, KY. Beginning in 1968, he also attended trade schools and college to acquire the skills of electrician, welder, telecommunications and ECG technician. He worked in many trades doing many different jobs. He did things such as: carhop, carpenter, welder, heavy equipment operator, truck driver, mechanic, auto body paint and repair, cable TV technician, as well as the jobs of foreman, field supervisor and crew leader.

Karen worked as a dietary clerk at Highland Regional Medical Center in Prestonsburg, KY, for nearly 12 years, at the time of this writing. She was also employed by Mrs. Ethel Cox at the Starfire Motel in Paintsville, KY, and Paintsville Cleaners and Laundry, also in Paintsville, KY. She was educated in the Johnson County School System and attended school at the old Buffalo School at Meally, KY, and Meade Memorial School at Boonscamp, KY. She attended Johnson Central High School in Paintsville, KY, and college at Prestonsburg Community College in Prestonsburg, KY, and Penn State in Pennsylvania.

DARLING - Donna Joyce Skaggs Darling was born in the Paintsville Clinic Hospital at Paintsville Apr. 9, 1949. She is the daughter of Golden and Emma Joy McKenzie Skaggs, and granddaughter of Ray and Beulah Lyon McKenzie of Johnson County and Everett and Lexie Skaggs Skaggs of Johnson County.

Donna's parents both grew up in Johnson County, KY. Donna's mother, Emma Joy McKenzie, was born at Keaton Jun. 27, 1931. Emma Joy's parents moved to Flat Gap where she attended grade and high school. She is a retired country store manager and a member of the Maverty Freewill Baptist Church. Donna's father, Golden Skaggs, was born at Gillem Branch Oct. 8, 1925. Golden graduated from Flat Gap High School and is veteran of WWII serving in the USN. After his tour of duty ended with the Navy, he enrolled at Mayo State Vocational School in Paintsville and became an electrician. He was a member of the International Brotherhood of Electrical Workers Local 317. Golden died Dec. 27, 1968, and is buried at Gillem Branch.

Donna has one sister, Doralene Skaggs Hicks of Blue Springs, MO (born Aug. 24, 1954) and one brother, Douglas Skaggs (born Jul. 11, 1958, died May 24, 1963). Douglas is buried in the M.O. McKenzie Family Cemetery at Flat Gap.

Gary and Donna Skaggs Darling

Donna's parents moved to Boyd County, KY, and Donna grew up there. She attended Cannonsburg grade school and graduated from Boyd County High School. Donna's first job was with J.C. Murphy in Ashland as a clerk. She later transferred to the Bookkeeping Dept. Donna became a pharmacy technician in 1981.

Donna married William Gary Darling in Clintwood, VA, Sep. 19, 1975. Gary is the son of William Lawrence and Helen Monzel Schmidt Darling of Rush, KY. Gary is retired from the International Union of Operating Engineers, Local 181.

Donna has one son from her previous marriage. Christopher Douglas Clevenger was born May 14, 1967, in Ashland, KY. Christopher is an eight year veteran of the USAF and participated in the Desert Storm conflict. He is a computer network systems specialist in Florida.

Donna is semi-retired from McMeans Pharmacy in Ashland. She enjoys arts and crafts, flower gardening, traveling, fishing and antique autos. Donna feels truly blessed to have such a loving family and so many good friends. *Submitted by Clista M. McKenzie Pelfrey.*

DAVIS - Beatrice Marie Davis (born in Van Lear, KY, Johnson County), daughter of George Washington and Verlie Fitzpatrick Davis. Brothers: Harold Leslie

Davis, Howard Hanford Davis, George W. Davis Jr. Sisters, Betty Margaret Davis and Christina Davis. Married Kenneth Borders (born in Lawrence County, KY) on Dec. 24, 1946. Kenneth, the son of McKinley and Goldie Castle Borders of Lawrence County, attended school in Lawrence County, Paintsville High School and Mayo Vocational School.

Beatrice attended grade school at Buffalo (first grade was a one-room school) then attended Meade Memorial High School, graduated May 1943; Mayo Vocational Business School, '44 and '45. Worked as a clerk/bookkeeper, bank teller and program assistant for ASCS. Likes to do crafts, working and planting flowers.

Carrier Row

On Aug. 12, 1943, during WWII, 48 men enlisted in the military from Johnson County, KY and 38 (including Kenneth) were signed to Co. 1239 U.S. Navy, Great Lakes, IL. After boot training they were shipped to Norfolk, VA and 18 men boarded the USS *Hornet* (others were sent elsewhere). On Mar. 20, 1944, the Carrier joined the 58th Task Force and fought in the South Pacific until the second bomb was dropped on the city of Nagasaki, Jun. 5, 1945. The ship was damaged by a typhoon, losing 30 feet of the bow. On Jun. 19, 1945, they returned to California for repairs. While in port for repairs, peace was signed on Sep. 2, 1945. After repairs the Carrier was used to transport troops from the South Pacific to the U.S. All 18 Johnson Countians were very fortunate to return home in March 1946. With no wounds, other than the woes of war.

Crewmen: Kenneth Borders, Paintsville, KY; Harold Leslie Davis, Meally, KY; Warth Goble, West Van Lear, KY; James Robert Stafford, Paintsville, KY; Ernest "Pete" Robinson, Thealka, KY; Russell Pack, White House, KY; Charles Ray May, Van Lear, KY; Glen Bland, Paintsville, KY; Clarence "Dock" Price, Whitehouse, KY; George Blanton, Volga, KY; Pete Colvin, Volga, KY; Escom Preston, Meally, KY; John McCarty, Van Lear, KY; Grath Trimble, Barnetts Creek, KY; Francis Lemaster, Staffordsville, KY; Jesse James Freeman, East Point, KY; Walter Childers, Whitehouse, KY; Harlie Sturgill, East Point, KY.

Balance of Co. 1239: Earl Conley, Charles D. Bailey, Walter Clay VanHoose, Charles Ted McKenzie, Sebert Wells, Robert Walters, Matthew Rowland, Ballard Meek, Curtis Meade, James Witten, Charles Johnson.

Kenneth received the Asiatic-Pacific w/9 stars, American Area, WWII Victory, Philippine Liberty w/2 stars and Presidential Unit Citation w/1 star. After service, most of his employment was with the coal industry. Princess Coal, David, KY, National Mine and Island Creek Coal, as a welder in shop and tipple, coal inspector and strip mine foreman. Hobbies: Likes attending car races, baseball and U.K. basketball. *Submitted by Bea Borders.*

DAVIS - Bracken Lewis Davis (born Sep. 11, 1838, died Dec. 1, 1921), born in Johnson County, son of Elias and Mary Elizabeth "Betty" Curtis.

Married Mary Elizabeth Conley, daughter of Thomas Conley.

Children: Manford Davis, E.P. "Leck" Davis, Lousine Davis, James Marin Davis, Charlie Davis, Julia Davis, Mary Elizabeth Davis, B.L. (son) Davis, Angie Davis, Leo Davis and Marie Alice Davis.

Bracken was reared in Johnson County and spent the greater part of his life on a farm on the Big Sandy River at the mouth of Buffalo Creek. In addition to farming he operated a ferry over the Big Sandy River. Also an attorney and active in political affairs of the county. He was possessed with a fine recollection. A member of the United Baptist Church. He and Mary are buried in Davis Cemetery at Concord, KY.

DAVIS - Elmon B. Davis, banker, farmer, teacher and community servant was born Dec. 17, 1916, at Flat Gap, KY. Elmon's parents were Crate Franklin Davis (born 1873, died 1950) and Gillie Fairchild Davis (born 1881, died 1945). He had four sisters and two brothers. Elmon lived his entire life on his birthplace farm, choosing to spend his life in the community and hills that he loved so much.

Elmon and Flora Davis, Apple Day 1973.

Elmon was educated in a one-room school at Flat Gap and graduated from Flat Gap High School in 1936. Raising hogs and cattle to earn money for college, he attended Bowling Green College. He later attended Morehead College, becoming a teacher in a one-room school in Johnson County.

During WWII, Elmon joined the Signal Corps of the U.S. Army. His specialty was radio repairman and mechanic. He served in Maryland, Florida, Missouri, Philippines, Guam and Hawaii. While home on Army leave in 1942, Elmon married his high-school sweetheart, Flora F. Davis. The couple established their home on the Davis family farm at Flat Gap. Elmon and Flora became the parents of three daughters: Linda Sue (born 1943), Sandra (born) 1946 and Elma Jean (born 1951); all teachers and librarians.

After the war Elmon became employed at Second National Bank (now Citizen's National Bank). He studied banking at the University of Virginia School of Banking and advanced from teller to vice-president at Citizens. After a banking career of 35 years, he retired in 1981. Elmon is remembered as a banker dedicated to serving the public and always striving to help the honest, hard-working county people.

Elmon was active in civic affairs working in the Kiwanis Club, Flat Gap Community development, PTA, Masonic Lodge and the Johnson County Library Board. He was also a board director of Foothills Telephone Co. and a Kentucky Colonel and Shriner. Elmon was also affectionately known as the "Mayor" of Flat Gap.

Elmon was prominent and long-standing in public service and is best known as the "Apple King." He was instrumental in beginning the Kentucky Apple Festival to celebrate the county's apple production and as a way to help Johnson County apple producers develop a market for their apples. The festival humbly began in October 1962, and has grown into a five day celebration that includes a week of old-fashioned fun as well as apple delicacies. The Kentucky Apple Festival has become a tourist event attracting thousands to Johnson County. It is second only to The Kentucky Derby in attendance.

Elmon was a faithful husband and father, a good provider, a diligent worker, an influential leader, a community servant and an excellent storyteller. He was a scholar in genealogy, an exceptional woodworker and an accomplished landscaper. Elmon was a dreamer, always planning a new project. Elmon was a man who touched the lives of many people. He relished learning, always striving toward a new goal. He was a strong man who was unafraid to take risks.

After a 10 year struggle with cancer, Elmon died Oct. 4, 1995, at his Flat Gap home. He is buried in Highland Memorial Cemetery at Staffordsville, KY.

DAVIS - Flora Finetta Davis, dedicated wife, mother, grandmother and great-grandmother, was born at Davisville in Lawrence County, KY, May 1, 1918. Flora was the 16th of 17 children born to Millard Albritton Davis (born 1874, died 1941) and Trinvilla Pack Davis (born 1878, died 1959). Her father was a farmer, who owned and operated a general store which included a post office that was near their home, for over 40 years. Flora is the only surviving child.

Flora was educated at Rocky Point, a one-room school near her home at Davisville. Later, she traveled by horseback to attend Flat Gap High School; graduating in 1936. She continued her education after high school at Booth Business College in Paintsville, KY.

In November 1942, Flora married Elmon B. Davis and to this union three daughters were born: Linda Sue)born 1943), Sandra (born 1946) and Elma Jean (born 1951). Flora was a dedicated wife at her Flat Gap home. She took great pleasure in being a full-time homemaker, supporting her husband's career for over 52 years. Flora created a warm home, welcoming Elmon's colleagues and business associates. She entertained with a personal warmth and friendly hospitality, an always welcoming host serving delicious dinners. Flora has an adventurous nature, and always accepted challenges. In her early years of marriage, Flora was a caretaker for first her ill mother-in-law and during the 50s for her father-in-law. While her husband worked in Paintsville, Flora became a determined contributor to the family income. She showed great effort, knowledge and skill in her farming and gardening. Flora raised cattle, hogs, Christmas trees, strawberries and potatoes. She also operated a pay fishing pond close to the family home.

Elmon and Flora Davis

Flora created a wonderful home. She is an expert at numerous things and takes special interest in running her household. Flora is a role model to her children- talented in writing, dress design, gardening, cooking, sewing, interior decorating and floral arranging. Flora instilled in her children a love for reading, and she devoted her life to encouraging them. "Be the best that you can be!" Flora was active in community life: supporting school functions in the Parent-Teacher Association, beautification and improvement in the Flat Gap Community Development Club and teaching Sunday school for over 25 years.

Flora is the ideal mother, sacrificing and encouraging her family. Her oldest daughter, Linda Miller, lives in Pittsburgh, PA, and graduated from Pikeville College and Duquense University. Sandra Chenault lives in Flat Gap, KY, and graduated from Pikeville College and Eastern Kentucky University. Elma Jean "Jeanie" Ferguson, also lives in Flat Gap, and graduated from Eastern Kentucky University and Morehead State University.

Flora's grandchildren include: Beth Ann Miller, Megan Chenault, Becky Burkett, Seth Ferguson and Timothy Ferguson. Flora's great-grandchildren are Hannah and Grant Burkett.

Flora became a widow in 1995, when Elmon

passed away after a long battle with cancer. She continues to live in her home at Flat Gap. At 81, she is a prolific reader and is fascinated by birds. She has created a haven for birds at her farm and is an avid bird-watcher, attracting the little creatures with a variety of trees, shrubs and flowers in the summer and feeding them daily in the winter. Flora can identify numerous species of birds, not only by sight but also by sound, recognizing the songs and calls of native Kentucky birds. Flora loves to surround her home with natural beauty. She devotes much of her time to home projects, designing and developing a landscaper's showcase. Flora prizes flowers for their shapes, colors and fragrances.

DAVIS - George Washington Davis (born Dec. 25, 1898, died May 26, 1997), born in Johnson County at Buffalo Creek, son of James Marion and Trinna Villa Arrowood Davis. Brothers: William Lee Davis, John C. Davis, James Marion Davis Jr. and Bruce Arnold Davis. Sisters, Lou Mintie Davis and Nancy Davis. Married: Verlie Fitzpatrick, daughter of Issac Henry and Miranda Penix Fitzpatrick, Dec. 22, 1922. George worked 51 years in the coal industry, Consolidated Coal Co., Jenkins and Van Lear, KY; Turner Elkhorn, Drift, KY. He and Verlie lived at Van Lear four years, moved to Meally, KY, and lived there until Verlie's death in 1977. George moved to Paintsville and lived there until his death.

Verlie was a role model for her children and grandchildren (10): Robert M. Rice II, George Keith Rice, Bettina Marie Rice, Robyn Leslie Davis, Harold Leslie Davis Jr., Deidra Denise Davis, Gina Leigh Davis, Erica Nicole Davis, Laura Davis and George Washington Davis III.

George also farmed, he loved to play the banjo, do wood crafts, watch baseball and U.K. Wildcat basketball.

George's grandparents were Bracken Lewis and Mary Elizabeth Conley Davis, George W. and Samatha Dillingham Arrowood. Verlie's grandparents were John and Amanda Short Fitzpatrick and Allen and Mary Stapleton Penix.

DESKINS & DOTSON - There is a saying that there were three subjects taught in the Pike County Schools during the economic slump of the 50s in the coal industry. The subjects were reading, writing and Route 23. That was certainly true of a young Gene and Ruth Deskins as they were forced to move from their childhood home to earn a living for themselves and their children.

Gene was the middle child of nine children born to Garrett and Erma Deskins. Ruth was the youngest of 10 children born to Frank Dotson and Rosa Hunt Dotson (daughter of Frank and Mary Taylor Hunt).

Leaving Kimper in Pike County, KY, in 1956, Gene T. Deskins and Ruth Dotson Deskins moved for a short time to Johnson City, TN, where Gene was an agent for the Commonwealth Life Insurance Co. He then transferred to Ironton, OH, and in April 1958, the family settled at 252 Second Street in Paintsville.

The couple and their growing family lived on Second Street for approximately four years before moving to Boyd Street in Bridgeford where they lived until 1964. They then built a home on the corner of Madison Avenue and Seventh Street where they currently reside.

The couple had four children: Brenda and Anna, twins (born Apr. 21, 1951, at Pikeville Methodist Hospital); Thomas Gene (born Oct. 29, 1956); and Mary Michelle "Shelli" (born January 1974).

Brenda is an elementary teacher in the Paintsville Independent Schools. In December 1972 she married businessman Robin Cooper, who was also a county commissioner, city councilman and later became mayor of Paintsville. They have two children, Johnathan Hunt Cooper (born Jun. 9, 1976) and Cassie Hall Cooper (born Nov. 8, 1978).

Anna is a 1973 graduate of the University of Kentucky and graduated from the University School of Law in 1988. In 1994 she was elected to the position of Commonwealth's attorney for Johnson, Martin and Lawrence counties. In 1973, she married businessman Charles T. Melvin Jr., who also was elected to the Paintsville City Council. They have three children: Emily Melvin Mooring (born Nov. 20, 1974); Charles T. Melvin III (born Jun. 30, 1977); and Lauren Michael Melvin (born Oct. 20, 1987).

Thom married Cherie Leigh Ramey and they have two children, Madison Elisabeth Deskins (born Sep. 17, 1988) and Taylor Caroline Deskins (born Nov. 6, 1992). Thom is employed as an agent for Commonwealth Life Insurance Co. and is a proprietor of businesses in Paintsville and Prestonsburg.

Mary Michelle "Shelli" is a graduate of the University of Kentucky and is attending Auburn University in Alabama to obtain a doctorate in clinical psychology.

Gene is an active member of the community. He has served many years in the First Christian Church on Main Street and during that time he has also served on the Planning and Zoning Commission for the city of Paintsville as well as being an active participant in other civic organizations. Ruth and Gene are very active not only in the community but in their children's lives.

DIXON - Paintsville founder, Henry Dixon (born 1774, died 1854), and his descendants have provided continuing and significant impacts on Johnson County since his arrival here in 1813. Henry's son, Martin (born 1805, died 1885), was an area millwright and blacksmith. He was noted for his mechanical talent and for his ability "to produce any device that was within reason, considering the tools and equipment of that time." (Mitchel Hall, Johnson County, KY, Vol. II, 1928, pp. 217.)

Garland Dixon Family

Martin's creative abilities were clearly passed down through the generations to his great nephew, Garland Dixon, son of Rolla (born 1893, died 1977) and Lillie Conley Dixon (born 1894, died 1990). Garland (born 1916) has gained notoriety in recent decades throughout the midwest as a result of his original Kentucky crafted wooden art sculptures.

A 1935 graduate of the Paintsville City Schools, Garland also has the unique ability to solve almost any mechanical challenge presented him and he used this talent in the drilling business. While working as a driller in Michigan, he met and married Aileen Frary (born 1922), daughter of Irving and Marian Frary of Dorr, MI. In 1942, he and Rolla operated the Dixon Drilling Co. in Johnson County.

In 1945, Garland and Oscar Evans entered into a partnership, creating Evans and Dixon Core Drilling Co., which served as a leader in the drilling business in Eastern Kentucky, Virginia and West Virginia for several decades.

While working, Garland's hobbies included flying, fishing and boating, although his seven-day week work schedule left him little time to enjoy them or pursue his artistic talents. However, following his retirement in 1975, he began developing his latent artistic talents and was named as a Kentucky craftsman, creating hundreds of original, beautiful bowls, vases and other wood products that have been bought and displayed throughout the nation.

His wife, Aileen, has also been an active member of the Johnson County community, serving as a PTA member, Cub Scout den mother, secretary of the county chapter of ARC and working with the board of the First United Methodist Church. She also worked as a secretary for the Paintsville Grocery Co. and also for Harry LaViers, president of Southeast Coal Co.

Garland and Aileen have two sons, Roger D. (born 1942) and Kenneth Ray (born 1948). Like many Kentuckians before them, both Roger and Kenny, following graduation from Paintsville High School, have spent their working careers outside the state.

Roger and his wife, Carolyn Carnes (born 1942), have two children, James Garland (born 1971) and Dana Marie (born 1975). Graduates of Morehead State University, both Roger (BA and MA, '64 and '65) and Carolyn (BA '64) continued their education at Western Michigan University in Kalamazoo, MI, where Roger received his doctorate in educational administration and Carolyn did master's level work in reading recovery.

Named the Michigan Advocate of the Year for At-Risk Children in 1998, Dixon retired from education that same year, following 22 years of service as a school superintendent in Michigan, including his last 11-1/2 years as the superintendent of the Mecosta-Osceola Intermediate School Dist. Carolyn also retired in 1998 as a reading recovery teacher in the Big Rapids Public Schools and as a RR Council representative for the state of Michigan.

Their children continue the educational tradition. James is currently a science teacher in the Hastings (MI) Public Schools. His wife, Tara Rueger Dixon (born 1969, died 1998), was a music teacher at the Kelloggsville Public Schools. They have a son, Bradley James (born 1997). Dana Marie is an elementary and middle school teacher.

Kenneth Ray is married to Gale Dawson (born 1949) of Louisa. They have two daughters, Melissa Rene (born 1972) and Mechelle Dawn (born 1975). A 1966 graduate of Paintsville High School, Ken received his BS degree in mechanical engineering in 1970 from the University of Kentucky and his professional engineer's license in 1975. Gale graduated from Lawrence County High School in 1967 and attended Mayo State Vocational School, graduating in 1969 with a degree in cosmetology.

After graduation, Ken took a position with Armco Steel Co. in Ashland, where he advanced to chief engineer in 1988. In 1990, he transferred to Armco's (now AK Steel Corporation) Corporate Offices in Middletown, OH, where he currently is serving as contract manager - project engineering. He and Gale reside in Loveland, OH.

Melissa graduated from Russell (KY) High School in 1990 and from Morehead State University in 1994 with a paralegal degree. She currently works for the Commonwealth of Kentucky in Frankfort and is a member of the Frankfort Community Orchestra and a local jazz ensemble.

Mechelle graduated from King's High School (King's Mills, OH) in 1993 and from the University of Cincinnati in 1997 with a degree in veterinary technology. She currently works for the Landen Veterinary Clinic in Landen, OH.

DIXON - Johnson County's Yeomen (A freeholder of a class below the English gentry, who worked his own land. One who provides "yeoman service" has been cited as providing exceptionally good or loyal service. Also described as: brave, sturdy and faithful).

Though not of the "gentry," the Dixon family has provided "good and loyal" service to the nation and to Johnson County in an unbroken line since Thomas Dixon, who died of smallpox while fighting for freedom for the colonies from Great Britain during the Revolutionary War.

Rolla and Lillie Conley Dixon

Thomas Dixon was the father of Henry (born 1774, died 1854), John and James Dixon. In 1813, according to family records, Henry and James settled in what was then Floyd County, KY. Henry and his wife, Joyce Farmer Dixon (born 1772, died 1856), located in Paintsville, while James briefly set up a home near the Forks of the Big Sandy River before shortly thereafter moving again to a new home on the Cumberland River in Harlan County. John located in Letcher County, where he died in 1847.

Like many settlers during the early years of the U.S., the Dixon brothers moved westward. Originally located in Ash County, NC, the family moved to Grayson County, VA, before settling in Eastern Kentucky, where they quit moving and set deep roots in the rocky mountain soil!

Henry and his family first appeared in the records of Floyd County in February 1816. At that time, he was a witness to the sale of some land on Big Paint Creek. His first record of land purchase was entered into the record Jul. 13, 1816. (Preston, Harold R., *"Henry and Joyce Dixon, Some Family Data and Their Burial Sites in the Old Town Cemetery."*) Although it wasn't until legislative action Feb. 24, 1843, that Johnson County was formed from the territory included in Floyd, Lawrence and Morgan counties, it was here that Henry Dixon and his descendants lived for most of the next two centuries.

Henry, according to chapter 554, page 787, Acts 1834, designed the plan ... "That the town of Paintsville in Floyd County ... be established." At this time, the Dixons (along with the Prestons, Franklins, Staffords, et al) were among the major landowners within the city boundaries. Henry owned the upper end of the town, possessing the land from College Street to "Hoss Mill Branch." (Ibid.)

Considered to be the founder of Paintsville, based upon having his land along Paint Creek surveyed and laid out in a plat, with lots sold to citizens of the community (Ely, William, *History of the Big Sandy,* 1887, "The county town of Johnson County as laid out in 1842 (1834) on the lands of the Dixons, one-half mile from the Sandy River, on Paint Creek." From *Johnson County, KY,* by Mitchel Hall, 1928, volume II, p. 242) Henry was also a well-known Baptist minister of his era and is noted for constructing the first house, a log cabin, in Paintsville. (Wells, J.K., *"A Short History of Paintsville and Johnson County, KY".*)

According to Mitchell Hall, in his 1928 text *Johnson County, KY, A History of the County, and Genealogy of Its 'People Up to the Year 1927'*, Volume II:

He was a man of most marked peculiarities. He was a fine fiddler and in his old days always took his fiddle with him to church, carrying his Bible under one arm and his fiddle under the other. He would introduce service by playing several tunes and then close in the same way. The novelty of such service always attracted the people, and the old man always gave them wholesome advice ... The brothers (i.e., Henry and James) were leading people of that section for nearly a half century. They owned large tracts of lands, and were in good circumstances. Their descendants are among the leading people of Eastern Kentucky ... He was one of the honored pioneer citizens of Johnson County."

Henry and Joyce, according to family and other genealogical records, had 13 children, including Andrew Farmer Dixon (born 1801, died 1881). Andrew married Abigail Kelly in 1834 in Johnson County and lived on Rush Fork of Tom's Creek all his life. Andrew and Abigail had at least six children, as cited in family records, including Isaac "Ike" Dixon.

Isaac (born 1839, died 1906) was one of several Dixons, including his brothers, Farmer and Joseph (n.b., who was too young to be drafted, but slipped off and enlisted regardless), who enlisted on the side of the Union forces during the War Between the States. According to Erie Dixon Van Hoose, Ike's daughter, he fought in several battles and was with Sherman on his famous march to the sea. He returned to Paintsville with five bullet holes in his overcoat and three in his hat, but he was never wounded. He told of having to sleep out in the open and waking many mornings with his blanket frozen to the ground. (Van Hoose, Erie Dixon, family conversations recorded on Apr. 9, 1953.)

Alonzo Dixon (born 1868, died 1944), one of Isaac and Ella May Dixon's 11 children, also lived on Rush Fork of Tom's Creek. He was well-known not only as a lay preacher in the Freewill Baptist Church, following in the footsteps of his great-grandfather, Henry, but also as a mountain healer of some repute. Alonzo, who learned the secret of healing mountain folk of infections and sores from a friend, Calvin Combs, provided comfort and health to his neighbors until his death in 1944. Alonzo died without passing on the secret of his healing powers to any of his five children. (Dixon, Rolla, *"The Mountain Healer", FATE,* October 1973, pp.56-57.)

One of those progeny, Rolla Dixon (born 1893, died 1977) worked as a coal miner and then lost his right leg in a drilling accident. Following that disability, he learned to drive one of the new motor vehicles just coming into Johnson County and bought a one-ton Maxwell Truck, one of the first trucks in Paintsville. He began a hauling service "Dixon's Transport" from the train depot to the business places downtown. Following the depression, he purchased a 732-acre timber farm in Morgan County. Using wood harvested from this property, he made and sold grave boards, highway stakes, picket fencing, lawn chairs and other wood products until shortly before his death.

He and his wife, Lillie Conley Dixon (born 1894, died 1990) had three children: Garland, Dorothy and Annabelle. In addition to raising the three youngsters, Lillie was a working member of the family, helping with the books, billings and other aspects of the business.

Members of the Johnson County branch of the Dixon family worked at a variety of occupations, ranging from drilling to farming to education to engineering. Additionally, continuing the tradition initiated in the U.S. by Thomas Dixon during the Revolutionary War and his grandchildren in the War Between the States, several members of the family volunteered to serve their country and participated in World Wars I and II.

Historically, while family members have rarely delved into public politics and similar roles, the Dixon family, for almost two centuries, has been a solid, contributing factor in the development and growth of Paintsville and Johnson County, providing "yeoman services" as citizens and neighbors. *By Roger D. Dixon.*

DOBSON - Willia Marie Dobson was born Sep. 13, 1925, in Johnson County, the daughter of W.A. "Willie" Frazier and Virginia "Virgie" Williams. Billie, as she was lovingly known by her family and friends, was the granddaughter of Theodore and Bertie (Williams) Williams, and Edward and Amanda (Pennington) Frazier.

Billie's parents were divorced when she was very young. Billie lived with her dad and helped him in his country grocery store while she attended school at Hager Hill. After selling the store and moving to Florida, he and Billie managed a motel until his death. At some point in her life, she married Larry Dobson who became a physician. After several years of marriage they divorced and Billie lived and worked in California. She worked as a beautician for the larger part of her life. At the time of her retirement she was employed as a travel agent in the Indianapolis, IN, area.

Billie loved to travel and was blessed during her lifetime to travel around the world, twice. She loved and enjoyed life and in the later years, enjoyed coming to the hills of Johnson County and visiting her family. She also called and spent much time talking with her cousins in the area.

Willa Marie Dobson

Billie was a generous, loving, caring kind of person. She died Monday, Mar. 8, 1999, in the Community East Hospital, Indianapolis, IN, after an extended illness. She is buried in the Williams Family Cemetery at Oil Springs in Johnson County, KY, where her cousins, whom she loved and who loved her can now visit her resting place. *Submitted by her cousin, Tobianna McCarty.*

DORTON - David Haden Dorton was born Dec. 19, 1890, at Red Bush in Johnson County KY, one of 14 children of William H. and Sarah Dorton. His work in the teaching profession was spent largely in Johnson County from 1912-17.

During WWI, he worked in the Ordinance Section of the War Dept. in Detroit, MI, and Cleveland, OH. He served in this capacity from 1917-21. In 1922, with a group of business associates, he began the organization of a new bank. He was elected assistant cashier in 1922, cashier in 1936, executive vice-president and cashier in 1944 and president in 1958. He served Citizens National Bank until his death in 1972.

Under his leadership, he brought the bank through the difficult days of the Bank Holiday of 1930. He was with the bank when it was converted to Second National in 1927 and when it became Citizens National Bank in 1959. He also served as president of the Kentucky Bankers Association from 1962-63.

Dave Dorton was an active civic leader and served on many commissions and boards in Johnson County and the Commonwealth. He was appointed as one of three commissioners for Paintsville Water and Gas when it was purchased by the city. Mr. Dorton was an active member of First United Methodist Church throughout his lifetime. His love for family, devotion to church, dedication to service and respect for his fellow man identified him as a rare personality. His service beyond self to his city, county, state and nation showed him to be a truly good citizen.

David H. Dorton

He was married to Flora Williams of Elna on Dec. 25, 1915. They had three children: David H., Oscar Trigg and Norma Jean.

David, an ophthalmologist, married Betty Batchlet of Ohio. They had one son, Michael and one daughter, Judith; O. Trigg, a banker, married Betty Marie Reynolds of Ohio. They had one son, Dennis Trigg and one daughter, Lynn Jane; Norma Jean married Mark Maggard in 1972. She has three daughters: Kathryn, Betty Ann and Jeannie Mayo.

DORTON - Oscar Trigg Dorton was born Jun. 15, 1920, in Detroit, MI, the son of David H. and Flora Williams Dorton. His family returned to Paintsville in 1923. Trigg graduated from Paintsville High School, received a bachelor's degree in commerce from the University of Kentucky and graduated from Rutgers School of Banking.

After serving as a lieutenant in the U.S. Army during WWII, he joined Citizens National Bank in 1945. During his service with the bank, he held the office of cashier, executive vice president and was made president in 1964. He held that office until his retirement in 1986.

Trigg has been very active in many community, area and state programs: president of Kentucky Bankers Association, 1976-77; president of Kentucky Chamber of Commerce, 1974-75; chairman of the Kentucky Independent College Fund; treasurer of the Big Sandy Community Action Program; board member of the Highland Regional Medical Center; past-president of the Lonesome Pine Council of Boy Scouts (receiving the Silver Beaver award); past-chairperson of the Mountain Mental Health Services. Also, an active member of Kentucky Rural Development Advisory Committee, Big Sandy Health Planning Council, Big Sandy Area Development Dist. Board, Paintsville Development Corporation, Region 11 Tourism Council and the Paintsville Gas and Water Commission.

O.T. Dorton

Trigg has been a friend to children and youth in our area through his involvement with regional educational programs. He served 12 years on the Paintsville Independent School Board, the Pikeville College Board, Lindsey Wilson College Board and the Development Board of the University of Kentucky. After many years of service to Prestonsburg Community College, he was made an emeritus member of the college board in 1999.

Trigg is an active member of the First United Methodist Church serving on the board, singing in the choir, teaching Sunday school and serving on the board of the Methodist Children's Home at Versailles.

Trigg is married to Betty Marie Reynolds of Columbus, OH. Their son, Dennis, is president of Citizens National Bank and is married to Jean M. Mollett. Their daughter Lynn Jane Mullins is a speech and language pathologist and is married to William C. Mullins.

He and Betty have three grandchildren: Andrew Dorton, Meridith and Macy Mullins.

Trigg Dorton is still active and interested in improving Paintsville, Johnson County and eastern Kentucky. He enjoys a good game of golf when time permits.

DORTON - William H. Dorton, son of Robert Fugate Dorton and Rhoda Horton Dorton, was born Jan. 4, 1853, in Scott County, VA. He was educated in the schools of Virginia. On Jan. 21, 1875, he married Esther Carter, and they moved to Slater, MO, where his mother, Rhoda, and stepfather were living. Four children were born to William H. and Esther while living in Missouri. Because of Esther's illness, they moved back to Rye Cove, VA, where she died and was buried beside their small daughter in Rye Cove.

On Jul. 1, 1885, William H. married Sarah E. Fletcher and with his three young children, they moved to Johnson County KY, joining his sister and her family who were already living there. Eventually, they settled at Red Bush, where all 11 of their children were born.

William H.'s livelihood included a country store, surveying roads, writing legal documents (deeds, wills, etc.), politics and law enforcement.

Meanwhile, the children were educated and taught good work habits with emphasis on good morals, proper behavior and religion. William H. and Sarah believed in strict discipline administered with good-natured humor. Theirs was a big happy family.

William H. Dorton

The honesty of the Dorton family was established the first day they arrived in Red Bush and two small boys learned a lesson. A young Dorton son and William's young brother-in-law went into "Uncle" Peter's (then a stranger) cornfield and confiscated enough corn to feed their horses (corn for horses was carried when people of that era traveled). A surprised "Uncle" Peter found at his door, the boys with twice as much corn as they had taken and an apology, while William H. Dorton waited at "Uncle" Peter's gate.

The descendants of William H. and Sarah Dorton's family included teachers, bankers, doctors, lawyers, engineers and business executives, who are sure that the training and discipline of their progenitors shaped their destiny.

Only two sons remained permanently in Johnson County. James R. "Jim" Dorton, who settled in Red Bush and was a natural gas station operator and farmer. He married Hettie Williams. Also, David H. "Dave" Dorton, who married Red Bush native, Flora Williams, became a resident of Paintsville where he was a prominent banker. *Written by Esther D. Williams.*

DUTTON - Bobby D. Dutton was born in Johnson County, KY, Sep. 3, 1936, to John Langley and Grace Ward Dutton. He was married in Martin County, KY, Mar. 23, 1961, to Donna Jean Kennedy. They have a daughter, Patricia Sue (born Apr. 14, 1963, at Paintsville, KY).

Bobby and Donna Dutton

Bob attended Meade Memorial School, but left in 1955 before he graduated and went to work for General Motors in Cleveland, OH. After he left Cleveland he returned to Johnson County and worked for Paintsville Heating and Cooling until he was drafted into the armed service in 1959. He was stationed in Kentucky and Georgia then went to Korea until his release in January 1961. After being discharged less than a year, he was recalled to active duty and stationed in Ft. Eustis, VA, until his final discharge in August 1962.

He left Johnson County in the fall of 1962 and moved to Columbus, OH, and went to work for Aire-Flo Heating and Cooling, after leaving this job he joined the Sheet Metal Union and began work for Dupont. He left Columbus in July 1974 and returned to Johnson County. After returning to school and earning his GED diploma he became sheet metal instructor at the Carl D. Perkins Rehabilitation Center and enrolled in Morehead College. He attended classes at night, sometimes driving two or three nights a week to Morehead, until he earned his degree, this was all accomplished at the age of 42.

After closing the sheet metal class he taught small engine repair for many years, then transferred to rehab engineering, where he designed and built equipment for rehabilitation clients. He was instrumental in helping schools and companies comply with the American with Disabilities Act, or better known as ADA, all over the state of Kentucky until his retirement Sep. 30, 1998.

He is a deacon in the Sulphur Springs United Baptist Church, Tomahawk, KY, where he is very active and also sings in a group at the church. He was saved at the Williams Road Freewill Baptist Church, Columbus, OH, Nov. 15, 1969.

Patty, his daughter, works at Citizens National Bank and is married to Tim Adams, a teacher at the Johnson County Middle School. They live in Paintsville with their children, Kyle Bradley (born May 29, 1982) and Kellye Michelle (born Jun. 28, 1986).

Donna, his wife, was born in Wyoming County, WV, and had a twin sister who was stillborn on Feb. 22, 1941. Her father, Tennis Kennedy, was killed in an automobile accident on his way home from work in the mines, at the age of 24. She moved to Kentucky with her mother and stepfather, Charles J. Hall, and attended Tomahawk Grade School and graduated from Inez High School in May 1959. She is a distant relative of the Hatfields, of the Hatfield and McCoy feud. Her mother is a third cousin to Devil Anse Hatfield.

DUTTON - Henly Clarence "H.C." Dutton was born Aug. 9, 1923, in Chatteroy, WV, to Elias Dutton and Josephine Diamond Dutton. After the death of his parents, when he was very young, he came to Johnson County to live with his Uncle John Langley Dutton and Aunt Grace Ward Dutton of Boons Camp. He had one brother, William Chester Dutton (born Oct. 21, 1924), who also came to Johnson County to live with his Uncle Ora Dutton and Aunt Beuna Mollett Dutton of Boons Camp. Chester married Merle Webb Aug. 28, 1943, the daughter of McKinley Webb and Bessie Miller of East Point. They were parents of four children who live and work in the Dayton, OH, area.

During WWII and at the age of 17 he enlisted in the Navy and was stationed in the South Pacific. After returning from the Navy he met and married Ellen Wells who was a few years older than him, now this in itself was something that just wasn't done in those days because he was only 19 and she was 35 years old, but this proved a lot of people wrong for the marriage lasted for 49-1/2 years. Ellen and Clarence married Sep. 4, 1943, and had one son named Robert (born 1947) who lived only a few days.

Clarence and Ellen both graduated from Morehead College and taught in the Johnson County school system for many years. He worked for Mayo School just before his retirement in 1982. He attended the Wells Chapel Methodist Church at Boons Camp, where he was very active and loved the church so much having served as pastor until he became disabled in 1996.

Clarence and Ellen Dutton

He also traveled many miles with the boy's basketball team at Meade Memorial School. He would tell many interesting stories of traveling to the different counties in Kentucky. About going to play the Inez Indians of Martin County who were the arch rivals of Meade Memorial School.

After retirement, he served on many committees throughout Johnson County and Kentucky. He helped many young people get scholarships to attend college and Mayo School. He was active in the Senior Citizens program of Johnson County and worked very hard in obtaining funds and items needed to get the program in operation. He and Ellen were very active in the Williamsport Volunteer Fire Dept. where he served as chairman of the board.

Ellen attended the John C.C. Mayo College of Paintsville and graduated from Morehead College in 1925. She taught many years in a one room school house and also at Meade Memorial School. Her parents bought the old Hicks house at Williamsport and she lived there until her marriage to Clarence. After marrying they moved to Dayton for a few years and then returned to Johnson County and moved in a little house at a place called Buzzard's Nest. They left there and moved just down the road to live with her mother and sister. They lived there until their death, Ellen's on Mar. 10, 1993, and Clarence on Feb. 9, 1998. They are buried in the Wells Family Cemetery at Williamsport, KY.

DUTTON - Sara Ellen Wells Dutton, whom we honor tonight, the daughter of Isaac and Mary Wells, was born in Williamsport, KY, in the home in which she presently resides. A landmark in Johnson County for many years, this home is said to be perhaps 150 years old.

In 1911, Mr. Wells' employment as mine foreman, moved the family to Hellier, KY, in Pike County. It is said that Ellen was very much a "Daddy's girl" in those early years and loved to follow her dad on the wagons. Perhaps it was fortunate that she did.

It's surprising that Ellen wasn't frightened away from her one and one-half mile daily trek to school by a traumatic experience that occurred during her first year in Pike County. Released from school early one day, the first grader decided to shorten the one and one-half mile trip home. A man, notorious for offering children rides in his wagon and then driving off quickly, leaving them in the dust clouds, stopped apparently offering Ellen a ride. Much quicker than he judged, and probably due to her experiences with her father around wagons, she was half-way up beside him when he jerked the wagon forward by flicking the team with the whip. Ellen was thrown under the wagon whose wheels barely missed her head but quickly rolled over her legs.

In 1918 the family moved to Whitehouse, then an up-and-coming mining town. Here Ellen attended third grade.

In 1919 another move sent her to Hurricane School for her years up to seventh grade. During that year Ellen and her sister, Melissa, went to Paintsville where they boarded with an aunt and attended Mayo College. These seventh and eighth grade years were under the instruction of Professor George Butcher.

Sometime during these teen years, Ellen experienced a pretty unforgettable prank inflicted by Hoy Preston. While playing tennis one day on the court behind the Wells' home, Hoy unluckily discovered a black snake. Although it is said by certain of her sisters that Ellen was a fun-loving tomboy and likely not above catching a snake herself now and then, we couldn't find out any more about this particular snake of Hoy's after his pet of the moment found itself being used as a necklace for Ellen.

Mrs. Dutton's high school instruction continued at Mayo, with the exception of her sophomore year in Pikeville, until after her junior year when she began her teaching career at South Williamson in Pike County.

High school and college years were completed at Morehead Normal School. At that time public schools were in session for only six months each year enabling Ellen to teach part of the year and finish her own education during the remainder of the year.

Her teaching career has been spent in the following places: Williamsport or Two Mile (for $42.00 per month); the head of Greasy where she rode horseback to and from a distance of eight miles each way; Rock House in Martin County; two to three years at Three Forks of Greasy and Hurricane; Paintsville; Buffalo School at Meally; and Meade Memorial.

Not only has she taught for regular school sessions but she has done summer work in Head Start and summer schools.

Along with dedicating her life to public education, she has also given herself to instilling spiritual values in her community through faithful service in her church and its related Sunday school and Vacation Bible School.

Her absence from the classroom will be hard to fill, someone will teach third grade next year, and the year after but I fear no one will really ever replace Mrs. Dutton in the room down the hall.

ESTEP & PELFREY - Beverly Pelfrey was born Apr. 23, 1949, in the Paintsville Clinic Hospital in Paintsville, Johnson County, KY, to William Hillard "Pat" Pelfrey (born Dec. 18, 1916, Morgan County, KY) and Clista Margaret McKenzie Pelfrey (born Dec. 26, 1932, Barn Rock, KY). Pat Pelfrey is retired after working many years as a pumper in the oil fields for Ashland Oil, Inc. Clista M. Pelfrey retired as supervisor of security from the Carl D. Perkins Comprehensive Rehabilitation Center at Thelma, KY.

Beverly (Pelfrey), Orville Paul, Monica Lynn and Daren Paul Estep.

Beverly was the second child in a family of four girls. Hilary Pelfrey was born Jul. 26, 1947, Marcia Rae Pelfrey was born Apr. 4, 1951, and Margaret Wynn Pelfrey was born Feb. 26, 1961.

The first five months of Beverly's life were spent with her family in Catlettsburg, KY. Then the family relocated to Keaton in Johnson County. Her school days began with first grade in the one room school at Keaton where eight grades were taught. That was the last school year for Keaton School, and second grade through high school graduation were spent at Flat Gap School. She graduated from Flat Gap in May 1967 and started her first job that summer in the office of Earnest G. Skaggs, MD at the Paintsville Clinic.

Beverly attended Berea College in Berea, KY, until 1969 when she married her high school sweetheart, Orville Paul Estep. Paul was born in Morgan County, KY, on May 1, 1947. They were married at the Mazie Baptist Church in Lawrence County, KY, Feb. 15, 1969, by ministers Herman Ross and Willard Bailey. Because of a lack of work in Eastern Kentucky Paul had obtained employment at Robbins and Meyers in Springfield, OH. While in Springfield, Beverly was employed by Spiegel, Inc. and as a teller at Security National Bank until March 1972 when Paul fulfilled a lifelong dream of becoming a Kentucky state trooper.

When Paul graduated from Trooper Cadet School in August 1972, he was assigned to the Pikeville Post so they moved to Wheelwright, Floyd County, KY. The next three years were spent in Floyd County - the last two and one-half years living at Price. Beverly was employed during that time at an insurance agency in Prestonsburg.

On Nov. 7, 1975, Monica Lynne Estep was born and about the same time Paul was transferred to Johnson County. In 1978, the couple bought property at Keaton which joined the property of Beverly's parents, and that remains "home" at this writing. On Sep. 18, 1979, Daren Paul Estep was born to complete the family.

Monica is a graduate of Johnson Central High School and Prestonsburg Community College and is married to Shawn Clay Spradlin (born Jul. 3, 1975). They reside in Floyd County, KY. Their daughter, Kelsey Lynne Spradlin, was born Jun. 2, 1998. Daren is a graduate of Johnson Central and is currently a student at Mayo Technical College in Paintsville, KY.

Throughout the years Beverly has been employed by the U.S. Census Bureau as an interviewer, by the Keaton Post Office as relief clerk, as a bookkeeper for an oil field contractor, as a secretary at the Carl D. Perkins Comprehensive Rehabilitation Center and the Dept. of Social Insurance and as payroll clerk and secretary to a local business owner.

Beverly has been a Christian since 1966 and is a member of the Flat Gap Baptist Church. She has been a Sunday school and Bible School teacher and participates in singing with other Christian friends at area nursing homes. She also loves to sing gospel music with her family in a group called Family Foundation. *Submitted by Beverly Pelfrey Estep.*

ESTEP - Orville Paul Estep was born in his grandparent's home (Alonzo Schyler Rice and Ella West Burchett Rice) in the edge of Morgan County, KY, May 1, 1947, to Richard Raymond Estep (born Feb. 21, 1919, deceased Nov. 24, 1978) and Nova Hester Rice Estep (born Feb. 11, 1920). Richard was known throughout the area as both "Red" and "Ray Bob" and was employed by the Kentucky Div. of Forestry at the time of his death.

Paul was the oldest of three sons, Danny Raymond Estep (born Jul. 15, 1948) and Johnny Randall Estep (born Apr. 19, 1952). Paul grew up on Stone Coal Road at Volga, KY, and attended school at Flat Gap. He graduated in May 1966. While still in high school, Paul worked during the height of the forest fire seasons each year as a dispatcher in the Forestry Office. During the summers he also mowed yards and did farm labor for neighbors to earn some spending money.

On Sep. 8, 1966, Paul entered the U.S. Army. He completed basic training and advanced individual training at Fort Knox, KY. In February 1967, Paul was stationed in Korea where he was trained as a dog handler. Guard dogs were trained to obey one "master," so Paul also fed and took care of his dog, Major. Major was a great friend to a country boy many miles from home. Paul was in Korea in February 1968 when the Pueblo was captured and his time there was extended for about 30 days. His military career was completed at Fort Hood, TX, and he received an honorable discharge in September 1968.

Orville Paul Estep

On Feb. 15, 1969, Paul married Beverly Pelfrey at Mazie Baptist Church in Lawrence County, KY, and they moved to Springfield, OH, where he worked repairing electric motors for Robbins and Meyers.

In March 1972 Paul was employed by the Kentucky State Police which had been his desire since the time he was a young man. He attended the State Police Academy in Frankfort and graduated as a trooper Aug. 11, 1972. He was assigned to the Pikeville Post and worked in Floyd County until late 1975 when he was transferred to Johnson County. He became a detective in July 1988 and continues in that capacity at this date.

Paul and Beverly are the parents of Monica Lynne Estep (born Nov. 7, 1975) and Daren Paul Estep (born Sep. 18, 1979). Monica is married to Shawn Clay Spradlin (born Jul. 3, 1975) and they have one daughter, Kelsey Lynne Spradlin (born Jun. 2, 1998). Daren is a student at Mayo Technical College in Paintsville, KY.

Paul became a Christian in 1966 and was baptized in Paint Creek near the Cold Springs United Baptist Church at Cuba, KY. This location is now about 60 feet deep as part of the Paintsville Lake, and Paul's birthplace is also under water. He is a member of the Flat Gap Baptist Church where he serves as trustee. He also enjoys singing gospel music. *Submitted by Orville Paul and Beverly Estep.*

EVANS - Everett J. Evans was born in Gallia County, southeastern Ohio, in 1882. He came to Paintsville in the early 1900s with a steam driven core drill to explore for coal. His interest in the mineral was the result of an early association with Henry LaViers and John C.C. Mayo. In the early 1920s he formed Evans Oil & Gas Co. and leased tracts of land in Johnson, Martin and Lawrence counties. His early drilling programs were successful.

Everett married a school teacher named Mabel Gee from near Grayson, KY, and they owned a home directly behind the Mayo Methodist Church on the present site of the Sunday school building. They had no children.

Oscar N. Evans, the youngest of the 12 children of a circuit riding preacher in Ohio came to Paintsville in the late teens and joined his brother, Everett. He kept the books of Evans Oil & Gas Co. and did the field supervision of drilling contractors. In 1925 he married Sara Ruth Frances, a nurse from southern Ohio. They had one son, Paul (born 1927).

Another brother, Leonard, spent several years in Paintsville in the 1930s and early 40s. While working in Whitesburg he married Sara Blair and they had two daughters, Mary Katherine and Francis, both of whom attended Paintsville High School. An employee of Ashland Oil & Refining Co., Leonard moved his family to Ashland in the mid 40s.

In the late 1930s, Everett became interested in coal reserves, and with Oscar as the leasing agent, he leased the coal on a large area in Floyd County which includes what is now the town of David on Middle Creek, west of Prestonsburg. To develop the property, a partnership was formed with Harry LaViers, president of Southeast Coal Co. and James Francis of Huntington, WV, then president of Island Creek Coal Co. The C & O railroad agreed to lay 12 miles of track to David, and in 1941, mining was begun by Princess Elkhorn Coal Co. This led to some additional mineral leases by the partnership in Knott, Breathett and Magoffin counties.

Everett purchased the Mayo properties in Paintsville during the depression. He was influential in getting the vocational school located on part of it, and he wanted to preserve the mansion. He later sold it to the Catholic Church, an organization with the resources to maintain the estate.

Everett died in 1951. Oscar continued to operate Evans Oil & Gas Co. until 1959 when he retired and moved to Florida. He died in 1979.

FAIRCHILD - Jessie Fairchild was the daughter of William Fairchild, a descendant of Abuid Fairchild (born 1875, died 1931?). Jessie was married to John Bayes, a farmer from Magoffin County, survived by one son Ray Bayes (born 1898, died 1976) in Dayton, OH. She also had a son, Dennie, who preceded her in death.

After John Bayes' death Jessie Fairchild Bayes married North J. Price (boatsman) and worked at Slone's Product House. North J. Price had been married three times earlier. To this marriage was born one daughter, Ruth Price (born Aug. 16, 1909).

Jessie Fairchild (Bayes) Price's sudden death at 56 left her husband; one daughter, Mrs. Floyd Gamboe (Ruth); son, Ray Bayes; one brother, Dr. John Fairchild of Inez, KY; and two Sisters, Mrs. Mary Bayes of Paintsville and Mrs. W.L. Fairchild of Flora, IL.

Ruth Price married Floyd Gamboe in 1924, only son of Hannah M. Risen and Edward C. Gamboe of Winchester, KY. Ruth was a lifelong resident of Paintsville. She possessed a genial personality, always gay and cheerful. She was active with her children in school activities. Her father died in 1936.

Floyd (Gam) was an avid fisherman, boat builder in his pasttime and worked for Kentucky & West Virginia Gas Company 44 years. Southside stations (natural gas) was his employment for several years. Floyd was born Oct. 15, 1902.

Jessie Fairchild (Bayes) Price

At Ruth Price Gamboe's unexpected death at age 51 (d. Nov. 10, 1960) at her home on Main Street, she was survived by her husband; four sons, James F., Edward P., Billie Ray and Gene David; one daughter, Mrs. George (Mary Sue) Shannon; two half sisters, Mrs. Vada Pendleton, New Boston, OH and Mrs. Clara Wells, Paradise, MT; and one half brother, Ray Bayes, Dayton, OH. Preceding her in death was one son, John William, and two daughters, Barbara and Betsy Gamboe.

Floyd Gamboe was a welder by trade and welded the natural gas line into Eastern KY. He lived at the family home on Main Street until his death in 1985. Ruth and Floyd's daughter, Mary Sue, now lives in the house.

Ruth's brother, Ray Bayes, married Ruth Ratliff and had one son, John, and one daughter, Jessie Bayes Poteet, Dayton, OH. Ruth Bayes and Jessie Poteet still live in Dayton.

Ruth and Floyd's son, James, had three sons and two dauthers. James married Mary Ezell, Hopkinsville, KY. Their son, Edward Price (Jake), had two sons, James L. and Eddie Ray, and one daughter, Susan and one stepson. Jake married Sally Gambill.

Their son, Billie Ray, married Tonya Bennett, St. Petersburg, FL. They have one son, Adam Corey.

Their son, Gene David, married Rosella Butcher. They have one daughter, Kathryn Ruth Coleman, Lexington, KY.

Daughter Mary Sue has no children.

FERGUSON - Buel Chester "B.C." Ferguson (bon Oct. 28, 1899, died Mar. 11, 1999), son of Thurman Ferguson (born Dec. 16, 1880, died Jan. 16, 1970) and Cynthia Hall Ferguson; grandson of James Powell Ferguson and Cynthia Lemaster Ferguson. Married Feb. 5, 1920, Georgie Price Ferguson (born Aug. 9, 1903, died Dec. 25, 1979), daughter of George Washington Price and Susan Hester Auxier Price (little is known about Susan Hester, an orphan, reared by the Tobe Auxier family at East Point).

B.C. was a third generation United Baptist ordained minister. He followed the footsteps of his dad and grandfather into the ministry by being obedient to God.

As a teenager B.C. began to work in the coal mines with North East Coal Co. at Thealka and Auxier. At times his pay would be 50 cents to 75 cents per day. Soon there was a market for coal. Salaries began to increase to $1.00 to $1.50 per day.

In 1919, this distinguished looking young man, residing with his parents at Red Bush, was told about a pie supper in the opposite end of the county. Seldom did he have extra money to spend as he was the oldest of nine children and helped his parents with the expenses of the family. Having just received his pay, and having very little left for himself, he decided to check out this pie supper. He rode the train to Buskirk and had no trouble locating the Thelma (one-room) school house where he was to attend his first pie supper.

Little did he know that another person was attending her first pie supper. She was a beautiful little blond teenager by the name of Georgie Price. She had come to spend the night with her oldest sister (Nora Johnson) and her husband (Charlie) in Thelma.

B.C. "Buel" and Georgie Price Ferguson

Evidently he did not buy a pie or he would have bought hers. Both were aware that the other was attending the same event. When the Johnson family returned home that night Georgie told her sister that "never in her life had she ever seen such a good looking young man." When her sister asked who it was she remarked, "I don't know his name." Georgie apparently made the same impression on B.C. because he started asking about her.

Six months after that gathering, B.C. and Georgie were married at East Point at the home of her parents, George Washington and Susan Hester Auxier Price, by Elder L.T. Preston.

This marriage was blessed with four children: James Earnest (born Nov. 1, 1920, died Apr. 9, 1981) married to Erma Lee McCain, no children to this marriage; Hester Elizabeth (born Jan. 4, 1923) married to Euel Preston, four children to this marriage; Roberta Louise (born Jan. 22, 1926, died Jul. 25, 1995) married Fredrick Munson, four children to this marriage; and Blanche (born May 9, 1933) married Johnny Hall, three children to this marriage.

In the 30s, during the depression, B.C. moved his wife and children to Wheelwright (Floyd County) where he had been hired by Inland Steel as a day laborer. Maybe because of the depression or for some unknown reason his wife, Georgie, became unhappy with the coal mining town. She and B.C. decided it might be best if she and the children returned home. Six months later Georgie and the children returned to the farm at Thelma. B.C. remained at his job in Wheelwright. But in 1934 the economy began to improve, and after being away from his family for two years, B.C. again moved his family back to Wheelwright.

He was asked to be on a committee to form a miner's union at Wheelwright. At that same time the position for mining foreman became available and B.C. was asked to take the exam. B.C. was uneducated, having only completed a few years of school, and knew he would need help to study for the exam. Robert Muire from Scotland, England, was in Wheelwright at that same time and became a mentor to B.C. He was widely known in Pennsylvania and Scotland for his knowledge of mining. Mr. Muire tutored B.C. and he passed the test for mining foreman, a position he held until retiring in 1965. He had worked in the mines for 43 years.

B.C. was also a member of the mine rescue team that was sent to Van Lear to help recover the eight men that were killed in an explosion at Mine 19.

In May 1933 he joined Concord United Baptist Church. In 1947 he was ordained as a minister of the gospel. In 1954 he was elected moderator of the Concord United Baptist Church. He served this church for 45 years. In addition to Concord, he also served other churches in the area. He was instrumental in organizing a United Baptist Church in Ypsilanti, MI. He also served as moderator of the Paint Union Association for 15 years. During his ministry B.C. conducted over 400 funerals.

B.C. was a member of F.A.M. Masonic Lodge for many years and served as master of the East Point and Wheelwright chapters.

B.C. liked to keep busy and took up the hobby of remodeling houses. In 1965 he built a house from the ground up in Meally, KY.

B.C. moved back to Johnson County in 1970.

He, Georgie and their friends, Cully and Hazel Sparks, made several trips to Arizona to visit friends. They also made many trips to Virginia to fish (something he loved to do). B.C. also loved gardening. He was referred to as a "gentleman gardener" in a *Paintsville Herald* article. He planted and tended a garden until 1997.

B.C. went home to be with his Lord, at the age of 99, on Mar. 11, 1999. He was ushered into the presence of the Lord with his family at his side. He loved preaching the gospel. He was a kind, caring, honest man ... "a special friend."

He is survived by his second wife, Sola; two daughters, Hester Preston, Lexington, KY, and Blanche Hall, Paintsville, KY; six step children; and one sister, Ann Hamilton of Detroit, MI. Also surviving are nine grandchildren, 16 great-grandchildren and many relatives and friends.

FERGUSON - Cossie Franklin Ferguson was born Jul. 22, 1899, near Flat Gap in Johnson County, KY. He was the third child of James Haden Ferguson (born Mar. 29, 1866, died Apr. 2, 1939) and Idabelle Mae Certain (born 1872, died June 1903) surviving to adulthood.

He attended Barnrock School. Cossie spent most of his early years with his uncle and aunt, Donnie and Catherine Ferguson Sagraves, working on the farm and learning blacksmith skills etc.

Cossie and Minnie Ferguson, Annabell, Willa Jean, Chester and Darleen.

Cossie met Minnie Gertrude Skaggs February 1928 during a revival meeting at Laurel Hill Primitive Baptist Church. Minnie was the daughter of Elder John Henry and Laura Bell Estep Skaggs of Lawrence County, KY. Cossie and Minnie were married May 17, 1928, by Elder J.H. Skaggs in Elliott County (on the ridge behind the bride's home on the head of Coal Creek in Lawrence County where the two counties met because the marriage license had been applied for in Sandy Hook, KY, in Elliott County).

Cossie and Minnie were the parents of six children: Eugene (born and died Feb. 9, 1929, interred at the J.H. Skaggs Cemetery on Coal Creek), Gloria Darleen (born Feb. 13, 1930) married Steward Ross, Willa Jean (born May 18, 1932) married Elwin Sagraves, John Haden Chester (born Mar. 26, 1935) married Darlene Johnson, Joseph Alonzo (born Jun. 6, 1941, died Jun. 7, 1944) and Edith Annabell (born Nov. 6, 1944) married Frederick Williams.

They lived in Lawrence County and Laurel Creek in Johnson County. He worked for different farmers until being employed by WPA, a Godsend for so many. Cossie was plagued by several illnesses, especially pneumonia, and was no longer able to work after Mar. 24, 1941.

Minnie went to Mayo Vocational School (1942) where she learned to read blueprints and micrometers, this helped her gain employment at Patterson Field, now Wright Patterson Air Force Base, Dayton, OH, which in turn led the family to Springfield, OH in January 1943, returning to Flat Gap May 1946. A short time before, Cossie, being told in a dream that Christ would be back for him in October, went to his eternal rest Oct. 2, 1946. He was interred at the Camant Cemetery at Flat Gap.

Minnie returned to Springfield, OH, April 1951. She retired from Omco Products Oct. 26, 1973.

Minnie was married to Rupert Sparks Mar. 29, 1952, by Elder J.H. Skaggs and reared his three sons as her own: Larry Eugene (born Dec. 2, 1939) married Janice Kelly; Farrell Dean (born Jun. 14, 1943) married first, Betty Downing and second, Sharon Ellis Guernsey; and Billie Douglas (born Mar. 30, 1946) married Carolyn Golden.

Minnie died Aug. 12, 1992, and was buried at the Camant Cemetery, Flat Gap, Johnson County, KY. Rupert lives at Cooper's Care Center in Springfield, OH.

Cossie and Minnie were members of the Old Regular Primitive Baptist Church.

FERGUSON - Ferdinand Ferguson was born about 1836 in Franklin County, VA, to Frances Ann Ferguson. His father's name is not known. Ferdinand came to Johnson County, KY, in the 1850s.

Ferdinand first married Margaret Williams about 1863 in Johnson County. Margaret (born 1842, died 1882) was the daughter of Thomas Williams and Susannah Ross Williams of Flat Gap.

Ferd and Margaret made their home on Upper Laurel Creek in the area of Gillium Branch and were the parents of 12 children: Thomas Manford (born Dec. 11, 1863, died Jun. 12, 1941) married Sebra Elizabeth Fyffe; James Haden (born Mar. 29, 1866, died Apr. 2, 1939; Lucas Perry (born January 1867, died Jan. 2, 1949) married Cynthia Alice Bailey; Susan Frances (born Sep. 28, 1870, died Jan. 28, 1944) married James Henry Fyffe; Alamander (born Nov. 1, 1868, died Apr. 9, 1957) married Malissa Conley; Mollie Alice (born February 1873, died Dec. 4, 1932) married first, Chilton Osborne and second, Harrison Grim; Noah (born Feb. 22, 1874, died Nov. 28, 1950); Lydia M. (born Sep. 1, 1875, died Jun. 23, 1957) married first, James S. Conley and second, Albert Bailey; Joseph (born August 1877, died Sep. 16, 1877); Katherine (born Sep. 11, 1878, died 1934) married Donnie Sagraves; Bobbie (born 1881, died 1883); and Malissa (born May 1881, died 1954) married first, Phillip Picklesimer and second, Sylvester Jones.

Margaret died about 1882 and was interred in the Camant Cemetery at Flat Gap. Ferdinand married second, Linnie Skaggs Certain, a widow with a daughter and a son, Sep. 22, 1882, in Johnson County. Linnie was born May 7, 1850, in Morgan County, KY, to John T. Skaggs and Margaret Holbrook. Ferd and Linnie were the parents of three children: Isaac Frank (born September 1883, died Oct. 10, 1918) married Virgie Bailey; William Henderson (born Apr. 6, 1885, died Oct. 29, 1943) married first, Tera Wright and second, Sarah Della Perry; and Ora M. (born Dec. 19, 1894, died Dec. 20, 1969) married Mary Lyon.

Hade Ferguson

Ferdinand died in 1911 and was interred in the Camant Cemetery at Flat Gap. Linnie died Sep. 12, 1924, and was interred in the Ferguson Cemetery on Travis Br. of Upper Laurel Creek.

Second Generation - James Haden Ferguson first married Idabelle Mae Certain Oct. 29, 1893, in Johnson County. Idabelle (born 1872) was the daughter of John and Linnie Skaggs Certain of Morgan County.

Hade lived on Upper and Lower Laurel Creeks and he and Idabelle were the parents of four children: Alonzo (born August 1894, died 1962) married Stella Craigs; Ollie (born February 1897, died Nov. 10, 1918) married Irwin Hitchcock; Cossie Franklin (born Jul. 22, 1899, died Oct. 2, 1946) married Minnie Gertrude Skaggs; and Monnie (born Feb. 22, 1902, died Aug. 7, 1982) married William Highie Bailey, first and Fred Vanhoose, second.

Idabelle died in 1903 and was interred in the Travis Br. Cemetery on Upper Laurel Creek. Hade married second, Louranie Pennington Jan. 7, 1904, in Johnson County. Lourannie "Granny Lou" (born 1878, died 1963) was the daughter of John and Cynthia Ellen Cantrell Pennington. NOTE: This family dropped the Pennington name in favor of Curtis after 1900. Hade and Lourannie were the parents of six children: Lunda (born Apr. 7, 1905, died Feb. 12, 1992) married Nollie Murray; Lura (born Jul. 4, 1907) married James E. McCoy; Mertie (born Jul. 2, 1910) married Noah West; Clyde (born Mar. 9, 1915, died Jan. 26, 1984) married Bulah Slone; Virgil Elwood (born May 1, 1918, died Nov. 13, 1984); and Hargus Lee (born Sep. 2, 1921, died Jan. 7, 1990) married Fern Clotine Boggs.

Hade died Apr. 2, 1939, and Lourannie in 1963, both were interred in the Camant Cemetery at Flat Gap. *Submitted by Steward David Ross.*

FERGUSON - William Girdie Ferguson was born Feb. 18, 1904, at Relief, KY (Morgan County). He was the son of Hansford Berry Ferguson (born 1877, died 1962) and Junie Attie Brown (born 1883, died 1954). He was one of six children and grew up helping his father on the family farm and logging. He was educated in a loghouse school at Relief.

On Jan. 13, 1925, he married Sally Ison of Moon, KY (Morgan County). They became the parents of three children: Mabel (born 1925, died at 9 months of "summer complaint" or dysentery); Edward Homer (born 1927), retired pipefitter living in Lorida, FL; and Norma Ethel (born 1929), merchant at Relief, KY, died of cancer in 1993.

In the 1930s Girdie became a merchant and opened a general store at Old Paint, KY, and later on the right hand fork of Blaine Creek in Lawrence County. His wife, Hazel, worked with him in the business.

In 1940s Girdie moved to Jeffersonville, IN, and was a welder in the shipyards. This job made him exempt from WWII service. Later, he moved to Houston, TX, continuing as a welder and then to Globe, AZ, welding in the copper mines.

Girdie and his family returned to Morgan County, KY, in 1947, and reopened his general store at Relief. In 1950, he bought property at Staffordsville on Rt. 172 near the present entrance to Paintsville Lake. Girdie established his home there with his store next door. It was at this location that Girdie and Hazel worked side-by-side and built a very successful business despite losing everything three times due to flooding of Paint Creek.

Girdie retired and closed his store in 1972. He enjoyed people and loved to garden and hunt. He attended the Church of God. Girdie died of a massive heart attack on Mar. 26, 1991, at Relief, KY. He is buried at Highland Memorial Cemetery and is survived by his son, Edward H. and six grandchildren: Michael K. Ferguson, Flat Gap, KY; Jan Branham, Worthington, OH; Tammy Morris, Cygnet, OH; Jeanie Hackworth, Relief, KY; Sam Brown, Relief, KY; and Derrick Brown, Cincinnati, OH.

FERGUSON - Sally Hazel Ison Ferguson, a descendent of Jenny Wiley, was born Dec. 20, 1903, in Moon, Morgan County, KY. She was the daughter of Dock Marion "Dockie" Ison (born 1869, died 1933) and Stella Sherman Ison (born 1868, died 1956). She had five sisters. Hazel was reared on Caney Creek at Moon working with her father in the fields of his farm. She attended a loghouse one-room school.

On Jan. 13, 1925, she married William Girdie Ferguson and to this union was born three children: Mabel (born 1925, died at 9 months of "summer complaint" or dysentery); Edward Homer (born 1927), retired pipefitter living in Lorida, FL; and Norma Ethel Brown (born 1929), merchant, died of cancer at Moon, KY, in 1993.

Hazel was converted and baptized in the New Salam United Baptist Church. In the 1930s, she helped her husband operate a general store, first at Old Paint, KY, and then at Blaine, KY.

In the 1940s, Hazel and Girdie moved to Jeffersonville, IN. Hazel was employed in a sewing factory, while Girdie became a welder. They later moved to Houston, TX, and then to Globe AZ.

The Ferguson family returned to their home in Morgan County, KY, in 1947, and reopened their general store. In 1950, they bought a store and house at Staffordsville on Rt. 172 near the present entrance to Paintsville Lake. Hazel worked along side her husband to build a successful business. They both retired in 1972.

Hazel loved to crochet, enjoyed making bedspreads, afghans and rugs. In her later years she was an invalid and died with complications from Alzheimer disease. She passed away Jan. 26, 1991, and is buried at Highland Memorial Cemetery at Staffordsville, KY.

William Girdie and Sally Hazel Ison Ferguson

Hazel is survived by her son, six grandchildren, 11 great-grandchildren and five great-great-grandchildren.

FRAZIER - Eugene Frazier was born Aug. 7, 1923. He was the fourth of 12 children born to Stephen Douglas and Emma Williams Frazier at Elna, KY, where he lived until young adulthood. His maternal grandparents were William and Lynn Witten Williams, and his paternal grandparents were Martin Luther and Clara Brown Frazier.

Eugene's father was an oil well driller and spent a lot of time away from home working in the oil fields. He and his siblings learned responsibility early while working on the farm and helping with household chores. His mother found time, however, even with a large family, to give each child much individual attention and to instill in them a love of books and learning. One of Eugene's fondest memories was of his mother reading to him. His formal education began in a one-room school next door to the family home at the head of Mud Lick Creek.

While still a teenager, Eugene, his father and other family members left the farm to work in the defense plants in Dayton, OH. On Apr. 27, 1943, he entered the Army to serve through the end of WWII, as did two of his brothers. He was promoted to sergeant and served the majority of his time at a base in Texas. He left the Army in 1946 after receiving various decorations and citations for his honorable service. He returned to Dayton to work at Wright Patterson Air Force Base until enrolling in college at Morehead State University where he was named to "Who's Who Among Students in American Colleges and Universities." He completed both a bachelor's and master's degree in education in four years at Morehead and returned to Johnson County to teach. In 1955 he served as teacher, basketball coach and principal at a four-room school in Thealka, KY, where he fell in love with and later married a young teacher named Helen Faye Castle, the daughter of Vern and Opal Preston Castle of Tutor Key. Within a few years they became the parents of two children, David Bryan and Karen Jean.

Eugene Frazier

In 1956, Eugene began teaching sixth grade at Paintsville Elementary, teaching for 11 years before becoming assistant superintendent in 1966. He served his last three years in education as superintendent before retiring in 1981. During this time he saw both his children go through the Paintsville School System from kindergarten through high school. Karen now teaches special needs children at Paintsville Elementary and David works in the mental health field in Lexington. Throughout his career, Eugene was dedicated to the field of education and loved working with the youth of Paintsville and Johnson County. Long after his retirement former students would approach him to recall fond memories of times spent in his classes. Students often recollected that "Mr. Frazier never raised his voice in class but we always knew we'd better do what he said." Teachers with whom he worked remember him as a fair and caring administrator who was always willing to listen to their concerns. He contributed to his community by serving on the Board of Directors of Mayo Technical School and as a member of the Rotary Club and regularly attended the First Baptist Church of Paintsville.

Eugene died Jan. 29, 1994, after a four year battle with lung cancer.

FRAZIER - Sanford "Sant" Frazier was born Mar. 24, 1898, in Paintsville, Johnson County, KY. He is the son of James Hiram Frazier and Martha Jane Crace. James and Martha had seven children all born in Johnson County, KY: William Alexander "Elick" (born Aug. 15, 1894), Alfred (born Nov. 16, 1896), Sant (born Mar. 24, 1898, died Jun. 6, 1968), Alta "Dolly" Frazier (born Mar. 14, 1901, died 1906), Julie (born Jan. 6, 1904, died Apr. 18, 1970), Flora (born Jul. 1, 1906) and Willard (born Sep. 2, 1908, died Apr. 18, 1912). Sant is the descendent of Henry Conley a Revolutionary War Soldier.

On Apr. 3, 1920, Sant married Evalena Lena Ward. They had six children: Carl Mitchel (born Jul. 5, 1921), Clyde Beacher (born Dec. 11, 1923, died Jan. 23, 1982), Gladys Jewell (born Sep. 12, 1925), Eula Mae (born Jan. 24, 1928, died Jun. 19, 1990), Juanita "Bon" (born Oct. 16, 1930) and Luther Lee "Luke" (born Feb. 10, 1936). All their children were born in Kentucky except for Luke who was born in Beaver, OH.

Sant was a very easy going individual. It took a lot for him to raise his voice or lose his temper. He had a very good sense of humor and loved practical jokes, especially if he was the one pulling the joke. He loved it when we had family reunions and all gathered to enjoy each other's company. You would always find him playing with the children. He would be the one holding the water hose and spraying water on anyone he could reach. He loved to eat, especially watermelon and chocolate pie. He was not very tall in stature, but stood tall in respect.

At the age of 21 he caught typhoid fever. He lost all his blonde hair and when it grew back it was extremely curly. When he was a little older he lost his hair again except for a ring that went from ear to ear only in the back. He said it was because he caught typhoid fever. If this was because of the fever, why did two of his sons (Carl and Luke) and three grandchildren (Eddie, Doug and Paul) also have this same trait?

Sant worked for the Sandy Valley Grocery Co. in Portsmouth, KY, and about 1929 moved to Louisa, KY, where he worked for Wheeler's Dairy. He moved to Beaver, OH, about 1933, where he farmed. He worked at the shipping yards in Baltimore, MD, during WWII. He returned home to farm and then tried working at NCR in Dayton, OH, about 1943-46. He missed the home place and moved back to Beaver for about two years and then returned to Dayton, OH, and worked at Curtis Cash. He retired from Curtis Cash. He had a small farm in Franklin, OH, that he worked on after retiring. He loved the outdoors and working with his hands. *By Nita Murray Lewis.*

Sanford "Sant" Frazier

FRAZIER & PENNINGTON - William Edward Frazier and Amanda Pennington were married in Johnson County Apr. 13, 1897. Ed was born in 1876, the son of William J. Frazier (born 1841, died 1921) and Zilphia Lemaster (born 1836, died 1910). William and Zilphia, it appears, were the parents of 11 children. They lived on or near Hargus most of their lives. They are buried in the D.J. McCarty Cemetery at Manila. They were referred to as "Pap" and "Granny." Granny was a mid-wife and a good "doctor." When there was sickness in the neighborhood someone would always say "Go get Aunt Zilphia."

William J. Frazier was the son of William Alexander Frazier (born 1818, died 1868) who married Apr. 29, 1840, in Clay County, Elizabeth "Betty" Woods (born 1819, died after 1880). Wm. Alexander was buried somewhere on Little Paint. Betty may have been buried in Elliott County. Zilphia was a daughter of Richard Lemaster (born 1807, died 1887) and Rebecca "Bexie" Christian (born 1813, died 1878). Richard and Bexie, along with a daughter, Elizabeth (Betty Dick) Lemaster, are buried in a cemetery near the Spice Cove Church.

Amanda was born in 1875, the daughter of George W. Pennington (born 1847, died 1929) and Mary Rebecca Young (born 1848, died 1937). George was probably born in Morgan County and Mary Rebecca in Lawrence County. George is buried in the Denver Hill Cemetery. Mary died during the 1937 flood in Kay-Ford, WV, and is buried there. I believe they were referred to as Grandpa and Grandma. They had 13 children.

George Pennington was the son of William Pennington (born 1816, died after 1880) and Martha Blanton (born 1816, died after 1880), who were married Dec. 8, 1836, in Floyd County. William was a son of Joshua Pennington (born 1790, died 1878-80) and Nancy Sparks (born 1795, died 1878). Martha was a daughter of George Blanton Sr. (born 1775, died 1850-60) and Martha Shepherd (born 1775, died 1850-60). We believe William and Martha (Blanton) Pennington, along with Joshua and Nancy (Sparks) Pennington, were buried in the Pendleton Cemetery which was moved to Johnson County Memorial Cemetery. Mary Rebecca Young was a daughter of James and Jane (Large ?) Young.

Ed and Mandy lived most of their early lives with his parents in or near Hargus. They were the parents of six children: W.A. "Willie" (born 1898) married Virgie Williams, had a daughter, Billie Marie; Mary Ellen "Dollie" (born 1902) married Arthur Lemaster, had two sons, Paul M. and Walter E. "Dick" Lemaster; Thurman (born 1905, died 1909) died with appendicitis; Alma (born 1907) married John R. Estep, they are buried in Indiana; Goldie (born 1909) married Frank Adams, their children were: Irene, Ralph and Mary; and Allie (born 1913) married Edgar Watson, their children were: Barbara Ann, Leonard Elmo and Patty. Allie and Edgar are buried in Lima, OH.

In 1921 Ed and Mandy moved to Jenny's Creek near Collista where they lived at the time of their deaths. Dollie died when Dick was a small baby and the two boys were reared by their grandparents at Collista. Ed was a farmer, he had a blacksmith shop and a mill. Mandy tended a large garden, sewed and made quilts, kept house, reared her grandchildren and made everyone welcome to come to visit or stay for the summer. She was a good neighbor in time of need. During the 1918/1919 flu epidemic she was away from home two weeks at a time helping her neighbors while Ed and William cared for their children. They roasted onions under the grate and gave them to the children to ward off the flu.

Ed died in 1944, Mandy died in 1945. They are buried in the D.J. McCarty Cemetery. As is "Little Thurman" and several members of Ed's family. Willie Frazier is buried in Florida; Dollie is buried in Denver Hill Cemetery; Frank and Goldie Adams are buried in Johnson County Memorial Cemetery at Staffordsville, KY. *Submitted by Barbara (Watson) Ryan.*

GAMBILL - Dan J. Gambill was born Oct. 6, 1910, in Johnson County. He was married to Anna Lee Johnson Feb. 18, 1931. Mr. Gambill taught in Johnson County schools for a number of years. He began his teaching career in a rural school on Chestnut Creek, where he was younger than many of his first pupils.

Dan J. Gambill

Mr. Gambill was first hired as an agriculture teacher at Meade Memorial High School at Williamsport, KY, where he taught, as such, into the late 30s or early 40s. He also coached basketball. Mr. Gambill went on to become principal at the Thealka and Buffalo Grade Schools in Johnson County, KY.

Mr. and Mrs. Gambill had four children. Their eldest, Ella Rose Gambill Daniels, was a former finance officer in the Johnson County Schools. Madge Gambill Williams married Forrest Roger Williams and became a mother and homemaker. They reside in Carmel Valley, CA. Their son, James Gambill, married Patricia Branham. He is a real estate broker and insurance agent in Paintsville, KY. Their youngest daughter, Donna Gambill Hamilton, became the wife of Johnson County school superintendent, Orville Hamilton.

The Gambills had four grandchildren: Nina Ann Williams, daughter of Madge and Forrest Williams; Chris and Kelly Gambill, children of James and Patricia Branham Gambill; and Lee Hamilton, son of Donna Lee and Orville Hamilton.

Dan J. Gambill passed from this life Nov. 6, 1993. He was preceded in death by his wife, Anna Lee Johnson Gambill, who died Dec. 14, 1991.

GAREY - Betty Evelyn Garey, the daughter of the late Homer D. and Ethel Conley Picklesimer, was born at Volga, KY, Sep. 10, 1929. Betty lived at Volga and attended the one room school at Ramey Branch. After graduating from Flat Gap High School as salutatorian in 1948, she lived and worked in Baltimore, MD, and retired in 1981 from Bethelhem Steel Corp.

While in Baltimore, Betty met and married her husband of 49 years, William Henry Garey. He is the son of the late George and Nettie Brehm Garey. They have no children.

Betty's mother, Ethel Conley Picklesimer, was born Mar. 27, 1890, in Johnson County, KY. Betty's father, Homer D. Picklesimer, was born Dec. 10, 1889, also in Johnson County, KY. They were married Jun. 19, 1909, and lived here all their lives. Her father was a song leader, farmer and sawmill operator. Her mother reared 10 children and in her later years, designed and made beautiful quilts by hand until her death at age 90.

Betty has seven brothers and two sisters: Walter L. Picklesimer (born May 18, 1910), Estill C. Picklesimer (born Sep. 30, 1912), Francis M. Picklesimer (born May 24, 1915), Juanita Bell (born Mar. 15, 1917), Hubert H. Picklesimer (born Sep. 18, 1920), Anna L. Monroe (born Sep. 14, 1923), Harry Hansel Picklesimer (born Nov. 26, 1925), Everett Willis Picklesimer (born Nov. 6, 1927) and Homer Picklesimer Jr. (born Dec. 7, 1932).

Betty Evelyn Garey

Betty currently resides in a log house on Stone Coal Road in Volga where her hobby is quilting. She teaches a children's Bible class at the Stambaugh Church of Christ where she is a member.

GARLAND - Reverend Charles Raleigh Garland was called to preach at the First United Methodist Church in Paintsville in 1936. As his family was driving to Paintsville from Benham, KY, a sad automobile accident occurred in which Mrs. Pearl Garland was killed. So Rev. Garland came to First Church with five sons. Charles R. Garland Jr., William E. Garland, Sidney Blythe Garland, Phillip Garland and Paul Garland. Rev. Garland later married Velma Plank Garland.

Two of the boys returned to Paintsville to make their homes following college and service in the Armed Forces. William Garland married Mary Grace Rice and they had two children, Rebecca and William Rice Garland.

Col. Sidney Blythe Garland married Janet Gwen Hyde. They had four sons: Sidney Blythe Garland II (born 1949), Richard D. Garland (born 1954) David Rees Garland and Robert Hyde Garland (born 1962).

GEIGER - Virgie Lee Hager Geiger was born in Paintsville Jun. 20, 1879, the daughter of Daniel Marion Hager and Jessica Vaughan Hager and the granddaughter of Gen. Daniel Hager and Violet Porter Hager and Henry S. Vaughan and Mary Turner Vaughan of Johnson County. Virgie had six brothers: Eugene Hayes Hager, Robert Barton Hager, Samuel Patton Hager, Benjamin B. Hager and Russell Hager; and one sister, Edna Hager.

In the first formal church wedding held in Paintsville at the First Methodist Episcopal Church, North, on Oct. 17, 1900, Virgie married Orville Cook Geiger (born Apr. 3, 1878, in Boyd County), one of eight children of Henry Alexander Geiger and Sophia Pollard Geiger. Cook's brothers and sisters were: Harry Geiger, James E. Geiger, Burwell S. Geiger, Forrest P. Geiger, Esther Geiger (Henthorne), George B. Geiger and Emma Geiger.

Virgie was educated in the public school of Paintsville and at a young ladies' seminary in Ashland. An accomplished pianist, she played piano accompaniment for silent films at the Arcade Theatre for many years. Following the rearing of her two children, Marion Braxton Geiger (born Sep. 4, 1903) and Dorothy Louise Geiger (Marsh) (born Oct. 31, 1908), Virgie was employed throughout most of her adult life by H.B. Rice Insurance Co. in Paintsville. In addition to being an active member of Paintsville's First Methodist Church until her death Jul. 13, 1958, Virgie was a charter member of the Paintsville chapter of the Daughters of the American Revolution.

Orville Cook Geiger began his career as a traveling salesman before the advent of the 20th century, riding horseback throughout the Big Sandy Valley selling merchandise to retail merchants in communities along the Levisa and Tug Forks of the river which they ordered from catalogs Cook carried in his saddlebags. Later, Cook became one of the first automobile dealers in Paintsville, selling Studebakers from his dealership on Bridge Street. Cook developed a close personal relationship with John C.C. Mayo and was active with Mayo in Democrat politics before Mayo's untimely death in 1914. He was one of the founding members of the Paintsville Rotary Club in 1922. Cook died in Paintsville Aug. 25, 1958, not quite six weeks after the death of Virgie.

Virgie Lee Hager Geiger

Virgie and Cook Geiger built a home on Euclid Avenue in 1907 which has been occupied by their descendants ever since.

GOODYEAR - Mary Kathleen Sparks was born Nov. 1, 1954, in Pontiac, MI. She is the eldest of three daughters born to Herman Howard Sparks (born Flat Gap, Johnson County, KY, 1924, died Knox County, OH, 1982, son of Elva Sparks and Tera McKenzie) and Sylvia Frances Ramey (born Ramey Branch, Davisville, Lawrence County, KY, 1931, daughter of James Isaac Ramey and Cassie Lettie Davis) and was reared in Delaware County, OH. She married Carl Eugene Goodyear in Delaware County, OH, Feb. 20, 1981, and has one beautiful daughter, Jenny Rose Goodyear (born Feb. 21, 1984, Knox County, OH).

A supporter for both paper and on-line resources, in May 1996, Mary K. became the U.S. GenWeb county representative for Johnson County, KY, GenWeb (http://www.usgenweb.org) and in September 1996 originated the Melungeon email list, where in 1997 she worked with others to create; 'First Union,' the first Melungeon research conference held in Wise, VA. She is a regular volunteer at the local LDS Family History Center in Mansfield, OH, and teaches or helps others teach genealogy subjects and land platting.

Garland family 50th Wedding Anniversary. Richard, Robert, Sid, Jann, Sidney II and David. [See Garland family history above center]

Mary K's love of Kentucky history has uncovered a wonderful diversified ancestry of English, Scotch-Irish, French Huguenot, Native American and Melungeon peoples. She is always 'Sincerely Searching' where her families have been found in Johnson County, KY, from Paintsville to Blaine in Lawrence County, KY, and from Fuget to the Big Sandy River. She is always looking for more information on the following families: Sparks, McKenzie, Salyer (two lines), Lemaster, Ramey, Remy (four lines), Davis, Cordial, Pack, Chandler, Wheeler (two lines), Borders, Nelson (two lines), Jones, Stanley, Slone, Vanover, Nickell, Rhoton, Pridemore, Parker, Hill, Estep, Thompson, Sellards, Lane, Jayne, Jane, Kearby. These families migrated into Johnson County from Virginia (Scott, Russell, Washington counties), West Virginia (Cabell/ Wayne County) and from North Carolina (Ashe, Surry counties). *By Mary K. Goodyear.*

Front: Carl Eugene and Jenny Rose Goodyear. Back: Mary K. Goodyear.

GREEN - The family Green is of English extraction. The Hundred Rolls of England, 1273 bear the names of Robert de la Grene and Warin de la Grene and the poll tax list of Yorkshire, England, 1379, bear the names of Petrus del Grene, Adam del Grene and Willenus del Grene.

George and Jane Lemaster Green

The family was numerous in the New England and southern colonies at an early date. Brothers, Giles and Enoch Green, were ancestors of a branch of the Green family who settled in the Big Sandy Valley region of Eastern Kentucky.

Giles Green (born in Virginia, about 1800, died in Johnson County, KY, circa 1876) was married first in Virginia to Katie Chandler (born about 1795 in North Carolina or Virginia, died in Johnson County about 1844). Giles married second to a widow Margaret "Peggy" Ghent Yates Mar. 14, 1846, who was born in 1807 in Virginia and died in Johnson County.

Giles and Katie Chandler Green had 10 children: Thomas Green, Elias Green (born in Kentucky, 1831), William Green (born in Kentucky, 1833), John Green (born 1838 or 1839), George W. Green (born 1841), Pasty "Martha" Green, Judy or Judith Green, Eliza Green, Sarah Green and David Green.

Giles and Margaret Ghent Yates Green had three children: Enoch Green (born 1847), Marcus Green (born 1849) and James M. Green (born 1852).

The 1850 U.S. census shows a female, Judea Green age 91, living in the Giles Green household. This lady is probably Giles' mother.

1. Giles Green married Katie Chandler.

2. George Green married Jane Lemaster. George Green was in the Union Army during the Civil War and was a prisoner at Andersonville, GA. This family story has always been told: George was one of the prisoners who prayed for water and a spring of fresh water broke out in the prison grounds, saving their lives.

2. George and Jane Lemaster Green had nine children.

3. Clista Margaret Green married Merdia Oliver McKenzie. See McKenzie history:

3. Ida Green married Nelson Lyon.

3. Sarah Green married Ora Holbrook.

3. Nannie Green married Hayden Hamilton.

3. George Green Jr. married Nola Williams.

3. Giles Green married Vinie Hill.

3. Henry Green married first, Alice Johnson and second, Lou Williams Thomas.

3. Lewis Green married first, Cora Bailey and second, Druzetta Cox.

3. Garfield Green married Ellen Lemaster.

See additional information in Clista Margaret Green McKenzie's history. *Submitted by William H. and Clista M. McKenzie Pelfrey.*

GRIFFITHS & PELFREY - Hilary Pelfrey Griffiths was born Jul. 26, 1947, in the Paintsville Clinic Hospital at Paintsville, KY, to William Hillard and Clista Margaret McKenzie Pelfrey. She spent the first two years of her life in Cattletsburg before moving to Keaton. Her parents and sisters: Beverly, Marcia Rae and Margaret Wynn; and their families remain at the Keaton homestead and at the McKenzie homestead at Flat Gap.

Hilary Pelfrey Griffiths

Hilary attended the one-room school at lower Keaton through the third grade. She and her sister walked to school. The school was heated with a coal stove, had a water bucket, outside toilets and all students packed their lunch. The students played games such as "round town" (softball), Red Rover, Mother May I? and other outside, physical games. School was not dismissed due to weather conditions.

She completed her elementary, junior high and high school at Flat Gap. She graduated in 1965. Following graduation, she completed her BS professional in home economics/consumer education at Berea College. Her practice teaching was done in a new round, "mod system" scheduling high school at Berea. She has completed a master's of business administration and has over 40 graduate hours above her master's.

She has been employed as a social worker, cooperative extension agent, teacher, nutrition director, planner, dietitian and currently teaches personal development in a juvenile correctional facility in Ohio. She maintains four professional license/certifications.

She married John Thomas Griffiths, son of Herman Adrian and Verna Mae Miller Griffiths from Huntington, IN. Hilary and John have lived in Kentucky and West Virginia, and have resided in Ohio for the past 23 years. They adopted a bi-racial daughter, Latisha Clista (born Jul. 31, 1978) when she was 2 years old. They are now the proud grandparents of a lovely granddaughter, Cherokee Alicia (born Apr. 23, 1998).

Hilary is a Kentucky Colonel, member of Eastern Star and has been an active member of the church, serving as youth advisor/teacher for many years. She has been selected to appear in the *Who's Who of Professional Educators* in their Year 2000 publication.

She has spent her life caring for others and attempting to show the world that God provides unconditional love and acceptance to all his children. *Submitted by W.H. Pat and Clista M. Pelfrey.*

GULLETT - Mae Gullett was born July 16, 1915, and on Dec. 24, 1929, she married Elvin Van Hoose at Barnetts Creek in Johnson County, KY. She remembers riding to her wedding atop a small mare. Crossing a frozen Paint Creek on a cold Christmas Eve, Mae and Elvin made their way to the home of United Baptist minister John Picklesimer for a ceremony to be witnessed by Elzie Picklesimer and Elvin's brother-in-law, Albert Lemaster.

They began their marriage living in Johnson County and working for local farmers. Their first child, Gladys Pauline, was born on Dec. 23, 1930, but died the next day -their first wedding anniversary. Mae and Elvin had seven other children born in Johnson County:

Anna Louise Van Hoose (born Feb. 5, 1932;

Harry Clayton Van Hoose (born Mar. 11, 1934, died Dec. 9, 1989);

Elvin and Mae Gullet

Dissie Ilene Van Hoose (born Mar. 29, 1936);

Doris Jean Van Hoose (born Mar. 5, 1938);

Mary Magdalene Van Hoose (born Mar. 23, 1940);

Verina Irene Van Hoose (born Aug. 14, 1942); and

John See Van Hoose (born Mar. 6, 1944).

Mae Gullett Van Hoose was the mother of eight children and grandmother of 24. Mae died Nov. 17, 1991, and is buried in Mutual, OH.

The Gullett line can be traced in America as follows:

10th generation - Mae Gullett (born Jul. 16, 1915, died Nov. 17, 1991) is buried in Mutual, OH.

9th generation - Harry B. Gullett (born Feb. 9, 1890, died May 6, 1939) and Mary Cantrell (born Apr. 18, 1890, died Jan. 15, 1959). Harry and Mary are buried on the family farm on Stone Coal, Johnson County, KY.

8th generation - Daniel P. Gullett (born Nov. 3, 1853, died Dec. 22, 1932), Melissa Jane Pratt (born June 1850, died June 1930). Daniel and Melissa are also buried on the family farm on Stone Coal, Johnson County, KY.

7th generation - Ira Gullett (born Oct. 8, 1820, died Jan. 15, 1901) and Lidia Elizabeth Pelphrey (born Aug. 10, 1825, died Jan. 3, 1894). Ira and Lidia are buried at the New Cemetery near the Paintsville Dam.

6th generation - William Gullett (born about 1775, died about 1845) and Tempy Hopper (born 1793, died Sep. 2, 1853).

5th generation - Daniel Gullett (born about 1755, died about 1813) and Mary (born about 1760).

4th generation - William Gullett (born 1730, died about 1800).

3rd generation - Abraham Gullett (born about 1715, died about 1758) and Susannah (born about 1705, died about 1785).

2nd generation - William Gullett (born Apr. 25, 1678, died about 1716) and Mary (born about 1685, died about 1716).

1st generation - William Gullett (born about 1645, died about 1705) and Susanna Mills (born about 1655, died about 1715). *Submitted by John See Van Hoose.*

HALL - Frank, the son of Judge Francis Preston (born Mar. 20, 1844) and Amanda Castle Spriggs (born Jan. 26, 1846). Amanda and Judge Francis were married Sep. 15, 1866.

Judge Francis was in the Civil War. He served in the 5th, West Virginia Inf. He was 19 when he volunteered for service. He received the Medal of Honor W.V. FT. Union soldier.

Judge Francis was the grandson of Reuben Preston (born 1817) and Lucinda Evans (born 1825), married January 1836. The great-grandson of Moses Preston Sr. (born 1762) married Fanny Arther (born 1774).

Frank F. Preston (born Apr. 12, 1888, Lawrence County, KY) married Dora Ann Hall, Mar. 27, 1918, Lawrence County KY. Dora b. Feb. 24, 1896 Magoffin County. Dora was the daughter of Harvey Hall and Emily Howard Hall. Granddaughter of Tommy Howard (died 1926) and Lidy Gullet. Great-great-granddaughter of Jim Howard Sr. and Liss Lemaster, Jarvey Hall and Mary Hackworth. Dora was from a family of four children: Ellen, Agnes and Cort Hall.

Frank was from a family of 12 children: Henry, Ella, Rose, Cora, Ramson, John, Edgar, Maud, Frank, Jay, Madison and Charlie. After Frank and Dora were married they moved to Thealka, KY, 1922. Frank worked in the mines for North East Coal Co. about 30 years.

In 1946 they bought a small farm at Horse Picture, Lawrence County, KY. They lived there until Frank died Mar. 31, 1967.

Frank and Dora had 11 children: Dixie Preston (born in Lawrence County, Aug. 19, 1911) married Edgar Charles Oct. 15, 1928. She had seven children: Magdaline, Mable, Dora Ellen, Elouisa, Robert (died at birth), Donald and Peggy. Edgar died 1968, Mable died June 1994. Dixie lives at Lovely, KY.

Frank and Dora (Hall) Preston

Dorthey Preston (born in Ohio, Jul. 27, 1914) married Everett Castle, Dec. 15, 1933. She had six children: Betty Ann, Bobby Ray, Elouise, Imogene, Mickle and Brenda; they live at Thealka, KY. Dorthey died January 1997.

Harvey Jay Preston (born in West Virginia, May 27, 1919) married Mildred Cook Jun. 17, 1944. They had two daughters, Karen Sue and Donna Jean. Harvey lives Columbus, OH.

Goldia Rae Preston (born Lawrence County, KY, Nov. 13, 1921) married Clyde B. Combs Oct. 6, 1945. She had three sons: Wendell Franklin (born Sep. 9, 1946), Harvey Bennett (born Jun. 11, 1949) and Donald Gregory (born Dec. 26, 1955). Goldia has three grandchildren: Erick Shayne, Matthew Allen and Amanda Dawn. Goldia lives in Columbus, OH.

Amanda Preston (born Feb. 4, 1924) married Donald VanHoose Jun. 8, 1942. She had two daughters, Barbra Joyce and Donna Fay. Donald died May 30, 1965. She later married Walsh Keener, Dec. 4, 1969. Amanda lives Westerville, OH. Walsh died.

Paul Preston (born Mar. 31, 1927) married Pauline Burchett, October 1949. They had four children: Pamela Kay (born Mar. 31, 1950), Patricia Lynn (born Oct. 16, 1952), Paula Jo (born Jan. 6, 1955) and Phillip (born Jul. 27, 1959). Phillip died February 1990. Pauline died Jun. 3, 1992. Paul later married Hilda Hewnson July 1993. They live at Thelka, KY.

Mitchell Preston (born Aug. 31, 1928) married Garnett Sue Jun. 3, 1949. They had two children, Susan and Mitchell Jr. They live in Florida.

Ellen Nora Preston (born Sep. 16, 1930, in Johnson County) married Lowell Cordial, Jun. 24, 1947. She had three children: Helen Rae, Lowell G. and David Lowell (died Aug. 22, 1976). Ellen is now married to Delmas Sorgent. They live in Columbus, OH.

Harvey Lee Preston (born Johnson County, KY, Jul. 13, 1933) married Ursla Newrath from Germany. They had five children: Bernard, Mickle, Clyde Steven, Rena and Karen. They live in Wisconsin.

Emily Agnes (born Jun. 3, 1936, in Johnson County, KY) married Charles Music, January 1953. She had four children: Lon Olen, Ruth Ann, Joyce and Kenneth Mickle. Emily divorced Charles. She married William Sparks Aug. 2, 1978, he died. Emily lives Dayton, OH. Joyce died.

Ernest James Preston (born in Johnson County, KY, Sep. 11, 1939) married Mary Barba in February 1960. They had five children: Jimmy, Cathy, Glen, Karen and Kelvin. Ernest James and Mary divorced. He is now married to Ruth E. Daniel Presonell. They live in Columbus, OH.

Frank and Dora's children went to H.S. Hawes, Community School, Thelka, KY. They attended all eight grades there. They all went to church at the Thelka Freewill Baptist Church. Harvey, Paul and Mitchell, played football for Paintsville Tigers at Paintsville High School. Ernest James played basketball for the Wildcats at Oil Spring High School.

Harvey was in WWII. He was in the Navy and served in the carriership *Wasp*; after it was sunk, he served in the *Lexington*. Frank and Dora are buried at Lowmansville, KY. *Submitted by Goldia R. Combs.*

HALL - James E. Hall "Jim" was born Apr. 2, 1927, in the Paintsville Hospital to Dr. Paul B. Hall and Blanche Ward Hall. Blanche was born Apr. 2, 1899, at Oil Springs in Johnson County, KY. Paul B. was born Jan. 21, 1897, on Davis Branch in Johnson County, KY. Their families lived on farms directly across the Levisa Fork of the Big Sandy River at the mouth of Davis Branch. Blanche and Bryan were married Sep. 25, 1922. She was a school teacher and he a physician in 1923.

Jim has one brother, Dr. Robert Ashley Hall, who was born in Johnson County Nov. 30, 1924. Jim grew up in Paintsville. He attended the Paintsville City Schools and graduated in 1945. He attended Centre College one year and graduated from the University of Louisville in 1950. Jim worked at the Paintsville Hospital from 1954 until retiring in 1995. Jim served in the USN from March 1945 until Jul. 31, 1946.

Jim was married to Violet Deane Barnett Jul. 31, 1957. She was born Aug. 6, 1933, in Floyd County, KY, and died Aug. 3, 1984, in Johnson County. She was born to Anna (Watsell) and John A. Barnett. Anna was born in 1899 in Coalton, WV, and John was born in 1886 in Michigan. Violet graduated from Wheelwright High School and attended Eastern State College. She was employed later by Nathaniel Hager CPA for 10 years. One child was born to Jim and Violet. Paula Anne Hall was born May 12, 1958, at the Paintsville Hospital.

Jim has been a member of the First United Methodist Church since 1940.

HALL - Paula Anne (Hall) Flora was born in the Paintsville Hospital May 12, 1958, the only child born to Violet (Barnett) Hall and James E. Hall. Violet was born in Floyd County, KY, Aug. 6, 1933, and James was born Apr. 2, 1927, in the Paintsville Hospital. Paula's parents met in the early 50s and were married Jul. 31, 1957. Violet worked for Nathaniel Hagar CPA and James worked at the Paintsville Hospital.

Paula Anne grew up in Paintsville. She attended grade school at Our Lady of the Mountains and graduated from Paintsville High School in 1976. She attended Morehead State University receiving an associate degree in corrections in 1981. Paula has been in the antique business for several years. She was married to George Aaron Flora at her grandparent's home in Paintsville Jul. 26, 1980. George was born in Georgetown, OH, Aug. 23, 1958, to Lyda Mae and Clyde Flora. Lyda Mae was born in Fleming County, KY, May 19, 1921, and Clyde was born in Bath County, KY, Apr. 17, 1919. George attended Fleming County High School and graduated from Morehead State University in 1981 with a degree in history and geography. He is presently employed by the Kentucky Environmental Protection Agency.

Paula and George have one daughter, Tyne Michelle, who was born at the Paul B. Hall Regional Medical Center Nov. 19, 1983. She is presently entering her sophomore year at Paintsville High School. She is a member of the Girl's Varsity Basketball Team.

Paula Anne is a member of the First United Methodist Church.

HARRIS - Oscar Warren "Tubby" Harris, was born Jun. 1, 1916, at Catlettsburg, Boyd County, KY, to Elijah Frank Harris and Erie Castle Harris. He was the only son of this family. He had four sisters: Bessie C. Harris, Alka Chandler, Helen Hazlett and Doris Ann Franklin.

Warren married Carrie Virginia Cecil, Aug. 15, 1936, at the Presbyterian church in Prestonsburg, Floyd County, KY. They are the parents of two sons, George Cecil Harris (born Sep. 29, 1941, in Paintsville, KY) and Tim Warren Harris (born Logan, WV, Nov. 27, 1952).

George C. Harris, attended Our Lady of the Mountains Academy, Paintsville, KY. Graduated Mullins High School, Pike County, KY. USN, U.S. Postal Service, Lexington, KY. Retired from this position. He lives at Winchester, KY.

Tim Warren Harris, Pikeville College Training School. St. Francis of Assisi Grade School, Pikeville, KY. Graduated Johnson Central High School, 1972. Pikeville College. Employed at Martiki Coal Corporation, Martin County, KY; Quentina Coals, Houston, TX; Utah International Energy (Radium) Riverton, WY; Commercial Testing and Engineering, Kenova, WV; Nesquehoning, PA; and Gary, IN. He lives at Portage, IN.

Warren is a graduate of Van Lear High School class of 1935, worked as a coal miner, mine foreman, Majestic Collieries Co., Majestic, KY; Consolidation Coal Co., Van Lear and McRoberts, KY; federal coal mine inspector, U.S. Dept. of Labor, Pittsburg, PA; Mt. Hope and Logan, WV; sub-district manager, Pikeville, KY, office.

Oscar Warren "Tubby" and Carrie Harris

Warren had on the job training, Texas A&M and attended Penn State. Taught mining classes, West Virginia Tech., Montgomery, WV.

Carrie was a payroll clerk for Majestic Collieries and dental assistant, at Logan, WV. Also a great house keeper and provider for her children.

Carrie was born Apr. 27, 1918, to Oscar Cecil and Ada Bellomy Cecil at Wellston, Jackson, OH. She had two brothers, John and George Cecil.

Warren is a Master Mason, writes for the Van Lear Historical Society and helps with the Johnson County Historical Society.

Warren and Carrie are members of the First Baptist Church, Paintsville, KY.

HAZELRIGG - William B. "Bill" Hazelrigg was born Nov. 18, 1918, in Johnson County, KY. He was the son of Harry Gordon Hazelrigg and Murah Bayes Hazelrigg. Mr. Hazelrigg's grandfather, Dr. F.M. Bayes, was an early doctor of note in Johnson County. Mr. Hazelrigg had one sister, Mary Frances Hazelrigg, who married Charles Stewart Baals, also of Johnson County.

Tommie Jean Kirk Hazelrigg, was the daughter of Conrad and Mildred Rule Kirk. She was born Jul. 26, 1918.

Bill and Tommie Jean were married in Johnson County, KY, Feb. 28, 1942, while Bill was a student of the University of Louisville College of Law. They had one child, Jean Hazelrigg Doyle, who was the wife of Lacy Owen Doyle. Jean and Owen were married Sep. 28, 1967. There were two children born of their marriage, namely, Kelly Doyle Griffith and Van Hazelrigg Doyle.

Bill graduated from his pre-law training at Western Kentucky University in 1943. He was an attorney for several years with the Veteran's Administration and served in several counties in and around Johnson County. He was also a service officer with the United States military. He was elected as Commonwealth Attorney for the 24th Judicial Dist. of Kentucky and served in that position for 12 years.

Bill then went to Frankfort, KY, to serve as state highway commissioner under the administration of former governor, Louie B. Nunn. Upon his return to Johnson County, he was elected as circuit judge for the 24th Judicial Dist. of Kentucky and served for eight years prior to his retirement.

Bill passed away Sep. 29, 1988, and is buried at the Richmond Cemetery near Paintsville, KY.

Tommie Jean is a retired school teacher. She taught for 20 years in the Paintsville and Johnson County school systems. Her father, Conrad Kirk, was a school teacher prior to becoming an attorney. It was as a school teacher that he met his wife, Mildred. Mr. Kirk was an attorney in Paintsville for many years prior to his last employment as an attorney for the former First Federal Savings and Loan Association in Paintsville. He served in that position until the time of his death.

Tommie Jean's mother, Mildred Kirk, was a secretary for Mr. Henry LaViers and South East Coal Co. for a number of years. She was also a legal secretary and court reporter of noted skill.

Tommie Jean's grandfather was Congressman Andrew J. Kirk.

HERNANDEZ - Margaret Louise Wells Hernandez was born Apr. 8, 1927, in Paintsville, KY. She was the only child of Gladys Ray Wells (born May 20, 1909, in Keystone, WV) and of Charles Jefferson Wells (born Oct. 14, 1905, at Boonscamp, KY). Gladys moved to Paintsville when she was 12 years old when her mother married Eugene Daniels in 1921. Gladys and Charles both attended Paintsville High School and were married in May 1926. Charles first worked at the family's wholesale business, Big Sandy Hardware Co., and Gladys later worked as bookkeeper for WSIP. Charles died Jul. 5, 1955, and Gladys Nov. 17, 1956.

Margaret grew up in Paintsville and graduated from Paintsville High School in 1945. She attended University of Kentucky from June 1945 until June 1948. She also attended summer schools at the University of Mexico in Mexico City until she married.

Margaret married Mariano Hernandez Jun. 19, 1948. At the time of their marriage he was studying civil engineering at the University of Mexico. He later was employed by the government as warehouse manager in the Dept. of Old Age Pensions. They lived in Mexico with their then three children until Margaret wanted to move back to Kentucky in 1957. There they had two more children and lived in Paintsville until 1960. They returned to Mexico City and stayed there until 1965.

Mariano was employed by the Big Sandy Hardware as catalogue manager until his death in 1975.

Margaret taught at Our Lady of the Mountains Academy but decided to return to the University of Kentucky to finish her college and get her degree in early elementary education which she did in 1979. She taught first grade one year at Flat Gap School and then moved to Lexington where she taught kindergarten at St. Agatha's School in Winchester. She taught there until 1985 when she and her youngest daughter, Mary, moved to Phoenix, AZ. Margaret taught first grade bilingual at El Mirage Elementary until her retirement in 1993. She now lives with her youngest daughter, Mary; her husband, Ron; and their two small children in Glendale, AZ.

Margaret Louise Wells Hernandez

HETTINGER - Sara Neal Hettinger was born to Frances Lee Welch and Ernest Neal, at Concord, KY, Feb. 17, 1934. Ernest always said she was his good luck charm, because he got a good job right after she was born. Sara had whooping cough at about 4 months of age and was very sick for a long time, but soon thrived when the disease left.

Sara grew up at Concord with her older sister, Mary Alice and a brother, Joe Grant. They lived on a farm, walked to the East Concord School, across a swinging bridge, over the Big Sandy River. She recalls the sideways sway to the bridge and how some of the boys loved to rock the girls on the bridge, as they were crossing it.

Active in 4H Club work, Sara was selected as state champion in foods preparation in 1949, when she attended the National 4H Club Congress held in Chicago.

Sara attended Meade Memorial High School and following graduation, she enrolled at Berea College for two years. She then enrolled at the University of Louisville and graduated from there in 1955, with a certificate in dental hygiene.

While at U of L, she met Dale Hettinger, from St. Cloud, FL. Dale graduated from U of L's dental program as a dentist. Sara and Dale both got jobs in Florida near Tallahassee and were married Dec. 31, 1955. They had three boys: Dale Neal (born Jul. 12, 1957), Frank Lloyd (born May 25, 1959) and Glenn Allen (born Sep. 19, 1963).

Dale entered the Army, as an officer and made a career of it. He retired as a colonel in 1984. He served two tours of duty, with his family, in Panama and was active in serving in Vietnam, as a dental surgeon.

Sara became quite a good artist, of the abstract school of art. Her art has been showcased in Los Angeles, Florida and New Mexico.

Sara Neal Hettinger

Involved in an automobile accident in 1964, Sara has suffered recurring pain and disability from the accident for the rest of her life.

Dale Neal Hettinger, her oldest son, has his own advertising agency, Lead Pencil Designs, in Los Angeles. Frank Lloyd acts and has many credits, as a stuntman in movies and commercials. Glenn Allen is a director and directs many commercials. All three boys live in the Los Angeles area.

Dale Neal Hettinger was married to Terri Eaton and they have two children, Kathyrn Marie and Joshua. Frank is unmarried at this time. Glenn Allen married Brigit Martinez and they have Jake Allen.

Sara and Dale currently reside in Las Vegas, NV.

HITCHCOCK - Marianne Hitchcock was born Nov. 24, 1971, in Columbus, OH. She lived in what became the Van Lear Historical Society when the owner was Bill Burke, her step-grandfather. She married Timothy J. Smith in Ohio and has two children.

Marianne's mother was Brenda Carol Hitchcock. Brenda married William "Buddy" Wesley Burke Sep. 16, 1975, in Dickenson County, VA. Brenda was born Feb. 28, 1955, in Johnson County, KY, delivered by Dr. Augustus D. Slone. Brenda was the third child of Thurman Hitchcock and Mary M. Young.

Thurman Hitchcock was born Mar. 11, 1916, in Johnson County to Grant and Jennie Lee Ward Hitchcock. Grant Hitchcock's parents were General Hitchcock and Mary Ann Frazier.

General Hitchcock, son of Parker D. and Sophia (Salyer) Hitchcock and Mary Ann Frazier, daughter of William J. and Zilpha (Lemaster) Frazier, married Sep. 20, 1883, in Johnson County, KY. They lived and died in Denver, Johnson County, KY. General (born Jun. 5, 1863, died Jan. 15, 1942) and Mary Ann (born Feb. 4, 1867, died Jun. 23, 1939) are buried side-by-side in the Sam Blair Cemetery located on Upper Twin Branch, Denver, Johnson County, KY.

General and Mary Ann had 11 known children:

1) William Alford (born 1885, died 1900).

2) David Jesse (born 1888, died 1977) married Elsa Colvin Jan. 6, 1915, in Johnson County. They had nine known children.

3) Benjamin Harrison (born 1890, died 1977) married first, Joshephine Caudill Oct. 16, 1913. They had six known children. He married second, Vergie Spradlin.

4) Grant Hitchcock (born 1892, died 1969) married first, Artie Blair Apr. 26, 1913. Artie died shortly after giving birth to twin boys, both boys died shortly after birth also. He married second, Jennie Lee Ward Sep. 4, 1914, in Johnson County, KY. (Grant and Jennie were Marianne's great-grandparents.) They had four children: Thurman, Burns W., O'Dessa and Lenzie B. Lenzie B. Hitchcock was killed in Italy while serving his country during WWII. He is buried in the Florence American Cemetery in Florence, Italy.

5) Mary Elizabeth (born 1894, died 1899).

6) Sarah Jane (born 1898, died 1969) married Oscar Arms Feb. 12, 1914, in Johnson County, KY. They had six known children.

7) James Edward (born 1900, died 1985) married Hannah Baldwin Sep. 5, 1919, in Johnson County, KY. They had four known children.

8) Alta Francis (born 1905, still living as of 1999) married Belva Baldwin Mar. 22, 1924, in Johnson County, KY. They have four known children.

9) Andrew Parker (born 1907, died 1907).

10) Dicie Alice (born 1908, still living as of June 1999) married Ray Baldwin in Johnson County, KY. They have seven known children.

11) Bessie Mae (born 1912, died 1990) married Dexter Blair Mar. 28, 1931, in Denver, Johnson County, KY. They had eight known children.

The Hitchcock family has been part of Johnson since before it separated from Floyd County. There are still several descendants of this family still living in Johnson County.

HITCHCOCK & YOUNG - Mary M. (Young) Hitchcock was born Oct. 16, 1933, in Johnson County, KY, to Rosie Thornsberry and Otto Young. She married Thurman Hitchcock Jun. 24, 1950, in Floyd County, KY. Thurman, born Mar. 16, 1916, in Johnson County, KY, to Jennie Ward and Grant Hitchcock, both of Johnson County, KY. She went to school in Van Lear where she lived until adulthood when she moved to Columbus, OH. She retired from Mt. Carmel Hospital in nursing. Thurman served in WWII where he received EAME Theater Ribbon w/5 Bronze Stars, American Theater Ribbon, Good Conduct Ribbon and WWII Victory Medal. He served under Co. F, 335th Engr. GS Regt. He worked at Danite Sign Co. until his death in March 1978.

Hitchcock Family. Back, L-R: Ronald, James and Phyllis. Front, L-R: Mike, Carol and Diane.

Children:

Diana (born November 1950, Johnson County, KY) married first, Larry Stout and second, Joseph Taynor III.

Ronald (born February 1953, Johnson County, KY) married Sheila Tillison.

Carol (born February 1955, Johnson County, KY) married William Burke. Both died Dec. 1, 1982, in Springfield, OH.

Phyllis (born July 1957, Johnson County, KY) married Christopher Sparks.

Michael (born December 1958, Johnson County, KY).

James (born February 1965, Franklin County, OH) married Leia Hoffman.

Rosie Thornsberry, born Dec. 1, 1909, to Cynthia Thornsberry and William Gibson married Otto Young, son of George and May Young, Oct. 3, 1923, in Floyd County, KY. Children:

Sylvia (born May 26, 1924, died Jul. 12, 1924, Johnson County, KY).

Katherine (born May 5, 1927, Johnson County, KY).

Foster (born Jul. 4, 1930, Johnson County, KY, died Jan. 2, 1997).

Mary (born Oct. 16, 1933, Johnson County, KY).

Eunice (born Feb. 3, 1941, Johnson County, KY).

Cynthia Thornsberry, born Sep. 27, 1891, in Floyd County, KY, to Mary Slone and Winston Thornsberry. No marriage date to William Gibson of Ravern, KY. Children:

Rosie (born Dec. 1, 1909, in Knott County, died Nov. 3, 1991, in Cols., OH) married to Otto Young, Glenn Shaver, Michael Columbo, Fred Smith.

Rebecca (born Mar. 23, 1912, in Knott County, KY) married Lace Trippett Sep. 14, 1926, in Floyd County, died May 15, 1997, Ohio.

Another child was born to Cynthia and William Slone- Name.

Beatrice (born Sep. 20, 1920, in Knott County).

Otto, born Jun. 22, 1901, in Johnson County, KY, to Mary Ann White and George Gallup Young. Otto lived out his life in Kentucky. He worked in the Van Lear Coal Mines for Consolidated Coal Co. until he retired an old man. He reared his four children after Rosie left home and went to Cols., OH, in about 1943. He was baptized in the Free Will Baptist Church in Van Lear where he attended church on regular basis.

HOLBROOK - Erma Nancy Holbrook was born Jan. 22, 1915, in Johnson County, Offitt, KY, to James Albert Holbrook and Nancy Rebecca Sparks. She was the third child born. There were four other children born to James and Rebecca. Erma was married to Edgar Ross May 5, 1939.

Erma Nancy Holbrook

They had four boys: James David (born May 27, 1940), Edgar Paul (born May 5, 1944), Ernest Ray (born Mar. 9, 1949) and Larry Joe (born Jan. 14, 1957).

Erma and Edgar settled in Lawrence County, KY, in the 1940s. Edgar was a carpenter and a welder. He had to work away from home to support his family, leaving Erma to keep house and raise the boys by herself.

They didn't have a modern house. They had a hand pump in the kitchen. They had a wood cook stove which made the house very hot in the summer time. When Edgar was home on the weekends the boys and he would cut wood for the stove. Erma would have to carry coal inside to fire up the stove. She would carry water from the creek across the road to wash clothes.

In 1957 Erma and Edgar moved to Columbus, OH. Edgar died Aug. 29, 1980. Erma took care of the youngest son who was disabled until she had a stroke and died Sep. 14, 1995. She is greatly missed by her children and grandchildren. Edgar and Erma are buried at Sunset Cemetery, Alton, OH.

Erma told of her brother, James Soloman Holbrook, playing football in high school. James was captain of the Louisa High School football team. Louisa High was playing Wayne, WV. During the game, after the completion of a play in the third quarter, James was walking away when three Wayne players tackled him (one on each side and one from behind) and James was injured.

Two of the Louisa players, Jim See and Bill Hinkle, carried him off the field. Immediately following the game he was taken to the River View Hospital at Louisa. James was transported by train to the C&O Hospital in Huntington, WV, on Sunday. He sustained spinal injuries, a broken neck and died of a head injury Oct. 6, 1924. James is buried at Smokey Valley Cemetery, Kentucky. *By James David Ross.*

HOLBROOK - Ambrose and Nancy Elam Holbrook migrated from Wilkes County, NC, in the early 1800s to Lawrence County, KY. Ambrose was born 1798 in Traphill, Wilkes County, NC, died Jan. 24, 1859, in Blaine, Lawrence County, KY. In October 1824 he had a deed for a 50 acre track of land on Blaine Creek, and Oct. 25, 1830, another for 175 acres on Blaine Creek, another on Mar. 8, 1833, for 100 acres on Cain Creek. There he reared his family of five children. They included farmers, merchants and doctors.

Harry Holbrook, Katherine Holbrook Hyden, Otto Hyden, Mathew Hyden, Lora Jane Hyde and Faye Virgie Holbrook.

They were 1) Ralph Wickliffe Holbrook (born Jul. 1, 1823, died Mar. 24, 1871, in Blaine, KY). He married Martha Ann Moore in 1865. He was a merchant in Lawrence County, KY.

2) William Rainer Holbrook (born May 15, 1825, died May 14, 1902, in Donnybrook, ND) married Nov. 3, 1850, to Pauline C. Prater of Morgan County, KY. He was engaged in the mercantile business.

3) Louisa Holbrook (born 1829, died Jul. 15. 1859) never married.

4) Dr. Campbell Rice Holbrook (born Oct. 31, 1830, died Jan. 2, 1923, in Stillwater, Payne County, OK) married first to Mary Ann Wilson, Jan. 19, 1862, in Owsley County, KY, she died in child birth. Married second on Sep. 12, 1872, to Nancy "Fannie" Holbrook, his cousin, in Wilkes County, NC. He had a total of 13 children. Campbell and his son, Ray, were doctors in Oklahoma for many years.

5) Ambrose Minton "Mint" Holbrook (born Sep. 16, 1836, died Jul. 28, 1906, at Blaine, KY) married Aug. 27, 1860, to Eleanor Jane "Nellie" Wheeler (born Feb. 23, 1843, died Sep. 30, 1904). She was the daughter of John R. and Rachel Lemaster Wheeler, who lived on the Hood's Fork of Blaine. Ambrose Holbrook was one of the wealthiest and most influential citizens in this end of the county. He owned 12 tracks of land ranging from five acres to 400 acres, he owned his own slaves, a saw mill, a gristmill and a general store. He deeded all 10 children each 100 acres of land.

Ambrose and Nellie Holbrook will carry the family name on down. Their 10 children were:

1) Dr. Winfield Scott Holbrook (born Jul. 19, 1861, died Sep. 19, 1902, Blaine, KY) married Jul. 3, 1880, to Mary P. Burton (born Oct. 14, 1860, died Dec. 3, 1935). Scott received his education under Professor Elam, there were about 75 men that made doctors or lawyers that came out of Professor Elam's lifetime of teaching. Scott was 25 years old in 1887 when he entered medical school. Four years later he graduated with an MD's degree, Jun. 18, 1891, a short successful life, he died 11 years later age 41.

2) Columbus Milton Holbrook (born Oct. 22, 1863, died Feb. 12, 1887) married Carrie Gambill May 30, 1886, they had one daughter (born and died Jan. 19, 1887); all three died within three weeks of each other with typhoid fever.

3) John James Holbrook (born Mar. 3, 1866, died Jan. 31, 1900) married Aug. 15, 1892, Polly Ann Hensley. Polly died Jun. 30, 1898. Both died within two years of each other. They had two boys who later lived in Chicago, IL.

4) Nancy Lee Holbrook (born May 18, 1868, died Jan. 9, 1901, in Lawrence County, KY) married Sep. 30, 1885, to John T. Moore. Five children born to this couple: Johnny, Hubert, Carrie, Nellie and Mable.

5) Mary E. "Molly" Holbrook (born Dec. 14, 1871, died Aug. 2, 1933) married Nov. 8, 1889, Rev. John Henry Stambaugh (born 1868, died 1939). One child, Fred M. Stambaugh, who was an attorney in Charleston, WV (born Oct. 2, 1890, died Jul. 9, 1949).

6) Ralph W. Holbrook (born Jan. 13. 1874, died Mar. 30, 1939, in Huntington, WV) was a teacher and was elected 1901 to county superintendent of Lawrence County. He married first, Oct. 8, 1894, to Cordial "Della" Johnson. Married second, Oct. 6, 1906, Lora M. Nickell. Eleven children in all.

7) Charles Russell Holbrook (born Mar. 17, 1876, died Jan. 31, 1942, in Ashland, KY) married first to Ruth Richardson (born May 28, 1897, died Apr. 2, 1997), divorced. Married second, Nora Blanche Gartin Nov. 20. 1899. Nora was born October 1881, died Apr. 20, 1913. Married third, Eliza (Webb) Green, Jan. 13, 1916. She was born 1891, died Jun. 1, 1917. Eliza was killed by lightning in her home at Blaine, KY.

8) Arminta P. Holbrook (born Nov. 22, 1878, died Oct. 6, 1929, in Chicago, IL) married Ecclestone C. Berry Aug. 11, 1897. He was born Nov. 1, 1872, died May 2, 1941, in Chicago, IL. They had six children: Earl, Herman, Russell, Eleanor, Helen and Charles.

9) Lydia Clay Holbrook (born May 31, 1881, died Aug. 21, 1906, age 25) never married.

10) Henry Chilt Holbrook (born Dec. 29, 1883, died unknown) married Ruth Kratzer, resident in Chicago, IL.

Dr. Winfield Scott and Mary Burton Holbrook will carry the family name on down. Their five children are:

1) Arnick C. Holbrook (born May 1882, died Feb. 18 1924, in Ashland, KY) married Virginia Mae Burke Oct. 16, 1909 (born Nov. 17, 1887, died Jul. 2, 1972, in Charleston, WV). Two children were born to this couple, William "Bill" Holbrook of Northridge, CA. He married Kathryn Elizabeth Story (dates unknown). George M. Holbrook of Charleston, WV, married Jun. 4, 1940, to Frances Kathryn Orth. They had three children: Timothy C. Holbrook, Nancy Jean Holbrook and Kathryn E. Holbrook. George was a retired newspaper man.

2) Ambrose Minton "Mint" Holbrook (born Mar. 6, 1883, died Oct. 20, 1976, in Paintsville, KY) married Martha Lee Adams Aug. 9, 1911. She was born Oct. 23, 1887, died Mar. 6, 1976, in Paintsville, KY. They had seven children: Gertrude Holbrook, Paulina Holbrook, Charles Irene Holbrook, Homer Holbrook, Nellie Holbrook, Mollie Holbrook and Blanche Holbrook.

3) Alta Norman Holbrook was a twin brother to Mint (born Mar. 6, 1883, died Jan. 28, 1956, at Ashland, KY) married Elizabeth "Eliza" Ramey Jul. 15, 1915. She was (born Sep. 18, 1890, died Jul. 16, 1928, in Fayette County, KY). Alta married the second time to Draxie Bartley.

4) Columbus Milton Holbrook (born Dec. 12, 1887, died Jul. 20, 1971, in Lacoochie, FL) married Clora Beatrice McGuire Oct. 3, 1910, in Magoffin County, KY. She was born Mar. 31, 1884, in Magoffin County, died Feb. 18, 1942, in Ashland, KY. They had two children, Milton Delmar Holbrook and William McGuire Holbrook.

5) Wild Wesky (born circa 1890, died 1902).

Alta Norman Holbrook will carry the family name on down. Alta had four children by his first wife and three children by his last wife. Children are:

1) Norman Woodrow Holbrook (born Apr. 18, 1916).

2) Winfield Scott Holbrook (born Sep. 18, 1918).

3) Harry Holbrook (born May 18, 1921).

4) Charles Holbrook (born Jul. 4, 1925).

Second family:

5) Chester Vernon Holbrook (born Jun. 22, 1928, died Feb. 14, 1990).

6) Raymond "Ray" Holbrook (born 1930).

7) Christine Holbrook (born Dec. 15, 1932).

Harry Holbrook and wife, Virgie Fay O'Bryan Holbrook, will carry the family name down. Harry (born May 18, 1921, at Louisa, Lawrence County, KY) and Virgie Fay (born October 1925, at Van Lear, KY) married Oct. 19, 1946. Three children:

1) Roger Leron Holbrook (born Sep. 1, 1947, died Jan. 14, 1969).

2) Harold Wayne (born Jun. 28, 1950, died May 4, 1954).

3) Kathryn Lynn Holbrook (born Feb. 16, 1955) married Otto Hyden Jun. 8, 1973. Otto was born Oct. 11, 1954. Two children, Matthew Brooks Hyden (born May 17, 1979) and Lora Jane Hyden (born Nov. 19, 1980). *Submitted by Harry Holbrook.*

HOLBROOK - William Pleasant Holbrook was my great-grandfather. He was born Aug. 8, 1860, in Johnson County, KY. He married Nancy Boggs May 27, 1881. They lived in Offitt, KY, in Johnson County. William Pleasant's father was Larkin Holbrook. His mother was Anne Hay. William died Jun. 19, 1937.

My great-grandmother, Nancy Bogg's mother, was Martha Terry. Her father was Alfred Boggs. Nancy was born Jul. 25, 1862, in Lawrence County, KY. She died Jan. 15, 1925. She is buried in Johnson County, Offitt, KY. Their children are: Sarah Ann (born May 15, 1883) married Clint Skaggs; James Albert (born Apr. 7, 1885) married Rebecca Emaline Sparks Feb. 23, 1905. James died Feb. 2, 1952, and is buried in Smokey Valley, KY; Cam (born March 1894) married Lulu Preston; Jena Bell (born Sep. 11, 1888) married Henry Seagraves; Della (born April 1892) was blind and never married; Hannah (born February 1897) married James Cochran; and Martha (born Jan. 27, 1889) married Henry Hayes.

House of William Pleasant Holbrook in Offutt, KY.

The photo is the home of William Pleasant in Johnson County, Offitt, KY. This is the house where my mother, Erma Nancy Holbrook, was born.

HORNE & WELLS - Allen Lee Horne was born Apr. 22, 1964, in Johnson County, KY, to Wilbure Lee Horne and Janet Sue (May) Horne. He was the oldest of five children, three sons: Allen Lee, Bryan Keith and Christopher K.; and two daughters, Anita Carol and Donna Denise. Allen was married in Floyd County, KY, to Billie Lee Wells on Jul. 29, 1995.

Allen Lee Horne and Billie Lee Wells Horne

He attended Johnson Central High School, Mayo College and Prestonsburg Community College, receiving diplomas in drafting and surveying. He is employed at Lowe's of Paintsville and holds the position as zone manager.

Allen has always been interested in sports and devotes his free time to his local bowling league and has recently taken up golf.

Billie attended Johnson Central High School and Prestonsburg Community College where she graduated from the business management program. She is employed by Dr. N. Roger Jurich in Prestonsburg, KY. She is the daughter of Elzie Wells and Fonda (Lowry) Wells. Elzie was a descendant of Richard Wells, a Revolutionary War soldier. Fonda's family was from Wayland, KY.

Allen and Billie live at Hager Hill, KY.

HORNE & HALL - Cecil Hall Jr. was born Jan. 3, 1962, the son of Cecil Hall Sr. and Marie (Goble) Hall. He has four brothers and four sisters: Alvis, Virgil, David, Jack, Mary Lou, Judy, Marthlene and Alice Marie. He has a daughter, Latondya Gail Hall (born Feb. 11, 1986). He is a welder by trade.

On Aug. 5, 1997, at Van Lear, KY, he married Donna Denise (Horne) Meade. Donna was born Apr. 10, 1967, Paintsville, KY, to Wilbure Lee Horne and Janet (May) Horne. She has three brothers and one sister: Allen Lee, Bryan Keith, Christopher K. and Anita Carol (Horne) Sexton. She also has a half brother, Donnie Horne and a half sister, Sandra Horne. She attended Paintsville High School and holds a license in cosmetology from Mayo College. She had previously married on May 25, 1983, in Clintwood, VA, to George Paul Meade, who was born Mar. 7, 1965, the son of Ernie Meade and Betty (Cantrell) Meade. They had three daughters: Janet Irine Meade (born May 25, 1984), Georgia Denise Meade (born Mar. 22, 1987) and Katie Ellen Jean Meade (born Aug. 6, 1990). Cecil and Donna live on #1 Hollow at Van Lear, KY.

Cecil Hall Jr. and Donna Denise (Horne) Hall

Cecil Hall Sr. was the son of John David Hall and Mary Alice (Adkins) Hall. John David Hall served as a constable for many years. Cecil Sr. worked in the coal mines all his life. He was working in "Bloody Breathitt" County when they fought to join the union. After working at Harmon Station, he last worked at the Van Lear Coal Tipple for James C. Witten. He was one of five children: Richard "Dick" who never married and worked in the mines and on the railroad; Bill owns a farm in Ohio where he lives; Bob; Nellie who married John Honaker and lives on a large farm in Texas.

Cecil Jr.'s. mother, Marie Goble Hall, was the daughter of Thomas Goble and Gypsy Blevins. Thomas Goble was from Auxier and worked in the Van Lear coal mines. The old Goble homeplace was on Goble Branch past American Standard. Marie was a homemaker and worked at the Star Fire Motel until declining health forced her to stop. She was one of seven children: Junie who lives in Springfield, OH; Virgil, married Alice. He served in the U.S. Army for many years; William married Darlene Tackett and lives in Ohio; Goldie married Proctor Webb and lives at Van Lear; Elvie married Walter Blevins and lives at West Van Lear; and Bertie.

HORNE & SEXTON - James Douglas Sexton was born Feb. 23, 1960, in Johnson County, KY, to Billy J. Sexton and Alma Mae (Branham) Sexton. He attended Paintsville High School and is employed by the city of Paintsville.

James Douglas Sexton and Anita Carol (Horne) Sexton

He married Anita Carol Horne, Jul. 4, 1982, at the Dewey Lake in Floyd County. The ceremony was performed by the Reverend Scott Castle. The wedding took place outside, during the Sexton Family Reunion. Park Rangers photographed the wedding as it was the first to be held at the park. The couple live on Frank Street in Paintsville and have two daughters, Jamie Lynn (born May 12, 1984) and Rebecca Carol (born Aug. 13, 1993).

He was one of 15 children born to Bill and Alma who all lived to adulthood, 13 sons and two daughters: Everett Lee, Bobby Gene, Arnold Michael, William Vencil, Johnny Bill, Larry Keith, Steve Ellis, James Douglas, Phillip Samuel, Ernie Ray, Gary Lewis, Albert Estill, Troy Stanley, Joyce Ann and Deloris. Bill Sexton was the son of Roy Sexton and Amanda (Franklin) Sexton. Alma was the daughter of Turner Branham and Sarah (Kirk) Branham.

Anita was born Nov. 21, 1965, in Johnson County, KY, the daughter of Wilbure Lee Horne and Janet (May) Horne. Janet was the daughter of Gail Edward May and Lucille Hitchcock May. Gail was the son of Willie May* and Leona Caudill. Leona was the daughter of Jesse Caudill and Mary Angeline Fairchild. Jesse was the son of Stephen Caudill and Jincy

Fairchild. Stephen was the son of Matthew Caudill** and Temperance Hitchcock. Mary Angeline Fairchild was the daughter of Aaron Fairchild and Mary Keeton. Jincy Fairchild was the daughter of Lowry Fairchild and Rachel Lemaster.

*See the *May Family Heritage* book by B. David May, Chapter II for more information on the May family.

**See *Appalachian Crossroads*, Volume II & III by Clayton Cox for more information on the Caudill family.

HORNE & KIRK - Bryan Keith Horne was born Jun. 23, 1968, in Paintsville, KY, to Wilbure L. Horne and Janet (May) Horne. He was one of five children born to this couple, three sons and two daughters: Allen Lee, Anita Carol, Donna Denise, Bryan Keith and Christopher K.

Bryan Keith and Nancy Mae Horne

He served in the Kentucky National Guard for six years, doing his basic training in Fort Leonard Wood, MO. Since moving to Ohio he has been employed by Mills Pride in Waverly, OH.

He first married Melissa Arms May 14, 1988. He married second to Nancy Mae Kirk, who was born in Scioto County, OH, the daughter of Bill Kirk and Margie (Biggs) Kirk. They have three daughters: Kasey Sueann (born Sep. 2, 1992), Kara Nicole (born Jul. 19, 1993) and Kindra May (born May 30, 1996). They live in Scioto County, OH.

His father was the son of Albert Horne and Ruby Gertrude (Bowen) Horne. Ruby was the daughter of Jack Bowen and Viola (Spears) Bowen. Jack was the son of James Bowen and Sarah Ann Dutton. James was the son of Daniel Bowen and Cynthia Mollett. Daniel was the son of Adam Bowen (born 1783, in Pennsylvania) and Rhoda Wooten (born 1788, in North Carolina, died 1855, in Johnson County, KY). Rhoda Wooten was a midwife and the daughter of Silas P. Wooten.

Viola Spears was the daughter of Lindsey B.L. Spears and Mahala Jane (Ward) Spears. Lindsey was the son of Wiley M. Spears and Elizabeth (Butcher) Spears, who married Dec. 12, 1846, in Johnson County. Elizabeth was the daughter of Jacob Butcher.

HORNE & PENNINGTON - Christopher K. Horne was born Feb. 16, 1970, at Paintsville to Wilbure L. Horne and Janet (May) Horne. Although his early years were spent on the Lower Twin Branch at Denver on Jenny's Creek, he grew up in Paintsville and attended the city schools. He is the youngest of five children: Allen Lee, Anita Carol, Donna Denise, Bryan Keith and Christopher K.

Christopher K. Horne and Betty Jewell Pennington

He married Betty Jewell Pennington when he was 19 and she was 16, Oct. 11, 1989, at Salyersville in Magoffin County, KY. She was born Sep. 17, 1973, the daughter of Chester Pennington and Brenda Kay (Meade) Pennington, and attended Magoffin County schools. Chris is employed at Meade's Auto Parts, Oil Springs, KY.

Chris's father, Wilbure Lee Horne was born May 11, 1942, the son of Albert Horne and Ruby Gertrude (Bowen) Horne. Albert was the son of Tom Horne (born February 1874) and Julia (Salyers) Horne Adams (born December 1878) who were married Oct. 24, 1895. Tom was the son of Thomas Horne (born 1845-47) and Elizabeth "Betsy" (Ratliff) Burkett Blanton. Thomas was the son of Thomas Horne (born about 1792, in Maryland), came to Johnson County about 1840. He married Nancy (Blair) Barnett, the daughter of Noble Blair, Jan. 30, 1842, in Floyd County, KY. Both had children from previous marriages.

HORNE & MAY - Janet Sue (May) Horne was born Dec. 4, 1945, on the Upper Twin Branch of Denver on Jenny's Creek, the youngest of four children born to Gail Edward May and Lucille (Hitchcock) May: Paul Edward (born Jul. 23, 1940) married Linda Mae Blanton; Jack (born Mar. 30, 1942) married Betty Ray Cantrell; and Patsy Lois (born Jan. 12, 1944) married Gene Arthur Butcher.

Janet Sue (May) Horne

There on Jenny's Creek she grew up and attended the Johnson County grade schools, Oil Springs High School and later Mayo Technical School. She lived in several places, including Washington, Ohio, Indiana and different places in Kentucky.

She was married to Wilbure Lee Horne Jun. 16, 1963, at Collista, KY, by the Reverend Charley Lemaster. To this union was born five children, three sons and two daughters: Allen Lee (born Apr. 22, 1964) married Billie Lee Wells, Anita Carol (born Nov. 21, 1965) married James Douglas Sexton, Donna Denise (born Apr. 10, 1967) married (1) George Paul Meade and (2) Cecil Hall Jr., Bryan Keith (born Jun. 23, 1968) married (1) Melissa Arms and (2) Nancy Kirk and Christopher K. (born Feb. 16, 1970) married Betty Jewell Pennington.

She moved to Paintsville in 1977 and has made her home on Frank Street for several years. She held a position with the Johnson County government as secretary to the Fiscal Court for six years, leaving in 1986. She has been the executive secretary to the president/general manager of Big Sandy Rural Electric since 1987. She has been active in the Johnson County Historical and Genealogical Society since its organization in 1983 and has compiled marriage records books, wills and other records for genealogical research.

Her parents were a talented couple. Lucille composed lyrics for songs and Gail would play the music while they sang. Her father could play any instrument by ear, and their home was always filled with music, friends and family.

Lucille (Hitchcock) May was born Feb. 20, 1914, in Johnson County to Benjamin Hitchcock and Vergie Spradlin. Benjamin was born Apr. 7, 1890, to General Hitchcock and Mary Ann Frazier. General was the son of Parker Hitchcock and Sophia Salyer. Vergie Spradlin was born May 16, 1891, the daughter of Solomon Spradlin and Mary (Castle) Gibbs Spradlin. Her first marriage was to Clinton Yates, whom she married Sep. 16, 1909. They had a daughter, Edna Mae Yates (born 1911).

Solomon served in the Union Army during the Civil War. He had a son and daughter from his first marriage to Harriet Moles, whom he married Jun. 29, 1857, in Johnson County. Mary and her first husband, John Gibbs, were married Feb. 1, 1872, in Johnson County. They had one child, a daughter, Maoma Gibbs (born Nov. 16, 1872). John Gibbs died in 1872.

Solomon and Mary, both widowed, married May 24, 1876, and had six children: Laura Ellen (born Nov. 4, 1877) married Albert Colvin; John H. (born October 1878); James Garfield (born Dec. 18, 1879) married Vergie Wiley; Rosa Bell (born November 1885) married James Francis; Vergie (born May 16, 1891); and Louverna (born Jul. 8, 1893) married (1) Elick Frazier, (2) Brandley Francis and (3) a Jenkins?

Most of Solomon Spradlins family is buried on the Denver Hill Cemetery on Jenny's Creek.

HOWARD - My name is Doris Ann Ward Howard (born Dec. 21, 1936). I was born at Boons Camp, KY, at home; Dr. Daniels was the doctor who delivered me.

My mother was Exer Wells, daughter of Shadrick Wells and Amanda Ward. She was born at Boons Camp, KY, Apr. 8, 1906. She had seven sisters and brothers: Exer Wells married Aaron Ward, Margaret Wells married French Holbrook, Sally Wells married Howard Sparks, Pauline Wells (Dutch) Malcome Shearer, Melvina Wells (Bob) married Wilber Daniel, Nancy Wells married Jack Vickers, Goldie, Shirley and Shadrick Wells (died young).

My father was Aaron Ward, son of Greenville Ward and Kate Wells. They had Aaron Ward married Exer Wells, Marshall Ward married Elsie Williams, Russell Ward married Willa Mae Wells, Lorenz Ward married Delia Preece, Ina Ward married Crit Hinkle, Lokie Ward married Albert Meek, Grace Ward married Langly Dutton and Jennie V. Ward married Raymond Preston.

Dad was born Jan. 16, 1897. They were married May 18, 1922. My Mom and Dad had the post office and grocery at Boons Camp, KY, for 43 years, lived there all their life. Helped out in the community. Every one knew and loved them.

My sisters were: Louise Ward (born Mar. 11, 1926), Doris Ann Ward (born Dec. 21, 1936) and Sandra Kay Ward (born Jun. 9, 1943). Louise Ward married Orville Penix. They had five children and lived at Boons Camp all their life: Halienna Yvonne Penix (born Apr. 6, 1947), Garry Wayne Penix (born Jul. 8, 1948), Scottie Aaron Penix (born Aug. 25, 1951) and Timothy Bryan Penix (born Nov. 23, 1956).

Doris Ann Ward married Robert J. Howard and they had three children: Deborah Lynn Howard (born Apr. 19, 1955), Darrell Dean Howard (born Apr. 26, 1956) and Daniel Keith Howard (born Sep. 16, 1958).

I lived here at Boons Camp until 1959. We moved to Dayton, OH, for work. Lived there for 40 years then we have moved back for the last five years. My husband has retired from Local #82. He was an electrician.

Sandra Kaye Ward married John Melvin Penix. They had five children: Eadie Denette Penix (born Aug. 19, 1959) married Timothy Price, Craig Byron Penix (born Dec. 9, 1961) married Reba __, Terry Lynn Penix (born Feb. 16, 1963, died 6 weeks old), Jacquline Penix (born Jan. 20, 1965) married Tony Fitch and Victor Penix (born Sep. 3, 1969) married Lisa Vanhoose.

HOWARD - In 1924 Lee and Alice Montgomery Howard and their 9-year-old daughter, Este Mae, moved from Magoffin County to Paintsville. They first rented a house in "Bristlebuck" while Lee found odd jobs, usually as a house painter. From Bristlebuck, they could see the quarry from which stone for the Mayo mansion and church had come.

When Lee began working for Sandy Valley Wholesale Grocery, he rented a house on Hencliff from Charlie Kirk. Alice's sister and brother-in-law, Ellen and Leander Blair, already lived on Hencliff. Another sister and her husband, Tella and Riley Lemaster, would also move there. It was a close-knit community where everyone helped their neighbor. The fire alarm, three gun shots, brought everyone running with pails of water.

The wholesale company asked Lee to run a grocery store that they were building beside his house. Instead, Lee asked Alice's cousins, Foster Rigsby and Minnifee Montgomery, to be the proprietors. Foster eventually moved this store to downtown Paintsville.

Lee and Alice celebrated the birth of their first

son, Lee Jr., on Jan. 20, 1925. Angie Marie Howard was born May 7, 1927. And on May 1, 1932, a second son was born. He was named Paul Harrison in honor of the attending doctor, Paul B. Hall, and a co-owner of Sandy Valley Wholesale, Harrison Wheeler.

As their family grew, Lee and Alice moved into five different houses on Hencliff before building their own house in the "Stafford Bottom." Most of the houses in the bottom were built along the creek bank and the remaining land was grassy pasture. The Howard house was the third to be built on the dirt lane known as Washington Avenue. Lee had bought several of the $200 lots which he later traded for lots on the other side of Broadway. He sold these for a tidy profit and used part of the money to buy the only car he ever owned. The WPA built a shed in Stafford bottom and broke up rocks to pave roads. Their supervisor was John Preston who later built his own home in the bottom.

It was around this time that the first concrete street, Broadway, was being paved, and the College Street Bridge was being built. Until then, there was only the swinging bridge at Hencliff, which had been deemed unsafe for cars, a swinging walk-bridge in Stafford Addition, that was ingeniously built using live trees for supports, and the iron bride at Bridgeford.

On Sep. 9, 1935, Edith Noretta Howard was born and on Jan. 20, 1941, Lee Junior's 16th birthday present was a sister named Mary Hazel.

Times were hard but Lee had his job and he and Junior were handy with their hands. They hunted small game and Lee always rented garden space, sometimes on a Tan Vat hillside and once as far away as Wittensville. Workers were paid 50 cents a day to help hoe the corn.

Sometimes, government commodities were handed out and the Howards received their share. But they shared in turn. In warm weather, each train whistle meant that hungry "hobos" would be knocking on the door and the Howards turned none away. At times, Alice and the "hired girl" found themselves cooking and washing dishes all day. Another harbinger of spring was the Gypsies. They camped in the bottom and the Howards allowed them to use their well. But great diligence was required to keep the Howard belongings from "evaporating" as well.

Lee Howard worked up to the day he died, Jul. 3, 1961. Alice is in her 100th year and still lives in the house on Washington Avenue.

HUGHES - 51 South Buckingham Avenue, West Van Lear, KY, is the residence of Shirley Jewel Slone Hughes, born Jul. 31, 1913, at Winifred, KY, to George Slone and Cora Castle Slone; she spent her childhood on the family's Franks Creek farm with her brothers and sisters: Dennis, Wayne, James, Clyde, Marietta and Ina. On Nov. 30, 1936, she married Clifford Donald Hughes at Paintsville, KY. To this marriage were born: Anna Ruth Hughes (born Mar. 17, 1940), George Dewey Hughes (born Oct. 5, 1942), Bobby Frank Hughes (born Sep. 12, 1945) and Edwin Earl Hughes (born Feb. 22, 1949), all at Paintsville, KY.

The family resided in Paintsville with all children graduating from Paintsville High School.

Clifford was in the plumbing business as well as freight hauling and moving business. He was civic minded, serving as City Council member in 1956, volunteer fireman, school bus driver and acted as Santa Claus for several groups at Christmas.

Clifford died Jun. 16, 1965. His funeral was held at Mayo Vocational School and was well attended by his many friends and admirers.

Anna Ruth married James Edward Tramel. They have two children, Michael Alan (born Nov. 30, 1959) and Sheryll Ann (born Nov. 27, 1964) and one grandson, Michael Ryan Tramel (born Jul. 10, 1991).

George Dewey married Lana Kay Johnson Jul. 31, 1965, at Clintwood, VA. They now reside in Springfield, OH. They have two daughters, Angela Renee Hughes Mercer (born Apr. 22, 1970) and Amy Lynn Hughes Mefford (born Nov. 26, 1976). They have two grandsons, Brandon Michael Mercer (born Mar. 2, 1994) and Gabriel Thomas Mefford (born Jun. 18, 1999).

Bobby Frank married Judy Lester. He died Nov. 5, 1994, at Huntington, WV, and was buried in Ironton, OH. Their daughter, Melissa Hughes Akers resides in Ironton, OH, with her husband, James Akers, and children, Bobbie Breann (born Jun. 26, 1991) and James Joseph (born Feb. 10, 1996).

Edwin Earl Hughes married Doris Jean Conley, daughter of Fical and Pauline Conley of Block House Bottom. Their children are Brent Edwin Hughes (born Oct. 30, 1970). Brent married Melissa Ward, daughter of Earl and Judy Ward. They have one son, Dustin Earl (born Dec. 8, 1989). Jeniffer Lynn Hughes (born Aug. 13, 1977) resides in Morehead, KY, and attends Morehead State University.

HUTCHISON - Bill, Mary Jane, Bob and Tom Hutchison moved from Akron, OH, to Wittensville, KY, in February 1979. The American dream made it possible for this family to move to Johnson County because their dream was to open the first McDonald's Restaurant in eastern Kentucky!

Bob, Mary Jane, Bill and Tom Hutchison, Oct. 5, 1979, opening day of McDonald's Restaurant.

Bill Hutchison was born May 27, 1920, and was reared in the Summit County Children's Home. Mary Jane was born Dec. 5, 1921, to Fred and Dora Darr. She was reared, along with her three brothers, by their mother after her father passed away in March 1933. Bill met his wife-to-be on Aug. 5, 1934, and married Mary Jane Jun. 1, 1941. By the end of that year Bill was part of the 82nd Abn. Inf. and served his country until the end of WWII. While he was away Mary Jane served her country working at the Goodyear Aerospace Center riveting parts and assembling brakes for the war planes.

Bill and Mary Jane were blessed with five sons: Billy James (born Feb. 12, 1947) resides in Akron, OH; Herbert Ray (born Apr. 17, 1949) resides in Crosset, AR; Eddie Leroy (born Aug. 25, 1950) resides in Akron; Bobby Mark (born Mar. 21, 1954) resides in Staffordsville; and Tommy Jay (born Feb. 10, 1957) lives in Pikeville. Mary Jane has since moved back to Akron but frequently visits her "home away from home" here in eastern Kentucky.

Bill held various positions before getting involved with McDonald's in 1959. Mary Jane worked in the food industry as well, associated first with the Firestone Country Club and then moving on to operate her own catering company. Bob joined the workforce at age 9 as a newspaper carrier but retired at the age of 14 to begin his career with McDonald's. Tom also started his career with McDonald's at the eager age of 14. In 1979 it was mutually agreed upon by McDonald's and the Hutchison family that eastern Kentucky, Johnson County and Paintsville would be their area of opportunity and their new home. They opened their first McDonald's on Oct. 5, 1979, during the Apple Festival weekend. The Hutchisons were advised by McDonald's to wait until after the festival to open but the people of Johnson County were excited to have a McDonald's so the family said "why wait?" To the best of their knowledge this was the only time that a business has officially opened its doors on Apple Day! At the time of Bill's passing on Jun. 20, 1986, the Hutchisons had opened three restaurants but Bob and Tom have since been blessed to have grown to a total of nine restaurants.

The Hutchisons owe their success to many individuals, families and organizations. Ray Kroc, for his vision and the opportunity to make a dream come true. Citizens National Bank and Trigg Dorton made it possible for the Hutchison family to obtain the necessary financing. Homer Short and family had the best location and were helpful in getting established. The James N. "Biz" and Robert Meek families assisted in getting the Hutchisons acquainted with the area. Most of all, without the ongoing support of the employees, customers and the communities in which they serve, it would be difficult to maintain the business. For this the Hutchisons are forever grateful.

ISAAC - Arlan Isaac was born on Aug. 9, 1937, in Wheelwright, KY. He was the second of six children born to Arthur and Bethel Isaac. He attended elementary and secondary schools in Wheelwright in Floyd County, leaving after his junior year to attend Alice Lloyd College. After graduating Alice Lloyd he attended UK for one semester and transferred to Morehead State University where he earned a BS degree in business, a master's in guidance and counseling and Rank I certification in supervision.

The Arlan Isaac Family: Arlan, Emma Lou and Shawn.

Arlan married Emma Lou Collins on Jun. 3, 1958. Emma Lou was born on Apr. 13, 1939, to Everage and Gladys Isaacs Collins. She was the third of five children. She attended elementary school at Topmost in Knott County. She boarded at Alice Lloyd and attended eighth through 10th grades. She returned home and finished high school at Wayland in Floyd County. She returned to Alice Lloyd to complete junior college, transferring to Morehead State University to earn a BA in education and a master's in education with an emphasis in library science.

Dan and Jill Isaac Imes and Emma Grace.

Emma Lou began her teaching career at age 18 in 1957 in first grade at Franklin-Monroe in Darke County, OH. Upon her marriage to Arlan, they moved to Slemp, KY, in Perry County where they taught at Leatherwood, Emma's second year and Arlan's first. The next eight years were spent teaching in Wheelwright. They moved to Van Lear and began teaching in the Johnson County School System in August 1967. Arlan served as guidance counselor at Oil Springs and Johnson Central and later served as testing coordinator for Johnson County Schools until he returned to Floyd County in 1986 as guidance counselor at Betsy Layne High School. He was in education for 35 years until he retired in May 1994. Emma served as school librarian at West Van Lear, Oil Springs, Meade, Central and

Porter Elementary Schools, completing 36 years in education before retiring in May 1994.

Arlan and Emma have two children, Jill Veronica and Shawn Arlan. Jill attended grade school at Meade, Porter and Central Elementaries. She graduated from Johnson Central in 1982. She earned her BA degree in education from Morehead State University where she met her future husband, Daniel Alan Imes, from Ashland, KY. They were married on Jul. 12, 1986. They both earned master's degrees in education from Western State University. They both teach in the Campbellsville School System in Taylor County. She teaches first grade and he is the band director and music teacher in the high school. They have one daughter, Emma Grace, who is a delight to her grandparents. Shawn attended grade school at Central Elementary and attended high school at Paintsville, leaving at the end of his junior year to attend PCC. He transferred to UK where he majored in accounting until he transferred to Morehead State University where he earned a BS degree in middle school education and a MBA degree. Shawn is involved in the stock market, serving as his own financial advisor. Shawn was a member of the Army National Guard for six years and was a cadet in ROTC while at UK.

The entire Isaac family became members of the First Baptist Church in Paintsville with Jill moving her membership to the Campbellsville Baptist Church after her marriage. They have been active in church activities for many years with Arlan currently serving as trustee. He is also active in the Paintsville Kiwanis Club, where he served as president for the 1997-98 year.

Although the Isaacs grew up and lived elsewhere for many years, they are proud to call Johnson County home.

ISAACS - Hobert N. Isaacs Sr. was born on Nov. 2, 1915, in Lawrence County, KY, son of Lewis Isaacs and LouVerne McKenzie Isaacs.

Hobert married Sarah Music on Dec. 24, 1935, at Nippa, KY. They had six children, who were all born in Johnson County: Bettie Annajine (commonly known as Lou Rissie) born Mar. 19, 1937; Phyllis Ann born Feb. 20, 1939; Ella Fay born Mar. 22, 1942; Janis Mae born Jan. 28, 1944; Hobert Jr. born Aug. 31, 1947; Thelma G. born Apr. 10, 1949 - stillborn.

Hobert worked many years at Stephen's Elkhorn Coal Co. before being laid-off in the early 1960s. He then moved to Wabash, IN, where three of his adult daughters were living. He was working at Wagner Industries when he had his first heart attack and had to retire, that was also when he was diagnosed with black lung disease.

Hobert's favorite hobby was family activities. He was an avid Cincinnati Reds fan. He also enjoyed gardening and had quite a green thumb. He and Sarah were very active in their church (Erie Street Freewill Baptist Church in Wabash, IN).

At the time of his death on Oct. 2, 1973, he had 11 grandchildren. There have been two grandchildren, and several great-grandchildren born since his death. His final resting place is in Lafontaine, IN, at the I.O.O.F. Cemetery.

Most of Hobert's family still reside in Indiana. *Respectfully submitted by: Hobert Isaacs Jr., Ella Fay (Isaacs) Slone and Janis Mae (Isaacs) Eytcheson.*

JAYNE & RULE - The Jayne and the Rule families were well established in neighboring areas of Johnson County by mid-1800s, representative of the agrarian society of that time.

Edgar Pleasant Jayne was born in Flat Gap, KY, 1913, son of Ernest Jayne (born 1879, died 1960) and Minnie Holbrook Jayne (born 1889, died 1967). The large family farm demanded long hours of hard work from Minnie and Ernest as well as their children: Leora Skaggs (born 1911), Edgar Jayne (born 1913, died 1998), Herschel Jayne (born 1915, died 1974), Carrie Jones (born 1917), James Jayne (born 1919, died 1978), Irene Gardner (born 1926) and William Jayne (born 1932).

Edgar P. and Jacqueline R. Jayne.

Ernest and Minnie Holbrook Jayne

The importance of education was emphasized to the children, influenced by the academic achievements of William Jayne, past principal, Enterprise High School, Flat Gap. Edgar's formal learning began in a one-room school, proceeded through Flat Gap High, AB and BS from University of Kentucky, and PhD from Washington University in St. Louis, MO, in 1950.

Ed filled a teaching-research position at George Washington University School of Medicine, Washington, DC, 1950-53. Soon after leaving his post in DC for the University of Connecticut, Edgar and Jacqueline Rule, Paintsville, KY, were married, 1954.

Ed's dedication to teaching and research led to success in his field of gerontology as he retired in 1978, a well published scientist, and chairman, Dept. of Anatomy, School of Allied Health Sciences, University of Connecticut, Storrs, CT.

Jackie's dad, Charles Tobias Rule (born 1877, died 1948), reared on his grandfather's farm in Johnson County, soon became one of the entrepreneurs furthering business development in Paintsville. In 1907, Tobe and Garnett Kirk (born 1889, died 1976), daughter of Elizabeth Goble Kirk and Judge A.J. Kirk, were married and established residence there.

Charles Tobias and Garnett Kirk Rule

Jeffrey and Sharon A. Jayne

Lauren Elizabeth and Michael David Jayne

Jackie's three sister's: Betsy Baker (born 1908, died 1985), Ruth Harris (born 1910, died 1982) and Virginia Southern (born 1913, died 1985); and one brother, Charles Rule (born 1918, died 1969), made for a fun-filled growing-up for the youngest Rule girl, Jacqueline Rule Jayne, (born 1927), who was extremely grateful for such tolerant parents!

After graduating from Paintsville High in 1945, attending Mayo and gaining experience working an assortment of jobs, Jackie's resumé included appointment to secretary-treasurer, Board member, of two private industry corporations in Washington, DC. In 1954, Jacqueline Rule married Edgar P. Jayne and was able to assist her husband in preparing research papers and grants, and reproduce needed anatomical illustrations.

During the worst blizzard in Connecticut's history (1958), Jeffrey Jayne decided now is the time to be born! While student and professor were in class, Jackie was a home mom and school and civic volunteer.

Jeffrey increased the family by bringing them Sharon Aderhold, married in Atlanta, 1983; children Lauren (born 1987) and Michael (born 1989). Ed, Jackie, Jeff and family lived in Georgia.

Life created many precious memories to share and comfort since Ed's death, Mar. 11, 1998. He was an exceptional person.

JAYNE - William E. "Bill" Jayne, a 10th generation descendant of William Jayne I (born 1618, died 1714) of Long Island, NY, was born Jan. 10, 1932, at Flat Gap, KY, the youngest child of eight born to his parents. All except one survived to adulthood. William's parents, Ernest Jayne of Flat Gap and Minnie Holbrook Jayne of Martha, KY, were married on Sep. 29, 1906. Other issues to this union were: Hazel (born 1908), Leora (born 1910), Edgar (born 1913), Herschel (born 1915), Carrie (born 1918) James (born 1921) and Irene (born 1926).

William and Georgia Jayne

William was married in Tacoma, WA, to Georgiana Borne of New Orleans, LA, on Apr. 27, 1954, while serving in the USAF. They became parents to two daughters and a son. Sue Ann was born in Tacoma, WA, on Feb. 3, 1955; Karen Lynn was born Apr. 25, 1954, in Abilene, TX; and David Ernest was born on Apr. 3, 1961, in Atlanta, GA.

After graduating high school at Flat Gap in 1951, William attended The University of Kentucky until joining the Air Force in 1953. While serving in the Air Force, he completed requirements for a Senior Air

Traffic Control Certificate issued by the Civil Aeronautics Authority (CAA) and worked at such airports as Tacoma, WA, Dhahran, Saudi Arabia, Adanna, Turkey and Abilene, TX.

After being honorably discharged from the Air Force in 1957, William took a position in Atlanta, GA, with the Federal Aviation Administration (FAA) as an air traffic controller, a career he followed until his retirement in Atlanta in 1997.

JENKINS & CASTLE - Alma Castle (born Sep. 25, 1932), daughter of James Charles Castle and Amanda Ella Caudill Castle, married Mar. 4, 1947 to Lloyd Jenkins (born Dec. 12, 1917) son of Green Jenkins and Clora Skaggs Jenkins.

Their children were:

Jerry Jenkins (born Feb. 13, 1949) md. Sue Williams, second Carol Jean Wayne; sons Billy Joe and Jerry Scott, daughter Kristy Amanda.

Larry Jenkins (born Jul. 25, 1953) md. Diane Rowe; daughter Tammy, son Kevin.

Jimme Darrell Jenkins (born Nov. 14, 1953) md. Lisa Sizemore; sons Jimmie Dewayne and Jimmie Darrell, daughter Melissa Ann.

Mary Lou Jenkins Brown (born Aug. 28, 1955) md. Paul Edwin Brown; son Pauld Edwin Jr., daughter Paula Sue.

Brenda Gaye Jenkins Carty (born May 27, 1963) md. Larry Ray Carty; son Adam Matthew (born May 17, 1982).

Terry Lynn Jenkins (born Aug. 20, 1965) md. Lisa Gamble; sons Christopher Lynn and Jason Oneal, daughter Brittany.

Eula Faye Jenkins Gamble (born Aug. 8, 1967) md. Michael Gamble; daughter Mika, son Michael Scott.

Jimmie Darrell Jenkins also has a son named Carl Shawn.

JOHNSON & REED - Eulah Lee Reed (born Apr. 27, 1899, in Oil Springs, KY), daughter of Benjamin Franklin Reed and Louise Wheeler, married in 1914 to George Otto Johnson (born Feb. 7, 1895, in Redbush, KY, died Feb. 16, 1963), son of Levi D'Estaing Johnson and Susan Catherine Conley.

Eula Lee Reed Johnson; Charles Larry Marsee

Levi was a farmer and Catherine was a housewife and a midwife in the Redbush area. They left Otto and Eulah 125 acres, the old farm house and the mineral rights to the property.

Eulah and Otto had three children: Charles Lasco Johnson (born on Christmas Day, Dec. 25, 1915, died Jul. 11, 1978), Virginia Wandalee Johnson (born Nov. 10, 1919, died Feb. 23, 1995) and Wilma Christine Johnson (born Nov. 2, 1926) all were born in Redbush, KY.

Otto earned a degree in mechanics at The Rahe Auto & Tractor School on Feb. 23, 1923, Cincinnati, OH. I believe he might have traveled by railroad train to school at that time, because they didn't own a car.

In 1925, Eulah and Otto Johnson bought their first car, a 1925 Moon car.

Otto was growing tired of farming the land and there was not enough automobiles in the area at that time to make a living at. So in 1939, Otto and Eulah sold the farm and one-half of the mineral rights to Willis Williams of Redbush.

They moved to the Hillsboro, OH, area where Otto worked on cars and Eulah had a greenhouse, which I believe she misses very much. Because she loves the family to bring her flowers for her birthday and holidays, even though her eyesight is about gone. They had to move sometime in the 1940s because the house burnt.

The hardest time for the family was when their son, Lasco, was drafted in WWII. They were afraid, as were so many families at that time, that their children would not return from the war. He served in the 101st Abn. Div.

In 1954 Lasco married Barbara Jean Riley of Crittenden County, KY. In December 1954, I was born in Covington, KY. My birth name was Charles Lasco Johnson Jr., named after my father. Mom and dad divorced in 1962. And she remarried Eugene Marsee, who adopted all three of us kids. I never lost the love I had for Lasco, my father, even though he didn't come around when I really needed him. You see I have always had a lot of medical problems. I have Fanconi's Syndrome (kidney disease). I always knew where the family lived so when I got out of high school in 1974, I found my father and his side of the family. I was very glad I did because I got to spend some time with him before he passed away in 1978.

I still see the family, and Grandma Johnson still quilts as she has done all her life, even though she can hardly see anymore. It must be habit that makes it possible for her to sew.

JOHNSON & RICE - Robert M. Johnson was born Apr. 29, 1903, in Johnson County, the son of Sampson Jobez and Martha Moles Johnson. He had three whole brothers: Stonewall, Martin (died in infancy) and Marion (died in infancy); two half brothers, Dave and Chris; four whole sisters: May (died in infancy), Arcie, Ella and Stella; and two half sisters, Hattie and Susan.

Beatrice Rice was born Oct. 30, 1910, in Floyd County, the daughter of Judd and Margaret Music Rice. She had five brothers: John D., Sam K., Thomas, Roy and Verlie; and three sisters: Vertrice, Lois and Avonell.

50th Anniversary, May 14, 1982. Left to Right: Beatrice Johnson, Marlene McNeil, Bob Johnson, Dean Johnson and Bonnie Bogan.

Bob and Beatty were married on May 14, 1932. Into this union were born three children: Marlene (md. Gene McNeil), Lowell Dean (md. Callie Daniel) and Bonnie (md. Lee Bogan). They have nine grandchildren and 10 great-grandchildren.

Robert Johnson homeplace, Hager Hill, KY, built circa 1850.

Robert retired from the Hager Hill Coal Tipple at the age of 72. He was a hard worker and always supplemented his income by hauling junk, farming, selling apples and trading. A shrewd businessman, Bob always enjoyed negotiating a deal and usually got the price he wanted.

Beatty was a full-time housewife and mother. She took great pride in her family and was never happier than when everyone got together. Mama Johnson always had a snack ready when the kids got off the school bus. She watched three generations get off the bus and was always ready to stop what she was doing and listen to stories about their day. Her front yard was frequently the sight of a neighborhood baseball game. She enjoyed getting to know the friends of her family and people of all ages would stop by to see Mama and Papa Johnson when they came back to Eastern Kentucky for a visit.

For many years, Bob and Beatty lived by the railroad tracks and people always knew they would be welcome when they stopped by the Johnson farm. The barn was always open if someone needed a place to spend the night and Beatty often remarked that she never knew who would show up for breakfast. She always had room for one more at the table and no one was ever sent away hungry.

Beatrice died on Jul. 10, 1990, from complications following a stroke. Fifteen months later, on Oct. 13, 1991, Robert followed his beloved wife in death. They are buried in the Johnson County Memorial Cemetery at Staffordsville, KY.

JONES - Nathaniel Tiller Jones (born circa 1771, Virginia) md. Nancy Ray in Amherst County, VA, on Nov. 17, 1794. By 1800 this family had migrated to Russell County, VA (current Scott County). In 1830 Nathaniel Jones moved his family to Floyd County, KY, where he and son, John Ray Jones, settled on Mud Creek, where they lived until almost 1860.

John Ray Jones married, circa 1829, Satira "Tera" Stanley and had the following children: Nathaniel Tiller, James, Claiborn, Ambrose, Lemuel G., William P., Tandy and Alina Jones.

Nathaniel Tiller Jones (born May 25, 1830, died May 6, 1920, Pike County) md. first, Mary Ann McCown, and second, Charity Cox.

James Jones (born Apr. 19, 1831, died Jun. 13, 1913, Floyd County, KY) md. Jul. 17, 1851, Pricey Blankenship and lived on Beaver Creek, Floyd County, KY.

Claiborn Jones (born circa 1832, Floyd County, KY) md. Elizabeth ??.

Ambrose Jones (born 1834, died Dec. 11, 1907) md. first, Mary Ann Blankenship and second, Martha Baldridge, and lived near McDowell, Floyd County, KY.

Lemuel G. Jones (born Mar. 9, 1838, died Mar. 10, 1920, Johnson County, KY) md. first, Elizabeth Hall Jul. 7, 1857, Floyd County, KY; married second, Jane Sparks, daughter of Elisha Sparks and Susannah Pridemore; and married third, Selina Crislip.

William Jones (born November 1839) md. Jul. 7, 1859, Lydia Salyer, daughter of Martin and Susannah Salyer.

Tandy Jones (born circa 1840, died 1864) died after being shot by James Patterson, a fellow Confederate soldier, who learned Tandy intended to enlist in the Union Army. Tandy married May 22, 1860, Susannah Sagraves, daughter of Joseph Sagraves Jr. and Nancy McDowell.

Alina Jones (born 1842, died Mar. 10, 1916) md. Jonathan Henry Salyer, son of Martin and Susannah Salyer. Alina and Henry Salyer had the following children: Malinda F. Salyer (born 1863); Satira M. Salyer married Andrew J. Castle Apr. 15, 1885); Martin "Mart" Van Buren Salyer (born Dec. 21, 1867, died Dec. 24, 1936) md. Nancy Jane Stapleton Jan. 28, 1892; John Salyer (born circa 1869); James H. Salyer (born April 1873) md. Virginia Belle Castle; Elizabeth Jane Salyer (born May 29, 1874); Ambrose "Booze" Salyer (born circa 1875) md. Nola Crider; Cora Ellen Salyer (born Dec. 22, 1878, died Jun. 15, 1914) md. Thomas Jefferson McKenzie, son of Henry McKenzie and Serena Vanover, May 27, 1899.

John Ray Jones remarried in 1845 at Pike County, KY, Phoebe Sturgill and had the following children: Francis, Martha, Littleton Bailey, Mary Jane, John Ray and Brownlow Jones.

Francis Jones was born about 1847.

Martha Jones (born Dec. 2, 1848) md. Jan. 9, 1865, George Washington Hopkins "Hop" Kimbler.

Littleton Bailey Jones (born Oct. 19, 1852, died Mar. 16, 1916) md. Apr. 26, 1871, Emmaline Salyer.

Mary Jane Jones was born Apr. 8, 1855.

John Ray Jones was born March 1859.

Brownlow Jones (born 1863) md. first, Caroline Brown and second, Eliza Jane Lemaster in 1904.

JONES & BORDERS - Kathryn Elizabeth Borders was born on May 14, 1908, in Allen County, KY, near the community of Trammel. She was the daughter and next to the youngest living child of John Wesley Landers and Ida Oliver Landers of Allen County, KY. Her name at birth was Elizabeth Catherine Landers. Her siblings were: Mabel Landers Lewis Willis, Ella Frances Landers Shaw, Leland Carson Landers, Orene Landers Liebtag and Opie or Fred Landers.

Katherine Elizabeth Borders Jones

At the age of about 4, Kathryn was orphaned and was placed in the Masonic Childrens' Home in Louisville, KY, by her oldest sister, Mabel. In 1914 she was adopted by Henry and Rebecca Borders of Paintsville, Johnson County, KY.

Kathryn attended the Sandy Valley Seminary in Paintsville and then the Eastern Kentucky Teacher's College, in Richmond, KY, where she received her teaching certificate. She taught school for 30 years in the communities of West Van Lear, Muddy Branch and Concord in Johnson County and was a retired teacher at the time of her death in 1964. She was teaching at West Van Lear, KY, when she met her husband, Terry Allen Jones. At the time, he was living in Van Lear, Johnson County, KY.

Terry was born on Jul. 28, 1908, in Jefferson County, AL, and was the youngest of three surviving children born to Margie Ellis Jones and Leroy Dalton. His siblings were Douglas Jones of Cape May, NJ; and Mary Lois Jones Hatcher of Fort Worth, TX.

Terry and Kathryn were united in marriage in November 1928, at the home of Henry and Rebecca Borders. They had three children who lived to adulthood, namely: Mary Rebecca Jones Lewis, wife of Paintsville attorney, Jack Lewis, and the first woman in the county to hold an elected office; and John and Henry Jones, identical twins and prominent physicians in Russell and Greenup counties of Kentucky. The Jones twins were born Aug. 5, 1933.

Kathryn died an untimely, accidental death on Nov. 22, 1964, and is buried beside her husband, Terry Allen, who died on Jun. 20, 1967. They are buried at the Porter Cemetery in Prestonsburg KY.

JOSEPH - Alice Joseph (born Jun. 27, 1884) was the only child of Woodson Joseph and Arminta Baldridge (md. Sep. 6, 1883). Alice was born in Johnson County. The family lived for a few years in the Puget Sound area of Washington. Upon their return to Kentucky the family bought a farm at Offutt, KY, where Alice lived until she married William Richard Richmond, Dec. 4, 1904. Alice and William lived in Paintsville for several years and then purchased a farm one mile east of Paintsville on what is now Rt. 40 east. They had five children: William Orville, John Woodson, James Gordon, Howard Estill and Myrtle. William died in 1945 and Alice managed the farm and reared her granddaughter, Esther Jean. Alice Joseph Richmond died Jan. 7, 1971.

Alice's father, Woodson Joseph, was born about 1865, the son (possibly adopted) of Nelson Joseph and Louisa McCoy (born 1850, Claiborne County, TN). Nelson and Louisa were married Oct. 8, 1863, in Magoffin County, KY. Woodson died Mar. 9, 1940.

Alice Joseph (Richmond)

Alice's mother, Arminta Baldridge (born Jun. 20, 1865, died Nov. 24, 1932) was the daughter of Levisa "Vicy" Brown (born May 27, 1824, Claiborne County, TN) and John Baldridge (born Dec. 16, 1822, Russell County, VA). Levisa and John were married in 1841. John died Jan. 30, 1901, and Levisa died Aug. 1, 1917. Both are buried on Mills Branch in Floyd County. Levisa was the daughter of Elizabeth Lee and Armster Brown. Armster fought in the War of 1812.

John Baldridge was the son of William Baldridge Jr. (born 1795, North Carolina, died after 1880, Abbott Creek, Floyd County) and (first wife) Hannah Estep. William and Hannah were married Mar. 12, 1818. Hannah's parents were Samuel Estep Sr. (born 1760, Rowan County, NC, died after 1840) and Mary "Polly" Lane, who were married Jul. 29, 1788, Green County, TN.

Samuel Estep Sr.'s parents were Thomas Estep Jr. (born Nov. 3, 1730, St. Margarets Parish-Arudel County, MD, between 1805-07) and Susannah Holmes (born Feb. 8, 1742, Fredrick, MD, died 1803, Rowan County, NC). Thomas Estep Jr. was the son of Thomas Estep Sr. and Mary ?. Susannah Holmes was the daughter of William Holmes Jr. and Honour Wells.

JUSTICE & DONALDSON - Quentin Roosevelt Justice and Annette Dale Donaldson Justice were married in the First Christian Church in Pikeville, KY, on Mar. 20, 1943.

Quentin was born in Pikeville, Pike County, KY, on Jan. 17, 1922, the oldest of three children born to Malcolm Finis Justice and Elsie Charles Justice. Quentin has two sisters, Lorraine Justice Robinson of Pikeville and Lucille Justice Pruitt, now deceased. He graduated from Pikeville High School in May 1940 and continued his education at Mayo State Vocational School in Paintsville as well as additional training in Lexington, KY, where he obtained expertise in communications.

Justice Family. Front Row: Daniel, Hunter Brooklyn, Gatha Dale, John L., Liddie R., Thomas and Brenda G. Justice. Back Row: Daniel Shannon, Annette, Joshua L. Quentin R. and Crystal G. Justice.

The day after his marriage to Annette, he entered the service and after being stationed at Camp Crowder, MO, for a year, was sent to the European Theatre of Operations where he served until his discharge in November 1945. Quentin began working in Pikeville for Southern Bell Telephone & Telegraph Co. (now Bell South) in February 1946. In November 1959, he was transferred to Paintsville, KY, as plant foreman. Quentin retired from the company in May 1985 where he had become a much revered manager of Central Office Operations.

Annette was born in Pikeville, Pike County, KY, on Aug. 16, 1922, the oldest of two children born to Albert Clarence and Laura Rebecca Pratt Donaldson. Laura born and reared in Virginia. After the untimely death of her mother (July 1926), Annette and her sister, Rebecca Jean Donaldson Baxter, lived with their "Granddaddy" and grandmother, the Rev. William Edward and Zola Dale Smith Donaldson, who, although originally from Alabama, was sent to Pike County, KY, in 1916 as a Presbyterian Sunday school missionary where he served for 25 years. He is still remembered with love by those who knew him. Annette has a half-sister and half-brother, Bobbie Donaldson Rogers and her twin, William Kyle Donaldson, who are children of her father and his second wife, the former Willie T. Thornbury.

Annette graduated from Pikeville College Academy in May 1941 and then entered Pikeville College where she completed one year in the department of business. After spending a short time working at Lexington Signal Depot in Avon, KY, and after their first child was born at Good Samaritan Hospital in Lexington, KY, Annette returned to Pikeville to live with Quentin's parents until he returned from the service. During that time Annette began working for Kentucky West Virginia Power Co. in Pikeville where she worked for eight years. After the Justices moved to Paintsville, Annette held varied employments: secretary to Paul W. Trimble, principal at Paintsville High School; city clerk under the administration of Paintsville mayor, John Chandler; payroll clerk for Paintsville Outerwear; State Farm Insurance clerk; and finally reporter for the Credit Bureau of Paintsville, last working in September 1985.

Quentin and Annette have three sons: Daniel Quentin Justice (born Aug. 5, 1944) md. Gatha Dale Robinson (born Mar. 6, 1944) Jan. 18, 1964. They reside in Pike County, KY, where Dan is employed with Appalachian Wireless. They have one son, Daniel Shannon Justice (born Jan. 11, 1966) and a granddaughter, Hunter Brooklyn Justice (born Apr. 7, 1994). Shannon works with John Michael Montgomery of country music fame.

Second son, John Laurance Justice (born Mar. 2, 1954). He married Liddie Renee Wells (born Dec. 2, 1956) Nov. 25, 1976, and they have one son, Joshua Lee Justice (born Jun. 8, 1978). They live in Pike County, KY, and John has worked for Southern Bell Telephone (now Bell South) since 1973.

Third son, Thomas Dale Justice (born Aug. 4, 1955) married Brenda Gale Cisco (born Jul. 3, 1958) Dec. 31, 1977. They have one daughter, Crystal Gale Justice (born Aug. 7, 1978). Tom started working for South Central Bell Telephone (now Bell South) in 1978 and was transferred with the company to Houston, TX, in 1980 where they are now living in Pasadena, TX.

Have Quentin and Annette really retired? The answer is a definite NO!!! They are the busiest couple in Johnson County in this year of 1999. They virtually "clean up the town" from picking up discarded trash to planting flowers in every vacant spot they can find. Also, they are very active members in the First United Methodist Church in Paintsville and can always find something that needs to be done at the church.

Quentin and Annette reside at 211 Preston Street, Paintsville, KY.

KEATON - Andy Paul Keaton was born Nov. 8, 1966 in Johnson County, KY (Paintsville Hospital) to Paul Emerson Keaton (b. Apr. 18, 1940 in Lawrence County, Martha, KY) and Emily Frances (Barker) Keaton) (b. Jun. 11, 1943 in Rowan County, Elliotsville, KY). His parents were married Jan. 14, 1961. He has one sister, Dana Karen (Keaton) Collett who was born on Feb. 20, 1962.

Andy, along with his family, spent the first four years of his life living at Keaton, KY, but later moved to the community of Red Bush only a few miles away. While growing up in Red Bush, Andy attended Flat Gap Elementary from which he graduated the eighth grade in 1980. He then attended and graduated as valedictorian from Johnson Central High School in 1984. After attending Prestonsburg Community College for two years and receiving an associate of science degree, he became the youngest person to be accepted to the University of Kentucky College of Dentistry. He graduated first in his class of 47 in 1990 having received his DMD.

Dr. Andy Paul and Jill Porter Keaton

Following graduation from dental school, Andy was an associate professor at the University of Kentucky College of Dentistry for one year. Also during this year, he worked at a private dental practice in Frankfort, KY. Not limiting his life to his dental career along, Andy attended Lexington Baptist College in Lexington, KY during 1990-1991 furthering his knowledge of the Holy Bible. Andy had been baptized at Red Bush in April 1986.

Desiring to further his dental education, Andy applied and was accepted to one of the top orthodontic programs in the nation, The University of Tennessee at Memphis in the fall of 1991. After having moved to Memphis, TN from Lexington, KY, Andy completed a three year residency program in orthodontics specializing in orthodontics and dentofacial orthopedics. After receiving his MS degree in Orthodontics, he returned to his beloved home of eastern Kentucky to start his practice in July of 1994. Andy began to practice in both Paintsville and Pikeville, KY, but soon had a third office in Prestonburg. In all of these three areas of eastern Kentucky, Andy was heavily involved in civic groups and community endeavors including United Way of Eastern Kentucky, The Kentucky Apple Festival, Christ Central Training School and Academy, Rotary Club, The Kentucky Mountain Dental Society, The Mountain HomePlace, and others.

On Jun. 20, 1998, Andy married Jill Elizabeth Porter, the daughter of Warren Jesse Porter and Jo Anne Porter of Flatwoods, KY. The marriage ceremony was at the First Baptist Church of Pikeville. Andy and Jill had met during dental school. Jill, also a dentist, was the coordinator of the dental hygiene program at Prestonburg Community College. Their daughter Emily Anne was born on Mar. 13, 1999 at King's Daughters Hospital in Ashland, KY. Andy and his family resided between homes in Pike and Johnson counties at the time of this writing.

KELLY - Mathias Kelly and his son, Frederick, were farmers in New River, NC. They brought their family to Johnson County, KY, where Wallace was born in September 1848 to Frederick and Patience. On Apr. 30, 1874, Wallace married Cynthia Bailey (born November 1853 in Johnson County). They had three sons and five daughters. Their son, Joel (born in November 1884), married Lily Collier and lived at Keaton, KY. Their children were: Lora, Edgar Harold and Chester Hager. Lily died at an early age when her youngest son was 17. Joel was a farmer and was often called to butcher cattle and hogs for his neighbors. He made sturdy knives from crosscut saws and made cane-bottom chairs by hand. He loved fishing, especially when his grandchildren accompanied him. He enjoyed vegetable and flower gardening. He died at age 85 in 1971.

Lora married Hurston Bailey and they reared three children: Peggy, Mary Margaret and Douglas. Harold never married. Hager married Rhoda Magdeline Rigsby, daughter of Henry and Laura (Boggs) Rigsby, on Sep. 2, 1939. They had a son, Clinton C., and a daughter, Barbara Sue. Hager worked almost 40 years in the Martha oil fields and was a Baptist minister. Maggie remains a homemaker.

Harold and Hager served in the Army in WWII. They both died in 1991. Lora died about 1993.

Clinton married Leatrice West on Jun. 11, 1960. Their children are Debra Annette, Sandra Lynn and Steven Clinton. Debra married Doyle Stratton and has a son, Corey, and a daughter, Kelly. Sandra married Thomas Cordle and has a daughter, Lindsay Catherine. Steven married Michelle Federer and has a son, Blake.

Sue married James Emory Bartrum on Sep. 3, 1966.

Although the Kelly homeplace is still maintained at Keaton, the family now has come full circle as Debra lives in North Carolina, where the history began.

KING - Henry Raymond King was born on May 4, 1899, in Paintsville, KY, to Samuel Porter King and Cynthia Fitch King. He had two brothers and three sisters. King Addition was named for his father Samuel Porter King. Samuel King also served as sheriff of Johnson County from Jan. 1, 1898-Dec. 31, 1901.

Henry Raymond King

Raymond spent his youth on the family farm located on the Big Sandy River. At that time there was no bridge to connect Paintsville and King Addition. Wagons came by their house to cross the river in order to get to town. When the river was up, young Raymond would use his boat to ferry the people back and forth, charging a nickel. Another enterprise involving a sister, was to catch logs that broke loose when being brought down the river from logging companies taking them to market. That brought a whopping fee of 10 cents a log. Raymond's tales of his childhood and the history of his neighborhood would entertain his grandchildren for hours.

He attended Paintsville High School until his junior year. Although he was encouraged by his parents to continue his education, he wanted to see what other opportunities might come his way. He loved baseball and played for P.H.S., mostly second base. Later he played on a company team where he was employed. This love for baseball carried over until his death. He was an avid Reds fan - WIN or LOSE - that was his team!

The WWI Armistice was signed just one day before he was scheduled to report for his physical. This exempted him from Military Service.

Raymond weighed coal and kept books for Consolidated Coal Co. in Jenkins, KY, until March 1939. He then transferred to Van Lear, KY, and retired from there in 1951. Later he was employed by the Community Food Market until June 1964.

Henry was married to Grethel Jordan on Apr. 15, 1925, in Jenkins, KY. They had one son, Tom Raymond (born Jul. 22, 1927). They also had two daughters, Phyllis Ann Miller (born Apr. 17, 1934) who now lives in Reistertown, MD, and Thelma Lavonne White (born Jun. 11, 1936). Tom and Thelma still reside in Paintsville, KY.

Henry Raymond and Grethel King were members of the First Baptist Church in Paintsville, KY. Henry was a deacon for many years and Grethel taught in the Sunday school. Grethel died Jan. 10, 1993. Four years later on Mar. 22, 1997, Henry passed away.

KING & CASTLE - James K. "Jim" Polk King was bon Mar. 25, 1883, the son of William and Polly King. On Aug. 10, 1910, he married Martha Ellen Castle (born Sep. 29, 1893), the daughter of Chilton and Leander Belle Curtis Castle. They were both from the Red Bush area of Johnson County.

Jim was a member of the United Mine Workers of America and paid dues for many years even though he was working elsewhere. He had worked around the mines for a while before becoming janitor at the Van Lear School. He also fired the furnaces of Consolidated Coal Co.'s office building and the Van Lear Clubhouse. He even found time to clear the hillsides and have as many as four garden spots at once. He continued gardening long after retiring, even though he was disabled. He would hoe while sitting down and scooting along the rows. When asked why he would work under such difficult conditions, he would say, "It makes supper taste better if you work hard."

Martha and James "Jim" King

Jim and Martha King reared three sons: William Edmon, Estill Jay "Jake" and Wallace Woodrow. All three excelled at football at Van Lear High School. Jim and Martha also reared four daughters: Ethel, Eva Lee, Malta and Anna Louise. All the children are now deceased with the exception of Estill Jay, who lives in the vicinity of Washington DC and Anna Louise, who is married to Burdette C. "BB" Kretzer Jr., and lives in the old family home in Van Lear.

Mary (Polly) King

Jim King supplemented his income by raising and selling vegetables. He grew them in homemade "hot beds" made from tunneling under the garden with open ended metal pipes and building fires at the entrances to the tunnels to heat the ground overhead. It also helped feed the extra five or six children they took in to raise even though they weren't their own.

Jim King died December 1968. Martha King died November 1973. Both are buried on Clubhouse Hill, Van Lear, KY.

KISTNER & SHORT - I don't know when he was born or where he was born, or when he died, but he was a school teacher in 1874 and a store-keeper in 1878. He also was a shoe cobbler, he made shoes for people. In his store he sold material to make clothing, too, besides groceries. We've got a ledger that he kept where he sold eggs for .06 cents a dozen and coffee for .25 cents a pound and lots of other stuff at low prices. He also was a Church of Christ preacher.

He was in a wheelchair but he didn't let that stop him from doing what he set out to do in life. He kept count of hour, many scholars he had in school but he didn't give their names. He wrote all of this with a quill which was a feather, and probably some might have been with a pen and ink at times too.

His wife, Louisa Short Kistner, was a homemaker. She made candles in a candle moll which we still have. I don't know when or where she was born, but according to some papers we have, she must have died around December 1931 of chronic heart disease.

They had about seven children: Walter Scott, Samuel Tillman, Sarah Margaret, Barbara Ellen, Melissa, June Kistner and another little girl but I don't

Louisa Short Kistner and Christopher Columbus Kistner

know what her name was. She died when she was small from what I assume.

But anyway Christopher and Louisa lived at a place called Short Branch, which used to be called Dead Fork Branch at Buffalo Creek at Meally, KY, in Johnson County, about five miles from Paintsville, KY. So both of them died and buried in two different graveyards. Christopher is buried down near the mouth of Short Branch and Louisa is buried on the hill above where they lived.

KISTNER & MUSIC - Samuel Tillman Kistner or Kestner they spelled it sometimes where he worked, and his wife Goldia Music Kistner. Samuel was called Sam. He was born in December 1876 and Goldie was born Nov. 20, 1905. They had eight children. Their names are: Walter Scott, Normia, Pauline, Ernest, Juney, Eliga, Bessie Mae and Billy Ray Kistner. Pauline and Billy Ray died while they were small.

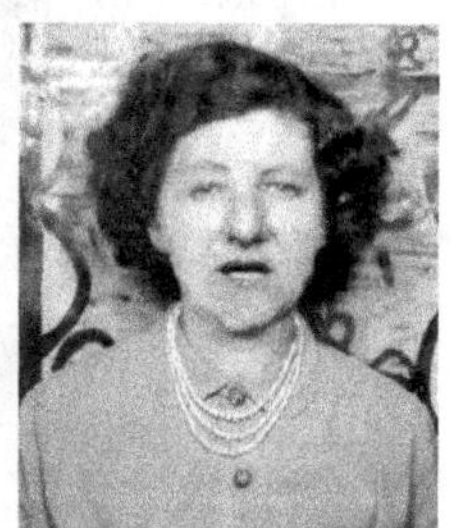

Samuel Tillman Kistner and Goldie Music Kistner

They lived on Short Branch at Meally on Buffalo Creek in Johnson County, KY. Sam used to walk across the hill from Short Branch to Van Lear in the winter time in his work clothes and work shoes when snow was on the ground and freezing cold to go to work in the coal mines, at the Consolidation Coal Co. at the Millers Creek Div. for a number of years. I guess he did that too in the summer time when the weather was steaming hot. He also would walk to Paintsville from Meally, KY, and back barefooted and it was about four miles each way. He was working at Mine Number 153 when the United Mine Workers Organized their union at No. 4170.

He was a good man and upheld the union and the lodge until the union went down in 1922. He also worked in 1929. He worked at other jobs like the WPA, at different places in 1936, and at Bobs Branch in Johnson County. He also helped build the Country Club House at Davis Branch at the golf course. He worked in 1940 and he supported his family till he got sick by taking a stroke and then died in December 1941 before the Black Lung came into effect, so he didn't draw any. He was buried upon the hill above where they lived.

Goldie was a homemaker, she cooked on a coal and wood stove and they burned it in a fireplace to keep warm in the winter time. Burned oil lamps at night with kerosene to see by. She also made lye soap in the summer. They took care of their children even though they had rough times they managed. Goldie died on Jul. 5, 1974, and was buried in the same graveyard where Sam, her husband was buried.

KISTNER & GREEN- Walter Scott Kistner was born Jul. 19, 1925, at Meally, KY, on Buffalo Creek in Johnson County. Viola Green Kistner, his wife, was born Aug. 26, 1930, at Crocked Creek near Peach Creek in Logan County, WV. They married May 1, 1949, at Peach Creek, WV, then came to Johnson County, KY, to live. They had five children. Their names are: Scotty, who died the same day he was born, Margaret, Delbert, Angie and Samuel Kistner.

William Scott and Viola Green Kistner, his wife.

Walter's dad, Sam, died when he was about 16 or 17 years old, so he had to work and help his mom, Goldie, raise five brothers and sisters younger than himself until he got married and had his own children. Then he continued working. He worked in Ohio on the railroad, and in canning factories and in New York picking cherries, apples, strawberries, eyeing potatoes and whatever else that needed to be done. He also worked on the golf course at Davis Branch, KY. He helped set up mobile homes in different places. He worked in the coal mines at Amherst Coal and Accoraville, WV, at Otseg, WV, and at Meally, KY, and probably other places too that we don't remember right now. He worked in the car factory in Michigan. He also worked for the Dept. of Highways in Johnson County, KY. He worked on a milk truck helping deliver milk at 3:00 o'clock in the morning.

He said where he worked in the mines in the winter time, where he would get wet and when he pulled his pants off they were froze so stiff that they'd almost stand alone by themselves. He also worked in grocery stores as a butcher and stock up boy and at other things. He had to go off to find work for there were no jobs he could get in Paintsville. While his wife, Viola, stayed home when she didn't work at public jobs herself to take care of their children. Walter helped with them too when he was home. He sure worked and took care of his family.

We reared a granddaughter whose name was Alicia Maynard until she married. We moved to Florida after Walter retired from the Dept. of State Highways in Kentucky and we still live in Bonifay, FL, in Holmes County. We've been married 50 fifty years on May 1, 1999.

We attend the Winterville Assembly of God Church, where we are members, at Bonifay, FL. We're happy, and all that keeps us going is tender loving care and serving the Lord. So we're hoping to meet all of our loved ones in Heaven when this life is over down here on earth.

KRETZER - Jason Ronald Kretzer was born Jul. 3, 1975, at Highlands Regional Medical Center to Kenneth Ronald and Joyce Britton Kretzer of Van Lear. Jason is the eighth of nine siblings. He graduated from eighth grade at Porter Elementary in 1989. As a student at Johnson Central High School, he was a member of the Chess Team, captain of the Academic Team and a member of the Beta Club. He graduated with honors in 1993 with a college preparatory diploma. After high school, Jason attended Morehead State University and later transferred to Harding University where be earned his BA degree in chemistry education in May 1999. Jason is currently employed as a junior chemist by Mineral Labs, Inc. in Salyersville, KY. Jason was baptized Jul. 29, 1995, at the Van Lear Freewill Baptist Church. Jason enjoys playing chess, advanced Dungeons and Dragons and Magic: The Gathering, as well as hiking and playing basketball, computers and reading/writing classical fantasy.

Laura Margaret Picklesimer was born Jan. 5, 1977, at Highlands Regional Medical Center to Homer Daulton Jr. and Linda Kay Brammer Picklesimer of Volga. She was the youngest of four children. She graduated from Flat Gap Elementary in 1990. She was baptized in May 1990 at the Highland Church of Christ. In high school at Johnson Central, Laura was a member of the Academic Team and held many offices in Future Homemakers of America including chapter president and state historian. She graduated as one of five valedictorians of the class of 1994 and was chosen as a National Merit Finalist. After high school, she attended Harding University, graduating Summa Cum Laude and earning a bachelor of social work degree in May 1998. Currently, she works as a service coordinator for children with severe emotional disabilities through the IMPACT program at Mountain Comprehensive Care Center in Prestonsburg. Laura enjoys hiking, sewing and reading Agatha Christie. She plans on pursuing her master's of social work degree through a University of Kentucky extended campus.

Mr. and Mrs. Jason Kretzer on wedding day, May 18, 1996.

Jason and Laura were married May 18, 1996, at the Paintsville Church of Christ with Keith Cozort performing the ceremony. The couple honeymooned at Jenny Wiley State Park and then lived in Van Lear until starting to college that fall. They lived in Searcy, AR, until they graduated and were able to secure jobs in their fields and move back to Johnson County in March 1999. They are members of Stambaugh Church of Christ. They currently live at Volga, where they plan to build a log home. At present, they have no children. Only a cat named Xerxes.

KRETZER - Burdette C. "BB" Kretzer Jr. was born Dec. 11, 1925, in Mordue (Madison County), WV. The son of Burdette C. Kretzer Sr. and Bertha McKnight Kretzer, he moved to Van Lear when he was six months old. His father worked for Consolidated Coal Co. in Van Lear for 24 years.

Louise and Burdette C. Kretzer Jr.

BB joined the Navy during WWII and served in the Pacific. On Aug. 8, 1945, while on leave from the Navy, he married Anna Louise King. Both were lifelong residents of Van Lear.

Anna Louise King Kretzer was born Mar. 22, 1928, to James K. Polk King and Martha Ellen Castle King. Louise Kretzer worked for G.C. Murphy Co. in Paintsville for years, winning numerous awards for her work decorating the storefront windows. She also sold Avon cosmetics and worked as a telephone operator for South Central Bell. She is a member of the Van Lear Freewill Baptist Church.

BB and Louise had five children. The eldest son is William E. "Bill" (born November 1947). Bill is married to Shirley Ratliff and they live in Winchester, KY. Their second son is Douglas A. Kretzer (born July

1949). Doug is married to Rhonda Hall and they live in Stanville, KY. The third child was B.C. "Binky" (born December 1951). Binky is married to Rene Hall and they reside in Thelma, KY. The fourth child, and only daughter, is Madonna June (born July 1953). Madonna is married to Reverend Steve Rose and they reside in Flat Gap, KY. Their youngest son is Kenneth David (born October 1959). David is married to DeDra McCarty and they call Van Lear home. At the time of this writing, BB and Louise have 10 grandchildren and three great-grandchildren.

BB attended Mayo State Vocational School and worked at several jobs during his lifetime. He worked in the coal mines, sold insurance, drove soft drink and potato chip trucks, loaded concrete blocks, delivered newspapers, did carpentry work, worked at and owned service stations, and worked for the Kentucky State Highway Dept. - all these while raising gardens, chickens, cows and hogs - whatever it took to provide for five children.

BB and Louise reside in the old Jim King home at the mouth of Sorghum Hollow in Van Lear.

LEMASTER & BLANTON - James Monroe Lemaster and Laura Belle Blanton issue: Merzie Lemaster (born Oct. 1892, Johnson County, KY, died Jul. 5 1977, at her daughter's home in Winifred KY) buried in the Lemaster Cemetery on Little Paint Creek, married Jan. 24, 1914, at James Lemaster's in Johnson County, KY, to Stephen Howard, died circa 1956, son of T.C. and Lydia (Gullett) Howard.

Madge Lemaster (born Jun. 27, 1894, died Feb. 20, 1899).

Hollie Lemaster (born Sep. 2, 1896, Johnson County, KY, died Oct. 29, 1973, in a Paintsville hospital) married Nancy Meade (born Jul. 15, 1897, Johnson County, KY, died Nov. 3, 1987, in Springfield, OH), daughter of Leck and Julia (Howard) Meade. Hollie and Nancy were members of the United Baptist Church, he being a member of the Low Gap Church for over 52 years. Hollie was a retired merchant and postmaster. Both are buried in the Lemaster Cemetery at Winifred, KY.

George Dewey Lemaster (born Jul. 8, 1898, Johnson County, KY, died Mar. 5, 1975, at his Winifred, KY, home, buried in the family cemetery, married Effie Lemaster, Johnson County, KY. George was a member of the United Baptist Church over 58 years.

Lileth Lemaster (born Sep. 1899, died circa 1943) md. Feb. 14, 1918, Roy H. Lemaster (see #1587), md. second, Andrew Stephen Howard.

Beckham Lemaster (born circa 1901, died circa 1930) md. Erie McKenzie.

Hasten Lemaster (born circa 1903) md. Feb. 7, 1925, in New Boston, OH, to Genoa Farley, daughter of Joseph E. and Rachel (Iderson) Farley. Hasten retired from Detroit Steel, New Boston, OH.

Eulah Lemaster (born circa 1906) md. Samuel Norman Stapleton, son of Robert and Martha (Cochran) Stapleton.

Beulah Lemaster (born circa 1906), twin of Eulah, married circa 1923 Lonza Reed (born Aug. 12, 1902) Colvin Branch, Big Paint Creek, Johnson County, KY, son of Asa J. and Elizabeth (Gullett) Reed. Lonza served as a Johnson County, KY, deputy clerk, merchant at Manilla, KY, and was an elder in the United Baptist Church. Elder Lonza was converted Feb. 1, 1921. He joined the old Fishtrap Church and was baptized Feb. 5, 1921. He was ordained in the Fishtrap Church Apr. 16, 1927. In 1940 he was moderator of the Fishtrap Church.

NOTE: From *LEMASTERS USA 1639-1965*, we found the following about Fishtrap Church: Joseph Lemaster (not identified in this series as a preacher) bought 300 acres on Feb. 20, 1841, from Alexander Pelphrey at Fishtrap. (Floyd County Kentucky Deeds.) Joseph Lemaster owned about 1000 acres near Fishtrap, but aside from farming he taught public school and was the pastor of the Fishtrap Baptist Church, about one mile from his large log house. He was a Baptist preacher for over 40 years. Once when a visiting preacher occupied his pulpit, the visitor in the course of his sermon said in a loud voice, "Who has the keys to the Kingdom of Heaven?" There was a prompt reply from on high, actually that of a drunk man lying on top of a cliff above the church house. The reply was, "Uncle Joe Lemaster, he has the keys to everything."

Junie Lemaster (born circa 1908, died circa 1928) never married.

An infant died at birth, Apr. 12, 1914, Johnson County, KY.

Murlie Mae Lemaster (born Oct. 28, 1912, Johnson County KY).

Sarah Myrtle Lemaster (born Apr. 1, 1915, Johnson County, KY) md. Willis Hitchcock.

Emeral Hay Lemaster (born circa 1919) md. Ruby Cantrell, daughter of James Cantrell.

LEMASTER - Johnnie H. Lemaster was born Sep. 22, 1937, on Joe's Creek, near Flat Gap, Johnson County, KY, to Plennie and Anna Tackett Lemaster. He was the sixth of 11 children, two died as infants and his brother, James Everett, died while being held captive during the Korean War. He has six sisters and one brother living at the present time.

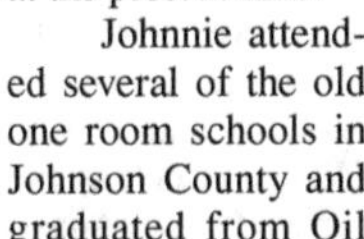

Johnnie and Judy Lemaster with granddaughter, Emily Taylor Bunch.

Johnnie attended several of the old one room schools in Johnson County and graduated from Oil Springs High School. After graduating from high school he worked at various jobs, Adam's Construction Co., Carroll Pelphrey's Auto Sales and fruit markets and a short time at Swan Rubber Co. of Carey, OH. He entered the Army on Nov. 3, 1960, and spent most of two years in Germany. Upon completion of his military obligation he again worked for Adam's Construction for a short time and for Vic McKenzie Drilling operations in Ohio. On Apr. 17, 1964, he went to work for Armco Steel Corp. in Ashland, KY, and just recently retired with 36 years of service.

Johnnie married Judy Groves, daughter of Claude and Dovie Groves, of Ashland, KY, on Mar. 15, 1966. They are the parents of two daughters, Tracy Renee (born Aug. 10, 1968) and Amy Elizabeth (born May 11, 1973). Tracy married David Bunch and they live in Lexington, KY, and have blessed Johnnie and Judy with two beautiful granddaughters, Emily Taylor (born Jun. 19, 1995) and Olivia Ann (born Jul. 24, 1999). Amy married David Russell "Rusty" Gray and they live in Ashland. Both Tracy and Amy graduated from Boyd County High School as did their mother, Judy. Tracy attended Eastern State University at Richmond and is at present a homemaker, her husband, David, works for Toyota Corp. in Georgetown, KY. Amy graduated from Ashland State Vocational Technical School and is a beautician, employed at Beau Monde Beauty Spa near Ashland. Her husband, Rusty, is employed by United Parcel Service at Cannonsburg, KY.

Johnnie's hobbies used to include hunting and fishing until an injury caused him to give up these sports a few years ago. He does some genealogy work and likes to study family history. He is a member of several historical and genealogy societies.

LEMASTER - John Lowell LeMaster was born Nov. 16, 1920, at Flat Gap, KY, to Bascom LeMaster and Florence Harris LeMaster. He was the youngest son of eight children born to his parents, descendants of Huguenots of France.

John was married to Mabel Fyffe LeMaster on Aug. 4, 1945. They were the parents of two sons, Link B. (born Oct. 30, 1946) and Johnnie Lee (born Jun. 19, 1954).

John Lowell Lemaster

John was a graduate of Flat Gap High School in 1939 and attended Pikeville College. September 1942, he was drafted in the Army for WWII. He served in the China-Burma-India Theatre until November 1945.

He attended Mayo Vocational School and trained for a welding job in the Pipefitters-Steamfitters Union. He worked as a welder on several construction jobs before spending the last 18 years at the Ashland Oil Plant at Catlettsburg, KY, before retiring.

He was an avid farmer, always gardening at the family farm at Franks Creek.

He is an active member of the Paintsville United Baptist Church where he serves as deacon.

His son, Link, earned his master's degree from Morehead University. He is employed by Leonard Lawson of Mountain Enterprises. He married Jane VanHoose LeMaster. She also received her master's degree from Morehead University and teaches primary education at Paintsville Elementary School. They have a son, Link Bryant, attending Pikeville College and a daughter, Carrie Maree attending Morehead University. They are all active members of the Church of Christ.

Johnnie "Peanut" graduated from Paintsville High School in 1973. In June 1973, he was the first round draft choice of San Francisco Giants Baseball Team. He married Debra Parsley LeMaster, bookkeeper and interior decorator. They have two daughters, Brandi Nicole and Amber Lea. In their double wedding, Brandi married Joe Collins and Amber married Craig Ratliff. Brandi is attending Medical School and Amber is enrolled at Morehead University. Amber and Craig are the proud parents of a son, Braxton (born Aug. 5, 1999). They are all active members of the Church of Christ.

LEMASTER - Mabel Fyffe LeMaster was born Oct. 8, 1922, at Keaton, KY, to Link Fyffe and Stella Wright Fyffe. She is the oldest child of six born to her parents of Scotch-Irish descent.

Mabel was married in Paintsville, KY, to John Lowell LeMaster on Aug. 4, 1945. They are the parents of two sons, Link B. (born Oct. 30, 1946) and Johnnie Lee (born Jun. 19, 1954).

Mable LeMaster

Mabel was a graduate of Flat Gap High School in 1940. After graduation, she attended Morehead University where she earned her AB, master's and Rank I degrees. She taught elementary school at Red Bush, Staffordsville, Keaton before coming to Paintsville second grade. She also served as elementary and high school counselor and assistant superintendent. She was very active in her profession for 32 years, serving as Federal Programs director, Head Start director, lunch room coordinator.

She loves cooking, arts and crafts, traveling and baseball. She is an active member of the Paintsville United Baptist Church and serves as president of the Ladies Fellowship Circle. She holds life membership in PTA, is a Kentucky Colonel, a home maker and many other civic organizations.

Her son, Link, earned his master's degree from Morehead University and is employed by Leonard Lawson of Mountain Enterprises. He married Jane VanHoose LeMaster who also received her master's degree from Morehead and teaches primary block at Paintsville Elementary School. They have a son, Link Bryant, an avid golfer, attending Pikeville College and a daughter, Carrie Maree, a four-point student attending Morehead University.

Johnnie "Peanut" was first round draft choice of San Francisco Giants when he graduated from High School in 1973. He married Debra Parsley LeMaster, bookkeeper and interior decorator. They have two daughters, Brandi Nicole and Amber Lea. In their double wedding, Brandi married Joe Collins, while Amber married Craig Ratliff. Brandi is attending Medical School and Amber is attending Morehead University. Craig and Amber are proud parents of Braxton Ratliff (born Aug. 5, 1999).

LEMASTER - Mae Lemaster was the daughter of James M. and Laura Blanton Lemaster. She was born Oct. 28, 1912.

Mae Lemaster

Mae was a delightful part of a family of 14 children. Merzie (born Oct. 4, 1892) married Stephen Howard; Madge (born Jun. 27, 1894, died at age 4); Hollie (born Sep. 2, 1896) married Nancy Meade; George D. (born Jul. 8, 1898) married Effie Lemaster; Lileth (born Nov. 10, 1899) married Roy Lemaster and Little Steve Howard second; Beckham (born Jun. 22, 1901) married Erie McKenzie; Hasten (born Nov. 4, 1903) married Genoa ?; Eulah (born Mar. 23, 1906) married Norman Stapleton; Beulah (born Mar. 23, 1906) married Lonza Reed; Junie (born Jun. 6, 1908, died age 19); infant son (born and died in April 1910); Mae (born Oct. 28, 1912) never married; Myrtle (born Apr. 1, 1915) married Willie Hitchcock; Emeral (born 1919) married Ruby Cantrell.

Mae had a rich background, the daughter of James M. Lemaster and Laura Blanton Lemaster; the granddaughter of Daniel P. and Phebe Bayes Lemaster, James McHenry Blanton and Sarah Jane McCarty; the great-granddaughter of Lewis and Martha Phillips Lemaster, Elijah and Margaret Rice Bayes, James H. and Mary "Polly" Davis Blanton, Nelson and Louisa Blanton McCarty; and the great-great-granddaughter of Eleazor and Machell Tackett Lemaster, Samuel and Phebe Hitchcock Rice Sr., George and Martha Shepherd Blanton, Elias and Elizabeth Curtis Davis and John P. and Clarissa ? McCarty.

She taught school, building fires, walking to work, later clearing the road to drive a jeep or car. Mae was truly a lady ahead of her time.

LEMASTER - Plennie Lemaster was born on Mar. 3, 1903, on Joe's Creek at Flat Gap, to Thomas Manford and Minerva Hitchcock Lemaster. He was the ninth of 12 children born to his parents, seven boys and five girls. Plennie, like most of his generation got very little formal education since all the boys were needed for labor on the farm. He only went to the third grade.

Plennie met Anna Tackett, daughter of John Franklin and Clara Blevins Tackett, and they were married on Jul. 25, 1927. Plennie and Anna had a rich heritage as their ancestors include the Lemaster, Tackett, Hitchcock, Blevins, Cantrell, Caudill, Picklesimer, Bayes, Shepherd, Conley, Blanton, Salyer, Christian, Owens and Shaver families, just to name a few.

Plennie worked at various jobs, coal mines, the railroad and at the end of the depression he was working on the WPA. He helped build several of the schools and gymnasiums that this program built in Johnson County. Although he worked at various trades he was really a sharecrop farmer. He would rent a farm and pay a portion of the crops to the landlord for rent. This sounds crude by today's standards but was an acceptable agreement in those days. Like most other families in those days they didn't have a lot but managed to take care of the family quiet well. There was always a cow for milk and butter and a hog to butcher and plenty of chickens and eggs. Plennie never owned an automobile or even learned to drive. He always kept a nice pair of mules, was a lifelong fox hunter and always kept a pack of hounds.

Plennie and Anna Tackett Lemaster

Plennie and Anna moved around quite often but lived all their lives in Johnson County. They reared a family of four boys and seven girls including one set of twins. Their first child, Wallace Franklin died shortly after birth in 1928. James Everett joined the Army at an early age and died in a POW camp in Korea in 1951. Roberta married Burl McCarty and lives on Rockhouse. Jessie Grace married Edward Cochran and they live in Fairborn, OH. Irene married Chester Auxier and they live at Red Bush. Johnnie, after graduating from Oil Springs High School, spent two years in the Army and has worked at Armco Steel in Ashland for 36 years. He married Judy Groves. Joan married Burt Blanton. Her twin, Jeanette, died when she was 2. Garland, after graduating from Oil Springs, married Valeeta Kestner. Garland worked for Bush and Burchett Bridge Building Co. for several years. Lillian married Jimmy Butcher. They are divorced and Lillian lives in Columbus, OH. Darlene married Jerry McKenzie and lives on Pickle Fork.

In 1953 Plennie and Anna bought a farm on Rockhouse where they lived the rest of their lives. Plennie died Dec. 6, 1985, from cancer and Anna had a stroke and was bedfast for the last four years of her life. She died Jul. 26, 1995. They are buried in Highland Memorial at Staffordsville.

LEMASTER - Rudolph Chandler Lemaster (born May 11, 1922, in Pleasant Township, Clark County, OH) married Aug. 23, 1945, in Marysville, OH, to Joy Evelyn Applegate (born Mar. 2, 1925, in Woodstock, OH).

He enlisted in the USAAC in Columbus, OH, October 1942 (WWII) and eventually earned his wings as a pilot, Jun. 27, 1944, at San Antonio, TX. He was discharged in October 1945 and entered the Ohio State University, January 1946 and graduated September 1948 with a major in accounting and a BS in business administration. He worked as an accountant for a property and Causality Insurance Co. for seven years, then transferred into statistics and pricing. He retired Dec. 31, 1986, as the vice president of the Actuarial Div.

His parents, Auta and Jessie Catherine (Chandler) Lemaster, were both born in Johnson County, KY. Dad, at Low Gap, Mar. 18, 1891, died Apr. 30, 1967, at Marysville, OH. Mother was born Jun. 9, 1894, at Chandlersville, KY, died Oct. 18, 1966, at Marysville, OH, both interred there in the Oakdale Cemetery. They were married Mar. 16, 1912, and started housekeeping in the Oil Branch, where his brother, Kenneth, was born Jun. 30, 1913. His parents moved to Plattsburg, OH, in 1918.

The Lemaster family French Huguenots spelled L'Maistree anglicized to Lemaster in the middle 1600s. They spent over a century in western Maryland then migrated to Amherst County, VA. Then to Spartenburg County, SC, then its Lee County, VA, or Knox County, KY. They arrived in what is known today as Johnson County, KY (formed 1843), out of Floyd, Lawrence and Morgan counties.

Two brothers, John and Eleazer, both settled in Johnson County prior to the 1810 census. John and his family settled along Big Paint Creek, while Eleazer settled at Volga. His direct descendancy is to John, but he also has two lines going back to Eleazor.

John was a trapper and farmer and when the game became scarce he and five of his sons and families moved to Missouri in the spring of 1842. John's wife, Frances Tackett, died Jun. 26, 1842, probably in Barry County, MO. John died there Sep. 16, 1846.

In May 1840, these members of Bethel Baptist Church received letters of dismissal to form Fish Trap Baptist Church: John and Frances (Tackett) Lemaster, Lewis and Martha (Phillips) Lemaster, Francis and Rachel (Reed) Lemaster, Joseph and Elinor (Wheeler) Lemaster, Joseph and Elizabeth (Lemaster) Williams. Fish Trap was organized Jul. 11, 1840.

Other members involved in the organization of Fish Trap were elder Ben Caudal, pastor and moderator from organization until March 1849, Alexander and Alce (Lemaster) Pelphrey, James and Mary Ann "Polly" Pelphrey (son of Alexander) who served as pastor and moderator from April 1849-November 1888.

Joseph's son, Isaac, is Rudolph's great-grandfather. Isaac married Mary Frances Barker of Morgan County but lived at Kenwood at Low Gap, KY.

Rudolph's grandfather is William Henry Lemaster, son of Isaac, who married Nora Alice Williams. Dad was the oldest of William Henry's family.

LEWANDOWSKI - The Lewandowski family came to Oaklawn Drive in Hagerhill in August 1991. Eileen (nee Markham) teaches communications at Prestonsburg Community College; Robert J. "Bob" is with Big Sandy Area Development Dist. Originally from Chicago, they've lived in Streamwood, IL (1965-73), Fond du Lac (1973-83) and Rice Lake, WI (1983-89).

L-R: Scott Jamison holding Taylor and Judi Jamison, Bob, Carol and Marc Cournouer, Eileen, Mary and Bob Waghorne.

Bob (U.S. Army 1960-62) attended De Paul University and University of Wisconsin. He has been active in Streamwood AMVETS and Haugen and Prestonsburg Kiwanis Clubs.

Eileen graduated from University of Illinois (AB 1963 in the teaching of speech 712). She spent many years teaching speech, math and English, coaching debate and forensics and adjunct college instructor. Her MA in speech communication is from Northern Illinois University (1973) and she's a doctoral candidate in the University of Kentucky College of Communications/Information Studies. She belongs to Leadership Kentucky Alumni, Johnson County Democratic Women's Club, East Kentucky Women in Leadership and participates in many community activities. Duties at

PCC have included the Appalachian Civic Leadership Project, Service Learning and AmericaReads. She is an associate of The Appalachian Center at U.K.

While living near Rice Lake, they owned and managed The Kamping Place on Devils Lake, a K.O.A. Kampground, and were members of Wisconsin Indian Head Country tourism region and Wisconsin Association of Campground Owners.

Their youngest daughter, Carol Dianne (Mrs. Marc) Cournoyer, joined the family in Kentucky after graduation (BSW 1990) from the College of St. Benedict in St. Joseph, MN. She worked for BSADD and the Big Sandy Family Abuse Center. Her internship in wellness management at Highlands Regional Medical Center's Wellness Center completed graduate studies at Ball State University in Muncie, IN. Carol and Marc married Jun. 24, 1996, at St. Michael's Church in Paintsville. Marc came to Kentucky as a volunteer with Christian Appalachian Project after graduation from the University of Rhode Island, worked with Mountain Comprehensive Care and Christian Appalachian Project's youth programs. The Cournoyers relocated (November 1996) to his native New England, for Marc's position, youth minister at St. Mary's Church in Groton. They live in Ledyard, CT, and have one daughter, Tessa Nicole (born Dec. 6, 1997). Carol is an administrative officer of The Spa at The Inn at Norwich.

The Lewandowskis' other two daughters, Judith Ann (Mrs. Scott) Jamison and Mary Catherine (Mrs. Robert) Waghorne, reside in Spokane, WA, and Western Springs, IL, respectively.

Judi, a violist with the Spokane Symphony and the Syringa String Quartet, is the mother of Taylor Eileen (born Jun. 25, 1995) and Lauren Regina (born Jul. 4, 1997). She is a graduate (BA 1986) of the Lawrence University Conservatory of Music (Appleton, WI), with a MS in viola performance (1989) from Bowling Green State University in Ohio.

Mary, an attorney, is the proud and happy mother of Maxwell Flynn (born Jul. 21, 1998). She, too, graduated from Lawrence University, earning her (BA 1987) degree in government. Mary worked in the securities industry before returning to De Paul University (Chicago) for her LLD (1996).

LEWIS - Ralph Lewis married Ann Prichard. He was a land owner of Eglwysilan, Wales and died there. The children of Ralph and Ann Lewis are listed in the Parish of Eglwysilan, Glamorganshire, Wales. Ann was the daughter of Richard Evan and Catherine Baset.

Their children were William Lewis born around 1636, Ralph Lewis, David Lewis and Susanna Lewis born around 1672.

William Lewis born ca. 1636, Eglwysilan Parish, Glamorganshire, Wales, married Ann Lewis, died ca. 1708, Newton, PA. William died ca. 1708-9, Newtown, PA. William and his wife Ann, came from Wales about 1686, and settled at Haverford Township, PA. They moved to Newtown, PA, where he and his wife died. They were both members of the Society of Friends (Quakers) Church.

Children of William and Ann Lewis were David Lewis, Lewis Lewis (born ca. 1674); Evan Lewis (born ca, 1677); William Lewis II (born ca. 1680); Seaborn Lewis (born ca. 1686 at sea).

William Lewis II, born ca. 1680, married 1st Gwen Jones on Aug. 27, 1704 in Gwyenedd Meeting House, Gwyenedd, PA. Married 2nd Lowery Jones on Jan. 7, 1717 in Gwyenedd Meeting House, Gwyenedd, PA. William died ca. 1731.

Gwen was the daughter of William John Jones and Jane Jones. Children of William and Gwen: Jephtha Lewis, Enos Lewis, William Lewis III, Nathan Lewis (born Sep. 21, 1705.

Children of William and Lowery Jones: Benjamin Lewis, Gideon Lewis I (born ca. 1710), Ann Lewis and Ambrose Lewis.

Gideon Lewis I (born ca. 1710). Probably more children than listed. Gideon Lewis II (born ca. 1730), James Lewis (born Aug. 9, 1736), Nathan Lewis and Theophilus Lewis (not proven).

Gideon Lewis II (born ca. 1730); children: Gideon Lewis III (born ca. 1765) and Elizabeth Lewis.

Isaac Lewis (born ca. 1773), North Carolina married Susanna Osborne. Isaac died ca. 1843. Their children were Jacob (No Fingered) Lewis (born ca. 1824), Gideon (Rock Creek) Lewis. Probably lived on Rock Creek, Isaac Jr. Lewis, William Lewis, Phillip Lewis and Rebecca Lewis.

Officer in the War of 1812. Isaac Lewis (born ca. 1773), George Lewis, James Lewis (born ca. 1779), Hiram Lewis, Richard Lewis (born ca. 1775). Nathan Lewis and Jacob (No Fingered) Lewis (born ca. 1824), married Delilah Robinson (born ca. 1824). Their children were William Preston Lewis, Isaac Lewis, listed in Floyd County, KY census 1880; Enoch Lewis (born 1847), David Lewis, John Cicero (Red Fox) Lewis (born Feb. 13, 1848), Sarah Lewis, Mary Lewis, Frank Lewis, Marion Lewis, Elbert Lewis, Laura Lewis, Dicy Lewis.

John Cicero (Red Fox) Lewis (born Feb. 13, 1848), Ash County, NC), married Martha Jane Graybeal (born Jan. 19, 1847, Ash County, NC, died Dec. 27, 1928). John died Jan. 9, 1929. John and Martha came to Kentucky about 1888. They are buried on their farm at Williamsport, near Paintsville in Johnson County, KY.

Their children were Callie Lewis (born Apr. 5, 1870, North Carolina, died Feb. 9, 1926; Avery Lewis (born ca. 1872, North Carolina) married Callie Preston; Eli Lewis (born ca. 1874, North Carolina) married Ina Estep; Walter Lewis (born ca. 1887, North Carolina) married Gypsie Robinson; Mona Lewis (born ca. 1878, North Carolina) married first to Harlan White and second to Carl Preston; Emma Lewis (born ca. 1882, North Carolina) married Henry Harmon; Roby Lewis (born ca. 1885, North Carolina) married Bulah Sanders; Hillary Lewis (born ca. 1880, North Carolina) married Marthia or Martha Hall; William Lewis (born ca. 1889, Kentucky) married Hattie Childers; Clyde Lewis (born ca. 1891, Kentucky) married first to Anna Nunnary, married second to Elizabeth Evans.

Frank Lewis (born Mar. 6, 1876, North Carolina) married 1st to Susan Meek, married 2nd, Cora Mollett (born Mar. 4, 1889, Kentucky, died Jun. 3, 1950, Kentucky), Frank died 1967, Johnson County, KY.

Their children were Oscar Lewis (born ca. 1898, died young); Mary Lewis (born ca. 1900, died young); Sarah Lewis (born ca. 1903, died 1970s); John R. Lewis (born ca. 1905). Children by Cora Mollett: Geneva Lewis (born ca. 1911, Kentucky, died 1937 of T.B.); George Lewis (born ca. 1913); Rose Lewis (born ca. 1915); Clyde Lewis (born 1917); Ethel Lewis (born 1919); Marthia (Martha Mae) Lewis; Walter Lewis (born Nov. 16, 1925); Ruth Lewis; Frank Jr. Lewis (born Dec. 23, 1934); Callie Lewis died young; Faye Lewis died at birth.

Walter Lewis born Nov. 16, 1925, Kentucky) married 1st, Louise Webb, 2nd, Daisy Dee Nicely (born Jan. 20, 1934, West Virginia, died Jun. 11, 1972, Cincinnati, OH).

Children by Louise Webb: Claudia Lewis (born ca. 1948); Keith Lewis (born 1950). Children by Daisy Dee Nicley: Pamela Lewis (born Oct. 25, 1953); Tracy Lewis (born Apr. 29, 1956); Geneva Lewis (born Sep. 16, 1961); Kelly Adrian Lewis (born Nov. 6, 1967).

LITTLE & RUSSELL - My mother, Rose Emily Schaus, was born in Ohio on Sep. 6, 1894. My father, Ed Alderson Russell, was born in Lawrence County, KY, on Jul. 29, 1886. They met in Catlettsburg, KY, and married in 1915. They lived at Thealka, KY, and later moved to Van Lear, KY, where Ed worked as a trackman in #5 mine for Consolidated Coal Co. Three children were born to this couple: Luther Clevland Russell, Ed Alderson Russell Jr. and Sarah Elizabeth Russell.

Luther Clevland Russell was born on Dec. 9, 1916. He married Ruth Wallen and they have three children: Luther Clevland Russell Jr., Roger Russell and Cherri Russell. Luther Jr. married Judy Slone. They have two sons, David and Jason. Roger married Tammy Slone, and they have two children, Dustin and Jesikah. Cherri married Danny Davis. They have four children: Brooke, Stephen, Aaron and Adam.

Ed Alderson Russell Jr. "Red" was born on Nov. 20, 1918. He married Winifred Merdith.

Elizabeth Russell was born on Nov. 11, 1920. She married Ervin Little and they have three children: Jerry Simpson, Carolyn Simpson and Stephen Little. Jerry married Sarah Hall, and they are the parents of two sons, Christopher and Todd. Carolyn married Robert Branham. They have three children: Ashley, Bradley and Dustin. Stephen married Susan Shaler. They have two sons, Alexander and Nathaniel.

Luther, Red and Elizabeth grew up in Van Lear and finished school at the Van Lear schools. They went to #5 school for four years and then to the lower schools until finishing high school. Later, all three Russells went on to work in the #5 company store. Luther and Red worked in the coal mines next. Then, WWII started, and Luther joined the Navy. Red entered the Marines. After the war, Luther lived in West Virginia for a while and then returned to west Van Lear, KY, where he lives today. His children all live nearby in the same area. Red lived in Michigan for many years before retiring to Lakeland, FL, where he lives today. Elizabeth lived in Wheelwright, KY, until her husband's death. She then moved to Betsy Layne, KY, where she lives today. She stays busy with church clubs, senior citizens organization and traveling. Her son, Jerry, lives nearby in Paintsville, KY. Her daughter, Carolyn, lives nearby in Pikeville, KY. Her son, Stevie, lives in Lexington, KY.

LYON - Con Lyon, son of Sherman and Lora Ellen Wallin Lyon, was born at Keaton, Johnson County, KY, Dec. 12, 1919. Con was born at home and was named after the attending doctor, Dr. Con Rice. Con has been a life long resident of Johnson County. He is one of four children born to Sherman and Lora. Con attended a one room school at Lower Keaton where the school day began with the pledge to the American Flag and Bible reading. He also became a welder by attending Mayo State Vocational School in Paintsville.

Con and Fredia Sowards Lyon

Con entered the U.S. Army on Oct. 7, 1942, and after the war ended he was discharged Jan. 13, 1946. He served in England, France, Belgium and Germany. He fought in the Battle of the Bulge. His unit marched for two days and nights and were finally met and transported by trucks to Marseilles, France.

Con married Fredia Sowards on Nov. 6, 1943, in Paintsville, KY.

Fredia (born Aug. 23, 1924) is the daughter of John Leonard Sowards (born Feb. 22, 1894, died Nov. 1, 1959) and Fannie "Sug" Roberts Sowards (born Jun. 27, 1896, died Mar. 19, 1978). Fredia attended both grade and high school in Paintsville.

Con and Fredia have two sons, Wayne (born Jun. 1, 1949) and Con Edward (born Feb. 18, 1960). They have five grandchildren and 10 great-grandchildren.

Con grew up on the family farm at Keaton and still owns part of the farm. Con's son, Edward, lives on the farm. Con always had a special interest in the farm animals. He and his brother, Kerlin, had a yoke of oxen they trained to work and also to be ridden. Con has maintained his love of horses and still owns one today.

He provided for his family by doing both welding

and mechanical work. Con worked for Oliver Jenkins for 18 years and for National Mines for 19 years. He retired in 1981. He and Fredia live at Sitka where they continue to enjoy their grandchildren, great-grandchildren, farm animals, gardening, reading and fox hunting. Con and Fredia are members of the Rock House Freewill Baptist Church.

Con loves people and is an entertaining story teller of happenings of the olden days. *Submitted by Clista M. McKenzie Pelfrey.*

LYON - Janieve Hamilton was born Jun. 25, 1925, at Keaton, Johnson County, KY, to John J. and Nancy Skaggs Hamilton. Nancy was born Oct. 24, 1899, in Morgan County, KY. John was born Sep. 10, 1891, in Johnson County, KY. John and Nancy met at church at Crocket in Morgan County and were later married on Feb. 2, 1923. They made their home at Keaton. John and Nancy are buried in Johnson County. The Hamiltons came from Ireland and first settled in Delaware, then in Pennsylvania and next in Virginia. Benjamin and Thomas Hamilton are Revolutionary War veterans. They came from Virginia to Kentucky and Thomas settled in Flat Gap, Johnson County, KY. Benjamin settled in Morgan County.

Janieve Hamilton Lyon

John J. Hamilton was a WWI veteran. He owned and operated a farm of 100 acres at Keaton. He also worked in the oil field at Keaton and at one time in a steel mill at Chicago, IN. His wife, Nancy J. Skaggs Hamilton, was a homemaker and the mother of five children. Janieve is the oldest; Fred Hamilton was born May 25, 1927; Arlene Hamilton was born Feb. 20, 1931; Bill Ivan Hamilton was born Sep. 2, 1933; and Estene Hamilton was born May 17, 1937.

Janieve lived at Keaton the first 22 years of her life. Janieve and her brothers and sisters attended a one room grade school at Upper Keaton. They grew up on the farm and learned how to keep house and do farm chores. They had many overnight visits from cousins and friends. They attended the local Baptist churches that were within walking distances. Janieve attended Flat Gap High School. She was blessed with wonderful grandparents, Franklin and Miranda Lyon Hamilton and William and Anna Ellen Ison Skaggs.

During WWII, Janieve worked in a defense plant in Ypsilanti, MI. After coming back to Kentucky, she became reacquainted with Kerlin Lyon and they married Aug. 29, 1947, at Paintsville. Kerlin was also born and reared at Keaton.

Janieve and Kerlin have three children with the first two being born while they lived at Keaton. Linda Carol was born May 20, 1948; Barbara Jean born Sep. 22, 1949; and Mark Kerlin born Oct. 4, 1959.

Janieve is a member of the Hoods Creek Freewill Baptist Church on Rt. 5 in Ashland, KY. She is a dedicated mother and Christian woman and was blessed to be a full time homemaker while her children were growing up. She provided transportation for her children to school and back before school bus service was established. Janieve and her husband continue to fully enjoy life as parents, grandparents and church workers. *Submitted by Clista M. McKenzie Pelfrey.*

LYON - Kerlin Lyon (born Mar. 14, 1922, at Keaton, KY) is the son of Sherman (born Dec. 25, 1871) and Lora Ellen Wallin Lyon (born Dec. 21, 1883). Both parents were born and reared in Johnson County. They had known each other several years before they started dating. Both were reared in church-going families. They were married Dec. 8, 1908, and both were members of the Red Bush Enterprise Church where Sherman served as deacon for several years. One responsibility of a deacon's wife was to bake unleavened bread for use with the communion/ foot-washing service.

Kerlin Lyon

Kerlin is the youngest of four children. His siblings are Beulah Lyon McKenzie (born Sep. 11, 1910), Tivis Lyon (born Mar. 8, 1915) and Con Lyon (born Dec. 12, 1919). Sherman owned a store, worked in the oil field at Keaton, and operated the 105 acre farm that they owned and where they also made their home. Lora Ellen was a homemaker, assisted with the store, took care of her children and her mother who lived with them. Lora was an avid Bible student and discussed Bible issues with her family and friends.

Kerlin grew up on the Keaton farm and enjoyed many overnight visits from cousins and friends. He had a great love for his own horse and was involved in taking care of all the farm animals and doing required chores. He attended the one room grade school at Lower Keaton and graduated from high school at Flat Gap. He had to walk through the hills from Keaton to Red Bush to catch the school bus.

Kerlin played basketball for the Flat Gap Greyhounds on the dirt court behind the school. There was no electricity, no running water and no cheerleaders. They did have wonderful, dedicated teachers who taught much more than reading, writing and arithmetic.

Kerlin joined the USAAF in September 1942, during WWII and served as a radar repairman in North Africa, Italy, France and Germany. During the time Kerlin was in the Army, his mother died. After his discharge, his first job was for Rural Electric Association stringing electrical wire up the hollow to the home place. Kerlin used a horse to pull the wire.

Kerlin courted the love of his life, Janieve Hamilton, and they married Aug. 29, 1947, at Paintsville. Janieve was also reared at Keaton, the child of John and Nancy Skaggs Hamilton. Kerlin and Janieve are the parents of three children: Linda Carol (born May 20, 1948), Barbara Jean (born Sep. 22, 1949) and Mark Kerlin (born Oct. 4, 1959).

Kerlin and Janieve are members of the Hoods Creek Freewill Baptist Church on Rt. 5, Ashland, KY. Kerlin worked for the C & O Chessie CSX Railroad as an electrical supervisor for 32 years. After his retirement in 1982, he and his wife, Janieve, have enjoyed many years working with their church, fishing, playing golf, traveling, spoiling grandchildren and loving family and friends. *Submitted by Clista M. McKenzie Pelfrey.*

LYON - The Lyon family was started in Scotland by Sir John Lyon of Forteviost. He was knighted in 1372 after he helped conquer Scotland from Normandy. The Lyon family began to build Glamis Castle about 1400. Sir John Lyon was made a Lord of Scotland, as a reward for his services, he was the first Lyon to occupy Glamis Castle. About 1767 the ninth Earl married an English heiress and assumed her family name of Bowes. Later the 13th Earl reinstated the name of Lyon by taking the name of Bowes-Lyon which is still in use today.

Landon and Nancy Skaggs Lyon

About 1770 Lord Lyon had four sons. It was the custom that the eldest son inherited the title and all the wealth, in order to compete with rival lords for prestige and popularity with the King. The younger sons had to make it on their own. The three younger Lyon brothers came to America from Scotland in the 1700s. The younger brothers: Andrew, Stephen and William Lyon, were apparently forced by their older brother to leave the place of their birth, Glamis Castle on Tayake in Scotland, and to come to America in 1772. This older brother married a Bowes. (Incidentally, the Queen Mother is a Bowes-Lyon and at 99 is the oldest living descendant of William Lyon Sr.) The present Earl, Michael Bowes-Lyon, the 18th Earl of Strathmore and Kinghorne is married to Isobel and they have three sons, the heir: Simon Patrick Bowes-Lyon, Lord Glamis; the Honorable John Fergus Bowes-Lyon and the Honorable George Norman Bowes-Lyon.

William Lyon Sr., after being forced to leave Scotland, was reported to be very resentful of this. He settled in North Carolina and had records falsified to show he was born there on Feb. 17, 1752. He married Magdilla Corbin in Culpepper County, VA. Magdilla was born in 1752 in North Carolina.

William joined the American Army and fought through the Revolutionary War under George Washington. After the war, he settled for a time in Wilkes County, NC, on the Yadkin River. William and Magdilla later moved to Kentucky and settled at the mouth of Keaton Fork in Lawrence County.

William and Magdilla had six sons and three daughters: William Jr., Lewis, John, James, Alexander, Jesse, Sarah, Mary and Francis.

1) William Lyon Jr. md. Nancy Skaggs.

2) Lewis Lyon md. Sine Grizzle.

3) John Lyon (born Feb. 10, 1776) came to Kentucky in 1824, and died Sep. 11, 1862, md. Mary Polly Holbrook.

4) James Lyon md. Nancy Large.

5) Alexander Lyon md. Sarah Sparks.

6) Jesse Lyon md. Frances Holbrook.

7) Sarah Lyon md. Lewis Sparks.

8) Mary Lyon md. John Holbrook.

9) Frances Lyon never married.

William Lyon Sr. died Apr. 15, 1847; Magdilla Corbin Lyon died in 1847. William Sr. and Magdilla are buried at Martha, in Lawrence County in the Holbrook Cemetery on the Con Rice farm.

See Sherman Lyon history also. *Submitted by W.H. Pat and Clista M. McKenzie Pelfrey.*

LYON - This Lyon history is to follow the lineage from 1372, Lyon family in Scotland to the 1999 Lyon family of Keaton, KY.

1) William Lyon Sr. (born in Scotland, Feb. 17, 1752) came to America as young adult, died Apr. 15, 1847, married Magdilla Corbin (born 1752, died 1847), both buried on the Con Rice farm in the Holbrook Cemetery at Martha, KY.

2) William's son, John Lyon (born Feb. 10, 1774, died Sep. 11, 1862), married Nancy Polly Holbrook (unable to locate place of burial).

Sherman and Lora Wallin Lyon, children Beulah (standing), Con in Sherman's lap, Tivis (standing), Kerlin (in Lora's lap).

3) John's son, William Lyon (born Mar. 10, 1811,

died Dec. 30, 1895), married Linnie Skaggs, both buried in the Lyon Cemetery at Keaton, KY.

4) William's son, Landon Lyon (born Mar. 10, 1853, died Jan. 23, 1938), married Nancy Skaggs, both buried in the Lyon Cemetery at Keaton, KY.

5) Landon's son, Sherman Lyon (born Dec. 25, 1879, died Dec. 7, 1954) married Lora Ellen Wallin, both buried in the Lyon Cemetery at Keaton, KY.

Sherman Lyon, son of Landon and Nancy Skaggs Lyon (born Dec. 25, 1879, at Red Bush in Johnson County, KY), grew up attending one room schools and country Baptist churches. He met Lora Ellen Wallin at church, while they were both young, and they fell in love and married Dec. 8, 1908. Lora was born in Morgan County Dec. 21, 1883, to Dr. Elihue Tivis and Martha Jane Pennington Wallin. Sherman was a farmer, oil field employee and a country store owner/operator. Lora was a wife, homemaker and mother. She developed refined skills in designing and constructing garments for both women and men. Lora was an avid Bible student and spent many hours in Bible study. Sherman and Lora loved to sing mountain hymns and ballads.

Sherman and Lora had four children: Beulah Lyon (born Sep. 11, 1910) married Ray McKenzie), Tivis Lyon (born Mar. 8, 1915) married Inez Ross, Con Lyon (born Dec. 12, 1919) married Fredia Sowards and Kerlin Lyon (born Mar. 14, 1922) married Janieve Hamilton.

In their early married life they lived at Paintsville and owned and operated a country store. They decided to return to the family farm at Keaton. Sherman and Lora were members of the Red Bush Enterprise Church. Sherman was a deacon there for many years. Lora always baked the unleavened bread that was used during Communion service.

Sherman and Lora are buried in the Lyon Cemetery at Keaton, KY. Lora's parents are buried in the Hamilton Cemetery at Red Bush on Ford Hamilton's farm.

The Lyon farm at Keaton is owned and occupied by one of Sherman and Lora Lyon's heirs. *Submitted by William H. and Clista M. McKenzie Pelfrey.*

LYON - Tivis Lyon was born in Paintsville, KY, Mar. 8, 1915, to Sherman and Lora Wallen Lyon. He attended Paintsville Elementary School and had Claudia Butler as his first grade teacher. When his parents bought a farm on Noisy Branch at Keaton, KY, Tivis attended and graduated from Flat Gap High School.

Tivis and Inez Ross Lyon

On May 30, 1936, he married his high school sweetheart, Inez Ross, of Franks Creek, KY. Their first child, Tivis Jay Lyon Jr., was born Jun. 9, 1937.

The Great Depression still lingered in much of the nation, so to support his new bride, Tivis hitchhiked to southern Ohio where he cut corn for 50¢ a day. With this income and farming the young family managed a happy if not affluent life.

Joe Allen Lyon, their second son, was born in February 1940. 1940 was also the year Tivis began work for Jenkins Drilling which was owned by Oliver Jenkins and "Ope" Roberts of Paintsville.

Because he was drilling for natural gas he was declared an essential worker and was not drafted in WWII. His brothers, who were drafted, persuaded him not to volunteer and that he was needed in the search for energy resources.

In August 1943 their third son, Russell Kerlin Lyon, was born near Red Bush, KY, as Inez was being taken to Paintsville for the impending birth. His birth certificate lists Paintsville as his place of birth.

In 1943 the family moved to Paintsville in order for their children to go to the Paintsville school system. Tivis Jr. also had Claudia Butler as his first grade teacher.

Michael Ross Lyon, their fourth son, was born Mar. 3, 1946, and their only daughter, Cara Lynn Lyon, was born Nov. 18, 1954.

In 1960 Tivis and Inez purchased a farm at the junction of Barnetts Creek Road and Route 40. They lived there until their deaths.

For many years Inez was well known for her special cakes and candies which provided a supplemental income for the family.

In 1970 Tivis retired from full time work and for several years worked part-time servicing gas and oil wells.

Both Tivis and Inez were members of the Staffordsville Free Will Baptist Church from 1956 until their deaths.

Inez succumbed to cancer Nov. 20, 1995. Tivis passed on Oct. 7, 1997. Their legacy is in their children and their families. *Submitted by Tivis Jay Lyon Jr.*

MAGGARD & HALL - Both J.C. and Sylvia Hall Maggard were born in 1897 in the Hindman, KY, area. However, their families moved to Magoffin County in the early 1900s.

J.C. left for Berea Academy when he was 14 and from there joined the Marine Corps during WWI and fought in most of the major battles that were waged in France.

J.C. and Sylvia Hall Maggard

After his return from the war he and Sylvia Hall were married. They went to the oil fields and found jobs; she as a cook and he as a tool-dresser.

With great frugality they saved the sum of $300.00 and moved to Paintsville. In Bridgeford they rented a very small store front building and began selling groceries. Being innovative, he bought a large walk-in refrigerator for meats which was the very first one in the town. With the success resulting from this risky purchase, he was able to move to the town proper. He had his nephew, Otto Pratt, and loyal employee, Norman Stratton, to continue to operate a grocery store where S. & S. Shoe Store was located on Court Street. He and Sylvia began a department store in the building that Malcom's Restaurant occupied.

By this time they had four children: Maxine, Faye, Mark and Bob. Without the help of Ludie Lemaster Preston to care for their children, they would not have had the freedom to pursue their business ventures. They were lucky!

They moved from the Malcom's location and opened a more high-style department store in the old Hotel Rule building where Maggard & Joseph is now located.

Being foresightful, they prepared for the coming economic depression. They had a sale that was planned by Mac Preston, father of Billy Marie Mason. J.C. said he was the greatest promoter in the country. After this successful sale, they opened a variety store with inexpensive merchandise. Also in this building, which incorporated the old Arcade Theatre, they had a grocery they named Home Cash Grocery.

In 1936 they bought the land and built the building that is now called the Murphy Building. In it they had a variety and a grocery store. Later they leased the building and sold the business to G.C. Murphy Co.

Never ones to idle, in 1939 they bought the Mountain Furniture Store on Court St. and in that building started Maggard's Furniture & Hardware which is today owned and operated by their grandson, Jim Stan Maggard, and his wife, Belinda.

During this period of growth J.C. owned and operated Home Cash Grocery, Sinclair Oil Distributorship, service stations, and bought and developed properties.

He loved his community and was active in its affairs. He was a member of the City Council, American Legion and was instrumental in building the American Legion Hall, a member of Kiwanis and a director of Citizens National Bank which was called Second National Bank at that time.

J.C. and Sylvia believed in education and the cultural arts. They insisted that all four of their children study piano and the girls - ballet, dance, voice, elocution and violin. They sent Mark and Bob to Riverside Military Academy for high school and sent all four children to good colleges. They also encouraged their children to serve their community.

J.C. and Sylvia lived for their children and always opened their home to their friends.

They lived long enough to see their children prosper. Mark was sole operator of Maggard's Furniture & Hardware until his retirement, Maxine was an elementary school teacher until her retirement, Bob was a major in the Air Force Intelligence until his retirement, Faye taught school for five years which she says were the happiest five years of her life.

Their grandson, Robin T. Cooper, following in the Cooper and Maggard tradition of community service, is now in his second term as mayor of Paintsville.

They have been blessed with 13 grandchildren, 23 great-grandchildren and two great-great-grandchildren.

Their lives were well spent. They served their families and their community. Sylvia, affectionately known as "Nanny," died at the age of 84 and J.C. died at the age of 87.

Their four children are: Maxine Maggard VanHoose married to L.O. VanHoose and they live in Cincinnati, OH, and Ft. Meyers, FL; Faye Maggard Cooper was married to the late John Ernest Cooper and lives in Lexington, KY; Mark Maggard is married to Norma Dorton Maggard and lives in Paintsville; Harold C. "Bob" is married to Barbara Stivers Maggard and lives in Indian Rocks Beach, FL.

MARSH & GEIGER - Dorothy Louise Geiger Marsh was born Oct. 31, 1908, in Paintsville, the daughter and second child of Orville C. "Cook" Geiger and Virgie Hager Geiger. She was the granddaughter of Daniel M. and Jessica Vaughan Hager of Paintsville and Henry and Sophia Pogue Geiger of Boyd County. Dorothy had one brother, Dr. Marion Braxton Geiger (born Sep. 4, 1903).

Dorothy Louise Geiger Marsh

On Jul. 8, 1926, Dorothy married Robert L. "Lee" Marsh (born in Wayne County, KY, Aug. 2, 1907). Dorothy and Lee had five children: Janet Louise Marsh (now Trimble) (born Jun. 12, 1927); Robert L. "Bob" Marsh (born Sep. 7, 1932); Virginia Carolyn Marsh (now Henry) (born Jun. 27, 1935); Franklin Hager Marsh (born Oct. 10, 1936); and Lawrence Braxton Marsh (born Mar. 13, 1939).

Dorothy was a 1926 graduate of Paintsville High School and the Ora M. Preston School of Music, where she became an accomplished pianist. She was active in many school events but excelled in basketball and music. She was a member of the Paintsville Comets basketball team which went to the state tournament in 1925.

Her brother, Marion, graduated from Paintsville High School in 1920 and from Georgetown College and Massachusetts Institute of Technology. He received his PhD in chemistry from the University of Michigan. Marion married Bonnie Castle Hart of Elizabethtown in 1928. Marion pursued his career in the chemical industry with Oldbury Chemical (later Hooker Chemical) in Niagara Falls, NY, eventually rising to executive vice president and general manager of the Oldbury Div. of Hooker Chemical. Prior to his retirement he served as a chemical projects specialist in Europe, Asia and Africa for the United Nations. Marion died on Jan. 4, 1986, survived by two daughters, Bonnie Geiger Loftus and Phyllis Geiger Miller.

Early in her career, Dorothy served as secretary for Paintsville High School and later entered government service with the Farmers Home Administration. She retired after 29 years of service on Oct. 31, 1969. In addition to her employment and the rearing of her five children, Dorothy was active in community life, including serving as pianist for many years for both the Paintsville Rotary and Kiwanis Clubs. For 45 years she remained active in First United Methodist Church of Paintsville and, later, in Clermont, FL.

Following her retirement to Florida, Dorothy remained active in community affairs as a volunteer for the Meals-On-Wheels program and a neighborhood center serving the needs of that area's migrant workers.

Dorothy died in Florida on Mar. 6, 1982, of complications arising from coronary by-pass surgery. She was survived by her five children, 21 grandchildren and six great-grandchildren.

MARSH - Franklin H. Marsh "Frank" was born in Ashland, Boyd County, KY, on Oct. 10, 1936, to Robert Lee Marsh and Dorothy Louise Geiger Marsh. Frank was one of five children. His brothers and sisters are: Janet Louise Marsh Trimble (Paintsville, KY), Robert Lee "Bob" Marsh II (Paintsville, KY), Virginia Carolyn Marsh Henry (Clermont, FL) and Lawrence Braxton Marsh (Buckeystown, MD). Frank's mother was born in Paintsville on Oct. 31, 1908, and his father was born in Wayne County, KY, on Aug. 2, 1907. Frank lived at 312 Third Street in Paintsville until after his graduation from Berea College in 1958 with a BS degree in business administration. He was also awarded a MS degree in international affairs from George Washington University and a M.Ed. in counseling from Penn State University.

Frank was married on Aug. 28, 1958, in Princeton, WV. He has three children: Jonathan Lee Marsh (born Aug. 28, 1963, in Yuma, AZ) currently living in Ocoee, FL; Mary Elizabeth Marsh Jensen (born May 29, 1965, in Camp Lejeune, NC) currently living in State College, PA; and Dana Louise Marsh (born Apr. 13, 1969, in Atlanta, GA) currently living in State College, PA.

Following his graduation from Berea College, Frank was commissioned a second lieutenant in the USMC where he served his country for 23 years, including several tours of duty overseas and a tour of duty in Vietnam. Frank retired in August 1979 with the rank of lieutenant colonel.

Following his retirement from the USMC, Frank began a second career, in 1981, working for Penn State University in the Undergraduate Admissions. He worked in several different positions including assistant director of admissions and coordinator of Information Systems. He retired from Penn State in 1992 and started his own consulting business, Marlan Associates. This business provided services to businesses and individuals in the areas of job search skills, resume writing and presentation skills.

In 1996, Frank moved back to his hometown of Paintsville and worked with his brother, Bob, for two years. In 1998 Frank was offered a position with Hazard Community College, Hazard, KY, as the director of Student Support Services. As of May 1999, Frank was still employed at Hazard Community College.

Frank enjoys playing golf, reading and working with his computer and hopes to retire, eventually, in Central Florida.

MARSH - Robert L. "Bob" Marsh was born in Paintsville, Johnson County, KY, on Sep. 7, 1932, the second of five children of Robert L. "Lee" Marsh and Dorothy Louise Geiger Marsh. Lee Marsh was born in Wayne County, KY, Aug. 2, 1907, the fourth son of W.T. "Dock" Marsh and Martha Lee Fairchild Marsh. Lee's father died prior to his birth and he was adopted by his uncle, Henry Frank Marsh, and his wife, Matilda Jane Marsh. Dorothy Louise Geiger Marsh (born in Paintsville Oct. 31, 1908) was the daughter of Orville Cook Geiger and Virgie Louise Hager Geiger.

Robert L. Marsh

Bob has two brothers and two sisters: Janet Louise Marsh (born Jun. 12, 1927) who married John Mark Trimble; Virginia Carolyn Marsh (born Jun. 27, 1935) who married first, Dan Williams, and second, Roger Henry; Franklin Hager Marsh (born Oct. 10, 1936) who married JoAnn Alvis; and Lawrence Braxton Marsh (born Mar. 13, 1939) who married Mary Bobanick. Bob was married three times: first, Betty Ruth Sammons, by whom he had one child, Brenda Sue (now Corona) (born May 5, 1951); second, Ruth Ellen Tackett, by whom he had two sons, Robert Lee Marsh III (born Feb. 20, 1959) and Thomas Keith Marsh (born Sep. 2, 1960); and third, Susan Jane Geer, by whom he had three children: Geoffrey Duncan Marsh (born Mar. 3, 1966), Jennifer Lynn Marsh (now Bingham) (born Apr. 9, 1968) and Pamela Ann Marsh (born Apr. 15, 1969).

Bob graduated from Paintsville High School in 1950 and began work immediately as an announcer with Radio Station WSIP. He continued his broadcasting career in Paintsville; Statesboro, GA; Owensboro, KY; Charleston, WV; and Baltimore, MD. In the intervening years he also served as assistant to the president of West Virginia Institute of Technology, Montgomery, WV, and as director of Educational Broadcasting of West Virginia Wesleyan College, Buckhannon, WV. Bob earned his BA degree from West Virginia Wesleyan College, majoring in history and English.

In 1966, Bob joined the staff of Baltimore County Executive (and later vice president of the U.S.) Spiro T. Agnew, serving as his administrative assistant and then co-campaign chairman of Mr. Agnew's successful campaign for governor of Maryland. In 1968, Bob was named executive director of the Maryland Physical Fitness Commission. In 1969, he joined three others in forming the public affairs consulting firm of McInerny, Marsh, Kilduff and Matthews in Washington, DC.

Bob returned to Paintsville in 1972 where he served as director of Public Relations for Mountain Comprehensive Care Center, the regional mental health agency. He later served as a member of the Paintsville City Council for three terms, chairman of the Paintsville Housing and Urban Development Commission, assistant to Johnson County Judge Executives James C. Witten and Wayne C. Blevins, executive vice president of the Paintsville-Johnson County Chamber of Commerce and executive director of Project 2000. In 1983, Bob founded and became president of the Paintsville Sesquicentennial Commission which planned and implemented a year long celebration of Paintsville's 150th founding in 1984.

In addition to creating the regional magazine *Highlands Magazine* in 1979, Bob is the author of *Agnew: The Unexamined Man*, M. Evans, New York 1971, *"And That's A Fact!"* pamphlet, 1982, *"And That's A Fact!" An Anecdotal History of Paintsville and Johnson County,* Gateway Publishing, Baltimore, 1998, *Tragedies and Disasters: Bad Things Happening to Good People in Paintsville and Johnson County,* publication date to be announced, as well as numerous articles and essays.

MATIJASIC - Thomas David Matijasic and Tammie Gayle Crider Matijasic were married in 1993 and have resided in Paintsville since 1996. Thomas was born in Youngstown, OH, in 1954. After receiving his PhD in history from Miami University (1982), he was hired as a professor by Prestonsburg Community College. Tammie was born in McDowell, KY, in 1968. She received her BA in elementary education from Morehead State University (1994) and is employed as a kindergarten teacher at Our Lady of the Mountain Catholic School in Paintsville. They are the proud parents of three daughters: Haley Jordan (b. 1994), Caitlin Nicole (b. 1996) and Julie Marie (b. 1999).

Matijasic Family: Haley, Thomas, Tammie and Caitlin.

Thomas is the son of Steve and Theresa Yochman Matijasic of Austintown, OH. Steve Matijasic was born in Pittsburgh, PA, in 1920 and worked as a shearman for the Youngstown Sheet and Tube Corp. He served in the 39th Regt. of the 9th U.S. Army Div. during WWII. He fought against the German Army in North Africa, Sicily, France and Germany, winning a Purple Heart, a Bronze Star, and a unit citation for bravery. His parents, Joseph (born 1874, died 1947) and Jennie Matijasic (born 1881, died 1963), immigrated to the U.S. from Croatia.

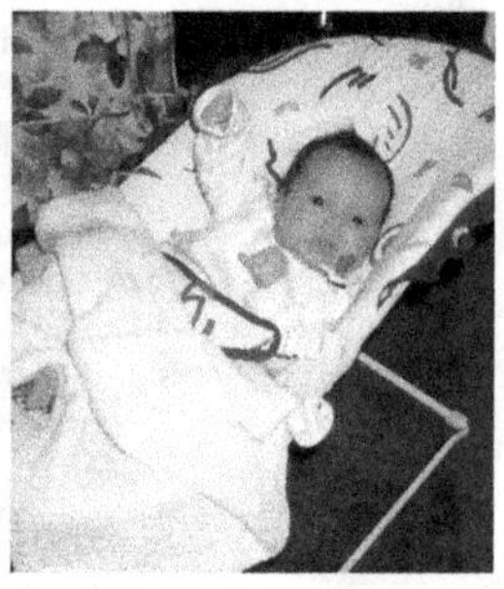
Julie Marie Matijasic

Theresa Yochman Matijasic was born on a farm in Milton Township, OH, in 1924. She worked as a clerk-stenographer for the federal government. Her father, John Yochman (born 1878, died 1936), was born in Stiavnik, Slovakia and worked for U.S. Steel in Youngstown, OH, after immigrating to the U.S. Her mother, Mary Markovich Yochman (born 1891, died 1971), was born in Hranovnica, Slovakia. She owned and operated a small dairy farm after the death of her husband.

Tammie is the daughter of Ottway and Thelma Wright Crider of the John's Creek area of Johnson County, KY. Ottway was born in Prestonsburg, KY, in 1949. After attending Mayo Technical School, he worked as a draftsman and surveyor. He is the son of Ottway (born 1924, died 1959) and Avonelle Prater Crider (born 1928, died 1996). Ottway Crider Sr. was born in Ottway, OH, and worked as a heavy equipment operator. Avonelle was a native of Lawrence County, KY, and she was employed for many years by Hobbs Dept. Store in Prestonsburg.

Thelma Wright Crider was born in Martin, KY, in

1952. She is the owner and director of TLC Daycare, the largest privately owned child development center in Johnson County. She is the daughter of Raymond (born 1926, died 1998) and Hattie Howell Wright (born 1932, died 1975). Raymond was born at Flat Gap, KY. He worked as a coal miner and coal truck driver. He was also well known along Left Beaver Creek in Floyd County as a Pentecostal preacher. Hattie was born along Frazier's Creek in Floyd County, KY.

MCCARTY - Burl McCarty was born Nov. 17, 1927, at Low Gap in Johnson County. He was the son of Hallack and Nora Curtis McCarty. He had five brothers: Ford, Walter Earl, Joe, Carl Chester and George. He had four sisters: Mary Ward, Helen Lemaster, Maxie McCarty and Norris Ann McCarty.

Burl and Roberta McCarty

Burl was married in Johnson County on Aug. 20, 1949, to Roberta Lemaster. She was the daughter of Plennie and Anna Tackett Lemaster. They lived most of their married life at Rockhouse in Johnson County where they built a new home. They had 11 children.

Karen (born Aug. 4, 1950) married Donald Colvin. They live at Oil Springs and have two sons, Kevin and Kriss. Kriss married Kim Picklesimer. They have one son, Justin.

Emma Faye (born Apr. 12, 1952) married Lifes Vanhoose Jr. They live at Denver and have two sons, Jason and Brian. Brian married Sharon Horne. They have two daughters, Heather and Rachel.

Danny (born Jun. 7, 1954) married Tobie Stapleton. They live at Collista and have three children: Cindy, Kelli and Mathew. Mathew married Jenni Parrett.

Janie (born Feb. 12, 1956) married Charles Rowland. They are divorced. They have two sons, Shawn and Shane. Janie lives in Florida.

Lenora (born Feb. 22, 1958) married Morgan Bowen. They live at Sitka. They have two children, Lisa and Scott. Scott married Jamie Davis. He has two children, Dekota and Shelby Lynn.

Shirley (born Mar. 20, 1960) married Van Gale Cope. They live in Woodland Estate, Paintsville. They have one daughter, Sara.

Johnny Gene (born Mar. 12, 1962) married Diane Hitchcock. They are divorced. His second wife is Eva Collier. They live at Hagerhill and have two daughters, April and Gena.

Debbie (born Aug. 31, 1964) married Bill Branham. They are divorced. They have two children, Billy Jr. and Amy. Her second husband is Gary Collins. They live at Staffordsville.

Jackie (born Oct. 21, 1967) married James Copley. They live in Tennessee and have three children: Jamie, Amanda and Christy.

Sheila (born Jan. 10, 1969) married Clarence Stapleton. They live at Baker Branch and have two children, Josh and Emily.

Brenda (born Jan. 29, 1973) married Jay Daniels. They live at Oil Springs and have one son, Brady.

Burl was a coal miner for about 30 years, until he became disabled with blacklung and had to retire. He loved to fish and work in the garden.

On Jun. 21, 1998, his work here was finished. He passed away on Father's Day at U.K. Medical Center in Lexington, KY, at age 70. He was laid to rest in the McCarty Cemetery at Low Gap, KY. *Submitted by Emma Faye VanHoose.*

MCCARTY - The Cartys who formerly lived in Russell County, VA, changed their name to McCarty when they settled in Floyd County, KY, approximately 1842. John P. Carty (born circa 1816, Russell County, VA, died Nov. 30, 1867) married Mar. 10, 1836, Harlan County, KY, Martha Clarissa Salyer, she died Aug. 30, 1886. Both buried old McCarty Cemetery, McCarty Fork, Johnson County, KY. Their children were: Nelson (born Jan. 30, 1839, Russell County, VA), Rebecca J. (born 1842, Russell County, VA), David J. (born Nov. 19, 1843, Kentucky died Oct. 20, 1919) and Minorva (born 1846, Kentucky).

James and Sarah McCarty

Nelson McCarty, the son of John P. McCarty and Martha Clarissa Salyer (born Jan. 30, 1839, Russell County, VA, died Sep. 20, 1915), married Jun. 2, 1856, Johnson County, KY, Louisa Blanton (born Sep. 27, 1838, died Apr. 16, 1919). Both buried Sand Suck Creek Road, Greenup County, KY. Their children were: John C. Brack (born Feb. 28, 1857, Kentucky, died 1937), Sariah J. (born Jan. 18, 1859) James H., Morhetta (born 1864, Kentucky), Susanna (born May 1867, Kentucky), Fred (born Apr. 22, 1879, died Nov. 14, 1963), Thomas Jefferson (born 1873, Kentucky), Allie Dicie and Mary E. (born 1865).

James H. McCarty (born Feb. 13, 1861, Johnson County, KY), the son of Nelson McCarty and Louise Blanton. He was a farmer by occupation and a United Baptist Church minister. The marriage records for James H. and Sarah Ellizabeth Coldiron Feb. 6, 1879, Wallis Bailey minister. She was born Apr. 18, 1864, the daughter of James H. Coldiron and Rebecca Blanton. Rebecca was the daughter of Rebecca Salyer and James Blanton. James H. McCarty was a member of the Low-Gap United Baptist Church when it was a log church. Later the church burned. He died Nov. 23, 1919, preaching his last words from First Timothy chapter 6 and 10th verse. Sarah died Jan. 27, 1947. They both are buried at the McCarty Cemetery located on McCarty Fork, Johnson County, KY. Their children were: Forest Winston (born Oct. 18, 1880, died Apr. 14, 1953) married Rosie Curtis (born Aug. 1, 1901), Oscur (born Jan. 8, 1883, died Mar. 11, 1967), Gracie (born Jan. 30, 1889, died Nov. 24, 1952), Clifton (born Dec. 1, 1890, died Dec. 11, 1963), Mattie (born February 1894, died 1981), Donna (born Oct. 7, 1896, died Jul. 31, 1985), Mollie (born Apr. 22, 1900, died Nov. 19, 1984), Dewey (born Jan. 14, 1903, died Jul. 12, 1930) and James (born Mar. 10, 1904).

Forest W. McCarty, son of James H., was a carpenter by occupation and a United Baptist Church minister. Rosa, his wife, was born Nov. 22, 1882, died Sep. 27, 1953. Their children: Virgil, Burley (born Apr. 28, 1904, died Feb. 3, 1985), Verna, Willie, Jay, Hager, Emery, Willis and James.

Burley McCarty, his occupation farmer, saw-mill, son of Forest W. McCarty, married Dora Salyer (born May 27, 1903, died Jun. 30, 1977).

James Forest McCarty, retired contractor, real estate, son of Burley (born Jul. 17, 1930, Upper Franks Creek, Johnson County, KY) married Loraine (Carter), three sons: Gregory, Jeffrey and Mark. *Submitted by James F. McCarty.*

MCCLOUD - Charles H. McCloud was born on Jenny's Creek in Johnson County on Apr. 23, 1916, to William Ireland and Hattie Conley McCloud. He was the youngest of five children born to this family. Two sisters, Myrtie Horn and Sophie Kimbler, as well as two brothers, Hershell McCloud and Beecher McCloud, preceded him in death. Charles himself died on Dec. 24, 1988, leaving one sister, Vivian Castle, who still resides in Paintsville.

Charles met Reta Moore, daughter of Scott Forrest and Stella McFadden Moore, in 1915, when they were both only 19 years of age. They were married in Salyersville, KY, on Feb. 1, 1936, and a son, Scotty, was born to them on Nov. 19, 1936. Almost six years later, on Mar. 1, 1942, another son, Mike, was born. Two daughters completed their family, Judy, on Jun. 28, 1944, and Lynn, on Oct. 13, 1947.

Charles was not an educated man, having left school during his eighth grade year. However, he was hard working and managed to support his family, while Reta maintained their home. Although their children may not have had everything they wanted, they certainly had all that they needed. One incident marred their happy home, however, when Michael was stricken with Tetanus at the age of 8. He survived through the heroic efforts of Dr. A.D. Slone, who kept a daily vigil at Mike's bedside in the Paintsville Clinic. As a result of this near tragedy, Charles and Reta both became Christians and remained faithful to their Lord until their death.

In the early years of their marriage, Charles worked as a coal truck driver. He then was employed by Leroy Slone at the Paintsville Produce Co., where he remained until 1969. Upon the death of Mr. Slone, the company was dissolved, and Charles was out of a job. Although his children were self-sufficient, Charles, being only 53 years old, started searching for other employment. He leased a grocery store, which had an apartment attached, from his brother, Beecher, and, in March 1969, Charles and Reta sold their home in town and moved to Stambaugh, KY. For several years, Charles also sold eggs wholesale to various businesses along the Big Sandy, leaving Reta to run the store, but later concentrated solely on his local business. They remained the owners of McCloud's Market until his death.

Their son, Scotty, is retired and resides at Nippa, KY. He is married to the former Patsy Barrett of Berea and has one daughter by a previous marriage.

Mike McCloud lives in Jacksonville, FL, where he is married, self-employed and the father of two daughters and one son.

Judy is married to Teddy Delong, part-owner in the Paintsville Dairy Queen. They are residents of Hager Hill and have three sons.

Lynn has remained in Paintsville since 1971, after living in Lexington, KY, during her education. She is married to attorney Michael Schmitt, and works as an accountant and payroll manager of Wells, Porter, Schmitt and Jones. They are the parents of two daughters and one son.

MCKENZIE & PELPHREY - On the banks of Paint Creek in a spot now covered by Paintsville Lake, there used to set a farm house with gardens, pastures, horses, cows, chickens and children all around. The children, seven in all, belonged to Malta (Rice) and Challie Pelphrey. The pretty little dark haired one born Apr. 23, 1929, was Betty. As the middle child, she was the one who looked after the three younger children while the three older children did their chores. She carried baby Mabel on her hip while chasing after and trying to keep her younger brothers, Jack and Robert, out of Paint Creek and out from under

Betty Pelphrey McKenzie

the horses' crushing hooves. Sometimes the younger ones would get so out of hand she would have to enlist the aid of the older kids. Agnes, Kelse (Bud - deceased at age 14 in 1940), and Ruby were always glad for a reason to chase down to the creek.

Betty and her siblings attended Clifton school, a one room school house located below Clifton Falls in the Fishtrap area of Paint Creek. They all later attended Oil Springs High School.

In 1949 Betty married James Orville McKenzie, the son of Cloma and Earl McKenzie of Flat Gap. They had three children: James Ishmael "Jim," Kathy and Scott. Betty, James and the kids lived most of their lives at Hager Hill. In 1991 James and Betty moved to Cross Creek in Staffordsville.

Betty devoted her young adult years to being a wife and mother. Then at the age of 35 she began her career as a Headstart teacher. She was soon known as the best Headstart teacher in Johnson County. All the parents wanted their child in Mrs. McKenzie's class at Oil Springs. Her good nature, positive outlook, strong work ethic, love for children and deep compassion for others are undoubtedly the reasons for her success as a Headstart teacher. She taught for 29 years and left an enviable legacy of success stories and positive outcomes for the children she taught.

Betty has been a member of Eastern Star since 1953 and is also a member of the Little Mud Lick Church of God and works as the bookkeeper for her husband's business. Her favorite hobbies are photography (of her grandchildren) and rose gardening. She has seven grandchildren and one great-granddaughter. Jim and his wife, Lois (Salyer), have Dewayne and his wife, Kim, who have a daughter, Baylee. Corey and Carla are Lois and Jim's other two children. Kathy and her husband, Charles Crigger, have one daughter, Mackenzie. Scott and his wife, Lesa (Milstead), have one daughter, Madison, and twin boys, Johnson and Kenton.

What Betty Pelphrey McKenzie has given to Johnson County is good loving care and instruction to its youngest citizens. Her influence will be felt for generations as the children of the children she reared and taught are still touched and influenced by her kind, compassionate and generous spirit.

MCKENZIE & LYON - Beulah Lyon born at Red Bush, Sep. 11, 1910. She is the daughter of Sherman and Lora Ellen Wallin Lyon. Sherman was born at Red Bush Dec. 25, 1871, the son of Landon and Nancy Skaggs Lyon. Lora was born in Morgan County, KY, Dec. 22, 1883, the daughter of Dr. Tivis E. and Martha Jane Pennington Wallin.

Beulah Lyon McKenzie

Beulah is the oldest of four children. Her siblings are Tivis Lyon (born Mar. 8, 1917), Con Lyon (born Dec. 12, 1919) and Kerlin Lyon (born Mar. 22, 1922).

Beulah attended Johnson County Schools in a one room school at Lower Keaton and Flat Gap High School.

Beulah married Ray McKenzie, May 6, 1930. Their first home was located at Barn Rock, KY. They decided to build a new home at Flat Gap on the McKenzie family farm. Their home was completed and they moved into it in 1935. Beulah was always a dedicated homemaker with special skills in hand embroidery and handmade quilts. Each of her children, grandchildren and great-grandchildren have a handmade keep-sake made especially for them. In her young married days, she grew a garden and canned vegetables for winter supplies, drew water from the hand dug well and carried it into the house for family use. Her work was done early and then there was time to read, play, or visit with neighbors.

Beulah and Ray have four children: Emma Joy (born Jun. 27, 1931); Clista Margaret (born Dec. 26, 1932); Daren Ray (born Jul. 31, 1934) and Jack Paul (born Feb. 28, 1942).

Beulah was converted and joined the Flat Gap Enterprise Baptist Church. She was baptized Feb. 20, 1938, and has remained a member there since that time. She was always progressive in her thinking and supported Bible study and Sunday school in the days when everyone did not approve of Sunday school attendance.

Beulah did not have a mother-in-law but she had a special love and respect for her father-in-law, Merdia Oliver McKenzie, who always treated her as a daughter. As he grew older, he paid many visits to Ray and Beulah's home in Ashland, KY. Sometimes both Beulah's and Ray's dads would make plans to visit at the same time and this was a special treat for everyone.

According to family history, one of Beulah's great-great-grandmothers was a Cherokee Indian. This has always been a source of family pride and each new baby is checked out to identify if they have any of the Cherokee looks.

Beulah has spent a great deal of time and effort in researching her family roots and has shared her records with many others. She has always taken great pride in her family and finds something good in each one. Beulah never fails to speak up if others try to be negative about the family. She has a special sense of pride in the family members that have served in the military and she supports the effort to buy U.S. made items first. Her love of her family and country is an inspiration to all who know her.

Strength and honor are her clothing; she openeth her mouth with wisdom; she looketh well to the ways of her household and eateth not the bread of idleness; her children rise up and call her blessed; her husband also and he praiseth her, she shall rejoice in the days to come! *Submitted by Clista M. McKenzie Pelfrey.*

MCKENZIE - Clista Margaret McKenzie was born Dec. 26, 1932, at Barn Rock, Johnson County, KY, the second child born to Ray and Beulah Lyon McKenzie. Clista was named after her paternal grandmother, Clista Margaret Green McKenzie. Clista has one older sister, Emma Joy (born Jun. 27, 1931) and two younger brothers, Daren Ray (born Jul. 31, 1934) and Jack Paul (born Feb. 28, 1941). Clista attended Johnson County schools and Morehead State College.

Clista Margaret McKenzie Pelfrey

Married to William Hillard "Pat" Pelfrey. They have four daughters: Hilary Griffiths Pelfrey, Beverly Pelfrey Estep, Marcia Rae Pelfrey Sumpter and Margaret Wynn Pelfrey Napier; four grandchildren: Latisha, adopted daughter of Hilary and John Griffiths; Monica Lynne Estep Spradlin and Daren Paul Estep, children of Beverly and Orville Paul Estep; and Kyle Ray Salyer, son of Marcia and Michael Salyer. They also have two great-grandchildren, Cherokee, daughter of Latisha and Kelsey Lynne, daughter of Monica and Shawn Spradlin.

Clista has been a Christian for 51 years and is a member of the Flat Gap Baptist Church. She was converted in a revival at Christian Union Enterprise Church at Keaton, held by Jiles Beculheimer and baptized in the creek at Keaton Mar. 18, 1948. Her greatest joy is serving Christ as her Lord and Savior and loving her family. She recently retired, as a facility security supervisor, after working at the Carl D. Perkins Rehabilitation Center from 1973-99. She is a Kentucky Colonel and a member of the National Rehabilitation Association. Other interests that have filled her life are playing the piano and guitar, reading and writing poetry, serving as Sunday school teacher, Bible school director, Christian Camp girls dormitory director, 4-H leader, Homemakers Club member, sewing, reading and collecting bells, garden birds, angels and Cape Cod dishes. Clista devotes two evenings a month to play the piano for a singing group at nursing homes in Johnson and Morgan counties. She plays piano for a gospel singing group known as "The Family Foundation." Since retiring Clista is researching her family roots.

Clista's children are an asset to the communities where they live and work. Hilary teaches personal development in a prison for juvenile felony offenders in Ohio. Beverly is an executive assistant to a private business owner in Johnson County. Marcia is Area 9 Kentucky Emergency Services manager for 10 counties located in Eastern Kentucky with an office in Floyd County. Margaret is a clinic coordinator for a Mental Health Agency located in Johnson County. The family philosophy continues to be that we serve Christ by serving others. All the family participates in the churches of their choice by attending Sunday school, Bible study, Bible school, worship service, special singing and fellowshipping other churches. The Pelfrey family has always had a strong focus centered on dedication to Christ as our Lord and Savior. *Submitted by W.H. Pat and Clista M. McKenzie Pelfrey.*

MCKENZIE - Clora Williams McKenzie was born Jul. 18, 1885 at the Noah Williams homestead at Mud Lick in northwestern Johnson County. Clora was the daughter of Hannah Frazier Williams. Hannah, the daughter of James (born 1929, died 1886) and Dolly Matney Frazier (born 1830, died 1897) was born Apr. 1, 1866 in the Flat Gap area. James and Dolly were born in Virginia.

Noah Williams Homestead in Mud Lick

Clora's father was Crayton Flinn Williams, born Oct. 9, 1863 at the homestead on Mud Lick. His parents, Noah H. Williams (born 1834, died 1912) and Ellen Webb Williams (born 1833, died 1906) were born in the Flat Gap area. Noahs father, Robert R. and grandfather, Robert S. were early settlers on Upper Laurel. Ellen was born in Scott County, VA and migrated to the Flat Gap area with her parents as a young child in the 1840s. Hannah and Crayton made their home with his parents on Williams Branch at Mud Lick. Sometime after 1865, Noah and Crayton enlarged and enhanced the original house that was a four-room log structure with a dog trot. They added a second story and a summer kitchen with a weaving and sewing room above. The two structures were connected by an open covered walkway both up and downstairs. The stairs were on the outside. Crayton and Hannah became the parents of five children. Erie (born Mar. 10, 1883) married May 6, 1902 to Eli Williams. She died May 30, 1974 in Georgetown, KY where they lived for many years. Ona (born May 29, 1884) married Dennis Williams on Oct. 3, 1902. She died Mar. 26, 1972 at her home on the head of Mud Lick.

Clora (born 1885, died 1965) married first, Albert McKenzie of Elna/Red Bush and second, Albert McKenzie of Cane Branch.

Ola (born Jun. 20, 1887) married Sandy Phillips and died Mar. 27 1971 at Lucasville where they had lived for 40 years.

Kendall (K.W.) Williams (born Jun. 27, 1892) married first, Laurie Bond and second, Ruth Music Price. Kendall lived all his life on the homestead and died there Nov. 23, 1975.

In early 1900 most of the household was stricken with Typhoid fever when the creek and branch flooded the open well. Crayton died Mar. 17, 1900. Hannah lingered until Nov. 13, 1900 weakened by the fever and the loss of her beloved Crayton. The five children were left in the care of grandparents, Noah and Ellen.

Hannah Frazier Williams and Crayton F. Williams holding their son, Kendall "K.W." Williams (before1900).

Clora met Albert McKenzie, the son of John and Survillar Sagraves McKenzie, as they moved through a common community. Bethel Church was a possible contact point. After their marriage, they set up housekeeping in the Red Bush area where Albert taught school.

Erie Williams (seated) and Ona Williams (before 1900)

On Jul. 14, 1909 their child, Neva Noel, was born. The young family moved happily through their days with frequent visits to family and church at Bethel. Albert consulted his brother-in-law, Eli Williams, concerning plans to further his education.

Noah Williams (before 1900)

On Jan. 3, 1912 these happy days were terminated. Albert died. His death was caused by a respiratory infection. During his childhood Albert had contracted polio. He walked with a limp and suffered chronic respiratory problems,

Clora and Neva were left with no visible means of support except for family members and their love. In August 1912, grandfather Noah died, Now the young adults had only each other for comfort and advice. For the next five years, Clora's siblings welcomed the young widow and the toddler into their homes where Clora was glad to be of help in household duties and Neva learned to love her many cousins as brothers and sisters.

Ellen Webb Williams (before 1900)

Clora also had ties to the McKenzie line. Her grandmother Ellen Webb, wife of Noah Willliams, was the daughter of George Washington Webb and Elizabeth McKenzie. Elizabeth and Oliver were siblings. The McKenzie family came to western Johnson County (the Elna-Red Bush area) from Fort Blackmore in Scott County, VA during the middle years of the 19th century. Albert and his brother M.O., were sons of John and Survillar Sagraves McKenzie. John was a son of Oliver and Matilda Strong McKenzie who made their home in the Elna-Red Bush area.

Included in the family were Hughie, David Jesse, William, John, James Henry, and a sister, Nancy, wife of John Egan. William lived in the Volga area around Stonecoal Creek. One of his sons was Lemuel who wed Mary Lemaster and settled in Cane Branch of Paint Creek near Fish Trap Church.

In 1917 Clora married again to a widower with the same name as her first husband, Albert McKenzie. This Albert was the son of Lemuel and Mary McKenzie of Cane Branch. Albert's first wife, Stella Burchwell had died in child-birth on Aug. 10, 1916. Twin daughters were born but one died and was buried in her mother's arms at the family cemetery now on the Paintsville Lake property, They were the parents of two other sons, Homer and Ford. The surviving twin, Ola, went to live with an aunt. After Clora and Albert married, Ola came home to be raised by Albert and Clora whom she still calls "Mom." On Apr. 30, 1919 Albert and Clora added Kendall ("theirs" to "his" and "hers"). While Clora kept the family, house and garden, Albert worked at blacksmithing and farming. He succeeded his father, Lemuel, as clerk of Fish Trap Church and served until his death of typhoid fever on Nov. 2, 1935. At the time of Albert's death Homer was married to Georgia Williams, daughter of Albert Williams, and Neva had married Arlyn Violet, son of John Violet. Ford later married Evelyn Hobson. Ola remembers this period as a time of apprehension and much extra work as Kendall was in the hospital with an emergency appendectomy. Ola tried to keep the farm running and go to school while Clora was spending her waking hours at the hospital.

L-R: Ola Williams and Clora Williams

Ola remembers the large crowd in the yard at her father's funeral in Cane Branch. According to the newspaper account "The spacious yard was packed to overflowing in respect and love for Albert and his family." The neighbors were very helpful in completing the harvest that fall. Ola remembers the winter of 1935-1936 as terribly sad and difficult physically. She recounts that she and Clora cried in mourning almost continuously.

Home of Albert McKenzie and Clora Williams in Cane Branch

In the spring of 1936, Ola married Morris Conley, son of John Dixon Conley. Clora and Kendall went to live with Neva and Arlyn in Ohio while the newlyweds stayed at Cane Branch. So again Clora had buried a beloved husband, lost a home, and been forced by circumstances to shoulder extra responsibilities. Clora did resume visiting her brother and sisters and their families for weeks at a time, but she always had a place of honor in Neva's home. The summer was an especially intense visiting time. Clora loved to attend Fish Trap and Bethel churches. Sacrament times were dear to her. This had always been a major social event for Clora, an opportunity to worship and to greet friends and relatives. In the summer of 1937, Neva and Arlyn presented Clora with her first grandchild, a girl, with whom she was to spend her remaining 25 years as a steadfast friend.

Clora and Albert's son, Kendall, served as an Army mechanic in Iceland during WWII. He married Alice Kent, daughter of John Kent, in Lucasville before he was drafted. After his safe return home, the couple added four children to Clora's growing line of grandchildren.

Clora lived with Neva, Arlyn and their daughter and son in Lucasville, keeping house and helping with child care after Neva resumed teaching in 1942. Clora was able to spend many weekends with her sister and to attend church at Candy Run where Ola's husband, Sandy Phillips, was moderator into the 1980s

Thus was the pattern established for the sunset of Clora Williams McKenzie's life. Her demeanor was always ladylike, her manner pleasant. She was plagued with arthritis and rheumatism as well, as high blood pressure toward the end of the days, but she persisted in household activities even though wheelchair bound,

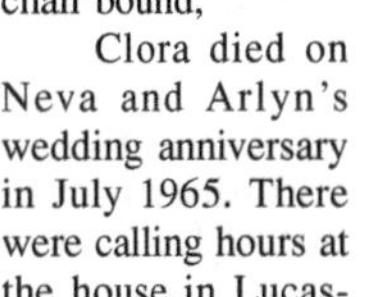

The children of Crayton and Hannah Williams: Ola Phillips, Clora McKenzie, Ona Williams, Erie Williams, Kendall Williams (seated) in the 1960s.

Clora died on Neva and Arlyn's wedding anniversary in July 1965. There were calling hours at the house in Lucasville where many friends expressed their sympathy. She was interred near her grandparents and parents in the Williams family plot on Mud Lick, within sight of the house where she had begun her journey 80 years earlier.

MCKENZIE - Daren Ray McKenzie was born Jul. 31, 1934, at Flat Gap, Johnson County, KY, to Ray and Beulah Lyon McKenzie. He is the third child born to Ray and Beulah. He has two older sisters, Emma Joy and Clista Margaret; and one younger brother, Jack. Daren attended grade school at Flat Gap. His family moved to Boyd County and he graduated from Boyd County High School, May 28, 1953. He played basketball and baseball while in high school.

Daren Ray McKenzie

Daren volunteered for military service in the Navy, Jul. 6, 1953. He was in basic training in Maryland. He entered Airman Preparatory training in Norman, OK. Upon graduation he attended school in Jacksonville, FL, and became an aviation electrician. Daren was transferred to Attack Sqdn. VA-25 and served in this capacity until his honorable discharge. He was based in Oceanea, VA, and served on four aircraft carriers. His first assignment was on the *Tycondaroga* in Cuba; the second was on the USS *Champlain* CVA 39, the third tour was on the largest aircraft carrier, the *Franklin D. Roosevelt* and the last tour was served on the *Intrepid*. His longest single assignment of six months was served on the USS *Lake Champlain*. Daren served four years of active duty and arrived home May 20, 1957. He was in the reserves four additional years. Daren was hired to work for Ashland Oil & Refining Co., Jul. 10, 1957, at the Catlettsbury #-1 Refinery.

Daren and Bonnie Lou Fraley (born Apr. 24, 1936) married Apr. 18, 1958. They had two children, Regina Rae (born May 4, 1959) and James Daren (born Aug. 5, 1960, died Aug. 22, 1962 of acute leukemia). He is buried in the Carter County Memorial Gardens. Regina Rae is a grade school teacher in Florida. Daren's second marriage to Karla Yonnne Porter, was Jul. 7, 1990. Karla was born May 26, 1952. Daren and Karla have one daughter, Lora Megan (born Feb. 3, 1991). Lora Megan is named after her great-grandmother, Lora Ellen Wallin Lyon. Daren was a foreman at the Ashland Oil Plant #1 for many years. After working 38 years for A.O.I., he retired in 1995. Daren enjoys fishing and playing golf.

He is a great supporter of the work done by the Shriner's organization. Daren joined the Mason's, Grand Lodge of Kentucky F & A M Poage of Ashland, York Rite, El Hasa Temple AAONMS of Ashland, Scottish Rite Freemasonry, Valley of Covington, Orient of Kentucky SJ, USA, El Hasa Temple Motor Corps, Ashland KY, Royal Order of Jesters Big Sandy, and El Hasa Oriental Band. As an active member of the Shriner's Marching Band he devotes many hours participating in their fund raising activities that support Shriner's Hospitals. Daren is also a member of the Ashland Elks 350, Loyal Order of Moose, Fraternal Order of Eagles, American Legion Post 76, Ironton Country Club, Ashland YMCA and has a life membership in the VFW 10017 and Amvets. He has been commissioned a Kentucky Colonel. He lives in another state but is a Kentuckian at heart and daily transports his young daughter to Kentucky to attend school. *Submitted by Clista M. McKenzie Pelfrey.*

MCKENZIE - Duane R. McKenzie was born on Apr. 2, 1953, in Litchfield, Meeker County, MN. His mother was Norma Olson (born Jun. 17, 1920, in Wykeham Township, Todd County, MN. His father is Donald McKenzie (born Mar. 6, 1920, in rural Annandale, Wright County, MN). They met when both their families farmed near Litchfield, MN. They married Nov. 20, 1942, in Litchfield, MN.

Duane R. McKenzie

His parents were from a family of four children. His mother's parents were Harold and Alma (Nelson) Olson of Swedish and Norwegian descent.

His father's parents were Oscar and Guida (Avery) McKenzie.

His Grandfather McKenzie's parents were Benjamin and Missouri B. (Kimbler) McKenzie, who came to Wright County, MN, to farm in the early 1890s. They were married on Feb. 21, 1891, at Cannon's Chapel in Johnson County, KY, near the town of Volga. Benjamin and Missouri (Kimbler) were born and reared in Johnson County, KY, and their families were from the Flat Gap and Volga area in Johnson County. Benjamin's father and mother were Lafayette McKenzie and Mary Ann Sparks from the Peter Cove Branch known as McKenzie Branch. Missouri's parents were John Wesley Kimbler and Thursey Ramey from Ramey Branch near Volga, KY.

He had one brother, David (born May 1, 1949, in Litchfield, MN, died there Mar. 1, 1961), had Cerebral Palsy.

Duane has always lived in Litchfield and graduated from the Litchfield Senior High School on Jun. 1, 1972. He is single and is an active member of Zion Lutheran Church and has sung in the adult senior choir for 30 years, also filing their music. He will be starting his 19th year singing with the Litchfield Male Chorus this fall. He has also been active in Meeker County politics.

He and his parents have taken many trips while he was growing up, some of the most special ones were their visits to Johnson County. His grandparents also visited there along with other McKenzie cousins and relatives from Minnesota and other states.

His dad retired in 1985 after being employed by the Economy Gas Co. as an accountant and office manager of this company for 39 years. His mother was employed by various stores among them being J.C. Penney, Ben Franklin and various dress shops. They are both active in church and volunteer work in Litchfield and enjoy retirement. He is self-employed as a groundskeeper and also does snow removal during the winter months. *By Duane R. McKenzie.*

MCKENZIE - Emma Joy McKenzie Skaggs Kazee was born Jun. 27, 1931, at the home of her grandparents, Sherman and Lora Lyon. She is the daughter of Ray and Beulah Lyon McKenzie. Ray and Beulah were both born at Red Bush, KY. Emma Joy is their oldest child and has three siblings: Clista Margaret, Daren Ray and Jack.

Emma Joy McKenzie Kazee

Emma Joy attended grade and high school at Flat Gap and later graduated in Boyd County. She married Golden Skaggs at Keaton, Feb. 14, 1948. Golden is the son of Everett and Lexie Skaggs Skaggs. Golden was born Oct. 8, 1925, at Red Bush and died Dec. 26, 1968. Golden was a Navy veteran, serving in WWII. He graduated from Flat Gap High School and Mayo State Vocational School majoring in electricity.

Emma Joy and Golden had three children: Donna Joyce Skaggs (born Apr. 9, 1949, in Paintsville) married William Gary Darling, Doralene Skaggs (born Aug. 24, 1956, in Ashland) married Dwight Hicks; Douglas (born Jul. 11, 1958, in Ashland) lost his life in a vehicle accident May 24, 1963, and is buried in the McKenzie Family Cemetery at Flat Gap on the Merdia Oliver McKenzie farm.

Emma Joy has three grandchildren: Donna's son, Christopher Clevenger and Doralene's children, Sandra Dawn Hicks and Zachary Alan Hicks.

Emma Joy later married Robert Calvin Kazee (born Oct. 14, 1927), the son of Curtis and Vergie Dove Kazee. Robert was member of the Baptist church, a brick mason and carpenter. He served in the U.S. Army during WWII and in the Korea Conflict. Robert died Jun. 24, 1984, and is buried in the McKenzie Family Cemetery at Flat Gap.

Emma Joy is a member of the Maverty Freewill Baptist Church and is a retired country store manager. She is a dedicated Christian, mother and friend and enjoys returning to Johnson County for visits at every opportunity. *Submitted by Clista M. McKenzie Pelfrey.*

MCKENZIE - George "Bill" Sherman McKenzie (born Dec. 6, 1931, in Johnson County, KY), son of Monroe and Nancy Cordle McKenzie, married Mar. 6, 1953, in Jackson County, OH, Ethel M. Culwell (born Aug. 14, 1932, in Johnson County, KY), daughter of Dennis and Exer Davis Culwell. Dennis was a minister of the United Baptist Church. The day they were married Bill and Ethel made their home in Johnson County, KY, where they would raise nine children. All of their children were born in Johnson County, KY.

George Sherman McKenzie Family. L. to R.: George, Jim, Kathy, Linda, Ollie, Stevie and Ethel McKenzie, standing. L. to R. Sitting: Billy, Monroe, Eddie and Tommy McKenzie.

Their children, grandchildren and great-grandchildren are the following.

1) Jimmie Darrell McKenzie (born Jul. 10, 1954) married Gwendolyn Jacqueline Stapleton, daughter of Wilmer and Sarah Roland Stapleton. Their children are: (a) Tina Raye McKenzie (born Mar. 22, 1975) married Joesph Cole, their children are Joesph Stephan Cole (born Dec. 8, 1994), Kailey Alissa Cole (born May 20, 1997) and Benjamin Noah Cole (born Jul. 23, 1998); (b) Clayton Darrell McKenzie (born Mar. 22, 1978); and (c) Sarah Rebecca McKenzie (born Nov. 6, 1982). Jim is currently the pastor of Sitka Freewill Baptist Church at Sitka, KY.

2) Linda Sue McKenzie (born Nov. 8, 1955) married Edgel Burchett, son of Delmer and Louvernia Castle Burchett. Their children are: (a) Misty Michael Burchett (born Apr. 6, 1974) married David Rigsby, their child is Harley Lee Rigsby (born Mar. 13, 1997) and (b) Dusty Lynn Burchett (born Feb. 24, 1980) married Londis Meek.

3) Tommy Lee McKenzie (born Aug. 15, 1957) married first, Edith Honeycutt, and second, Lora Lynn Watson Fairchild. His children are (a) Randy Scott McKenzie (born Feb. 29, 1976) married Julie Darst, their child is Randy Scott McKenzie (born Sep. 8, 1996); (b) Valerie Marie McKenzie (born Feb. 1, 1978) married John Morris, their child is Dakota Ryan Morris (born Nov. 21, 1996); (c) James Allen Fairchild, stepson (born Jan. 23, 1980); (d) Jessica Raye McKenzie (born Jul. 15, 1981); (e) Thomas Lee McKenzie (born Dec. 6, 1981); and (f) Brian Keith "Keifer" McKenzie (born Aug. 7, 1984).

4) Kathy Mae McKenzie (born Apr. 24, 1959) married first, Lawrence Ratliff; second, Lovonne Davis; and third, Tommy Mollette. Her children are: (a) Stanley Steven Ratliff (born Dec. 15, 1977); (b) Tiffany Fayne Davis (born Jun. 16, 1981); and (c) Alicia Vonne Davis (born Sep. 15, 1982).

5) Stevie Wayne McKenzie (born Dec. 2, 1960).

6) Billy Ray McKenzie (born Oct. 31, 1961) married Anita Louise Keefer, daughter of George and Mae Louise Wheeler Keefer. Their child is Brandon Ray McKenzie (born Jun. 9, 1984).

7) Eddie Jay McKenzie (born Jul. 31, 1963) married Gretta Jean Fraley Cox Daniels, daughter of Chester and Ruth Fraley Butcher. Their children are, (a) Ryan Douglas Daniels, stepson (born May 26, 1986) and (b) Danielle Rashelle Jaye McKenzie (born Feb. 17, 1993).

8) Ollie Francis McKenzie (born Mar. 29, 1965) married Richard Boyd, son of Richard and Jeanette Sindle Boyd, assistant pastor at Walnut Grove Freewill Baptist Church at Lowmansville, KY. Their child is Richard Sherman Boyd (born Dec. 17, 1982).

9) Monroe Dennis McKenzie (born Jul. 25, 1966) married Vicki Lynn Keefer, daughter of George and Mae Louise Wheeler Keefer. Their children are: (a) Christipher George McKenzie (born Feb. 20, 1990); (b) Dakota Alexandra Keefer McKenzie (born Mar. 3, 1993); and (c) Nicholas Wayne McKenzie (born Jul. 17, 1995). *Information provided by George and Ethel McKenzie. Submitted by Vicki Keefer McKenzie.*

MCKENZIE - Henry Patrick McKenzie (born Sep. 15, 1833, Scott County, VA), son of James Henry and Frances (Estep) McKenzie, arrived in Floyd County, KY, in 1837 (today Johnson County) grew up on Tom's Creek (today Sitka), KY, married first Mar. 4, 1853, Johnson County, KY, to Sarah Jane Bayes, daughter of Elijah and Margaret (Rice) Bayes, died Dec. 4, 1857. Issues: Margaret F., James Elijah and William M. McKenzie.

Henry married the second time Sep. 11, 1858, in Johnson County, KY, to Serene Ann Vanover (born Jan. 2, 1833, in Ashe County, NC). She just arrived in Johnson County from Russell County, VA, with her stepfather and mother, Joseph and Catherine (Vanover) Estep. Henry reared his family on the Hood Fork Precinct near where he was reared. In 1860 his uncle, William McKenzie, lived next door to Henry and by 1870 his mother-in-law was only three households away. Issues: Henry Patrick md. Victoria Murray; Levicy md. Francis Marion Kimbler; George M. md. Martha Caldwell; Sarah Catherine md. Franklin Backinridge Salyer; Martellia E. md. John Creed Calwell; Thomas Jefferson md. (first) Missouri Fairchild, (second) Cora Salyer, (third) Lou Caudill; Newton S. md. Arizona Sparks; Jethroe md. Victoria Cantrell; Jacob R. (twin to Jethroe) died Sep. 13, 1887. Henry and Serene were members of Coal Springs United Baptist Church.

Henry joined the Confederate Army Dec. 14, 1861, at Camp Recovery, near Prestonsburg, KY, in Co. K of the 5th Kentucky Inf. He served as a private and fought in the Battle of Middle Creek. The battle resulted in a loss for the Confederates and retreated to Virginia. Henry and several of his comrades remained in Kentucky and were declared deserted on Jan. 16, 1862, and returned to Johnson County and served as a pro-confederate guerrilla until the fall of 1862. On Sep. 24, 1862, he rejoined the 5th Kentucky Inf. at Salyersville, KY, and was appointed musician for Co. F. He took part in the Kentucky campaign which resulted in the confederate defeat at Perryville. On Oct. 1, 1862, he was transferred to Capt. William Field's Company of the Kentucky Partisan Rangers. However on Nov. 30, 1862, the muster roll listed as "cut off by the enemy." Then on Oct. 30, 1863, almost a year later, he joined Co. D of the 14th Kentucky Inf. USA at Louisa, KY. He served the remainder of the war in this unit. About 100 years later in 1962 a crate came in via C & O Rail address to H.L. and Elzie H. McKenzie, it was the Civil War marker with his name Henry McKinza, Co. D 14th Kentucky Inf. Henry died Sep. 10, 1887, and was buried in Joseph Estep Cemetery on Cuba Point, Fuget, KY.

Serene died Aug. 24, 1910, at her son, Henry "Hensock," on Mudlick near Flat Gap, KY, and was buried near her husband. *By Reva Fern (McKenzie) Rose.*

MCKENZIE - Henry Patrick McKenzie II (born Dec. 30, 1862, on Tom's Creek (today Sitka) KY, the son of Henry Patrick McKenzie Sr. and Serene Ann Vanover, married Apr. 1, 1885, to Victoria Murray (born Jan. 10, 1867, on Puncheon Creek, Kerz, KY), the daughter of George Washington Murray and Dicy Salyer.

Young Henry, as he was called, was a tall man of six feet and two inches, weight about 175 pounds or less, bony type structure. As a young man sparking on Puncheon Creek the boys in the area would like to have fun, gang up on Henry, so one day Henry took off his sock and filled it with sand, thus ended the fun session and from that day forward Henry earned the name "Hensock" even his four sons carried "sock" after their first name. Henry was a self-educated man, only attended school to the fourth grade, was well read in history, current events and the Bible. A man who lived and reared his family by the Golden Rule. He was a sawer at a saw mill, many said he could count the footage as the lumber fell from the mill, and a farmer.

He purchased a 100 acre farm on Mudlick, Rt. 172 near Flat Gap, KY, in early 1900, where he reared his family. Issues: Flora Frances md. Elmer Jones, issues: Lavena, Ova Dexter, Cova Frances, Edith, Emma, Deloris and Virginia Victoria; Ira Patrick md. Stella Sparks, issues: Hazel, Neva and Eula; Nora Ellen md. Roscoe Salyer, issues: Marvin, Myrtle, Hoadley, Chester, Earl, Troy, Ochel, Orville "Jr." and Charles Ray; Harry Littleton "Dock" md. Mollie Kimbler, issues: Harry Jr. and Garnet; Charles Howe md. Olive Castle, issues: Venice Dee and Wanda Charlene; Elzie Hayden md. Roberta Elizabeth Young, issues: Imogene, Betty Jean, Reva Fern, Henry Patrick III and Janett Louise; Dixie Lee md. Wade H. McKenzie, issues: Robert Charles, Lois Jacquline, Betty Joy, Vivian Josephine, William Henry, Ival Lorraine, Douglas Howard, Ellis Bond, Melvin Ray and Stella Faye (twin); Ival md. Herbert Blair, issues: Henry Franklin, Patricia Ann, Regina Kaye and Gary Neal.

Henry died Feb. 9, 1951, at home, Flat Gap, KY. Services were at the homeplace, Saturday, Feb. 11, 1950, with Reverend Willard Wilcox and Harry Salyer and songs were sung by the Tom's Creek quartet, prayer by Clyde Conley. Then laid to rest at Sparks Cemetery, Spark's Branch, Flat Gap, KY. Victoria died Apr. 10, 1956, at her daughter's, Ival Blair, Five Forks, Louisa, KY. Services were held at Louisa, KY, by Bruce Daniel and Harry Salyer then laid to rest beside her husband. *By Reva Fern (McKenzie) Rose.*

MCKENZIE - Jack McKenzie was born on Feb. 28, 1942, at home in Flat Gap, KY, to Ray and Beulah Lyon McKenzie. Jack's birth was attended by Dr. F.M. Picklesimer of Paintsville. Jack is the youngest of four children, having two sisters, Emma Joy Kazee and Clista Margaret Pelfrey; and one brother, Daren Ray McKenzie.

Jack McKenzie

When Jack was very young his family moved to Keaton to care for his great-grandmother. Jack began his formal education in the one room school at Keaton. He has since earned two college degrees. His father was employed by Ashland Oil & Refining Co. at the Cattletsburg plant and the family moved to Boyd County. Jack graduated from Ashland City schools and attended the University of Kentucky extension for two years majoring in business. Jack worked for Ashland Oil & Refining Co. during this time.

Jack and Ellen Kay Arthur were married in January 1963. They have three children: William Raymond, Elizabeth Charlene and Paula Kay. They also have six grandchildren.

In 1965 Jack joined the Navy and served 10 years as an electronics technician/instructor/special projects logistician. In the Navy Jack received 132 weeks of electronics training after which he developed and taught an additional 40 weeks of communications and electronics courses. The first four years in the Navy were served at Naval Air Station Oceana, VA, working in the Aircraft Maintenance Dept. The next six years were served at Patuxent River Naval Test Center in Maryland in Fleet Air Recon. Sqdn. Four (VQ-4) as an instructor and special projects logistician. VQ-4 is a communications platform that provides a strategic link from the Joint Chiefs of Staff and the president to the Nuclear Forces of the U.S. The platform uses a dual antenna with one being five miles in length and a 200KW transmitter with the nuclear submarines around the world. VQ-4 is a part of the community called TACAMO.

In 1975 Jack left the Navy for employment with Rockwell International located in Texas as an instructor and logistician. While at Rockwell Jack attended night school at Grayson County College and the University of Texas at Dallas to complete his formal education in business and science.

At Rockwell International, Jack has developed another 60 weeks of communications and electronics courses. As a logistician engineer, Jack has provided the planning resources necessary to field new military systems around the world.

Jack and his wife, Kay, live in Plano, TX, and take every opportunity to enjoy their church, grandchildren and to return to visit the hills of Eastern Kentucky that they still consider home. Their future plans include retirement to the community of Jack's birth, Flat Gap, Johnson County, KY. *Submitted by Clista M. McKenzie Pelfrey.*

MCKENZIE & ESTEP - James Earl was born Jun. 20, 1904, on McKenzie Branch at Stone Coal in Johnson County to James David (born Sep. 18, 1865, died Jan. 22, 1942) and Laura May McKenzie (born Oct. 15, 1868, died Sep. 12, 1911). Earl had six brothers: Powell, Oscar, Halleck, Charles Haston, Beldon and Frank; and five sisters: Ella, Lula, Ollie, Buelah and Maxie. They were all born in Johnson County, KY. James David was the son of Oliver Brown McKenzie and Martha Jane Blanton.

James Earl and Cloma Estep McKenzie

Laura was the daughter of Mary Ann Mahan and Sam May. Cloma was born Sep. 14, 1908, on Patterson Creek at Flat Gap in Johnson County to Scott Estep (born Jan. 15, 1878, died Mar. 7, 1953) and Carrie Belle Collinsworth Arnett Estep (born Aug. 25, 1884, died Oct. 14, 1954). Cloma had two brothers, Charlie Jay and Glenn; and one half brother, Taylor Arnett. She had one sister, Hazel and one half sister, Flora Estep Cantrell. Scott was the son of Ambrose Jay and Elizabeth Jane Holbrook Estep. Carrie was the daughter of Edward and Ellen Risner Collinsworth of Magoffin County, KY.

Both Earl and Cloma attended one room schools, he at McKenzie Branch, she at Patterson Creek. They met while attending church at Joe's Creek in Johnson County and were married on Aug. 26, 1926, at Volga, KY, in Johnson County by E.H. Prater. Earl worked as a mail carrier and in the 1950s he and Cloma owned and operated a store on Patterson. He worked for the Kentucky State Highway Dept. until 1959 and was also a farmer. Cloma was a housewife and homemaker and kept very busy rearing six children.

Earl and Cloma had two sons, James O. and Charles A.; and four daughters: Betty, Phyllis, Donlyn and Gail. Their children gifted them with nine grandchildren, 13 great-grandchildren and one great-great-grandchild.

Cloma and Earl were members at the Bethel United Baptist Church located at Flat Gap until their deaths. Earl passed away on Jul. 10, 1967, at the age of 63. Cloma died Dec. 22, 1990, at the age of 82. They were buried in the family cemetery on Patterson Creek where they had lived all their lives.

Earl and Cloma were the descendants of early pioneer families who came to Johnson County from Virginia and helped to settle the area.

MCKENZIE - A man as steadfast and true as the rock of Gibraltar and as kind-hearted and gentle as a saint was born on May 22, 1927, in Johnson County at Flat Gap. "He is as fine a gentleman as there is anywhere." "He is a man you can always depend on to keep his word." "If you ask him a question he may not give you the answer you want but he'll tell you the truth." "He was never afraid of hard work." These quotes are typical comments about this man.

James O. McKenzie

This good man is James O. McKenzie. He is the oldest of six children born to Cloma (Estep) and James Earl McKenzie of Flat Gap. He spent his boyhood on the family farm at Patterson Creek. His elementary school was taken at Patterson Creek Elementary School. He graduated from Flat Gap High School in 1948. His high school career was interrupted by a two year stint in the U.S. Army, six months of which he spent in Japan. In spite of the interruption, he returned to school determined to earn his high school diploma.

Following high school graduation he married Betty Pelphrey, daughter of Challie and Malta (Rice) Pelphrey. James and Betty have lived all their married life in Johnson County and now live in Staffordsville.

They had three children. Jim owns D and L Trucking Co. Kathy is a speech pathologist. Scott is an auditor for the state treasurer's office in Frankfort.

James became a truck driver in 1948 when he began working for Farmers Supply in Paintsville. In 1952 he transferred to Big Sandy Hardware where he drove a tractor-trailer for 24 years until 1976. By that time he had become involved in Kentucky's coal business and was buying, leasing and selling coal mined here in the mountains. He began his own trucking company called Thunderbolt Trucking in 1980. With the help of his wife, Betty, he manages a small fleet of trucks which transports coal to plants and factories. Recyclables such as steel, aluminum, copper and brass are trucked to sites all over the eastern U.S. James works side by side with his older son, Jim, and they run their trucking companies from "The Lot" on U.S. 23. Together, with occasional help from Jim's sons, Dewayne and Corey, this father and son works as a team which has provided jobs for our community, coal for our electricity and recycling services for our environment.

At the age of 72 years, James O. still works from daylight to dark managing the business at the truck lot. Sometimes he takes time off to entertain his grandchildren: Dewayne and wife, Kim, and great-granddaughters: Baylee, Corey, Carla, Madison, Kenton and Johnson McKenzie and Mackenzie Crigger.

What this man gave and is still giving to Johnson County is years of hard and honest work for his family and community. He reared a family of people who believe in God, the American Dream and Kentucky.

MCKENZIE - John McKenzie was born in Scotland in 1780 and came to the USA about 1785. He settled in Virginia, married Ellen Boggs (aka) Martha Patsy Cox (born 1784 died 1845). John died in 1837 and he and his wife are buried in Virginia. John's son, Oliver McKenzie (born 1813 in Virginia), married Matilda Strong (born 1814, in Scott County, VA).

John and Survilla Segraves McKenzie

Matilda was the daughter of John and Hannah Quillen Strong. John Strong was the son of Thomas and Anna Fields Strong. Oliver and Matilda came to Kentucky in 1855. Oliver died May 17, 1878. Oliver and Matilda are buried at Elna, Johnson County, KY.

Other siblings of Oliver, seven of whom settled in Kentucky. James Henry (born 1803) married Francis Estep, settled at Tom's Creek; William (born 1805) married Barbara Estep, settled at Stone Coal; Nancy (born 1808) married John Egan, remained in Virginia; Elizabeth (born 1810) married George W. Webb, settled at Flat Gap; David Jesse (born 1811) married first, Cynthia Estep and married second, Ann Saunders, settled at McKenzie Branch; John (born 1815) married Nancy Wilhite, settled in Boyd County; Hughie (born 1817) married Martha Patsy Webb, settled at Patty Flats.

Oliver and Matilda Strong McKenzie are the parents of the following children, also listed are their children's spouses: Henry md. Lisa Hill; Dora md. Melissa Salyer; James Elbert md. Cynthia Jayne; Asberry md. Nancy Evelyn Williams; Aaron md. Edith Stapleton; Elza md. first, Oma Pelfrey, md. second, Polly ?, from England; Rebecca md. Richard Coffee; Sarah Elizabeth md. Stephen Lemaster; Phebe E. md. Richard Hamilton; Melissa Anna md. Thomas Salyer; Nancy J. md. Joe Gullett; John McKenzie md. Survilla Segraves. John and Survilla are buried in the McKenzie Cemetery on the Merdia Oliver McKenzie farm at Flat Gap, Johnson County, KY.

Listed are the children of John and Survilla Segraves McKenzie and their children's spouses: Merdia Oliver McKenzie md. Clista Margaret Green; Sebastain McKenzie md. Allie Blanton; Albert McKenzie md. Clora Williams; Landio McKenzie md. Clara Hill; Emma McKenzie md. Charlie Woods.

Victoria McKenzie died at age 12 and is buried in the cemetery, near her grandparents, Oliver and Matilda Strong McKenzie, located at Elna, KY. See additional McKenzie family history under Merdia Oliver McKenzie records. *Submitted by Clista M. McKenzie Pelfrey.*

MCKENZIE - Jimmie Darrell McKenzie (born Jul. 10, 1954, in Johnson County, KY) on Aug. 4, 1974, married Gwendolyn Jacqueline Stapleton (born Aug. 13, 1959), daughter of Wilmer and Sarah Rosetta Rowland Stapleton. To this union three children were born.

Tina Raye McKenzie (born Mar. 22, 1975) married Joseph Stephen Cole, son of Jesse Eugene Cole and Anita Gaye Daniels, Sep. 4, 1993. To this union was born three children also: Joseph Stephen Cole II (born Dec. 8, 1994), Kailey Alissa Cole (born May 20, 1997) and Benjamin Noah Cole (born Jul. 23, 1998).

Clayton Darrell McKenzie (born Mar. 22, 1978) graduated from Johnson Central High school and attended Cumberland College for two years and finished his education at Morehead State's campus in Prestonsburg.

Sarah Rebecca McKenzie (born Nov. 6, 1982) plans to finish High School at Johnson Central and go to college and major in communications.

Joseph, Joseph II, Tina McKenzie and Kailey Cole; Rebecca, Jackie and Clayton McKenzie.

Jim worked as a carpet installer for many years. He also worked in the coal mines for two years. In the year 1999 he is currently employed as an insurance agent at American General in Paintsville, KY. Jim was called to preach the gospel in 1983. He began his ministry at Sitka Freewill Baptist Church and in 1985 became pastor, which is his current position today at Sitka Freewill Baptist Church. *Submitted by Jackie Stapleton McKenzie.*

MCKENZIE - Merdia Oliver McKenzie, son of John and Survilla Segraves McKenzie was born Apr. 7, 1873, at Red Bush, KY, and died Apr. 24, 1964, at his home at Flat Gap, KY. Merdia married Clista Margaret Green Jan. 19, 1901. She is the daughter of George and Jane Lemaster Green. Clista was born Apr. 9, 1879, and died Oct. 26, 1914. Merdia Oliver and Clista Margaret are buried in the McKenzie Family Cemetery at Flat Gap, KY., located on the farm they owned.

Merdia Oliver and Clista Margaret Green McKenzie. Children: Goldie, Ray and Nelson.

Merdia and Clista had three children: Goldie Mae McKenzie (born Apr. 25, 1905, at Red Bush, KY, died Feb. 25, 1946, at home at Flat Gap, KY) was single; Ray McKenzie (born Jan. 22, 1907, at Red Bush, KY, died Jun. 5, 1980, in Kings Daughters Hospital in Ashland, KY) married Beulah Lyon; and Nelson McKenzie (born Aug. 7, 1909, at Flat Gap, KY, died Jul. 25, 1973, at home at Flat Gap, KY) married Vertrice Castle.

Merdia was educated in Johnson County Schools. The first school he attended was known as a "Blab" school, meaning that all reading was done aloud. He attended the Flat Gap Academy and became a teacher. He taught school in Johnson County for 32 years. In his early teaching days he taught at a one room school and his older students went into the near-by woods to gather wood to use to heat the classroom. There was no teacher's retirement in those days. Merdia was also a farmer and owned a saw and grist mill that he and his sons operated. He was a carpenter and he taught school during the day and built his new home in the evening hours. He hand-crafted display shelves for his grandchildren and great-grandchildren. Merdia presented a baby ring to each new great-grandchild when they were born. These rings are precious keepsakes. He was also a watch repairman. Merdia was widowed at a young age and left with three children to rear alone. He never married again.

Merdia was a great lover of music and played old time fiddle tunes, such as *Cripple Creek*, *Wildwood Flower*, *Listen To The Mockingbird* and *When The Roll Is Called Up Yonder*. He and his son, Ray, played for country dances during Ray's young days.

Merdia became a born-again Christian about 1928 and joined the Flat Gap Enterprise Baptist Church where he served as clerk for many years. He was richly blessed with the much deserved love of his former students, children, grandchildren and great-grandchildren. As he grew older he always dressed himself in his Sunday best to be ready for his "surprise" birthday party each April 7th. He treated every person he met with great kindness and respect and was loved not only by his family but all who were blessed to know him. *Submitted by Clista Margaret McKenzie Pelfrey.*

MCKENZIE - Monroe Dennis McKenzie (born Jul. 25, 1966, in Johnson County, KY), son of George "Bill" and Ethel McKenzie, married Oct. 19, 1985, at the Chandlersville Church, Chandlersville, KY, Vicki Lynn Keefer (born Mar. 1, 1970, in Franklin County, OH), daughter of George and Mae Louise Wheeler Keefer. Monroe has followed in his father's footsteps and is a coal miner. He currently works for Coalburg.

Monroe Dennis McKenzie Family

Children of Monroe and Vicki are: Christipher George McKenzie, named after both his Grandpas (born Feb. 20, 1990, in Johnson County, KY); Dakota Alexandra Keefer McKenzie, named after her mother (born Mar. 3, 1993, in Johnson County, KY); and Nicholas Wayne McKenzie, named after his Uncle Steve (born Jul. 17, 1995, in Johnson County, KY).

They reside in Johnson County, KY, and attend the Sitka Freewill Baptist Church.

MCKENZIE - Nelson McKenzie was born Aug. 7, 1909, at Flat Gap, KY, to Merdia Oliver and Clista Margaret Green McKenzie. He died Jul. 25, 1973, at his home at Flat Gap. He is buried in the McKenzie Family Cemetery on the home place.

Nelson, Vertrice (Castle) and Debra Ruth McKenzie.

Nelson attended school at Flat Gap. He earned his living by farming and driving a Johnson County school bus. He farmed with a team of horses that powered the turning plow, drag, mowing machine and hay rake. Some of the hay cuttings were stored in the barn loft. The remainder was stacked around a tall pole and left outside. This was called a haystack. Nelson and his father operated the grist and saw mill owned by the family.

Nelson married Vertrice Castle (born Dec. 29, 1928). Nelson and Vertrice had one daughter, Debra Ruth McKenzie (born Mar. 20, 1949). Debra Ruth married Clifford Dale Kemp (born May 21, 1943, in Canada). They have four children: Kelly Gyne, Richard Paul, Christopher Eugene and Patricia Ruth. Debra Ruth no longer lives in Kentucky. She and Cliff make their home in Huntertown, IN, where they are involved in their church and loving their grandchildren.

Vertrice is married the second time to Jim Hayes and lives in Ohio. She returns to Johnson County at every opportunity to visit with her dear family and friends. *Submitted by Clista Margaret McKenzie Pelfrey.*

MCKENZIE - Ray McKenzie, son of Merdia Oliver and Clista Margaret Green McKenzie, was born Jan. 22, 1907, at Red Bush, KY. He died at Kings Daughters Hospital in Ashland, KY, Jun. 5, 1980. He is buried in the McKenzie Family Cemetery at Flat Gap, KY, located on the Merdia Oliver McKenzie family farm where Ray grew up. Ray's parents bought the farm at Flat Gap and moved there about the time Ray was 2 years old. He attended Johnson County Schools and Morehead State College. As he grew up he learned how to farm, cut timber, operate the steam powered boiler that powered a saw and grist mill owned by his dad. He later, along with the help of his dad, built his own family home on the McKenzie farm. This home is currently occupied by Ray's granddaughter, Margaret Wynn Pelfrey Napier.

Ray and Beulah (Lyon) McKenzie

He played many musical instruments with the guitar being his favorite. He and his dad played for country dances with Ray attaching a harmonica to the neck of his guitar and playing both instruments at the same time. He read music well and also played the piano and organ.

Ray was very skilled in playing baseball and played on the Big Sandy team. He also played on a Morehead College team that won a State Championship. His best plays were made as first baseman but he played other positions as well.

When Ray was ready to go to high school, he went to Paintsville and stayed with his Aunt Clora Williams McKenzie and attended school there until the high school was established at Flat Gap. He then returned home and graduated with the first graduating class at Flat Gap High School in 1930. After attending Morehead College he taught at Flat Gap, Upper Franks Creek and a two room school at Lower Keaton. His annual pay for teaching school was $344.47.

Ray and Beulah Lyon were married May 6, 1930, by Rev. J.D. Marcum in Louisa, KY. They had four children: Emma Joy (born Jun. 27, 1931); Clista Margaret (born Dec. 26, 1932); Daren Ray (born Jul. 31, 1934); and Jack Paul (born Feb. 28, 1942).

Ray decided to leave the teaching profession, therefore, from Apr. 8, 1943-Apr. 6, 1944, he served as an auxiliary to the Military Police of the Army of the USA at Ashland Oil Refining Co. at Cattletsburg, KY. He received an honorable discharge and began his employment for A.O.& R. as boiler operator. Ray continued in this profession until his retirement at 65 in 1972. He was critically injured in an explosion at work in October 1971, however he survived and lived for several years. He loved to fish and camp and to hunt quail and squirrel. Ray and Beulah bought a home in 1954 in South Ashland and Beulah has continued to live there after Ray's death. *Submitted by Clista M. McKenzie Pelfrey.*

MCKENZIE - Thomas Jefferson McKenzie, son of Henry Patrick McKenzie and Serena Vanover, was born Dec. 18, 1873, in Flat Gap, Johnson County, KY. Tom was a carpenter and lived his entire life in Johnson County.

Tom married first, his first cousin, Missouri Fairchild, on Oct. 14, 1890, daughter of Moses Fairchild and Catherine McKenzie. Tom and Missouri had two sons, William W. McKenzie (born Jan. 2, 1891, died Jan. 7, 1891) and Wiley P. McKenzie (born Jan. 16, 1892, died Feb. 11, 1892). Both William and Wiley are buried next to their mother in unmarked graves on Joe's Creek, near Flat Gap.

Tom married second, May 27, 1899, Cora Ellen Salyer (born Dec. 22, 1878), daughter of Jonathan Henry Salyer and Alina Jones. Tom and Cora had the following children before Cora's early death on Jun. 15, 1914: Georgia Ann McKenzie (born Aug. 14, 1899, died Nov. 11, 1906), Erie Pennsylvania McKenzie (born Feb. 25, 1900, died Dec. 6, 1904), Nianzie R. McKenzie (born Jul. 3, 1902, died Aug. 12, 1903), Estell McKenzie (born Mar. 19, 1908, died Jul. 17, 1910), Osker McKenzie (born Feb. 24, 1912, died Feb. 12, 1913), Bessie McKenzie (born May 3, 1914, in Flat Gap, Johnson County, KY, died Jan. 28, 1987, and buried Authy Daniels Cemetery, Johnson County, KY) married Con Lemaster; Tera McKenzie (born Apr. 20, 1906, in Flat Gap, Johnson County, KY, died Nov. 11, 1986) married Elva Sparks, Feb. 2, 1924, in Paintsville, Johnson County, KY, son of Jesse Sparks and Jemima Ellen Lemaster.

Thomas Jefferson McKenzie married third, Lou Sparks and they had one child, Rinnie McKenzie (born Sep. 16, 1918, died Mar. 10, 1919), buried in the Authy Daniels Cemetery, Daniels Branch, Johnson County, KY.

Thomas Jefferson McKenzie died Jun. 16, 1950, in Paintsville and is buried in the Sparks family cemetery on Sparks Branch, near Flat Gap, KY. *By Mary K. Goodyear.*

MCKENZIE - Thomas McKenzie was born Apr. 25, 1833, in Virginia. He died Feb. 6, 1915, dates found on his headstone. He lived on Drake. He was married to Lizzie Rose Fyffe. She was born Feb. 22, 1836, and died May 5, 1899, dates found on her headstone.

Thomas McKenzie house

Lizzie was the daughter of Thomas Fyffe and Rhoda Fyffe. Thomas was a blacksmith. His children are: William (born Mar. 1, 1861, died Mar. 11, 1934); John (born circa 1863); Rhoda (born Sep. 23, 1864, died Jan. 24, 1957) was married to William Marion Ross Mar. 19, 1893. Rhoda and William Marion are my great-grandparents; Martha (born circa 1867); Sarah born (circa 1868); Meredith (born circa 1872); and James (born Apr. 12, 1876). *By James David Ross.*

MCKENZIE - The Staffordsville-Johnson County area has lost a great man, Ervin W. McKenzie, better known to his many friends and family as "Wade," will long be remembered.

What is a Father and Friend?

A father and friend is someone thoughtful, understanding, dear and kind that lets you ask a lot of him and never seemed to mind. He's someone, who will listen to the things you talk about, give you advice, or well-earned praise and always help you out. He's someone to admire and love the whole year through - at least that's what a father and friend is if he's at all like Dad.

Wade McKenzie

Wade was born on May 24, 1927, in Johnson County to Kitty (daughter of Schuyler and Rosie 'Witten' Rice) and Roy Lee (son of Phoebe J. 'Fairchild' and John McKenzie). His mother was a housewife while his father was a mail carrier for many years. He was the youngest of seven children. He had four brothers: Hobert (born Oct. 10, 1911) married Lora Blanton, Marvin "Tom" (born Oct. 19, 1915) married Sipp Williams, John Schuyler (born Nov. 19, 1918) married Edna Lee Reed and Charlie (born Jun. 22, 1921), killed in France during WWII on Jun. 20, 1944). He had twin sisters, May and Fay (born Feb. 6, 1912) who died in infancy.

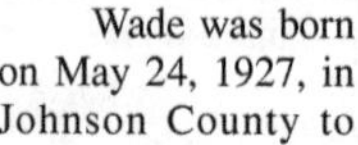

He was married in Magoffin County to Edna Earle (daughter of Nancy Evelyn 'Blair' and Morton Griffith) of Hager Hill, KY, on Jul. 16, 1945. To this union three daughters were born: Carolyn Jane of West Liberty, KY, married Paul Arch Keeton; Connie Jean of Nippa, KY, married Clarence Scarberry; and Cathie Lynn of Staffordsville, KY, married Harold Gene Hall.

Wade attended one-room schools at Ramey Branch and Clifton in Johnson County. He never graduated from high school; but his knowledge was by no means limited.

He grew up in the community of Stone Coal at Volga, KY, and lived there approximately 28 years. Wade was a hard worker all of his life. His first job was at Big Sandy Hardware at the age of 16 driving a delivery truck. From there he answered the call of duty to his country, by serving two years in the Army. Upon returning, he went to work for Hardware Charlie delivering gas. He worked at Preston Funeral Home driving an ambulance, as well as being in many funerals. He later took over his father's mail route from Paintsville to West Liberty. Wade also worked on the pipelines in Illinois, Indiana, Michigan, Ohio and Pennsylvania before he went to work for himself hauling and delivering hay in Johnson County. When coal started booming, bigger trucks came into the picture. He started his own trucking company with six trucks hauling coal down Route 23. He served as one of Johnson County's commissioners for four years. This was his last public job. Upon retiring, he was a night watchman with Bizzack Construction for 13 years.

He was a member of Ramey Branch Community Church, Volga, KY. Serving as deacon and trustee.

Dad was a man that went at every thing he did whole-heartedly. He enjoyed life, and no one was a stranger to him. His favorite pastime was fishing, he had the patience of Job, and he truly enjoyed this until his sudden passing on Mar. 27, 1996. He is buried at Highlands Memorial Park at Staffordsville, KY.

This is our tribute to him, our father and friend. *Written by Carolyn Keeton.*

MCKENZIE - William Oakley McKenzie (born Oct. 4, 1917, in Johnson County, KY, died May 10, 1947) was a sawmill worker. He was the son of Hollie McKenzie and Missie Stapleton McKenzie. Oakley was married to Mary Magdaline Holbrook on May 6, 1939. She was the daughter of James Albert Holbrook and Rebecca Emeline Sparks Holbrook. Rebecca was born Jan. 29, 1922, in Louisa, KY, and died Jan. 10, 1987. Mary Magdaline is buried at Pleasant Hill Cemetery in W. Jefferson, OH.

Oakley and Mary's children are: William Ray (born May 16, 1940, Lawrence County, KY) married to Carolyn Kitts; James Donald (born Jul. 31, 1943, Lawrence County, KY) married to Phyllis Brigner; Oakley Marvin (born Aug. 21, 1945, in Lawrence County, KY) married Betty Lou Strawser on Aug. 20, 1965; and Barbara Jane (born Dec. 6, 1947, in Lawrence County, KY) married Robert Phillips. *By James David Ross.*

William Oakley McKenzie

MEDDINGS - Charles Lawrence "Jinks" Meddings was born in Tayes, Putnam County, WV, Apr. 17, 1894. He was the eighth child born to Patrick Henry Meddings and Mary Ellen (Nelson) Meddings. In 1910, his parents made the move from West Virginia to Van Lear, Johnson County, KY, bringing with them their teenage son, Lawrence. As soon as he was old enough to work inside the mines, he began working for Consol. He felt he was getting in on the ground floor as the company was still in the process of building this modern coal town. Evidently, this was correct, as he remained in Van Lear until his death.

Lawrence and Minnie with their family at J.H. Feltner 4-H Camp, Fishtrap, Manila, Johnson County, KY.

In 1915, Lawrence met and married Minnie McCarty, from Louisa, Lawrence County, KY. Minnie was the daughter of George Washington and Mary Elizabeth (Clark) McCarty. In those days, there could be no better place for a young couple to establish a home. This was a new company with modern ideas. Salaries were good and the company offered many opportunities. Thus began another Meddings family in Van Lear.

Lawrence and Minnie renew their vows on their 50th anniversary in 1965

This marriage was blessed with four children: Charles Huffman (born 1916), Beatrice Elouise (born 1918), Wayne Anderson (born 1922) and Virginia Maxine (born 1925). All four children were born in Van Lear and attended Van Lear schools.

As soon as Huff was old enough to work inside the mine, he followed his dad's footsteps and began underground for the coal company. He was a young man with a good job, making big money and was truly happy.

Our country was in a state of unrest. The U.S. initiated a military draft so America's young men would be trained to defend our country. Being single, in good mental and physical health, Huffman was in the first call of Johnson County men to be drafted into the U.S. Army, June 1941.

Huff found he liked the service life. He chose to make a career soldier. He had remarked to friends that he never intended to go under the hill in a coal mine again, he had found a "Home in the Army." Only seven months later, Dec. 7, 1941, changed the lives of so many of our young men ... Pearl Harbor Day. Huffman was already being trained for whatever was ahead for our military.

Although he liked Army life, he always stayed close to his family and friends in Johnson County. Everyone looked forward to his next furlough.

December 1959, his parents were informed by the U.S. Army, that M/Sgt. Charles Huffman Meddings was critically ill, in Madrid, Spain. Military doctors had performed emergency surgery that date, thinking it to be routine ulcer surgery. They did inform the family, he would be flown to the States and hospitalized near the family as soon as his condition would allow him to be transported.

Practically simultaneous another report came, post-op test had changed the previous diagnosis of ulcer to cancer. Again, they reported the urgency to fly him stateside to be near his family and special medical attention. Huffman only lived 10 days after surgery. He died in Madrid, Spain. He never became strong enough to be transported to the U.S. His remains were escorted home by the military. His funeral was in Van Lear and he was laid to rest in the Highland Memorial Cemetery, Staffordsville, KY.

After Beatrice completed school, she married her high school sweetheart, Mearl Meade, son of Jeff and Ida Meade. There were three children born to this marriage: Charles Thomas, Betty and Mike. As the Consolidation Coal Co. began to close out in Van Lear, Bea and Mearl, along with many others from the area, moved to North Manchester, IN, seeking work. Soon Mearl's health began to fail. His parents, as well as her parents, were getting older and not well. They returned from Indiana after seven years. Mearl suffered a massive heart attack in 1974. He is buried in Highland Memorial Cemetery, Staffordsville.

Beatrice still lives in Van Lear and spends most of her time doing church work. She is an active member of the First Church of God in Paintsville. She is also a great-grandmother with pictures.

Just as Wayne became a young man, he compared a career in the mines to a military career and followed in his brother, Huff's path. Wayne served two terms in the Army, enlisting twice. He spent 18 months of the second enlistment as a Prisoner of War in a German Prison Camp, during WWII.

After returning from the war and some rest and recuperation at home, Wayne traveled to Illinois seeking work. He found work and also found a wife, Ina Scholl. There were two sons born to this marriage. Wayne was stricken with cancer and expired in 1992. He is buried in McHenry, IL, where he and Ina had established their home and reared their family.

Shortly after completion of school Virginia "Jenny" also went to Illinois. She met and married Richard Doherty. They had four children. Dec. 7, 1998, Jenny died of cancer. She is buried near Wayne in Illinois.

In the 40s Lawrence was diagnosed with cancer near his ear. At that time there was very little treatment available. In order to save his life, he had radical and disfiguring surgery. Although he was not really well the 20 plus surviving years he kept his jovial personality. He truly loved everyone. He was a pleasure to be around.

Lawrence and Minnie were both active Christians and will always be remembered for their work in The Little Mission Church in Van Lear. Both are buried in the Highland Cemetery at Staffordsville, KY.

MELVIN - Charles T. Melvin was born on Dec. 13, 1923, in Johnson County to Roy and Stella Robinson Melvin. The oldest of six children, he graduated from Paintsville High School in 1941 with 39 other students.

After high school, he enlisted and served in the Armed Forces for four years. During WWII, he was stationed at Guadalcanal and the Philippines. Upon his return home, he began working for his father in the grocery business and soon established his own grocery business in which he was active for over 50 years contributing generously to community and local organizations and events.

In 1945, he married Opal Williams. Opal, who was instrumental in assisting him in developing a retail grocery business is also an avid golfer. They had two children, Charles T. Melvin Jr. and Kimberly Melvin.

Charles "Chuck" Melvin Jr., who began as a grocer with his father, is currently an active businessman and is involved in many community and philanthropic events as well as serving on the board of the Paintsville Country Club. He is married to Anna Lou Deskins, elected commonwealth's attorney for the 24th Circuit in 1993. They have three children: Emily Ann Melvin Mooring, a student at the University of Kentucky School of Law; Charles T. "Ty" Melvin III, also a student at the University of Kentucky; and Lauren, a seventh grader at Paintsville Middle School. Chuck, Anna and their children attend the First United Methodist Church.

Kimberly is married to James Michael Lauffer, a local businessman involved in the gas and oil drilling industry. Kimberly has been an active and full-time member of the Booster Club at Paintsville High School for many years. They have three children: Seth, who attends the University of Kentucky; Will, a junior at Paintsville High School; and Clara, a fifth grader at Paintsville Elementary.

Charles T. Melvin served three terms on the Paintsville City Council and has served as a member of the Paintsville City Utilities Board. He is also a 50 year member of the First United Methodist Church.

Like his father before him, his love of family and horses continues to this day, and having instilled the same in his grandchildren, you might find Emily and Ty, both well-known equestrians like their grandfather, at the Tennessee Walking Horse Celebration or other horse shows throughout the year in the southeast.

MELVIN - Roy Melvin (born Apr. 12, 1898) was the son of John and Ida Stafford Melvin. John Melvin was the son of George and Martha Baldwin Melvin from Orange County, NC. Martha was also from North Carolina. Ida's parents, George Washington Stafford and Susan Turner, were both from Johnson County.

Roy attended the Paintsville Public School System and finished the eighth grade. As was often the custom at that time, Roy quit school to work full-time and help support his family.

At age 23, Roy married Stella Robinson, daughter of Enoch and Nancy Music Robinson. Enoch was Paintsville's chief of police during the 1930s. Along with his brother-in-law, Bill Robinson, Roy owned and managed the Busy Bee Restaurant on Main Street during the 1930s. In the late 30s and 40s, Roy owned and operated a grocery store beside the Southside Bridge on Main Street. In the late 50s and 60s, Roy owned and managed a trailer park and grocery on West Third Street. Later he converted this grocery into a furniture store.

Roy and Stella had six children, four sons and two daughters: Charles T. Melvin, local businessman married to Opal Williams from Wayland in Floyd County who attended Paintsville High School; Leroy Melvin, pharmaceutical salesman married to Nancy Snow, a social worker from Lexington, KY; John Walter who died at age 5; Patsy Carrol Melvin, a community leader and wife of Circuit Judge James A. Knight; Shirley Melvin, teacher for 30 years with the Johnson County School System, wife of Roger D. Short, retired assistant director of the Carl D. Perkins Rehabilitation Center; and David Powell Melvin, a Paintsville merchant now employed with the IRS.

During his career, Roy also served as a Paintsville city councilman, was known for his great love of horses and his generosity to people throughout the community during troubling times. Many recall the assistance he gave to their families when money was scarce. A highly successful businessman, Roy was known and beloved as a "character" and made many contributions to Paintsville and Johnson County.

MONTGOMERY - Mother: Eva Penix Montgomery (born Feb. 4, 1907, in Magoffin County, KY, died Jun. 9, 1963). Father: Willie "Buttermilk" Montgomery (born 1905 in Martin County, KY, died in 1974). I don't recall how or where my parents met, but they married in Johnson County on Oct. 18, 1924. Daddy was what you would call a contract painter and brick layer. Mommy stayed at home and took care of us kids and the upkeep of the home. Mommy was the daughter of Roscoe and Loudena Litteral Penix. Daddy was the son of Jim and Lizzie Keaton Montgomery. On the other Montgomery side my great-grandparents were Thomas Anthony and Betz Smith Montgomery.

Willie "Buttermilk" and Eva Penix Montgomery

Children: Louise Montgomery (born Oct. 13, 1925, died May 10, 1992), Juanita Montgomery (born Mar. 31, 1927, died Jun. 2, 1979), Marvin Montgomery (born Jun. 24, 1930), Richard Montgomery (born March 1931, died Sep. 11, 1934), Charles Montgomery (born Nov. 4, 1932, died Sep. 2, 1972), Glen Montgomery (born Apr. 27, 1933), Patsy Montgomery (born Jul. 9, 1938) and Joseph Montgomery (born Feb. 23, 1944, died Aug. 13, 1994). My parents also reared one grandchild, Frances A. Collins (born Jan. 28, 1944). Frances is the daughter of my sister, Louise.

We moved from Southside to Bristle Buck to Stafford Bottom, then we moved to Williams Branch. All of these places were part of Johnson County. In the early 1940s we moved to Blackberry, now known as Sixth Street. That is where we all grew up and all of us attended the old Paintsville School. *Prepared by Patsy C. Montgomery and Norma J. Holbrook.*

MOLLETT - Stella Ward, daughter of Exer Baldridge and Elias Ward of Williamsport, and Forest Mollett, son of Sarah Jane Spears and Jerry Mollett of Tomahawk, were married in Meally on May 15, 1937, and moved into a little house Forest built on the Left Fork of Two-Mile Creek. From this marriage were born three daughters: Exer Jane (Pass) on Sep. 13, 1938, Elizabeth (Flashner) on Feb. 8, 1941, and Jean Marie (Dorton) on Apr. 14, 1953. Later there were seven grandchildren: James J. Pass Jr., David Forest Jacob Flashner, Carl Forest Pass, Ruth Evelyn Pass (Walton), Evan Douglas Flashner, Lori Jo Flashner and Andrew Trigg Dorton. Although they began their married life in Williamsport and lived there at several times in their early married life, they resided mainly in Paintsville with some short intervals in Lima, OH, until they returned to Williamsport in 1977 in preparation for their retirement. This retirement together was short-lived, as Stella died a year and a half later.

Forest and Stella Mollett

Stella graduated from Meade Memorial High School and attended Georgetown College for two years, majoring in foreign languages. She returned to Williamsport to marry Forest and teach school on Hurricane Creek in Johnson County. She worked intermittently over the next several years while raising her family. In 1955 she returned to teaching in the Johnson County Schools while completing her bachelor's degree in education at Morehead State University. Most of her teaching career was accomplished at West Van Lear School and Porter Elementary where she was well-known for her skill in teaching reading and math. Even though she retired from teaching in 1977, she continued to be involved with Porter School until her death in January of 1979.

Forest was mainly a self-educated man. His mother used to tell tales of the practice he did on the early automobiles at her front gate. This mechanical skill served him well in later years, as he became legendary among International truck owners both in Johnson County, KY, and Lima, OH. His natural talents were supplemented by training programs he completed at the International Harvester Company in Fort Wayne, IN. After retiring in 1972 from Big Sandy Motor Co. in Paintsville, he worked part-time for several years for Roberts and Jenkins Drilling Co. and worked at woodcraft and quilting. Neighbors, family and friends brought him many pieces of machinery and furniture to repair or other problems to solve. He remained active in these pursuits until his death at 83 on Dec. 11, 1995.

From 1954 until their deaths, Stella and Forest were active members of the First Christian Church. Forest also served as a deacon and was chief volunteer handyman.

Following Stella's death, Forest married Elizabeth Daniels Davis on Jun. 30, 1979, merging two families consisting of 10 children and numerous grandchildren and great-grandchildren. They enjoyed a happy union for 16-1/2 years interacting with their extended family and continuing to pursue their interests in traveling, crafts, quilting, visiting family and attending church.

MORRIS - Patricia R. Baldwin was born Feb. 25, 1936, at Paintsville, Johnson County, KY, the fifth child born to McKinley and Nova Holbrook Baldwin.

Patricia, or Patty as she was nicknamed, was first married in 1951 to R. Hancock. On Jun. 4, 1957, she married Ernest Morris Jr., who was born the eldest son of Ernest Sr. and Bessie Huffman Morris on Jan. 9, 1928, in Greenup County, KY.

Patty and Ernie are the parents of two children, Robert Keith Morris (born Sep. 20, 1952) and Patricia Brett Morris (born Mar. 20, 1973).

Patty attended Paintsville Elementary, Paintsville High School, and Mayo Technical School where she became proficient in shorthand and typing. She began her profession as a legal secretary for the law firm of Wheeler & Wheeler (John and M.O. Wheeler) and then followed Ernie's career with him in the U.S. Army, being stationed at different posts in the States as well as living in Paris and Fountainbleu, France, for one tour of duty, until Ernie retired from the military in 1967.

In May 1967, Patty started her career as a court reporter, doing freelance work for some of the attorneys in and around Paintsville and reporting for the Workers' Compensation Board in several counties. She continues to do reporting work in the Eastern Kentucky area. After retiring from the military in 1967, Ernie worked in several federal government programs until he retired from public works.

The Morrises lived for a number of years on Fourth Street. In 1979 they moved to Fifth Street where they continue to live.

MULLINS - Jesse Ollen Mullins was the second child born to William Henry and Elizabeth "Liz" Rose Mullins on Feb. 12, 1907. His life began at Keaton,

KY, on the Ole Rose farm of his ancestors. Although his health was poor at a young age, in time, he became a pillar of strength of the large Mullins family. It was Jesse who became the second father to the family of 12.

Jesse and Glenda

Jesse married Glenda Mae Hill in August 1931. She was born in October 1911 to Forrest and Laura Belle Williams Hill at Relief, Morgan County. As a youngster, Glenda loved attending school. She always told about getting a dollar for attending school every day—nor was she late for books. A remarkable feat, as she departed each day before daybreak in all kinds of weather for this long journey.

Jesse and Glenda had four daughters: Jessie, Mary, Willamae and Deborah. All attended Lower Keaton Grade School and Flat Gap School.

Jessie married Charles Loechler and this union produced five daughters: Cherryl, Terri, Melissa, Yvonne and Christi. This family lives in Ohio. Jessie received a cosmetology degree from Mayo Vocational School.

Deborah, Willa, Mary and Jessie Mullins.

Mary Margaret married John Jones and lives in Thatcher, AZ. She graduated from Morehead State University with a home economics degree. She retired after 33 years of teaching in Indiana, New Mexico, Eastern Kentucky Rehab Center and Arizona. Her stepson, Mark, lives in Tennessee and Mike and wife, Paula, live in Tucson, AZ.

Willamae has one daughter, Kristen Bailey Preston. For many years she lived at Keaton and worked at Flat Gap Elementary. She now resides in Arizona. Willa graduated from Flat Gap High and attended Morehead State and Western New Mexico State University.

After graduating from Flat Gap High School, Deborah met and married Scotty Hamilton. She and Scotty have a daughter, LeAnna Hamilton Vaughn, and a son, Jesse Brandon. This couple resides in West Liberty, Morgan County.

Jesse was grade school educated mainly in Keaton Grade School. His early work experiences come from farming, roust about oil lease work and running a barber shop in Morehead in the late 20s and early 30s. After marriage to Glenda, he held an oil pumpers job for Ashland Oil Co., until he became a pipe fitter. He pursued this profession until his retirement in the 1970s. Although grade school educated, he was educated mechanically to a degree of perfection obtained by only a few who follow trade work. He improvised jigs and other labor saving devices on his jobs. He was noted for his swing making from a pattern he created 50 years earlier.

Whatever success Jesse may have achieved, Miss Glenda Mae was a supportive backbone in this union. She had the talent to be a farmer, carpenter, nurse, seamstress, short order cook, cleaning service and a bodyguard—most of all she was a Class A mother.

For 30 years they lived in the ole Mott House at Red Bush. Jesse was almost 90 years of age at his death and Glenda soon followed at the near age of 87. They were members of the United Baptist Church.

MULLINS - The first generation consists of the William and Oscar Mullins families. Ralph William (born 1905) married Esta Ferguson, a farmer and pipe fitter. Jesse Olen (born 1907) married Glenda Hill, farmer, pumper, pipe fitter. Mortmer Proctor (born 1909) married Bulah Nickell, oil producer. Charlie J. (born 1911) married Area Capps, farmer, pipe fitter, Berea Grad. Basil Thomas (born 1913) married Finetta Hamilton, school administrator. Polly Margret (born 1915) married Henry C. Huff, housewife to Army man. Maude Belle (born 1918) married Estil R. Hay, housewife, lives in Ohio. Pearl Fritz "Mutt" (born 1919) married Myrtle Ferguson, farmer, pipe fitter. Harold W. (born 1923) married Louise Melton 1946 in Baltimore, MD. I played football for Paintsville High, Lynch High, Duke University, Morehead State and coached at Wheelersburg High, pipefitted in Ohio. Now widowed, lived in Wheelersburg since 1953. Bobby Elwood (born 1928) married Mageline Hill, lawyer in Paintsville until his death. Sara Elda (born 1922) died at birth. Boyd Woerh (born 1930) died 1997 on an oil battery tank. Oscar Winson and Ollie May. Okie Regional married Desie Skaggs. Sadie Leatha married Claude Hutchinson. Clive Winson never married. Murl Justin married Salyers.

Those that served in the Armed Forces in WWII were: Clive for two years, Murl in Navy for four years, Pearl Fritz "Mutt" four years and Harold W. Navy two years.

MULLINS - Keaton, KY lies in the northwest corner of Johnson County, that flows into Big Blaine Creek and about four and one half miles water shed. It is bounded on the northwest by Lawrence County and on the southeast by Morgan County. Pioneering stock from western Pennsylvania and Virginia peopled it. It was aligned with Mulengeons and Cherokee Indians. The Mullins Clan were of no different.

The first Mullins to settle on Keaton was William Henry Mullins (born Feb. 10, 1883) and his brother, Oscar Winson, and sister, Sarah Mullins. Each married into the Thomas Rose and Rhoda Fyffe family. William Henry Mullins married Leona Elizabeth Rose in 1905 in Pickaway County, OH. Oscar Winson married Ollie Mae Rose, both are daughters of Thomas Rose and Mandy Gambill. Sarah married Benjamin Rose, son of Thomas and Rhoda Fyffe. Thomas Rose, son of William Rose of Lawrence County was the first to get a land grant of 500 acres on Keaton in 1840. The estate is still owned by the great-great-grandchildren of C.C. Rose and Mae Tencher.

The pioneering clan of the Keaton began probably with William Mullins who signed the Mayflower Compact. I know that William Mullins Jr. (born 1740) md. Christina and was the father of Rev. John Mullins who fought the Battle of Stony Mountain. He was captured by the British and was carried to England as a prisoner. He returned to the United States about 1791 and married Nancy Gentry in Hallifax, VA. His oldest son Daniel (born 1799) md. Nancy Demartin. Their youngest son Elihue (born 1858) md. Margaret McKenzie (born 1854) in Johnson County.

Elihue and Margaret married in Paintsville and moved to Bear Creek in Boyd County. Their issue: Sarah (born 1875), Oscar Winson (born 1880) and William Henry (born 1873). When dad was seven weeks old Elihue deserted the family and disappeared. According to the Carter County Census of 1910, he had remarried and nine issue. I know only their names and dates birth. Elihue was reared in Johnson County by his older sister, Mary Dean Mullins and James Pelphrey (1950/60/70 Census).

The first generation consists of the William Henry and Oscar Winston Mullins families.

William Henry Mullins family included:

1) Ralph William (born Jun. 6, 1905) md. Esta Ferguson Jul. 15, 1925, daughter of Luke Ferguson and Alice Bailey. Ralph was a farmer and pipefitter. He died Jun. 26, 1963

2) Jessie Ollen (born Feb. 12, 1907) md. Glenda Mae Hill, daughter of Forrest B. Hill and Laura Belle Williams.

3) Mortimer Proctor (born Jan. 9, 1909) md. Beulah Nickells, daughter of Edward Lee Nickells and Mary Myrtle Fallen.

4) Charlie John (born Apr. 21, 1911) md. Feb. 18, 1938 to Aria Capps. He was a graduate of Berea College.

5) Basil Thomas (born Apr. 21, 1913) md. Oct. 22, 1942 to Finetta Hamilton, daughter of Charlie P. Hamilton and Macy Bond. He was a graduate of Berea College and University of Kentucky.

6) Polly Margaret (born Mar. 6, 1915) md. Henry C. Huff.

7) Maude Belle (born Aug. 3, 1918) md. Estil R. Hay, son of Henry Hay and Pearlie Phillips.

8) Pearl Fritz "Mutt" (born Nov. 14, 1919) md. Myrtle Ferguson, daughter of Roby Ferguson and Mandy Ferguson.

9) Harold W. (born Jan. 22, 1923) md. Louise Melton, 1946, in Baltimore, MD. He played football for Paintsville High, Lynch High, Duke University, Morehead State and coached at Wheelersburg High School.

10) Bobby Elwood (born Jan. 26, 1928) md. Magdalene Hill, daughter of Van Buren Hill and Carrie Ferguson. He practiced law in Paintsville until his death.

11) Sara Elda (born 1922) died at birth.

12) Boyd Worth (born Oct. 19, 1930) died in 1997.

The Oscar and Ollie Mae Rose family included:

1. Okie Regional (born Dec. 31, 1906) md. May 18, 1927 to Desie Skaggs, daughter of Corneliss Skaggs and Carrie Osborn.

2. Sadie Leatha md. Claude Hutchinson on Mar. 3, 1925.

3. Clive Winson never married.

4. Murl Justin (born Jul. 2, 1921) md. Maxine Salyer on Nov. 21, 1945.

Those who served in the armed forces during WWII were Clive (2 years), Murl (Navy, 4 years), Pearl Fritz "Mutt" (4 years) and Harold W. (Navy, 2 years).

The Sarah Emily Mullins and Benjamin Rose Family include Proctor Rose and Willard Smith.

MUNSON - Hazel Vivian Meek Ward Munson was born Mar. 27, 1914, in Whitehouse, KY, daughter of Maud Sagraves and Davis Meek. Her maternal grandparents were Samantha Nickell Justice and Greenville Sagraves and paternal grandparents were Susan Butcher and Aaron Meek, all descendants of early eastern Kentucky pioneers. Hazel's brothers and sisters were Earl, Gladys (Gambill), Leslie, Herman, Thurman, her twin brother, Roma and Delores (Sparks).

Hazel Meek Ward Munson 80th birthday picture.

Davis Meek was a coal miner at Whitehouse where the family lived in a yellow company owned house. Hazel's parents were very active in the Methodist Church where they taught Sunday school and Maud played the organ. Hazel remembers her mother waking up the children on Sunday mornings and then walking down the row of houses calling out to others to get ready for church. Hazel graduated from the eighth grade in Whitehouse. After her mother became ill the family moved to Thealka and Maud entered Golden Rule Hospital in Paintsville where she died on Christmas Day, 1929. Sometime after her mother's death, Hazel enrolled in Paintsville High School as a freshman where she was elected homecoming queen. Shortly after that event she left school to keep house for her father and her younger siblings.

When she was 20 years old, Hazel met John

Calhoun Ward II of Offutt, KY, at a church meeting. (John's parents were Amanda Melvina Mollett and John Calhoun Ward. His maternal grandparents were Nancy Butcher and Benjamin Mollett and paternal grandparents were Sarah Hicks and William Jefferson Ward.) He was recently discharged from the USN and was attending Pikeville College. They married and he left school to work on his father's farm. Their first child, Helen Melvina, was born in Thealka. John and Hazel then moved to St. Louis, MO, where John was a radio operator on a government ship on the Mississippi River. He later worked with the CAA and they moved throughout the midwest where their other children: Virginia Ann, Carole Sue, John Calhoun III and Bert David were born. In 1944, John re-enlisted in the USN for a short tour of duty as a radio operator in Hawaii, and the family moved back to Paintsville to be near their relatives. After John's discharge they returned to Colorado.

In later years, John retired from the Santa Fe Railroad and moved back home. He died on Jan. 2, 1975, in Paintsville and is buried in the Ward Family cemetery at Tutor Key. Hazel retired as assistant director of the La Junta Senior Citizens Center in Colorado where she was extremely popular as an enthusiastic and imaginative leader in planning activities and programs. She married Dale Munson.

"Grandma Hazel" loves day tripping throughout Colorado with her husband, Dale, and being with her children, 25 grandchildren, 34 great-grandchildren and one great-great-grandchild. She keeps "home" alive by telling old stories, singing the old songs such as "*Put My Little Shoes Away*" and by sharing her memories of growing up in the beautiful Kentucky hills.

MURRAY - Arnie Murray was born May 22, 1919, at Meally, KY, the oldest child of Arby and Anna Lee Preston Murray. Arby's parents were Bethlehem "Bethley" Murray and Unis Selesta "Lesta" Preston. Anna Lee's parents were Ide Lee Preston and Elizabeth "Lizzie" Childers. Bethley Murray's ancestry goes back to Thomas Murray, a Revolutionary War veteran. Lesta Preston and Ide Lee Preston can trace their family back to Moses Preston, another Revolutionary War veteran. Lizzie is also a descendant of Moses Preston and Abraham Childers.

Arnie and Dixie (McKenzie) Murray

Arby and Anna Lee reared their children at Meally until about 1936 when they bought a farm at Beaver, OH, and moved their family of seven boys there. Their only daughter, Elizabeth, was born in Jackson County, OH. Their other sons are Arvin, John Bethley, Robert Lee, Hobert, Samuel and James E. Murray.

Arnie enlisted in the Army in 1941 as a private in the infantry. He was wounded in 1944 by machine gun bullets, and honorably discharged on Mar. 29, 1945. On Apr. 7, 1945, at Paintsville, KY, he married Dixie Ellen McKenzie. They met at the home of Charlie and Lestie Preston where she was employed. Dixie was born Feb. 23, 1914, at Volga, KY, the daughter of John Burns McKenzie and Cynthia Alice Fairchild. Burns was the son of John T. McKenzie and Julia Witten. Alice was the daughter of Andrew Martin Fairchild and Cynthia Ellen Hitchcock. The McKenzies, Fairchilds, Wittens and Hitchcocks all came to Johnson County in the early 1800s.

Arnie attended Mayo State Vocational School at Paintsville. Some of his occupations were carpenter (an occupation he toiled at for many years), construction work, Preston Funeral Home and retired from Goodyear Aerospace Corp. as a tool and dye maintenance man.

Arnie was converted and baptized in 1949 at Buffalo United Baptist Church at Meally, KY. He was an ordained minister. He and his family moved to Beaver, OH, in 1962 after the death of his father. He moved his membership to Pine Creek United Baptist Church and was the moderator at the time of his death on Apr. 18, 1982.

Dixie was a quiet, mild mannered and caring person. She loved to sew and quilt. She made many beautiful quilts that she quilted by hand. She was an exceptional cook and many people enjoyed being in her company. She passed away on Aug. 15, 1990.

Arnie and Dixie had three daughters: Alice Jeanette and Wanda Sue were born in Paintsville, and Lois Ann was born in Ashland, KY. Alice graduated from Jackson High School and attended Ohio University for two years. She worked in Columbus for two years before she married James Lewis Lauderback and had four children: Christy Ellen Lauderback (born 1969, died 1971); Amy Catherine married Fred Berdean Cox (they have two daughters, Heather Nicole and Brittany Lynn); Stacy Sue married Shannon Lee Vance (one daughter and one son, Victoria Ellen and Dakota Shannon); and Michael Arnie. Alice is an amateur genealogist and worked in a restaurant for about 15 years, seven as the manager. At present she is employed at a nursing home in Waverly. She is the secretary of Jackson County Chapter of the Ohio Genealogical Society since 1980.

Lois graduated from Jackson High School and went to work in Columbus, where she met her husband, Emerson Montgomery. They have three children: Gregory Scott married Anita Montgomery (one son, Colton Scott) then Greg and Anita divorced and Greg married second to Amy Snider (one son, Caleb Gregory); Stephanie Ann is married to John Paul Jones (two daughters, Cassandra Ann and McKenzie Dawn); Kevin Emerson is employed at Chillicothe, OH. Lois is a licensed dietitian at a nursing home in Waverly.

Wanda graduated from Jackson High School and went to work at G.C. Murphys for about 15 years, first as a clerk, then as an office worker. Then went to work at Revco (now CVS) where she is presently employed as a pharmacy tech. She was converted and baptized at Beaver Valley United Baptist Church. She enjoys reading and cross-stitch. *Submitted by Alice Murray Lauderback.*

MURRAY - Robert Lee Murray was born Apr. 6, 1926, in Meally, Johnson County, KY. He is the fourth son of Arby Murray and Anna Lee Preston. Arby and Anna Lee Preston Murray had eight children: Arnie (born May 22, 1919), Arvin (born Feb. 2, 1922), John Bethley (born Jan. 23, 1924), Robert Lee (born Apr. 6, 1926), Hobert (born Oct. 1, 1928), Samuel (born Jul. 9, 1931), James E. (born Apr. 8, 1936) and Elizabeth (born Oct. 28, 1938). Arby is the son of Bethley Murray and Unis Lestie Preston. Robert Lee is a descendant of Thomas Murray and Moses Coby Preston, both are Revolutionary War Soldiers.

He moved to Beaver, OH, when he was about 9 years old. When he crossed the Ohio River he was so scared, he felt as if he was moving into a foreign county. The land looked quite different. He was use to the beautiful, rolling mountains and now he saw flat farm lands that looked so strange. He worked for Sunshine Biscuit and Tempken Roller Bearing. Then on Aug. 22, 1944, he was drafted into the U.S. Army and discharged on Jul. 3, 1946. After returning home from WWII he returned to the civilian work force and was employed by Frigadaire until 1976 at which time he retired.

Robert Lee Murray Family

On Apr. 11, 1944, he married Gladys Jewell Frazier. To this union were born three children: Helen Louise (born Jan. 22, 1951), Jeanita "Nita" (born Oct. 17, 1953) and Steve (born Sep. 9, 1957) all born in Dayton, Montgomery County, OH.

Helen married Lowell Prater Wright on Feb. 14, 1971, and had three children. They are now divorced and Helen is married to Robert Powers. Kenneth Shane Wright (born Sep. 3, 1972) married Deana Michelle Worden on Apr. 1, 1995, and had two children, Breana Ashley Wright (born Mar. 12, 1996) and Taylor Shae Wright (born Aug. 10, 1973). Shauna Mae Wright (born Aug. 10, 1973) had two children, Jacob Daniel Blackburn (born Jan. 15, 1993) and Georgia Mae Blackburn (born May 19, 1999). Seth Jason Wright (born Aug. 8, 1977) married Melissa Ann Beach on Jun. 30, 1998, and have one child, Kenneth Blake Wright (born Sep. 3, 1997). Seth and Missy are expecting their second child at any time.

Nita married Loren David Lewis on Feb. 3, 1973, and had three children. They were divorced in 1987. Angela Crystal Lewis (born Oct. 9, 1974) married Sean Michael Thomson on Sep. 6, 1996, and Andrea Beth Lewis (born Feb. 9, 1978).

Steve married Kathy Lynn Moore on Feb. 27, 1982, and had three children: Chad Robert (born May 31, 1985), Nina Kristen (born Jul. 24, 1987) and Eric Steven Murray (born Jun. 15, 1996.)

Robert Lee was converted Mar. 18, 1957, baptized Apr. 21, 1957, and joined the Beaver Valley Church in Beaver, OH. In 1959 he was called by God to preach. He was ordained as a minister, October 1965. He is now a member of Lebanon Church in Kentucky. He has devoted many years for the preaching of God's word. He loves fishing, hunting, gardening and spending time with his family. *By Nita Murray Lewis.*

MUSIC - Mary Rebecca Jones Lewis Music was born on Apr. 15, 1930, in Johnson County, KY, the oldest child and only daughter of Kathryn E. Borders and Terry Allen Jones. Her brothers, John Oliver Jones and Henry Allen Jones, twins, were born Aug. 5, 1933, at the Golden Rule Hospital in Paintsville, KY.

Rebecca Jones Lewis Music

They graduated from Paintsville High School and Centre College in Danville, KY. In 1956 they received degrees from the University of Louisville School of Medicine. John is currently a physician in Boyd County, KY; and Henry is a physician in Greenup County, KY. A third brother, Roy Douglas Jones, died in infancy. Rebecca was salutatorian of the 1947 class of Meade Memorial High School at Williamsport, KY. She later received business training at Mayo State Vocational School. On Sep. 30, 1947, Rebecca married Jack Leighton Lewis, son of Corby Dempsey and Avery I. Lewis Jr. in Johnson County,

KY. Together they reared four daughters: Mary Lou, Anne, Jennifer and Lisa. After her husband's untimely death from the complications of a brain tumor on Jun. 6, 1987, Rebecca remarried to Mr. Burnett Music on Apr. 5, 1996, in Clintwood, VA.

After her business training, Rebecca worked as a legal secretary for her husband, Jack Lewis, and as a court reporter for various judges throughout the state. Additionally, she was the 24th Judicial Circuit Court reporter under Hon. W.D. Sparks and Hon. William B. Hazelrigg.

As official court reporter for the 24th Judicial Dist. She once described her job as "a lot of drudgery," but she followed by saying that it afforded her the opportunity to meet many interesting people and to experience "life in the raw." One of the highlights of her career was her work on the infamous "Cedar Chest Murder" in which she collaborated as author on a feature story for a leading detective magazine.

In addition to her job as court report, Rebecca, was also active in numerous community and civic activities. She was elected president of the Kentucky Court Reporter's Association. She served as president of the Johnson County Historical Association for two years and was twice elected to the Paintsville Board of Education (1966-74). During her tenure on the Paintsville Board of Education, she served in all offices, including chairman and vice-chairman. In 1969 she was elected chairman of the East Kentucky Region (South) of the Kentucky State School Board Association. In that capacity she worked for the progress of state and local education.

Rebecca was honored in 1974, to serve as district governor of the Kentucky Federation of Republican Women. As such, she represented a 22 county district and was one of only seven governors chosen from the entire state. She also served in different capacities as a member of the Johnson County Republican Women's organization.

As one of three women on the Johnson County Planning Commission, she helped to institute the "Green Box" system of garbage collection, which was designed to supplement private trash collection in the county.

Additionally, Rebecca served as a Sunday school teacher for Intermediate Girls for many years at the Bridgeford Mission of the First Baptist Church and held various positions with the Women's Missionary Union.

Rebecca recently completed eight years as president of the Meade Memorial Alumni Association and is currently working on a committee of the Johnson County Historical Association to publish a history of Johnson County, KY.

NEAL - Ernest D. Neal was born Oct. 22, 1899, at Pine Knot, KY, to Joseph and Mary Elizabeth Roberts Neal. He was one of seven sons and three daughters. The Neal family came into south-central Kentucky about 1800.

Ernest D. Neal

He attended school at Marshes Creek, until high school. He joined his sisters at Berea Academy and enrolled in Berea College for three years with a major in agriculture. While at Berea, he met Frances Lee Welch, who was attending Normal School for Teachers in the summer of 1923. They corresponded for a few years and were married at Paintsville, KY, Apr. 9, 1928.

Ernest went to work for General Motors at Pontiac, MI, in 1926. Frances and he were married and lived there when the depression hit and lost his job in 1930. They returned to Paintsville, KY, and he worked carpentry until 1934. He installed cabinets in the old G.C. Murphy building on the corner of Main and Court Streets.

In 1934, President Roosevelt started a program to help people feed themselves by learning to grow their own food. He was hired to teach people to work the land for a living. This program became the Farmers Home Administration, which made loans and helped people to own and work their farms effectively. Ernest worked for the government until 1947. He decided to make the farm at Concord his main source of income.

He and Frances worked as a team. They raised chickens and milked Brown Swiss cows. Running the milk route, delivering milk, eggs and produce provided the income. Frances did sewing and upholstery. He did the heavy work and she washed milk bottles and bottled the milk, candled eggs and packed them into cartons. They were honored for the outstanding job as Master Farm Family in 1952 in Kentucky by *The Progressive Farmer* magazine, and *The Courier Journal.*

Ernest used the farm at Concord as his laboratory. He was always experimenting to find better ways of doing things and growing new varieties for higher production. He was honored as Master Green Pastureman in 1950 and several other years. He consistently grew more corn per acre than any other farmer in Johnson County. He was proud of the cleanliness of his Grade A natural milk. It was so free of bacteria, it wouldn't clabber for buttermilk.

He milled his own corn on the farm and took care of all the daily activities until 1964. Health problems with emphysema caused him to sell the chickens and cows and spend the winters in Florida. He just changed his product from the land. He set out and grafted 300 orange trees on three and one-half acres for fruit. Each year he took orders before he left Kentucky and shipped back.

Ernest died Dec. 13, 1976, at Orlando, FL. His remains rest in the family cemetery at Concord, KY, in the ground he so carefully tended when he was alive.

NEAL - Frances Welch Neal was born at Meally, KY, Jan. 13, 1904, to Ulysses Grant and Sara Susan Wells Welch. She had four brothers and one sister. Descended from the Green Wells branch of the Richard Wells family, who came to Kentucky from Maryland about 1800.

Frances Welch Neal

Frances learned womanly skills, making biscuits and cooking at an early age. She learned to sew and made clothes for herself and her mother. The family lived near the Halls and Wards at Concord and played and went to school together. They made their own tennis court. Frances liked to tell about popping corn and one of the Hall boys grabbing the dishpan and all the others chasing him. She attended school at Concord and then walked about three miles into Paintsville to attend Mayo Academy. She graduated from Mayo Academy in 1922. She attended Berea College Normal School for teachers the summers of 1922 and 1923. She taught school as her first job at Van Lear Schools and Thealka. When at Van Lear, she rode horseback or stayed with her Aunt Mary Jane Watson.

She met Ernest Neal from Pine Knot, KY, at Berea College during the summer of 1922. They corresponded for a few years and then he came to Paintsville. They married at the home of Dr. James A. Wells on Apr. 9, 1928. Her bridal bouquet was a bunch of violets, hand-picked by her sister, Mary Mae Welch Kazee. She and Ernest moved to Pontiac, MI, where he worked for General Motors putting wood panels into car doors.

Frances and Ernest Neal had three children: Mary Alice (born Jan. 17, 1930, at Pontiac, MI), Sara Elizabeth (born Feb. 17, 1934) and Joe Grant (born Sep. 1, 1935, in Johnson County, KY). The depression caused Ernest to lose his job in 1930 and they moved back to Johnson County. Frances had bought her grandparents, Thomas Jefferson Welch's, 1888 log house and one acre of ground with her teaching money. They bought out heirs of the original tract until they had 41 acres of hill and bottom land. The C&O Railroad went through the farm in 1903 and opened up the Big Sandy Valley to rail moving the products of the land. The original bridge was replaced in 1998 across the Levisa River of the Big Sandy.

Frances volunteered with the Extension Service as a 4H Club leader in 1933 and continued for 37 years. She was active in the Homemakers Club for 62 years and was honored when selected as a Master Homemaker of Kentucky. Many of her former 4H girls were active in the King Addition Homemakers' Club.

Frances operated a sewing shop and did alterations, draperies, upholstery and chair caning. She was a woman with many skills, many learned through the homemakers club. She did a lot of quilts in her 94 years as she started doing them at age 12 for the next 81 years.

Frances Neal was a member of the Mayo Memorial Methodist Church and had many positions in the Sunday school. She was very proud of the perfect attendance years. Frances passed away Sep. 18, 1998, at home in Tangerine, FL, at age 94. She joined three generations of grandmothers buried in the Welch-Neal Cemetery at Concord.

NEAL - Joe Grant Neal was born Sep. 1, 1935, in Johnson County, KY, to Ernest and Frances Welch Neal. He was the youngest of three children: Mary Alice (born 1930) and Sara Elizabeth (born 1933), all who survived to adulthood.

Joe Neal

He attended East Concord School, Thealka School and graduated from Meade Memorial High School in 1953. Graduated from Berea College in 1957 with a BS degree in agriculture. He was a member of the college track team four years. After graduation he taught agriculture, chemistry and science at Jackson Township High School in Westport, IN. He coached junior high basketball two years and one year his team won the county championship in 1961. In 1958 he entered the U.S. Army for two years and served as a clerk typist with the rank of specialist fourth class and received an honorable discharge.

He taught one more year before leaving teaching to work with Southern States Cooperative, Inc. of Richmond, VA. He started at Somerset, KY, as a training manager. He met his wife, Thresa Doris Godby, at Somerset and they were married Aug. 12, 1962, at Somerset, KY, at Pleasant Hill Baptist Church where they were members. They were parents of two children, Theresa Lynn (born Oct. 7, 1963, at Somerset, KY) and Steven Grant (born Jun. 7, 1966, at Glasgow, KY). Southern States Cooperative provides a service to all farmers in the southeast U.S. Joe's career would span some 37-1/2 years until he retired in February 1999. He was a store manager at Somerset, Danville and Horse Cave, KY. In 1969 he was promoted to mechanical systems supervisor for all of Kentucky and part of West Virginia. This job called on his teaching experience as he worked with 19 locations training the employees in sales and installation of the farm equipment and buildings.

He was very active in his profession and was promoted into the construction management department in the central office of Southern States. He would hold several jobs in that department over the next 17 years and retire as manager of engineer and construction in February 1999.

He has moved back to the childhood farm where he grew up and is renovating the house that his father, Ernest Neal, built in 1933 from some materials from the original log house built in 1888 by Thomas Jefferson Welch, Joe's great-grandfather. His hobbies are fishing, hunting, golf and doing wood working projects. His daughter, Theresa Lynn, was married to Mathew Reed Ward from Auburn, AL, on Oct. 11, 1986. They met at the University of Kentucky where Theresa was awarded a BS degree in computer science. They have one son, Thomas Reed (born May 14, 1994), and live in Madisonville, KY. Steven Grant married Mindy Arvo of Upper Marboro, MD, Oct. 28, 1995. Steven earned an associate technician degree at DeVery Institute of Atlanta, GA. They have one daughter, Carmella Rose (born May 7, 1999), and live in Tucker, GA.

NEAL - Mary Alice Neal was born to Ernest and Frances Welch Neal Jan. 17, 1930, at Pontiac, MI. She moved back to Johnson County, KY, when 3 months old to the log house where her great-grandparents lived before their death at Concord Community. She was the oldest of three children of Ernest and Frances, Sara Elizabeth (born 1934) and Joe Grant (born 1935).

Mary Alice Neal

Mary Alice was an early 4H member. Her mother, a 4H leader, took her to J.M. Feltner 4H Camp when she was only 3 years old. She was active in the 4H club until going away to college. She was a member of the Mayo Memorial Methodist Church for many years and still attends when back in Paintsville on visits.

She attended East Concord School, Meade Memorial High School and graduated from Berea College in 1949 with a degree in home economics. She worked as a dietitian at King's Daughters' Hospital in Ashland, KY, where she met James W. Smith, she later married. Mary Alice and James W. Smith were married in Bluefield, WV, Mar. 2, 1952. They had three children: Scott David (born Feb. 17, 1954), Nancy Susan (born Feb. 29, 1956) and Craig Stephen (born Dec. 6, 1957).

Scott David Smith has his own business in Kalispel, MT; Craig Stephen Smith works as foreman for Montana Rockworks in Kalispel, MT; and Nancy Susan Smith Dennison works as chief financial officer for a hospital that gives long term care at Whitehall, MI.

Mary Alice was a teacher in Johnson County, KY, at Denver, Oil Springs and Meade Memorial schools. She retired from teaching in 1994 at Lifestream Academy, a school for emotionally disturbed children in Leesburg, FL.

Mary Alice is known for her sewing and designing skills. She had her own business of interior design in Florida and has made thousands of garments during her career as a seamstress.

Following her divorce from James W. Smith in 1979, she returned to her maiden name. She writes and sings her own songs and has a book of poetry in progress. Most of the singing she does is acappella.

NEWMAN - James Thomas Newman was born May 2, 1927, in Paintsville, KY. Parents were John Gainey and Leona Auxier Newman. James attended Paintsville City Schools, where he graduated from high school in 1945. He joined the USN and served two years. During that time, he served aboard the USS *Keokuk* and USS LSM-175. After discharge, he attended Thomas More College, where he received his BS degree in 1951. He attended graduate school at UK in 1951-52.

James Thomas Newman

James married the former Florence Arbogast Jun. 14, 1952, in Fort Mitchell, KY. The couple had four children: Sue Ann, James Thomas Jr., Paul Gainey and John Auxier, and have three grandchildren.

Mr. Newman was employed by the Paintsville Grocery Co., where he was president and general manager from 1959-81. He was then employed by Southeast Coal Co. as safety director, until 1994.

Mr. Newman was city councilman for three terms, and served as mayor. He joined the Paintsville Fire Dept. in 1942 as a volunteer, and is still active, serving as safety officer.

Mr. Newman has been City-County Civil Defense director since June 1956, being appointed by Mayor Ralph Preston, and County Judge Joe Radcliffe. He is still in this position at this date as the director of the Emergency Management Agency.

In 1971, when the Emergency Medical Technician Program was initiated, he taught the seventh class of EMTs in the state of Kentucky.

Mr. Newman was president of the Kentucky Wholesale Grocers' Association, Kiwanis Club, Toastmasters and the Big Sandy Coal Mining Institute. He was admitted to the Paintsville High School Life Honor Roll in 1983, and was selected Citizen of the Year by Beta Sigma Phi Sorority in 1979, and Kiwanian of the Year in 1965.

He has received letters of appreciation from the Army Corps of Engineers, President Richard Nixon, President Lyndon Johnson and Governor Louis Nunn, for his work during disasters and emergencies.

Mr. Newman has been a member of the American Legion and of the Knights of Columbus for over 50 years. He has been a lifelong member of St. Michael's Catholic Church, where he has served on the Parish Council, and was instrumental in the planning of the present church building.

OSBORNE & SALYER - Alice Mae Salyer was born Dec. 3, 1917, at Flat Gap, KY, in Johnson County to parents, Kendrick and Beulah Salyer, at the home of Monroe and Alice Salyer, her paternal grandparents.

Beatrice Osborne

Mae's mother, Beulah Salyer (born Aug. 8, 1900), was the daughter of Manford and Mary Ann Bunyard who lived on Salyers Branch at Volga. Beulah was the mother of five children, housewife and a friend to all. At the close of every day Beulah breathed a sigh of relief when the last buggy of coal was dumped and waited anxiously for her husband, Kendrick, whom she dearly loved, to get home from the mines. Mae's father, Kendrick (born Feb. 11, 1894), was a coal miner and a lumberjack.

Fred and Mae Osborne and daughters.

Alice Mae, her twin sister, Mary Fay, sisters Marie (born Feb. 4, 1920), Tera (born Oct. 18, 1925) and brother, James Manford (born Feb. 4, 1928), grew up on Salyers Branch at Volga. All attended McKenzie Branch School where Mae was proficient in art. Mae drew pictures of subjects and buildings having Miss Maude Vaughn as her visiting teacher and John Fred William's appreciative recognition.

Mae married Fred Osborne Sep. 14, 1935. Reverend George Brown performed the ceremony at the home of Mae's parents. Fred was born Sep. 21, 1914, to Bertha Jane Osborne (born Jan. 29, 1880). Fred's grandparents were John Henry and Ellen Boggs Osborne. John Henry was born Oct. 9, 1849, and Ellen was born Jun. 16, 1845.

In school Fred won prizes for memorizing poetry. His favorite poem to recite was "*The Little Ant Going to Jerusalem*," learning this poem at Ramey Branch School when his teacher was Hazel Davis. Fred played the harmonica. *Little Moses, You Are My Sunshine* and *Maple on the Hill* were favorite tunes.

Fred and Mae were the parents of three daughters: Beatrice Lenore (born Jun. 11, 1936), Goldie Maxine (born Aug. 7, 1937) and Opal Ernestine (born Mar. 1, 1940). All three daughters attended the one-room McKenzie Branch School being third generation students. After completing elementary school Fred and Mae's daughters graduated from Flat Gap High School during the time when their father was employed as a school bus driver for the Johnson County Schools.

Mae and her daughter, Beatrice, live on 172 in the home Fred helped build in 1957. Beatrice graduated from Morehead State University Aug. 4, 1966, with a degree in elementary education. She is a retired Johnson County teacher. Her interests are walking, reading, bible study and attending church. Beatrice and her mother are faithful members of the Upper Room International Pentecostal Church at Paintsville.

Beatrice was very ill when she was 13 months old. Being a preacher and musician her great-uncle, Harry, prayed and walked the floor one night when all hope was gone. This early experience continues to influence her life today. One of Beatrice's unforgettable memories was witnessing her father's conversion, healing and baptism at the Brownie Hole near Route 172.

PACK - Bessie Jane (Meddings) Pack (born 1891, died 1974), a pioneer lady. Having just successfully completed the required years of schooling to qualify for a teaching position of that period, Bessie one day dreamed of teaching. The next day she would plan her future around working for the coal mining company where she had grown up. Her mother was the manager of the company boarding house and her father was the keeper of the mule barn and all of the male persons in her family worked in the mines. On other days, at her age she probably dreamed of that mythical 'Prince on the White Horse.' She was still not settled on her future plans.

What she had not foreseen was the prosperous coal company in her home town, Detroit (Putnam County), WV, now offered new employees $1.50 per day as compared to the usual $1.00 per day being paid coal miners elsewhere.

In this vast flow of new people to her home town

was an intelligent, good looking, well dressed 17-year-old young gentleman from Martin County, KY, named James Arthur "Jim" Pack, who the company favored and put to work immediately.

Bessie holding Helen, their youngest child and Jim in the back seat. Bill is at steering wheel, Hazel in center and Troy on passenger side.

Bessie and Jim met at the town croquet court. Jim had remarked that she was the prettiest young lady he had ever seen. Learning that her brother was Clyde Meddings, whom Jim worked with, Jim became a very close friend of Clyde, with hopes of knowing Bessie better.

This must have been the correct strategy as on Christmas Eve, 1907, Jim and Bessie were married at the home of her parents, Patrick Henry Meddings and Mary Ellen (Nelson) Meddings, in Kanawah County, WV.

Soon after the birth of their first child, Willie Alvie "Bill," Oct. 9, 1908, news continued to reach them about the many opportunities with Consolidation Coal Co. in the modern coal town being constructed in Van Lear (Johnson County), KY.

In 1910, Bessie, with their baby, accompanied her husband to Kentucky. Arriving in Van Lear, her husband was hired at once but they found there were no available houses. The prospective mining families were arriving faster than the construction crews could build houses.

She had always lived in a mining town and had always had access to the "company store," which was like a modern 19th century mall. She had never lived where the most modern of utilities were not available as per that period of time.

Housing being scarce, her husband took her and their small son to his home place in Milo, Martin County, KY, to await the completion of their new house in Van Lear. Comforted in the knowledge that his sister, Mahala (Pack) Maynard, and many of his family would be her neighbors, he returned to Van Lear to begin his new employment. Bessie and their son, approximately 3 years old, remained in this two room log house with 'zero' convenience.

Hazelgreen "Hazel" chose not to wait for the construction crew to finish the new house and for her dad to move them to Van Lear. She was born Aug. 19, 1911, at the old Pack home place, Joe Branch, Milo, Martin County, KY.

Soon their company house was completed and the new baby and mother, along with big brother, were able to move. Once again Bessie had electricity, running water plus all of those comforts afforded by the 'Company Store.'

All the time she was in Martin County she kept letters going to her West Virginia kin to join her in Kentucky. She wanted them to share in this good life in this land of hope as she planned to move her young children there.

First came her parents, bringing with them her young teenage brother, Charles Lawrence "Jinks" Meddings. Lawrence later met and married Minnie McCarty from Louisa, Lawrence County. All of these remained in Van Lear until their death many years later.

An older sister, Effie, along with her husband, Otto Fowler, soon came to Van Lear. One by one, her older brothers: Stanley, John, George and Clyde, began to bring their families to Van Lear.

She was truly a pioneer lady. Not yet 20 years old, having blazed the trail and looking on the bright side, seeming to forget the bad times, she encouraged others to follow.

To the marriage of Bessie and Jim Pack were eight children: Willie Alvie "Bill" (born 1908, died 1974), Hazelgreen "Hazel" (born 1911, died 1994), Charles Troy (born 1913, died 1981), Helen Marie (born 1916, died 1997), Lillian Mae (born 1920), James Arthur Jr. (born 1924), Mary Elizabeth (born 1927) and Paul Douglas "P.D." (born 1932, died 1996).

She assisted her husband in the development of the Pack-Grumbles Subdivision, King Addition. Re: *Misc. Inst. Book* 4, page 454, in the Johnson County Court Clerk's Office.

They built their home in this subdivision and moved there in 1928. She also operated a "Mom & Pop" grocery store adjacent to her home. Bessie was an active member of the Van Lear Missionary Baptist Church, where her husband, Jim, was a deacon. Later, they moved their church membership to the First Baptist Church in Paintsville.

She was a charter member of the King Addition Homemakers Club which was organized in her store. They also held their monthly meetings and workshops there. The King Addition Club was the first homemakers club organized in Johnson County. It is still a very active club.

Even with her busy lifestyle, Bessie always kept in touch with her two sons who served in the military by writing long letters from home. Jimmie was a Marine in WWII and P.D. was in the Air Force during the Korean conflict.

Bessie never failed to let everyone know she was a Republican. She was very proud of that fact. She would further inform all, that she voted the first time women were allowed to vote and had never failed to vote since that day. She was very pleased to serve as a Republican election officer for King Addition for many years.

She was known to family, neighbors, friends and the general public as "Mom Pack."

Feb. 23, 1946, her husband, James Arthur Pack Sr., died and she remained in the home place until her death on May 6, 1974. Both Bessie and Jim are buried in the Pack Family Cemetery, Pack Hill Drive, overlooking the home they built together in 1928.

The Pack's often laughed about staying on the road so much, they couldn't get home in time to milk the cow ... therefore they sold the cow ... so they could enjoy their family outings.

PACK & WHEELER - Elizabeth Wheeler Pack was born Feb. 28, 1897, on Lower Laurel Creek of Flat Gap, Johnson County, KY, the daughter of William "Henderson" Wheeler and Eliza Jane (Phillips) Wheeler. She died Dec. 22, 1993, at Boyd County, KY.

Elizabeth and Tracy Pack

The family moved to Franks Creek at Winifred when she was 6 years old. She attended a one-room school. She first taught in 1916 after completing the eighth grade at Paintsville and obtaining a two-year teacher's certificate. She attended Sandy Valley Seminary and Mayo College and Normal School. She continued teaching in rural schools which started and ended earlier. She returned to high school each year for a half year, graduating from Paintsville High School in 1925. She attended Pikeville Jr. Presbyterian College, Morehead State Teachers College and Eastern State Teachers College. She taught six years in Johnson County schools and 42 years in Paintsville City Schools, retiring in 1965.

She married Albert Tracy Pack Feb. 9, 1923, at Paintsville. They met when she was teaching school at Rock House near his home. Tracy Pack was born Nov. 21, 1892, at Wilbur, Lawrence County, KY, the son of Leander and Hessie (Davis) Pack. He died Oct. 6, 1989, in Boyd County, KY. Tracy and Elizabeth are buried at the Marvin Sparks Cemetery, Lawrence County, KY. Tracy served in WWI from 1918-19. Tracy founded and operated the Big Sandy Livestock Market.

Tracy and Elizabeth lived in Paintsville and were devout members of Paintsville United Baptist Church. They had one child, Helen (born Jun. 3, 1925). Helen graduated from Paintsville High School, attended Pikeville Junior College and received her AB degree from Marshall University, Huntington, WV, in 1962. She taught her first year in a two-room school at Wittensville, two years at Paintsville Grade School and 27 years at Kenova Grade School, Kenova, WV, retiring in 1984. She married Samuel Forrest Colvin Jan. 2, 1946, at Paintsville. Samuel was born Jul. 6, 1914, at Manila, Johnson County, KY, the son of Samuel Forrest Colvin and Julia Jane (Blanton) Colvin. Samuel served in WWII, graduated from Mayo State Vocational School and retired from the Huntington Veterans Hospital in 1973 after working there 23 years. He is an ordained United Baptist minister.

Helen and Samuel have two sons, David Forrest (born Jan. 28, 1948) and Samuel Tracy (born Nov. 5, 1950), both in Paintsville.

David married Marcia Patricia Roesch, daughter of William R. Roesch and Helena (Foros) Roesch Jul. 14, 1973, in Morgantown, WV. David and Marcia have two children, Alicia Brook (born Oct. 26, 1974) and Nicholas Forrest (born Feb. 14, 1978).

Samuel Tracy married Prudence Carol Olmstead, daughter of Frank S. Olmstead and Phyllis E. (Jones) Olmstead, May 23, 1987, in Kenova, WV. They have two sons, Andrew Brock (born Sep. 2, 1990) and Samuel Franklin (born May 4, 1992).

PACK - Herschell Pack was born Nov. 1, 1919, at Lowmansville, KY, to Henry and Rebecca Murray Pack. He served four years in the Marine Corps with a tour of duty on Okinawa. He returned home in May 1946 and married Herma Lee Castle. They had two daughters, Marilyn and Joan. He was a graduate of Oil Springs High School, Ashland Community College and Morehead State University. He spent 40 years in the Johnson County School System as a teacher and principal. He was active in the Republican Party, an avid hunter and member of the Masonic Lodge.

Herschell Pack

The daughters followed in his educational footsteps. Marilyn is a graduate of Oil Springs High School, Prestonsburg Community College, University of Kentucky and the University of Louisville School of Medicine. She is director of pediatric surgery of medicine at Wake Medical Center in Raleigh, NC. Professor of surgery medicine at University of North Carolina, North Carolina Chapel Hill.

Joan is a graduate of Johnson Central High School and the University of Cincinnati. She works with the school system as Family and Children First coordinator, licensed professional clinical counselor and certified prevention consultant. By Herma Pack.

PACK - James Arthur Pack Sr., "a man before his time." James Arthur Pack was born May 16, 1890, in Milo, Martin County, KY, to Thomas Pack and Elizabeth (Haney) Pack. He was the oldest of two children. His sister Mahala "Haley" Pack was born three years later, Jan. 8, 1893. Their mother, Elizabeth, died when Jim was 12 years old and his sister was 9.

Just prior to the move to Van Lear, James A. Pack and brother-in-law, Clyde Meddings, prepare for work, 1909.

Being a healthy young man of 17, already accustomed to honest hard work, he believed it was time to be on his own. When he learned of the need for men to work in the coal mines, he left Kentucky with high hopes for the future and his financial plans set.

Arriving in Detroit, Putnam County, WV, he was immediately hired, with a starting salary of $1.50 per day as compared to the $1.00 per day in his home state. The knowledge of this escalated pay was his reason for traveling out of state.

In a short time Bessie Jane Meddings caught his eye. On Christmas Eve 1907, Jim and Bessie were married in the home of her parents, Patrick Henry Meddings and Mary Ellen (Nelson) Meddings. Marriage license are recorded in Kanawha County, WV.

Through the remaining years of their life together, also to her shy embarrassment, he would often affectionately remark in 'jest,' "I had a full time job paying $1.50 per day and had saved $15.00 ... did she marry me for my money?"

Consolidation Coal Co., known for establishing good towns and good working conditions for their employees, had begun to construct a model coal company in Van Lear, Johnson County, KY, in 1909. This constant report of the "Coal Boom" in Eastern Kentucky made Jim's decision to return to Kentucky with his young family.

Jim became an employee of Consolidation Coal Co. in 1910. The vast flow of new employees was greater than houses could be constructed. Jim placed his wife and small son, Bill, in his old home place in Martin County until their house could be built in Van Lear. Before their house was completed their second child arrived. When the family settled in their new home in this land of great expectations, there was also a baby daughter, Hazel.

As coal mining and marketing conditions improved, Consol increased the wages so that it was possible for men who were willing to work could earn as much as $5.00 per day.

As a potential for large profits for the company and the employees, a contract was offered on one mine in Van Lear. Jim was awarded this contract under the supervision of J.R. "Jack" Price, manager, who came to Van Lear from Pennsylvania in 1919.

Having already worked 10 years for the company, Jim was allowed to recruit his men from those he had worked with and knew to be "good and willing" workers.

Being of strong physical, mental and spiritual constitution, Jim Pack, along with this group, was so successful that some envy and jealousy began to surface from a few disgruntled employees. A few salaried employees realized these ordinary hard working men of many nationalities and colors, were earning more than they. Therefore, at the close of the contract date, this contract was not renewed, nor was it offered again.

During this time, Jim noticed a 'bottle neck' when unloading the mine cars. The process was requiring far too many men to lift and tilt the mine car to unload the coal when it reached the outside. Jim drew a diagram, along with his written suggestion of an improved lever or latch with a plan to easily tilt the cars. He brought this to the attention of the American Car Co. They listened. Engineers worked on Jim's suggested mechanism. It was soon perfected and is still being used on the modern mine cars of today.

While attending a revival service at the Missionary Baptist Church in Van Lear, Jim and his wife, Bessie, accepted the Lord and vowed to live for Him the remainder of their lives. Although he worked long hard hours in the mines, he always found time to be active in his church. He served many years as deacon and Sunday school superintendent and often music director.

In the 1920s, Rev. S.D. Grumbles and Jim pooled their assets and purchased a portion of King Addition from Sam King in Paintsville and developed the Pack-Grumbles Subdivision which was located on both sides of the Garrett Highway, two miles east of Paintsville on Route 40. This being recorded in *Misc. Inst. Book* 4, page 454, Johnson County Court Clerks office.

In July 1928, he moved his family to their newly constructed home in this subdivision.

He continued to work in Van Lear. At that time, he, as well as many men, walked from King Addition to Meally, walked across the hill via Dicey Fork or Fitch Branch to Van Lear, worked their shift (which was many more than eight hours) then returned home the same walk. Also other men walked from Boons Camp and Williamsport via the same route.

During the seasons of 'slack work' at the mines, which were beginning to be frequent, Jim always managed to have a truck he would use to move families from the coal town to other places, many times out of state, etc. He also utilized this time to contact several schools and businesses in Ohio. He delivered their winter supply of coal. On his return trip he would bring to Johnson County loads of fruit and vegetables, hay or corn. These same contacts and contracts provided his family income during the "Depression Years."

In the 1930s he was diagnosed as having diabetes which came as a terrible blow to him and to his family. At that time, even his local doctors knew very little about the proper treatment for a diabetic.

Jim was an unsuccessful Republican candidate for jailer in 1933. He was defeated by his good friend and former Van Lear neighbor, Powell Williams.

In the mid 30s he bought and operated two underground mines, one at Riceville and one on Tom's Creek, DBA/Paintsville Coal Co. Inc. He started as truck mines but began to branch out with contracts to ship coal by rail, thus requiring a tipple and railroad site in Jennies Creek. As his company began to grow, his health began to fail. He sold to Tilson Coal Co. but remained as superintendent of the Riceville operation.

His goal regarding the coal mining industry was to get the coal moving again in Johnson County and then to make a move on the coal at his old home place in Martin County and get the coal moving there. He felt that coal was going to boom, but was not yet aware of surface and strip mining techniques. He paved the way for those to follow a few years later when the Eastern Kentucky Coal Boom did come with modern equipment, mountain top removal, etc., making millionaires of many Eastern Kentucky entrepreneurs. Again, a vast number of people began to move here as work was again plentiful in the coal fields.

James Arthur Pack Sr. was truly 'A Man Before His Time.'

By this time Jim was showing many side effects of diabetes. Feb. 23, 1946, he suffered a fatal heart attack at an early age of 55 years. He was buried in the Pack Family Cemetery, Pack Hill Drive, overlooking his home and subdivision he developed.

Besides his widow, Bessie Meddings Pack, he was survived by eight children: Willie Pack, Wheelwright; Mrs. Hazel Gullett, Owensboro; Mrs. Helen Patton, Mrs. Lillian Arrowood and James Pack Jr., City; and Mary Elizabeth and Paul Douglas, at home. Thirteen grandchildren and one sister, Mrs. Mahala Maynard, Stidham, also survived.

PACK - Thomas Pack (born 1843, died 1934). Father, George Pack (born 1824, died 1865), son of Samuel Pack and Jane Brown. Mother, Anna (Fannin) Pack, daughter of William Fannin and Jane Penix.

Thomas was the first child (of 10 children) born to this marriage. He had four brothers as follows: Noah (born 1846), Arthur (born 1848), Solimon (born 1850) and Uriah (born 1854). Uriah married Arminta Caudill.

His five sisters were Lydia (born 1852) married William Preston; Charlotte (born 1856); Thursday "Thursy" (born 1858) married Lefner Castle; Unice "Eunice" (born 1862); and Mary (born 1864).

Thomas Pack and granddaughter Mary Elizabeth Pack

The following Civil War record appears, "*PRESIDENTS, SOLDIERS & STATESMEN,*" Volume II, page 1209, publisher H.H. Hardesty, published 1896.

"Thomas Pack was born in Martin County, KY, Jun. 25, 1843, and was a son of George Pack who was born in Floyd County, KY, and died in Martin County, KY, Dec. 25, 1865. His mother, Anna (Fannin), was born in Virginia and died in Martin County, KY, in 1871, aged 52 years. He was married Dec. 22, 1883, to Elizabeth Haney who was born in this (Martin) county Mar. 27, 1859. They have two children, James A. (born May 16, 1890) and Mahala (born Jan. 8, 1893). Mrs. Pack was a daughter of William Haney who was born in this county (Martin) and died here in 1876, aged 60 years; her mother, Rebecca (Moore) was born and also died in this county (Martin) in 1874 at the age of 61 years. Besides the two children born to our subject and wife, they have reared three children: Elizabeth, John A. and Tamsy Nealy. Comrade Pack was engaged in farming when he enlisted in the Federal army in 1862, aged 18 years; he was enrolled as a private in Co. G, 14th Kentucky V I, 2nd Bde., 1st. Div., 23d A. C. He was wounded at Pine Mt., Jun. (corrected in ink to January) 22, 1864, and again June 12, same year at Pumpkin Vine Creek. He was treated in hospital for wounds a short time; he was given a leave of absence of nine days; he was taken prisoner Jun. 22, 1864, but made his escape while the bullets were flying thick and fast; he participated in the engagements of Middle Creek, Cumberland Gap, Tazwell, Licking, Lookout Mt., Buzzared Roost, Resaca, Kinston, Dallas, Pine Mt., Cass Station, Pumpkin Vine Mt., Chattahoochee River and several others; he was honorably discharged at Louisa, KY, Jan. 21, 1865. Prior to his enlistment he served three months in service. Comrade Pack has been constable of this county (Martin) and deputy sheriff for 16 years, he is highly esteemed in this county and resides in Inez, KY."

The correction of dates of injuries were surely that of Thomas Pack, as these notes were made from his personal volume. To his family and those who knew him best, this book rated second only to his Holy Bible, which he studied daily.

After the death of wife, Elizabeth, the mother of his two small children, he married a second time to Nancy Jane (maiden name unknown). She was a Justice, by a previous marriage. She brought two (maybe three) Justice children to the marriage. Thomas and Nancy Jane had no children by their marriage. Nancy

Jane Pack is buried in the Pack-Webb Cemetery, Milo, Martin County, KY.

When his health started failing he tried to lighten his work load and began to retire. Approximately 1924, he came to reside with his son, James Arthur Pack, and family at Van Lear.

By this time, much of the population of Van Lear was families from many counties. They not only were learning to speak English, they were also seeking history of our country. Telling his Civil War experiences to these eager to learn people was a great way to retire. He also enjoyed public speaking regarding these activities and the "hi-lite" of these invitations seemed to be the many times he was asked to speak to the students at the schools. The students were just as eager to hear as he was happy to share his story.

He still had a daughter, Mahala (Pack) Maynard, her husband, Lace, and other grandchildren in Martin County so he returned often to visit them as well as check on his farm and property there.

Thomas moved to Paintsville in 1928, along with his son and family and remained there until his death, Mar. 1, 1934. His remains were laid to rest between his two wives who preceded him in death, in the Pack-Webb Cemetery, Milo, Martin County, KY.

The following is a hand written love letter Thomas wrote, October 1883, to Elizabeth "Lizzy" Haney two months before they married, December 1883. Because of the age difference of Thomas and Lizzy, and she was rearing three Nealy children (orphaned by her deceased sister) evidently her family and friends were advising her to not marry. The marriage must have worked well. They had two children of their own and Thomas continued to raise all the children after Elizabeth's death, Mar. 11, 1902.

As the following hand written letter is now 116 years old it is quiet faded and difficult to read. However the penmanship and wording are so beautiful it is interpreted as follows:

Oct. 17, 1883
Inez, Martin County, KY

Miss Lizzy

The morning being fair and the air calm and serene I take pleasure in writing you this message to inform you that I have not forgotten you. Owing you all the kind appreciation and love that could be bestowed on any lady. It appears to me that I never get an opportunity of seeing you any more. I want to have the pleasure of meeting with you soon.

The long absent days from you appear as months to me. I hope the time will soon come when I will not be severed from your pleasant face. I hardly know how to write at present, not knowing whether my last letter was appreciated by you or not.

Lizzy, it appears to me that every thing that can oppose our talking is at work with all the energy they can against us.

So I will close by saying I remain your affectionate lover until death and wishing that your days on earth may be many and happy and that pleasures many and happy moments may all ways be your fortune.

Thomas Pack

PATTON - Goodale Patton was born at Sublett in Magoffin County, KY, Mar. 16, 1906, to Reece Patton and Carrie Arnett Patton. Reece was born Mar. 10, 1869, to Thomas Patton and Armina Houndshell Patton. Carrie Arnett Patton was the daughter of Reuben Arnett and Emaline Patrick Arnett. Reece and Carrie Patton and Thomas and Armina Patton are buried at Sublett, KY. The Cemetery is on a hilltop overlooking a beautiful valley. A peaceful breeze is most always blowing.

Goodale's brothers were Thomas Patton, Dexter Patton and Camdon Patton; and his sister was Flossie Patton May. Thomas worked as a farmer and self employed logger. He was murdered while hauling logs. Reece and Carrie lived in Paintsville for a few years as well as Magoffin County.

Goodale, Gertrude, Oakley, Bromley, Donald and Franklin Patton.

Goodale married Gertrude Marie White (born in Brave, PA, Nov. 26, 1908). Gertrude was the daughter of Franklin Claude White, son of John H. White and Fannie Cutter White of Green County, PA, and Hannah Matilda Gump White, daughter of Leonard Gump and Jane McGumphy Gump of Green County, PA. Gertrude had a sister, Thelma White Morehouse, and two brothers, John White and Arville White.

Goodale and Gertrude are buried in Mayo Cemetery in Paintsville. Franklin Claude and Hannah Matilda Gump White are buried in Highland Memorial Cemetery at Staffordsville, KY. Arville White is buried in Texas, John White in Virginia and other White ancestors are buried in Pennsylvania.

Goodale and Gertrude were the parents of Oakley Patton, Bromley Patton, Donald Patton, Franklin Patton and two sons who died in infancy. Goodale was employed by the Kentucky West Virginia Gas Co. and worked at the station on Hencliff or Southside in Paintsville.

Goodale died suddenly in 1957 and Gertrude reared Franklin and Donald alone. She was employed by the famed "Tiger Drive Inn" and other "Good Food" locations in Paintsville. She spent several years in the Volga, WV area, but returned to Paintsville about 15 years before her death.

PELPHREY & LEMASTER - Brooks Pelphrey (born Oct. 29, 1906, at Staffordsville, KY, in Johnson County, died Mar. 8, 1987) was the son of Amos and Laura Sturgill Pelphrey.

He had two sisters, Donnie and Grace, and one half-sister, Chala Blanton. He had three brothers: Fred, Burt and Val, and two half-brothers, Leck and George Blanton.

Swonnie (born Apr. 2, 1909, at Barnetts Creek in Johnson County, died Apr. 3, 1954) was the daughter of Alfred and Hattie LeMaster of Barnetts Creek. She had four sisters: Lexie, Lessie, Francis and Tressie. She had seven brothers: Richard, Garland, Edward, Elmer, John, Frank and Herbert.

Both Brooks and Swonnie attended one-room schools, she at Barnetts Creek, and he at Staffordsville. They met at Barnetts Creek Church and were married May 4, 1928, at Paintsville by John W. Butcher.

Brooks worked for Toral Franklin in Franklin's store and post office at Staffordsville. Also he worked on the farms. Swonnie was a housewife and mother to nine children. Six sons: William K., James H., Bob, Jack, John and Kenny. Three girls: Jane, Freda and Edna.

Brooks and Swonnie were members of the Union United Baptist Church until their deaths. Both are buried in the Dixon Cemetery at Staffordsville.

Brooks married Mae Davis LeMaster in 1958. He worked for the Paintsville Grocery from 1965 until retiring in 1972.

PELPHREY - James Richard Pelphrey Sr. was born Sep. 20, 1933, at Van Lear, Johnson County, KY, a small coal mining community about five miles from Paintsville, KY. His dad was a coal miner, Milford Pelphrey Sr., and his mother was Rosa Blair Pelphrey. His parents were originally from Barnetts Creek, KY. He was the fifth of 10 children.

Jim, at an early age had much ambition and showed signs of becoming a very wise businessman. He was a graduate of Van Lear High School and attended Morehead State College. He entered the USAF Dec. 4, 1954, completing his tour of duty, Oct. 22, 1957.

Upon leaving the Air Force, Jim began working for Daniels Dairy, which was later sold to Meadow Gold Dairy, a division of Beatrice Foods, Inc., becoming assistant manager. While with the dairy, he acquired two Standard Oil service stations, one in Paintsville and the other in Prestonsburg, KY. Along with his dairy job and service stations, Jim held sales positions with Life of Kentucky Insurance Co., the Blue Grass Meat Provision Co., and was also a distributor for the Bunny Bread Co. These were the first of his business ventures of which there were to be many.

Rheumatoid arthritis forced Jim to sell his businesses and relocate to Phoenix, AZ, 1966-1967. There he worked as a sales representative for the Atlantic Richfield Oil Co., thus gaining more knowledge of the oil business.

Jim returned to Paintsville in 1967 and purchased an Ashland Oil service station in downtown Paintsville. He became a partner in 1969 in Pelphrey Auto Sales, Inc. at Prestonsburg. Also in 1969, Jim joined Arnett Supply Co. in Paintsville, a wholesaler of petroleum products, as an employee and partner. From this partnership Jim became an agent/distributor for the Standard Oil Co., founding Pelphrey Supply Co., Inc. and Pelphrey Auto Parts, Inc. on Depot Road in Paintsville in 1970. He ran these businesses very successfully for many years, later becoming a Chevron jobber covering five eastern Kentucky counties, and opening 20 convenience stores in Kentucky and Ohio, forming the Jim's Stop and Shop, Inc. chain. He had by then relocated his bulk plant and opened his first Stop and Shop on Highway 23 North, between Paintsville and Prestonsburg. Besides the Chevron jobbership, Jim was a Marathon Oil Co. jobber and acquired the Williams-Nickel Oil Co. in Morehead, KY, the Lykins Oil Co. in Vanceburg, KY, and the Park Oil Co. in Ravenna, KY, gaining multiple stations and land holdings. On Oct. 1, 1995, Jim sold his oil business and convenience stores to the Coleman Oil Co. of Pikeville, KY.

He was a member of the Van Lear Masonic Lodge and a former director of the Paintsville-Johnson County Chamber of Commerce.

On Aug. 28, 1992, Jim announced his intent to purchase a controlling interest in The Bank Josephine in Prestonsburg, Floyd County, KY. On Dec. 20, 1992, this acquisition was approved and he became chairman of the board of The Bank Josephine. The bank was established in 1891, making it the oldest bank in southeast Kentucky, with assets of $120,000,000, and the only bank in the U.S. named for a woman. Later he acquired all the outstanding stock making him the sole owner of the bank. On Sep. 30, 1997, Jim sold The Bank Josephine to Citizens National Bank of Paintsville.

Jim, through the years as an entrepreneur, had bought and sold many commercial and residential properties. He was once owner of the Starfire Motel and Heart O' Highlands Motel and Restaurant in Paintsville. Upon selling Heart O' Highlands Motel, Jim retained a portion of the property and established Highland Plaza, a group of apartments and retail spaces. He then formed Pelphrey Investments, L.P., whose offices are now located in Highland Plaza.

Jim stayed active in business until his untimely death, Apr. 11, 1998. He fought a courageous and secretive battle with cancer as aggressively as he had lived.

"Work" was Jim's hobby, he loved work and the challenge of a business deal. He had an uncanny ability of remembering a name, always calling everyone by their first name. His smile was contagious and the secret to his success. Probably no man had a better knowledge of the people of this area or more business experience than did Jim Pelphrey.

Jim was married at Paintsville, Johnson County,

KY, to Nicky Carol Wetzel, on Oct. 17, 1953. Jim and Nicky were married 44 years and were the parents of James Richard Pelphrey Jr. (born Jul. 20, 1959), Paul David Pelphrey (born Oct. 14, 1961) and Jane Ann Pelphrey (born Sep. 17, 1967). They also were the grandparents of Diana Nicole Daniels (born Dec. 18, 1989), Madalynn Louise Pelphrey (born May 16, 1994), Matthew Scott Daniels (born May 27, 1994) and James Dalton Daniels (born Dec. 10, 1998).

Pelphrey Investments, L.P. is now managed by Nicky, Jim's wife, and Jim's three children, together with businesses and investments of their own.

PELPHREY - Mairiam Lilly (Pelphrey) Loring, the eighth of nine children, born Dec. 25, 1930, at Van Lear, KY, near the Bradley Crossing to Alta (LeMaster) Pelphrey. The LeMasters were French. Many fled France in 1639 on record of their arrival in America, they came to America as stowaways, indentured servants or under false identities. They lived on the eastern edge of Zechiah swamp near Bryantown, MD, for over a century before starting their westward migration.

Front Row: Rosemarie, Jewell, Mairiam Lilly, Howard and Norris. Back Row, Left to Right: Otchel, Eula, Dad Elzie, Freda, Mom Alta Lemaster Pelphrey, VanLear Bradley Crossing.

My parents met at his oldest brother's home, Edward and Martha (Grim) Pelphrey. Alta LeMaster was a housekeeper for them. Born Jan. 14, 1893, Kenwood, Johnson County, KY, died Feb. 26, 1967. Elzie Pelphrey was born Nov. 16, 1897, Sitka, Johnson County, died Mar. 25, 1977. They were married Mar. 9, 1916, at Edds by Tom Jeff Collins. He always talked of his parents coming from Old Virginia on his mother's side, the Fletchers. His great-great-great-grandfather was full blooded Cherokee Indian. His name was Alexander Sire Horse. His wife was Ledunia Wills. No information about them.

My mother was a housewife, a wonderful cook and mother. Dad was a farmer, hunter, fisherman, carpenter and a UMWA member. Van Lear Chapter 5835 Kentucky coal miner at #1, 2, 3, 5 and Weeksbury mines. This is where he was when he quit the mines and moved to Ohio.

My brothers and sisters: Opal (born Jul. 12, 1914, died Feb. 25, 1937), Freda (born Feb. 2, 1917, died Feb. 1, 1987), James Edward Pelphrey (born Jun. 24, 1919, died Jun. 27, 1919), Otchel (born Apr. 10, 1921, died Sep. 23, 1997), Eula (born Mar. 1, 1923, died Apr. 5, 1980), Rose Marie (born Apr. 15, 1925, died Oct. 11, 1997), Jewell (born Apr. 6, 1928), Mairiam Lilly (born Dec. 25, 1930) and Howard Norris Pelphrey (born Mar. 12, 1934, died Feb. 20, 1996).

We moved from Van Lear when I was just a baby to the Oil Branch. We later moved back to Van Lear by the railroad tracks at the Bradly Crossing. I attended first through fifth grade there in Van Lear. Then we moved to West Van Lear. I went two years there. Then the family relocated to Galloway, OH, where my father worked on the John Galbreath farm. I went one year at Alton Hall School. Again the family moved into Columbus, OH. At age 16 I quit Central High School to attend Cosmetology School, which upon graduation at age 17, Oct. 23, 1948, I became Mrs. John Harley Loring. My first job was the Purity Cone Co. I thought I was rich clearing $25.00 a week.

Our daughter, Sharen Elaine Loring, was born Jun. 2, 1950, in Cleveland, OH. My husband worked for the Swift Packing Co. in the smokehouse. We moved back to Columbus when she was 2 years old. She married Bernard Louis Grove on Aug. 28, 1968, and she gave birth to "B.J." Bernard Louis Jr. on Nov. 25, 1969. He wed Brandy Lee Smith May 11, 1996. They have one daughter, Bailey Shane Grove (born Feb. 17, 1996). They divorced May 7, 1998.

John and I both worked in factories until he later went with the Iron Workers Local 172. From there he retired May 1983. I continued to work at Anheuser-Busch Inc. and retired Feb. 25, 1991, and have enjoyed working on my genealogy. *By Mairiam Lilly Loring.*

PELFREY - Margaret Wynn Pelfrey Napier was born in the Paintsville Clinic, Paintsville, KY, Feb. 26, 1961, to William Hillard Pelfrey and Clista Margaret McKenzie Pelfrey. She is the youngest of four girls. Her sisters are Hilary Pelfrey Griffiths, Beverly Pelfrey Estep and Marcia Rae Salyer Sumpter.

Margaret was married to Timothy Dwayne Napier Jul. 25, 1989. Margaret was a 1979 graduate of Johnson Central High School in Paintsville, KY. She graduated from Morehead State University in 1982 with a bachelor of social work. She continued her education by obtaining a MA degree from Morehead State University in 1988.

Margaret Wynn Pelfrey Napier

She has worked extensively with abused children and adults. She began her career by working for the Cabinet for Human Resources, Dept. for Social Services, where she worked for over seven years. In 1994 she accepted a position for Mountain Comprehensive Care Center, Paintsville, KY. She provided mental health treatment for victims of abuse. In 1997 she was promoted to the coordinator of the Johnson County Clinic.

She is a Kentucky Colonel and was selected into the *Who's Who of Women Executives*. In her spare time Margaret enjoys vegetable and flower gardening. She values handmade and family-made items. She enjoys making craft items for family and friends. She is an avid cook and always likes to try new foods and recipes. She loves to camp at state parks and enjoys the scenery of plants and animals.

Margaret volunteers her time to help the community. She was involved in the Paintsville Lions Club and the Lend A Hand Organization. She is a supporter of the Mountain Arts Center in Prestonsburg which strives to promote the talents of local residents. She also supports the amphitheater located at the Jenny Wiley Sate Park at Prestonsburg, KY.

Margaret was active in music as she was growing up by taking piano lessons, playing first trumpet in Johnson Central Marching Band and also in Morehead University Marching Band.

Margaret was saved at a young age and currently sings alto in a singing group known as "The Family Foundation."

Margaret currently makes her home at Flat Gap in the house built by her grandfather, Ray McKenzie, and her great-grandfather, Merdia Oliver McKenzie. *Submitted by Clista M. McKenzie Pelfrey.*

PELFREY & MCKENZIE - Marcia Rae Pelfrey was born Apr. 4, 1951, in Paintsville, Johnson County, KY, to William Hillard "Pat" Pelfrey and Clista Margaret McKenzie Pelfrey. She was the third of four daughters. Marcia is the granddaughter of Ray and Beulah Lyon McKenzie and Forest Lee and Rinda Cox Pelfrey.

Marcia married Earl Samuel Sumpter (born in Bell County, KY, and raised in Virginia) in Johnson County, KY, Aug. 6, 1996. Marcia has one son, Kyle Ray Salyer (born Mar. 8, 1981, in Huntington, WV), from a previous marriage. Sam has two children from a previous marriage, Earl Samuel Sumpter Jr. and Kristi Michelle Sumpter.

Sam and Marcia R. Pelfrey Sumpter and Kyle Ray Salyer.

Marcia attended school at Flat Gap, then college at Marshall University and Prestonsburg Community College. She is also a candidate with the Kentucky Certified Public Manager's Program. She works for Kentucky Div. of Emergency Management as the Area 9 manager, covering 10 counties in Eastern Kentucky. Sam, a staff sergeant, is employed by the KYARNG as a support service specialist.

Her son, Kyle, graduated from Johnson Central High School in 1999 as an honor student and plans to become an attorney.

Marcia was commissioned an admiral of Kentucky Waterways on Apr. 5, 1973, by Governor Wendell T. Ford and as a Kentucky Colonel on Apr. 5, 1988, by Governor Wallace G. Wilkerson.

Marcia, Sam and Kyle make their home at Keaton and attend Flat Gap Baptist Sunday school and church.

PELFREY - William Hillard "Pat" Pelfrey. The first records available show the Pelfrey family living in Germany in the seventh century. During a revolt they fled to England, then came to Plymouth, MA, in 1626. Some settled there and others made their way to Maryland, Virginia and Kentucky. John Pelfreys, of Virginia, raised his family there. One of his sons, William (born 1764), was in the Revolutionary War. He came to Floyd County in 1804 and settled on the waters of Paint Creek. This area became Johnson County in 1843 when Johnson County was formed. William's son, John Lewis Pelfrey, married Katherine Ferguson and their son, John Pelfrey, married Amanda Brown. John and Amanda had a son, William Thomas Pelfrey, who married Nancy Brown. William and Nancy are Pat's grandparents.

Clista M. (McKenzie), William Hillard "Pat" Pelfrey Hilary, Beverly, Marcia Rae and Margaret Wynn Pelfrey.

William Hillard Pelfrey was born at Mima, Morgan County, KY, Dec. 18, 1916, to Forest Lee and Rinda Cox Pelfrey. William Hillard was nicknamed "Pat" at an early age. Pat's grandparents are William Thomas and Nancy Brown Pelfrey and John Allen and Cora Cantrell Cox. William Thomas Pelfrey made his home in Johnson County the last 20 years of his life. Pat is one of 13 children born to Forest Lee and Rinda. Listed in order of their birth: Grettie, Emerson, "W.H. Pat," Grace, John, Ellis, Nannie, Gladys, Thelma, Forest Jr., Chester, Betty and Robert Lee.

Pat attended one room grade schools in Morgan and Lawrence counties and received his high school diploma in Johnson County. As an adult he worked for an oil company for seven years, pulling oil wells with a team of horses. In 1939 he went to Radford, VA, and worked in the Hercules Powder Plant. His next job was in Baltimore, MD, for Bethlehem Steel.

Pat entered the U.S. Army Jan. 26, 1943, and served in the Pacific Theatre with the 180th Chemical Div. Two platoons went overseas and landed at New Caledonia. He served with the Navy Seabees and the Americal Div. in the Solomon and Philippine Islands. Pat's rank was sergeant at the time he was honorably discharged Dec. 22, 1945. The 180th Chemical Div. continues to meet for a reunion each year.

After his U.S. Army years he worked in Dayton, OH, for a short period of time, just prior to being employed by A.O.&R. Pat married Clista M. McKenzie and they have made their home at Keaton for 50 years. They have four daughters: Hilary, Beverly, Marcia Rae and Margaret Wynn. Pat was employed by Ashland Oil and Refining Co. for 33 years, until his retirement in 1982. He was active in Community Development Club work and was a 4H leader for 20 years. Pat is a devoted husband, father, Christian, a lifetime member in the Kentucky Parent Teachers Association, a Kentucky Colonel, genealogist, historian and a member of the Johnson County, Magoffin County, Big Sandy, Eastern Kentucky Genealogical/Historical Societies. He has been instrumental in having gravestones set at several Revolutionary and Civil War veterans unmarked graves. He has contributed a great amount of information from his personal records, compiled by reading cemeteries and research, in Johnson and surrounding counties. He has visited with many elderly people to gather and record unwritten family histories. Pat has shared family tree information with many school children and adults tracing their family roots. He was a Sunday school teacher and Sunday school superintendent for many years. Pat was listed in the 1982 publication of "*Who's Who in Kentucky Genealogy.*" *Submitted by William H. and Clista M. Pelfrey.*

PENNINGTON - James R. Pennington was born Dec. 12, 1829, to Joshua and Nancy Jane Sparks Pennington. Joshua was born in Virginia about 1789. Nancy Jane was born about 1790 in Virginia. James R. Pennington came to Kentucky from North Carolina. He died Oct. 28, 1924, at his daughter's home at Red Bush, KY. He is buried at Red Bush, KY.

He served in the Confederate Army with Capt. Fields' Co. (Partisan Rangers) from Nov. 20, 1862-Jun. 30, 1865. His grave is honored with a Civil War government marker.

James R. Pennington

James was married twice, his first marriage was to Nancy Fairchilds. She was the daughter of Joe and Katherine Lark Fairchilds. James and Nancy had eight children: Martha Jane, who married Dr. Elihue Tivis Wallin; Charolette, who married 1) Haden McKenzie, 2) John Wells; Ida, who married William McCarty; Katherine, who married Benn Pratt; Bud, died young; William, who married Cynthia Curtis; Nathan, who married __ Church; and Phoebe, who married Loranzo Holbrook.

James was married the second time to Jane McCarty Coldiron and together they had three children: Leander "Lee," who married Elizabeth Fraley; Etta, who married Raleigh Ison; and Abialum "Abner," who married __ Conley.

James was an old-time "fiddle" player and enjoyed playing for family and friends.

Family history handed down reports that when James and Jane were aged and physically unable to care for each other they agreed for each to go to one of their children to live out the remainder of their days. At this time James moved to the home of his daughter, Phoebe, and remained there until his death. *Submitted by Clista M. Pelfrey.*

PICKLESIMER - Homer Picklesimer was born Dec. 7, 1932, in Johnson County, KY, to Homer D. and Ethel Conley Picklesimer. He is the youngest of 10 born to his parents, and all of them survive until this day.

Homer, Linda (Brammer), George, Jonathan, Jeanette and Laura Picklesimer.

Homer was married to Linda Kay Brammer Nov. 5, 1966, at the Fairborn Church of Christ, Fairborn, OH, by Dan Wright. They are the parents of four children: George (born Oct. 27, 1961, adopted in 1971), Jonathan (born Jul. 9, 1971), Jeannette (born Aug. 19, 1972) and Laura (born Jan. 5, 1977).

After attending a one and two room school at Ramey Branch, Homer graduated from Flat Gap High School in 1951 as valedictorian. He attended Freed-Hardeman College, Henderson, TN, 1951-54 where he majored in Bible and graduated with honors. In 1958 he graduated magna cum laude from Harding College, Searcy, AR, as a biblical language major. He taught in Athens Bible School, Athens, AL, in 1958, 1959. In the early 1960s he attended summer schools at Morehead State College for an area of concentration in elementary education. He has taught in various Johnson County Schools for 33 years and retired in 1989. In the meantime, he has preached at the Stambaugh Church of Christ since 1960 and has worked with other Churches of Christ in Johnson, Floyd and Magoffin counties. He also likes to boat, fish, work on cars and surf the internet.

Linda Kay Brammer was born Feb. 27, 1941, to Allen T. and Genevieve E. Brammer in Ironton, OH. She is the second of four daughters. She attended grade school in Fairborn, OH, where she graduated from Fairborn High School in 1959. Afterwards she enrolled in Carniege Institute in Cleveland, OH, for medical laboratory training. Further training was obtained from working in various hospitals. She is now a certified medical laboratory technologist. After working for various doctors and hospitals in Eastern Kentucky, she is now employed at Hope Family Medical Center, Salyersville, KY.

Jonathan Samuel graduated with top honors from Johnson Central in 1989. He attended Harding university and graduated magna cum laude in 1994 with a BS degree in mathematics. From Arkansas State University he received a MS degree in mathematics. He computer networked and taught at Crowley's Ridge College, Paragould, AR, and Cascade College in Portland, OR. Presently he is a computer support services specialist at Harding University. He married Sharon Culpepper in 1994.

Jeannette Elizabeth graduated with honors from Johnson Central in 1990. She attended Harding University and graduated cum laude in 1995 with a BS degree in biology. She has done mission work in Romania and has worked for an environmental company in Portland, OR. Recently she has worked for Redd, Brown and Williams Real Estate in Paintsville, and is currently studying environmental law at Northern Kentucky University.

Laura Margaret graduated with top honors from Johnson Central in 1994. She attended Harding University and graduated summa cum laude in 1998 with a BS degree in social work. She married Jason Kretzer in 1996 at the Paintsville Church of Christ. She is currently employed at Mountain Comprehensive Care Center in Prestonsburg as a service coordinator for severely emotionally disturbed children.

PRESTON - Author Lee Preston (born Dec. 8, 1901, at River, KY), was the second son born to William and Myrtle Spears Preston. Known to many in the Johnson County area as A.L., he met and eventually married Matilda Daniel, born the second daughter of Luther and Savillar Preston Daniel, also of River, KY, Apr. 1, 1900. Author Lee and Matilda married at Paintsville Sep. 24, 1921, and soon made their home approximately one mile south of the River post office on a small 36 acre farm of hillside and bottomland.

Author Lee and Matilda Daniel Preston

Author was a coal miner for most of his life, spending much of his time in the mines of Offutt, Van Lear and Red Jacket, WV. Author was known to be a member of the Offutt Oddfellows Lodge and still was in possession of his ceremonial regalia at the time of his death. Matilda and he were blessed with eight children, three of which preceded them in death.

Richard (born August 1924) was only 2 years old when diphtheria took his life.

Clarence, the first born child, was 14 when he was injured internally and bled to death at home in bed.

Six other children were born to the Prestons including: Opal, of Baltimore, MD (born Jun. 14, 1923); Clifford (born Nov. 27, 1926, died Nov. 17, 1982) was a longtime Big Sandy RECC employee; James (born Oct. 14, 1929, died Apr. 27, 1965) was a coal miner residing in Matewan, WV, when he was killed in a roof fall; Claude, of McViegh, KY (born Oct. 4, 1931) is retired from mining; Robert, of Dayton, OH (born May 21, 1934) is retired from General Motors Corp.; and Verona Mae "Ronnie" of Ashland, KY (born Mar. 21, 1936). Fifteen grandchildren, 18 great-grandchildren and two great-great-grandchildren have been born to the extended family at the time of this publication.

The family enjoyed many holidays and weekend visits to the farm at River where A.L. was known to take grandsons "shottin" with his .22 caliber rifle into the Levisa Fork of the Big Sandy. Targets of the day were usually floating logs that resembled snarling alligators, but sometimes an unlucky groundhog would stumble into the line of fire.

Matilda, or "Tildy," as she was called by friends, was always busy at the wood cookstove, preparing yet another fine feast of soup beans, corn bread, fried chicken, pork or salmon cakes. Usually the first to rise, her coffee and biscuits could wake visitors from even the deepest slumber. Matilda, who became ill during a common flood of the Levisa Fork, died at the old Paintsville Hospital on Euclid Ave. on Apr. 24, 1972.

Author, or A.L., enjoyed his retirement by reading nearly every western novel the Johnson County library came to acquire, and visiting with friends and relatives of the Johnson County area, died of heart attack at Paul B. Hall Hospital on Jul. 6, 1985.

Both are buried beside Clarence and Richard in the Daniel Cemetery on Wiley Branch Rd.

PRESTON - Barbara Lyon Preston was born Sep. 22, 1949, in Paintsville, KY, to Kerlin Lyon and Janieve Hamilton Lyon. A sister, Linda Carol Lyon, was born May 20, 1948, and a brother, Mark Kerlin Lyon was born Oct. 4, 1959.

Barbara was married in Raceland, KY, Dec. 18, 1967, to Rodney C. Mattingly. They are the parents of one son, Matthew E. Mattingly (born Nov. 29, 1974).

Barbara was divorced in 1979 and married Kenneth P. Preston in Flatwoods, KY, Mar. 21, 1980. Ken has one son, Chad E. Preston (born Dec. 17, 1974).

Barbara Lyon Preston

Barbara was a graduate of Russell High School in Russell, KY, in 1967, and attended Ashland Community College in Ashland, KY. She has worked for Ashland Oil, Inc. from July 1970 to the present time. For 10 years she was an executive secretary for Valvoline Oil Co. and is presently an executive secretary for Ashland's corporate medical director.

Her husband, Ken, is a graduate of Morehead State University, Morehead, KY, and has been employed by AK Steel from 1970 to the present time.

Barbara's hobbies are hiking, bicycle riding and reading. She is a member of Raceland Christian Church in Raceland, KY.

Barbara's son, Matthew, is a graduate of Eastern Kentucky University, Richmond, KY, with a BS in manufacturing technology. He is employed by AK Steel, Ashland, KY. Barbara's stepson, Chad, is a graduate of the University of Kentucky, Lexington, KY, with a BA in journalism. He is employed by the Chamber of Commerce, Cincinnati, OH.

PRESTON - Ben Preston was born in Johnson County, KY. He was the youngest son of Eliphus Preston and Nancy Jane Grimm. Other siblings of Ben are: John F. (born 1842), Jefferson (born 1847), Charles (born 1848), Laura (born 1852), Francis M. (born 1855), William W. (born 1856), Amanda (born 1858), Winfield (born 1861), Sarah J. (born 1867) and Lewis C. (born 1868).

Ben married Mary Louise Roberts in Johnson County, KY, May 17, 1889. Mary was the daughter of Horace Roberts and Martha Jane Cooper. Ben and Mary resided and raised their family in Johnson County. Their children are: Angelina (born 1896), Martha (born 1897), Brookie (born 1899) and Mary (born 1903).

Ben was a farmer and coal miner until his untimely death in 1904 of a fever. His widowed wife moved her family to Catlettsburg, KY, to be near her family, she died there in 1949.

Angelina married William Ambrose Spence in 1914, she died in 1968. Martha married John Pack in 1915, she died in 19??. Brookie never married, he died in 1955. Mary married Tom Lanham, she died in 1981.

PRESTON - Isaac David Preston "I.D." was born Sep. 3, 1888, on Two-Mile Creek in Johnson County, KY. He was the sixth of 10 children born to General Lafayette and Julina Pack Preston. He married Nomi Malta Howe in Johnson County on Sep. 30, 1908. Malta was a daughter of James Henry and Minta Spears Howe; she was born Mar. 24, 1891, on Rock House Branch in Johnson County. The couple went to housekeeping on Boyd Branch in the mining camp located at Thealka. Virgil, the first child, was born here while I.D. worked in the coal mines. Malta's family moved to Mason County circa 1912. I.D. and Malta, along with other members of the Howe family, made this move as a joint venture. I.D. and Malta, along with their first born son, returned to Johnson County about 1913 and settled on Two-Mile Creek where the remainder of their children were born. The couple were the parents of eight children, in order of their birth, they were: Virgil Wadsworth, Edith, Neva Leona, Paul Richard, Charles Edmund, Harold Lloyd, Betty Dean and Patty Ann. Charles Edmund died in infancy with the other seven living into adulthood.

I.D. died at the age of 88 in Boyd County, KY, on Oct. 10, 1976. Malta died at the age of 86 at the home place on Two-Mile Creek on Jul. 22, 1977. They were laid to rest in a family cemetery on the home place at Williamsport. Their bodies, along with their daughter, Edith, and two sons-in-law, were exhumed and re-interred in the Highlands Memorial Park at Staffordsville in the fall of 1998.

Isaac David and Malta Howe Preston with their seven children. From youngest to oldest, they were: Patty Ann, Betty Dean, Harold Lloyd, Paul Richard, Neva Leona, Edith and Virgil Wadsworth.

Virgil Wadsworth became a teacher as a young man and began that career in a one-room school at the head of Greasy Creek. His teaching career ended as the head teacher in the Van Lear Grade School in 1941. At that time, he resigned and enlisted in the USAF. Shortly before his ordered movement to Europe during WWII, he married Edith Boyles. After the conclusion of the war, Virgil and Edith settled in Cincinnati where Virgil assumed an occupation in private industry, and Edith continued her career as a teacher. They had one daughter named Joan Elizabeth.

Edith became a teacher in the Johnson County School System and continued in that role in the said county until her retirement in the early 1970s. She was a graduate of Pikeville College. Edith first married James Short; Jim died in 1951. Edith took Lloyd Hill as her second husband. Edith had no children. She died May 25, 1975, in Huntington, WV, and was buried in a new family cemetery at Williamsport.

Neva Leona married Mitchell Wallen, and the couple settled on Two-Mile where they operated a country store for many years. Mitchell was appointed postmaster at Williamsport and served in that capacity until his retirement. This couple had two children who were named Howard Wendell and Lois Avonell.

Paul Richard, a graduate of Morehead State University, also became a school teacher. He first taught in a two-room school called Three Forks of Greasy. Paul's teaching career was also interrupted by WWII. He entered the U.S. Signal Corps and served in the European Theater of Operations. At war's end, he returned to Johnson County where he resumed his career as a grade school principal and teacher. In the summer of 1959, he and his family moved to Vero Beach, FL, where he and his wife, the former Emily Burke, resumed their teaching careers. After their retirement, they continued to live in that locale. They had one son named Paul Richard.

Harold Lloyd, a graduate of Morehead State with both a baccalaureate and master's degree, also became a teacher and administrator in Johnson County. He began his teaching career at the one-room Hurricane of Greasy School in 1948. During the next two years, he taught and served as head teacher in the grade schools at Thelma and Buffalo. In 1951, he was drafted into the Army and served in personnel work at Fort Knox during the Korean Conflict. He returned to the Buffalo School in the summer of 1953 where he taught and served as head teacher until the summer of 1959 when he was named principal of the 12-grade school at Meade Memorial. When the county high schools were consolidated in 1968, he was selected as a co-principal for the new Johnson Central High School. In the summer of 1975, he left the principal's position at the high school and moved to the central office to become the secondary supervisor of instruction. He maintained that position until he retired in 1989. Harold married Marthalene Phelps, his high school sweetheart, in 1951. Marthalene worked for South Central Bell as a telephone operator until the birth of their second child in 1959. The three children of this couple were Martha Sue, David Bruce and Cheryl Ann.

Betty Dean married Virgil Wallen, a salesman for the Big Sandy Hardware. The couple built a home on land owned by Betty's parents. Later, Betty and Virgil bought the family homeplace. Virgil died at his residence in 1983. Betty continued to live in their homeplace at Williamsport. The couple had one son who was named Warren Kevin.

Patty Ann graduated from Meade Memorial High School in 1951 and went to Cincinnati to live with her older brother and seek employment. Shortly after her arrival, she met Noel Schwartz who would later become her husband. After their marriage, Noel and Patty settled in Dayton, OH. Noel was employed at Wright Patterson Air Force Base as a civil service employee. Noel retired in 1989. The couple bought a second home in Barefoot Bay, FL, where they reside during the winter months. They had two sons named Robert Francis and Barry Preston.

Living in the Past

When Kentucky was established as a state in June 1792, the mountains of Eastern Kentucky were virtually wilderness, traveled only by lone hunters. Soon afterward, permanent settlers did begin to show up in the mountains. They came mostly from Virginia and North Carolina. The Virginians entered Kentucky through Pound Gap, while the North Carolinians came through Cumberland Gap.

As a child I heard talk of the hardships, faced by these first settler-cold weather, inadequate housing, short supplies, bears eating the pigs, wolves the sheep, hawks, foxes and eagles eating the chickens, and many other problems that can now only be imagined. Out of this struggle for survival came a way of life that persisted right up until the early years of the present century. At that time, inroads made by the coming of the trains and automobiles resulted in social upheavals, which caused the termination of the old-time agricultural economy, and the introduction of an industrial economy based on coal mining.

I grew up on Two-Mile Creek, at Williamsport, KY, in Johnson County. Until the age of 15 years, I lived in a log cabin with a shed kitchen. We then moved into a more modern home, built by my father and grandfather. This new home had tow stories and was weather boarded and painted.

At one time, my mother was postmistress of the Williamsport post office. Father and grandfather built the post office she used.

Two-Mile Creek was dammed up to provide waterpower for a gristmill owned and operated by Washington Ward, one of my uncles. Mr. Ward stoneground, Hickory King corn and buckwheat, into meal and flour for the people in the community. For a toll he dipped a "toll box" into the hopper each time it was filled to remove for himself a portion of the corn or wheat. The box was calibrated so that the volume of grain removed was exactly equal to the volume expansion of the grain caused by the grinding process. Thus anyone taking a one-bushel turn of corn to the mill would, after payment of toll, always take home one bushel of meal. The millers always claimed toll was "made by the Mill."

The people in the community utilized the millpond on Two-Mile Creek as a recreation facility. In the spring it was fishing hole. In the summertime it became a swimming hole, and in the winter it became an ice skating rink. The tow banks of the pond were used for growing watermelons, peanuts, and sorghum cane. It was here that we cut bamboo for fishing canes and for arrow shafts. Here grew the elderberry bushes, which furnished berries for our elderberry jelly and for the hollow pipe we used when making popguns and squirt guns with Barlow knives. Sections of the elderberry bush made a good pipe for collecting maple sap to make maple syrup.

The members of the Preston family were fortunate in being the owners of an almost untouched forest primeval called Rocky Cove. This proved to be of great value for the family. There they found the many types of wood needed for their construction projects and for handicrafts, such as basketry and chairmaking, where special woods with special properties are required. Much of the family food came from this forest, not only as game animals but also in the form of black and white walnuts, hickory nuts, chestnuts, "serviceberries," pawpaws, "possum grapes," summer grapes, huckleberries, mountain teaberries, wild cherries for jelly, maple sap for maple syrup, and bee trees for honey. After the tree was cut and honey collected, the bees were transported home; to be put into black gum hives.

Among the medicinal herbs the Preston family collected at Rocky Cove were Mayapple, ginseng, and yellow root. Needless to say Rocky Cove served as a recreation area for the family. For example, there was a large cave here where my Boy Scout Troop held their powwows at night with light provided by burning pine knots.

Under the firm tutelage of a legendary teacher, George Butcher, I graduated from the eighth grade at the John C.C. Mayo College at Paintsville in May 1925. One month later I took and passed the county examinations for schoolteachers. In July of that year, I began work as a schoolteacher of the one room school at the head of Greasy Creek. When school was out I continued my education at Morehead State Normal School (which later became in turn, Morehead State Teachers College. Morehead State College and finally, Morehead State University). I graduated from Caney Junior College in 1934.

At a recent alumni homecoming for students of Meade Memorial High School at Williamsport I was singled out for special honors-being the only survivor of the original Meade Memorial Faculty.

PRESTON - Ralph B. "Tiny" Preston was born Nov. 9, 1907, at Emma in Floyd County to Forrest B. and Alice Leslie Preston. He was the oldest of four children. He had one brother, Thomas J. Preston, a professional engineer and two sisters, Marguerite Preston Jones and Polly Preston Gorman, who were both former teachers in Johnson County. Polly later became appointment secretary to two governors, Bert Combs and Ned Breathitt. Tiny is the only one living. He has a half-brother, Joseph Jackson Preston, living in Seaman, OH. All five Prestons grew up in Johnson County and graduated from Paintsville High School. His father, Forrest, was active in the coal business, politics and had the first automobile agency with Fonnie Daniels and established the Big Sandy Dairy which Ralph took over and ran for 40 years. At one time it was the largest milk producer in Johnson County.

"Tiny" married Lillie May Witten Nov. 8, 1929. They had two daughters, Alice Eleanora and Patricia Ann. Alice married Norvin L. Bourne Jr. of Harrodsburg, KY. They reside in Ashland, KY. Alice graduated from Paintsville High School, Morehead University and the University of Kentucky. She taught in the Johnson County and Paintsville School System and retired from Russell Independent Schools. Her husband retired from Ashland Oil. Pat, also a UK graduate, taught in Johnson County and retired from the Paintsville School System after having taught 35 years.

Ralph's wife, Lillie May, was the daughter of Edgar Witten and Ida Litteral Witten. Edgar had a hardware and furniture store in the old Herald building and on the corner of Second and College where Williams Floral is now located.

Ralph Preston and Lillie Mae Witten Preston

"Tiny," as Ralph was called by many, spent eight years as a Paintsville city councilman and was mayor for 10 years. He is a veteran of WWII, a master Mason, a Shriner, a past president of the Rotary Club, a Kentucky Colonel and a past member of the Prestonsburg Community College Advisory Board. He is a member of The First United Methodist Church.

"Tiny" was mayor when President Lyndon Johnson visited in 1954. Honors he has received are many. Among them outstanding service to the people of Paintsville presented in 1984 by the Paintsville Sesui Contenival Charter Night Banquet. The Harmon Station Chapter of the DAR honored him on Jun. 14, 1989, for outstanding community pride and endeavor. He was *Citizen of the Year* in 1993 presented by Beta Sigma Phi Sorority. He was presented a key to the city of Paintsville and honored by the city with a reception at the Paintsville Country Club on Aug. 14, 1985, by then Mayor Robert Wiley.

"Tiny's" devotion to the city of Paintsville was most evident during the 1957 flood. As mayor, he spent many sleepless hours along with Jim Tom Newman and other volunteers at the Command Center directing help to those in need, while suffering major damage to his own home and dairy farm.

QUALLICH - Pamela and Patricia Volota, twin daughters of Geneva Wells and Steve Volota, were born Mar. 24, 1951; a stillborn girl named Diane Marie on Jul. 25, 1961 and a son John Steven Volota, born Mar. 20, 1963. Diane Marie Volota was buried in the family cemetery in Johnson County, KY at Daniel's Creek, Rt. 3 across from Ben and Anna Wells homestead.

Pamela Volota, born Mar. 24, 1951 in Cleveland, OH, is a Euclid Sr. High School 1969 graduate and Cleveland State University 1973 graduate. She received a bachelors of arts degree in social service and worked as a caseworker at the Cuyahoga County Welfare Department before becoming a clinical social worker at St. Lukes' Hospital in Cleveland. She is presently working at Parma Community General Hospital as a clinical social worker in Parma, OH. She is 5'3" tall, fair skinned, and has blue-gray eyes and blond hair. Pamela developed asthma after childbirth, which was most likely inherited from the Clark line of her family. She resides in Parma, OH.

Thomas John, Patrick Michael and Pamela Volota Haynish

She married Thomas John Haynish, a Catholic, on Nov. 30, 1985 at Lake Shore Christian Church, Euclid, OH. He was born Feb. 12, 1950, the son of Adolph Haynish and Dorothy Mravitz who reside in Parma. He is a St. Francis De Sales School Graduate and a Padua High School 1968 graduate. Tom went into the Navy and played in the Navy Band before graduating from Cleveland State University with a bachelor of arts degree in communications. Besides being musically talented with the piccolo and saxophone, he also has a beautiful tenor singing voice. Tom and Pam divorced in 1992.

Their son, Patrick Michael Haynish, born Mar. 7, 1988, is blond haired, brown eyed, and fair skinned. Patrick attends St. Charles Catholic School in Parma, OH, excelling in all his subjects, especially music and is presently learning to play the saxophone. He has exercised induced asthma.

Patti Volota, Heather Ann and Douglas Anthony Quallich

Patricia "Patti" Volota, born Mar. 24, 1951 in Cleveland, OH, is a Euclid Sr. High School 1969 graduate and Cleveland State University 1973 graduate with a bachelors of arts degree in fine arts. She got a part time job three months before graduation in the CSU Graphics Dept. and received the full-time job at graduation as an artist. After working there for eight years, Patricia went to Premier Industrial Corp, now known as Premier Farnell, LLC where she became a computer design artist producing catalogs, brochures, business cards, etc. Patricia is 5'1-3/4" tall, dark skinned, with light brown hair and hazel eyes. She has been involved with the Wells Family Association for several years and is presently a member of their historical committee.

Pat married Douglas Anthony Quallich, who was Tom Haynish's best friend from high school, on Sep. 24, 1988 at Lake Shore Christian Church, Euclid, OH and resides in Parma. Doug was born May 17, 1949, the son of Mildred Duchoslav and Leonard George Quallich Sr. and was educated at St. Francis De Sales School in Parma, OH and Padua High School (1968 graduate). He was dark skinned, brown eyed and 5'9" tall. A devout Catholic, he was a very intelligent, talkative, loving father and husband who touched many lives. Douglas had a sense of humor, and a talent for being a very good listener, analyzing people and situations. He didn't give advice but gave people all their options to help them decide for themselves how they would plan to solve their problems. Working in his father's pattern making shop as a teen, after high school he went into the trades to become a machinist, tool and die maker, and co-owner of a company called Independent Die & Mfg. Co. Inc. His father's family came from Metzenseifen, Austria-Hungary. Doug died Sep. 20 and is buried near the entrance of Sunset Memorial Park (Grave 6, Lot 164, Section 1-A), which is located at 6265 Columbia Rd., North Olmsted, OH. He passed away four days before his 10th wedding anniversary from a rare genetic disease called CPT II Defiency, a type of Mitachondrial Disease.

Doug and Patti met Easter April 1976 after attending the Easter Vigil Mass where Tom Haynish was singing in the Men's Choir at St. Francis De Sales Church. Their 10 years of friendship became a dating relationship March 1986.

After two years of marriage they had a baby girl named Heather Anne Quallich born Saturday Nov. 3, 1990 at Parma Community General Hospital, Parma, OH. Heather attends St. Francis De Sales School and Church in Parma, OH and excels in all her subjects especially art, math, science, and vocabulary. She is very bright, talkative and always ready to smile and makes friends easily. Heather has light brown hair, blue eyes, dark skinned, and has a slim build.

Heather Ann Quallich and Patrick Michael Haynish

John Steven Volota, born Mar. 20, 1963 in Euclid, OH, is a 1981 graduate of Euclid Senior High School. He received a bachelors of arts degree in geology and Spanish in 1986 from Cleveland State University and presently works at Sherwin Williams Company as a chemist. John has volunteered some of his time helping Habitat for Humanity build homes for the poor and has an interest in carpentry and home construction. He spent two summers in San Juan, Puerto Rico teaching English to Spanish students and during college he lived for several weeks with a family in Mexico. During junior high he was on the varsity track and wrestling teams and during college on the varsity fencing team. John is fair skinned, 5'9" tall, has blond hair, and hazel eyes. He is presently not married and is residing in Parma.

RATLIFF - Topsy Ratliff was born Apr. 28, 1900 in Johnson County. He was the son of Leander and Hattie Selvage Ratliff. He was married in 1920 to Leona Fairchild. She was the daughter of Millard and Ella Johnson Fairchild. They met at the Rockhouse Freewill Baptist Church. They lived on Rockhouse near Barnett Creek. In 1943 they sold their house and bought a big farm at Denver. Then in August 1948 Leaona became ill and passed away at a Paintsville Hospital. She was the first person to be buried in the Topsy Ratliff Cemetery at Denver. They had 11 children. Their son Charles was killed in a house fire at Denver in 1956.

Topsy and Leona Fairchild Ratliff

Add married Ruth Vanhoose. They were divorced. His second wife was Judy Salyers. He died in 1990.

Obie married Iva Joy Horne. Obie died in 1988.

Lee married Ella Mae Vanhoose. He died in 1984 and Ella Mae died in 1994.

Jay married Janice Thatcher. They are divorced. His second wife was Holli (last name unknown).

Ova "Bub" married Betty Swank they are divorced.

Gladys died when she was a child.

Dicie married Lifes Vanhoose. He died in 1997.

Dixie married Roy Blair. He died in 1993 and Dixie died in 1999.

Ella married Freddie Hitchcock. He died in 1975. Ella's second husband was Elmon Ratliff.

Hattie married Paul Thatcher. He died in 1982.

Topsy married again in 1949 to Ruby Vanhoose. She was the daughter of Earl and Ethel Taylor Vanhoose of Muddy Branch, KY. They had 10 children, including a baby named Andy that died as an infant.

Topsy Ray married Kathy Vanhoose, they are divorced.

Earl Thomas married Gail Franklin, they were divorced. He died in 1998.

Hollie married Judy Clark.

Lawrence married Kathy McKenzie. They were divorced. His second wife was Debbie Vanhoose.

Andy married Kay Smith.

Clark died at his Denver home in 1991.

Ollie married Artie Southern.

Martha married Danny Castle. They were divorced. Her second husband was Rosco Kidd.

Mary married Odie Davis. He died in 1985. Her second husband was Gary Pennington.

Ruby died in 1990.

Topsy was a coal miner and a farmer. He was proud of his farm and worked on it very hard.

On Sunday he walked to church. He stopped to talk to everyone he saw along the way. Old people say they loved to hear him shout in church. He was a good Christian man.

When he died on Aug. 12, 1970 at age 70, he was survived by 18 children and many grandchildren. He was buried beside his first wife, Leona, in the Topsy Ratliff Cemetery at Denver. *Submitted by Dicie Vanhoose.*

RICE - Cora Bell Rice (born Oct. 11, 1881) was the second daughter of Patrick G. Rice and Mary Jane Rice. Her grandparents were Harrison Rice and Sarah "Sally" Rowland and her great-grandparents were Martin R. Rice and Malinda Davis who resided on the head waters of Jeney's Creek, Johnson County, KY. Her maternal grandparents were Alexander Rice and Lucy Barnett who was the daughter of Elias Barnett and Nancy Blair who married about 1826. Elias was the first pioneer to carry the first overland letter to California. He at that time was assigned to drive an ox team from St. Louis, MO, with the Bidwell-John Bartleson Party to California. He was chosen to carry the first letter to Dr. Marsh or Gen. Sutton who were already there. This story is interesting to read. All of his kin should read this story.

Cora Bell Rice

My mother's maternal grandparents were Dr. Isaac Rice, who was a Civil War medical soldier who also has an interesting life history. He married Celia Connelley who was a granddaughter of Capt. Henry Connelley and Ann McGreggory. Capt. Henry was a Revolutionary soldier from Guilford, NC, who came to Eastern Kentucky sometime after the Revolutionary War. My mother's parents were both descendants of two separate Rice families in Johnson County, KY.

My mother, Cora, was unquestionably one of the greatest mothers that ever lived. She was a mother who was always there when one of her children stumped his or her toe or stumbled and fell bloodying its nose. She was there to soothe and wipe away all tears and hug it until the last whimper faded away. She taught discipline, to listen, to obey and not to back talk. She saw to it that not any of the children ever went hungry or cold. She with the help of the children raised a garden to have food to be prepared and conserved for wintery days. She sewed and made warm clothing for the children to attend school. She saw to it that the children studied their homework and were in bed early to be ready for the next day's activities. She defended them when they were right and disciplined them when they were wrong. With these objectives in mind each child knew his limitations. There never was over punishment. Occasionally one would get a spanking but not until that child had a chance to explain his reasons for being offensive.

Mother was a mother who believed a right was a right and a wrong was a wrong. She was a living example of what she taught. Her theory was instilled in every one of her children from infancy to adulthood. Those teachings remained in the lives of each of her children. If one child went astray, it always returned. She was a good wife and a loving and caring mother and was loved dearly by all of her children. This was exemplified on that day, Jul. 26, 1941, when the children stood by her bedside and heard her say "I love all of my children" and shortly thereafter, they (the children) watched the last round of blood moving through her veins to her heart and she smiled and breathed the last breath. God took her without any struggle or resistance. The children bid her good-bye. The nurses came and pulled the sheet over her face. Every saddened heart walked away. *Written by Ruth Salyer*

RICE & RIVERS - Alger Rice, son of George W. and Sarah Blair Rice, was born at Leander, Johnson County, KY on Jun. 13, 1897. He married Bertha M. Rivers, daughter of Winfield and Doshia Rice Rivers, of Middle Fork of Jennie's Creek, at Denver, KY, on Jun. 25, 1920. Bertha was born on Feb. 6, 1902. They lived on the homestead at Leander until 1964, when they moved to West Van Lear.

Alger and Bertha were truck farmers and occasionally he worked for road construction crews and at other public works. They sold plants, eggs, chickens and various other produce to the people in Paintsville. He was a deacon at Liberty Baptist Church and they attended when the door was open. Both taught Sunday School there for many years.

Alger died at his home in West Van Lear on Aug. 11, 1968. Bertha died Oct. 17, 1989, in a Nursing Home in Xenia, OH.

They had two sons: Harold Morton was born at Leander on Nov. 14, 1922. He graduated from Jennie's Creek High School at age 16 and attended two years at Morehead State Teachers College and taught in a one-room school in Johnson County for two years. He then went to Dayton, OH and worked as a draftsman for a brief time before he volunteered for the Air Force in World War II. He served on Tinian Island in the South Pacific and was there when the *Enola Gay* left there and dropped the first atom bomb on Japan.

After the war he finished his education (BS in 1949 and MA in 1955) at Western Kentucky State College in Bowling Green on the GI Bill. After graduation he came back to Johnson County and became drafting instructor at Mayo Vocational School (now Mayo Technical College). He later became principal of all the regional technical high school classes in a five-county area. He retired in 1982 with 36 years in education including his 3-1/2 service years in the Air Force.

A long-time victim of Alzheimer's disease, he died in the Veteran's Hospital at Lexington, KY on Jun. 6, 1996. He is buried at Highland Regional Memorial Park at Staffordsville.

He married June Baxter, of South Hill, Butler County, on Jun. 17, 1950. June, daughter of Ervin Estill and Lura Beliles Baxter, was born Aug. 13, 1925. Like her spouse, June was a 1949 graduate of Western. She taught in Butler County, Waterman, IL, and spent 32 years as Paintsville High School Librarian. Both Harold and June were active members of Liberty Baptist Church at Denver. He was deacon, Sunday school superintendent, church treasurer. June taught Sunday school, became church treasurer after her husband's death, and is active in association and state Baptist committees.

Bertha and Alger's second son, Arnold Lee, was born at their home on Jennie's Creek on Nov. 16, 1926. A graduate of Jennie's Creek High School, he served in the U.S. Army in France during World War II. He married Barbara Taylor (born to Bert and Brida Castle Taylor, Staffordsville, on Oct. 14, 1933) on Jun. 30, 1954.

Barbara and Arnold Lee live in Dayton. He

retired in 1989, having worked 42 years with Delco Division of General Motors. Barbara retired in 1989 from Wright-Patterson Air Force Base in Dayton.

Alger and Bertha's grandchildren are all college graduates. Harold's children are Catherine Mattingly (born Feb. 2, 1952 in Paintsville) a librarian at Barret Traditional Middle School in Louisville, married to Marvin, who is an electronics engineer with Johnson Controls, Patricia Ann (born Aug. 10, 1955 in Paintsville) an art teacher in Kings Middle School in Edmonds, WA, a suburb of Seattle, and Stephen Harold (born Mar. 13, 1965 in Paintsville) Clifton, VA, who is a band director at West Potomac High School in Alexandria, VA. He is married to Wendy Margaret Blanchard who is an account executive with PMI Mortgage Insurance Company in the Washington, DC area.

Arnold Lee's children are LaDonna Sue Lally (born Dayton, OH, July 27, 1955) a CPA who works for the Princeton (NJ) Hospital, married to Robert, a financial consultant, vice-president and treasurer of Aegis Insurance Service in New York City, and Debra Lee (born Dayton on July 26, 1959) who manages the Child Health Research Center, University of Texas Center in Galveston, TX. She is married to Stephen Pyron, who has his own automotive business in that area.

Great-grandchildren are: Jennifer Mattingly (born Louisville, KY, Nov. 29, 1976) who is currently a student at Savannah College of Art and Design in Savannah, GA. She has one son, Thomas Eric Guthrie, born on Feb. 15, 1999.

Justin Mattingly (born Louisville, Jul. 3, 1980) is a welder with Jeffersonville Boat Works in Jeffersonville, IN.

Andrew Michael Rice, Clifton, VA, who was born Mar. 15, 1997.

Shelby Marissa Rice, Clifton, born May 25, 1999.

Robert Lally, Princeton Junction, NJ, born Jun. 22, 1984.

Stephanie Lally, born Jun. 29, 1988.

Katharine Elizabeth Pyron, Houston, TX, born Dec. 13, 1990.

Alexandra Nicole Pyron, Houston, born Jan. 18, 1993.

Though Alger, Bertha and Harold are dead, the rest of the family, from Seattle, Houston, Princeton, Washington, DC, Louisville and Dayton, have continued to meet for a meal at June Rice's home in Paintsville sometime during the Christmas season each year.

RICE & SALYER - James Rice and his wife, Nancy Catherine Salyer, resided in Johnson County their entire lives. James was a farmer. They had a total of 13 children, 12 survived. The youngest, Addie Ethel (born 1890, died 1960) was my mother. James and Nancy lived good lives, never realizing that they were descended from prominent roots.

James and Nancy Catherine Salyer Rice

The Salyer family is being written of by another author. Nancy's mother was a Conley and that family traces back to the Connellys of Charlestown, SC. The Connellys were a merchant family with activity along the east coast. Henry was born in Pennsylvania where his parents were conducting family business. Henry Connelly was a hero of the revolution as the head of a militia unit of cavalry (South Carolina). Militia units were usually inferior to regular units, but Henry's unit was the exception. His unit fought with distinction in the southern campaign in several battles, including the Battle of Cowpens. He married Ann MacGregor in 1774. He is buried in Oil Springs, Johnson County.

James Rice's father was Martin M. Rice (born 1808, died 1879). Martin is believed to have been born in Floyd County, KY (Note: Johnson County was carved out of several counties, including Floyd). His father is unknown as he was born prior to his mother's marriage to John Fitzpatrick. Martin M. married Sallie Menix (born 1808/10, died ??), nee Stone. Sally married into the Menix family and is confused by some with a Sally Menix born of the Menix family.

Martin M.'s mother was Fanny Rice (born 1784/90, died 1872), the sister of Martin Rice (born 1782/88, died ??) and John Rice (born 1786, died ??). The three were the children of John Rice (born 1756\62, died 1786) and Patsie Fleming. The elder John reputedly had emigrated from Wales. Fanny and her brothers moved from the Roanoke, VA area after the reputed death of their father, John Rice (born 1756\62, died 1786), by Indians. They migrated down the Wilderness Trail and crossed the mountains at Cumberland Gap, arriving in Floyd County, KY.

Martin M. Rice's wife, Sally Stone, was the daughter of John Stone (born 1779/83, died 1859). He married Deliley Maynard (born 1781/2, died 1859). John and Deliley were born in Wilkes County, NC. John was the son of Cutberth Stone (born 1755/8, died 1844), and Deliley was the daughter of James Maynard (born 1750, died 1852). Both are Revolutionary War veterans. John and Deliley migrated with Cuthbert and family into Floyd County. The migration moved over an Indian trail along the state line west to the Wilderness Trail and they crossed the mountains at Pound Gap into Kentucky.

James Maynard's ancestry is controversial, but there is prevailing evidence that his father was Henry Maynard. There is solid evidence that Henry married Larrede Hammond of Anne Arundel County, MD. Larrede's ancestry is a wonder to behold. Her family traces to the Howard's of Anne Arundel County and then to the Douglas of Scotland and over 4,000 recorded ancestors in Europe including royalty.

Cuthbert Stone was born in 1755/8, likely in Maryland, but moved to central Virginia early in life. He is a direct descendant of Governor William Stone, the first colonial governor of Maryland. His uncle, Thomas Stone, signed the Declaration of Independence. He traveled to St. Marys County, MD, where he enlisted in the 7th Maryland Regiment (headquartered in Baltimore) of the Continental Army. He served in the Southern Campaign, and was severely wounded at the Battle of Cowpens (1780), near Spartansbug, SC. He was left on the battlefield for dead. There were no military hospitals at that time and the wounded recuperated in private homes or with the Quakers who were opposed to the fighting. He recuperated and briefly served as a militia courier.

He met Sally and was married by the younger Reverend Muelke, a circuit rider, in an open field near Spartansburg on Mar. 17, 1784. The field was the site, a few years later, for the Skull Shoals Baptist Church, which is in existence today. The field was owned by William Sisson (wife, Sarah Lowen) and they had as one of their children, Sarah (born 1766/9), who is surely Cuthbert's wife.

Cuthbert and Sally moved briefly to Montgomery County, VA (1789), but finally settled in Wilkes County, NC. They are reported in the 1790 census. They had eight children: John: (my ancestor), Enoch, Solomon, William, Margaret, Jean (or Jane) and Cuthbert.

John Stone, as stated above, married Deliley Maynard before leaving Wilkes County. After residing in Floyd County, they moved to Greenup County where they died of typhoid fever.

My mother, Addie, Ethel Rice Collins never dreamed that she had multiple ancestors who fought in the Revolution. Nor could she dream that the family lines through Larrede Hammond lead to the royal houses of Europe. *Submitted by Charles M. Collins.*

RICE - My grandfather James Albert "Squire" Rice worked saw mills in Johnson County, when oxen pulled the logs. He served a term as a magistrate in Johnson County, thus the nickname. My other grandfather, William Calhoun "Uncle Billy" Bowe, operated a farm at Wittensville. He once was a partner in Kennard (cq) & Bowe in Paintsville. He and Ben Combs operated Combs & Bowe, grocery and post office, at Wittensville. Uncle Billy sold produce from a Ford rumble seat in Paintsville. He became known as the "Cucumber King" of Johnson County. He owned stock in many early companies in Paintsville.

My father lied about his age and started working in the Van Lear mines at age 14. He also once operated for a brief spell a restaurant/pool room in Paintsville, where I was born Nov. 7, 1924. My mother lived with her parents at Wittensville, where her mother, Lou Witten Bowe had several relatives. Lou's brother Argales Witten married my father's sister, Minnie, and thus the connection came about.

Our family lived first in Music Hollow, then moved to Slate Row just across from the elementary school I attended. I earned letters in baseball, basketball and football at Van Lear High School. I hit a crazy hook shot from the right corner to defeat Oil Springs on the road; other than that, I don't remember any heroics.

After WWII broke out in December 1941, an Army recruiter came to the school seeking seniors to enroll in a Signal Corps school at Mayo State Vocational School in Paintsville. Several of us enlisted and were excused from further high school work, but allowed to return and graduate that year. I quit the Signal Corps and enlisted in the Marines in 1943, spending 2-1/2 years in the South Pacific and occupied Japan.

My father worked in the Van Lear mines until near the end of World War II, when he operated truck mines for his brother Jim at Garrett in Floyd County. Mom remained in Van Lear until after the war when she moved the family to Garrett. After a discharge from the Marines, I joined them there and worked for a while in my uncle's truck mines; meanwhile I enrolled in Kentucky Wesleyan College under the GI Bill of Rights, transferring the following year to the University of Kentucky. During summer breaks and Xmas holidays, I continued to work in the mines, doing everything from loading shooting, timbering, laying track and even driving the ponies.

After receiving my journalism degree in 1951, I worked as city editor of the *Mountain Eagle* at Whitesburg. I moved the following year to *The Hazard Herald*. The next stop came in 1953 when I became police court reporter and eventually an investigative reporter for *The Lexington Leader*. In 1962, the newspaper named me its sports editor. I joined the University of Kentucky as assistant sports information director five years later and became the department head in May 1969. I retired in 1989 as an assistant athletic director.

Published books include: *The Wildcats: A Story of Kentucky Football, Kentucky Basketball's Big Blue Machine, Joe B. Hall, My Own Kentucky Home, The Wildcat Legacy, and Adolph Rupp: Kentucky's Basketball Baron. Also contributed to A History of the Southeastern Conference, A Pictorial History of Kentucky* and *The Kentucky Encyclopedia.*

Attended national sports editor seminar at Columbia University. Kentucky area correspondent for *Time-Life-Fortune* magazines. Kentucky editor of *Religious News Service* and *Tobacco Magazine*.

Recipient of 1971 Churchmen's "Sportswriter of the Year" award. Manager of the 1978 NCAA Mid-East Regional Basketball Tournament.

Only person to serve two consecutive years as president of the Southeastern Conference Sports Information Directors Association. Chairman of the Basketball Hall of Fame Committee. Currently columnist for *The Cat's Pause* and editor of *The Orange Peal*, newsletter of the Port Orange (FL) Elks Lodge 2723. Earned "Best in the Nation" award for special publications (1983) Football Brochure Cover (1984).

Sister Leveda married Henry Wells, also a Van Lear High graduate, who lived on Daniels Creek. They now reside in South Point, Ohio.

Randy earned his bachelor degree at Kentucky Wesleyan College and did advance work at the University of Kentucky. He is a retired math teacher living in Philadelphia.

Jim earned an engineering degree at the University of Kentucky. He retired after traveling the world for General Electric.

Darrell starred in basketball at Pikeville College. He taught at Johnson Central before his death.

Bob has retired from International Harvester in Indiana. All five Rice brothers served in the armed forces.

RICE & BORDERS - Our family history, as we know it, goes back to John Borders, a Hession soldier during the Revolutionary War. He married Catherine Elizabeth Sellards, sister of Jenny Wiley. John died around 1815 at Wild Goose Shoal in Kentucky.

Their son Hezekiah, born in Virginia, moved to Kentucky in 1804. He was a farmer and tavern keeper at the mouth of Lost Creek at Borders Chapel. He and his wife Frances "Fanny" Davis (daughter of Joseph Davis Jr. and Margaret Hays), donated the Borders Chapel Methodist Church, built in 1825. Hezekiah died in 1857 and Fannie in 1845. They are buried in the Border's Chapel Cemetery.

Top Row, L-R: Guy W. Rice, Julia Ella (Borders) Rice, Mabel (Rice) White, M. Bert Rice, Front: Birdie (Flynn) Rice, Charles A. White, Lois L. White, Rose (Lais) Rice (ca. 1924/25)

They had eight children, including Joseph, born 1817 in Kentucky. He married in 1839 to Julia Ann Brown (born 1820), daughter of Frances Asbury Brown and Edith "Edy" Preston, and granddaughter of Thomas C. Brown and Nathan Preston. Their youngest child was Julia Ella, born 1861.

Julia Ella married Elliott Milton Rice, born 1855, son of Martin R. and Mary "Polly" Hannah. They were married at the home of Joseph Borders in Paintsville. Elliott was the senior partner in the E.M. Rice and Brother Mercantile. Elliott died at the age of 37, and is buried in Old Town Cemetery. Of their five children, Robbi and Donnalson died in infancy, leaving Guy Wycliffe, Milton Bert and Mabel.

Guy, born 1880, graduated from University of Kentucky in 1901 with an engineering degree. He was appointed by President Taft to inspect the building of the Panama Canal. In 1908 was awarded the contract as chief engineer for the construction of the Goose Valley Irrigation Project in Lake County, OR. He moved to Oregon, taking Julia Ella, Bert and Mabel with him. Upon completion of this project in 1918 he married Bridie Flynn from Ireland. They moved to California where Guy was engineer for several railroads. He later became manager of the Escrow Department at Security Pacific Bank in Los Angeles. He was the subject of article written by Dale Carnegie. He was a Mason, Elk and avid golfer. Bridie died in 1946 and Guy in 1954. Both are buried in the family cemetery in Ashland, Oregon, with Julia Ella who died in 1947.

Bert, born 1884, was a graduate of the University of Kentucky. He was an avid fisherman and wrote for *Field and Stream Magazine*. He died in 1956 and is buried in Ashland.

Mabel, born 1888, graduated with a degree in science from the Sandy Valley Seminary, in Paintsville. She became a teacher in New Pine Creek, OR. In 1918 she married Charles A. White, soloist with Chicago Opera Company. In 1913 he returned to Lakeview, OR as a watchmaker, jeweler and conductor. He continued singing, accompanied by Mabel, an accomplished pianist. In 1921, daughter Lois was born, and in 1925 the family moved to Ashland, OR where daughter Agnes was born. Charles purchased a jewelry store and was the "certified watch inspector" for the Southern Pacific Railroad. He continued his prowess as a cellist, vocalist and conductor. He was a Royal Arch Mason; both Charles and Mabel belonged to the Eastern Star. After Charles' death in 1936, Mabel managed the jewelry store until it sold in 1945. She died in 1967. Both are buried in Ashland.

RICE - Robert M. Rice, known as Bob, was born Aug. 7, 1929 in Johnson County at Sitka, KY to Louie Rice and Thelma Slone. Bob is the grandson of Charles and Sola May Rice. Charlie Rice was a merchant and farmer. He established the Freewill Baptist Church at Sitka. Sola May was a retired postmistress. At a very early age Bob's mother and father divorced. He and his sister Mary Edith stayed with their grandparents.

Bob's father was in the coal business. Louie served in the Army during WWII and fought in the Battle of Guadalcanal. Guadalcanal was referred to as a "hell hole." Louie's rank was technician 5 and his discharge states his duty was well done.

Robert and Betty Rice

Bob graduated from Meade Memorial High School, joined the Air Force and served overseas in Europe and South Pacific in WWII and Korean War. His rank was staff sergeant. After his discharge he went to the University of Kentucky. Later he attended Mayo State Vocational School, studying radio communications and electricity. Bob married his high school sweetheart, Betty M. Davis in 1950. Betty was born Aug. 8, 1929 at Meally.

Betty is the daughter of George W. Davis Sr. and Verlie Fitzpatrick. She is the granddaughter of James M. Davis, who was a blacksmith and pastor of the Church of Christ at Meally, KY. Betty's great-grandfather Bracken L. Davis was a lawyer and run a ferry boat on the Big Sandy River. Betty has two sisters, Beatrice M. and Christina; three brothers: Harold, Howard and George W. Jr.

Betty graduated from Paintsville High School in 1947. She attended the University of Kentucky and graduated from Mayo Vocational School of Business Administration and Cosmetology. Betty has owned her own beauty business for 32 years.

Betty and Bob lived in Columbus, OH about three years before moving to Florida. Bob worked as a technician at Cape Canaveral Missile Center. During a visit back to Paintsville, George Ramey (principal at Mayo School) asked Bob to set up and teach an electronic class. This caused the school to receive more funds from the state. The name was changed to Mayo State Vocational Technical School. Bob retired with 31 years teaching. He was known to be the best in the state.

Bob and Betty raised three children. All three graduated from Paintsville High School. Robert M. II attended University of Kentucky and Mayo School taking drafting. He works at Marrow Bone Development on heavy equipment. He is also a civil engineer. Bob II has two daughters, Melanie Lynn (deceased) and Alysha Dawn. He now lives at Lovely, KY.

George Keith attended Mayo School in electronics. He served 3-1/2 years as specialist E-5 in the Army. He was in Seoul, Korea and was on a baseball team. Keith lives in Nashville, TN, pursuing a music career.

Bettina Marie attended Transylvania College on a basketball scholarship and graduated from University of Kentucky. She lives outside of Dallas, TX in Plano. She is manager with Applied Materials. Bettina is married to Charles Ensor of Mt. Sterling. They have one son, Matthew Alexandera Rice Ensor.

Bob and Betty have taken active parts in the community. They live near the city park in Paintsville, KY.

RICE - Vicki Marcella Crace Rice was born on Jul. 7, 1952 in Johnson County, KY to Harry Wilson Crace and Veva Mae West Crace. She has one brother, John Phillip Crace, who was born Apr. 17, 1948.

Vicki attended Oil Springs School until Johnson Central High School was created in 1968. She graduated in 1970. She was very active in many school activities. After graduation from JCHS, she attended Mayo State Vocational School when she received her cosmetology license.

Vicki married Payne Rice Jr. on May 1, 1971. They have two children, namely Chad Wilson Rice (born Dec. 22, 1971) and Joni Michelle Rice (born Apr. 17, 1978). Chad is married to Stephanie Meade and they have one son, Bryce Parker Rice (born Feb. 28, 1999).

While Payne was attending Cumberland College, Vicki worked at Lyon Sewing Factory and then for Cumberland College. After returning to Oil Springs in 1975, Vicki worked at various secretary jobs. In 1979 she worked for the district judge and in 1987 Vicki was elected for the job of Johnson Circuit Court Clerk.

Vicki is a Christian and member of the Oil Springs United Methodist Church. She is on the board of directors of Paintsville Kiwanis, president of Lend-A-Hand Foundation, Inc., past-president of Oil Springs PTA, Oil Springs Youth League, Johnson County Republican Women, current vice-president of the Kentucky Circuit Clerk's Association. She has also been a member or chairperson of various committees in the clerk's association.

RICHMOND - Unoka Clark Richmond (born Oct. 21, 1878, died Feb. 15, 1970 in Johnson County, KY) was one of 11 children born to Samuel Clark and Susannah Wells Clark. She was a small woman of about 4'10" weighing about 120 pounds with a fair complexion. She married Oct. 31, 1894 to Samuel Buchanan Richmond (born Oct. 9, 1870, died Sep. 15, 1907 in Johnson County, KY). They were farmers and at Samuel's death, Unoka's life was hard for she was left with three children and pregnant with another (which she lost plowing). They had the following children: Fanny Richmond Wells (born 1895, died 1970); Susannah Richmond Wells (born 1897, died 1982); Willie Bill Richmond (born 1899, died 1971).

Unoka (Nokre) Clark Richmond

After the death of her husband, Unoka Clark never married again but farmed, raised livestock and fresh vegetables of which she transported by horse back to the mining towns to sell so she could buy her stables for the family. She and the children raised everything else to eat and she sewed their clothes.

She was a very unique little woman in that no matter how many of her grandchildren came to visit her, she always showed an interest in them asking how they were doing in school and making them feel important. Unoka's three children gave her 22 grandchildren and 33 great-grandchildren and scores of great-great-grandchildren. Unoka lived to the ripe old age of 92 and was loved and respected by all of her children, grandchildren and great-grandchildren.

Unoka loved the land and was her happiest when she was at work on her little farm. She was very independent with strong values and did not waver from her beliefs throughout her life. She made her own medicine by gathering wild herbs but did see a doctor in later years. She never was in the hospital as a patient until the night before her death where she was taken with the flu. She made the statement "they are killing me now" when they removed her flannel gown and put a hospital gown on her. It was evident that the shock of it all brought on a heart attack and she died the next morning at age 92. Unoka is buried in the late Ben Wells family cemetery, Rt. 3, Van Lear, KY. Her husband Samuel Richmond is buried on the Richmond Cemetery at Johns Creek.

RICHMOND - William Richard Richmond was born Aug. 9, 1878 at East point, KY. He was the son of John W. Richmond (born May 16, 1839, Edinburgh, Scotland, died Sep. 20, 1879, East Point, KY) and Susan Angeline Auxier (born Mar. 22, 1849, East Point, KY, died Aug. 3, 1890). Susan and John were married May 16, 1864. They are both buried in the Richmond Cemetery at Van Lear, KY.

William R. Richmond, John W. Richmond, Alice Joseph Richmond, Myrtle Richmond, Howard E. Richmond, James G. Richmond and W. Orville Richmond

William's mother, Susan Angeline, was the daughter of Samuel Auxier II (born Aug. 7, 1791, Russell County, VA) and Agnes Wells (born Dec. 7, 1820, Russell County, VA). Agnes was the second wife of Samuel (married May 2, 1838 in Floyd County). They lived at Block House Bottom in Johnson County, where Samuel died Dec. 13, 1883. Agnes was the daughter of Susannah Hutcheson and Richard Wells. Agnes died in 1908. Samuel Auxier II was the son of Sarah "Sallie" Brown and Samuel Auxier I.

William's father, John W. Richmond, was the son of James Richmond (born Dec. 20, 1816, Stevenston, Scotland, died Sep. 8, 1861, Block House Bottom, Johnson County) and Margaret Buchanan (born Oct. 19, 1818, Eaglesham, Scotland, died prior to 1851 in Renfrew Province, Scotland). Margaret and James were married in Scotland Jun. 8, 1838. Margaret was the daughter of Helen McCullock and James Buchanan, both of Scotland. James Richmond was the son of Isabella Fraser and John Richmond of Scotland.

Dec. 4, 1904 William married Alice Joseph, daughter of Woodson Joseph and Arminta Baldridge Joseph. William was a school teacher, surveyor and farmer. He surveyed many of the streets in Paintsville. William bought a farm one mile east of Paintsville and resided there until his death July 26, 1945. Alice died Jan. 1, 1971.

The children and descendants of Alice Joseph and William R. Richmond are as follows:

William Orville, married Julia Hatcher, children: Rebecca, William and David.

Howard Estill, married first, Elaine Smallwood, child: Esther Jean, married Douglas M. Titlow and their children are William and Michael). Howard married second, Reathel Daniels.

James Gordon, married Edith Blanton, child: Alice Jane married Jim Marien.

John Woodson, married first, Monnie Blanton and second, Mildred Price, children: Paul Richard and Charlotte. Charlotte lived only a few days. Paul R. married Wilma Bush and their children are Amber and Melissa. He married third, Mary Pack James and has stepson Calvin James. Calvin married Margie Alexander and has children Samantha and Andrea.

Myrtle married first, Phillip Jenkins and second, Ray Holbrook. No children from either marriage.

RIGSBY - Ruth Castle was born in Johnson County on Oct. 16, 1925 to Eula Daniel Castle and Russell Castle. Eula was born in Johnson County on Feb. 25, 1908 and Russell was born in Johnson County on Apr. 20, 1907. Russell during his lifetime worked as a coal miner and as a blacksmith. They were married in 1924.

Ruth had four sisters: Ruby, Rusha, Roberta and Janet Sue, and four brothers: Richard, Ray, Ralph and Robert. She has resided in Johnson County all her life.

She married W.L. Rigsby on Dec. 25, 1944 and had three children: Leneda, William Franklin and James Michael. She joined the United Baptist Church on Feb. 25, 1951 and was an active member of the United Baptist Church Women's Auxiliary and the Eastern Star.

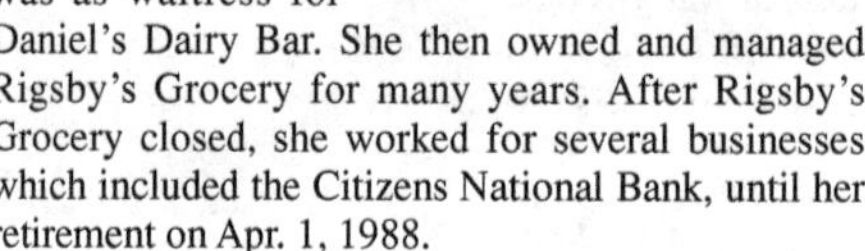

W.L. and Ruth Castle Rigsby

She attended a one-room school for grades 1-8 at Mingo. She graduated from Meade Memorial High School on May 22, 1945.

Her first job was as waitress for Daniel's Dairy Bar. She then owned and managed Rigsby's Grocery for many years. After Rigsby's Grocery closed, she worked for several businesses which included the Citizens National Bank, until her retirement on Apr. 1, 1988.

She and her husband currently reside in Paintsville.

RIGSBY - William LeFrance "W.L." Rigsby was born in Paintsville, Johnson County on Jul. 6, 1926 to Gladys Colvin Rigsby and Foster Franklin Rigsby. His mother was born in Johnson County on Apr. 18, 1910, and his father was born in Magoffin County on Apr. 25, 1897. F.F. moved to Johnson County around 1924, where he went into the grocery business at Hencliff. It was there he met Gladys and they were married Apr. 24, 1925.

W.L. had one sister, Juanita Rigsby Kerr, who was born Dec. 7, 1931. He grew up in Johnson County and lived there until 1940, when his family moved to Greenup, KY, where they owned a grocery store. The family moved back to Johnson County in 1942.

He served during WWII from June 1945 until October 1946 and was stationed in Germany during his active duty time which included guarding prisoners at the Nuremberg War Crimes Trials. On Dec. 25, 1944, he married Ruth Castle Rigsby. They were married in Paintsville by Lonza Reed and had three children: Leneda (b. Nov. 7, 1945); William Franklin (b. Apr. 23, 1949); and James Michael (b. Aug. 23, 1954).

He joined the United Baptist Church in 1957, and was ordained a minister in 1972. He has been an active member of KYCH and Eastern Star.

He attended the Paintsville City Schools, except for one year when he lived in Greenup. That year in Greenup was very memorable because Jesse Stuart was his principal and it was also the year Pearl Harbor was bombed. He also attended both the University of Kentucky and Morehead State College, but did not graduate.

The first job he ever held was working for his dad in the grocery business and at the same time he was an usher for the Royal Theater. Other jobs he held included fire chief for Paintsville, salesman for Sealtest, worker for Meadowgold Dairy, worker for Maggard and Joseph Furniture, and owner/operator for Rigsby Grocery. He retired in 1985 from the Carl Perkins Rehabilitation Center where he had taught appliance repair. After his retirement he worked as a self-employed appliance repairman until 1990.

He and his wife currently live in Paintsville.

RIGGSBY & MCKENZIE - Watha Malcom Riggsby (born Nov. 19, 1905, Johnson County, KY, died Oct. 10, 1969) married Ethel May McKenzie on Apr. 19, 1926 in Johnson County, KY. She was born Aug. 19, 1911 in Johnson County, KY, daughter of John McKenzie and Julie Ann Dials of Johnson County, KY.

Children: Elwanda (born Nov. 18, 1932 in Johnson County, KY) married Jun. 1, 1949 in Johnson County, KY to Chester V. Sparks (born May 29, 1929) son of Hannah Ferguson and Mart Sparks of Lawrence County, KY. Elwanda married second to Ellis Lowe. Children: Watha (born Dec. 13, 1949 in Johnson County, KY) married Letha Adkins Oct. 9, 1970. Chestina (born Mar. 3, 1952 in Johnson County, KY, married Raymond Stoops Sep. 27, 1968. Danny (born July 31, 1953 in Cols, OH). Christopher (born Oct. 31, 1954 in Marysville, OH) married Phyllis Hitchcock Nov. 4, 1972. Lisha (born July 28, 1960 in Johnson County, KY) married Alfonzo McCoy Jerry Dowell and Richard Hendershott.

Willa Faye (born Sep. 28, 1927 in Johnson County, KY, died May 3, 1952) married Lowell Fyffe Apr. 16, 1952 in Johnson County.

Wathalene and Pamela.

Watha Riggsby was born in Johnson County, KY and lived his whole life there. Working as an oil driller nearly all his adulthood was how he raised his family. He was a great father and husband that minded his own business and expected others to do the same. Peoples first impression of him was that he was a mean man because of the expression he always had on his face but in fact he was a very respected and well like man. He promoted his education by reading a lot, his favorite was westerns. Watha was the son of Thomas Riggsby and Sarah Melissa "Sal" Rose.

Thomas (born 1878 in Lawrence County, KY, died March 1960 in Johnson County) married "Sal" Rose on Aug. 27, 1904 in Johnson County. Sal (born Nov. 28, 1877 in Johnson County, died March 1947 in Johnson County) was the daughter of Thomas C. "Bud" Rose and Mary Gambill.

Children: Watha Malcom Riggsby and Mary Rebecca "Molly" (born Jan. 17, 1909, died 1964) married Henry French.

Thomas Riggsby was the son of John "Boots" Riggsby and Rebecca Elizabeth Eldridge (born 1840 in Elliott County KY). John "Boots" (born 1849 in Lawrence County, KY, died 1909).

Children: Thomas (born 1878) md. Sarah Melissa Rose; Jess (born 1888, died 1972) md. Emma Baker; Henry (born 1882) md. Laura Boggs; Crede (born 1886) md. Lonzo Riggsby; Rose (born 1875) md. George Kelly; Susie (born 1884) md. Merdie Kelly; Amanda (born 1889) md. Faris Sagraves; Mary (born 1870) md. Plesent Collier; Sena (born 1879) md. Tom Skaggs; Rhoda (born 1879).

ROBERTS - Grandparents of Reecia, Douglas, Nancy, Daniel and 17 other grandchildren were Verner "Vern" K. Roberts, one of seven children (born Feb. 6, 1885, died July 31, 1970) and Nevada "Vada" Spradlin

Roberts (born May 3, 1885, died Jan. 2, 1968) lived in Paintsville most of their lives. Vern was a carpenter, painter and paper hanger. They made their home in the upper part of town on a farm. Later, they moved their family to "Stafford Bottom," as we called it, which in time became avenues and streets.

Vern and Vada Roberts, grandparents

Vern and Vada had a large corn field and they raised hogs, which they slaughtered themselves. Vada made her own lye soap in a large black kettle over an open fire. At one time Vada Laundered uniforms for the "3 C Camp for .25 cents each. Occasionally, Vada or "Ma" would take the grandchildren with her to pick "greens" in the bottom field. Old man bacon-collard, dandelion are a few.

We remember the apple trees in the front yard which grew the sweetest Grimes Golden Delicious apples. The children were never allowed to pick an apple off the tree. If one should get brave enough and start to pull an apple, a voice would come from above "no." We thought it was "Jesus;" it was Ma, standing on the front porch above us, with a little smile on her face. The apples meant food on the table in the winter time, apple butter and applesauce.

All the grandchildren and a few of the great-grandchildren remember "Pa," as we called him, whittling, as he sat in a rocking chair that he built. There would be shavings all around Pa's chair. Once Pa whittled a wheelbarrow and a wagon, the size of his hand. They were perfect.

In the late 30s and early 40s, Vern and Vada opened a general store on their property but had to close due to World War II.

Vern and Vada had 12 children, one is still living. Parents of Vern were Daniel C. Roberts (born 1863) and Carrie Melvin (born 1868). Vada's parents were Dan Spradlin and Sarah Blair Spradlin. Love to our grandparents from your grandchildren.

ROSE - The first of the Rose clan to settle on Keaton, Johnson County was Thomas Rose (born 1814-20 in Lawrence County) and Rhoda Fyffe (born 1814-15). Thomas was the son of William Rose (born 1775 in Wilks County, NC) and Agnes Burchett (born 1834 in Wilks County, NC). Thomas married Rhoda Fyffe, daughter of John Fyffe Sr. and Francis Burchett. William Rose was son of John Rose and Rachel Sparks. John Rose was son of John Rose Sr. Rachel Sparks was daughter of William Sparks, both were born in or about Wilks County, NC.

Note: Agnes Burchett and Francis Burchett were sisters. Francis Burchett married John Fyffe Sr. The sisters made Thomas Rose and Rhoda Fyffe first cousins. Their issues together were the dominant settlers of Keaton.

William Rose and Agnes Burchett family:

1. Thomas Rose md. Rhoda Fyffe.

2. Hosea Rose.

3. William "Buck" Rose, born ca. 1815/16 in Surry County, NC, was killed during Civil War.

4. Nancy Rose md. Dury Rigsby, a farmer.

5. Sallie Rose.

Thomas Rose and Rhoda Fyffe family:

Elizabeth Rose (born 1836, died 1899) md. Henry Thomas McKinzie.

John Rose md. Perlina Fyffe (born 1840/41).

William Rose.

Sallie Rose md. Steve McKinzie.

Nancy Ibbie md. Benjaman Diles.

Thomas Chilton "Bud" Rose (born Mar. 13, 1850, died Jun. 13, 1919) md. Mary Mandy Gambill (died Apr. 30, 1931), daughter of John Gambill and Rena Boggs.

Anna Rose md. Jessie Bryant.

Benjamin Rose md. Sarah Mullins.

Thomas Chilton "Bud" Rose and Manda Gambill family:

1. Rena Rhoda Francis Rose (born Feb. 12, 1875, died 1941) md. Manford Lyons on Nov. 23, 1899. Children: Vernie/Nora, Clifford, Ruie, Esta, Noah and Thomas. They raised Everett Lyons. Tommy killed Esta accidentally.

2. Jeanettie (born Mar. 12 1876, died Apr. 6, 1906) md. George Nelson Evans. Their children are as follows:

a) Proctor James Evans (born 1897, died 1965) md. Neva Meade daughter of Dr. Paris Meade of Flat Gap, KY. Proctor was a dentist in Blaine until 1923; in Lynch, KY until 1944; and in Ashland, KY until his death in 1965. Their children were Paul Wathin, dentist, and Evaline Georgene, MD doctor, Ashland and Lexington, KY.

b) Neva Evans md. Harrison Osborn. Their children were Wendell (born 1923) who served in WWII and Jeanine Osborn (born 1933).

c) Erie Malinda Evans 1901 md. Jerry Thomas Bailey. She was a housewife and J.T. a preacher and farmer. Their children were Jewell Evlyn md. Raleigh Lemaster; Lowell Andrew; Edna Hildrith; Sally Wiladene md. Foster C. Skaggs; James Holman; Thomas Lurray; Jannette Lorell.

3. Sarah Melissa Rose (born Nov. 23, 1877, died Mar. 24, 1947) md. in August 1904 to Thomas Rigsby, son of Dury Rigsby and Nancy Rose. Their children were Waltha Malcom and Mary "Molly" Rigsby.

4. Mary A. Mollie "Moll" Rose (born Aug. 20, 1879, died Oct. 13, 1964) md. Mar. 9, 1899 to Charlie Lyons. He was a Baptist preacher and they lived in Ashland, KY with their children: Bessie, Ethel, Bonnie and Hazel.

5. Ollie May Rose (born Apr. 1, 1881) md. Oscar Winson Mullins. Their children were Sadie Letha, Okie Reginal, Clive Winson (never married) and Murl Justin.

6. Elva (born Feb. 28, 1885, died May 11, 1962) md. Leo James Skaggs on Dec. 11, 1911. Their children were James Purcy, Paul Thomas and Edger Allen Poe Skaggs.

7. Leona Elizabeth (born Mar. 8, 1886, died Aug. 11, 1966) md. William H. Mullins. Their children were Ralph William (born 1905 in Ohio) md. Esta Ferguson; Jessie Ollen (born 1907) md. Glenda Hill; Mortimer Proctor (born 1909) md. Beulah Nickells; Charlie John (born 1911) md. Area Capps; Basil Thomas (born 1913) md. Finetta Hamilton; Polly Margaret (born 1915) md. Henry Clay Huff; Maude Belle (born 1918) md. Estill Russell Hay; Pearl Fritz (born 1919) md. Myrtle Ferguson; Harold Winston (born 1923) md. Louise Melton; Bobby Elwood (born 1927) md. Maggie Hill; Note: Sarah Elda (born 1921, died at birth) and Boyd Worth (born 1930 died on an old tank in 1937).

8. Jessie Merida Rose (born May 2, 1888, died Jan. 27, 1961) md. Ida Ferguson on Feb. 16, 1910. They had one child, Shirley.

9. John Thomas Reginel (born Aug. 11, 1892) md. Martha Susan Skaggs on Feb. 22, 1912. Their children were Ishmal, Garna and Thomas.

10. Maude Bell (born Aug. 12, 1899, died Jan. 27, 1942) md. William H. Terry (born Mar. 25, 1908) and had Mandy (died young); md. second Noah Fyffe and had Noah Elmo. Noah was killed in 1932. John Fyffe was his brother.

11. Lusette Rose (born 1891) md. Noah Skaggs. Their children were Ivan, Hurchel, Polly Amber, Glayds, Hurston and Leo.

12. Esta Evaline (born Jan. 3, 1895, died 1997) md. John Thompson. Their children were Darrell, Urslie, Opal and Polly Sena.

13. Charlie Chilton (born Jan. 24, 1897) md. Mae Tencher. Their children were Maureen Evelyn, Mary Martha and Elizabeth Ann. Fred Harold was born first and is the last of this Rose clan.

All the above were born and raised on Keaton. C.C. was the youngest and was a farmer, pipefitter, merchant and the geneolgist who researched this information. H.W. Mullins was his nephew.

ROSS - On Jun. 5, 1949 Charles and Dorothy "Moore" Ross began their lives together. Refford Trimble, then Johnson County Judge, united the young couple after a 10 mile walk and a continued bus ride from Flat Gap into Paintsville that summer more than 50 years ago.

Charles was the eldest son born to Glen and Bertha Dixon Ross of Johnson County, on Jun. 5, 1931. He was the second of 10 children. Dorothy was born Apr. 9, 1925, the daughter of James and Melissia "Rigsby" Moore.

For the first 9-1/2 years, the couple lived in both Plain City and Columbus, OH and then later returned to their home state of Kentucky. Charles and Dorothy became the proud parents of five children: Nieda, Naomi, Joe, Viola and Velma. All five of whom attended Flat Gap Elementary, as well, Nieda graduated from Flat Gap High, with each of the remaining four attending and graduating from Johnson Central High School. Dorothy stressed the importance of school, encouraging her children to further their education, since the opportunity wasn't as openly available to Charles and herself. Among the five children nearly 50 cumulative years of perfect attendance was achieved.

Charles and Dorothy Ross

Dorothy took on the job as mother and housewife, while Charles farmed and worked in produce. Their success came from endless days of hard work and a supportive, loving Christian family. Charles and Dorothy continue to be active in the church community. Alongside being encouraging parents they are both loving grandparents and great-grandparents.

ROSS - David Ross Jr., a farmer, and the son of David Ross Sr. and Margaret Vanbibber. He was born Feb. 26, 1824 Lawrence County, KY. He married Mar. 4, 1853 to Martha Jayne of Flat Gap, KY. She was the daughter of Henry Jayne and Sarah Sparks. Martha was born 1834 and died Jan. 5, 1897. David died Mar. 26, 1893. Their burial place is Jayne Cemetery Flat Gap, KY, Johnson County.

David and Martha had 14 children: Mary Jane (born 1854) md. Joseph W. Williams of Johnson County; Daniel (born Mar. 12, 1855) md. Ellen Fannin; Sarah Ellen (born Apr. 13, 1856) md. Clark Fairchild; Elizabeth (born Jan. 26, 1858) md. Thomas Bailey; James H. (born 1860); Joseph born Mar. 3, 1861; William Marion (born Dec. 9, 1862) md. Rhoda McKenzie Mar. 18, 1893. William died Jul. 5, 1937; Jefferson D. (born 1864); David M. (born 1866) md. Elizabeth Fairchild; Elephus (born 1869) md. Cova Gremsley Apr. 2, 1908; Plyman (born 1872) md. William Shaners; Stephen (born Nov. 4, 1874) md. Mary Jane Kazee Sep. 29, 1898; Alminta (born 1876) md. Harrey Sagraves.

ROSS - David Ross Sr. (born ca. 1760 in North Carolina) md. Margaret Vanbibber ca. 1810 in Clai County, TN. David and Margaret were among the first settlers of Flap Gap, KY (1818). They lived on Little

David Ross Jr. Sons (L-R): Steve, Elife, Dave, Jeff, William and Joe

Laurel, a place known as Drake. Margaret was born ca. 1792 in Lee County, VA. She died after 1860 in Johnson County, KY. David died ca. 1861 in Johnson County, KY.

They had nine children: Susannah Ross (born Mar. 31, 1810) md. Mar. 31, 1836 to Thomas Williams; Dorcus Ross (born ca. 1817) md. Dec. 21, 1837 to Nicholas Sparks; James A. Ross (born Oct. 10, 1819) md. Sarah Lyon Feb. 24, 1842; Robert R. Ross (born ca. 1820) md. Feb. 18, 1847 to Alsy Osborn; David Ross Jr. (born Mar. 4, 1824) md. Mar. 4, 1853 to Martha Jayne; Mary Ross (born 1827) md. Oct. 1, 1853 to Daniel Jayne; Joseph Ross (born Aug. 14, 1828) md. Mar. 25, 1855 to Verlina Dobyns; Catherine Ross (born May 29, 1829) md. Allen Stapleton; Stephen Ross (born Sep. 6, 1830) md. Apr. 26, 1864 to Angeline Williams. *Submitted by James David Ross.*

ROSS - David William Ross was born Oct. 20, 1971 to James David and Rosa Faye Carter Ross in Franklin County, OH. David was married in Columbus, OH to Jennifer Louise Root on Jul. 3, 1993.

David William Ross, Jennifer Louise Root, Tyler Scott, Conner James, Jarred Blaine

Jennifer's parents are Ernie and Carrie Root. Jennie was born May 14, 1970 in Ohio. David and Jennie are the parents of three boys: Tyler Scott (born Jun. 7, 1992); Conner James (born Aug. 6, 1994); Jarred Blaine (born Sep. 16, 1996), all in Columbus, OH.

David likes Nascar racing and wood crafting. Jeenny likes cake decorating. *Submitted by Rosa Faye Ross.*

ROSS - Deborah Faye Ross was born May 3, 1963 in Franklin County, OH to James David and Rosa Faye Carter Ross. Deborah was married at Franklin County, OH to Daniel James Maynard on Sep. 11, 1982.

David, Dava, Debbie and Danielle Maynard

Daniel is the son of Jack Stover and Opal Maynard. Dan was born Apr. 28, 1961. Dan and Debbie are the parents of two daughters: Danielle Nicole (born Feb. 3, 1984) and Dava Ashley (born Jan. 11, 1986). Debbie works for Martin Marietta and her hobbies are taking care of her Quarter horses and gardening.

Dan works for Nationwide Ins. Co. His hobbies are riding his Harley motorcycle and showing his Quarter horse named Cotton. *Submitted by Rosa Faye Ross.*

ROSS - Edgar Ross (born Mar. 4, 1918, Skaggs, KY, died Aug. 29, 1980) married May 5, 1939 to Erma Nancy Holbrook at Mazie, KY. He is buried in Sunset Cemetery, Alton, OH.

Erma Nancy (born Jan. 22, 1915, Offit, KY, died Sep. 14 1995), daughter of Albert Holbrook and Rebecca E. Sparks.

Edgar Ross Family (Back): Susan, Velma, Stacey, Deanna, Dan, Marilyn, Paul, Carol, Ray. (Middle): Faye, David, Erma, Joe, Jimmy. (Front): Zac, Paula, Debbie, Danielle, Chris, Michael and Johnny

Edgar's occupation was a welder and Erma was a housewife. They lived in Lawrence County, Maize, KY until 1957, then moved to Columbus, OH. They raised four boys: James David (born May 27, 1940); Edgar Paul (born May 5, 1944, died Mar. 4, 1988); Ernest Ray (born Mar. 9, 1949); Larry Joe (born Jan. 14, 1957). *Submitted by James David Ross.*

ROSS - Ernest Ross was born Sep. 3, 1911, died Oct. 21, 1946. He was the son of Jesse David Ross and Nola Francis Hay Ross. He was married to Taxi Bailey born Apr. 3, 1910. She lives in Paintsville, KY. Their children are Mavis Ernestine (born Jun. 27, 1932), married Sep. 4, 1954 to William Joseph (born Aug. 13, 1937), Buford (born Mar. 8, 1940), Mary Francis (born Jan. 8, 1947) married Nov. 14, 1964. *Submitted by James David Ross.*

ROSS - James David Ross was born May 27, 1940 in Lawrence County, KY to Edgar Ross and Erma Nancy Holbrook Ross. James was married at Liberty, IN to Rosa Faye Carter on Nov. 14, 1957. Rosa is the daughter of George Jay Carter and Elsie Smith Carter. Rosa was born Jun. 9, 1941.

James David and Rosa Faye Ross

They are the parents of four children: James Lee (born Nov. 10, 1959); Susan Renee (born Dec. 18, 1961); Deborah Faye (born May 3, 1963); and David William (born Oct. 20, 1971), all in Franklin County, OH.

James works at Midwest Distribution Warehouse. He likes gardening, Nascar racing, Kentucky UK basketball and his six grandchildren. He resides in the Columbus, OH area. His father was born in Johnson County, KY and his mother was born in Offitt, KY.

His wife is a Honda of America associate. She likes genealogy and enjoying her grandchildren. *Submitted by Rosa Faye Ross.*

ROSS - James Lee Ross was born Nov. 10, 1959 in Franklin County, OH to James David and Rosa Faye Ross. James was married in Myrtle Beach, SC to Carol Perritt on Jun. 8, 1984. Carol's parents are Linton and Emily Miller. Carol was born Nov. 24, 1959.

James was in the Air Force, stationed at Myrtle Beach, where he met Carol. They have one son, Christopher David Ross (born Apr. 29, 1982). They reside in Columbus, OH. His interest's are Nascar racing. He is currently in the process of building a race car. He works at Ralston Industries in Columbus and Carol works for Aetna Insurance Co. *Submitted by Rosa Faye Ross.*

James Lee and Carol Perritt Ross with their son, Christopher David

ROSS - Jesse David Ross was born Dec. 19, 1893 Skaggs, KY, died Jun. 30, 1956. His burial place is Princebranch, KY. He married Aug. 20, 1910 to Nola Frances Hay daughter of William Asa Hay and Sally Fannin. Nola was born Mar. 31, 1893, died Aug. 9, 1977 and is buried in Sandy Hook, KY.

Edgar, Louella, Wilmer and Jessie

They had six children: Ernest (born Sep. 3, 1911, died Oct. 22, 1946, married Taxie Bailey; Idis (born May 30, 1914, died Nov. 23, 1923; Edgar (born Mar. 4, 1918, died Aug. 29, 1980) married Erma Nancy Holbrook May 5, 1939; Louella (born Jul. 11, 1924, died Jun. 9, 1982) married William "Bill" Markley; Wilmer (born Jul. 31, 1930, died Feb. 13, 1986) married Phyllis Blair; Jesse David Jr. (born Aug. 3, 1933) married Oct. 6, 1956 to Nelley Peters. Jesse was a blacksmith and had a shop in one of the side buildings. *By James David Ross.*

ROSS - Joseph Ross was born Aug. 14, 1828 at Flat Gap, KY to David and Margaret VanBibber Ross. He was the eighth of 10 children. Joseph married Verlina Dobyns Mar. 27, 1855 in Johnson County. Verlina (born Feb. 26, 1836) was the daughter of William and Elizabeth Minix Dobyns of Virginia. By the time of his marriage to Verlina, Joe with his younger brother Stephen, had procured 360 acres of land on the east side of Lower Laurel Cr. below Flat Gap. The lower half became Joe and Verlina's home and farm. Stephen made his home on the upper half.

Joe and Verlina were the parents of nine children: Francis E. (born Dec. 5, 1855, died Feb. 9, 1928) married Henry Daniel; Mary Virginia (born Mar. 3, 1858, died 1938) married Samuel B. Williams; William Harrison (born Aug. 30, 1861); Nancy Jane (born Aug. 11, 1863, died Jan. 9, 1877); Margaret Elmira (born Dec. 16, 1866, died May 13, 1932) married Daniel B. Williams: George W. (born Mar. 10, 1870, died Mar. 10, 1870); Robert M. (born May 8, 1872, died Aug. 8,1945) married first, Surilda A. Evans and second, Mattie Snodgrass; Marion Steward (born May 4, 1876, died Sep. 21, 1952) married first, Margaret Lemaster and second, Della Wheeler; Flora Etta Helen (born Apr. 26, 1879, died Jul. 26, 1970) married William Hayes Sparks.

Joe died Jan. 14, 1914 and Verlina Sep. 5, 1914. They were interred on the point above their home.

Cora Williams and William Harrison Ross (1936)

2nd Generation: William Harrison Ross married Cora Alice Williams Apr. 9, 1885 in Johnson County, KY. Cora (born Oct. 2, 1868) was the daughter of Noah H. and Ellen Webb Williams.

Harrison and Cora were the parents of 10 children: Lonnie (born Feb. 16, 1886, died Mar. 7, 1910; Plura Alda (born Apr. 5, 1889, died Nov. 16, 1905); Noah Steward (born Feb. 2, 1892, died Jul. 26, 1947) married Eliza Mae Travis. Elva Jane (born Nov. 21, 1893, died Jul. 4, 1917) married Luther Wellman; Mason A. (born Aug. 28, 1895, died Jun. 13, 1965) married Lester Williams; Mitchell E. (born Aug. 28, 1895, died Sep. 24, 1968) married first, Lena Boggs, second, Junie Williams and third, Esta Boggs Evans; Dewey J. (born Oct. 8, 1898, died May 1, 1970) married Louella Grim; Oscar Merrill (born Apr. 8, 1902, died Apr. 5, 1935) married Jessie Williams; Glenn (born Jun. 8, 1905, died May 9, 1985) married Bertha Dixon; Della Frances (born Oct. 13, 1907, died Aug. 15, 1986) married Gusta Sparks.

Harrison and Cora lived several years on Joe's farm on Lower Laurel, eventually buying the lower 80 acres of the farm. Then in 1918 they bought the farm across the creek from W.H. Kelly where they lived for the remainder of their lives.

Harrison farmed, taught school, blacksmithed and made legal whiskey. These skills served him well. He passed them to his sons and they served them as well.

Harrison died May 8, 1940 and Cora Dec. 24, 1945. They were interred on their farm on Lower Laurel Cr. below Flat Gap. *Submitted by Steward David Ross.*

ROSS - Lonnie Farish Ross (born Feb. 16, 1886, on Lower Laurel Creek below Flat Gap, died Mar. 7, 1910. He was the eldest son of William Harrison Ross (born Aug. 30, 1861, died May 8, 1940). Harrison married Cora Alice Williams Apr. 9, 1885. Cora was born Oct. 17, 1868 to Noah H. and Ellen Webb Williams.

He began his formal education at Beech Branch, a one-room log school on Jul. 24, 1893. His first teacher was M.L. Ross. He grew to be a handsome young man. Many pictures found in the family collection proves this statement.

Lonnie and a friend, Ben Cox, left Johnson County to find fame and fortune by working their way west. A postcard received by his brother Mitchell postmarked Feb. 1909, from Hartline, WA, said he was working on a wheat ranch. Lonnie moved on to Leavenworth, WA, where he found employment as a fireman for the Great Northern Railway Company clearing snow from tracks in the Cascade Mountains. The avalanche that took his life is still the worst snow disaster in the U.S., according to a book titled *Northwest Disasters*, written by Ruby El Hult. Lonnie was one of the few able to dig out of the snow and wreckage only to die of injuries and exposure. The body was shipped back to Paintsville by train. His twin brothers, Mitchell and Mason, met the train with a wagon and a team of horses to claim the body. What a difficult assignment for two 15-year-old boys to claim the body of one they admired so much. Lonnie was laid to rest in the Ross Cemetery on Laurel Creek below Flat Gap.

ROSS - Mitchell E. Ross was born Aug. 28, 1895, Laurel Creek, Johnson County to William Harrison Ross (b. Aug. 30 1891) and married Apr. 9, 1885 to Cora Alice Williams (b. Oct. 2, 1868), daughter of Noah H. and Ellen Webb Williams.

Mitchell married first, Lena Boggs (b. 1897) and they were the parents of one son Harry Ray (born Apr. 25, 1915, died May 5, 1993). He married second, Junie Williams (born 1895, died Sep. 2, 1923). To this union was born a daughter Dorothy on May 1918, a son Denzel was born Jul. 15, 1920, and a stillborn son on Jul. 31, 1923. His third marriage to Esta Boggs Evans (born May 1, 1893, Cains Creek near Blaine, Lawrence County) bore four children: daughter Nola Ilene (born Feb. 3, 1926); daughter Loetta (born Nov. 25, 1928); daughter Willie Alice (born Sep. 21, 1931); and a son Mitchell Darrell (born Apr. 8, 1935), were all born in Johnson County, Laurel Creek, below Flat Gap.

Mitchell had many professions such as, farmer, sheep raiser, coal miner and country store owner/operator. He also made sorghum molasses, butchered his own meat, and various other things to keep food on the table during the Depression years. He was an avid fox hunter as many were in those days. He was a board member of the Beech Branch School, Johnson County, where he had attended as a child. All his children, save Darrell, also attended. In March 1938, they moved along with the last five children to Waverly, OH, where he made his living as a farmer. During WWII he worked in a defense plant making gun powder.

He donated a portion of his land and helped build the Straight Creek Enterprise Baptist Church located in Pike County, OH. Both he and his wife were members. Mitchell died Sep. 24, 1968 and Esta died May 23, 1975. They were both laid to rest in Mound Cemetery, Piketon, OH.

ROSS - Steward Ross was born Feb. 19, 1923 on Franks Creek near Flat Gap in Johnson County, KY to Noah Steward Ross and Eliza Mae Travis Ross. He was the oldest of three sons: John Denver died at the age of 2; Henry Clyde, born May 14, 1933 and died from a motorcycle accident Aug. 29, 1987.

Steward married Gloria Darleen Ferguson in Paintsville, KY on Apr. 12, 1947 by Elder Lonza Reed. She was born Feb. 13, 1930 on Drakes Fork near Flat Gap in Johnson County, KY to Cossie Franklin Ferguson and Minnie Gertrude Skaggs Ferguson. She was the second oldest of six children, four of whom survived to adulthood.

They are the parents of two daughters, Carol Lynn (born Apr. 8, 1948) and Deborah Lee (born Jun. 29, 1950) both born in Waverly, OH, and three sons: Steward David (born Nov. 13, 1951); Joseph Denver (born Sep. 11, 1953) and Timothy Denzel (born Aug. 11, 1956), all born in Springfield, OH.

Steward attended school at Hoods Fork, Upper and Lower Franks Creek, Beech Branch and Flat Gap prior to his family moving to Winchester, OH in 1941 where he graduated in 1943. He enlisted in the U.S. Army in the spring of 1943 and left for basic training before commencement exercises at Winchester High School. Serving in North Africa, India, Burma and China until 1946. After his marriage, he farmed for a while in Waverly, OH, by 1951 he was working as a machinist and later as a toolmaker in Springfield, OH.

Steward and Darleen Ross

Retiring from Morris Bean Co. in 1985 with 32 years service.

Darleen attended school at Flat Gap until her family moved to Springfield, OH in 1943, where she attended Roosevelt Jr. High and Springfield High School. Due to the failing health of her father, the family returned to Flat Gap a few months prior to his untimely death on Oct. 2, 1946. She began working in 1965 for the Springfield Local School District as a cook and in 1966 started driving a school bus. Retiring in 1990 with 25 years service.

Steward and Darleen are long time members of the Hickory Grove United Baptist Church of Jesus Christ at Mechanicburg, OH where Steward is a deacon and served several years as clerk.

They maintain the house on Darleen's home place on Lower Laurel Creek just below Flat Gap, Johnson County, KY. This house, referred to as the "Old House" was the place for family vacations for Steward, Darleen and their five children for many years. Now the "Old House" serves as a get-a-way and for their own family reunion each Memorial and Labor Day holiday weekend. The "Old House" is an important link for their children, grandchildren and great-grandchildren to their Kentucky heritage.

ROSS - Susan Renee Ross was born Dec. 18, 1961 to James David and Rosa Faye Carter Ross in Franklin County, OH.

Susan Renee Ross

She works for Big Bear Stores in Columbus, OH. She enjoys cooking, yard sales, soap operas and her nieces and nephews.

ROSS - William Marion Ross was born Dec. 9, 1862, BarnRock, KY in Johnson County and died Jul. 5, 1937. His burial place is Princebranch Skaggs, KY.

William Marion Ross and Rhoda McKenzie Ross

William married Rhoda McKenzie (born Sep. 23, 1864 Conley Creek, KY) on Mar. 18, 1893. Rhoda died Jan. 24, 1957. She was the daughter of Thomas McKenzie and Lizzie Rose Fyffe. William bought a farm on Princebranch, Skaggs, KY.

They had two children, Jesse David (born Dec. 19, 1893) and Lexi (born Sep. 25, 1902, died Sep. 26, 1902). *By James David Ross.*

ROWLAND - Robert Lee Rowland "Bob" (born Apr. 8, 1931, Chicago, IL) married Sep. 8, 1951 in Hopkins, MN to Barbara Rowland (born Dec. 7, 1931, Minneapolis, MN). They have three children: Daniel (born 1954, Minneapolis, MN) married Joyce Olsen; Nancy (born 1956, Minneapolis, MN) married Phillip Chitko; Michael (born 1958, Minneapolis, MN) married Deborah DesJardin. Bob was a barber for several years until he decided to change occupations. He attended the University of Minnesota obtaining a bachelor of science degree in chemical dependency. Bob became director of chemical dependency treatment centers in Minnesota, Virginia and Wisconsin.

Now retired, he owns Amicus Counseling Service in Roseville, MN. His parents were Daniel Clifford Rowland (born Nov. 5, 1906, Sauk Center, MN) and Sybil Eloise Bixler (born Oct. 2, 1907, Lismore, MN). Daniel's parents were Joel Benjamin Rowland (born Apr. 22, 1885, Holdingford, MN) and Elizabeth Maria Gram (born Jul. 13, 1886, Buffalo, MN). Joel's parents were Santford Rowland (born May 12, 1850 in Paintsville, KY) and Rachel Watson (born Jun. 23, 1845, Prestonsburg, KY). Santford's parents were Daniel R. Rowland (born 1811 ca. Washington County, VA) and Emily Lemaster (born 1820 Floyd County, KY).

Daniel's parents were John Rowland (born between 1765-75 Washington County, VA) and Ellender Remy (born ca. 1780 in Virginia).

John Rowland lived all his life in Washington County, VA. He served in the 70th Regiment of the Virginia Militia for Washington County, VA. John bought 200 acres of land from Hezekiah and Jamina Fairchild for $600 on Sep. 17, 1806. It was located on the south side of the South Fork of Holston River. This was located in the part of Washington County that later became Smyth County in 1832. He married Sep. 19, 1799 to Ellender Remy (Ramey).

They had eight children: Michael (born ca. 1800) md. Nancy Stwart on Jul. 11, 1822 in Washington County, VA; Catherine (born ca. 1802) md. Ransome Suite in September 1822 in Washington County, VA; Ryland (born ca. 1804) md. Polly Stewart on Jul. 22, 1823 in Washington County, VA; John (born ca. 1805) md. Edith Isemary in 1827 in Washington County, VA; Armstrong/Armsted (born ca. 1806) md. Polly; Santford (born ca. 1808) md. Catherine __ in 1827; Rememberance (born ca. 1809) md. Daniel Pelfrey on Nov. 21, 1837 in Floyd County, KY; Daniel (born ca. 1810) md. Emily Lemaster on Nov. 21, 1837, Floyd County, KY.

According to the 1810 Washington County, VA census, all children were born before 1810 census. In addition to raising their own children, they raised twin boys, Owen and Ephriam Ramy (born May 14, 1814). Their parents, who died suddenly, were Owen Ramy (brother of Ellender) and his wife Mary Bryan (Briant). John became legal guardian Aug. 20, 1816.

After Johns death, Ellender stayed in Washington County, VA until 1830 according to Virginia tax records. When she and the unmarried children: Daniel, Rememberance, Owen and Ephriam, moved to Floyd County, KY so she could be near her sister Catherine (Remy) and brother-in-law Stephen Wheeler. She arrived in time to be recorded in the 1830 Floyd County, KY census.

Ellender was the daughter of William and Eleanor (McCarty) Remy. John's last will and testament was made Dec. 20, 1821. Every thing was left to Ellender. Upon her demise everything to be divided evenly among the remaining children. No death records or probate records have been found for her. However, in 1837 her children Santford and Daniel made a marriage bond for their sister Rememberance rather than Ellender. It is suspected she was no longer living.

Possible parents of John, John Rowland. His siblings: Margret (born 1777) md. James Bruce ; Mary Rowland (born ca. 1780) md. James Fleenor on Oct. 22, 1799; Thomas (born ca. 1782) md. Mary Charp/ Sharp on May 18, 1809. All marriages were in Washington County, VA. *Submitted by Barbara Rowland of Folsom, CA.*

ROYALTY - Martha Davis Royalty was born Oct. 24, 1926, in Paintsville, KY to Harry Davis and Hazel Williams Davis. One other daughter was born to this union, Helen Davis Neal on Jan. 12, 1930.

Hazel Williams Davis was born Sep. 3, 1901 to James Marion and Jennie Vaughan Williams in Volga, KY. Harry Davis was born Dec. 4, 1881 to Daniel and Martha Jane Rule Davis in Paintsville, KY. Harry Davis and Hazel Williams met while Hazel attended John C.C. Mayo College and they were married, Jan. 25, 1925. These families, Davis and Williams were descendants of early settlers to Johnson County.

Hazel Davis was a teacher at John C.C. Mayo College and was one of the youngest to enter the teaching field at this time. After her marriage, she became a farmer's wife.

Martha Davis attended Hyde-Hopkins Kindergarten in Paintsville under the direction of Amanda Mollette Holbrook. Her education continued in this private school until third grade.

A memorable one-half school year was attending a two-room school in the community where she lived, Staffordsville. The teacher was her uncle, Sankey Williams. She graduated from Paintsville High School. Two years were spent a Center College in Danville, KY. After graduating with a degree in library science from University of Kentucky, Martha came to Irvine, KY as librarian at the local high school.

It was here she met and married E.P. Royalty. Mr. Royalty who was a native of Estill County, attended University of Kentucky before serving in the Army during the Korean War. He then returned to Irvine to join his father in the family business.

To this union three children were born: Robert Davis on Jun. 18, 1953; Elizabeth Park on Feb. 19, 1955 and Charles William on May 23,1960

Since retirement she has enjoyed traveling, playing golf and flower gardening. Time is devoted to church and its activities. She is also involved with industrial development in the county. Other interests are, member Four Seasons Garden Club, Estill County Retired Teachers, Pi Chapter Delta Kappa Gamma (educational group), and the Estill County Country Club.

SAGRAVES - Donnie Aire Sagraves was born Feb. 26, 1882 two and a half miles below Flat Gap on Little Laurel Creek in Johnson County, KY. He was the eldest son of seven children born to William Henry (born Jan. 31, 1856, died Mar. 2, 1939) and Armilda Jane Williams Sagraves (born Jul. 20, 1860, died Jul. 19, 1941). They were married Feb. 5, 1880 by Elder James Collins.

Donnie's siblings were: Proctor M. (born Aug. 17, 1884, died Mar. 11, 1940); Noah H. (born Sep. 5, 1890, died 1948) md. Virgie Williams; Ellen Jane (born Aug. 17, 1892, died November 1975) md. Hendrix Kelly; Crayton Glen (born Mar. 12, 1895, died May 1971) md. Jennie Goodlett; Ashley Ward (born Nov. 29, 1898, died Nov. 29, 1952) md. Addie Evans; Bula M. (born Aug. 26, 1903, died Aug. 14, 1908).

Donnie, Lassie and Kate Segraves

Donnie attended old Beech Branch School with Mrs. John M. Williams teacher. Donnie was a self made veterinarian and always ready when needed. He owned a dog, Carlo, so well trained he was depended on to take messages or lunch to Donnie in the fields when necessary.

A pair of "pliers" were always at the ready for Donnie to extract a tooth if someone came by with a toothache or loose tooth. His knowledge of herbs and roots was also applied often when he heard a complaint of arthritis, stomach ache, or whatever, he would come to the rescue with a herbal mixture to take care of the problem or make it better until a real doctor could come.

Donnie was also known for the stories (bear tales) he was always ready to tell to all children that would listen, very few didn't, causing young and old alike to refer to him as "Uncle Donnie." He reminded one of the scripture in the Bible where Jesus says "Suffer little children to come unto me." Donnie was a member of Bethel United Baptist Church at Flat Gap, KY.

He was married to Malissa Evans Mar. 10, 1900. After she died he met and married Katherine "Kate" Ferguson on Dec. 18, 1901. They were the parents of one daughter, Lassie Alka (born Aug. 3, 1903, died Nov. 12, 1979) md. Jesse Sparks. They had also had one grandchild, Paul J. Sagraves (born October 1932, d. December 1948).

Katherine was born Sep. 11, 1878, died 1934) to Ferdinand Ferguson (born September 1836, died 1911) and Margaret Williams (born 1842, died 1882). They were married in 1864. Katherine suffered with asthma and epilepsy. Uable to read, a nephew read the bible "And if thy wife doith not obey thee whip her then if she doith not obey thee whip her much." Kate replied, "Now Ferd, you know that's not so!" Kate was very instrumental in the nurturing of her nieces and nephews. Katherine was a member of Laurel Hill Primitive Baptist Church.

Donnie and Kate lived on Beech Branch of Laurel Creek portion of the farm passed to him through his father, grandfather, Tommy Sagraves and great-grandfather Joseph Sagraves.

Later he shared wit and wisdom with family and friends at Red Bush, Flat Gap and Springfield (OH) before his demise in 1971. He and Kate are buried on Beech Branch.

SAGRAVES - Elwin Eugene Sagraves was born Oct. 26, 1929 two and a half miles below Flat Gap, Johnson County, KY. His mother was Addie Melinda Evans, daughter of James H. and Ara Sagraves Evans. Addie was born Jul. 7, 1903 on Big Laurel Creek in Johnson County, KY. Elwin's father, Ashley Ward Sagraves, was born Nov. 29, 1898 in the same house where Elwin was born on that part of the farm owned by Elwin's great-great-grandfather Joseph Sagraves. Elwin's parents were married Nov. 15, 1924 by Elder Bill Skaggs. Elwin's father made his living on the farm inherited from his father and mother, William H. and Armilda Williams Sagraves.

Elwin and Willa Jean Sagraves

Elwin was the third son of six children: James Elmo (born Aug. 24, 1925) md. Pauline Parker; Woodrow Wilson (born Aug. 17, 1927) md. Vinelia Rose; Ellis Tommy (born Apr. 10, 1932) md. Maxine McKenzie; Deloris Ara (born Dec. 21, 1933) md. Dexter Blair; Dallas Thurman (born Mar. 8, 1936) md. Sarah Alice Cox Slone.

Elwin attended Beech Branch and Flat Gap Schools. Having no desire to farm he tried water well drilling, garage work, and running a saw mill before entering the US Army, Jun. 13, 1951. He served one year in Korea before returning home nine days before his father's last fight with cancer, Nov. 29, 1952. Ashley is buried in the family cemetery on the hill in front of his home.

Elwin was discharged Mar. 13, 1953. Was married to Willa Jean Ferguson Mar. 18, 1953 in Springfield, OH by Elder John Henry Skaggs.

Willa Jean was born May 18, 1932 on Drakes Fork of Laurel Creek, Flat Gap, KY. Her parents were Cossie Franklin Ferguson (born Jul. 22, 1899, d. Oct. 2, 1946) and Minnie Gertrude Skaggs Ferguson (born Oct. 22, 1908, died Aug. 12, 1992). They were married May 17, 1928 in Elliott County by Elder John Henry Skaggs.

Willa Jean attended school at Flat Gap, Lagonda Grade School and Roosevelt Jr. High in Springfield, OH, returning to attend and graduate from Flat Gap High School Apr. 27, 1950. She also went to Mayo Vocational School. She retired from National City Bank, Springfield, OH Jan. 3, 1990. Elwin retired from Navistar, Jan. 1, 1987 with 30 years service.

They are the parents of two children, Gregory Elwin (born Oct. 25, 1956) md. Rhonda Davis. He works for Honda Inc. of Marysville. Beverly Joan (born Jul. 18, 1960) md. Paul R. Collins. Beverly got her BS plus in education at Ohio University, Belmont County, OH. She teaches at Barnsville Middle School, Barnesville. OH.

Elwin and Willa Jean are members of Straight Creek Enterprise Baptist Church where he has served as trustee and deacon.

SALYER - The Salyer family, which is well known in portions of Eastern Kentucky and Western Virginia, had its origin in Southern France where generations of them have lived for centuries. The best researchers claim that the name goes back 2,000 years to the time of Julius Caesar. The tribe 'Salye' held province, a portion of Southern France, despite the legions of Julius Caesar. In France the name is written Salier and pronounced Salye or Salyer. Today the spelling of the name differs so much that it sometimes loses its original spelling. The correct spelling is Salyer. The history of the emigration of the members of the family came into England and Ireland in the early 1600s. Many members of the family claim they are of Irish descent but this is due to the fact they just came to America from Ireland having their earlier origin in France. They are of Huguenot descent which may account for their having settled in South Carolina in the early 1700.

The first account of the name Salyer was William Salyer (Sallier). The name is found spelled various ways such as: Sallyar, Sallyards, Sallier and Salyer. William appeared on Long Island, NY in 1656. He was a tailor and weaver by trade. He married Sarah Davis, daughter of Foulk Davis, a Welshman. He held some town offices and probably was born about 1630 and died before 1703. He is evidently the emigrant ancestor of all the Salyer family in Brookhaven, Long Island and will be remembered as the hometown of the original Salyer family. They resided on Long Island for well over a century.

It is believed by many that Benjamin K. Salyer, the progenitor of all the Salyers of Western Virginia and portions of Eastern Kentucky, is descendant of William Salyer, the weaver and tailor who settled in Brookhaven, Long Island in 1655 or 1657 and who had a son Charles Salyer born about 1672 in Brookhaven, Long Island. Charles married Mary Jones about 1692 and had several children. The oldest child was named Benjamin, of which is thought to be Benjamin K. Benjamin about the age of 21 bought land in southernmost part of New Jersey and sold it. It is surmised from this transaction that Benjamin kept going south and settled in South Carolina.

There is record of Revolutionary soldiers by the name of Salyer in both the north and south. Benjamin K. Salyer had sons in the Revolutionary War. In keeping with the characteristics of his race and in a course of time, Benjamin K. became a wealthy planter of the colony of South Carolina and also acquired land in North Carolina, before he died at Fuilford Court House in that colony in 1754. Family records handed down stated he died as a result of falling from his horse while riding over his estate. There seems to be no record of his wife, but there is record of his sons. They are namely: Benjamin Jr. born about 1730 in North Carolina, Zachariah, John and Isaiah.

Benjamin Salyer Jr. served in the Revolutionary War as a private soldier under General Greene and was in the famous retreat from the Dan River and was wounded in the campaign. His death in 1781 was attributed to the war wound. There is found no mention of his wife but his sons, William and Zachariah, have numerous descendants in Eastern Kentucky. Benjamin K.'s sons, Zachariah and Isaiah, both have descendants in Eastern Kentucky. John, son of Benjamin K., we do not know much about.

Zachariah, Benjamin K.'s son, served in the Revolution and was with General Washington in the dire winter of 1777 at Valley Forge. Zachariah had descendants in Eastern Kentucky but most of his descendants stayed in Virginia. Zazhariah and his wife had several children of whom Samuel was the best known. Apparently this family lived most of their lives in Russel County, VA. Samuel married a Castle who was the daughter of Joe Castle. Joe is said to have been the founder of Castlewood about 1767. He was of the famous band known as the "long hunters." Samuel Jr. lived an interesting life as most records show. He was born 1793 and lived to be 117 years and died on Thacker Branch in Wise County, VA in 1911. He married Lydia Culbertson, daughter of Tyree and Mattie Vicars.

Col. Logan N.H. Salyer, son of Samuel Jr., served with Gen. Lee and surrendered with him at Appomatox on Apr. 9, 1865. He organized a company of 101 Confederates at Gladeville (now Wise County, VA) and he, also, was the builder of the second permanent residence in Prince's Flats, now Norton, VA. Col. Salyer spent all the latter part of his life at Whitesburg, KY, where he was a noted lawyer and federal judge for the Eastern District of Kentucky. He died in 1916 at the age of 86.

Benjamin K. Salyer Jr. whose name is among 10 on a monument to Revolutionary soldiers at Paintsville, KY, had two sons, Zachariah and William, who have numerous descendants in Floyd, Magoffin and Johnson counties. Zachariah served in the war of 1812. He probably grew up in Russell County, VA and came to Floyd County in the 1820s and settled in the section set off as Johnson County. William settled in Floyd County. Both brothers had large families and several members of the families went west to Missouri, Texas, Arkansas, California and some remained here in Eastern Kentucky. The city of Salyersville, the county seat of Magoffin County was named for Samuel who was the state legislator in 1860 from Magoffin County. There is a city in Trinity County, CA named Salyer of which was named for Charles Marshall Salyer born 1888, son of Henry Salyer, and who is a grandson of David J. Salyer of Johnson County, KY.

Isaiah Salyer's descendants settled here in Floyd County in the part of which was set off as Lawrence County, KY. His son, David Jesse Salyer, settled on Barnetts Creek, Johnson County, Kentucky. He was widely known as a merchant and livestock dealer. He had two sons to die in the Civil War. They are buried in the Salyer Cemetery at Barnetts Creek, Johnson County, KY.

During World War I and World War II, the Salyer name was well represented. Many of them gave their lives for the defense of their country. They served with honor and dignity. John Marshall Salyer, born in Johnson County, received his elementary and secondary education at Paintsville, KY, a graduate of the University of Kentucky and has a medical degree from Vanderbuilt University. He gave 20 years service to his country and now is retired from the services. Today he and associates have a clinic in San Ana, CA and perform open heart surgery. All across the U.S. the name Salyer is well represented as teachers, doctors, ministers, farmers, and there are others not as fortunate.

In conclusion, one will have to say the Salyer family has served the country with honor and dignity.

SALYER - Addison M., better known as Add or Addie, was small in stature weighing about 168 pounds at the time of his death. His childhood days were on the left fork of Barnetts Creek, Johnson County, KY. He never knew what motherly love really meant because his mother died when he was about 9 years old. She died in 1884. His father remarried shortly thereafter to a woman for whom the children did not care about and which is a natural instinct for them. My father spent a good deal of the time with his grandparents, William Caudill and David Salyer, both living nearby in the same community. He often made the statement of his grandmother Caudill "that she was the best lovable woman that ever lived." He had great respect for both grandmothers.

Education in those days was hard to get. He went to school in a one-room schoolhouse roughly furnished and heated. He mastered the three Rs and excelled in them. He was very intelligent. The only community activities were school gatherings and church going. They, also, had what they called singing school that was held at nighttime. The school activities consisted of adding, spelling bees, humorous programs which were made up of short plays, humorous speeches and pie suppers held at nighttime. His teacher, John H. Picklesimer, tried to get him to continue his education but at that time he couldn't see how he could. Times in those days were hard. In the latter 1890s, he, with other neighbors, went to Kansas where he found work on a farm for $16.00 per month for a Mr. Beckett. He worked in and around Olathe, KS, until he decided to return to Kentucky for the girl he wanted to marry. He married Oct. 11, 1901 in Johnson County, KY, but his wife persuaded him not to return to Kansas, but to settle here in Johnson County, KY. He and his young wife started housekeeping at Denver, KY.

Addison Salyer

In 1908, Patrick G. Rice, his father-in-law, decided to leave Johnson County for Lewis County, KY. He sold his farm to his son-in-law, Addison M. It was at this farm where my father and mother reared their family. It was a large farm approximately 450 acres. He operated the farm with the help of his sons, dealt in real estate and various financial enterprises. He was a good citizen, deacon of the Liberty Baptist Church at Denver, KY, the oldest Baptist Church in Johnson County, KY. He reared a large respected family which has exemplified itself in life. His wife, my mother, was responsible for all the life values that were instilled in each of the children. She was always at hand when that child needed love and understanding. She was a good wife, a loving and faithful mother and was loved dearly by all of her children. She and my father are laid to rest in the Hyden-Music Cemetery, Hagerhill, KY, to wait for Judgment Day. *Written by Ruth Salyer.*

SALYER - John Marshall Salyer, MD, Col., US Army Corps (Ret) was born Oct. 25, 1911 in a one-room log cabin at Volga, Johnson County, KY to Manuel and Bessie (Williams) Salyer. The father, Manuel Salyer, was a rural school teacher with a salary of $29.50 per month. Marshall attended a one-room school and graduated from Paintsville High School in 1930. After high school, he was employed by the Atlantic and Pacific Tea Co. for one year in order to provide savings of minimal funds for college entrance. He entered the University of Kentucky, Lexington, KY in September 1931 (Pre-Med curriculum) and attended three school years and two summer terms. During two of those academic years, he conducted early morning, 4:00 a.m. eight mile trek, paper route (*Lexington Herald*) to defray most of the college expenses. In meantime, he enjoyed membership in the Lamba Chi Alpha Social Fraternity.

In the spring of 1934 he applied to three medical schools: Duke, Tulane and Vanderbilt, and was accepted by all. He accepted Vanderbilt after discussions with his UK professors and Nashville was closer to his home state, Kentucky. He entered Vanderbilt University School of Medicine in September 1934. He was issued an AB degree from University of Kentucky in 1935 after completion of the first year at Vanderbilt. He graduated from Vanderbilt in 1938 with a MD degree. He served as an exterm during his senior year at the Tennessee State Penitentiary where he gained a great deal of clinical experience and minimal monetary benefits.

His surgical and medical post graduate training before and during and after World War II included.

Vanderbilt University Hospital; Fitzsimons Army Hospital, Denver, CO; University of Colorado; College of Medicine and the University of Minnesota.

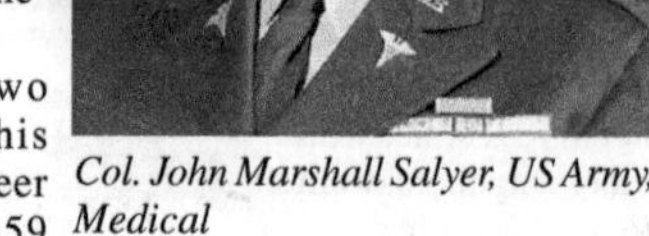
Col. John Marshall Salyer, US Army, Medical

The two phases of his surgical career from 1939-59 was Regular Army Medical Corps, where he attained the rank of full colonel at age of 39 and, from 1939-78 a partnership practice in thoracic and cardiovascular surgery in Orange County, CA.

On retirement from the Medical Corps in 1959, he was Chief of the Department of Surgery, Fitzsimons Army Hospital where he served three tours of duty between wars, a total of 15 years.

He served 31 months (World War II) in India and Burma with the 73rd Evacuation Hospital and was also commanding officer of the unit for four months prior to deactivation in Burma in August 1945.

For a period of two years he served as the surgical consultant for East Command during the Korean Conflict, a bloody war where 54,000 of the troops lost their lives; about 88% were saved that was forwarded to the medical facilities, some being the four forward Mash Units.

He had about 900 doctors under his direction regarding assignments and surgical care policies of the wounded and evacuations to the US Hospitals located in Japan.

At Fitzsimons, during the summer of 1947 and 1948, Dr. John M. directed the annual physical examinations on retired Gen. Dwight D. Eisenhower. By 1948 Eisenhower was convinced that he should abstain from cigarette smoking. He obeyed but after about two years, he resumed his smoking. (Information by a letter from Mrs. Eisenhower). He had different occasions to provide consultations, surgical care and professional advice to many high ranking Army and Air Force commanders and personnel during and after World War II and Korean War. For example some were Gen. Joseph Stilwell in China, Burma and India Theater; Gen. Mark Clark during the Korean Conflict. Lt. Gen. Hubert Harmon, Maj. Gen. James E. Moore and others.

Following are some of his surgical achievements during his professional career.

1) Performed the first direct vision open heart surgery at Walter Reed Army Hospital, August 1954.

2) Performed the first open heart surgery in a Service Hospital (Fitzsimons) 1955.

3) Performed the first open heart surgery in orange County, CA at St. Joseph Hospital, June 1961.

4) Implanted one of the first cardiac pacemaker on the West Coast, August 1961.

This is only a few of the good humanitarian deeds Dr. Salyer has done for his country with honor and dignity. He, who is in poor health and his wife Sally (who died this February 1999), resides at Indian Wells, CA near Palm Springs, CA.

Dr. John Marshall Salyer first married ca. 1939/40 to Nancy K. Kennedy, a niece of Col. George F. Aycock.

Two children were born to this union: Barbara Ann (born ca. 1942) and John R. Salyer (born ca. 1948).

SALYER - Ruth Salyer of Staffordsville, Johnson County was born Jan. 3, 1916, Johnson County, KY, and was a graduate of Western Kentucky State University, Bowling Green, KY. with a BS degree in administration and supervision and a MS degree in library science from The George Peabody College in Nashville, TN and Rank I from Eastern Kentucky State University, Richmond, KY. She began her teaching in 1938 in a one-room school at a very minimal salary. From the one-room school, she was promoted into high school. In high school she taught English and was librarian at Meade Memorial High School and head librarian at Johnson Central High School until retirement in 1986. During two summer sessions she taught library science at Morehead Kentucky State University.

Her educational association memberships were KEA, Kentucky Library Assoc.; Big Sandy Historical Society, Magoffin County Historical Society, Johnson County Historical Society, Kentucky Historical Society and Kentucky Retired Teachers Assoc. She is a member of the First Baptist Church, Paintsville, KY. After retirement, she authored and published a book, *The Blair Families And Their Related Families of Johnson County, KY* and she also compiled *The Census Reports of Johnson County from 1850-1920.*

Ruth Salyer

Her Ancestry: She is the daughter of Addison M. Salyer who was born in 1874 Baronets Creek, KY and died in 1956. He married Oct. 24, 1901 Core Bell Rice (born 1881 in Johnson County, died 1941). Both parents are buried in The Hyden-Music Cemetery, Hager Hill, KY, a point over-looking the valley that was once the battle-ground during the Civil War. The cemetery itself was the spot where breastwork was thrown up for protection while a battle was fought across the valley at another point between the forces of Gen. Marshall's Army and Gen. Garfield's Army.

Ruth grew up in the Salyer family who lived on a large farm on Lower Middle Fork of Jenny's Creek, Johnson County, KY. Her father operated a farm, dealt in real estate and also had interest in other diversified financial enterprises. He was a good citizen, worked for the improvement of his community and a deacon of The Liberty Baptist Church, Denver, KY. He and her mother reared a large respectful family which has exemplified itself in life. Ruth grew up with her brother and sisters doing chores on the farm under the supervision of their mother, a dedicated and loving mother who taught her children a right was a right and a wrong was a wrong. Her mother was always there when one of the children needed her. This was the kind of environment that Ruth grew up in. Ruth had different opportunities to leave Johnson County for advancements such as Washington, DC in civil service during WWII and to Indianapolis, IN Civil Service Naval Depot and after receiving her MS degree in library science from Peabody, she was offered a permanent position as librarian at Morehead Kentucky State University, but she felt a greater need to remain in Johnson County to help educate and improve children lives in the school system of Johnson County, KY. She chose a career and remained single instead of marrying and rearing a family.

The early ancestors of the Salyer's came into Eastern Kentucky about 1820 from Russell County, VA. The Salyers who settled in Russell County, VA, migrated from North and South Carolina. At this point there is a question from where and how the Salyers came into the United States. The earliest known Salyer in the US was found on Long Island, NY. His name was William Salyer (born ca. 1630, died before 1703) who appeared there in 1656. He was a tailor and weaver by trade and married to Sarah Davis, daughter of Foulk Davis, a Welshman. At this point no effort will be taken to trace the history of the Salyer families. All across the U.S. the name Salyer is well represented as teachers, doctors, ministers, farmers and there were others not as fortunate; but in conclusion, one will have to say the Salyer family has served their country with honor and dignity.

SAMMONS - Merida Lorene Haar was born on Mar. 16, 1947 in Marysville, KS to Frederick Max Haar and Bessie Lorraine Wiley. She is the oldest of five born to her parents, all of whom survived to adulthood. Lorene was married in Clintwood, VA to Walter Wathen Sammons on Aug. 25, 1964 and divorced in 1990.

They were parents of two sons, Douglas Dwayne (born Nov. 17, 1965, in Paintsville, KY) and David Wayne (born Feb. 6, 1969, in Newport News, VA). Lorene attended Paintsville City Schools, Class of 1965. She was a member of First Baptist Church, Paintsville. She relocated to Newport News, VA in 1966 where her husband was employed with the Newport News Fire Department. She pursued further education at Thomas Nelson Community College where she was a member of the Phi Theta Kappa Honor Fraternity and a National Dean's List student. She and her family later moved to a local suburban community, Poquoson, VA, where both sons graduated from Poquoson High School.

Lorene was employed for 10 years with the Peninsula Baptist Association of Virginia as administrative secretary. She served on the committee for developing a state Baptist secretary organization, as well as the first secretary to the Virginia Baptist Secretaries Association and was a member of the National Association of Southern Baptist Secretaries. She was a member of the American Institute of Professional Bookkeepers for a number of years.

Merida Lorene Haar Sammons Wright

Her community involvement included serving on the board of the Seaman's Friend House, a ministry to seafarers who frequent the port of Newport News. She was listed as a Distinguished Community Leader in The International Directory of Distinguished Leadership.

She later married Harold Dean Wright, son of the late Leo and Mary Strickland Wright. They formed a construction company, Lorene serving as president and treasurer. The greatest percentage of their work involved the Newport News Redevelopment and Housing Authority. Harold and Lorene retired to Loris, SC, near Myrtle Beach, at the end of 1996. He pursues his hobby of fishing and continues as a carpenter on a small scale. Lorene is a decorative painter and teaches at a local craft business and does computer accounting in her home for small businesses.

Douglas Sammons resides in Dallas, TX. He graduated from the Automotive Training Institute in Virgnia Beach, VA; continued his education in Texas, and is now a full-time student of prosthetics and orthodics at the University of Texas, Irving.

David Sammons traveled several places doing seasonal work after high school graduation; attended Devry Institute in Dallas, TX, and married Apr. 24, 1997 to Tiffany E. Florence, born Apr. 11, 1969, daughter of Robert H. and Linda M. Florence, Bountiful, UT. They have a son, Christopher David Sammons (born Jun. 16, 1998). They reside in Bountiful. David is completing his degree in computer science this year.

SAMMONS - Russell Sammons was born on Mar. 27, 1908, in Johnson County, KY to John and Minnie Price Sammons. He was one of nine children born to this couple. Russell lived his entire life in Johnson County with most of it being in the Meally Community.

On Aug. 21, 1931, Russell married June Dills and to this union five children were born: Russell L. on Jun.

14, 1933; Avonell on Aug. 11, 1935; Charlene and Arlene on May 5, 1939; and Geraldine on Aug. 26, 1944.

Russell started to work when he was 15 years old. His first job was helping blast the "River Narrows" between King's Addition and Buffalo which is now Route 40 East. He later worked in the mines at Van Lear and David, KY. In the mid-1940s, Russell changed his profession. He became a fruit and produce salesman and covered much of Eastern Kentucky as his territory. First, he worked for the Fred Caudill Fruit Company which later became the A&R Fruit Company and finally became Pratt Fruit Company. For many years, in addition to his sales work, he assisted in purchasing from the Huntington, WV, Fruit and Vegetable Market, the fruit and vegetables sold by his employer. Russell was well known for his pleasant disposition and ability to converse with anyone. Although Russell received limited formal schooling, he was well educated in that he was an avid reader as well as one who was always attempting to learn something new. His family remembers him as one who could accomplish anything he set out to do. His acquired skills included all phases of construction work, auto and mechanical repairs and several other self-taught skills.

Russell Sammons

After Russell retired, he was able to travel and visit his children who were in Cincinnati and Dayton, OH and Atlanta, GA. He also became very involved with activities at his church.

At the time of his death on Aug. 3, 1979, he was survived by his wife, June, four of his children (Avonell preceded him in death) and five grandchildren. Russell L. and his wife, Margaret, live in Cincinnati, OH; Charlene and her husband, James, live in Dayton, OH; Arlene lives in Xenia, OH and Geraldine and her husband, Gerry, live in Marietta, GA.

Russell was very much a family man, a good neighbor and a person who was loyal to Johnson County.

SCHMITT - Mary Katheryn Schmitt was born in Paintsville, KY on Mar. 30, 1925 to German C. Wells and Cora Blair Wells. Her parents were both natives of Johnson County, where they owned and operated Wells Shoe Store in downtown Paintsville for over 40 years.

Mary was the only daughter and youngest of four children born to the Wells family. One brother died in infancy, while another, Eldridge D. Wells, lived until 1977. Frank A. Wells Sr., the oldest brother, resides at Flat Gap, KY with his wife, Ann Williams Wells.

In 1941, at the age of 16, Mary graduated from Paintsville High School. She went on to receive a bachelor's degree from Kentucky Wesleyan College in 1945, majoring in political science and history. She met Joseph John Schmitt, the son of a Pennsylvania oil driller, while still in high school. Joe was born in Paintsville in 1921, but his family transferred several times before moving back to the area in 1940. After his return from service with the Marine Corps in the South Pacific, Mary and Joe were married on Apr. 17, 1945. Their life together was short-lived, however, as Joe was suddenly stricken with polio and died on Oct. 21, 1951. During their six year marriage, three children were born: Michael Joseph on May 23, 1946; Nancy Catherine on Dec. 17, 1947; and Ruth Meyers on Aug. 23, 1951.

Following her husband's death, Mary taught at Van Lear High School for three years before becoming a social worker with the Kentucky Department of Social Services. For over 30 years, she was a champion of children's rights. At the time of her retirement in October 1987, she was supervisor of the five county Big Sandy District. In addition to being a successful career woman, Mary reared her three children, all of whom have remained in the area.

Her son, Michael, is a graduate of the University of Kentucky College of Law. He is a partner in the firm of Wells, Porter, Schmitt and Jones in Paintsville, and is married to the former Lynn McCloud. They have one son, two daughters and two granddaughters.

Her daughter, Nancy, is employed at American Standard and married to James Tackett. They live at Sitka, KY and are the parents of two sons and one daughter. They also have four grandchildren.

Ruth, Mary's second daughter, also works at American Standard. She lives in Prestonsburg with her husband, Roy Roberts and their son.

Although retired, Mary K. Schmitt still remains active. She enjoys several hobbies, and regularly attends Mayo Memorial Methodist Church.

SCHMITT - Michael J. Schmitt is the son of Mary Katheryn and the late Joseph John Schmitt. He was born in Paintsville, KY on May 23, 1946, and was the first of three children. Both of his parents were also born in Paintsville. Mike has two sisters, Nancy Tackett of Sitka, and Ruth Roberts of Prestonsburg.

Lynn Schmitt is the daughter of the late Charles and Reta Moore McCloud. She, too, was born in Paintsville on Oct. 13, 1947. Her parents were both natives of Johnson County and raised four children. Her brother, Scotty, lives at Nippa, and her sister, Judy, is a resident of Hager Hill. Lynn's other brother, Mike, left Paintsville at an early age and now resides in Jacksonville, FL.

Mike and Lynn met while attending Paintsville High School. They began dating in December 1962, became engaged during college, and married in Lexington, KY on May 18, 1968 upon Mike's graduation from the University of Kentucky. Lynn graduated from UK the following semester, then began working as an auditor for the Kentucky Department of Revenue in Frankfort. During this time, Mike attended law school and their first daughter, Kelly, was born on Nov. 9, 1969.

Mike had a natural affinity for the law, graduating near the top of his class, as well as receiving various honors. Although he had not planned on practicing law in his hometown, he changed his mind shortly before graduation and joined J.K. Wells and John Porter in their law firm in 1971.

While Mike became settled in his law practice, Lynn worked for the Kentucky Division of Unemployment Insurance in Prestonsburg until they were expecting their second child. When Kimberly was born on Mar. 2, 1973, Lynn stayed home to raise their children. On Jun. 16, 1976, their third child and only son, Joseph, was born. When the children were all in school, Lynn began working at the law firm as an accountant.

Since 1971, the law firm of Wells, Porter, Schmitt and Jones has grown from three to nine attorneys, two paralegals, as well as several other administrative employees. Mike is a very successful trial attorney, specializing in insurance defense, education law and employment law.

Their daughter, Kelly, lives in Paintsville and is married to Michael Colvin. She is employed by the Kentucky Department of Vocational Rehabilitation as a rehabilitation specialist. They have two daughters, Olivia and Sarah.

Kimberly is employed by Norton Hospital as chief clinical dietitian. She is married to Michael Cooley and is a resident of Louisville, KY.

Joe will receive a degree in Computer Information Services from Morehead State University in the spring of 2000. He is engaged to be married to Stephanie Wheeler of Staffordsville in July 2001.

Mike and Lynn have been married 31 years and have had a very successful and happy life. They are members of Mayo Memorial Methodist Church. In addition to their home in Paintsville, they own a house at River, KY, where they spend many weekends and holidays with friends and family.

SCHROYER - Dorothy Dixon was born on Mar. 9, 1918, at Nippa, KY, the second child of Rolla and Lillie Conley Dixon who were married on Jul. 12, 1914, by Colfax Butler at Staffordsville, KY. Her parents met as children in a one-room school taught by Lillie's father, John Milton Conley.

Dorothy's older brother is Garland Dixon (born Mar. 16, 1916) and was married to Aileen Frary from Michigan on Jun. 3, 1941. Dorothy's younger sister is Annabelle Dixon, born Jan. 9, 1920, who married Buell Daniel on Feb. 11, 1940, and lives in Michigan.

Dorothy first lived on State Street in Paintsville, close to Paint Creek. The house burned when she was a young child, and the family moved to a four room house on the corner of Pine St. and Broadway. The house had several additions over the years, and was occupied by the Dixon family until the death of Lillie Dixon in 1990.

Dorothy was educated in the Paintsville schools on Second St. There were no school buses at the time, and, with a trip home for lunch, she walked four miles daily. In addition to her regular chores at home, she worked as an extra in the evenings at Maggard's 5&10 Cent Store, which later became G.C. Murphy Co.

Upon graduation from PHS in 1938, Dorothy worked at Murphy's and attended Booth Business School, which later became Mayo School. During World War II, she joined the US Navy WAVES and went by railroad to basic training at Hunter College in New York City. After completing basic, she worked in the Bureau of Ships in Washington, DC, as a clerk. Dorothy received an honorable discharge in 1946 at the end of the war. On Jul. 24, 1946, she married Kenneth Alton Schroyer from Pennsylvania who was a US Navy Seaman working as a welder at the Anacosta, MD, Shipyards.

Marcia and Charla Helton

Dorothy Dixon Schroyer and Kenneth Alton Schroyer

The couple moved to Ft. Lauderdale, FL, and Dorothy graduated from Broward Business College where she was a member of PiRhoZeta Sorority.

Shortly before the arrival of their only child, Marcia Gail, in 1950, the Schroyers moved to Paintsville. Dorothy began working for Southern Bell in 1955 as a switchboard operator. An active member of the Communication Workers of America, she served as an officer and union steward. She retired as a Central Office Foreman's Clerk in 1983 with over 32 years service, receiving several commendations for outstanding and courteous service. She worked through the Flood of

1957, being transported by row boat and amphibious vehicle to lodging down the street in the Hearld Hotel.

After his Navy service, Kenneth worked as a welder in strip mines in Magoffin County, KY and Ohio. He then worked for the U.S. Corps of Army Engineers in Louisville and Huntington, welding on locks and dams on the Ohio and Kentucky Rivers, retiring in 1984 at age 77.

When their daughter Marcia was a child, Dorothy was an assistant leader in her Girl Scouts troop. She is a member of the First Baptist Church in Paintsville and a Kentucky Colonel. Also, Dorothy is a charter member of the Women in Military Service Memorial Foundation where her name is proudly displayed with others in the Women's Memorial at Arlington Cemetery in Virginia. She and Kenneth are the proud grandparents of Charla Gail Helton, Winchester, KY, whose father, Charles T. Helton, died while in service to our country in 1993.

The Schroyers are residing in Paintsville.

SHEPHERD - Alice E. Shepherd was born Oct. 3, 1912 to Walter H. Shepherd and Mary E. Ruch Shepherd at Sharon Hill, PA. Alice's father was born Feb. 2 1883 and was a carpenter. Her mother was born Nov. 12, 1882 and they were married Jan. 26, 1910.

Alice had one brother born Jul. 4, 1918 and died Jul. 23, 1980. Alice attended Sharon Hill Grade School eight years with a classroom for each grade, then graduated from Upper Darby High School in 1930. She worked some during the summer in a department store in Philadelphia, and later worked 11 years in an insurance company. She attended Philadelphia Bible College for three years in the evenings. She was never married.

In May 1941 Alice came to Dessie Scott Children's Home at Little, Breathitt County, KY to help there in different ways—office work, cooking and caring for some preschool children.

While helping with cooking one day, a couple of half gallons of home canned beans were opened. The beans smelled so bad to her, she thought they had spoiled, but later she was told it was pickled beans. Alice had never heard about or seen pickled beans before, but it was too late to explain—they had been thrown out.

Alice Shepherd

After a devastating fire that closed the Children's Home, Alice and Sophia Van Horn were invited to work with the youth in Johnson County. They moved in October 1942 to Flat Gap, KY.

During the almost 57 years here, Alice has been teaching many children and adults the Bible; working in daily Vacation Bible Schools and Bible Camps. She always encouraged children to complete the Bible lessons and earn one week vacation at Camp Nathanael in Knott County, KY. Sometimes her job included helping with the Johnson County Health Department work visiting in schools to keep immunization records. These visits provided many opportunities to teach God's Word.

There have been many enjoyable times with friends and neighbors. It is good to see how many young, and older ones too, that Alice taught about God's grace who now are teaching school and working in other professions.

Alice's 57 years in Johnson County have been a living testimony to many people.

SKAGGS - Arlene Skaggs was born Apr. 4, 1926 at Barn Rock, KY to Andrew Edward and Ova Kelly Skaggs. Andy Skaggs, known as a hard worker, owned a farm at Drake and one at Barn Rock. Besides farming, he once carried mail on horseback from Flat Gap to Barn Rock, hauled coal with a team and wagon, worked for other farmers, was a share cropper on the Lafe Skaggs farm, cleaned dug wells for individuals and local schools, and in early days, he worked in the Martha oil field. Ova was a reader, seamstress and quilt maker. When the children found school subjects difficult, she read textbooks aloud to them and then entertained them by reading *Silas Marner, Little Women* and other novels as they begged for one more page to be read to them.

The Skaggs Family: Andy, Ova, Arvin, Arlene, Earl and Granny Fern

Arlene attended Drake School in grades one through seven. She graduated from Flat Gap High School in 1943 in the middle of World War II. Half the young men who would have graduated that year were already enlisted. Fairel Bailey, Junis Moore, Robert Sturgill, John M. Wheeler and Edgar Green were permitted to remain in school. After graduation, each joined our armed forces. The 1943 female graduates were Jeanetta Conley, Pauline McKenzie, Hermalee Sparks, Mertie B. Fyffe, Mary L. Barber, Geneva Salyer, Inez Lyon and Arlene Skaggs.

While attending high school, Arlene rode a black pony. The road was well known to Sid as Arvin rode him to high school before that. The pony was sheltered in the school barn. Some students fed their steeds at noon, but Sid stayed fat from morning and night feedings at home. After Arlene graduated, Sid was sold to Ernest Jayne to be used in the coal mines. Earl rode a mule when he was a freshman and was then able to buy a good mare for school.

Arlene and her brothers, Arvin Skaggs (born 1921) and Earl Skaggs (born 1929), all graduated from Morehead State University with majors in English. All had double majors and all taught other subjects as well as English in Johnson County schools. Arvin, Arlene and Earl also taught at Barn Rock and other one-room schools. Arlene attended summer school at UK in the early 1950s. She taught at Meade Memorial High School during 1947-52. During this time, she lived in the home of Walter and Daisy Pack and assisted George Walter Pack with his school work before his graduation and subsequent enrollment in Morehead State University. At Meade, Miss Skaggs taught many outstanding pupils. Their attitude is unparalleled. Wendell Wallen became a distinguished student, class president, athlete and coach. Many good students and athletes come to the minds of Meade faculty members. Among them are Minnie Kirk, Les Houston, Walter Ward Jr., Joyce Hale, Bob Banks, Devon Meek, Helen Boyd, Barbara Wells, Wilma Spradlin, Doug Wallen, Betty and Billie Sturgill, Paul V. Preston for his Christian ministry and the late Carl Blair for capable leadership as president of the Class of 1952.

Fourteen years of teaching at Flat Gap School began in 1954 and ended in 1969 when three Johnson County High Schools merged with Van Lear Independent School and became Johnson Central High School. Miss Skaggs taught mostly English IV, Journalism and Mass Communications Media at JCHS from 1969-80.

Arlene reared her beloved niece, Alice Skaggs, who in 1962 became her adopted daughter. Alice attended Johnson County Schools and Morehead State University. After leaving a secretarial position at Mayo State Vocational School, she is now field office secretary for Mine Safety & Health Administration, US Department of Labor at Martin, KY. Alice Skaggs Kestner and her husband, Delby A. Kestner, have a son, Cody Wayne Kestner, born Jan. 6, 1992.

Arlene was baptized by the Rev. Lafe Skaggs in 1944. She is a believer in Christ and a member of Point Pleasant Enterprise Baptist Church where the Rev. J.W. Beculheimer opened the doors of the church to her during a Saturday morning service.

For most of her now 73 years, she has lived in the same location near Flat Gap. Following her retirement from teaching, she remains a busy person with varied interests.

SLONE - John and Elizabeth (Parker) Slone and their family were in Scott County, VA, in the 1850 census. In 1860 they are in Johnson County, KY. Family tradition says they walked through, bringing their things with them on the back of an old blind mare. The family settled on Slone Branch.

Marvel Slone Family. Seated, L-R: Nora, Rosamond, Marvel, Elizabeth, Margaret, Minerva. Standing: Monroe, Isaac, Proctor, John, Marion William and David.

John and Elizabeth's known children are: Margaret md. Joshua Bayes; Serena; Jasper md. Mary Bayes; William md. Sarah Rhotten; George md. 1) ? and 2) Martha Lemaster; James md. Jemima Pack; Marvel md. Elizabeth Wheeler; Nancy md. Louis Salyer; Emeline md. James Lemaster; Minerva md. William Lemaster; Mary md. John Borders; and there may have been other children.

Elizabeth died March 1890 and John died December 1895. Both are buried in the old Slone Cemetery and have large stones. John also has a Civil War marker.

On Jul. 19, 1869, John's son, Marvel (born 1847), married Elizabeth Wheeler (born 1852). She was the daughter of William and Elizabeth Borders Wheeler. Their children were: Mary (born and died 1870), Amanda (born 1871) married Charles Fitzpatrick, Isaac (born 1872) married Alice Pennington, Margaret (born 1874) married Guy Dixon, Daniel (born 1875) married 1) Laura Castle and 2) Jemima Castle, Minerva (born 1876) married Charlie Ross, William (born 1877) married Pearl Pack, Lucina (born 1878, died 1884), John (born 1879) married Mary Ross, James Monroe (born 1880) married 1) Minnie Sparks and 2) Jane McKenzie, Marion (born 1881) married Alice Bryant, Genora (born 1882) married Biram Daniels, Cynthia (born 1884) married Jay Adams, Rosamond (born 1885) married Franklin Craft, Proctor (born 1887) married Laura Harris and Virgie (born 1888, died 1890).

Marvel and Elizabeth's son, James Monroe, married 1) Minnie Sparks, daughter of William and Martha Salyers Sparks. Their children were: Virgil (born 1901) married Augusta Slone, Marion (born 1903) married Ruie Conley, Lola (born 1905) married Hobart McKenzie, Amanda (born 1907) married Irvin Castle and Evan (born and died 1911).

After Minnie died in 1913, James Monroe married Jane McKenzie. Their children were: Clarice (born 1915) married James Pelhprey, Clarence (born 1917) married Dorothy Stambaugh, Reginald (born 1919) married Ruby Fairchild, James (born 1926) married Nancy Rice and Bobbie Jean (born and died 1928).

J.M. Slone operated a saddle, harness and shoe repair shop in Paintsville for many years. He was well known for his saddles and other leather work.

Isaac Slone was the jailer in Paintsville around 1920.

William Slone operated the produce house in Paintsville.

William's son, Darwin, was one of the doctors at the Golden Rule Hospital. *By Jean Slone McCarty.*

SPARKS - Jesse Sparks was born Nov. 26, 1875, the son of William Sparks and Martha Salyer, of Upper Frank's Creek (now Sparks Branch) near Flat Gap, Johnson County, KY. Jesse married Jemima Ellen Lemaster on Aug. 7, 1895, in Johnson County, KY, at J.M. Lemaster's. Ellen was the daughter of James Monroe Lemaster and Martha Slone of Johnson County, KY. Ellen died Mar. 26, 1952, and is buried next to Jesse in the Sparks Cemetery on Sparks Branch. Jesse was found dead, setting up against the corner store in Flat Gap on Dec. 25, 1936.

Edward Frazier, Amanda (Pennington) Frazier and daughter Allie. Other unknown.

Jesse and Ellen had six children: Elizabeth, Tera, Ethel, Elva, William Logan and Ova Jay.

Elizabeth Sparks died young and single.

Tera Sparks (born 1896, died 1957) is buried in the Lemaster Cemetery, on Frank's Creek alongside her husband, Jerry Cordial. Tera and Jerry turned the Upper Frank's Creek Schoolhouse into a dwelling and lived there for a while.

Ethel Sparks (born December 1899) married Elzie Murray, son of Henry Murray and Samantha Sparks. Ethel and Elzie lived in Delaware County, OH, where they are buried in the Sunbury Memorial Gardens.

William Logan Sparks (born about 1907) married Ema Murray. William Logan was beat to death with a sled standard on Puncheon Fork and Ema remarried to Harry Sparks.

Ova Jay Sparks (born Jul. 29, 1913) married Lucille Colvin. Ova was killed in a mining accident on Puncheon Fork Aug. 14, 1967.

Elva Sparks was born Dec. 9, 1903, and died Oct. 25, 1974. Elva married Feb. 2, 1924, in Paintsville, Tera McKenzie (born Apr. 20, 1906, died Nov. 11, 1986), the daughter of Thomas Jefferson McKenzie and Cora Ellen Salyer. Elva farmed for his cousin, Oak Sparks, on the over 600 acres which later became the Paintsville Lake dam site and history village, at Barnetts Creek. Elva and Tera had five children.

Herman Howard Sparks (born Dec. 16, 1924, Flat Gap, died Mar. 18, 1982, Knox County, OH) married first, Imogene Preston and had a son, William Charles Sparks. He married second, Sylvia Frances Ramey (born Sep. 11, 1931, on Ramey Branch, Lawrence County, KY), daughter of James Isaac Ramey and Cassie Lettie Davis. Herman and Sylvia had three girls: Mary Kathleen md. Carl Eugene Goodyear, Margie Annette md. Jack Lusby and Bonnie Elaine md. Paul Armstrong.

Elwanda Sparks (born Jun. 30, 1926) married first, William Clayton and second, Ralph Holland and had the following children: Margaret Stapleton, Tim Clayton, Brenda Clayton and William Clayton.

Mervin Elwood Sparks (born Sep. 11, 1934, died Sep. 16, 1934).

Jesse Thomas Sparks (born Mar. 20, 1936, died Mar. 23, 1936).

Magdalene Sparks (born May 28, 1938) married Bradley Burton. *By Mary K. Goodyear.*

SPARKS & HITCHCOCK - Phyllis Jean Hitchcock-Sparks is the daughter of Mary M. Young and Thurman Hitchcock. She was born Jul. 21, 1957, in Johnson County. Phyllis was born in a car on the highway in Paintsville, KY, called "The Harry Davis Curve." Times were always rough and money was hard to come by in Kentucky. After being turned away from the Paintsville Hospital for lack of insurance and money, they were on their way to Thurman's mother's house when her fourth child was delivered in the car by Mary herself. Mary is the daughter of Rosie Thornsberry and Otto Young. Her father, Thurman, is the son of Jennie Ward and General Grant Hitchcock, all of which were born in Johnson County, KY. She lived on Daniels Creek where she went to school in a one room school house taught by Mrs. Hopskin and Van Lear where she went to school for a short time at the Van Lear Elementary School until the family moved to Columbus, OH. Phyllis has two children.

Christopher V. Sparks and Phyllis Sparks

Phyllis married Christopher V. Sparks (born Oct. 31, 1954, in Marysville, OH), son of Elwanda Riggsby of Johnson County and Chester V. Sparks of Lawrence County, KY, on Nov. 4, 1972, in Dickenson County, VA. She moved to Columbus, OH, when she was 6 years old where she finished school and is now working for Southwestern City Schools. Christopher is the owner/operator in his trucking business. They now reside in Grove City, OH.

Children: 1) Tawana Lee (born Jun. 18, 1975, in Franklin, OH) married Johnny Leo Hopper Jun. 20, 1997. One child, Jeanna Lastarr Hopper (born Mar. 27, 1998). 2) Chrissy Lastarr (born Mar. 13, 1978, in Franklin County, OH) has one child, Christopher Thomas Douthitt (born Mar. 20, 1999).

Mary M. Young (born Oct. 16, 1933, in Johnson County) married Thurman Hitchcock Jun. 24, 1950, in Floyd County. Thurman was born Mar. 11, 1916, in Johnson County.Children as follows:

1) Diana (born Nov. 9, 1950, in Johnson County) married first, Larry Stout and second, Joseph Taynor III.

2) Ronald (born Feb. 2, 1953, in Johnson County) married Sheila Tillison.

3) Carol (born Feb. 28, 1955, in Johnson County, died Dec. 1, 1982, in Springfield, OH).

4) Phyllis (born Jul. 21, 1957, in Johnson County) married Christopher Sparks.

5) Michael (born Dec. 21, 1958, in Johnson County).

6) James (born Feb. 4, 1965, in Franklin County, OH) married Leia Hoffman and Sheila Dalgarn.

Elwanda, daughter of Ethel McKenzie and Watha Riggsby, and Chester Sparks, son of Hannah Ferguson and Mart Sparks of Lawrence County, KY, married Jun. 1, 1949, in Johnson County, KY.

Children: Watha (born Dec. 13, 1949, in Johnson County, KY) married Letha Adkins Oct. 9, 1970.

Chestina (born Mar. 3, 1952, in Johnson County, KY) married Raymond Stoops Sep. 27, 1968.

Danny (born Jul. 31, 1953, in Cols, OH).

Christopher (born Oct. 31, 1954, in Marysville, OH) married Phyllis Hitchcock Nov. 4, 1972.

Lisha (born Jul. 28, 1960, in Johnson County, KY) married Alfonzo McCoy, Jerry Dowell and Richard Hendershott.

SPARKS - Ronald Keith Sparks was born Sep. 4, 1937, in Johnson County, KY, to Charles Richard "Dickie" Sparks and Delores Jean Meek. He was the second born of four children, the only son.

Ronald lived a few years in Thealka, KY, while his father worked for the North East Coal Co. Before starting his school years, his parents moved to Paintsville, on Preston Street. He went to Paintsville grade school. In his second year of high school, he left school and joined the USAF. In the meantime Ronald's parents moved from Paintsville, KY, to Marion County, OH, where his mother passed away.

Ronald met a young lady in Marion County in 1957. His mother worked with her at Murphy's Dept. Store. Her name was Sharon Lee Huntsman. Ronald and Sharon were married Dec. 14, 1958, at New Bloomington, OH, in Marion County. Of this union two sons were born, Richard Maurice Sparks (born Dec. 14, 1959, at Wright-Patterson Air Force Base, Dayton, OH) and Michael Keith Sparks (born Apr. 13, 1962, at Donaldson Air Force Base, Greenville, SC).

Ronald retired from the USAF, July 1975 after almost 21 years of service. He worked six years for Super X Drugs as an assistant manager. Then he went to work for Pinkerton Security and Investigations Service. He was with them until he retired in 1995.

Ronald is a member of the LaRue Baptist Church in his hometown of LaRue, OH. He is also a member of American Legion Post 101 in LaRue. He and Sharon are avid campers and love spending as much time with their grandchildren as possible. Ronald also loves to work on his genealogy.

Ronald's parents were natives of Johnson County, KY, as were his grandparents, Fred Sparks and Sarah Castle. Fred's parents were Nelson Sparks and Calista Ward. Nelson's parents were William Jayne Sparks and Elizabeth Hager, they came to Johnson County from Greenup County in the mid 1850s.

SPARKS - Solomon Sparks was born in 1866 in Kentucky. He died 1909. He was buried in the Hay-Sparks Cemetery in Lawrence County, Martha, KY.

Solomon Sparks and Nancy Ann Hay

He was married to Nancy Ann Hay, daughter of John J. Hay and Rebecca Skaggs. Nancy was born May 15, 1869, in Lawrence County, KY. She died Jun. 18, 1947. She was buried in the Hay-Sparks Cemetery.

Solomon's father was Solomon Sr. His mother was Phebe Sparks.

Solomon and Nancy's children are: Martha Manda Sparks, Rebecca Emeline Sparks, John Martin Sparks, William M. Sparks, James Frank Sparks, Noah

E. Sparks, Ulysses S. Sparks, Virgil L. Sparks, Emory A. Sparks and George W. Sparks.

SPRADLIN - *no bio submitted, photos only.*

Hamilton Spradlin, mail carrier.

Rev. James Spradlin

STAGGS & BUTCHER - Sheila R. (Butcher) Staggs was born Sep. 3, 1965, in Johnson County. She was the third child of Patsy (May) Butcher (born Jan. 12, 1944, in Johnson County) and Gene Arthur Butcher (born Oct. 1, 1942, in Johnson County).

Sheila's parents met when her mother, Patsy May, came from Jennys Creek to Daniels Creek to care for her great aunt who had had a stroke. Sheila's father, Gene's family, were neighbors of Patsy's great aunt. They began dating soon after meeting and continued to date for over a year. They were married Jun. 23, 1962, and resided on Daniels Creek in Johnson County, KY.

Sheila (Butcher) Staggs

Sheila's father was employed with the railroad in Ohio and Michigan for a time. For many years he worked for Paintsville Heating and Roofing Co. in Paintsville, KY. Sheila's mother was a homemaker for several years before she took a position with the U.S. Shoe Corp. in Floyd County, KY.

Sheila had two sisters and one brother.

Sherrie Lynn (Butcher) Anderson (born Apr. 28, 1963, in Johnson County) currently resides in Baldwin, MI, and is employed by the Baldwin School System.

Ricky Eugene Butcher (born Sep. 23, 1964, in Johnson County, where he is currently living) is employed by East Kentucky Hydro Seeding Co.

Vonda Lois (Butcher) Stidham (born Sep. 14, 1966, in Johnson County, where she currently resides).

Sheila lived in the Daniels Creek area of Johnson County until she moved to Cincinnati, OH, in 1996. Some of the most memorable events in Sheila's life were the family trips taken each year to many different states. She attended Porter Elementary School and graduated from Johnson Central High School in 1983. Later she attended Mayo State Vocational School. She was employed by Dr. Jerry Fraim in Paintsville, KY, until she moved to Cincinnati, OH, where she is currently employed by DA-Lite Screen Co., Inc.

She married Terry Lee Staggs, Dec. 23, 1997. Terry was born Feb. 15, 1961, in Cincinnati, OH, to Marvin Staggs and Shirley (Cramer) Porter. He is an employee of Time Warner Inc.

Sheila has three children: Brandon Morrison (born Mar. 18, 1985), Krystle Morrison (born Jan. 5, 1988) and Ashlie Morrison (born Sep. 13, 1992).

STAPLETON & TRIMBLE - Manasseh Stapleton was born Mar. 5, 1882, and died Oct. 17, 1947. He was the son of the late John and Sara Stapleton of Red Bush, KY. He was a farmer and he married Julia E. Trimble.

Julia E. Trimble Stapleton was born Mar. 19, 1879, and died Feb. 11, 1957. She was the daughter of the late William and Cynthia Reed Trimble. She was a homemaker.

Mannaseh and Julia Trimble Stapleton

They resided at Fuget, KY. They had five children: (1) Gracie J. Stapleton Cantrell (born 1902, died 1959), (2) Versie L. Stapleton McKenzie (born 1905, died 1982), (3) William Alvie Stapleton (born 1910, died 1995), (4) Iva Stapleton Witten (born 1913) and (5) Dennis Hager Stapleton (born 1917). Four of their children moved to Michigan where their families reside today. William remained in Kentucky.

They are buried in the Patty Flat Cemetery in Johnson County.

STAPLETON & DAVIS - Tera Ethel Davis Stapleton was born Nov. 4, 1913, to the late Trinvilla Pack (born 1878, died 1959) and M.A. Davis (born 1894, died 1940) of Davisville, KY. She was the 13th child of 17 children. Her mother was a homemaker and her father was the local storekeeper and post master at Davisville.

Growing up at Davisville, she attended an one-room school and she eventually graduated from Flat Gap High School in 1932. She attended Morehead State Teachers' College and the University of Kentucky. She taught in an one-room school for nine years before becoming a full-time homemaker. Many former pupils called her a "natural born" teacher. Her love of children and learning were evident throughout her life.

Tera Ethel Davis Stapleton

She married William Alvie Stapleton of Fuget, KY, Nov. 17, 1934. They lived at Carrollton, KY, for a short period before returning to Johnson County where they resided at Staffordsville. They later moved to Richmond, KY (1967), where he had accepted a new position at Eastern Kentucky University.

They had two children (twins), Diana Lynn and David Lee, who were born Sep. 30, 1946, at the Golden Rule Hospital, Paintsville, KY.

She loved to write poetry. She was active with various poetry societies. The subjects of many of her poems reflected her upbringing and adult life. She won many awards for her poetry on the local, regional and state levels.

As a member of the First Baptist Church, she taught Sunday school while living in Johnson County. As a member of the First Baptist Church in Richmond, KY, she was very active in the Women's Missionary Union.

She resided in Richmond, KY, with her family until her death of heart disease and diabetes Mar. 24, 1983. She was buried in the Richmond Cemetery, Richmond, KY.

STAPLETON - William Alvie Stapleton was born Jul. 14, 1910, at Fuget, KY, to the late Julia Trimble (born 1879, died 1957) and Mannaseh Stapleton (born 1882, died 1947). He was the third child of five children. His mother was a homemaker and his father was a farmer.

He attended one-room schools in Johnson and Morgan counties, often riding his mule to get there. After graduating from Flat Gap High School in 1932, he attended Morehead State Teachers' College and graduated from the University of Kentucky (1941) with a degree in vocational agriculture. He also did postgraduate work at Morehead.

William Alvie Stapleton

He married Tera Ethel Davis, daughter of the late Trinvilla Pack and M.A. Davis of Davisville, KY, Nov. 17, 1934. They had twins, Diana Lynn and David Lee, who were born Sep. 30, 1946, at the Golden Rule Hospital, Paintsville, KY.

They resided at Carrollton, KY, for a short period before returning to Johnson County. They resided for many years at Staffordsville near the Barnetts Creek Bridge before moving to Richmond, KY, in 1967 where he had accepted a position at Eastern Kentucky University.

As an educator, he served as a vocational agriculture teacher, sponsor of the Oil Springs Chapter of the Future Farmers of America Chapter and a principal. He served as superintendent of Johnson County Schools from 1957-67. He served as Bursar at Eastern Kentucky University from 1967-77.

He had been active in various teachers' organizations and served as president of the Eastern Kentucky Education Association. Even upon retirement in 1967, he remained active with educational issues by being involved with the Kentucky Retired Teachers' Association on the local, district and state levels.

On the community level, he was a member of the Kiwanis Club and was a 50 year member of the Masonic Lodge #381, Paintsville, KY.

He successfully pioneered some broad and far-sighted community projects for Johnson County that were not included in his regular duties and activities as a vocational agriculture teacher. Under his leadership, programs concerning forestry, soil conservation, water resources and land reclamation were initiated and nurtured. He was responsible for the organization of the Johnson County Soil Conservation Dist.

He loved people; he never met a stranger. This quality was reflected throughout his educational career and community activities. Even when he moved away from Johnson County, he still had the people of Johnson County at heart.

In appreciation for many years of faithful service, the Oil Springs Future Farmers of America alumni paid a special tribute to Mr. Stapleton by honoring him at an Oil Springs School Reunion in the early 1990s. The special plaque presented to him stated: "The Steps of a Good Man Are Ordered of the Lord."

He resided in Richmond, KY, with his daughter until his death, due to complications of heart disease, May 3, 1995. He was buried in the Richmond Cemetery, Richmond, KY.

STIDHAM & BUTCHER - Vonda Lois (Butcher) Stidham was born Sep. 14, 1966, in Johnson County, the youngest of four children born to Gene Arthur Butcher and Patsy Lois (May) Butcher. Her father, Gene Arthur Butcher, was born Oct. 1, 1942, in Johnson County. Her mother, Patsy Lois (May) Butcher, was born Jan. 12, 1944, in Johnson County, also.

Vonda's parents, Gene and Patsy Butcher, met in 1960 and dated until they were united in marriage Jun. 23, 1962. They reside at Daniels Creek in Johnson County, KY.

Vonda's father was employed with the railroad in Ohio and Michigan for a time. For many years he worked for Paintsville Heating and Roofing Co. Her mother was a homemaker and then worked for many years at the U.S. Shoe Corp. in Floyd County, KY.

Vonda has two sisters and one brother: Sherrie Lynn (Butcher) Anderson (born in Johnson County, KY, Apr. 28, 1963) currently resides in Baldwin, MI, and is employed by the Baldwin School System.

Ricky Eugene Butcher (born in Johnson County, Sep. 23, 1964) currently lives at Hager Hill, KY, with his wife, Sandy (Hannah) Butcher, and two children, and is employed by East Kentucky Hydro Seeding Co.

Sheila Rose (Butcher) Staggs (born in Johnson County, Sep. 3, 1965) currently resides in Mason, OH, and is employed by DA-Lite Screen Co.

Vonda currently resides on Daniels Creek in Johnson County, KY. She lived in Michigan during 1985-87. She attended Porter Elementary School at Hager Hill and Johnson Central High School in Paintsville, where she was in the graduating class of 1984.

She was united in marriage to Victor Lee Stidham at Paintsville, KY, Sep. 4, 1985. Victor was born Apr. 11, 1962, in Lagrange, IN, to Russell Stidham and Birdie (Shepard) Stidham. Vic is a certified welder and is presently employed by Little River Pipeline Co. in Virginia. He spent many years working for Eastern Kentucky Pipeline Co., also as a welder.

Vonda and Victor Stidham have two living children and one deceased child: Heather Nichole Stidham (born in Johnson County, Apr. 23, 1989); Tiffany Dawn Stidham (born in Floyd County, Mar. 24, 1997); and Chad Lee Stidham (born Jun. 17, 1993, in Huntington, WV, passed away Jun. 21, 1993). He was buried in the Gene Butcher Cemetery on Daniels Creek in Johnson County, KY.

TAYLOR - This heritage began with the birth of Bascom Taylor (born Nov. 10, 1886) and Jenettia Robinson (born Apr. 28, 1895). They were married Aug. 16, 1911 and to this union six children were born: Baby Taylor (deceased), Molly, Earl, Mabel, Recettia and Curtis.

Bascom and Jenettia Taylor

Mollie (born 1912) married Darley Caudill Dec. 21, 1934. They had seven children: Baby Caudill (deceased), Lee Edward, Billy Ray, Glen Richard, James Russell, Dan Alvin and Brenda.

Lee Edward married Marlene and had two children, Deborah and James Edward and four grandchildren. He is now married to Rudy.

Billy Ray married Georgene and had seven children: Michael, Kathy, Billie, Anita Sue, Nancy Lynn, Toni and Melissa, and nine grandchildren. Billy Ray is deceased.

Glen Richard has two sons, Brian and John. He is married to Kathy.

Dan Alvin is deceased.

James Russell had one daughter, Leighann, and one grandchild. He is married to Lola.

Brenda married Steve Crossman and has three children: Jonathan and twin girls, Danielle and Meghan. Millie died in March 1968.

Earl was born in 1914 and married Donna. They have two daughters, Debbie and Donna. Debbie has one son, James Jacob "J.J." Donna has two children, Natosha and Miranda.

Mable was born in 1916 and married Eperson Daniel Dec. 15, 1934. They had five girls: Maryetta, Nancy, Ruth, Janice and Phyllis. Maryetta married Elmer Sebastian. They have four children: Dwayne, Patti Goffe, Karen Lightfield and Beth Koonce. They have 11 grandchildren.

Nancy married George Littrell and they have one daughter, Kim Wilson, and two grandchildren.

Ruth married Richard Pressnell and they had two daughters, Melody and Machell. She has one grandson. Richard is now deceased and Ruth is married to Ernie Preston.

Janice married Joe Barnett and they had one son, Daniel Allen. She has two grandchildren. Janice was married to Paul Stir who is now deceased.

Phyllis married Jerry Cochram and they have two children, Roger and Linda Tyree, and two grandchildren.

Mabel later married Rufus Crutcher. She died in December 1967.

Recettia was born in 1918 and married Theodore "Jack" Daniel Jun. 6, 1936. They had six children: Baby Daniel (deceased), Beatrice Joylene, Paul Dencil, Roger Dean, Theodore Darrel and Connie.

Bea married Hubert Collins. Paul married Cathy and they had one daughter, Lisa. Roger married Phyllis; Ted married Janet and they have twin boys, Andrew Theodore and Benjamin Elliott. Connie married Mike Cook and they have one daughter, Leslie Ann.

Curtis (born 1923) married Gay on Apr. 28, 1945. They have one daughter, Ellen. Ellen married Bill and they have children, Rachael and Richard.

TITLOW - William Bernard "Bill" Titlow was born in 1911 at Charleston, WV. He was the son of Jacob Titlow (born 1877, Pennsylvania) and Lennie B. Waugh (born 1886, Straight Creek, Carter County, KY).

Wm. "Bill" was a miner and worked for the Princess Elkhorn Coal Co. at David, KY. He married Amma Robinson, daughter of Thomas Robinson and Arminta Goble. William "Bill" and Amma had three sons:

William B. "Billy" married Gloria Kipps. Children, Lisa and Corinne.

Douglas M. "Mickey" married Esther J. Richmond. Children, William B. "Wil" and Michael D. "Mike."

Richard D. married first, Connie Black and married second, Chris Ramey. Child, Adam J.

William "Bill" Titlow and Amma Robinson Titlow, 1941.

Wm. "Bill" and Amma were residents of West Van Lear until his death in a mine accident at David, KY, July 1967.

William's father, Jacob, moved from Pennsylvania to Charleston, WV, and married Lennie Waugh, who is possibly the daughter of John Waugh. Lennie's mother was a Belieu, first name not known. The family moved to Franks Creek at Flat Gap, KY, and were living there in 1944 when Lennie died. Jacob moved to West Van Lear, KY, to live with his son, John, and died there in 1951. The children of Jacob and Lennie B. Waugh Titlow are: Gus, William B., Lillian, John, Evelyn, Sue, Vida, Charles, Harry and Mary Opal.

Amma Robinson was for many years a nurse at the Paintsville Hospital and is now retired and lives at West Van Lear, KY. Amma's father, Thomas Robinson, was born Jan. 10, 1879, and died Mar. 31, 1956, at West Van Lear. Amma's mother, Arminta Goble, was born Dec. 25, 1879, in Johnson County, and died in 1972 at West Van Lear. Arminta's parents were Lucinda Baldridge (born June 1846, Floyd County) who in July 1870, Johnson County, married Comodore Goble (born May 1849, Washington County, VA). Comodore was the son of Mary Jane Perry (born May 1825, in Tennessee) and John M. Goble (born February 1821, in Virginia), who were married Sep. 11, 1845. John died between 1900 and 1901. John's parents were Elizabeth Music and Isaac Gobble (name later became Goble). Isaac's parents were Elizabeth Linder and George Gobble.

Lucinda Baldridge was the daughter of Nancy Emeline Gillespie (born 1825, Virginia), second wife of William Baldridge Jr. (born about 1795, North Carolina). Nancy and William were married Mar. 23, 1843, Pike County, KY. Nancy's parents were William Gillespie and Mary (?Arnett).

The children of Thomas Robinson and Arminta Goble Robinson are: Jim, Manche, Amma, Ollie, Manda, Elizabeth, Tom, Curtis and Oakie.

TRIMBLE - Billie Jean Trimble Newman was born Nov. 3, 1931, to James H. and Lillie Beecher Roberts Trimble in Paintsville, KY. She had one sister, Ernestine Trimble (born Dec. 16, 1932), who married Donald B. Trimble.

The summer before she was to start school she was very ill and her parents did not send her to school until the next year when her sister was ready. Uniquely, they went all through school together and graduated from Paintsville High School in 1950, as co-salutatorians. Both then attended Mayo State Vocational School in the business department. Billie Jean worked at First Federal Savings and Loan Association and Ernestine was secretary at Paintsville City School.

Billie Jean met Earl B. Newman from McDowell, KY, while they were both attending Mayo State Vocational School. They were married Feb. 25, 1956, at the First Baptist Church of Paintsville, where she had been an active member since 1944. At that time, he was employed by Big Sandy Motor Co. in the body shop. In September 1956, he started working for Ashland Oil, Inc., holding various positions for the next 38 years.

Their daughter, Anita Earle, was born Dec. 4, 1959, and son, Gregory Cliff, was born Jan. 4, 1962, in Paintsville.

In January 1968, Earl was transferred to Mansfield, OH, where he later became division superintendent until 1984.

Anita and Greg graduated from Ontario High School in 1977 and 1980, respectively.

In 1982, Anita graduated from Bowling Green State University, Bowling Green, OH, with a double major in elementary education and learning disabilities. She went job hunting in the Tampa, FL, area and since then has been employed by the Hillsboro County Board of Education. She was first a teacher, but after receiving her master's in educational administration, is now a principal in Plant City, FL.

On Jul. 2, 1983, she married Edward F. Mason, from Ottawa, OH, whom she met while attending college. He graduated from the University of Southern Florida, and is a high school drama teacher in Brandon. They live in Valrico and have one daughter, Mara Elaine (born Jul. 18, 1988).

Greg attended the Mansfield Branch of Ohio State University and North Central Technical College before starting to work for Ashland Oil, Inc., in May 1983, in Owensboro, KY. On Aug. 13, 1983, he married Carla Jean Craze, his high school sweetheart, who was a graduate of North Central Technical College secretarial department. In November 1984, he was transferred back to Mansfield where he still works. Carla is a legal secretary/office manager for a local law firm.

On Aug. 5, 1985, Breinn Elyse was born and on Jul. 30, 1987, Bryan Gregory was born.

In January 1984, Earl was transferred as division superintendent to Ferriday, LA, and they lived in Natchez, MS, until early 1989, when he took early retirement, moving back to Mansfield. The retirement lasted less than a year, when he was asked to come back to work and go to Owensboro, KY, where he worked until retiring again in 1993.

They started spending their winters in Florida at that time, and in 1995, bought a condo in Daytona

Beach Shores, FL, on the beach, where they spend most of their time, except a few months in the summer back in Mansfield. They always have, and still do, enjoy boating wherever they happen to be.

TRIMBLE - Carless D. Trimble was born Mar. 11, 1870, in Johnson County, KY, to John Garfield and Matilda Van Hoose Trimble. Carless died Oct. 29, 1919, in Montgomery County but his body was returned to Johnson County for burial in the old Trimble family cemetery on Pickle Fork.

L-R: John Trimble (son of Carl), Mae Trimble (daughter of Carl), John Hall (husband of Mae), Minnie McCoy Trimble (wife of John), Laura Picklesimer Trimble (wife of Carl) and Laura Trimble Pelphrey (wife of Deal).

He married Laura Alee Picklesimer, daughter of Nathaniel and Mahala Conley Picklesimer. Laura was born Nov. 11, 1890, in Johnson County and died Jul. 27, 1961, in Indianapolis, IN.

After the birth of their fourth child, Carl and Laura moved from Johnson County to Mt. Sterling in Montgomery County, KY.

In 1929, Laura and several of her children moved to Indianapolis where she is buried.

Carless, known as Carl to his family and friends, was a farmer and livestock dealer and often traveled around the county buying and trading cattle and then selling the cattle at market.

Carl and Laura had the following children:

Iva (born May 14, 1892, died around 1970) married Ernest Hall (born Nov. 5, 1892).

Ova (born Nov. 3, 1893, died around 1979) married Arthur Welch (born Aug. 4, 1894, died Aug. 31, 1965).

Mae (born Apr. 12, 1898, died Mar. 17, 1993, in Indianapolis, IN) married John Hall.

John (born Jan. 6, 1900, died around 1975) married Minnie McCoy.

Carroll (born Dec. 8, 1906, died Apr. 7, 1983) married Bertha Centers.

Grace (born Feb. 22, 1909, died Dec. 7, 1969) married Sheldon Pattison.

Rucker Jim (born Apr. 22, 1911, died Oct. 14, 1986) married Iva Centers Apr. 15, 1933. Iva was born Aug. 23, 1914, and died Oct. 20, 1984. Iva attended high school at the Winchester Academy, a Church of God school in Winchester, KY. She played basketball and was called "Dimples" while she attended school there.

Paris Nelson (born Dec. 5, 1913, in Montgomery County, died Jan. 3, 1998, in Bloomington, IN) married Olive Davis Sparks Mar. 25, 1939, in Louisville, KY. Olive was born Jul. 14, 1917, and died Nov. 8, 1998, in Bloomington, IN.

Sterling Sid Hart (born Nov. 18, 1916, died Nov. 10, 1983) married first, Alice Marie Parker. They had six children. He married second, Barbara Jean Davis and they had one child.

TRIMBLE & PATTON - David Lawrence Trimble and Kimberly Patton Trimble were married at the First United Methodist Church in Paintsville, KY, May 12, 1988.

David was born in Paintsville, Johnson County, KY, Jun. 19, 1960, the third of four children of John Mark and Janet Louise Marsh Trimble. He has one sister, Ann Wade Trimble Wallen (born 1958) and two brothers, Mark Wesley Trimble (born 1956) and Phillip Lee Trimble (born 1962).

David graduated from Paintsville High School in 1978 and from the University of Kentucky in 1982 with a bachelor's degree in business administration.

Kimberly Dawn Patton Trimble was born in Pikeville, Pike County, KY, May 29, 1964, the only child of Donald Patton and Billie Earleen May Patton.

Kimberly graduated from Allen Central High School in 1982.

David and Kim have two children, Benjamin Donald Trimble (born 1982) and Lauren Alexandria Trimble (born 1990).

David and Kim, and their family, currently reside in Paintsville, KY, where both are part owners of Computers Plus, Inc. a computer service business. Prior to working with Computers Plus, Inc. David was employed by Citizens National Bank of Paintsville as a consumer lending officer and Kimberly was employed by Underwriters Safety and Claims of Paintsville as a claims adjuster.

In addition to their careers at Computers Plus, Inc., David and Kim are members of the First United Methodist Church in Paintsville, KY, and actively involved in Paintsville City School activities. David is a current member of the Paintsville City Council where he is serving his third term in that office. David is a past member and past president of the Paintsville Kiwanis Club. Kimberly is actively involved in the Paintsville PTO where she has served as vice-president and currently serves as treasurer.

TRIMBLE - Ernestine Trimble was born Dec. 16, 1932, in Paintsville, KY, to James H. and Lillie Beecher Roberts Trimble. Her sister, Billie Jean Trimble Newman, was born Nov. 3, 1931. Both sisters graduated as co-salutatorians from Paintsville High School Class of 1950 and they were both active members of the First Baptist Church of Paintsville.

Ernestine lived in Paintsville for 23 years until her marriage in Lexington, to Donald Bert Trimble of Oil Springs, on Jan. 27, 1956. After graduating from Paintsville High School in 1950, she graduated from Mayo State Vocational School business department in August 1951, and worked as secretary-treasurer of the Paintsville City Schools until her marriage.

Donald B. and Ernestine Trimble

Her husband, Donald B. Trimble was born Jan. 11, 1930, at Barnetts Creek, KY, to Newton and Ethel Rice Trimble, the youngest of three sons. His brothers were Leon Franklin Trimble (married Joan Wheeler Trimble) and Nevin Rice Trimble (married Mildred Ashley Trimble). A sister, Charlene Trimble, died in infancy. Donald's mother died when he was 10 months old, and he was reared at Oil Springs, KY, by his grandparents Dr. Grant and Lou Sina Caudill Rice. His father, Newton, married Mary Elizabeth West, and they had three daughters: Joyce Ann Trimble Ross, Doris Jean Trimble Ball and Elma Carol Trimble Williams.

Charles Brian, Donna Jeanne Kelsey, Michelle and Kristin Nicole Cook.

Donald graduated from Oil Springs High School in the class of 1948. He was in the U.S. Army during the Korean Conflict from 1951-53, stationed in Korea. After their marriage, he and Ernestine lived in Lexington, until he graduated from the University of Kentucky in 1957. Then, they moved to Chillicothe, OH. They were parents of two children, Donna Jeanne Trimble Cook (born Apr. 21, 1961) graduated from Union Scioto High School, Chillicothe, OH, in the class of 1979, and from Ohio University, Athens, OH, in the class of 1983, with a business degree with an emphasis in accounting and certification as a secondary education teacher. She is the budget analyst at the Veterans Affairs Medical Center, Chillicothe, OH, where she has worked for 15 years. She was married Jun. 7, 1986, to Charles Brian Cook, also a 1979 graduate of Union Scioto High School, who graduated from Ohio State University, Columbus, OH, with a master's degree in agriculture. Charles works at Thomson Consumer Electronics, Circleville, OH, and is also a farmer. They have two daughters, Kelsey Michelle (born Apr. 25, 1992) and Kristen Nicole (born Dec. 11, 1995). Dean Alan Trimble (born Oct. 3, 1964, died Oct. 5, 1964) was buried at Highland Memorial Park in Staffordsville, KY, next to his maternal grandparents, Jim and Beecher Trimble.

Donald Trimble was a corrective therapist at the Veterans Affairs Medical Center in Chillicothe, OH, for 31 years, retiring in 1988. He died May 6, 1993, after a brief illness following surgery and was buried in Rowland Memorial Cemetery in Chillicothe, OH.

Ernestine has worked for 25 years at Chivaho Federal Credit Union at the VA Medical Center, Chillicothe, where she is still employed as a loan officer. She is an active member of the Chillicothe Baptist Church.

TRIMBLE - James H. "Jim" Trimble was born Sep. 23, 1989, to Sherman and Margaret Shellie Williams Trimble. Jim was not an orphan boy, as stated in an old Johnson County History Book. His father was born Sherman Trimble Ramey to Taylor and Susan Trimble Ramey. At the death of his mother, Sherman was reared by his Trimble grandparents, James and Susan Tackett Trimble, therefore, he went by the name of Trimble, instead of Ramey. Sherman Trimble served, 1914-18, as Johnson County jailer. Jim was the oldest of four children. Moncie married Vint Davis, Birdie married Hervie Stambaugh and Doris Trimble married Maxie Stapleton.

Jim was married to Lillie Beecher Roberts Trimble Aug. 6, 1921, in Johnson County. She was born in Johnson County to Hiram and Tallahassee Stafford Roberts on Dec. 6, 1890, and was the oldest of nine children: James Espa Roberts, Sherman R. and Clarence Coy Roberts, who died in infancy, William Everett "Judge" Roberts, Marvin Roberts, Sheila Roberts, who died at age 17, Gladys Roberts Kennard and Lucille Roberts Johnson. Beecher was first married at age 16 to Norris Williams, who died in a train accident in Jenkins, KY, while working for the railroad. They were married for 10 years.

James H. and Lillie Beecher Trimble

Jim and Beecher were the parents of two daughters, Billie Jean Trimble Newman and Ernestine Trimble. Billie Jean was born Nov. 3, 1931, and married Earl B. Newman of McDowell (Floyd County), KY, on Feb. 25, 1956. Ernestine was born Dec. 16, 1932, and married Donald Bert Trimble of Oil Springs, on Jan. 27, 1956.

They had four grandchildren: Anita Earle Newman Mason, Gregory Cliff Newman, Donna Jeanne

Trimble Cook and Dean Alan Trimble (deceased); and five great-grandchildren: Breinn Elyse Newman, Bryan Gregory Newman, Mara Elaine Mason, Kelsey Michelle Cook and Kristen Nicole Cook.

Jim served in the U.S. Army in France during WWI, and was Johnson County coroner, 1950-62. He was employed many years at the Paintsville Funeral Home. Jim and Beecher were members of the Third Street Freewill Baptist Church. Jim died May 26, 1964, in Paintsville, and Beecher died Jul. 5, 1970, in Chillicothe, OH. They and their infant grandson, Dean Alan Trimble, are buried in Highland Memorial Cemetery at Staffordsville.

TRIMBLE - John Mark Trimble was born Jan. 7, 1854, in Johnson County, KY, to William Henry "Bill Dodger" Trimble and Clarinda Ellen Picklesimer. John Mark died Nov. 5, 1925.

He married Clarinda Francis Spradlin, daughter of William H. Spradlin and Mahala Conley, on Mar. 25, 1876, in Johnson County. Clarinda was born Apr. 8, 1860, and died May 25, 1941. John Mark and Clarinda had 15 children, all born in Johnson County: Mantford, Bertha, Della, Lindsey, Elzie, Dennis, Elmer, Mahala, Bruce, Daniel Boone, Harry, Shella, Winston "Wince," Quince and Clara.

John Mark and Clarinda Francis Spradlin Trimble, circa 1924, Barnetts Creek.

John Mark was in the general merchandise business on Barnetts Creek for 40 years. He was also a successful farmer, producing large amounts of honey and sorghum. At times he had 10 to 15 work hands employed and John Mark's wife, Clarinda, had to cook for all of them. During WWI, John Mark and Clarinda had six sons in the military at the same time, but they all returned safely. In the last years of his life, he bought the George B. Rice farm at Hager Hill, where he lived at the time of his death.

John Mark and Clarinda raised a large, well-known, family and some of their descendants still live in Johnson County. Two of their children became sheriff of the county.

Their first child, Mantford, died as an infant.

Bertha married Crate Davis of Johnson County.

After Della's husband, Leonard Caudill, died in 1934, she married Arthur Hubbard.

Lindsey never married and died at the age of 31 from appendicitis.

Elzie Jack made a living as a soldier, a live stock dealer, a taxi driver, and, at times, in the real estate business. He was married seven times, but his longest marriage was to Oma Craft, who he married in 1914.

Dennis died when he was less than a year old.

After Elmer's first wife, Lillie Etta Picklesimer, died around 1910, he married Terra Barnett and lived near Jackson, OH, where he owned a jewelry store.

Mahala married Albert "Byrd" Preston.

Bruce, who married Norsie Reed, was the postmaster at Staffordsville for many years.

Boone, the sheriff of Johnson County from 1950-54, married Rosa LeMaster in 1924. After Rosa's death in 1945, Boone married Eula Patrick.

Harry, who married Bessie Lee Adams, worked for the Columbia Fuel and Gas Co. in Pikeville, KY.

Shella married Howard Sebastian Coldiron and lived in Westerville, OH.

John and Clarinda's son, Wince, became a well known Federal revenue agent, was a member of the fiscal court of Johnson County, and was very active for the improvement of the roads of the County. Additionally, Wince was elected and served from 1958-62 as sheriff of the County.

Quince worked for many years in the aircraft industry with North American Rockwell Corporation. Quince married Lessie LeMaster.

Clara was a gifted homemaker and made many beautiful knitted and sewn items. She married Sam Levy.

TRIMBLE & MARSH - John Mark Trimble and Janet Louise Marsh Trimble were married at the First United Methodist Church in Paintsville, KY, Feb. 10, 1956.

John Mark Trimble and Janet M. Trimble

John Mark was born in Barnetts Creek, Johnson County, KY, Jan. 10, 1927, the fourth of six children of Bruce C. Trimble and Norsie Ellen Reed Trimble. He has three brothers and two sisters: Davis Reed (born 1921), Granvil C. (born 1922, died 1997), Georgene Trimble McKenzie (born 1924), Paul Wade Trimble (born 1928) and Lorene Trimble Fraim Carney (born 1930).

John Mark graduated from Oil Springs High School in 1945. After graduation he joined the U.S. Army and was stationed from 1945-47 in the European Theater. On his return from service, he entered Morehead University where he was awarded a BA degree in January 1952.

Janet was born in Paintsville, Johnson County, KY, Jun. 12, 1927, the first of five children of Robert L. "Lee" Marsh and Dorothy Louise Geiger Marsh. She has three brothers and one sister: Robert Lee "Bob" Marsh (born 1932), Virginia Carolyn Marsh Williams Henry (born 1935), Franklin Hager Marsh (born 1936) and Larry Braxton Marsh (born 1939).

Janet graduated from Paintsville High School in 1945 and earned her BA degree from Berea College in 1949 majoring in psychology and English.

John Mark and Janet have four children: Mark Wesley (born Oct. 26, 1956), Ann Wade (born Aug. 1, 1958), David Lawrence (born Jun. 19, 1960) and Phillip Lee (born Jun. 11, 1962). Theirs is a very close-knit family with all of the children residing in Johnson County with the exception of Mark Wesley and his family who live in Huntington, WV.

John Mark and Janet are both very active in the First United Methodist Church in Paintsville where John Mark has been an usher for many years and Janet a tenor in the church choir. They have both chaired or been members of various committees in the church as well as in community organizations.

Since their marriage, John Mark and Janet have worked together in several joint self-employment ventures. Over the years they have owned and operated the Tiger Drive-In, the Family Store, the Credit Bureau of Paintsville, John Trimble Insurance Agency and Computers Plus, all located in Paintsville, KY.

In 1998 John Mark and Janet sold their interest in the computer store to two of their sons, David and Phillip, and an employee, Brett Higgins.

John Mark and Janet are now both retired and living at 108 Euclid Avenue in Paintsville.

TRIMBLE - Leon Franklin Trimble was born Sep. 8, 1921, in Oil Springs, KY, to Newton Trimble and Ethel Mae Rice. Leon was the oldest of three sons born to his parents, but also had three half-sisters born to step-mother, Mary Gartin. After his mother's death he resided with his grandparents, Dr. and Mrs. Grant Rice, and attended Oil Springs High School until he graduated in 1940. He received an electrical engineering degree from University of Kentucky, at Lexington, June 1948 and a degree in management science from Stevens Institute of Technology in Hoboken, NJ, in June 1965.

Joan and Leon Trimble, 50th anniversary, Mar. 13, 1994.

He was a fighter pilot, flying P-38s in the U.S. Army Air Force during WWII (assigned as aviation cadet to class 43G). He served in the Panama Canal Zone and Hawaii.

Leon was married in Johnson County, KY, to M. Joan Wheeler on Mar. 13, 1944, and they are parents of a daughter, Diana Lynn (born Sep. 22, 1951) and a son, Delbert Lee (born Jul. 11, 1957). Both born in Poughkeepsie, NY. Diana Lynn married Charles E. Kearns of Pennsylvania on Dec. 23, 1979, and a daughter, Krystle Lili Kearns was born Nov. 4, 1985, in Chico, CA. Delbert Lee was married to Penny Messer on Jul. 5, 1983, and has step-sons, Jonathan Scott Redwine and Anthony Todd Redwine. Delbert Lee received a degree from Miami University in Oxford, OH, and is an IRS agent in Cincinnati, OH. Leon's daughter, Diana Lynn, graduated from Dutchess County Community College in Poughkeepsie and at this time is a masseuse at Positive Touch, Chico, CA.

Joan Wheeler graduated from Oil Springs High School, class of 1942 and attended Mayo Vocational Business School, Paintsville, KY. During war time she worked as accountant for Paintsville Wholesale Grocery Co. in Kentucky, a civil service employee for Signal Corps in Dayton, OH, and Army Air Force employee in Clovis, NM. While Leon completed college she worked in the accounting department at the U.S. Public Health Service Hospital, Lexington, KY.

After college, Leon was employed as an electrical engineer for International Business Machines. He and Joan lived and worked in Cincinnati, OH, until a transfer to the Poughkeepsie/Hyde Park, NY, area in 1950. He was a manager at IBM for 38 years until retirement in 1986. When a student he was a member of the Ancient Mystic Order of Rosae Crucis. He was an avid golf and tennis player and attended the Hyde Park United Methodist Church. He was also active with Hyde Park Meals-on-Wheels program. Leon died of a heart attack Dec. 7, 1996. His body was flown to Columbus, OH, and interred in the Rowland Memorial Cemetery in Chillicothe, OH, where he is buried beside his brother, Donald B. Trimble.

TRIMBLE & ARMS - Mark Wesley Trimble and Teresa Arms Trimble were married at the First United Methodist Church in Paintsville, KY, Jun. 18, 1977.

Mark Wesley was born in Paintsville, Johnson County, KY, Oct. 26, 1956, the first of four children of John Mark and Janet Louise Marsh Trimble. He has one sister, Ann Wade Trimble Wallen (born 1958) and two brothers, David Lawrence Trimble (born 1960) and Phillip Lee Trimble (born 1960).

Mark graduated from Paintsville High School in 1974 and from the University of Kentucky in 1979 with a bachelor's degree in civil engineering.

Teresa Arms Trimble was born in Paintsville, Johnson County, KY, Jan. 6, 1957, the first of two children of Morris L. "Tony" and Helen Irene Blair Arms.

She has one sister, Toni Arms Fraley (born 1962).

Teresa graduated from Johnson Central High School in 1975.

Mark and Teresa have three children: Gina Michelle Trimble (born Jun. 24, 19__), Rachel Ann Trimble (born Jul. 10, 19__) and Mark Richard Trimble (born Jul. 23, 1986).

Mark and Teresa, and their family, currently reside in Huntington, WV, where both are employed at Huntington Steel, a regional steel supplier and fabricator. Prior to moving to Huntington, Mark and Teresa opened Mark W. Trimble Engineering, Inc. (1986) a Paintsville business providing consulting engineering and surveying services to the region. Mark W. Trimble Engineering, Inc. in partnership with Terry L. Simmons, Architects, of Lexington, KY, formed Simmons-Trimble Architectural/Engineering also provided architectural services to the region. Mark also served one term as Johnson County surveyor and was special advisor to the county judge-executive.

In addition to their careers at Huntington Steel, Mark and Teresa are actively involved in church and civic activities. Members of First United Methodist Church, Huntington, Mark, Teresa and their children are involved in the youth and choir programs of the church. Mark is a member of the West Virginia Society of Professional Engineers, Huntington, where he is a chapter officer, a member of the Kentucky Association of Professional Surveyors. Mark is licensed as a professional engineer in Kentucky, Ohio and West Virginia and as a land surveyor in Kentucky and West Virginia. Teresa is actively involved in the children's school activities, such as PTA and as a volunteer.

TRIMBLE - Newton "Newt" Trimble was born Nov. 5, 1897, at Barnetts Creek, KY, to William Henry and Sara Alice VanHoose Trimble. William was born Nov. 25, 1862, and died Sep. 13, 1941. Sara was born Mar. 14, 1860, and died Apr. 6, 1932. Newton's brothers and sisters were: Boe, Floyd, James V., Pierce, Thurman, Laura Trimble, Sudie Ealey. Newt died Mar. 12, 1965.

Newt was married two times, first to Ethel Mae Rice, daughter of Dr. Grant and Lou Sina Rice of Oil Springs, KY, on Oct. 9, 1920. Ethel was born Oct. 9, 1904, and died Nov. 28, 1930. She was buried in the Preston Cemetery at Barnetts Creek, KY. Dr. Rice was born Dec. 31, 1872, and died Apr. 18, 1970. Mrs. Rice was born Jun. 27, 1875, and died Mar. 17, 1957. They were married Nov. 19, 1897. Ethel's brothers and sister were: Wayne, Wade, Kelly, Eddie, Carl and Hazel (Mrs. Eschel) Rice.

Newton and Ethel Trimble and children in the 1920s.

Newt and Ethel's children were: Leon Franklin Trimble (married Joan Wheeler), Charlene Trimble died in infancy and was buried in the Preston Cemetery at Barnetts Creek, Nevin Rice Trimble (married Mildred Ashley) and Donald Bert Trimble (married Ernestine Trimble). Their grandchildren were: Diana Lynn Trimble (Charles) Kearns, Delbert Lee (Penny) Trimble, Teresa Lou Trimble, David Keith (Anna) Trimble, Donna Jeanne Trimble (Charles B.) Cook and Dean Alan Trimble (deceased). Their great-grandchildren were: Krystle Lili Kearns, Rebekah Anne, David Nevin and Hannah Noel Trimble, and Kelsey Michelle and Kristen Nicole Cook.

Leon Trimble died Dec. 7, 1996, in Hyde Park, NY; Nevin Rice Trimble died Aug. 18, 1980, in Dayton, OH; and Donald Bert Trimble died May 6, 1993, in Chillicothe, OH.

Newton and Mary Trimble

Newt was married the second time to Mary Elizabeth West, daughter of Enoch Spencer "Spencer" and Stella Patrick West, on Oct. 22, 1932. Mary was born Apr. 9, 1911, and died Oct. 27, 1999, at Morehead, KY. Spencer West was born Mar. 24, 1880, and died in 1958. Stella West was born Jul. 16, 1881, and died in May 1951. Mary's sister and brothers were: Rhoda Hay, Parker, Claude, Barton, Eddie, Lee, Noah and North West.

Newt and Mary's children were: Doris Jean (John) Ball, Joyce Ann Ross and Elma Carol (Homer) Williams. Their grandchildren were: Anita Gail Ball (Jeffrey) Hammond, Derri Lea Ball (Henderson) Hicks, Shela Rae Ball (Steve) Gilley, Lisa Renee Ball (David) Williamson, John Kyle Ball and Kelia Ann Ross (Gary) Hay. Their great-grandchildren were: Tina Marie Freeman, Sarah Beth Hammond, Lisa Renee Wells (Eddie) Lyons, Matthew and Stephanie Gilley, Emily Renee Williamson and Heather and Daniel Rupert. Their great-great-granddaughter was MacKenzie Nicole Wells.

Newt and Mary lived at Redbush, KY, and later moved to Blaine, KY, and lived there many years. They were members of Old Blaine United Baptist Church at Blaine. Newt retired from Ashland Oil after about 35 years of service.

Mary later married Luther Gartin of Blaine, in October 1967. Luther died Jan. 10, 1988. Mary, then lived with her daughter, Doris Jean Ball, in Flatwoods, KY, and for several years with her daughter, Joyce Ross, in Chillicothe, OH, and later, with her daughter, Carol Williams, in Morehead, KY. Newt and Mary were buried in the Louisa Cemetery at Louisa, KY.

TRIMBLE - Phillip Lee Trimble was born in Paintsville, Johnson County, KY, Jun. 11, 1962, the fourth of four children of John Mark and Janet Marsh Trimble. He has one sister, Ann Wade Trimble Wallen (born 1958) and two brothers, Mark Wesley Trimble (born 1956) and David Lawrence Trimble (born 1960).

Phillip graduated from Paintsville High School in May 1980. In September 1980 he enrolled at Prestonsburg Community College where he attended for three semesters. He then transferred to Mayo State Vocational Technical School in Paintsville where he successfully completed an associate degree in electronic data processing in May 1983.

Phillip Trimble and daughter, Amy.

On Apr. 17, 1980, Phillip was married to Willa Jean "Jeanie" Blevins, daughter of Robert and Betty Blevins of Burnt Cabin in Paintsville. Two children were born to this union, Ami Nicole (born Oct. 4, 1980) and Brandon Lee (born Jan. 27, 1986). The marriage was dissolved in March 1990.

In July 1983, Phillip, with the assistance of his parents, John Mark and Janet Trimble, opened Computers Plus, a computer retail store located at 241 College Street in downtown Paintsville. In 1998, Phillip, along with his brother, David, and another associate, Brett Higgins of Salyersville, purchased the business from Phillip's parents. Phillip and his associates have transformed Computers Plus from a small virtually unknown retail establishment into a national presence in the service arena with alliances among well-respected Fortune 500 companies throughout the U.S. and abroad.

Phillip's hobbies include sports, movies and playing the drums. Although his two children reside with their mother in Prestonsburg, KY, his son, Brandon, spends most every weekend at his father's home at 203 Second Street in Paintsville where they enjoy playing ball and serious fishing.

TRIMBLE - Winston "Wince" E. Trimble was born Sep. 7, 1896, in Johnson County, KY, to John Mark and Clarinda Francis Spradlin Trimble. He lived at Hager Hill, in Johnson County, where he died May 31, 1973.

Wince's first wife, Gypsie Stapleton, daughter of Abraham and Mary Walker Stapleton, died in 1942. Wince's second wife was Hannah Jean Ward, daughter of John M. and Mary Sammons Ward. Hannah was born in 1904 and died about 1990. Neither marriage produced any children.

Winston "Wince" Trimble

In the early 1920s, Wince lived with his sister and brother-in-law, Sebastian and Shelly Trimble Coldiron, in Columbus, OH, where he worked as a conductor on the city trolley car system. Some time later, he moved back to Johnson County where he served, for several years, as a Federal revenue agent charged with hunting down moonshiners in Eastern Kentucky. At one time, Wince was a member of the Johnson County Fiscal Court and became active in the improvement of County Roads. He was also elected to the office of Johnson County sheriff and served from 1958-62. Although as a revenue agent, Wince became somewhat of a legend, and was generally referred to as being "relentless" by any moonshiner meeting up with him, he, nonetheless, had many friends and was loved and respected by most everybody in the county.

VANHOOSE & OSBORNE - Ernestine Osborne was born Mar. 1, 1940, on Salyers Branch at the home owned by Homer Salyer where her parents lived. Ernestine is the daughter of Fred and Mae Osborne of Volga, KY. Ernestine's parents met at church and married at the home of Kendrick and Beulah Salyer on Sep. 14, 1935.

Ernestine attended McKenzie Branch School, Flat Gap Elementary and Flat Gap High School graduating in the class of 1958. Ernestine graduated from Mayo State Vocational School where she majored in business. After graduation she became employed as a secretary for the Johnson County Extension Office in Paintsville on Sep. 1, 1960, and continues her work there.

James O. and Ernestine VanHoose

Ernestine married James O. VanHoose Nov. 24, 1960. They were married at the home of his grandparents, Mart and Selina Ward VanHoose by Reverend Florida Lyons.

James is the son of Proctor and Hazel May VanHoose. James was born Jul. 18, 1935, at Thealka, KY. He has two brothers, John Martin (born Jan. 25, 1937) lives in Little Rock, AR, and Larry Gene (born Oct. 21, 1947) lives at Wittensville, KY; and a sister, Sandra Jane Harlow (born Mar. 28, 1952) lives at Paintsville, KY. A brother, Phillip Roger VanHoose (born May 31, 1943) died of cancer Apr. 30, 1996, and is buried at the Highland Memorial Cemetery at Staffordsville.

James' father, Proctor VanHoose was born Sep. 13, 1913, to parents, John and Lou Lyons VanHoose. James' mother, Hazel May VanHoose, was born Jun. 12, 1915. Her parents were Mart and Selina Ward VanHoose of Thealka, a northeast coal mining town.

James attended Thealka Elementary School, Paintsville High School and served in the U.S. Army as a medical technician during the Korean War.

James is a Christian and a member of the First Freewill Baptist Church on Third Street in Paintsville where he has been a faithful member for seven years. James is recently retired from the Bank Josephine of Prestonsburg.

James and Ernestine live on Route 172 at Volga where Ernestine spends her spare time cooking fabulous meals and tending her garden, flowers and fruit trees. Like her father, she is smart and thrifty. Ernestine's father was a farmer, cattle trader, merchant and passenger bus driver. When her father, Fred Osborne, closed his grocery store, he burned the store records, so his children would never know the people still owing for merchandise purchased on credit.

VAN HORN - Sophia Moore Van Horn was born Sep. 15, 1912, in Montgomery County, PA. Her father, Horace Miller Van Horn, was born Oct. 14, 1888, in Philadelphia, PA, and her mother, Caroline Blanche Curtis, was born at Oaklands Ranch in Douglas County, Sedalia, CO, Nov. 3, 1889. Her parents met at the ranch where Horace went for meals when he was working with a crew on the highway and Blanche was waiting on the workmen around the table. They were married Nov. 19, 1911. Although Sophia's parents never lived in Kentucky, they did visit here. Her parents were mainly occupied by dairy farming. They took up a homestead in sagebrush country on the Great Divide, 25 miles northwest of Craig, CO, and raised grain.

Sophia Van Horn

Sophia had two brothers, Charlie (born Jun. 5, 1914) and Van Jr. (born Nov. 29, 1920). Her one sister, Mary, was born May 12, 1922. The family moved many times and the children attended schools in Colorado, Pennsylvania and New York. Sophia attended one room schools at Sedalia and the homestead, Thornton, PA, had a two-room school with eight grades. Sophia graduated from West Chester (PA) High School in 1931. She studied a three year nursing course at Media Hospital in Pennsylvania and graduated in 1936. Her first job as a nurse was private duty nursing in homes and at hospitals.

Sophia was never married.

Sophia came to Little, Breathitt County, KY, in April 1940 where she worked at a mission home called the Dessie Scott Children's Home. In October 1942, she came to Johnson County, KY, with Alice Shepherd with whom she had been working in Sunday schools, Vacation Bible Schools and Bible camp work at Camp Nathanael, Knott County, KY. Sophia began working as a part time nurse at the Johnson County Health Dept. and throughout the years, has made many nursing visits to sick or hurt neighbors' homes day and night.

While working in Breathitt County at the Children's Home, there was a cow to milk and chickens to care for, etc. Without a man to regularly do these chores, it became one of Sophia's part time duties. One day the cow was in her stanchion waiting to be fed and milked when she "went wild" and tried to get out, she kicked, jumped around, stamped and snorted. Sophia finally got the cow loose so she could go outside, and a snake came out too, from the cow's feed bin.

One night there was a terrible clatter of hens in the chicken house. Workers were all in bed asleep, so Sophia got dressed, got a flashlight, a hoe for a weapon and went to the chicken house. Hens were on the roost, but under one roost she saw two beady eyes on a hen's back. It was a weasel, eating on that hen and she was fighting to get loose, but the weasel hung on. Sophia rammed at him with the hoe, he came out on the hen's back as the hen came out the door. Sophia tried to hit the weasel, but he got away and the hen got hit, and had to be killed. What a night!

Since coming to Johnson County in 1942, Sophia has enjoyed the jolly good friends and neighbors. Many have come to know the Lord as Savior, some older and many young ones. Several young men who were taught by Sophia and Alice Shepherd are preaching and teaching the Word of God; young women have been teaching Sunday school and Vacation Bible School; and some have been playing the piano for services here and other places where they have moved. There are many teaching in public schools, and one has gone to Africa as a missionary nurse.

Sophia is very thankful for all who are making it part of their schedule to teach Bible truths to children and others in Kentucky. The Lord is SO good! *Submitted by Sophia Van Horn.*

VAN HOOSE - Jan Fransse Van Hoesen (born in 1608) was a sailor for the Dutch West Indies Co. He was recruited by this company to settle in New Amsterdam, along the Hudson River, now in the state of New York.

Jan Fransse married Voikje Junaens in Amsterdam, Holland May 15, 1639, and soon sailed for the New World. After arriving, he must have decided that being a sailor was not a good career for a family man, because he started learning the baking trade from his captain.

He lived in Fort Orange, on what would now be the northeast corner of today's Broadway and State Streets of downtown Albany, NY. Jan Fransse started dealing in land. Records list him as a land commissioner for the Dutch West Indies Co.

Levi Van Hoose, 1795-1857

In 1662 he bought land from the Indians for 500 guilders in beavers. This tract along the Hudson River would include the present city of Hudson and half of Columbia County, NY. After his death in 1667, the land was divided among his children: Frans, Junaen, Styntje, Anna, Maria, Catharina, Johannes, Jacob, and Volckert.

The son, Johannes Van Hoesen, was born in 1655 in Fort Orange and lived and raised his family in the Kinderhook area, Claverick, NY. He married Jannitje De Ryck and they had 11 children. One of his sons, also named Johannes Van Hoesen, was born 1697. This Johannes married Elizabeth Laux and moved their family to Berks County, PA. Neighbors in this community were the Boones and Bryans. Word of good land in western North Carolina must have attracted the Van Hoesens, Boones and Bryans to the Yadkin River area. Away from the Dutch-German communities the spelling of Johannes Van Hoesen became Anglicized to John Van Hooser. They had a son, John Van Hooser (born 1723), who married Hannah Cheek. They raised their family by the Pee Dee River in North Carolina. Their son John Van Hoose (Van Hase), was born April 5, 1762, and is the granddaddy of all of the Eastern Kentucky Van Hooses. A Revolutionary War soldier, he served as a private with George Rogers Clark's Illinois Regt., a band of 175 Virginia riflemen who won the U.S. Rights to the whole Northwest Territories in the Battle at Vincennes.

John C. Van Hoose, 1819-1888

He married Mary Bryan, a daughter of William Bryan. Through his service to his community, John Van Hoose earned the title colonel and to this day is known as Col. John Van Hoose. His name is on the DAR monument at the Johnson County, KY, Courthouse and in 1989 his descendants placed a new tombstone on his grave at White House, KY.

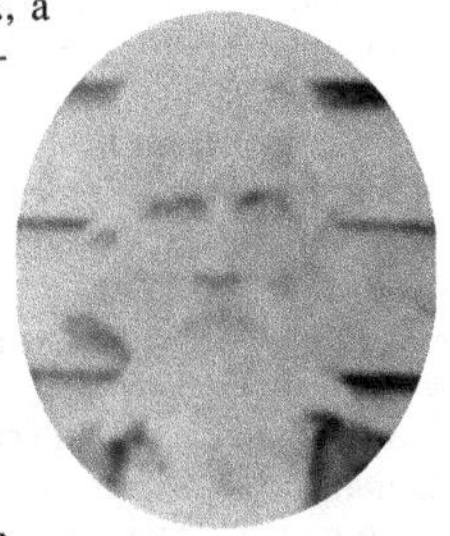

Levi J. Van Hoose, 1842-1942

Elvin Van Hoose is a descendant through Col. John's son, Levi. Levi was born Mar. 22, 1795, and married Sarah Clark. Levi's grave was moved to New Cemetery when the Paintsville Dam was built and marked by his descendants. They had a son John C. (born Jun. 15, 1819). John C. married Almira Keesee and is buried in Lewis County, KY. John C. and Almira had a son, Levi Jasper (born Feb. 19, 1842). Levi Jasper married Malissa Salyer and they had a son, John William, on Sep. 3, 1877. John William married Lou Anna O'Bryan. Levi Jasper, Malissa, John William and Lou Anna are all buried in the Old Pelphrey Cemetery on Cliffton Branch. John William and Lou Anna are the parents of Elvin (born Jan. 7, 1911). Elvin married Mae Gullett (see the Gullett family) and had eight children born in Johnson County: Gladys Pauline, Anna Louise Muncy, Harry Clayton, Dissie Ilene Sherman, Doris Jean Jones, Mary Magdalene Williams, Verina Irene Dygert and John See. Elvin and Mae moved to Ohio where Elvin was a carpenter and farmer. Elvin died Jun. 7, 1996, and is buried in Mutual, OH. *Submitted by John See Van Hoose.*

John W. Van Hoose, 1877-1942

Elvin Van Hoose, 1911-1996

VAUGHAN/VAUGHN - Like many other families who migrated into Johnson County, KY after the mining town of Van Lear was established by Consolidation Coal Company in 1910-14, the family of Anthony Wayne Vaughan and America MacBrayer Vaughan had several male members represented there, including my father, James, his brother, Everett, and his brother-in-law, John Hammond.

Grandfather Anthony Wayne Vaughan was born in Wayne County, VA (now Cabell County, WV) Oct. 17, 1848, he was the seventh of 10 children of James and Susannah Wilson Vaughan. In 1863, as a boy of 15, he worked with his father who was employed by the Union Army to care for horses at a federal post in South Point, OH, on the north side of the Ohio River, James' father, Thomas owned a sizable farm, but he and his wife, Nancy Ford Vaughan, left most of their property to their son, Thomas II. Around 1858, James and his wife relocated across the Big Sandy River in Lawrence County, KY. It was from this location that James and his son, Anthony Wayne, commuted down river to their work at the confluence of the Big Sandy and Ohio at South Point.

Our first Vaughan of record in this country is William (born around 1750), described as a "Welshman who traded with Indians." Around 1772, he married Fereby Benton (born ca. 1750 North Carolina, died May 1950 in Madison County, AR). In a deposition given in 1892 by Benjamin Vaughan in support of claims for Indian citizenship, he stated that Fereby Benton Vaughan was his grandmother. Her maiden name was Fereby Benton whose mother's maiden name was Looney, who was Cherokee by blood. Fereby married William Vaughan in the "Old Cherokee Nation in Tennessee," After service in Lord Dunmore's War in 1774 in David Looney's company, William acquired land in Russell County, VA, then migrated on to Hawkins County, TN, where he and Fereby remained for a time before going on to northwest Arkansas where they and most of their children settled, their eldest, Thomas, remaining in Virginia.

My great-great-great-grandfather William and his wife Fereby had at least seven children, including their first-born, my great-great-grandfather Thomas (born 1773), John (born 1774), Samuel (born 1776), Daniel (born 1787), William II (born 1789) and Elizabeth (born 1790). All of these birthdates are approximate.

Around 1793, Thomas married Nancy Ford (born ca. 1776), daughter of John and Betsy Hill Ford of Virginia. To this union 12 children were born: John (born 1794), Elizabeth (born 1796), Jane (born 1800), Martha (born 1802), Nancy (born 1804), Phoebe (Ferabe) (born 1806), William Tyler (born 1808), Lucinda (born 1813), my great-grandfather James (born 1814), Christiana (born 1816), Thomas II (born 1819) and Abraham (born 1822).

James (born 1914) married Susannah Wilson, daughter of James and Sarah Mountz Wilson, ca. 1833 in Boyd County, KY. They had 10 children: Goodwin (born 1834), Mary Jane (born 1836), Allen T. (born 1840), Lucinda (1841), Rebecca Belle (born 1842), Cassia (born 1846), my grandfather Anthony Wayne (born 1848), Hugh (born 1851), Jackson (born 1854) and Mary (born 1859),

On Oct. 21, 1871 in Carter County, KY, Anthony Wayne Vaughan married the daughter of William McBrayer, America, who was born Mar. 31, 1848. This union was blessed with 13 children: Lou Ella (born 1872), Charles (born 1873), Ida (born 1875), Susan Jane (born 1876), Esther Ann (born 1878), Daisy (born 1879), my father James (born 1881), Allen Toby (born 1883), William M. (born 1885), Howard (born 1887), John (born 1889), Daniel Everett (born 1892) and Anthony Wayne II (born 1893).

My father, James (born 1881), married 1st, Ella Hammond (born 1888), on Feb. 27, 1910. To this union were born two children, George Willis Vaughan (born Aug. 17, 1912) and Ida Mae Vaughan (born Oct. 16, 1914). James was working in Van Lear when Ella died suddenly on Mar. 7, 1918. On Sep. 9, 1919, James married 2nd, Frances Lynk (born Jan. 22, 1892), daughter of John and Lyda (Burgraff) Lynk. This writer, James E. Vaughan (born Dec. 7, 1925) is the only child of this union.

Following the death of his first wife, James returned to Ashland and remained there in the employ of C&O Rwy, returning with his second wife (my mother) and three children to Van Lear in 1920 through 1924. At that time he and his family shared a double house with his brother, Daniel Everett Vaughan, and his wife, Maude, and their children, Charlene and Maurice. The family of the brother of James' first wife Ella, John Hammond, was then employed as a foreman at Consolidation Mine #152, and they lived in what was known as "Silk Stocking Row" across from the Van Lear Central Schools.

James returned to Ashland and for a time operated a small coal mine with his father at Winslow near what is known as "Number Eight." In 1928, he and his family returned to Van Lear where his three children entered the Van Lear public school system, When George decided he wanted to enter the mines in 1930, James quit his job as a foreman to take his son into the pits and show him the ropes, George returned to school to graduate with the Class of 1932. On Jul. 15, 1935, a methane gas explosion in Consolidation Mine #155 took the lives of nine miners, including that of James Vaughan. The other miners were Roy Murray; brothers, Bill and Charley Kretzer; Shirley Hereford, Honus Gool, Durwood Litz and (the youngest at 21) Virgil Clay. A plaque in their memory is now on display in the Miners' Room of the Museum.

Following his father's death, George Vaughan remained in the employ of Consolidation Coal Company as the family's sole breadwinner. Ida Mae entered nurses' training at Saint Elizabeth's in Covington following her high school graduation in 1934. With war raging in Europe in 1940, George joined a number of other Van Lear boys in an electronics training school operated by the Army at Avon near Lexington, transferring to the Army Signal Corps the following year. He served in Europe and was caught up in the Battle of the Bulge, along with his cousin Johnny, son of our Uncle John Vaughan). My mother and I moved to Ashland in 1942, where she died from cancer in August of that year. I finished high school at Ashland, and entered Michigan State College in the summer of 1943, remaining there until I entered the Navy V-5 pilot training program in October of that year. Following further V-12 and NROTC duty, I was released from active duty in 1946, returning to Oklahoma University to complete degree work, where I met my future wife. Wanda Lee Rice, daughter *of* Thomas Lee and Samantha Rice of Delaplaine, AR, and I were married Feb. 14, 1949. After working as manager of Radio Station WMBM on Miami Beach, FL, we came to Arkansas and settled in 1955, remaining there as teachers, farmers and writers. We have no children. Brother George and his wife Nora (Revis) Vaughan have no children. Our sister, Ida Mae, married James Jacobs in 1943. They had two children, Melane (born May 17, 1944) and James "Skip" (born Jul. 19, 1952). Ida Mae passed away in 1993 and is buried in Los Angeles where she resided for 40 of her 69 years. George died in 1996 at age 83 and is interred at South Lebanon, OH.

Other male members of the family of Anthony Wayne Vaughan worked in the mines of eastern Kentucky: John and his sons, Delbert and Hubert, at Garrett in Floyd County, and Anthony Wayne II, who lost his life in a mining accident in February 1923 at Wolf Pen, KY. Daniel Everett and Howard served in the U.S. Army during World War I. Everett later became a federal mine inspector, a job he held at Pikeville in 1935 when his brother, James, was killed at Van Lear. All three of his sons: Maurice, Warren and Eugene, served in the military during World War II, Warren losing his life in Army action in Europe on the second day of January 1945.

In 1960, a series of articles in the *Floyd County Times* put me on the trail of the origins of William Vaughan (born 1750, died 1840) and his part-Cherokee bride, Fereby Benton (born 1750, died 1859). This led me to our distant cousin, Lewis Vaughan, and his family research, ultimately resulting in personal visits to the Vaughan homeplace (1450-1775) at Tretower, about 30 miles north of Cardiff in southern Wales. A great deal of ancient history concerning this family is found in my book, *Vaughans in Wales & America*, and in Lewis Vaughan's book, *Vaughan Pioneers*, both now available from Higginson Book Company, 14 Derby Square, Salem, MA.

VIOLET - Neva Noel McKenzie was born Jul. 14, 1909, at Red Bush in Johnson County, KY. She was the first, and only child, of Albert McKenzie, schoolteacher and Clora Williams.

Arlyn and Neva McKenzie Violet, 1956.

In January 1912, Albert died leaving Clora and Neva dependent on Clora's grandfather, Noah Williams, and her sisters and brother for shelter and support. For the next five years, Clora and Neva made their home with the various family members. Neva became a member of each family; her cousins became nearly as close as brothers and sisters.

In 1917, Clora remarried to Albert Mackenzie of Cane Branch near Manila. Albert was a descendant of William of the Volga Community. Clora or Neva was never aware that they were of the same family. Clora's great-grandmother was Elizabeth McKenzie Webb who was a sister of William. Neva's father, Albert, was the grandson of Oliver and Matilda of Elna-Red Bush. William, Oliver and Elizabeth were members of the McKenzie clan that migrated from Fort Blackmore (Scott County), VA. The entire family settled and farmed in the northwestern section of present-day Johnson County.

Now Neva was part of a "real" family. Albert had three children: Homer, Ford and Ola, whose mother and twin had died at her birth in August 1916. In 1919, the family was joined and completed by the birth of Hula Kendall, son of Albert and Clora. Neva was very happy as a member of this family. Fish Trap United Baptist Church and Colvin Branch School were centers of her social world. Neighbor's Blantons, Salyers, Auxiers, Colvins, McCartys, VanHooses, Stapletons and Davis were integral parts of life. When Ford and Neva reached high school age (1924), the family rented a home in Paintsville where Clora kept house and sent her children, as well as cousins Ray McKenzie and Eulas Williams, to Paintsville High. Neva attended there for two years before moving to Morehead State abnormal where she studied home economics. For three years, 1927, 1928 and 1929, Neva divided her time between winter term at Morehead and teaching in one-room schools in Johnson County. In 1927, she taught at Hurricane School on Barnetts Creek for $60 for the seven-month term. She also had to pay room and board. In 1928 Neva taught at Pigeon School; in 1929 she began the term at Colvin Branch School before her Uncle Sandy Phillips lured her to a teaching position in the Scioto County, OH, schools. She was by now the proud owner of a 1928 Chevy coupe. Neva taught in the Lucasville Valley Elementary School until she married in July 1932.

On Jul. 5, 1932, Neva married Arlyn Violet, a native of Lucasville. In that time period in Ohio, married women were not employed as teachers, so Neva did seasonal work at Martings in Portsmouth, but primarily being a homemaker.

In 1935, Albert died and soon Clora and Kendall came to Lucasville to make their home with Arlyn and Neva. Two children were born to the family, Sue Ann in 1937 and Jon Albert in 1939. Clora's assistance as a housekeeper and childcare helper were needed and appreciated.

The advent of Pearl Harbor created a shortage of teachers in public schools. Neva was re-employed at Lucasville Valley as a first grade teacher. In 1950 she received her BS degree in education from Rio Grande College in Ohio. She was employed at Lucasville until 1965, the year that Clora died.

Neva and Arlyn relocated to Columbus, OH, where she taught in the Whitehall schools until her retirement in 1974.

Neva loved to cook and entertain at meals. She enjoyed playing bridge, fishing, painting in oils, watercolors and chalk. She enjoyed gardening and belonged to the Lucasville Garden Club. Neva belonged to Delta Kappa Gamma, American University Women, Business and Professional Women and the United Methodist Church at Lucasville and Church of the Redeemer in Columbus.

In 1971 she and Arlyn purchased their second and final home in East Columbus. Arlyn passed away in August 1979. Neva remained in the house in her role of matriarch, homemaker, hostess and neighbor. At her death in June 1988 she left her son and daughter surviving as well as six grandchildren. Her first great-granddaughter was born in August 1988 and bears her middle name.

VOLOTA - Geneva Wells Volota, the oldest daughter of Susanna "Anna" Richmond and Benjamin Harrison Wells of Daniels Creek, Johnson County, KY, was 11 lbs. when she was born at home in Van Lear by a midwife on Nov. 11, 1916. She was also the shortest out of 10 children standing at five feet tall and was of the Protestant faith, belonging to the "Disciples of Christ," Lake Shore Christian Church in Euclid, OH. She died Saturday, Aug. 14, 1993, from a heart attack at Parma Community General Hospital, Parma, OH, after suffering for five years from stomach cancer. Short in stature, five feet, with light brown hair and hazel eyes, she was pleasant, humble and made friends easily. She often said that she aged 10 years with premature gray hair when becoming a mother of twin girls who would often cry at the same time. She said that she threw up her hands once and exclaimed, "I only have two hands." In her later years she stopped coloring her hair and it was snow white like her father's. She and her husband, Steven Volota, are buried in the Westwood Abbey, South Wing on the Chapel Floor Section 7A, at Sunset Memorial Park, 6265 Columbia Rd., North Olmsted, OH. Originally she was buried temporarily in the Garden Mausoleum until the new wing was complete in the Westwood Abbey.

Back, L-R: Patricia and Pamela. Front, L-R: John Steven, Geneva "Wells" and Steve Volota.

Since she dropped out of school at the eighth grade to help care for her family who had become ill with small pox, she educated herself by reading and learning on her own. Geneva always felt a little inferior and encouraged her children to further their education. She, however, did go to Mayo Vocational School before she came to Cleveland, OH, at age 26 in 1943, during WWII and lived with her friend, Ethel Moore (from Johns Creek). They worked at Chicago Pneumatic in the machine shop and for recreation they went for walks, cycled, ballroom danced, roller skated weekly and went to the beach. Ethel Moore, who married James (Jimmy Campbell), now lives in Madison, OH. She said also that Geneva seemed to have nightmares and one time when they stayed the night while visiting Ethel's sister in Kentucky, she was yelling in her sleep thinking a man was standing at the head of their bed. She said that Geneva did the cooking for the five girls that lived in their apartment and one morning (or they thought it was morning) she woke everyone up and said that breakfast was ready. Ethel said that she felt so tired as they sat down to eat, glancing out the window she wondered why so many people were on the street at 5:00 a.m. in the morning. Then they heard on the radio that it was 11:00 p.m. at night. They always kidded her about that and ate the breakfast at 11:00 p.m. anyway, it was good for she had homemade biscuits. Ethel mentioned that the neighborhood was safe in those days and they slept with the windows, which had no screens, wide open.

Geneva met her future husband, Stephanus "Steve" or "Steven" Volota (Wolota), at the Aragon Ballroom on West 25th. She wasn't interested in going out with him at first and made excuses like ... I have to bake an apple pie. However, he was persistent and told her that he wasn't going to ask her anymore if she didn't go out with him, so she did. They married Jul. 1, 1950, at Euclid Avenue Christian Church at East 93rd and Euclid Avenue. The beautiful greenish stone church still stands by Cleveland Clinic Foundation.

Steven "Steve," the oldest son of his mother's (Catharina <Catherine> Kudlik <Kudlyk>) second marriage was born Oct. 17, 1915, in McKees Rocks, PA, and died Feb. 18, 1997. He was raised Greek Catholic, resided on 64 Orchard Street in Preston, McKees Rocks, PA, and was a blond when young, dark brown haired when older, a dark complexion and blue-gray eyes. When he died he still had a lot of dark color hair. His father, Joannes "John" Wolota (Volota), and his mother were from a small town called Lisko near Sanok, that was in Austria before the world wars. It is presently in the southern tip of Poland. Her first marriage was to Josef "Joseph" Baraniewicz at St. Mary's Greek Catholic Church in Allegheny County, PA. Marriage certificate #1154 Series G. Josef met with his accidental death Tuesday, Nov. 23, 1909, at 11:25 a.m. when a train in McKees hit him, Rocks, PA. Death record Nr. R.L. #967. They came to America in the early 1900s. His mother was about 14 years old when she immigrated to America. Steve did not know any English when he began school since only Ukrainian was spoken in the home. His mother spoke English, Ukrainian and Polish. Steve's siblings were Marie, Mike, Anna, Josephus "Joseph" and Helena "Helen" Volota who was the youngest. Helena "Helen," Marie and Anna never married. His mother's first marriage produced two children, Catherine and Tony Baraniewicz. Catherine married Matthew Radko. Joseph drowned in the Ohio River near his home.

Steve was in the Army twice, before WWII in Hawaii and then during the war in the Philippines. When stationed in Hawaii he was a sergeant and taught soldiers boxing. He lived in New York City, went to radio and television repair school in Erie, PA, and had a carpentry apprenticeship. After WWII, he worked at the trucking docks in Cleveland until he got a full-time job at TRW, Euclid, OH, where he stayed until retirement at 65 years of age.

They moved from East 93rd in March 1953 to 456 East 274th Street, Euclid, OH, where they remained until their death. Their children are twin girls, Pamela and Patricia (born Mar. 24, 1951); a stillborn girl named Diane Marie (born Jul. 25, 1961); and a son, John Steven Volota (born Mar. 20, 1963). Diane Marie Volota was buried in the family cemetery in Johnson County, KY, at Daniel's Creek, Rt. 3, across from Ben and Anna Wells' homestead. *Submitted by Patricia Volota Quallich.*

WALLEN & TRIMBLE - Charles Ervin Wallen and Ann Wade Trimble Wallen were married in Paintsville, KY, Apr. 25, 1980. Charles "Charlie" was born at Chestnut in Johnson County, KY, Aug. 8, 1956, the seventh of eight children of Loretta Boyd Wallen Blair and Leslie Wallen. He has three sisters and four brothers: Sue Wallen Nichols (born 1944, died 1988), Jimmy Wallen (born 1946), Sandra Wallen Pack (born 1949), Leslie Jr. Wallen (born 1951), Eddie Wallen (born 1952) Sharon Wallen Helton (born 1955) and Willie Blair (born 1965).

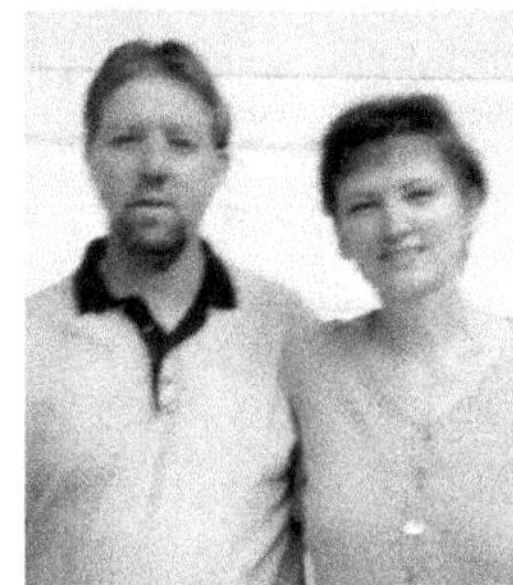

Charles and Ann Wallen

Charlie graduated from Paintsville High School in 1974. Soon after graduation he worked a short time for F.S. Vanhoose Lumber Co. but in August 1976 he began employment with CSX (formerly C&O) Railway Co. where he is currently employed as foreman on the eastern seaboard of the U.S. Charlie is an avid deer hunter during his leisure time.

Ann was born in Paintsville, Johnson County, KY, Aug. 1, 1958, the second of four children of John Mark Trimble and Janet Marsh Trimble. She has three brothers: Mark Wesley Trimble (born 1956), David Lawrence Trimble (born 1960) and Phillip Lee Trimble (born 1962).

Ann graduated from Paintsville High School in 1976. After high school graduation, she attended Eastern Kentucky University in Richmond, KY, and Prestonsburg Community College in Prestonsburg, KY. After their two children were born, Ann decided to continue her education. In May 1991 she was awarded an RN degree from Ashland Community College in Ashland, KY. After working a short time at Three Rivers Medical Center in Louisa, KY, and Paul B. Hall Medical Center in Paintsville, KY, she was offered employment with Johnson County Home Health where she worked from April 1993-April 1999. She is currently working with Dr. Michael Lyons, orthopedic surgeon, in Paintsville, KY.

Charlie, Ann and their two children, Leigh Ann (born Apr. 12, 1981) and Justin Brent (born Jun. 24, 1984), live at 100 Poplar Hill Drive, Staffordsville, KY.

WALLEN - Howard Wendell Wallen was born Dec. 25, 1932, in Johnson County, KY, to Mitchell Wallen and Neva Leona Preston. He has one sister, Lois A. Wallen Webb.

Howard Wendell Wallen Family. L-R: Howard, Wendell, Jewell, Lisa and Michael.

Wendell was married in August 1951 to Jewell Ward. Jewell was the daughter of Marshall Ward and Elsie Music Ward. She has four sisters and two brothers.

Wendell and Jewell have three children and five grandchildren.

Howard married Deborah L. Elkins. They have two children named Dustin Mitchell and Olivia Nicole.

Michael married Teresa Lynn Barber. They have one son by the name of Joseph Michael who married Chasidy Russell.

Lisa Michelle married Hubert James Senters. They have two children named McKenzie Danielle and Morgan Taylor.

Wendell and Jewell graduated from Meade Memorial High School. Wendell continued his education at Pikeville College where he graduated in 1953. He started his teaching career at Hammond, and from there, he moved to the Meade Memorial School. He later graduated form Morehead State University with an AB and master's degree, as well as continuing the Rank I Program for teachers and administrators. He worked for the Johnson County Board of Education for 38 years as a coach, teacher and administrator. In his 11 years of coaching at Meade Memorial, he served as a coach for basketball, baseball and cross country. He was also the basketball coach at Johnson Central for seven years. In basketball, he had a won/loss record of 385 to 178 with 11 District and four Regional Championships. He was elected to the Kentucky High School Athletic Hall of Fame. Jewell is a retired U.S. postmistress.

All three children of the couple graduated from the Johnson Central High School and Morehead State University. Howard is currently serving as superintendent of the Pikeville Independent School Dist. Michael is a vice-president for Daugherty Petroleum, Inc. of Lexington, KY. Lisa is a certified public accountant and resides in Versailles, KY.

Wendell and Jewell began housekeeping at Williamsport and have continued to live in that locale to the present time. Wendell's hobbies are fishing, gardening and woodworking.

WALLIN & PENNINGTON - This Wallin history was partially researched by Clyde Wallin Jr., son of Clyde and Verlie Stewart Wallin. Clyde Jr. is the grandson of Clarence Wallin, who is a brother of Lora Ellen Wallin that married Sherman Lyon. Some records of the Wallin family are reported to have been lost during the Civil War when the court houses were destroyed in Lee and Scott County, VA. The Wallin family came from England and first settled in Virginia. We find Wallin spelled several different ways. Walling appears to be the original correct spelling. Elisha Walling's name can be found in various documents and military records as Wallen, Wallings, Wallens and Walden. Some of our ancestors are listed in the 1890 Johnson County tax list as Wallen, others of this same family are listed as Wallin.

Dr. Elihue Tivis and Martha Jane Pennington Wallin.

During 1746-86 large numbers living in Virginia, hunted through southwest Virginia, east Tennessee and Eastern Kentucky. They were known as long hunters because their hunting trips would last for as long as one and one-half years. The most noted long hunters are Elisha Walden, William Carr, William Crabtree, James Aldridge, William Pitman and Henry Scaggs. We are sure that our Wallin family is a descendent of this same Elisha Walden.

1. Harvy Trigg Carter Wallin married Margaret "Peggy" Lawson. Their children are: Conley Wallin married Helen Williams, daughter of David and Lydia Webb Williams; Fuget Wallin married Telitha Williams, daughter of David and Lydia Webb Williams; James Wallin married Sarah Legg.

Elihue Tivis Wallin (born Oct. 15, 1856, died Oct. 24, 1893) married Martha Jane Pennington Aug. 28, 1879. Martha Jane was born May 12, 1862, and died Sep. 30, 1951, daughter of James and Nancy Fairchilds Pennington. James Pennington came to Kentucky from North Carolina and was in the Confederate Army during the Civil War.

Dr. Elihue Tivis and Martha Jane Pennington Wallin are buried at Red Bush in the Hamilton Cemetery on the Ford Hamilton farm. Several years after Elihue Tivis' death, Martha Jane, at age 38 years, was married the second time to Merdia Evans, 57 years of age. They had no children together.

Elihue Tivis Wallin became a medical doctor, attending the Kentucky School of Medicine in Louisville, KY. This school educated a large number of physicians from 1850 through its merger with the University of Louisville in 1908. While Elihue Tivis was in medical school, he contracted tuberculosis and eventually it took his life.

Elihue Tivis and Martha Jane had these children.

1. Clarence McCellan Wallin (born Jul. 15, 1880, died Dec. 2, 1962) married Ella Dixon at Elna, KY, Aug. 5, 1903.

2. Loranze E. "Jence" Wallin never married.

3. Bernard Wallin married Stella Riggsby.

4. Lora Ellen Wallin married Sherman Lyon. See records in Lyon family history.

5. Corneilas Hood Wallin (born May 1, 1889, died May 31, 1982) married Bessie Fyffe Oct. 24, 1894.

Elihue Tivis and Martha Jane were members of the Cold Springs United Baptist Church until their deaths. Martha Jane lived to an old age and was known to her family and neighbors as "Granny." She had a special love for small children and was never cross with them. She really preferred that they never be corrected in her presence. Granny Martha lived to be 91 years old. *Submitted by William Hillard and Clista Margaret McKenzie Pelfrey.*

WALTER FAMILY - The forefather of the Walter Family of Johnson County was John Calvin Walter, a son of Israel and Elizabeth "Betsy" Holbrook Walter. Israel never lived in Kentucky. He was killed in a brandy distillery explosion near Wheeler's Ford (now St. Paul) in Russell County, VA ca. 1815-18. Betsy married Stephen Wheeler and moved to Blaine, Floyd County (now Lawrence County), KY about 1818. Israel and his family lived at Dockery, Wilkes County, NC before moving to Virginia about 1802.

John Calvin Walter, son of Israel and Elizabeth Holbrook Walter, was a Confederate Soldier, 13th KY Cav. 1863-1865

Israel and Betsy had six known children: 1) William, married to Elizabeth Woods; 2) Robert Bruce, married to Louisa Ascoth Swetnam; 3) Elizabeth, married to Winfrey Holbrook; 4) John Calvin, married first to Judah Ward and second to Sara Winfred Gambill; 5) Mary "Polly," married to James Graham; 6) Sarah "Sally," married to James Barnard.

John Calvin Walter, who was born Jan. 2, 1807, and died in August 1880 was buried at Tutor Key, Johnson County Cemetery. He was married twice, first on May 13, 1830, to Judah Ward, who was born on Feb. 25, 1816. She died in Johnson County ca. 1837-41. She was a daughter of Shadrack and Vina (Hilton) Ward. John Calvin and Judah had three sons: Shadrack W. Walter, Winfrey Holbrook Walter and John M. Walter. About 1843, John Calvin left his sons with his parent-in-laws and went to Dockery, NC, where he married Sarah Winfred Gambill. They had one child: James Paris Walter. Sarah and James Paris never moved to Kentucky. They remained at Dockery where Sarah is buried in the Pisgah Cemetery. John Calvin volunteered for military service, enlisting as a private in the Confederate Army at the age of 54 and serving until the war was over.

(5) Mary "Polly" Walter married James Graham and had the following known children: Louvina, William Walter, Lafayette, Martin Van Buren, Greenville A. Graham, Larkin Madison, Emily Jane, James K., Marcus N. and Mary E. Graham. This family lived in the Cherokee section of Lawrence County, KY: and (6) Sarah "Sally" Walter married James Barnard on Nov. 24, 1821.

Winfrey Holbrook Walter, son of John Calvin and Judah (Ward) Walter, was born on Aug. 22, 1833, in Johnson County, KY, and lived at Offutt, Thelma, and Flat Gap. He died on Apr. 1, 1914 and was buried at Flat Gap, KY. He married on Oct. 11, 1854, Elizabeth Preston, a daughter of James "Coby" and Lavina (Murray) Preston, and a great-granddaughter of Moses Preston, a veteran of the Revolutionary War, and Fanny (Arthur) Preston, who lived and are buried at Ulysses, Lawrence County, KY. Elizabeth was born on Nov. 25, 1840, in Johnson County and died Aug. 29, 1934, at Thelma, Johnson County, and is buried at Flat Gap next to her husband.

Winfrey Holbrook Walter and wife Elizabeth (Preston) Walter

Children in front, L-R: Lawson Wadsworth Walter, Guffie Clayton Walter. Others L-R: Rev. Lafayette Walter, Ralph Waldo Walter, Cullie Bee Walter, Nancy Hetta (Daniel) Walter

Winfrey and Elizabeth had 15 children: Lavina married Psalmist David Spears; James Preston married Sarah Francis Daniel; John M. married Nannie Preston; Shadrack W. married Martha Sagraves, Judah married Richard M. Butcher; Dr. William Jefferson married twice, first to Margaret Elliot and second to Mary Elizabeth Syck; Ulysess Simpson married Mary Suzanne Mollett; Rev. Lafayette married Nancy Hetta Daniel, a sister to Sarah Frances Daniel; Elizabeth married Columbus Borders Wheeler; Exer married Hansford Preston; Mary Ellen died at the age of 14 years unmarried; Dr. Edgar Poe married first, Mousie

Williams and second, Ada Walker; Clora Della married first, Robert Nelson Cox, second, Elbert Davis and third, Julius Dick" Spears; Vinton Walter died at age 15 days; and Susie married James L Preston.

Rev. Lafayette Walter, son of Winfrey Holbrook and Elizabeth (Preston) Walter was born on Apr. 30, 1872, in Johnson County, KY, He was married on Jul. 4, 1890 in Johnson County, KY to Nancy Hetta Daniel who was born Nov. 19, 1870, at River, Johnson County, KY, a daughter of Wyatt A. and Merinda (Lyon) Daniel of River, KY and a granddaughter of Jesse and Ann Francis (Holbrook) Lyon of Martha, Lawrence County, KY. Nancy died at Ashland, KY on Mar. 10, 1950, and was buried at River next to her husband.

Lafayette was a well-known United Baptist preacher in the Big Sandy and Southern Ohio area. In addition to his church duties, in his early life he was a school teacher, a farmer, a store owner, and a building contractor. In 1905, he purchased 250 acres on Brushy Creek in Lawrence County, KY, and built a fine home where he was to live until the fall of 1917. He ran for county judge in 1917 but was defeated by 21 votes. On Oct. 30, 1917, he sold his farm to Amos Cordial and moved to Chillicothe, OH, where he had purchased a 150 acre farm and leased another 375 acres. In 1921, he moved to Ashland, KY, where he opened a grocery store and became a building contractor. Later, he purchased his father-in-law's farm at River, Johnson County, and lived a couple of years before purchasing a farm at Glade, Jackson County, OH, where he remained until his death on Sep. 12, 1929, of typhoid fever.

Lafayette and Nancy had seven children:

Dr. Cullie B. Walter (born Mar. 24, 1892, in Johnson County, KY) lived at Wilbur, Lawrence County, where he attended the public schools. He later attended Professor G. Milton Elam's Academy at Blaine. He graduated first in his class in 1912 at the Louisville College of Dentistry. After graduation, he returned to Lawrence County, where he set up practice at Blaine for a short period of time before moving his practice to Louisa. His office was across from the courthouse which he built and bears his name. In World War 1, he volunteered his services and was commissioned a lieutenant. After service, he returned to Louisa where he remained until Mar. 1, 1923, when he sold his practice to Dr. Elbert Skaggs and moved to Ashland, where he became a major real estate developer. In 1929, he moved to San Antonio, TX, where he again practiced dentistry. He died on Jun. 14, 1979, and is buried in San Antonio. He married Mary Esta Holbrook, who was born on Nov. 1, 1889 at Skaggs, Lawrence County, a daughter of Pleasant W. and Rutha (Skaggs) Holbrook and a granddaughter of Hargis and Fannie (Stambaugh) Holbrook and Lewis C. and Nancy (Lester) Skaggs. Esta died on May 10, 1971, and is also buried in San Antonio. Cullie and Esta were the parents of two children: Opal, who was a school teacher and never married; and Anita Eileen, who married Sam Vaughan and had two children, Kay and Douglas. Sam and Anita lived in Dallas, TX.

Ralph Waldo Walter (born Apr. 19, 1894, in Johnson County, KY, died Sep. 1, 1981), the second child of Lafayette and Nancy, is buried at Ashland, KY. Ralph was married first on Apr. 20, 1914, to Lena Eliza Burgess (born Sep. 8, 1895, at Wilbur, Lawrence County, KY), a daughter of Ben and Rosa (Davis) Burgess. Lena died Nov. 16, 1937. Ralph and Lena were the parents of one child, Ernest Graydon Walter, who married Margaret Cordle, and they had three children: Rosemary, Gary Dean and Ernest Graydon Jr. This family lives at Ashland, KY. Ralph married second on Feb. 16, 1927 to Eunice Jane Thompson (born Sep. 3, 1903 at Jettie, Lawrence County, KY). She was a teacher for many years in the Ashland Public School System. Ralph was a veteran of World War I and worked most of his life for Kitchen and Whitt Wholesale Grocers at Ashland. Ralph and Eunice had two children, Ralph Thompson and Ruth Modean Walter.

Guffie Clayton Walter (born Mar.26, 1898 in Johnson County, KY, died Aug. 11, 1961), the third child of Lafayette and Nancy, is buried in the Ashland Cemetery at Ashland, KY. He married first, Dollie Hayes (born Jan. 7, 1900, at Wilbur, Lawrence County, KY) and they had three children: Grace Milton, Cullie B. and Alvia Pauline Walter. Guffie married second on May 6, 1943 to Masil Garnet Halsey (born May 12, 1912) and they reared her nephew, Rodney Moss. Guffie was a veteran of both World War I and 11. He worked for the Semet Solvay Company at Ashland, KY.

Paul Walter (born Apr. 20, 1900, and died Mar. 31, 1901), the fourth child of Lafayette and Nancy is buried on his father's old farm at River, KY, which is now commonly known as the London Stapleton farm.

Lawson Wadsworth Walter (born Jan. 22, 1903 at River, Johnson County, KY), the fifth child of Lafayette and Nancy, moved to Wilbur, Lawrence County, KY, with his parents when he was a little over 1 year of age. He lived the last 33 years of his life at Ashland. He died there and is buried in the old Williams Cemetery. He attended the rural schools of Lawrence County, KY, Normal School at Louisa, Ashland High School and Ashland Business College. He was a farmer and an accountant for the Ashland Ford Motor Co. for a number of years.

Lawson Wadsworth Walter and Lora Thelma (Chandler) Walter

He married Lora Thelma Chandler on Jun. 1, 1929 at Waverly, OH. She was born at Charley, Lawrence County, KY, on Jan. 31, 1908, a daughter of John Henry and Nora (Hayes) Chandler and a granddaughter of Wesley Thompson and Alafair (Brown) Hayes and William Washington and Sarah Ann (Wheeler) Chandler, and a great-granddaughter of John and Elizabeth (Thompson) Hayes, James and Catherine (Daniel) Chandler, Archibald and Melinda (Francis) Brown, and Joshua Roman and Kesiah (Pack) Wheeler, all residents of Johnson County at one time. Thelma received her early education from John Hayes School at Charley. She moved with her parents to Beaver, OH, in 1920 and attended the public schools of Pike County, OH. She attended college at Wilmington College and graduated from Morehead State University. She taught in the rural schools of Scioto County, OH, the Catlettsburg Public Schools and the Boyd County Public Schools. She is active in genealogical research and has co-authored four books: *The Chandler Family of Eastern Kentucky, A Genealogical Record of the Descendants of Bazeal Hayes of Charley, Lawrence County, Kentucky*, and *A Genealogical Record of the Descendants of Israel Walter, Volumes I and II.*

Lawson Wadsworth Walter and Lora Thelma (Chandler) Walter

Nora (Hayes) Chandler and husband John Henry Chandler, grandparents of Theodore B. Walter Sr.

Lawson and Thelma are the parents of seven children, to wit: Marquis de Lafayette, John Paul, Wendell Jack, Richard Brockton, Norida Nan, Theodore Bronston and William Grady Walter. Marquis de Lafayette was born Sep. 12, 1930 at Beaver, OH. He is a retired teacher, having received his formal education in the public schools of Ashland, KY, Ashland Junior College and Marshall University (BA) and Morehead State University (MA). Prior to his retirement, he taught and coached in the public schools at Hillsborough County, FL, and Fairview and Russell, KY. He married Betty Jo Runyon on Jun. 12, 1951. She was born at Ashland, KY, a daughter of James "Jack" Vernon and Gertrude (Beverly) Runyon. Lafayette and Betty Jo have eight children: John Randolph is single and is a geologist at Tampa, FL; Marquis de Lafayette II, married Pamela Stapleton and they have three children: Angela, Cristin and Matthew. They live at Lexington, KY. Jacqueline married Aaron Dale Burke and they had two children: Russell and Amanda. They live at Ashland, KY. James Lawson married Amy Albright, and they live at Cincinnati, OH. They have two children, Anna Lora and Bonnie Elizabeth. Beverly Jo married Carl Coats. They have one child, Zachary. They live at St. Petersburg, FL. Daniel Chandler married Rebecca Daniel. They have two children, Ryan and Samantha Walter. Daniel's second marriage is to Melissa Bledsoe. Mary Beth, the eighth child of Lafayette and Betty Jo, is a physical therapist and lives in Louisville, KY.

John Paul, the second child of Lawson and Thelma, was born at Beaver, OH, on Oct. 19, 1932. He owned and operated J&S Jewelry at Ashland, KY before retiring. He attended the public schools of Ashland and Ashland Junior College. He married Sylvia Maxine Peery on Dec. 31, 1952. She was born Sep. 17, 1933, at Ashland, KY, a daughter of Hobart Thomas and Easter (Daniel) Peery. John served in the US Army, 76th Tank Battalion, llth Airborne Division, 1953-55. John and Sylvia are the parents of four children: Cynthia Jeanne married Randall Warren Elkins. They have one child, Adam. Paul Gregory married Vickie Bush and they have one child, Morgan; Timothy Peery married Leslie Alexander. Gregory and Timothy are twins. Greg and Tim are graduates of the University of Kentucky and are certified public accountants. Philip Michael married Paula Atkins, and they have two children, Michael and Andrew. Philip is a graduate of the College of Business and Economics, University of Kentucky, and they live at Ashland, KY.

Wendell Jack, the third child of Lawson and Thelma, was born Mar. 24, 1935, at Ashland, KY. He married Virginia L. Lanthorne on Jun. 15, 1962, at Ashland, KY. She was born Oct. 21, 1939 at Ashland, KY, a daughter of Norman and Virginia (Swan) Lanthorne. Jack attended the public schools of Ashland and Morehead State University. He served in the US Navy, 1954-56 on the USS *Salem* in the 6th Fleet in the Mediterranean and in the Far East aboard the USS *Baltimore*. He was employed with Ashland Oil, Inc. before retirement. Virginia attended the public schools of Ashland and graduated from the University of Kentucky, College of Education. She is a teacher in the Ashland Public School System. Jack and Virginia are the parents of four children: Wendell Jeffrey is a graduate of the University of Kentucky School of Journalism. He worked as a copy editor for the *Lexington (Kentucky) Herald-Leader* newspaper before becoming a free-lance writer. He is married to Roberta Reece and they have one son, Reece. Roberta taught in the Fayette County School System. They now live in Nashville, TN. Bruce Edward is single and lives in Ashland, KY. He is a graduate of the University of Kentucky College of Business and Economics. Patrick Scott married Shelia Keeney and they live in South Point, OH where Shelia is a teacher. Amy Leigh married Steve Alley who is a fireman. Amy works for the Unity Baptist Church.

Richard Brockton, the fourth child of Lawson and Thelma, was born at Ashland, KY on Jul. 6, 1937. He married Carole Lynn Webb on Oct. 1, 1957 at Ashland, KY. She was born at Ashland on Nov. 20, 1937, a daughter of Jay B. and Elizabeth (Porter) Webb. Richard attended the public schools of Catlettsburg, Morehead State University and University of Tampa. He was employed by Ashland Oil, Inc. at Catlettsburg before retirement. Richard and Carole are the parents of four children; Natalie Lynn married Jack Rife and they have two children, Tessa and Rachael Joyce. Natalie is a graduate of Morehead State University. Richard Brockton II is single and a graduate of Morehead State University. Elizabeth Suzanne married Robert Gonzalas and they have two children, Rex and Thor. Nancy Elaine married Shannon Coleman and they had two children, Jay and Randi. Nancy's second married is to Johnny Spaulding and they have one child, Sidney Spaulding.

Norida Nan, the fifth child of Lawson and Thelma, was born Apr. 24, 1940, at Ashland, KY. She married Bob Herbst Nipp on Sep. 20, 1963, at Ashland, KY. He was born Dec. 2, 1936, at Ashland, KY, a son of Curtis and Isabelle (Herbst) Nipp. Bob is a graduate of the University of Kentucky and the University of Cincinnati. He is employed by the Armco Steel Corporation at Ashland, KY. Norida attended the public schools of Catlettsburg, Ashland Community College, and the University of South Florida. Norida and Bob are parents of three children: Bob Herbst II, a graduate of the University, and married to Julia Ann Benton; William Christopher, a graduate of the University of Kentucky and the University of Connecticut, and married to Jennifer Ann Clancy. William and Jennifer have two children, William Christopher Jr. and Abagail Elizabeth; John Charles a graduate of the University of Kentucky. John is married to Sheri Mechille Oliver. They live at Tupelo, MS where John is a stock broker.

Theodore Bronston, the sixth child of Lawson and Thelma, was born at Ashland, KY, on Sep. 10, 1943. He attended the public schools of Catlettsburg, KY, and graduated in 1965 from the University of Kentucky, College of Education, and in 1970 from the College of Law. He is an attorney in Lexington and a partner with the law firm of Todd & Walter. He is a past president of the Kentucky Genealogical Society, having been one of the founding charter members. He is also active in the Masons, having served as president of the Masonic Temple Association of Lexington from 1983-86. He has co-authored four genealogical publications with his mother, Thelma, on the Hayes, Chandler and Walter families of Lawrence County, KY (see above for titles). On Aug. 7, 1965, Ted married Patricia Lynne Wilson (born Nov. 13, 1944 at Chester, PA), a daughter of Arnold and Kathleen (Howard) Wilson. She is a granddaughter of George Edward and Mellie May (Carter) Wilson and a great-granddaughter of Mordiaci and Vashti (Jarrell) Wilson, and Strother J. "Dock" and America (Prince) Carter, all residents of Lawrence County during their lifetime. Patricia "Patsy" received her BA and MA from the University of Kentucky, College of Education. She was a counselor at Tates Creek Senior High School at Lexington before retirement. Ted and Patricia are parents of one child, Theodore Bronston II (born Feb. 5, 1984 at Lexington, KY).

William Grady, the seventh child of Lawson and Thelma, was born Nov. 5, 1945, at Ashland, KY. He attended the public schools at Catlettsburg, KY. He received his BA from the University of Kentucky, College of Education, and his MA from Morehead State University. He is a teacher and a coach at Russell High School at Russell, KY. He married Carol Sue Barcello on Dec. 9, 1967 at Lexington, KY. Sue was born at Kenova, Wayne County, WV, on Nov. 12, 1946, a daughter of Manuel and Rosemary (Null) Barcello. She is employed with Ashland Oil, Inc. in their travel department. Grady and Sue are the parents of two children, William Grady II (born Aug. 10, 1968 at Lexington, KY), a graduate of Paul Blazer High School and University of Kentucky, College of Education. He taught English at Tates Creek Senior High at Lexington, KY and is now the editor of *Kentucke Magazine*. He is married to Jena Pillion; Dwight (born Oct. 14, 1972) is married to Melissa Kazee. Dwight and Jena have one child, Casey Marie Walter.

Dean Emerson Walter, the sixth child of Lafayette and Nancy was born Oct. 22, 1905, at Wilbur, Lawrence County, KY. He died Dec. 3, 1987, at Ashland, KY and is buried in the Rose Hill Mausoleum at Ashland. He was married first to Cynthia Jane Ball (born Oct. 13, 1906, in Lawrence County, KY and died Apr. 15, 1990, at Huntington, WV. Dean and Jane were married Dec. 24, 1928. They later divorced. They had three children: Joanne Exer Walter married Aldophido Frank Smith on Jun. 30, 1949. They have four children: Nancy Jane, Karen Jo, Sharon Ann and Franklin Keith Smith. Dean Emerson Jr., the second child of Dean and Jane, was married twice, first to Antionette Kurban on Jun. 1, 1956. They had one child: Michael David Walter. Dean Jr. married second Betty Francis Baker and they had two children: Joseph Bradley and Judith Dee Walter. Dean Emerson Walter married second, Sadie Mary Daniel on May 23, 1940 at River, Johnson County, KY, a daughter of Henry Ashbury and Rebecca (Blevins) Daniel and a granddaughter of Wyatt A. and Merinda (Lyons) Daniel. Dean worked in the automotive sales industry most of his life, first for McGuire Motor Co. at Ashland, then at Bruce Walters Ford at Pikeville, and later he owned and operated his own Walters Ford Agency at Prestonburg, KY.

Thelma Gladys Walter, the seventh child of Lafayette and Nancy, was born Jan. 22, 1911, at Wilbur, Lawrence County, KY. She died Mar. 9, 1980, and is buried in the Highland Memorial Park at Staffordsville, KY. She was married on Sep. 19, 1928, to Ervin Wallen (born Oct. 19, 1908 at Henreitta, Johson County, KY), a son of William and Gypsie (Murray) Wallen. He died Oct. 17, 1982 and was buried next to his wife.

Wyatt A. Daniel and Merinda (Lyon) Daniel

Nelle (Walters) Dickison Lafayette Walter

Thelma and Ervin were the parents of six children: Nancy Geraldine Wallen (born Jun. 9, 1929 and died Jul. 19, 1960). She was married on Jan. 3, 1947 to Ora Quinton Sparks (born Jan. 13, 1919, and died on May 16, 1960). They had no children. Thelma and Ervin's second child was Anna Myraleen Wallen (born Dec. 20, 1931) who married on Apr. 5, 1954, Edwin Shane Walters (born Oct. 1, 1927). They are the parents of five children: Edwin Shane Jr., Linda Carol, Valorie Kay, Susan Ann and Pamela Ann

Standing L-R: W. Jack Walter, Theodore B. Walter Sr., Bob Herbst Nipp, Richard B. Walter, John Paul Walter, Lafayette Walter, Wm. Grady Walter. Seated L-R: Virginia (Lanthorne) Walter, Patsy (Wilson) Walter, Norida Nan (Walter) Nipp, T. (Chandler) Walter, Carol (Webb) Walter, Sylvia (Peery) Walter, Betty Jo (Runyon) Walter, Sue (Barcello) Walter

Walters. This family lives at Tallahassee, FL. Douglas Graden Wallen, the third child of Thelma and Ervin, was born Dec. 30, 1933, at River, Johnson County, KY. He was married on Jun. 7, 1953, to Betty Lou Sturgill (born Aug. 17, 1934). They are the parents of three children: Beverly Ann, Barry Douglas and Mary Elizabeth Wallen. Doug and Betty live at Boons Camp, KY. Edgar Poe Wallen, the fourth child of Thelma and Ervin, was born Mar. 9, 1937 at Auxier, KY. He was married Sep. 1, 1956, to Lou Hazel Banks (born Jul. 12, 1936). They had one child, Susan Michelle Wallen (born May 16, 1975 and died in an automobile accident Aug. 6, 1986). Ed received his doctorate of ministry at Luther Rice Seminary. He is a minister in the Baptist Church at Hueytown, AL. Karen Gail is the fifth child of Thelma and Ervin Wallen. She was born Feb. 17, 1947 at River, Johnson County, KY. She was married Mar. 30, 1968, to Ronald Edward Holliday (born Sep. 8, 1938). They are the parents of three children: Nancy Anne, Melissa Lynn and Chad Edward Holliday. This family lives at Ft. Myers, FL. David Anthony Wallen is the youngest child of Thelma and Ervin. He was born on Oct. 9, 1950, at River, Johnson County, KY. He is married to Jane Burgess and they have three children: Emily Jane, Beth Burgess and Joseph David. David is a Kentucky State Trooper. David and Jane live at Louisa, KY.

Theodore B. Walter II, Sadie Mary (Daniel) Walter

L-R: Theodore B. Walter II, Patricia (Wilson) Walter, Theodore B. Walter Sr.

Additional Notes: Merinda Lyon was born in 1833 in Lawrence County, KY. She died in 1898 and is buried in the Daniel Cemetery at River, Johnson County, KY. She was married in Lawrence County, KY to Wyatt A. Daniel (born 1834 in Johnson County, KY, and died 1914). Wyatt was a son of Isom and Polly (Borders) Daniel. Merinda Lyon was a daughter of

Jesse Lyon (born Apr. 12, 1789 in North Carolina), and Anne Frances Holbrook, a daughter of William and Agnes (Collier) Holbrook. Jesse and Anne Frances were married Jul. 17, 1814. Jesse and Anne Frances were from Dockery, Wilkes County, NC.

L-R: Wendell Jack Walter, John H. Walters, Douglas G. Wallen

William Lyon, father of Jesse, was born Feb. 17, 1752, in Culpepper County, VA, and died Apr. 15, 1847. William married Magdaline Corbin, mother of Jesse who was a daughter of John and Frances (Fant) Corbin. William Lyon and William Holbrook were veterans of the American Revolution, and they are buried along with their wives in the Lyon-Holbrook Cemetery at Martha, Lawrence County, KY.

WALTERS - Clark F. Walters was born Jul. 18, 1887 in Johnson County, KY to George N. Walters and Mariah Louise King. He was married to Hattie Blair Dec. 24, 1912. She was the daughter of Franklin Pierce Blair, Attorney at Law and Nancy Catherine Adams.

Mr. and Mrs. Walters were the parents of three daughters: Louise Weldon, born Jul. 19, 1915, Georgemary born Mar. 19, 1923 and Nancy Catherine born Aug. 25, 1926.

Mr. Walters was employed by Standard Oil Co. in 1922 and retired in 1952. He was a member of First Baptist Church of Paintsville, KY, serving as deacon, superintendent of the Sunday School Department, president of Brotherhood, and at the time of his death he was serving as recording secretary of the Paintsville church and treasurer of Enterprise Association.

Mr. Walters served on the Paintsville City Council several terms, and during that tenure the city purchased the Paintsville Water Works and the City Gas System. He served as Paintsville City Treasurer until his untimely death.

Mrs. Walters taught school from 1911 until 1920 when she chose to become a full-time homemaker. She was a member of First Baptist Church, Paintsville, KY, where she taught Sunday School and was president of Women's Missionary Society. She also served as vice president of Northeastern Region of Kentucky Baptists and trustee of Magoffin Baptist Institute.

Two of Mr. and Mrs. Walters daughters lived in Houston, TX. Louise is president of Stockdale, Inc. She has four children: Harriet Louise Marsala, Dr. Hope Lucinda Stockdale, H.L. "Ridge" Stockdale Jr. and Joseph Shields Stockdale II.

Nancy was personnel director of Houston Libraries until her death on Aug. 28, 1979. She had two children: Ann Clark Kazee and Robert B. Kazee Jr. Georgemary was co-owner of Wellman Hardware, Louisa, KY, until she retired in 1990. She had three children: Ann Adams Hall who died in infancy, Gayle Walters Thacker who died in 1964, and Joel Preston Thacker.

Mr. Walters died on May 30, 1966 and was buried in Mayo Cemetery.

WALTON & WELLS - Manford Walton, born Aug. 2, 1927 in Johnson County to the late Chester and Lucy DeLong Walton. He is 5'8" tall, black hair, blue eyes and fair complexion. His father, Chester Walton (born Feb. 22, 1898, died May 3, 1931), the son of George Washington and Margaret Addis Walton. of Wellston, OH. Chester came to Eastern Kentucky in 1925 seeking work, married Oct. 4, 1926 Lucy DeLong (born Aug. 3, 1908, died Jul. 18, 1985), the daughter of Marion and Viola Wells DeLong, Lucy was about 5' tall black hair and olive complexion.

Mary F. Wells Walton, Manford Walton

Manford Walton, served 5-1/2 years in the military one year in Japan and four years in Germany. He was discharged from Fort Knox, KY in November 1951, married Mary Frances Wells (born Sep. 27, 1932) the daughter of Benjamin H. and Susana Richmond Wells. Mary is 5"5" tall with hazel eyes and auburn hair. They married on Dec. 27, 1951. Manford retired from Chevron Oil Inc. in 1985.

Manford, Mary Wells, Timothy A. and Bradford Walton

They have two sons, Bradford (born Nov. 17, 1952) and Timothy Alan (born Aug. 9, 1958), both graduated from Russell High School. Brad graduated from the University of Kentucky with a master's in structural engineer. He presently owns and operated Walton's Engineer, Lexington, KY. He married Jul. 31, 1983 to Katherine A. Adams of Sulpher, KY, who is an attorney for the University of KY. They have no children.

Timothy attended the University of Kentucky and graduated from Ashland Vocational School as a electronic technician. He works for Kentucky Education Television in Central Kentucky. He married in Chicago, IL, on Aug. 9, 1996 to Nancy S. Leach of Ashland, KY. They presently reside in Morgantown, KY, where his wife Nancy is employed with Semitone Corp., Morgantown, KY. They have no children.

Mary Frances Wells Walton, was with the Third National Bank in Ashland before returning to College and graduating from Morehead State University with a degree in social work. She worked for the state of Kentucky as a child protection worker, Foster Care-Adoption before taking a position with Eastern Kentucky University where she worked for five years before retirement in 1995. In her position with EKU she trained or coordinated training for Social Service Staff in the Fivco Big Sandy District.

Manford and Mary are active in the Wells Family Association. Mary serves as co-editor with Tommie Cochran for the Wells Family Association family newsletter. They are members of the Advance United Methodist Church, Flatwoods, KY both having served in many different positions in their church. Mary presently serves as delegate to the Conference, Official Council Pastor Parish committee and Finance Committee for her church. Member of United Methodist Women. She is active in K-wood Homemakers and the YMCA.

Manford works with the Shriners transporting children to the hospital in Lexington and Cincinnati. He previously served in different capacities of his church and served for eight years as city commissioner of Bellefonte serving head of several departments including four years as Police commissioner. The Walton's reside on Mt. Savage Drive, Bellefonte, KY where they have lived for 38 years.

WARD - Roma G. Ward, the seventh of nine children, was born on Oct. 4, 1892 in Johnson County, KY to Colba Ward and Frances Preston Ward who were residents of River, KY. Roma's great-grandfather, William Ward, moved from Russell County, VA in 1805 when he was about 13 years old. He married Elizabeth Meek in 1816 and they made their home at River, KY.

Roma G. Ward

After serving in the Army in France during World War I, Roma returned to Johnson County to attend school to complete his education. He became a teacher in the Johnson County School District teaching in a one-room school house. After teaching for several years, he became a foreman with the WPA during the depression years. When this job ended, he began working for the U.S. Postal Service in Cincinnati. Even though he was employed away from Johnson County, he still maintained his farm at River, KY and was on the farm as much as possible. In 1948, he was transferred to a position with the Postal Department in Ashland, KY. He was employed there until he retired in January 1958.

Roma married Gladys McFadden, the daughter of Ross and Monnie McCarty McFadden in 1935. They were the parents of four daughters: Nila Jean, Frances Sue, Karen Lynn and Roma Lou. His daughters, Nila Jean and Frances Sue graduated from Meade Memorial High School.

Roma died Aug. 4, 1962 of a heart attack while working on his farm. A few months after his death, Gladys sold the farm and moved to Ohio to be near her two older daughters. The two younger daughters, Karen Lynn and Roma Lou, graduated from high schools in Ohio and they still reside there along with Frances Sue. Nila Jean resides in Lexington, SC, and is retired from employment with the Federal Government.

WARD & WHEELER - Wiley Ward was born Dec. 1, 1904 at Boones Camp, Johnson County, KY, the son of Abisha "Bish" Ward and Martha Branham. His paternal grandparents were Greenville Ward and Hannah Butcher; his maternal grandparents were Exer Ward and Joseph Branham. He died May 16, 1986 at Flat Gap, KY. He attended school at Boones Camp and Mayo Normal School, Paintsville.

Wiley Ward and Velma Wheeler Ward

He married Velma Wheeler, Sep. 23, 1932, in Williamson, Mingo County, WV. He taught school at Rockhouse in 1923 and Trace Fork in 1924, both in Martin County. In 1925 he taught the upper grades in a two-room school at Buffalo (Meally), Johnson County, with his sister, Nellie, teaching the lower grades. Following this he was employed with United Fuel and Gas Company of Maryland working throughout Kentucky, West Virginia, Virginia and Maryland. At the onset of the depression he began farming and farmed for over 50 years in the Franks Creek area of Flat Gap. He won several farm awards including the District Master

Pastureman Award.

In addition to farming he was employed by the Soil Conservation Service for a short period during the late 40s and early 50s. Throughout the latter 50s and 60s he worked for the Agricultural Stabilization and Conservation Service (ASCS) of Johnson County where he eventually became farm field supervisor. He was an avid reader throughout his life, something that was taught and encouraged at an early age by his mother to all her children.

Velma Wheeler was born Feb. 9, 1906 on Lower Franks Creek of Winifred, now Flat Gap, Johnson County, KY the daughter of William "Henderson" Wheeler and Eliza Jane Phillips. She died Aug. 26, 1993 in Hawthorne, Los Angeles County, CA. Her paternal grandparents were William "Daniel" Wheeler and Mary Salyer and her maternal grandparents were William Powell Phillips and Margaret Sparks. She was a life-long member of Bethel United Baptist Church. Velma and Wiley are buried at Camant Cemetery (also known as Old Fields), Lower Laurel Creek of Flat Gap.

She attended grade school in the one-room school at Lower Franks Creek transferring to Paintsville schools in the seventh grade. She began her teaching career at Little Paint in 1924 when she was 18. Like others of this time, she taught and attended school at intervals usually teaching in rural schools and returning to high school for half a year after the term for rural schools had ended. She graduated from Paintsville High School in 1926 and attended Morehead College beginning in 1927. She taught various schools throughout the county including Little Paint, Three Forks of Greasy, Clifton, Sugar Grove and Lower Franks Creek retiring after 27 years. She was an active 4-H Club leader for many years.

Wiley and Velma had two children, Phyllis Edra, born Nov. 6, 1934 and Daniel Keith, born Feb. 4, 1936. Both graduated from Flat Gap High School-Phyllis in the Class of 1953 and Daniel Keith in the Class of 1954. Danny attended Pikeville College and served nine and a half years in the U.S. Air Force with overseas assignments in South Korea and Spain. He currently lives in Waterford, MI and works for General Motors Corporation in Pontiac. Phyllis graduated from Mayo State Vocational School. She married Leonard "Bud" Burton in Long Beach, CA. They spent a number of years living and working in Thailand and are now retired and living in Los Angeles, CA. *Submitted by Phyllis (Ward) Burton.*

WEBB - Elize Hatcher "John" Webb was born Dec. 13, 1903, the fifth child of Grant and Helen Bowe Webb in Paintsville, Johnson County, KY. The Webb family moved to Hugo, OK in 1909 where John received his education. His older sisters married and moved to California and in 1926 John and his friends followed and found jobs in Gerber, CA with Southern Pacific Railroad and in the farming industry.

Elize Hatcher Webb

John married Iris Hunter Nicholson, Jul. 25, 1927 in Sacramento, CA. They lived in Gerber, CA where their children: Mildred Elaine, John Grant, Elizabeth Joy and Carolyn Janice Evedell were born.

In 1934 they moved to Westwood, Lassen County, CA where Frances and James were born.

John worked for the Red River Company at a variety of jobs. In the early 40s, John began building houses and selling them in Westwood and Susanville.

The Walker Family sold Red River Lumber Company to Fruit Growers Supply who almost immediately began closing mill operation and John moved his family to Susanville, Lassen, CA. After moving to Susanville, John worked the rest of his life constructing and remodeling houses.

John built or remodeled homes for each of his children at one time or another. He built the family vacation cabin at Eagle Lake, built and helped his wife Iris operate the Webb's Drive-Inn in Chester, CA.

He was a life time member of the AFL-CIO Carpenter's Union. He was an expert building tilt up concrete forms, we can all still see the first prison, the Main Street, "Old Safeway Building," Lassen College and Lassen High buildings.

It has been said that John had his hammer on almost every house and building in the Susanville area.

John loved to dance. In Westwood their home was often the Party Place. A band was setup in the porch off the living room and folks square and round danced the night away accompanied by good food and games for the children.

His home was always open to anyone. He never failed to offer food or drink and always good cheer.

One time in Westwood the circus came to town and there was no place to accommodate the "Fat Lady." Dad got a couple of friends and they cleared up a room in his house and constructed a bed strong enough to accommodate the "Fat Lady." Morale of the story, no one in John's knowledge would be without the necessities of living if even for just a night.

After his first wife passed away, John married Katherine Ellen Mercer Chandler (a widow) who had been a family friend for years, we called her Murphy. They had 17 wonderful years together. *Written by Frances Hemphill, daughter and submitted by Carolyn J. Danford, daughter.*

WEBB - Frank B. Webb was born Dec. 16, 1911 in Johnson County, KY, son of William Leonard Webb and Pearl Short Webb of Meally, KY. The Webbs operated a country store at Meally, KY and in the 1930s operated a dry goods store on Main Street in Paintsville, KY. Frank and Elva Spears born Jan. 28, 1916, daughter of Wilbur Spears and Ella Wiley Spears of Hager Hill, KY were married May 11, 1938, at Auxier, KY by Spurgen Hunnicutt.

Frank B. Webb and Elva Spears Webb

Frank attended a one room school at Meally. He graduated from Van Lear High School in 1933 and graduated from Morehead State College with an AB degree in 1936. In 1947 he graduated from The University of Cincinnati, OH with an MA in education and supervision.

In 1939 he became principal of Jenny's Creek High School, and later served as principal at Mead Memorial High School and Oil Springs High School. He also was assistant principal of Johnson Central High School. In 1950 he became supervisor of Johnson County Schools. He served for 43 years in Johnson County Schools. Elva completed eight grades at Hager Hill, graduated from Paintsville High School in 1933, from Booth Business College in 1935, and from Morehead State College. She taught in Johnson County for 27 years. The Webb's have two daughters, Phyllis Ann Young, Bellbrook, OH and Barbara J. Lavender, Hager Hill and five grandchildren: Dr. Timothy R. Lavender, Michelle Robinson, Brenda Mckee, Suzan Starkey and Gail Sharrod .

Frank and Elva are both members of the Paintsville Church of Christ. Frank serves as an elder of the church.

WEDDINGTON - Hershel Kenneth Weddington, son of Leonidas "Lee" and Dora Alice (Blair) Weddington was born Feb. 6, 1909 at Leander, KY and died Mar. 3, 1993 in Highland Hospital. He was buried in Johnson County Memorial Cemetery.

Hershel, Ethel and Loretta Weddington

Hershel met and married Ethel Blair, daughter of Alfred Harlan and Rosa Lee (Caudill) Blair. Ethel was born Nov. 1, 1909 at Denver, KY, and died Jun. 7, 1994 in Paul B. Hall Medical Center. She was buried in Johnson County Memorial Cemetery beside her husband of 63 years. They took their marriage vows seriously and lived a devoted happy life together. They were both members of Beechwald United Baptist Church at Leander.

Hershel and Ethel spent their entire life living in Johnson County. They began housekeeping in West Van Lear, where Hershel was employed in Van Lear Coal Mines.

Their first child, Loretta, was born Nov. 22, 1929. Not only was this the first child of Hershel and Ethel, it was the first grandchild of Harlan and Rosa Lee Blair.

In 1932 Hershel and Ethel moved to Jennies Creek near his birthplace at Leander. They remained at this address the rest of their life. She was the Leander News reporter for the *Paintsville Herald* for over 25 years.

Loretta attended the Buckhorn School and Jennies Creek High School graduating in 1946. She graduated from Pikeville College with a teaching certificate and began teaching first grade at Jennies Creek consolidated Elementary School at Leander. She attended Morehead University earning an AB degree in education in 1957. After eight years teaching at Jennies Creek, Loretta moved to New Carlisle, OH in 1956, and began teaching in Bethel Local School, Tipp City, OH. She retired in 1982 and returned to Leander, KY, where she cared for her parents until their deaths in 1993 and 1994. She still resides at the home place.

The second child of Hershel and Ethel was delivered by midwife Callie Vaughn, Oct. 9, 1933 and was named Opal Evelyn.

Opal attended Buckhorn School through 8th grade. She attended Oil Springs High School graduating in 1950. Opal continued her education at University of Tennessee earning her degree in nursing. She is retired and lives in Knoxville, TN with her husband R.B. Bundren, who is a retired private detective. They are the parents of five children: Michael Kenneth Bundren (born Apr. 14, 1953); Sherry Ethel Bundren (born May 29, 1954); Canny Edward Bundren (born Sep. 1, 1955); Teresa Ann Bundren (born Jul. 15, 1956, died Sep. 20, 1994) and Mary Evelyn Bundren (born Nov. 11, 1957).

Hershel and Ethel reared Michael Kenneth Bundren from the age of three months. He attended Jennies Creek Consolidated School and Oil Springs High and graduated from Johnson Central High School in 1970. Mike married Christine Jarrells from Columbus, OH. Mike and Chris live at East Point, KY.

The third and last child of Hershel and Ethel is Kenneth Elwood who was born Jan. 30, 1945. Kenneth attended Jennies Creek Consolidate School and graduated from Oil Springs High School in 1962. He attended Mayo School and graduated as an electrician. After spending three years in the Army in Germany he returned home and married Joyce Castle. They reside in Saline, MI. He is a retired electrician and Joyce is employed at St. Joseph Mercy Hospital as case manager.

WELLS - Alex Samuel Wells (born Sep. 23, 1937), the youngest of Benjamin and Susana Richmond Wells 10 children. Alex was active in sports as a young man playing basketball and baseball throughout his high school years. He was a good looking man of 6'2" tall, blue eyes, light brown hair and fair complexion. He was known for his strength. He fought in the Golden Glove Boxing Tournament while in high school.

He entered the military after graduating from high school and after his discharge went to Cleveland, OH to find work. He returned to Kentucky to work in heavy equipment for a strip mining company. He had a sawmill and timbered after leaving the mines, until becoming disabled. Alex married Susan Goble, of Martin County, KY at the age of 29.

Alex Samuel, Ben, Susie, Goldie Vertrice, Anita, Alex and Bernita Wells

Alex has seven children, Sheri Lynn Wells (born Nov. 4, 1966 in Beckley, WV); Anita Kay Wells (born Jul. 12, 1967); Vernita Lynn Wells (born Jun. 21, 1968); Alex Samuel Wells Jr. (born Jul. 5, 1972); Bernita Wells (born Apr. 5, 1975); Goldie Ann Wells (born Oct. 16, 1982); and Benjamin Joshua Wells (born Mar. 10, 1984). Sherri married Norman Bennett (born Oct. 7, 1966) and they reside in Lexington, NC. They have no children.

Anita Kay Wells (born Jul. 12, 1967 in Johnson County, KY) married Craig Faith in 1988 after their divorce, he was killed in an auto accident. Anita and Brad Longsworth have one son, Cody David Longsworth (born Aug. 30, 1993) and reside in Calvert City, KY.

Vernita Lynn Wells (born Jun. 21, 1968 at Highland Regional Hospital) married Richard Wilcox on Mar. 12, 1988. They have three children: Caleb Lee Wilcox (born Dec. 5, 1991); Amber Nicole Wilcox (born Dec. 4, 1993); and Nathaniel Lee Wilcox (born Feb. 10, 1998). The family is active in the Freewill Baptist Church and reside in Van Lear, KY.

Alex Samuel Wells Jr. (born May 5, 1972 at Highland Regional Hospital) married on Dec. 5, 1992, to Melissa Conley (born Nov. 19, 1974), the daughter of Winfrey and Sharon Witten Conley. Alex is employed for a coal company and Melissa is employed for Brian Cumbo, attorney in Martin County, KY. Alex and Melissa have two daughters, Hope Alexander Wells (born Jul. 21, 1994) and Lakin Dawnielle Wells (born Jan. 18, 1997). Alex and Melissa reside on Rt. 3, Van Lear, KY.

Bernita Wells (born Apr. 5, 1975 at Highland Regional Hospital) entered the U.S. Army and is stationed in Texas. She served two six month terms in Saudi Arabia. Bernita has one child, Marcus Nathaniel Wells (born Nov. 30, 1998). She has enlisted in the Army for two more years.

Goldie Ann Wells is a Junior at Johnson Central High School. She is a honor student and was selected as an All-American Scholar, which is awarded to those with academic excellence. Goldie is very athletic and plays ball for her school and is an excellent shot when it comes to deer hunting. She got her first deer during the 1998 deer season in Johnson County.

Benjamin Joshua Wells is a sophomore at Johnson Central High School. Ben is active in baseball and loves hunting. He usually gets his limit when deer season is in.

Alex and Susie reside at Rt. 3, Daniels Creek, with Goldie and Ben.

WELLS - Arnold Wells was born Feb. 27, 1936 at Slagle, WV to Charles Wells and Hazel (Daniels) Wells. He is the youngest of three children born to his parents.

Arnold Wells

Arnold was married in Johnson County, KY, to Betty L. Grimm on Nov. 21, 1961 and they are the parents of two children: Arnold Kevin (born Jan. 26, 1963) and Anita Kimberly (born Jul. 4, 1965).

Arnold is a graduate of Paintsville High School with the Class of 1955. He attended Pikeville College on a basketball scholarship and later transferred and graduated from Eastern Kentucky University with a BS degree in accounting. He successfully passed the uniform certified public accounting examination and became a partner in the accounting firm of Helton, Butler and Wells, CPA's, that later changed the name to Wells & Company, PSC. The firm has prospered and served the clientele of Eastern Kentucky for the last 35 years.

Arnold's son, Arnold Kevin, graduated from Paintsville High School and Eastern Kentucky University and became a certified public accountant and works with the firm of Wells & Company, PSC. He married Deana Dotson and has fathered a daughter named Chelsea Paige.

Arnold's daughter graduated from Paintsville High School and attended Eastern Kentucky University. She was accepted into the Southern School of Optometry at Memphis, TN. There she met and married Mark Nordin. They are optometrists and own Nordin Eye Center, PSC with locations in Paintsville, Prestonsburg and Salyersville. They have two sons, Mark Elliott and Bradley Andrew, and one daughter Victoria Leslie.

WELLS & HARRISON - Benjamin "Ben" Harrison Wells (born Feb. 14, 1891 at East Point, KY, died Feb. 26, 1959 at Paintsville Hospital) was one of eight children born to Alexander Morgan Wells (born 1885, died 1937) and Polly Peery Wells (born 1868, died 1905). Ben had black hair, blue eyes, fair complexion, 5'8" tall and was known for his strength. A man that enjoyed a good joke and having fun. He never seen a stranger. He married Feb. 5, 1916, to Susana "Ann" Richmond (born Nov. 8, 1897, died Feb. 10, 1982), the daughter of Samuel Buchanan Richmond and Unoka Clark Richmond.

Benjamin H. and Susana Richmond Wells (1917)

Ben was a farmer and machinist in the mines. He worked both at North East and Consolidate mines until they worked out. His wife Ann was a merchant, operating a general store for approximately 20 years on Daniels Creek until retirement in 1956. Ben worked in the mines and farmed where everything was raised for their large family. Ben was a craftsman in that he could do anything that he put his mind to. Ann was very artistic and gifted in writing poetry, sewing, gardening, canning and preserving of all types of the things that was raised by the family. There were always plenty to last all winter plus feed visitors during the year. They always raised a large patch of cane to make their own sorghum with some left to sell. Farm life for the family was a team effort—everyone worked and knew what their jobs were and never asked questions. The parents never had to worry about the chores being done because the children were taught early responsibility. Ben and Ann had a strong work ethic and passed this onto their children and grandchildren. The children and grandchildren inherited many of their talents and several of the children and grandchildren are known artists today.

Ben and Ann Richmond Wells had 10 children: Geneva Wells Volota (born Nov. 11, 1916, died Aug. 14, 1993); Bennie Wells Jr. (born Mar. 2, 1918, died Jan. 15, 1960); Jeanette Wells (born Jan. 30, 1920, died May 10, 1982); Nevard Wells (born Mar. 27, 1922); Betty Wells Brown (born Sep. 20, 1924, died Jun. 8, 1980); Polly Wells Collins (born Jan. 2, 1927); Minnie Sue Wells (born Aug. 27, 1930, died Jan. 4, 1992) Mary Frances Wells Walton (born Sep. 27, 1932); Emma Delores Wells Adkins (born Mar. 3, 1935); and Alex Samuel Wells (born Sep. 23, 1937). Ann told her daughter Mary that Ben loved children and was excited each time she became pregnant.

Ben and Ann Richmond Wells are buried in the Wells Family Cemetery Rt. 3, Daniels Creek. Their daughters, Betty Wells Brown and Minnie Sue Wells, are also buried there. Bennie Wells was buried there to but was moved later by his children to Brick Union Cemetery, Lloyd, (Greenup County) KY, after his wife Jaunita died so they could be buried together. Geneva Wells Volota is buried in the mausoleum at Sunset Memorial Park, 6265 Columbia Rd., North Olmsteade, OH. Jeanette Wells is buried at Highland Memorial, Paintsville, KY.

Nevard Wells, Alex Wells, Polly Wells Collins and Emma Wells Adkins reside on Rt. 3, Van Lear, KY. Mary F. Wells Walton resides in Ashland (Bellfonte) KY.

WELLS & GOBLE - Bennie Wells Jr. (born Mar. 2, 1918 in Johnson County, KY died Jan. 15, 1960 in Greenup County, KY) was one of 10 children of Benjamin and Susana Richmond Wells. Bennie was a good looking man of 5'7," blue eyes, fair complexion, weighing 170 pounds. Bennie was very adventurous in that as a young man, he went hoboing across country. Bennie entered the U.S. Army on Jun. 14, 1949, at Fort Knox, KY. His military occupational specialty was field lineman and pistol-sharpshooter. He served as corporal in Battery C, 19th Field Artillery Battalion and was in Normandy, Northern France, Rhineland battles and campaigns. He earned the decorations and citations of EAME Theatre Ribbon w/3 Bronze Stars per We Go #33/45; American Defense Service Medal. During World War II he served with Gen. Patton's Third Army. After serving five years, he received an honorable discharge on Jul. 3, 1945, at Camp Atterbury, IN.

Bennie and Juanita Goble Wells

Upon returning from the military Bennie attended the Mayo State Vocational School. He married Juanita Goble (born Aug. 4, 1926, died Aug. 7, 1994 in King Daughters Hospital, Ashland). They married on Feb. 15, 1946, the daughter of Carl and Bertha Collins Goble. To this marriage four children were born: Patricia Ann Wells, Jerry Wells, Gerald Ray Wells, and Sandra Lee Wells. Patricia (born Dec. 15, 1946) married on May 29, 1971 to Kermit Womack (born Feb. 2, 1947), they have one son, Robert Wayne Womack (born Jan. 16, 1987). They reside in Greenup, KY. Patricia is involved in her son's school activities and serves as treasurer of the Wells Family Association, Inc. One of her favorite hobbies is genealogy. Jerry Wells (born Mar. 8, 1948) married Connie Craft and they have one son, Jerry Michael Wells (born Apr. 19, 1974), who lives in Greenup, KY. Gerald Ray Wells (born Sep. 30, 1949) married Vicky Corns and they have two daughters, Dawn M. Wells Jude (born Sep. 29, 1971) and Lisa Wells Stumbo (born Dec. 18, 1974). Gerald and Vicky divorced and he resides in Johnson County, KY. Sandra Lee Wells (born Feb. 12, 1959) is an invalid and in the South Shore (KY) Convalescent Home.

Juanita Goble Wells never worked out of the home but became a full time mother and homemaker. She remarried after the death of Bennie to Oscar Carr and was widowed again some years before her death. Juanita was buried at Brick Union Cemetery, Lloyd, KY. Their children removed their father's grave from the family cemetery, Van Lear to Brick Union Cemetery beside their mother.

WELLS - Betty Wells (born Sep. 20, 1924 in Johnson County), the daughter of the late Benjamin H. and Susana Richmond Wells. Betty was a beautiful woman with blonde hair, blue eyes, fair complexion and 5'7" tall. Betty married Feb. 15, 1944, to Eyvand Brown (born Jun. 4, 1925, died Jan. 11, 1999), the son of Roy and Emma Arrowood Brown. Betty was in failing health and had open heart surgery in December 1979. She died on Jun. 8, 1980, at the age of 56 years old. She is buried in the Wells Family Cemetery on Rt. 3, Daniels Creek.

Betty Wells

There were three children born to this marriage: (1) Janet Sue Brown (born May 28, 1946), who married Bill Clifton of Van Lear. Sue and Bill had four sons: Vinson and Keith who were stillborn, Billy Clifton (born Sep. 20, 1974) and Robert Clifton (born Dec. 23, 1976). They reside in Wabash, IN.

(2) Anna Lois Brown (born May 11, 1948), married Harold Meade of Paintsville. Ann and Harold had three sons: twins, Tony and Todd (born Jan. 22, 1970) and James Craig (born Oct. 12, 1972). The children all attended Paintsville school system. Todd graduated from Eastern Kentucky University and married Lisa Cox from Maysville, KY. Todd and Lisa have one daughter, Madison Haley Meade (born Jul. 8, 1997) and they reside in Paintsville. Tony married first Malenda Spence and second, Coletta Harris and divorced. James Craig is not married and is in the Marines Reserve. Anna and Harold divorced and she is married to James Wilson and they reside in Columbus, OH.

Uyvonia Carol Brown (born Nov. 8, 1950), married on Jun. 22, 1968 to Roger Ray from Floyd County and they had two children, Roger Ray Jr. (born Sep. 3, 1969) and Shantel Ray (born Feb. 19, 1975). Carol and Roger are divorced and she reared her children by herself. She married on Apr. 19, 1996 to Charles Roy Burchett (born Jan. 2, 1959) and they reside in Prestonsburg, KY. Roger Jr. married Allison Skeann and they divorced having no children. Roger works in Columbus, OH where he resides. Shantel married Charles Castle of which one son was born, Gregory Patrick Castle (born Feb. 18, 1997). She and Charles are divorced and she resides in Prestonsburg.

James Edsel Brown (born Feb. 28, 1953) married Regina Sheryl Slone and he adopted her son, Jimmy Lee Slone (born May 31, 1975). James and Sheryl divorced and he has not remarried. He presently resides with his son, Jimmy Lee in Floyd County.

WELLS - Charles C. Wells was born Aug. 18, 1934, in Paintsville, KY. The son of Charles J. and Elizabeth (Rice) Wells. He graduated from Millersburg Military Institute in 1953 and is an alumnus of Transylvania University. Upon the death of his father in 1955, Mr. Wells returned home to manage the family business.

In 1957, he married Carlos E. Horn, the daughter of Carl R. and Eleanor (Spurlock) Horn of Prestonsburg, KY. They have one son, Charles B. Wells, who resides in Georgetown, KY.

Mr. and Mrs. Wells worked diligently to develop a small propane business into one of the largest dealerships in Eastern Kentucky. Operating under the name of Hardware Charlie Gas Co., by 1996 the company operated in nine counties, serving over 3,000 customers. They retired from the business in May 1996.

In 1970 and 1971, he received the highest honor which can be bestowed by his peers by being elected president of the Kentucky Propane Association. In 1981, Mr. Wells was elected to the board of directors of the Citizens National Bank and in 1996 was elected chairman of the board of the bank. He was chairman of the Board of Southern School of Osteopathic Medicine, which became the Pikeville College School of Osteopathic Medicine. Mrs. Wells is active in many civic organizations and is a director at the Mountain Arts Center in Prestonsburg, KY.

In an effort to preserve local records, Mr. Wells has compiled and published the following genealogical reference books. *Records of Johnson County, KY-1850; Vital Statistics of Johnson County, KY. 1843 to 1904* and *Annals of Floyd County, KY. 1800 to 1826.*

WELLS - Herman Wells (born Mar. 18, 1928) was one of five children born to Elmer and Pearl Hamilton Wells of Johnson County, KY. Herman married on May 18, 1949 to Jeanette Wells (born Jan. 30, 1920), the third of 10 born to Benjamin and Susana Richmond Wells. They resided in Johnson County where Jeanette taught school for eight years. They moved to Cleveland where Herman found employment with Precision Metal Smith and Jeanette became a full time wife, mother and homemaker.

Herman and Jeanette Wells

They are the parents of two sons, Ronnie Gene Wells (born Mar. 25, 1950) and Donnie Dean Wells (born Jun. 18, 1952). Herman and Jeanette returned to Kentucky before the boys entered school. They owned and operated a grocery store at East Point, KY until their retirement. Jeanette took a position with the education system as coordinator of the Head Start Program, where she worked until she quit due to health reasons. Jeanette died on May 10, 1982 from congested heart failure at Our Lady of Bellfonte Hospital in Ashland, KY. She was buried at Highland Memorial Cemetery in Staffordsville, KY. Jeanette was active in East Point Christian Church and the Eastern Star. Herman is active in the Masonic Lodge at east Point and the Shriners. The State Highway Department took the Wells property and they moved to Van Lear where Herman presently resides.

Ronnie and Donnie attended Paintsville High School where both were active in sports. Ronnie played football and baseball and upon graduating, he and Mary Lou Lewis (born Dec. 29, 1950) were married on Jun. 29, 1970). Mary Lou and Ronnie both were attending Morehead State University when their son, Jonathan Jared (J.J.) Wells (born 1971), was born. They both graduated from MSU and Ronnie had the franchise on Giovanni's Pizza and then taught school and coached ball at Johnson Central High School, while Mary Lou attended Louisville Law of which she graduated. Ronnie and Mary Lou divorced and Ronnie later married Diane Slone who had one son, Greg Slone (born 1972), and he and J.J. were like brothers as they grew up on the farm. Greg married and settled in Bowling Green, KY, and has one child, Kaitlyn Chevenne Wells (born May 4, 1998).

Donnie Dean Wells attended Paintsville High School where he was on the football team. When he was 16, he was in a freak accident that left him half paralyzed from the chest down. Donnie required much more care from his father and mother who were totally dedicated to him. Donnie met Linda Vaughn of Johnson County and they married in 1978 at Wise, VA. Linda entered the Nursing Program at Prestonsburg Community College where she graduated and worked for both Paul B. Hall Hospital and Highland Regional Hospital. Throughout this marriage, Donnie was in and out of the hospital and Linda nursed him back to health. Donnie died on Jan. 23, 1996, when his kidneys failed him. Donnie was buried at Highland Cemetery in Staffordsville, KY, by his mother and paternal grandparents.

WELLS & ADKINS - James Noah Adkins (born Mar. 27, 1930 in Johnson County, KY) was one of five boys born to Edward and Bertie Wells Adkins. James entered the military service on Mar. 1, 1951, and received his basic training at Camp Penix, VA. He served in Munich, Germany and was discharged on Feb. 15, 1953. James married Emma Delores Wells (born Mar. 3, 1935), the daughter of Benjamin and Susana Richmond Wells. James and Emma both have dark eyes, James has olive skin and Emma is fair and both had dark brown hair. Both their children inherited their father's olive skin and dark eyes. James and Emma lived and worked in Cleveland, OH for several years before returning to Kentucky and buying the farm of the late Ben DeLong where they presently reside.

James and Emma, Delores Wells Adkins

James was employed with Park Drops Ford while in Cleveland. After returning to Kentucky he was employed with Consolidated Coal Company. James and Emma do light farming and raise their own vegetables and fruits for the winter. Emma is a wonderful cook and enjoys trying new recipes. James jokes saying that he taught her everything that she knows. Emma is a well-known artist in the area and has won many ribbons and awards for her work.

James and Emma have two children, Vicky Ann Adkins (born Sep. 22, 1957), who is employed for Vanhoose Lumber Co. She married John Patrick McCoart (born Aug. 22, 1953) of Van Lear. John and Vicky have two children, Aric Russell McCoart (born May 16, 1977), who is serving in the U.S. Navy and Erin Susana McCoart (born Aug. 21, 1981), who graduated from Paintsville High School in May 1999 and will be attending Prestonsburg Community College in the fall of 1999.

Vicky Ann was 11 years old before her brother was born. James Edward Adkins (born Sep. 22, 1968) graduated from Johnson Central High School and married Margo Cantrell. They divorced and he then married Amanda Morton of which one daughter was born, Kelcie Page Adkins (born Aug. 12, 1993). James and Amanda divorced and he married Lisa K. Rogers (born Aug. 8, 1964) of Mt. Sterling, KY. James and Lisa reside on Music Branch, Van Lear, KY. There have been no children born to this marriage.

WELLS - Jarrod J. Wells was born on Dec. 9, 1970, in Boyd County, KY, to Ronnie G. Wells and Mary Lou Lewis (Wells, Chandler, Barton). His parents Mary Lou Wells and Ronnie G. Wells were married in Johnson County, KY on Jun. 26, 1970. Ronnie is the son of Herman Wells and the late Jeanette Wells of East Point, KY in Johnson County. Mary Lou is the daughter of Rebecca Lewis (Music) and the late Jack L. Lewis of Paintsville, KY. Jack died on Jun. 6, 1987, and is buried in Porter Cemetery in Prestonsburg, KY.

Jarrod J. (J.J.) Wells

J.J.'s father, Ronnie's paternal grandparents were Elmer Wells and Pearl Hamilton Wells, both are deceased and buried in Johnson County, KY. J.J.'s mother's maternal grandparents were A.I. Lewis and Corby Dempsey Lewis, both of whom are deceased and were buried in Highland Memorial Cemetery in Paintsville, KY.

J.J. graduated from Paintsville High School where he was active in sports, playing baseball and football. He was elected to the all-star area football team. His interests include hunting and fishing. He is currently employed in McLean, VA, outside Washington, by Lucent Technologies, after completing a course at Mayo State Technological School in Paintsville, KY, in June, 1998.

J.J. was married to Stephanie Johnson, of Auxier, Floyd County, KY, on Jun. 23, 1998, at the home of his father, Ronnie, and stepmother, Diane Slone Wells, in Johnson County, KY. Stephanie is the daughter of Larry Johnson and Debbie Johnson, of Auxier, KY.

On May 4, 1998, Kaitlyn Cheyenne Wells was born to J.J. and Stephanie in Floyd County, KY.

WELLS SR. - John Britton Wells Sr. was born 1880 at Boonscamp, KY, the son of Charles J. and Margaret (Arrowood) Wells. Orphaned at an early age, John and his brother, Jake Wells, went to live with their grandmother Butcher. Due to her advanced age, she was only able to care for them a short time. John and Jake then went to live with their Uncle Jacob Wells. When of age, the brothers set up house keeping for themselves.

John began courting Jennie Ward, the daughter of prominent Offutt merchant William J. and Sarah (Hicks) Ward. After obtaining reluctant permission from Mr. Ward, the couple were married at Offutt, KY in 1902. John and Jennie began married life on Greasy Creek at Boons Camp.

For a time, John and Jake hauled railroad ties for the new rail line being built down the Big Sandy by the C&O Railway. It was not long before John and Jennie opened a general store and eventually the Post Office at Boons Camp. It was here at Boons Camp that four of their five children were born: Vina, Charles Jefferson, John Britton Jr. and Sarah Margaret.

In 1918 the family moved to Paintsville where their fifth child, Irene, was born. Mr. Wells purchased a part interest in the Big Sandy Hardware Company and over a period of time bought control of the company. Under his management, the company soon outgrew its location and a new and larger building was constructed on Main Street. It should be noted that in all Mr. Wells undertakings he had the assistance of his wife, Jennie, herself an able business woman.

Mr. Wells was one of the leaders of the community, serving on the City Council and various civic organizations. He was elected president of the Second National Bank of Paintsville, later to become Citizens National Bank in 1929, and served as president until his death in 1958.

WELLS JR. - J.B. Wells Jr. was born Jul. 4, 1914 at Boonscamp, KY, the son of John B. and Jennie (Ward) Wells. In 1917 the family moved from Boonscamp to Paintsville and it was here that he received his education.

Mr. Wells' first marriage was to Patsy Phillis and they had one child, Patricia Jane. His second marriage was to Miss Martha G. Hayman, of Lexington, KY. From this union there were four children: John B. Wells III, Mary B. Wells, Martha D. Wells and Jennie B. Wells.

Over ensuing decades, Mr. Wells was elected six times mayor of Paintsville. When first elected in 1940, Mr. Wells was the youngest Mayor in the United States. Under his stewardship, the city obtained the reputation of being one of the most progressive cities in southeastern Kentucky. His major accomplishments included the purchase of the city gas and water system, the development of a city park and playground, complete with swimming pool, the construction of affordable municipal housing, a $300,000 water filtration plant, the initiation of garbage disposal services and an urban renewal program.

During World War II, he volunteered for the Army Air Corps. After his discharge from service, Mr. Wells, returned to Paintsville and resumed duties as mayor.

J.B. continued his public service as Rural Highways Commissioner under Governor A.B. Chandler. Returning to private life, he became CEO and president of the Big Sandy Hardware Company. Under his able leadership the company became the largest wholesaler of its kind in the region. He retired from the company in 1980.

Once again, his talents were called upon when he was asked to become the executive director of the ailing Paintsville Housing Authority. Under his leadership the existing units were brought into compliance and the 150 apartment Senior Citizens Complex was built and opened for occupancy in 1982. At his second retirement in 1992, Mr. Wells was honored by the Federal Housing Authority as having the best local Housing Authority in the Commonwealth of Kentucky.

Still feeling he could be of service to his fellow citizens, Mr. Wells volunteered to guide visitors at the Mountain Home Place, which he did until his health forced a third and final retirement in 1996.

The citizens of this area are truly indebted to Mr. Wells for his efforts in improving the quality of life for the region.

WELLS III - John B. Wells, III was born Jun. 11, 1946, the son of J.B. Wells Jr. and Martha G. Hayman. He is married to Terrie A. Barrier, daughter of Hobert and Mildred (Barnes) Barrier of Monticello, KY. They have three children: John B. Wells IV, Jacob B. Wells and Joshua H. Wells.

Mr. Wells attended Deerfield Academy, received his BA in American history at Columbia University, his MA in history at the University of North Carolina and received his MBA degree from Vanderbilt University.

In 1966 and 1967 he served as an intelligence operative for the U.S. Navy during the Vietnam War.

From 1969 through 1971 he was director of Historic Sites Survey for the state of North Carolina. In 1972, he returned to Paintsville to assist his father in the operations of the Big Sandy Hardware Company. On the retirement of his father in 1980, Mr. Wells was elected CEO and president of the company, which position he currently holds.

His community service includes one term on the Paintsville City Council, an appointment as the city's mayor pro-tem. He has served as president of the Paintsville Kiwanis Club, chairman of the East Kentucky Veterans Referral Center, president of the Big Sandy Chapter of the Sons of the American Revolution and commander of the General Humphrey Marshall and Captain William Green Wells camps of the Sons of Confederate Veterans.

Mr. Wells has always had an active interest in preserving the local history of eastern Kentucky. He has taught an evening history class at Prestonsburg Community College and currently at Morehead University, Prestonsburg branch. He is the founder of the first Sons of Confederate Veterans Camp in Eastern Kentucky, was responsible for the erection of the only monument in eastern Kentucky which honors Confederate soldiers from the mountains.

In preserving the local history of the area, Mr. Wells is co-author of 10th Kentucky Cavalry, CSA, both Confederate Military units being recruited from the mountains of eastern Kentucky.

WELLS - Minnie Sue Wells (born Aug. 27, 1930, died Jan. 4, 1994) is one of 10 children born to Benjamin and Susana Richmond Wells. Minnie graduated in the class of 1950 from Van Lear High School and went to Cleveland, OH where she worked in a local bank. Minnie returned to Kentucky and attended Morehead State University and taught school for several years.

She married Charles Rollen Wells on May 13, 1954 in Lawrence County, KY. They had four children: Phillip Wells (born Feb. 28, 1955); Katherine Sue Wells (born May 18, 1956, died Aug. 31, 1983); Lisa Gail Wells (born Oct. 27, 1960); and Charles Rollen (Chuck) Wells Jr. (born Feb. 24, 1963).

Minnie Sue Wells

Minnie and Charles resided in Defiance, OH until their separation and she returned to Kentucky to be near her family. They divorced when Chuck was a toddler. Minnie had a hard life trying to raise the four children by herself, but her mother was a great support system for the family. Minnie was known for her apple pies of which she always baked for the annual Apple Day in Johnson County. She sometimes baked as many as 100 pies for Apple Day.

Kathy married Ray Collins and had one son, Ray Collins Jr. (born 1975). Kathy was a child diabetic and died on Aug. 31, 1983 in University Kentucky Hospital at age 27. Kathy was in failing health the last 10 years of her life and her mother Minnie was always there for her to help with her young son, Ray. After her death, Ray, lived with his father until his high school years when he stayed with friends and his uncle.

Phillip Wells married Vicky Corns and they had two children Darla Wells (born Mar. 24, 1981) and Phillip Jason (DJ) Wells (born Sep. 29, 1982). Phillip and Vicky divorced and Phillip and his two children reside on Daniel Creek. Phillip was employed in the mines in West Virginia until he was stricken with diabetes and ended up in the hospital losing his vision for a time. Phillip is disabled and resides with his two children on Rt. 3, Van Lear, KY.

Lisa Gail Wells married Donnie Horn of Marin County, KY and they have two children, Dustin Bradley Horn (born 1981) and Brandi Michelle Horn (born July 1984). Lisa and Donnie reside in Louisa, KY and Lisa is a mother, wife and homemaker. Donnie is employed for Columbia Gas, Inc. Dustin graduates from Louisa High School in May 1999 as an honor student and plans are to attend college in the fall of 1999 but has not picked the school he will attend yet. Brandi Michelle is an 8th grader and has maintained straight A's all through the years. She is also a member of the school band.

Charles R. "Chuck" married a Pike County girl named Kim and they have two children, Rhianna Kenzi Wells, age 8, and Charles Joseph Wells, age 6. Chuck and Kim divorced in 1997 and Chuck and his two children reside on Rt. 3, Van Lear, KY. Chuck is employed in Prestonsburg, KY at a service station.

WELLS - Nevard Wells (born Mar. 27, 1922) was the fourth of 10 children born to the late Benjamin H. and Susana Richmond Wells. Nevard was a good looking young man with black hair, brown eyes, fair complexion and 5'9" tall. Nevard entered the military on Dec. 2, 1942 and during World War II served in the South Pacific, in New Guinea and Leyte. He was shot while in the military and his mother received the Purple Heart. After the war, Nevard was discharged on Jan. 6, 1946 with an honorable discharge. After returning from the war he attended Mayo Vocational School. Nevard worked in the mines before going to work for the state of Kentucky with Department of Reclamation where he worked until his retirement in 1985. Genene attended Morehead State University and taught school in Johnson County School System. She owned and operated a restaurant on Rt. 3 until her retirement.

Nevard Wells

Nevard married Genene Wells (born December 1930), the daughter of Willie and Lutie Collins Wells. There were two sons born to this marriage, Garold Wendell Wells (born Aug. 30, 1948), who married on Jun. 8, 1967 to Carol Sue Hall (born Dec. 6, 1947). They have three children.

Wendell Lee Wells (born Jun. 2, 1968) is not married and is assistant manager of Wal-Mart's in Cambridge, MD.

Deidra Renee D.D. Wells (born Dec. 24, 1970) is married to Ken Lawson and they have one daughter, Hollie Lawson (born Feb. 26, 1998). D.D. is a cosmetologist but since the baby came she chose to be a full-time wife, mother and homemaker.

Justin Blake Wells (born Mar. 7, 1986) is a 7th grader in the Johnson County school system.

Dwayne Wells (born May 1, 1951 in Paintsville) graduated from Prestonsburg High School and married on Jan. 2, 1970 to Jenny Ann Sammons (born Oct. 9, 1950). Dwayne and Jenny divorced. Two children were born to this marriage.

Kimberly Dawn Wells (born Nov. 27, 1970) married James Bryon Clevenger and divorced. She married Ron Cline from Martin County and they had one daughter, Logan Alexander (born Oct. 15, 1993). Kim and Ron divorced and she married Keith Harris from Floyd County and they have a son, Kethon Harris (born Oct. 27, 1998). Kim and Keith reside in Floyd County, KY.

Christopher Wells (born Nov. 27, 1974) graduated from Johnson Central High School and resides in Lexington, KY. He is employed with MCI in Winchester, KY.

Dwayne married Geraldine Morrison, the daughter of Mr. and Mrs. Jackson Morrison. One son was born to this marriage, Nevard Jackson Wells (born 1987, died 1987). He is buried on the Morris farm at Johns Creek.

Nevard and Genene reside at the old Samuel Clark farm on Rt. 3, Daniels Creek, Van Lear, KY.

WELLS - William Green Wells was born in Scott County, VA, in 1818, the son of Richard and Susanna (Hutchinson) Wells. He migrated to Kentucky with his family about the year 1824, where they settled on Daniels Creek in what is now Johnson County. On Jan. 15, 1839, William married Mary Butcher, the daughter of Jacob Butcher.

William Green and Mary (Butcher) Wells had 13 children: Richard M., Moses, Aaron, William A., Susannah, M.L.K., Sarah, Nancy J., John P., Charles J., Jacob G., Mary and Julia. Of their eight sons, four served in the Confederate Army and one in the Union Army. Four were farmers, two were lawyers, one was a merchant, one became a teacher, two served as elected county officials, one served in the Kentucky General Assembly and four became postmasters.

William Green Wells

Mr. Wells developed a reputation as a hard worker and shrewd businessman. By 1857, he owned over 6,000 acres located on the waters of Daniels Creek, Greasy Creek and Rockcastle Creek. In 1857, he traded his land on Daniels Creek for acreage on the right fork of Greasy Creek and set up his residence.

In addition to being a merchant and farmer, Mr. Wells became a minister in the Methodist Episcopal Church South, a lieutenant in the local militia and a county doctor. Politically, Dr. Wells was a staunch Democrat. During the War between the States, he cast his lot with the Southern Confederacy. Traveling to Virginia, he enlisted Nov. 21, 1862 in Co. E, 54th Virginia Infantry. He later affiliated with Co. E of the 5th Kentucky Infantry. Captured in Morgan County, KY in 1862, he was sent to Camp Chase, OH as a prisoner of war. Exchanged in 1863, Dr. Wells returned home to Johnson County, where he formed his own Partisan Ranger Company and was commissioned a captain. His unit was active until the end of the war. Dr. Wells surrendered at Charleston, WV on Jun. 12, 1865.

Dr. Wells reopened his store and continued the practice of medicine. He also continued to minister to the spiritual needs of the community. In 1872, he was appointed as one of three commissioners to select a county seat for the new county of Martin. It was his suggestion that placed the county seat at its current location of Inez, KY.

Dr. Wells passed away on the family farm on Greasy Creek in 1887 and is buried in the old Ward Cemetery at Offutt, KY. Later his grave was moved to the J.B. Wells Cemetery in Paintsville, KY.

WHEATLEY - John Burns was born Sep. 17, 1860 in Wise County, VA. At age 19 he was brought to Johnson County, KY by Thomas Jefferson Mayo to live in his home as a tutor for his seven children.

Professor John Burns Wheatley and Miranda "Ma" Wheatley

On Jan. 12, 1883, in Johnson County, John married Miranda Brown ("Ma Wheatley" as she was known) from Morgan County. To them was born seven children: May Wheatly (born February 1886); Hebert Wheatley (born March 1888); Jimmy Grant (February 1890); Virgil Oakley (born Jul. 4, 1896); John Brown (August 1898); and Bill Wheatly (born 1900).

John, through his son, Virgil Oakley Wheatley, had three grandchildren: Larry Joe Wheatley, Willodean Wheatley Caudill and Wanda Wheatley Bowling, through whom he had three great-grandchildren: Virgil Gene Bowling, Susan Kelly Caudill Dye and Phillip Morris Caudill. He had one great-great-grandchild, Henry Harrison Dye.

Leander Brown, brother-in-law of John Burns Wheatley, sitting on Main Street

John, through his son, William Wheatley, had a name sake who gave him three great-grandchildren: Hilda Jean Wheatley, William Burns Wheatley and Leila Kay Wheatley.

Prof. Wheatley and his wife Miranda lived in Paintsville and operated the oldest hotel in the area, known as the Dennison Hotel. John taught school in Paintsville and surrounding counties. He was principal of Paintsville's graded school and became the first superintendent of Paintsville schools. He inaugurated the first annual commencement exercise May 19, 1893. Its first two graduates were James W. Turner and Fred Howes.

John taught the Teacher's Institute of Martin County in 1895 and was associated in conducting the Teacher's Institute of Johnson County in August of that same year. John was also principal of Willard, KY grade school for a year.

The following are the glowing recommendations of some of the institutions where John worked:

"John B. Wheatley who taught Teacher's Institute of Martin County, KY, last year 1895 is to me well known both as a gentleman and a polished scholar. It gives me great pleasure to testify to his ability as an instructor. He is an honest, earnest and conscientious worker. He gave more than satisfaction while with us, and I am proud to recommend him to any and all county superintendents who may desire to employ him."

Yours,
W.T. Cains, County Superintendent
Inez, KY.

"I speak from experience and can say I take pleasure in recommending for your favorable consideration, Prof. J.B. Wheatley, as an earnest, able and energetic institute instructor."

G.V. Daniel, Supt., P.S., J.C.

"It gives me great pleasure to state that Prof. J.B. Wheatley, Principal of the Paintsville Graded Schools, Paintsville, KY, was associated with me in conducting the Teacher's Institute of Johnson County, KY, in August 1895. Mr. Wheatley is a cultured, Christian gentleman; he is a born teacher whenever his time to talk came, the institute gave him the most marked attention. His work was very much appreciated by the teacher of above institution. It has seldom been my privilege to meet a young man for whom I have as a great respect, both as a teacher and as a man."

J.C. Willis, President
Southern Indiana Normal College

Professor Wheatley is believed to have passed away in the early 1900s, possibly 1904. He was in his early 40s when he died.

WHEATLEY - Virgil Oakley Wheatley was born on our country's birthday, Jul. 4, 1896 at East Point, KY. He died Oct. 3, 1967, Paintsville, KY during the week of the Johnson County Apple Festival. Virgil was one of several sons and a brother to one sister,

Mae (Wheatley) Layne. Mae was a court stenographer.

Virgil's parents were Miranda (Brown) and Professor John Burns Wheatley. Virgil's father was the second superintendent of the Paintsville City School System and later was given Honorary First Superintendent of the Paintsville City School System and was inducted in the Centenarian Hall of Fame.

Virgil's father came from Wise County, VA. His father was a relative to the famous Jenny Wiley. Virgil's father died in mid-age of life. The late well known pianist in our area, John Grant Wheatley, was Virgil's nephew, his brother's son, James Grant Wheatley.

Virgil's mother was from Kentucky. Her mother was a Hill and married Nathan Brown. His mother lived to be around 90 or over.

Virgil graduated from Sandy Valley Seminary at Paintsville, KY, on May 17, 1917 (date taken from original diploma). Fourteen months after his graduation he went to Huntington, WV, and enlisted in the U.S. Marines. He served during World War I in France. After his military time was over he came back home. During that time he traveled some, then later on in life he was introduced to Myrtle Blair and at his age of 42 and her age of 24 they were married on Mar. 10, 1939 at Paintsville, KY, and started their small family later on in life.

Virgil worked different jobs during that time and later was hired by Ben H. Cox of First Federal Savings and Loan Association of Paintsville, KY (now called Family Federal), to hold the position of parking attendant until his death.

Myrtle (Blair) Wheatley was born Jun. 2, 1914 in Magoffin County, KY and was the eldest daughter out of nine children of Louise (Litteral) and Oscar Blair. All of Myrtle's sisters and brothers were born at Magoffin County, KY. The girls were born before the boys in that family. Myrtle's family moved from Magoffin County, KY to the head of Van Lear, KY up a small hollow called Hurt Hollow (now days is called Pea Vine). Myrtle's father was manager of a mercantile store that was located up the head of Hurt Hollow, which his brother Burns Blair owned. Also, Myrtle's father worked in the Van Lear Mines, that was her father's main reason to move to Van Lear.

Myrtle's grandparents on her mother's side were Mary Jane (Rice) and Milton Litteral from Magoffin County, KY.

Myrtle's father was from the head of Jenny's Creek, Johnson County, KY. Her grandparents on her father's side were Mary and Britton Blair from the head of Jenny's Creek, Johnson County, KY. Her father's mother, Mary, was a full blooded Cherokee Indian. Myrtle is a relative to the country singer, Loretta Lynn, on her father's side of the family through the Ramey's side.

Later on, when Myrtle's father abandoned the family, Myrtle had to take the lead as the main supporter and help provide for her mother and younger sisters and brothers. She had to quit school at a very young age and work at various jobs to help with the hard situation they had fallen into since her father had abandoned the family.

Myrtle was hired by Ben H. Cox of First Federal Savings and Loan Association (which is called Family Federal now a days), to work along side Virgil as parking attendant. Myrtle was hired in 1958 and retired in 1982. She was also hired later by Robert M. Conley of First National Bank to work side by side for both lots.

They had two girls: Willodean Wheatley and Wanda L. Wheatley. These two girls were born and reared at Paintsville, KY.

Willodean married Henry Morris Caudill of Stambaugh, Johnson County, KY, the son of the late Johnson County Tax Commissioner, Kelly Caudill and Hazel (Vanhoose) Caudill. They had two children, Susan Kelly Caudill and Phillip Morris Caudill.

Wanda married Gene Bowling of Booneville, Breathitt County, KY. He was the son of Harlan and Lottie (Deaton) Bowling. They had one son, Virgil Gene Bowling.

Wanda won the title of Miss Johnson Fair Queen, September 1967, a few weeks before her father died, she was sponsored by Maggard's Furniture Store. That was the last year for the Johnson County Fair which was replaced by the Johnson County Apple Festival.

These two girls of Virgil and Myrtle Wheatley presently reside at Stambaugh, KY, with their husbands. Willodean also has our mother, Myrtle, at home with them.

This information compiled by Wanda L. (Wheatley) Bowling, given to her by her loving parents and other events she witnessed in her life.

WHEELER - Charles Wesley Wheeler (born Nov. 3, 1875 at Franks Creek in Johnson County, KY) was the son of Henry Clay and Urina Elizabeth Wheeler. His parents moved to Rock House Fork of Hoods Creek in Johnson County when he was about 2 years old. They then moved to Rock House Creek, Magoffin County, KY when he was about 5. When we moved to 137 Main Street, Paintsville, KY in 1921, his parents were owners of Wheeler Grocery in a large building, where the Paintsville-Johnson County Library is now located.

Charles Wesley Wheeler and Elizabeth Jayne Wheeler

Dad was in the early oil and gas boom in Magoffin, Morgan, Johnson, and Lawrence counties. As early as 1917, there was a lease between dad and Joseph L. Bond, Oil City, PA, Somerset Oil, Cumberland Pipe Line. He owning in Jack Hunley Lease, No. 5294. A.J. Tackett Lease and in 1924 incorporated Wheeler-Lemaster Lease.

Elizabeth Jayne (born Jul. 20, 1879), probably middle or lower Laurel, Johnson County, KY, daughter of Henry Harrison and Pelina Ellington Jayne. She was married to Charles Wesley Wheeler on Feb. 3, 1893, by Preacher John Wesley VanHoose. They were both members of Paintsville United Baptist Church and are buried in the Mayo Cemetery. They were parents of nine children: Loula Wheeler Kennard, Henry Melvin Wheeler, Henry Harrison Wheeler, Sherman Clay Wheeler, Rouie Wheeler Ramsey, Dola E. Wheeler, Dona W. Wheeler, Johnnie Wheeler and Myrtle Wheeler Minix, the only living child of our parents.

Their children and their descendants are the only heirs, and inherit from their estate, forever. *Submitted by Myrtle Wheeler Minix.*

WHEELER - Charles O. "Buzzy" Wheeler was born Oct. 22, 1922 in Paintsville, KY to Charles Orion and Olga Auxier Stapleton Wheeler. His father, the son of D.J. and Pauline Cooper Wheeler, was an electrician for Kentucky and West Virginia Gas Company. His mother, the daughter of George B. and Emma Ward Staplton, was actively involved in community and civic affairs and served as Grand Worthy Matron for the Paintsville Chapter of the Eastern Star, president of the Harmon Station Chapter of the DAR and National DAR Parliamentarian, and president of the Republican Women's Club.

Buzzy, a 1941 graduate of Paintsville High School, attended Marshall University on a sports scholarship before enlisting in the U.S. Marine Corps where he valiantly served as master staff sergeant in the South Pacific Campaign.

Upon his return home he married Jeanne Miller on Dec. 29, 1947. She was the daughter of Robert Lee Miller, a barber and local businessman, and Lucille Reynolds Miller Gilkerson, a businesswoman. She graduated from Paintsville High School in 1946 and attended Lindonwood College in Missouri and Eastern Kentucky State College. They had four daughters: Melinda (born Nov. 8, 1948); Sarah (born Aug. 21, 1950); Jennifer (born Sep. 4, 1955); and Amanda (born Aug. 27, 1960).

Charles O. "Buzzy" Wheeler and Jeanne Miller Wheeler

Buzzy, a magnanimous and gregarious personality was prominent in county and state politics and was a highly successful businessman and philanthropist. He served as Johnson County Court Clerk from January 1950 until December 1966. When first elected, he was the county's youngest elected official. When running for his second term as clerk, he was elected by the largest majority of votes ever cast in Johnson County up to that time.

In 1958, Buzzy established Wheeler Lumber Company and was a successful building contractor. He also established, owned, and operated Pride Motel and Restaurant in Paintsville as well as having land holdings and gas and oil properties.

Buzzy was actively involved in politics on a state level and held many positions in the Kentucky Republican Club. In 1968, in the administration of Governor Louie B. Nunn working with the Kentucky Department of Highways until 1972.

A sport's enthusiast, Buzzy was instrumental in establishing Paintsville's Little League Program and sponsored many teams throughout the years. Buzzy's favorite pastimes included horse racing, Tennessee walking horses, cooking, dancing, singing and composing songs. He was also a member of the Masonic Lodge of Paintsville. His political slogan, "A friend to all" was a fitting tribute to this man who devoted his life to helping others.

After a long illness, Buzzy passed away from lung cancer and complications from rheumatoid arthritis on Jun. 2, 1984. Jeanne, his widow, retired form the Kentucky Department of Social Insurance in 1988 and still resides in Paintsville.

Their daughter, Melinda, is the Director of Pretrial Services with the Administartive Office of the Courts in Frankfort, KY, and has two children, Michelle Pursell of Indianapolis, IN and Melissa Bingham of Crittendon, KY. Sara, is the crime victim's advocate with the Commonwealth's Attorney's Office for the 24th Circuit, a column writer for several Eastern Kentucky newspapers and has two stepchildren, Tara and James Raymond Hopson, of Paintsville. Amanda is an officer with National City Bank in Indianapolis, IN. Jennifer passed away from cancer on Jan. 2, 1999. She was a drug and alcohol counselor within the state correctional facilities in Fairfield, OH. She is survived by a son, Joshua Wheeler Castaneda. The Jenny Wheeler Memorial Arts and Drama Scholarship has been established in Jennifer's name to assist young people in Johnson County who wish to pursue a career in the arts.

Buzzy has two sisters, Peggy Wilson of Franklin, TN (children: Ann Gordon of Atlanta, GA and John Christopher of Knoxville, TN) and Barbara McPherson of Paintsville, KY (child, Jan M. Ball of Huntington, WV)

WHEELER - Jesse's father's name was James, deceased 1804. Jesse Wheeler, a Revolutionary War soldier was born in 1750 and his son, Stephen Wheeler was born in 1780. They were the first Wheelers of this family to be living in Johnson County. They are both buried in the Concord Cemetery. William Remy Wheeler (born 1810) was the first to be born in Kentucky in then Floyd County. His son, Stephen, was the father of Henry Clay Wheeler (born 1854).

Henry Clay and Urina Elizabeth Wheeler

He was the first business man in our family in Paintsville, KY. He founded the Wheeler Grocery in about 1910 on the corner of Main and Church Streets where the Johnson County Library is now located. Their lovely old two-story home was up the street in the 500 block, where Bell South has a large parking lot.

Henry Clay was married to Urina Elizabeth Wheeler. They are buried in Buckingham Cemetery, Depot Road. They had three sons: William Sanford, Greenville Monroe and Charles Wesley Wheeler. 1817 annals, Floyd County, page 152, are James Sr. and James Wheeler Jr. which is now apparently Lawrence County, KY. They are the ancestors of Urina Elizabeth Wheeler. Her father was William B. Wheeler and he married Judea Green. *Submitted by Myrtle Wheeler Minix.*

WHEELER - Our first Wheeler to arrive in America was Stephen Moses Wheeler (born about 1695 in England). He had two sons William Wheeler (born 1727) married __ Jayne, and James Wheeler (born 1735) married Abigail Jayne. We descend from both sons. Our lines combine with John Ramey Wheeler (born Aug. 19, 1820 in Lawrence County, KY), son of James Harrison Wheeler and Elizabeth Ramey (John Ramey Wheeler being a direct descendant of William Wheeler) and Catherine Wheeler (maiden also) (born Apr. 21, 1832), in Johnson County, KY, daughter of William Ramey Wheeler and Elizabeth Borders. (Catherine being a direct descendant of James Wheeler). Catherine and John Ramey Wheeler were married by her maternal Grandfather Rev. John Borders.

May Louise Wheeler and Family. Victor and Shannon Moore, Anita and Vicki Keefer

Oliver B. Wheeler (born Apr. 19, 1854 in Lawrence County, KY), son of John Ramey and Cathrine Wheeler, married Amanda Terry (born Feb. 9, 1857 in Lawrence County, KY), daughter of John and Sarah Hannah Terry.

Joshua Miles Wheeler (born 1877 in Lawrence County, KY) was the son of Oliver B. and Amanda Terry Wheeler. He married on Sep. 28, 1899 in Johnson County, KY to Jamima Historia Chandler (born 1882), daughter of Isaac and Lucina Wheeler Chandler. She being from Chandlersville, KY. They resided on Brushy Creek in Lawrence County, KY.

Troy Deard Wheeler (born Apr. 23, 1902 in Lawrence County, KY), son of Joshua and Jamima Chandler Wheeler, married Nina Alice Craft (born Sep. 26, 1905 in Johnson County, KY), daughter of Franklin Pierce and Rosamond Victoria Slone Craft. They resided on Brushy Creek in Lawrence County, KY.

May Louise Wheeler (born Aug. 1, 1939 in Lawrence County, KY), daughter of Troy and Nina Craft Wheeler, married first, Stewart Moore and second, George Lawrence Keefer. Mae would move to Columbus, OH at the age of 18 with her first husband. All her children were born in Franklin County, OH. She would later move back to Brushy Creek of Lawrence County with her children, and still resides there today.

The children and grandchildren of Mae Louise Wheeler are: Victor Stewart Moore (born Sep. 27, 1958) married Tina Manter Applegate, daughter of Harry and Eloise Manter. Children of Victor are Joseph Frederick Applegate, stepson (born Jul. 25, 1975) and Tiffany Shiree Moore (born Dec. 27, 1979 in Franklin County, OH).

Vaughn Shannon Richie Moore (born Jun. 16, 1962) married Georganne Bowman Humphries, daughter of Fred and Georgie Neel Bowman. Children of Shannon are Jack Dean Humphries, stepson, (born May 3, 1976) and Joshua Vaughn Moore (born Feb. 9, 1984 in Cleveland, OH).

Anita Louise Keefer (born Jun. 10, 1965) married first, Billy Ray McKenzie, son of George "Bill" and Ethel Culwell McKenzie. She married second, Michael Dean Sturgill, son of Bobby and Kathleen Castle Sturgill. Children of Anita are Brandon Ray McKenzie (born Jun. 9, 1984 in Johnson County, KY) and Elizabeth Kathleen Louise Sturgill (born Sep. 28, 1997 in Boyd County, KY).

Vicki Lynn Keefer (born Mar. 1, 1970) married Monroe Dennis McKenzie, son of George "Bill" and Ethel Culwell McKenzie. Children of Vicki are Christipher George McKenzie (born Feb. 20, 1990 in Johnson County, KY); Dakota Alexandra Keefer McKenzie (born Mar. 3, 1993 in Johnson County, KY); and Nicholas Wayne McKenzie (born Jul. 17, 1995 in Johnson County, KY). *Submitted by Vicki Keefer McKenzie.*

WHEELER - William "Daniel" Wheeler was born Mar. 6, 1836 in Lawrence County, KY to William Remy Wheeler and Elizabeth Borders. He was a grandson of Stephen Wheeler and Catherine Remy. He died Sep. 8, 1904 and is buried at the Daniel Wheeler Cemetery located on the family farm. He was a farmer and had his own farm on Shop Branch, Lower Franks Creek of Flat Gap (the old Winifred Post Office).

Daniel married first, Mary Salyer on Dec. 30, 1852, in Johnson County, KY. Mary Salyer (born Nov. 17, 1836 in Lawrence County, died Jul. 30, 1881 in Johnson County) is buried at the Wheeler Cemetery on Lower Franks Creek of Flat Gap. She was the daughter of John Salyer and Margaret (Jayne) Salyer.

Daniel and Mary had the following children: Mahala Angeline (born Sep. 23, 1854, died ca. 1922) married Merchant (March) Kestner on Nov. 10, 1880; Greenville Powell (born Nov. 5, 1856, died Nov. 26, 1936) married Melvina Alice Wheeler on Nov. 27, 1873; Benjamin R. (born Sep. 13, 1858, died Feb. 25, 1941) is buried at the Becky Lemaster Cemetery, Lower Franks Creek of Flat Gap. He married (1) Martha Salyer on Nov. 4, 1880, (2) Martha Rice on Nov. 6, 1889 and (3) Cynthia (Segraves) Williams on Dec. 19, 1903; Marion Frances (born Jun. 2/07?, 1860, died Aug. 19, 1866; Elizabeth "Margaret" (born Mar. 27, 1862, died May 2, 1911) married James P. Hall on Aug. 17, 1876; William "Henderson" (born Apr. 7, 1864, died Jun. 19, 1929) married Eliza Jane Phillips on Dec. 12, 1884. They are both buried at Camant (Old Fields) Cemetery, Flat Gap; Samuel Sherman (born Jun. 2, 1866, died Jun. 1, 1944) married Zelphia Hensley on Jan. 10, 1888. They are both buried on Patterson of Joe's Creek of Flat Gap; Cynthia Jane (born Aug. 3, 1868, died Jan. 3, 1957) married Deeleenee Wheeler on Jul. 15, 1886. They are both buried at Rush Twp., McDermott, OH; Darcus Rose (born Mar. 27, 1871, died Oct. 24, 1965) married Sanford Bays. They are both buried at Everett, WA; Nancy Catherine (born Nov. 10, 1873, died Sep. 29, 1966) married William Lewis Murray on Jan. 24, 1889. They are buried in Eaton, CO; Noah Santford (born Dec. 4, 1872/1875?, died Dec. 4, 1872/1875?) is buried at Becky Lemaster Cemetery; and Dora Ethel (born Nov. 20, 1877, died Nov. 12, 1965) married Luke P. Williams on Jul. 10, 1895. They are buried at Luke Williams Cemetery at Shop Branch, Lower Franks Creek.

William "Daniel" Wheeler

After Mary's death, Daniel married second, Anna Lemaster on Dec. 2, 1881. Anna Lemaster (born Jul. 27, 1841 in Lawrence County, died Oct. 11, 1924 in Johnson County) is buried with her husband at the Daniel Wheeler Cemetery. She was the daughter of William and Sara (Ghent) Lemaster. Daniel and Anna had two children, Lewis Henry (born Aug. 31, 1882, died Sep. 29, 1952) married Maude Naomi Chandler on Jul. 19, 1906. They are both buried in Wheelersburg, OH; and Sara Jane (born Aug. 1, 1887, died Sep. 14, 1973) married Allen Fora (Firey) Bishop in December 1908. They are buried at Castle Cemetery, Rt. 201, Lawrence County, KY. *Submitted by Phyllis (Ward) Burton.*

WHEELER - William "Henderson" Wheeler (born Apr. 7, 1864 in Johnson County, KY), son of Daniel Wheeler and Mary (Salyer) Wheeler. He died Jun. 19, 1929 at the Golden Rule Hospital in Paintsville. He was the grandson of William Remy Wheeler and Elizabeth (Borders) Wheeler. His maternal grandparents were John Salyer and Margaret (Jayne) Salyer. His paternal great-grandparents were Stephen Wheeler and Catherine (Remy) Wheeler. Henderson married Eliza Jane Phillips on Dec. 12, 1884 in Johnson County.

Eliza Jane Phillips (born Oct. 5, 1866 in Johnson County, KY) was the daughter of William Powell "Bill" Phillips and Margaret Sparks. (William Powell Phillips served with the Union forces, 14th Kentucky Infantry, Co. B, during the Civil War). Eliza was a granddaughter of Iredell (Ardell) Phillips and Mary "Polly" (Evans) Phillips and Nicholas Sparks and Darcus Jane (Ross) Sparks. She died on Oct. 16, 1939 at Paintsville.

William Henderson Wheeler and Eliza Jane (Phillips) Wheeler

Henderson and Eliza had the following children: Myrtie (born Oct. 7, 1885, died Jul. 9, 1921) married Paris Murray on May 10, 1914; Bascom Cromwell (born Oct. 16, 1887, died Sep. 2, 1934) married Alice Chandler on Dec. 23, 1908; Gracie Myrtle (born Mar. 13, 1890, died Mar. 20, 1891 at 12 months) is buried at Camant Cemetery; Zella (born Oct. 26, 1892, died Dec. 7, 1979) married James "Bert" Hall on Dec. 20, 1910; Elizabeth (born Feb. 28, 1897, died Dec. 22, 1993) married Albert "Tracy" Pack on Feb. 9, 1923; William "Bill" Taylor (born Sep. 4, 1899, died Mar. 14, 1970) married Helen Mitchell on Jun. 25, 1930; "Sophia" Margaret (born Mar. 10, 1902, died May 11, 1983) married Arnold L. Williams on Apr. 28, 1928; Velma (born Feb. 9, 1906, died Aug. 26, 1993) married Wiley

Ward on Sep. 23, 1932; and Thelma "Dot" (born Sep. 8, 1907, died Dec. 9, 1944) married Shady Kenneth Preston on Oct. 19, 1929. The five youngest children graduated from Paintsville High School. Velma and Thelma attended Morehead State Teacher's College and Elizabeth, Pikeville, Morehead and Eastern. All taught for varying lengths of time in county schools with Elizabeth teaching first in county schools and later at Paintsville for many years.

The first 22 years of their married life, Henderson and Eliza lived on Lower Laurel of Flat Gap where all of their children were born except for the last two. Velma and Thelma were born on Lower Franks Creek at Winifred, after the family moved there sometime around late 1905. At Winifred, Henderson ran a small country store and mill and was a farmer. He was a postmaster of the Winifred Post Office for a period of time. Henderson and Eliza were devout members of the Bethel United Baptist Church at Flat Gap. Henderson was clerk at Bethel from 1917 until his death in 1929. Both are buried at Camant Cemetery, Flat Gap, Johnson County, KY.

WILEY & HAAR - Bessie Lorraine Wiley (born Oct. 29, 1925 in Pike County, KY), daughter of Merida "Bud" Wiley and Carrie Stapleton Wiley. She was the 11th child of 12. She was married to Frederick Max Haar on Jun. 7, 1946, in Richmond, VA. He was born Aug. 13, 1927 in Marysville, KS.

They were parents of four daughters and one son: Merida Lorene (born Mar. 16, 1947 in Marysville, KS; Fred (born Apr. 18, 1948 in Marysville, KS; Linda Sue (born May 25, 1951 in Paintsville, KY); Becky Jane (born Apr. 18, 1953 in Lawton, OK); and Mildred (born Mar. 28, 1954 in Lawton, OK).

Bessie L. Wiley

Bessie moved to Paintsville with her parents in the late 1930s during her teen years and attended Paintsville City Schools. She took her first job in 1943 at Brown's Potato Chip Company which was located in the Herald Hotel Building. She married and traveled to the midwest with her husband who served in the U.S. Army. She returned to Paintsville in 1954 to raise her family when her husband was sent to Germany. They were divorced in 1957.

She was employed by the state of Kentucky at the Mayo Vocational Technical College cafeteria until her retirement in 1987. She and her children lived in a C&O Railway company house between the railroad and the Big Sandy River and later moved down the road (now called River Road) to dwell beside her father in a rather modest home he had built.

Mrs. Ocie Crace and Mrs. Ruby Wright were responsible for taking the children to Sunday School at the Bridgeford Mission, a ministry of First Baptist Church in Paintsville. It was through this exposure in their young lives that the Haar children found the spiritual strength that sustains them to this day. Bessie's children were active in the programs of the First Baptist Church in Paintsville. Her children graduated from Paintsville High School.

Lorene married Walter Sammons and moved to Newport News, VA, later to Poquoson, VA, where her two sons graduated and have gone on to further their education: Douglas in Texas, studying prosthetics and orthodics, and David in Utah, studying computer science. David is married and has one son.

Lorene attended college in Virginia. She worked for 10 years with the Peninsula Baptist Association. She now resides in Loris, SC with her second husband, Harold Wright, and is semi-retired.

Fred lives in Van Lear, KY and has been employed in the mining industry for many years. He served in the U.S. Army as a paratrooper medic. During Vietnam he earned the Purple Heart, Silver Star and the Cross of Gallantry, along with other awards. His two children, Delisa and Fred live in Lexington, KY. Delisa is a registered nurse, married and has one son. Fred is attending the University of Kentucky.

Linda Sue lives in Kaufman, TX, and is married to Gordon Roberts and has no children. She is an executive secretary.

Becky Jane is married to Raymond Brinkley. She is a registered nurse and resides in Suffolk, VA. They have no children.

Mildred lives in Dallas, TX, is single and teaches in the city school system. She graduated from Cumberland College and earned her master's degree from the University of Louisville.

The Haar children carry a sense of pride, loyalty and strength just as portrayed by their great ancestor, Jenny Wiley. Jenny's traits of perseverance and strong character, as well as faith in God have been evident through the years as life has molded, shaped and formed. It is their prayer that these fine attributes will be carried on for many more generations. *Submitted by Lorene H. Wright.*

WILEY - Merida "Bud" Wiley (born Jan. 8, 1890 at River, KY, died Jul. 25, 1966 at Paintsville, KY), married on Jun. 14, 1906 to Carrie Stapleton (born Jan. 6, 1887 at River, KY, died May 1, 1959 in Paintsville). Merida married second, Alice Daniel Lyon (died Mar. 3, 1971 in Urbana, OH). Merida, a retired C&O Railway employee, was a minister of the United Baptist Church and a member of Lodge No. 381 F&AM.

Bud and Carrie Wiley

They had 12 children:

1) Ella Wiley (born Apr. 28, 1907 at River, KY, died May 25, 1931) never married.

2) Ola Wiley (born May 17, 1909, River, KY, died Nov. 6, 1974, Paintsville, KY) never married.

3) Esta Wiley (born and died Jan. 13, 1911 at Lookout, KY).

4) Effie Wiley (born Dec. 31, 1911 in Paintsville) married Delbert Copley on Jan. 16, 1932. They had one daughter, five grandchildren, 11 great-grandchildren and one great-great-grandchild. Effie resides in Van Lear, KY. Her husband died at age 90 on May 23, 1999.

5) Virgil Wiley (born Oct. 5, 1914, died Sep. 20, 1915).

6) Dorothy Wiley (born Feb. 25, 1915 in Lackey, KY) married James Delbert Mullins. They had four children, six grandchildren, and five great-grandchildren. Dorothy is widowed and resides in Bristol, TN with her daughter Jeanette.

7) Howard E. Wiley (born Nov. 18, 1916 in Lackey, KY, died Apr. 4, 1971) married first, Myrtle Webb and second, Lillie Marie Pelphrey. He had five children, seven grandchildren, and six great-grandchildren; The eldest daughter, Frances Anne Jarrell currently serves on the Paintsville City Council.

8) Piney Wiley (born Oct. 11, 1918) married first, Otis Small and second, H.G. Beadles. She has five children, and four grandchildren. Piney resides in Cumberland, MD. Son, Eddie Small lives nearby in Keyser, WV.

9) Lanceford Clyde Wiley (born Jun. 26, 1920 in Pikeville, KY and died Jun. 22, 1995 in Poughkeepsie, NY) married first, Jane Shine and second, Alberta Gresey. He had three children and four grandchildren.

10) Clarence E. Wiley (born Dec. 4, 1923 in Pikeville, KY) married first, Verna May Sturgill and second, Oma Cockrell. He has two children, seven grandchildren and three great-grandchildren. Clarence and Oma live in Oklawaha, FL.

11) Bessie Wiley (born Oct. 29, 1925 in Pikeville, KY) married Frederick Max Haar. They have five children, four grandchildren and two great-grandchildren. Bessie lives in Newport News, VA.

12) Madge Wiley (born Jun. 15, 1929 in Shelbiana, KY) married Arnold Jennings. They have three children and four grandchildren. Madge resides near Cattletsburg, KY, and is widowed.

Merida moved his family from Pike County to Paintsville in 1938 and resided in a C&O Railway company house located between the railroad and the Big Sandy River across from the big coal tipple on Depot Road. The family later moved further down the road, now known as River Road. He and Carrie were affectionately known as Mamoo and Papoo by their 26 grandchildren. He was an interested, involved citizen of the community. He served on the Paintsville City Council in 1948 and 1949. He was employed by the C&O Railroad, beginning as a water boy and retiring as a section foreman with more than 50 years service. He loved his family and cherished the great history of his predecessors, the admirable Jenny Wiley being one of them. He and Carrie are buried in the Gambill Cemetery in Thelma, KY. *Submitted by Lorene H. Wright, a granddaughter.*

WILEY - Howard E. Wiley (born Nov. 18, 1916 in Lackey, KY) to Merida "Bud" Wiley and Carrie Stapleton Wiley. He married Lillie Marie Pelphrey on Mar. 1, 1943. Marie was born Feb. 3, 1923 at Barnett's Creek to Clarence and Cordia Lee (May) Pelphrey. They produced five children.

Howard E. Wiley and Lillie Marie Pelphrey Wiley

1) Frances Ann Wiley (born Jul. 15, 1945 in Paintsville, KY) had two sons, William Donald Jarrell and Ronald Howard Jarell. Don has four daughters and one son.

2) Carrie Lee Wiley Cinnamond (born Jan. 10, 1947 in Paintsville, KY). She produced one daughter, Cara Cay Cinnamond Hood and one son, Cade Coleman Cinnamond. Cara has one daughter.

3) Mary Margaret Wiley Pack (born Sep. 12, 1949 in Lompac, CA) She produced one son, William Michael Pack, and one daughter, Heather Renee Pack Sunseri. Heather has one daughter.

4) Judith Nell Wiley Backus (born Jan. 3, 1953 in Paintsville, KY.)

5) William Michael Wiley (born Jul. 18, 1955 in Heidberh, Germany). Mike has one daughter, Amber Lynne Wiley.

Howard graduated from Pikeville High School in 1935. He was a member of the Speech and Debate Team. He also played football for Coach Hatcher in 1935. They had an undefeated squad and won the Big Sandy Valley Conference Championship for the first time. Charles Wesley (Dutch) Ishmael also played on his team and he went on to play for UK and the Detroit Lions pro team.

After high school he attended Kentucky Christian College for a year and then went to work for the C&O Railroad. After threats of war, he joined the Army where he served 24 years and was a World War II veteran.

After retiring from the Army, he returned to Johnson County and was very active in umpiring the Little League and high school sports.

Howard died Apr. 4, 1971 and Lillie followed in death on Aug. 29, 1979.

WILLIAMS - Members of the Duell Williams family need travel only a few miles to visit the grave of a direct ancestor, Phillip Williams, a Revolutionary War soldier (born 1753, died 1848). Phillip came from Virginia via North Carolina to Kentucky about 1814. He is buried in what is known as the Old Indian Graveyard on Misery Mountain at the mouth of Stone Coal in the community of Volga beside his Cherokee Indian wife.

Phillip's oldest son, Robert S., born in North Carolina in 1788 and died in Kentucky in 1851, was the father of Hardin H. Williams. Hardin (born 1818, died 1888), established a homestead in what is now the community of Red Bush (on the Briar Fork of Big Laurel Creek). Through land patents and purchases, he put together a farm of 1,125 acres. Hardin, a farmer and circuit riding preacher, and his wife Elizabeth Picklesimer Williams, daughter of Abraham Picklesimer, became the parents of five sons and five daughters.

Hardin H. Williams

Hardin's youngest son, Dr. Buell Green Williams (born 1862), inherited the family farm and married Lydia Reed (born 1867), daughter of William and Lydia Rice Reed.

Buell G. Williams, M.D., University of Tennessee, practiced medicine from his home in Red Bush. In 1898 both he and his wife contracted typhoid and died within one month of each other, leaving an orphan son, Charlie H. Williams (born 1889, died 1956), then 9 years old.

Charlie then went to live with relatives, eventually making his home with his Uncle and Aunt, George W. and Ida Reed at Low Gap. Here, he learned moral values and was sent to school. When he was 16, he returned to his Red Bush home where he lived with a caretaker cousin, until at age 19, he married Effie Hill (born 1888, died 1949), daughter of John Wallace and Nancy Ellen Ferguson Hill of Morgan County on Feb. 9, 1909.

Effie became a mid-wife, walking or riding side-saddle near and far, never refusing to serve a patient or demanding to be paid. Charlie drilled water wells, farmed, and built and operated a grist mill. With mail-order instructions, he built the community's first radio. Together, without charge, they made most of the coffins and responded to any other community need. In 1917, Charlie joined in the development of a newly discovered oil and gas field in the area which lasted for a number of years. Later, they also operated a general store.

In 1920 they joined the Red Bush Regular Baptist Church where Charlie served as "clerk" (secretary-treasurer) for many years.

Two children were born to the family: Dixie (born 1909, died 1995) and Duell (born 1911). Dixie chose not to marry and spent most of her adult years in Miami, FL where she was a real estate broker. Duell married Esther Dorton, daughter of James R. and Hettie Williams Dorton in 1933. He was instrumental in founding Foothills Rural Telephone Coop and was the Foothills manager for its first 25 years. He retired in 1975. Esther was a teacher in the schools of Johnson County for 30 years. She retired in 1972 after 20 years of service at Flat Gap School.

Esther and Duell have continued to live on the Red Bush farm of their ancestors. They are parents to three daughters: Marilyn, Carolyn and Leonora; grandparents to 10; and great-grandparents to 17, all of whom are proud to share this heritage.

WILLIAMS - Kenwood, which doesn't exist anymore, was once a real place with real people. It was a place where everyone knew your name; it was home to the Joseph Williams family for over 100 years. Today, Kenwood is only a memory with almost no trace that it was once a thriving community. Due to the events of World War II and the building of the Paintsville Dam, the lives of the people who once called this land home was changed forever.

Home of Elephus and Minerva Williams on the porch. Sarah Elizabeth VanHoose, Minerva VanHoose Williams, Eliphas Turner Williams and Leora Jewell Dutton

Our Williams Roots grew very deep into Johnson County soil. The first of the Williams clan to settle in Johnson County, KY was Joseph Williams born in Wythe County, VA. He married Elizabeth Lemaster. Lewis was the first born of their 12 children. Rev. James Pelphrey married Lewis and Margaret Salyer in the Fish Trap Church in 1851. They became the first deacons of the Coal Springs Baptist Church. Later they organized the Spice Cove Enterprise Church in 1876. Joseph, Elizabeth, Lewis and Margaret are all buried in the Spice Cove Cemetery. The building is gone and the cemetery is now over grown with weeds.

Sometime after 1851, Lewis and Margaret acquired property on Low Gap and the community of Kenwood was established. Lewis built a big house behind what we knew as Aunt Fannie's house. When one of Lewis's children got married he gave each of them a few acres of land to build a house.

Manerva VanHoose Williams

Lewis's son, Elephus married Manerva VanHoose. They were my grandparents and their property was in a prime location at forks of the road. All the neighbors in the neighborhood were relatives. Their land, which ran along Big Paint Creek, had rolling hills with some flat land and even a waterfall. There was a high swinging bridge that you could walk across but the most fun was to wade in the creek. The terrain along the creek was the most tranquil and peaceful spot on earth. There were cliffs with rhododendrons, ferns and hollyhock. The family cemetery had to be moved before the dam could be built. The graves of grandmother, uncles and aunts as well as other relatives were moved to Johnson County Memorial Cemetery at Staffordsville. Today, part of our grandparent's property is under water from the Paintsville Dam.

Grandpa's farm at Kenwood about 1970. Elephus and Manerva Williams

This land served their purpose for many years. But in my father's generation, they could no longer live off the land. They had to go elsewhere to find work. My father got his start from the WPA Program during the depression. He helped to build the Oil Springs High School Gymnasium when I was in elementary school. My parents were Brenford Williams and Ethel Salyer. They were once members of the Fish Trap Church. When my father retired as a carpenter foreman at the age of 65, they moved to Winter Haven, FL. They are buried in the Auburndale Cemetery in Florida.

Agnes Avonell, Paul B., Brenford and Ethel, Darrell and Harold Williams

I am the first born of my generation, Agnes Avonell Williams. I was born in the Pea Rat Cantrell House in Dick Town at Fuget, KY in Johnson County. My brother and I spent a lot of time with our grandparents who lived just across the creek.

My formal education began in a one-room school on McKenzie Branch. My first teacher was John Fred Williams. I graduated from Oil Springs High School in 1944 and moved to Dayton, OH to do our part for World War II. After the war, we moved to Ashland, KY so I could attend Ashland Junior College. I started my teaching career in Catlettsburg, KY. I married Charles Prince and we had a son, William David Prince. We moved to Winter Haven, FL when our son was 7 years old. I graduated from Florida Southern College in Lakeland, FL. I retired from teaching after 27 years of service.

Josie Williams and husband Roy Patrice (returned from war)

After my husband died, I remarried and changed my name to Mrs. Robert Shakespeare. We now make our home in Naples, FL.

My son, William David Prince was born in Ashland, KY. He graduated from Florida Atlantic University in Boca Raton, FL and went on to earn two more master's degrees. He lives in Orlando, FL and is looking forward to his retirement after his teaching career.

WILLIAMS - On Jan. 31, 1805, in Washington County, VA, Lydia Wheeler married Joseph Williams. This Joseph Williams died before reaching Kentucky, but Lydia and two of their three children arrived in Floyd County about 1815. The widow married Daniel Pelphrey in 1819.

Her son, Joseph Williams married Elizabeth Lemaster on Aug. 18, 1827 and had 12 children. The first born was Lewis Williams who married Margaret Salyer in 1851. Lewis and Margaret became parents of nine children. Their first born was Benjamin S. Williams (born 1853) who first married Permelia Josephine Williams. Before she died in 1894 they had six children. Benjamin S. taught school at Joe's Creek School and in Morehead, Rowan County. He had a store and his second wife, Miranda Hamilton, ran the Kenwood Post Office.

Ruth and Benjamin J. Williams

Benjamin S. and Permelia's fifth child was Warner Lucas Williams born in 1889. The boys of this generation could not make a living in Kentucky, so Warner left Johnson County with his friend, Mervin Daniels, for Columbus, OH about 1910. Both young men became machinists. Warner married an Italian girl in 1912 and had three children: Florence, Pauline and Benjamin Jack.

Benjamin joined the 102nd Infantry Division during World War II, and served in the European Theater. He returned to work at Curtis Wright after the war and retired from Rockwell International in 1983. He married first, Mary V. Watkins and had two children, John Gary and Pamela Jill. He married second in 1972 to Ruth J. Keller. They greatly enjoy Benjamin's Kentucky roots.

WILLIAMS - Scottie Williams was born on Jun. 18, 1923 at his home at Elna in Johnson County, KY. He was born as Sidney John Scottie Williams and was one of seven children born to Albert Williams and Nineavah Stapleton Williams. Albert was the son of Sanford Williams and Lue Reed Williams. Nineavah's parents were Johnny Stapleton and Sarah McKenzie Stapleton. Scottie was married to Tera E. Salyer on Nov. 2, 1942 at the Foster Rigsby Grocery in Paintsville, KY.

Scottie and Tera Salyers Williams

Tera Williams was one of five children born in Johnson County. She was born Oct. 18, 1925 to Noah Kendric Salyer and Martha Buelah Salyer. Kendric was the son of James Monroe Salyer and Mary Anne Bunyard.

Scottie and Tera Williams are the parents of 15 children consisting of six sons and nine daughters. The sons include Sidney Nevada, Tennessee Montana, Buddy Boyed, Samuel Sherwood, Maxwell Benjamin, and Timothy Howard. Of the daughters, Texas Rose and Eadith Loraine died as children. The remaining are Edith Elaine, Violet Georgene, Lola Lee, Lila Bea, Rachel Buelah, Alberta Lorene, and Thelma Darleen. Eleven of the children were born at their home on Williams Creek at Flat Gap, KY. The last four were born in the Paintsville Hospital. As of 1999, they have 25 grandchildren, six great-grandchildren, five step-grandchildren and three step-great-grandchildren.

Scottie was enlisted in World War II and discharged in August 1944. He then received training as a mechanic on the GI Bill. He left Kentucky to work in Springfield, OH where he was employed by Steel Products, an engineering company, for 30 years. He retired in 1980.

After retiring, he was the first volunteer for the Corps of Engineers of Paintsville Lake. At the age of 62, he rode on horseback twice a week around the lake spotting fires, trash dumping, and the occasional drunks in speedboats. He was given the name Lone Ranger of the Lake.

Scottie was also known as Rev. Scottie Williams, ministering for 42 years for the United Baptist Church. He went home to be with the Lord on Feb. 18, 1996.

While working in Ohio, Scottie could only come home to Flat Gap, KY on weekends as weather permitted. Tera was left to raise their many children. Tera lives through her children and has seen them through school, marriage, and the birth of her grandchildren. She is proud of the fact that all of her children graduated high school and many of her grandchildren plan to pursue a secondary education.

Tera is a prominent part of all family gatherings which are held at least four times a year. The greatest joy her grandchildren receive from her is the telling of the good old days before computers and video games.

Her greatest gift to her children has been her wisdom and lessons of high morals and honor to spouses and others. She also taught them to always trust God. All of her children and grandchildren still reside in Johnson County.

WILLIAMSON - Aulden Williamson, better known as Aud, was born Jun. 28, 1908, in Johnson County, KY, the son of Ale and Mary Ann Wells Williamson. His occupation was mining. He won many mine safety awards and also helped in rescue efforts.

He married Julia Music, daughter of Arch and Della Preston Music, Apr. 8, 1928. They lived mainly in the Van Lear area.

Their marriage was blessed with seven children: Aulden Williamson Jr., Freelin Williamson, Wodridge Williamson, Reatha Lou Williamson, Gerald Ray Williamson, Gwendolyn Williamson and Betty Sue Williamson.

Mr. and Mrs. Williamson, 50th Wedding Anniversary

Aulden Williamson Sr. passed away in the year of his 60th wedding anniversary, Dec. 21, 1988.

WITTEN - Francis Marin Witten was born Apr. 18, 1866 in Johnson County, KY to John Wesley Witten and Lydia Ramey. He was married Feb. 17, 1892 to Sarah Catherine "Kit" Ward (born Mar. 8, 1871, died Aug. 6, 1928), daughter of Andrew Jackson Ward and Lydia V. Litteral.

Francis Marion "Frank" Witten was a physician and surgeon, practicing in Johnson and Magoffin counties. He graduated from law school in 1901, but did little work as an attorney other than to help others to obtain their pensions.

Dr. Frank and Kit Witten were the parents of Clara who married Charles Mahan, P. French "Bill" Witten married Hazel Risner, Emma married Taylor Meade and Thelma married a Slone. P. French "Bill" Witten was Chief of Police of Paintsville for several years.

Dr. Francis Marion Witten

Dr. Witten died Nov. 6, 1938. Dr. Witten, his wife, daughters, Emma and Thelma, and five children who died at an early age are buried in the Judge Litteral Cemetery at Oil Springs, KY. *Submitted by Mrs. Francis "Mary" Witten.*

WITTEN - William Pitt Witten was the first Witten in Johnson County. When he arrived in the Paintsville area in fact, there was no Johnson County. Records show that he married Charlotte Hackworth, from Pike County, in 1819 in Floyd County. William had left his parents in Tazewell County, VA, where they had lived for several years.

The Wittens came to Tazewell County from Pulaski County, VA and before that from Maryland. The first Witten in America was with the House of Calvert. They came from England settling in Baltimore, MD in 1643.

William Pitt Witten and his wife, Charlotte, settled a few miles northeast of Paintsville in what is now Wittensville. I'm sure it was named in his honor. Their children were John, George Hamilton, Isaac, William Pitt Jr., Thomas, Francis "Frank," Rebecca, Melinda, Nancy and Susan.

During the Civil War, William had five sons who served in the Union Army: John, George Hamilton, William Jr., Thomas and Frank. They joined the 14th Kentucky Volunteers, Co. K at Louisa, KY and served in Kentucky and Tennessee with Sherman's forces in Georgia. Undoubtedly, the most traumatic battle for them was at Kenesaw Mountain, for after the battle was over, Thomas found Frank's dead body on the battlefield.

George Hamilton was captured and became a prisoner of war. He had been assigned to a small patrol doing forward surveillance, when they were attacked by Southern forces. Although they were out-numbered, more than 10-1, they held their position for two days before they were finally captured. He was taken to the infamous Andersonville Prison in Georgia. Of the approximately 54,000 prisoners confined at Andersonville during its 15 months of operation almost 13,000 died, primarily of starvation and dysentery. George was one of the lucky ones—he survived. After the war was over, he returned to Johnson County by steamboat. It landed at Paintsville, where Paint Creek runs into the Big Sandy.

William Pitt and George Hamilton both lived their entire lives and are buried at Wittensville. A veteran's monument marks George's grave.

I don't know all of the branches of the Witten family. I know George Hamilton's branch, because he was my great-grandfather. George was a farmer, but also a Church of Christ preacher. He also served as representative in the Kentucky State Legislature. He married Martha Butler. Their children were William Wilk Witten who married Rachel Stambaugh, Mary Witten married Troy Stambaugh, Florence Witten married Julius Burchett, Dr. George Witten married Mary Williams and Frank Witten married Mint Butler.

Wilk Witten and his wife Rachel lived at Stambaugh. He was a farmer, a Church of Christ preacher and served on the Johnson County School Board. Their children were Naomi Witten who married Roy Stambaugh, Anna Witten married Lon Arrowood, Raleigh "Ham" Witten married Virla Johnson and Earl Witten married Tera Lemasters. This brings us up to the 1890s.

WHITE & YOUNG - Mary Ann White (born Nov. 19, 1864 in Lawrence County, died Dec. 17, 1948 in Johnson County), daughter of Elizabeth Daniel and Paris White, married George Gallup Young, son of Mary Burton and Harrison Young, on Mar. 24, 1881 in Lawrence County. George was born Apr. 17, 1863 in Johnson County, KY.

Young Family L-R: Monroe, Tom, John, Gilbert, Bill, Bradley, Bert, Ott. Front: Mr. and Mrs. Young.

George and Mary Anne's children were:
1) Monroe (born Jan. 4, 1884, died Oct. 20, 1954) married Hattie Murray on Feb. 16, 1904 in Johnson County.
2) John (born Nov. 7, 1884, died May 26, 1950) married Borders on Jan. 31, 1929 in Johnson County.
3) Thomas (born Feb. 26, 1887, died Jun. 6, 1955) married Terrie Daniel on Dec. 7, 1905 in Johnson County.
4) Alonzo (born Feb. 7, 1888, died Feb. 7, 1889).
5) Gilbert (born Jun. 26, 1889, died Mar. 13, 1983) married May Salyer on Jul. 13, 1906 in Johnson County.
6) William (born Jan. 15, 1891, died Nov. 14, 1960) married Flossie Daniel on Sep. 30, 1917 in Johnson County.
7) Gracie (born Oct. 26, 1892, died Mar. 10, 1894 in Johnson County).
8) Bradley (born Mar. 12, 1893, died Oct. 21, 1982) married Ada Conley on Nov. 23, 1918 in Russell, KY.
9) Mary Florence (born Oct. 20, 1895, died Oct. 18, 1896 in Johnson County).
10) Bert (born May 8, 1899, died Oct. 9, 1966) married Malvery Davis on Dec. 16, 1919 in Johnson County.
11) Otto (born Jun. 22, 1901, died Sep. 13, 1982) married Rosie Thornsberry on Oct. 3, 1923, He married first to Pearl Tackett and third to Myrtle Evans.

The family has been much respected and appreciated for the hard work they produced for the Consolidated Coal Company. Pictured above is a photograph that The Coal Company took of the family while all of the family member's were employed by Van Lear's Consolidated Coal Company. Statement on the bottom of the picture is as written:

"We present with pleasure the family of Mr. and Mrs. George Young all of whose name appear on the Van Lear payroll as good and faithful employees of our company."

YOUNG - Timmy Young was born on Mar. 31, 1958 in Paintsville, KY to Hershel and Lorene Blevins Young. He is the fifth of six children born to his parents.

His father, Hershel, born May 21, 1929, is the son of Ben and Mollie Caudill Young. He worked as a miner until he was disabled. His mother, Lorene, born Mar. 26, 1929, is the daughter of Herbert Chum and Dixie Simpson Blevins.

Tim graduated from Johnson Central High School in 1979 with a Vocational-Technical Diploma. After his high school graduation, Tim worked for Magic Mart as a stockman and Terry's Office Supply as a route salesman and a machine repair technician before starting to work in 1989 for the Carl D. Perkins Job Corp. in Prestonsburg, KY where he teaches electricity. In 1989, he was licensed as a master electrician. Tim also served as commissioner from August 1991 to January 1994 for the city of Van Lear when it was re-incorporated. Tim is also the owner and operator of his business, Young Business Machine Repair.

He was married at Mayo Memorial United Methodist Church in Paintsville, KY, to Connie Jean Butcher, on Jun. 24, 1976. They are the parents of one daughter, Tymsone Machelle, born on Jul. 14, 1978.

His wife, Connie, was born Sep. 8, 1957, in Paintsville, KY. She is the daughter of Elmer and Anna Ruth Jones Butcher. Elmer (born Feb. 13, 1924) is the son of Melvin and Ida Bowling Butcher. Elmer worked as a miner until his retirement in 1986. Anna Ruth (born Feb. 14, 1931) is the daughter of William Kirkpatrick and Mina Mae Evans Jones. Connie graduated from Johnson Central High School with honors in 1975 with a Vocational-Business Diploma and graduated from Mayo Vocational Technical School with a Business Diploma in 1976. After graduation she worked for Luginbyhl and Associates, an accounting firm, in Prestonsburg, KY and then for Mountain Comprehensive Care Center in Paintsville, KY. She is employed at Mayo Memorial United Methodist Church.

Tim, Connie and Tymsone Young

Their daughter, Tymsone, was born at Pikeville Methodist Hospital in Pikeville, KY. She attended Porter Elementary School and graduated from Johnson Central High School in 1996 with a College Preparatory Diploma and attended Prestonsburg Community College. She is currently employed as a crew supervisor at Hardee's of Paintsville. Tymsone is engaged to Christopher Shawn Williams of Collista, KY. Shawn is the son of Tim and Wanda Williams. Submitted by Connie Young.

John M. Conley sawmill at Greenrock, Kentucky, circa 1911. Ralph Conley, sawdust boy, right foreground. Billy O'Bryan and Chandler Woods on right of picture. H.P. McKenzie, slender one in center with mustache (under shed.) J.M. bought timber from Dan Davis and sold crossties and lumber to Dawkins Lumber Co., which was used in constructing B.S. and K.R. Railroad from Ivyton, Kentucky to C. & O. Railroad near Paintsville, Kentucky.

Index

I

J

K

L